DECOLONIZING AFRICAN KNOWLEDGE

Addressing the consequences of European slavery, colonialism, and neo-colonialism on African history, knowledge, and its institutions, this innovative book applies autoethnography to the understanding of African knowledge systems. Considering the "Self" and Yoruba Being (the individual and the collective) in the context of the African decolonial project, Falola strips away Eurocentric influences and interruptions from African epistemology. Avoiding colonial archival sources, it grounds itself in alternative archives created by memory, spoken words, images, and photographs to look at the themes of politics, culture, nation, ethnicity, satire, poetics, magic, myth, metaphor, sculpture, textiles, hair, and gender. Vividly illustrated in color, it uses diverse and novel methods to access an African way of knowing. Exploring the different ways that a society understands and presents itself, this book highlights convergence, enmeshing private and public data to provide a comprehensive understanding of society, public consciousness, and cultural identity.

TOYIN FALOLA is Professor of History, University Distinguished Teaching Professor, and the Jacob and Frances Sanger Mossiker Chair in the Humanities at the University of Texas at Austin. He had served as the General Secretary of the Historical Society of Nigeria, the President of the African Studies Association, Vice-President of UNESCO Slave Route Project, and the Kluge Chair of the Countries of the South, Library of Congress. He is a member of the Scholars' Council, Kluge Center, the Library of Congress. He has received over thirty lifetime career awards and sixteen honorary doctorates. He has written extensively on African knowledge systems, including *Religious Beliefs and Knowledge Systems in Africa* (2021), *African Spirituality, Politics and Knowledge Systems: Sacred Words and Holy Realm* (2022), and *Decolonizing African Studies: Knowledge Production, Agency and Voice* (2022). He is also the series co-editor for Cambridge University Press's series *African Identities*.

AFRICAN IDENTITIES: PAST AND PRESENT

GENERAL EDITORS

Toyin Falola, *The University of Texas at Austin*
Carina Ray, *Brandeis University*

African Identities: Past and Present offers scholars a unique publishing platform for exploring the multivalent processes through which collective identities have come into being. Books in this series probe the work that African identities have been made to do, the varied investments that historical and contemporary actors have made in them, and the epistemological dilemmas and intellectually fraught politics of writing about such contingent categories of being. The focus on African identities makes clear the series' commitment to publishing histories of the complex and ongoing processes of identity formation through which Africans have taken on shared senses of being. This series calls upon its authors to unpack the flexible, fluid, contingent, and interactive nature of collective African identities, while also exploring how historical actors have alternatively sought to delimit, expand or otherwise challenge the boundaries of such identities.

DECOLONIZING AFRICAN KNOWLEDGE

Autoethnography and African Epistemologies

TOYIN FALOLA
University of Texas, Austin

Shaftesbury Road, Cambridge CB2 8EA, United Kingdom

One Liberty Plaza, 20th Floor, New York, NY 10006, USA

477 Williamstown Road, Port Melbourne, VIC 3207, Australia

314–321, 3rd Floor, Plot 3, Splendor Forum, Jasola District Centre, New Delhi – 110025, India

103 Penang Road, #05-06/07, Visioncrest Commercial, Singapore 238467

Cambridge University Press is part of Cambridge University Press & Assessment, a department of the University of Cambridge.

We share the University's mission to contribute to society through the pursuit of education, learning and research at the highest international levels of excellence.

www.cambridge.org
Information on this title: www.cambridge.org/9781009048934

DOI: 10.1017/9781009049634

© Toyin Falola 2022

This publication is in copyright. Subject to statutory exception and to the provisions of relevant collective licensing agreements, no reproduction of any part may take place without the written permission of Cambridge University Press & Assessment.

First published 2022
First paperback edition 2025

A catalogue record for this publication is available from the British Library

ISBN 978-1-316-51123-7 Hardback
ISBN 978-1-009-04893-4 Paperback

Cambridge University Press & Assessment has no responsibility for the persistence or accuracy of URLs for external or third-party internet websites referred to in this publication and does not guarantee that any content on such websites is, or will remain, accurate or appropriate.

For
Adanna and Damilare Bello, One Union, Blessed Future
and
Kaosarat and Ibrahim Odugbemi, May Allah's Blessing Be
Upon You.

CONTENTS

List of Figures		*page* ix
Notes on Language and Orthography		xiv
Preface		xv
Acknowledgments		xviii

	PART I Introduction	1
1	Prologue: My Archive	3
2	Autoethnography and Epistemic Liberation	19
	PART II History, Fictions, and Factions	43
3	Narrative Politics and Cultural Ideologies	45
4	Memory, Magic, Myth, and Metaphor	70
5	A Poetological Narration of the Nation	99
6	A Poetological Narrative of the Self	125
7	Satire and Society	151
8	Narrative Politics and the Politics of Narrative	183
	PART III Visual Cultures	203
9	Sculpture as Archive	205
10	Textiles as Texts	282
11	Canvas and the Archiving of Ethnic Reality	327
12	Yorùbá Hair Art and the Agency of Women	373
13	Photography and Ethnography	414

	PART IV	**Conclusion**	451
14		Self, Collective, and Collection	453
		Bibliography	482
		Index	506

FIGURES

Unless otherwise stated, all images are either traditional works or the author's own photographs.

9.1	Acrobatic dancers	page 207
9.2	Egúngún Abale mask	208
9.3	Ọ̀rúnmìlà Baba Ifá	211
9.4	Homage to Ìyálọ́jà	214
9.5	Witchcraft mask I	215
9.6	Ọlọ́jọ́ festival mask I	216
9.7	Ọlọ́jọ́ festival mask II	217
9.8	Drummers mask	218
9.9	Egúngún mask	219
9.10	Fiber ware and mask	220
9.11	Metal mask	221
9.12	Wooden mask	221
9.13	Witchcraft mask II	222
9.14	Èṣù Ologo	222
9.15	Èṣù Oníkóndó	223
9.16	Èṣù Rogodo	224
9.17	Èṣù Mẹta I	225
9.18	Èṣù Ẹlẹ́gbárá I	226
9.19	Èṣù Mẹta II	227
9.20	Èṣù Láàlú Ògiri Òkò	228
9.21	Èṣù flautist	229
9.22	Ère Ìbejì	230
9.23	Odùduwà	231
9.24	Oṣé Ṣàngó	232
9.25	Ọya (wife of Ṣàngó)	233
9.26	Yemọja	234
9.27	Òṣun	235
9.28	Ògún	236
9.29	Ajere Ifá (Olúkòso)	237
9.30	Ajere Ifá (Olúmeye)	238

9.31	*Arugbá Ṣàngó*	239
9.32	*Ògún Lákáayé*	240
9.33	City drummers	241
9.34	*Fúrá* seller (contemporary art figure)	242
9.35	Contemporary art figure	243
9.36	Contemporary art figure	244
9.37	Mother and child motif	245
9.38	Motherhood abstract figure	246
9.39	Motherhood abstract figure	249
9.40	Motherhood abstract figure	249
9.41	Motherhood abstract figure	250
9.42	Ifẹ̀ head (wooden)	253
9.43	Terracotta head	254
9.44	Ifẹ̀ head (bronze)	254
9.45	Asante art	255
9.46	Contemporary art	256
9.47	Contemporary art	258
9.48	Beaded *Oṣé Ṣàngó*	258
9.49	*Kòríkòtò Òrìṣà Èwe* I	259
9.50	Homage	262
9.51	Contemporary art Ia	264
9.52	Contemporary art Ib	264
9.53	Contemporary art Ic	265
9.54	Contemporary art Id	266
9.55	Black warrior	267
9.56	Beaded crown (contemporary)	269
9.57	*Ifá* divination tray	271
9.58	*Èṣù Ẹlẹ́gbárá* II	272
9.59	*Jagunjagun (Ọbàtálá)*	273
9.60	*Arugbá Ṣàngó* I	275
9.61	Kneeling figure (contemporary)	276
9.62	*Arugbá Ṣàngó* II	277
9.63	*Ìyá Ìbejì* (mother of twins)	278
9.64	*Igbá Ọpẹ́*	279
9.65	*Kòríkòtò Òrìṣà Èwe* II	280
9.66	*Kòríkòtò Òrìṣà Èwe* III	280
9.67	*Onílù* (drummer)	281
10.1	*Dànṣíkí*	300
10.2	*Dànṣíkí*	301
10.3	*Agbádá*	302
10.4	*Bùbá* and *Ṣòkòtò*	302
10.5	*Agbádá* and *Fìlà*	303
10.6	*Agbádá Yẹbẹ* I	304

LIST OF FIGURES

10.7	*Agbádá Yẹbẹ* II	305
10.8	*Agbádá* (Five Knives)	306
10.9	*Bùbá/Ṣòkòtò/Fìlà* (Five Knives)	306
10.10	*Bùbá* and *Ṣòkòtò* type I	307
10.11	*Bùbá* and *Ṣòkòtò* type II	307
10.12	Short-sleeve *Dàṅṣíkí*	308
10.13	*Dàṅṣíkí* type (*Gbáriyè*)	308
10.14	*Ṣòkòtò Kẹ̀ńbẹ̀*	309
10.15	*Aṣọ ẹbí*	310
10.16	Hunter	311
10.17	Woman's clothing ensemble	312
10.18	*Yèye Falola*	312
10.19	Dress with beads on *Abetí ajá* (a type of *Fìlà*)	313
10.20	*Àdìrẹ* type I	318
10.21	*Àdìrẹ* type II	319
10.22	*Àdìrẹ* type III	319
10.23	*Àdìrẹ* type IV	320
10.24	*Àdìrẹ* type V	320
10.25	Various types of women's cloth	325
10.26	*Fìlà*	326
11.1	Path to the Town	332
11.2	Soweto	332
11.3	*Yemọja*	333
11.4	*Ọ̀sun* I	334
11.5	*Ọ̀sun* II	335
11.6	*Obìnrin omi*	336
11.7	*Ètùtù*	337
11.8	*Ìmúra*	337
11.9	Yèye Bisi Falola	338
11.10	Ọ̀jọ̀gbọ́n Toyin Falola	339
11.11	*Sisí Èkó*	343
11.12	*Iwin*	344
11.13	Isola Ológbojò	347
11.14	Dolapo Falola	348
11.15	*Ìmọ̀*	349
11.16	Ọ̀jọ̀gbọ́n Isola	350
11.17	Toyin Falola Jr.	352
11.18	*Agbékòyà*	355
11.19	*Èyò*	355
11.20	*Ògún* I	356
11.21	*Ọmọdé mẹta ń ṣ'iṣẹ́*	356
11.22	*Ọdún*	357
11.23	*Fúrá*	358

LIST OF FIGURES

11.24	Onílù	360
11.25	Ìdí Ìlẹ̀kẹ̀	362
11.26	Pópó Ibadan	363
11.27	Àdánwò	363
11.28	Ọjà Bódìjà	364
11.29	Olú Awo	365
11.30	Ṣàngó I	366
11.31	Ṣàngó II	367
11.32	Ọbàtálá	368
11.33	Ògún II	369
11.34	After market	372
12.1	Ońilé gogoro	375
12.2	Pàtẹ́wọ́ (modern Mohawk)	378
12.3	Ṣába (modern zip)	379
12.4	Korobá	380
12.5	Ṣùkú àdìmọ́lẹ̀	380
12.6	Ṣùkú ọlọ́gẹ̀dẹ̀	381
12.7	All-back	382
12.8	Dídì	382
12.9	Òjòkòpetí (modernized)	383
12.10	Pàtẹ́wọ́	387
12.11	Ṣùkú (Made with all-front)	387
12.12	Dídì (weaving) and Bíba (braiding)	388
12.13	Dídì (weaving with attachments)	388
12.14	All-back Obama patterned with modern Dídì	393
12.15	Basket weaving	393
12.16	Kóòmù/Ìyarun (comb)	396
12.17	The process of hair making	396
12.18	Hair-making process	397
12.19	Kíkó with black thread	397
12.20	Kíkó with black ribbon	398
12.21	Kòlẹ́sẹ̀	399
12.22	Doughnut (Ṣùkú)	399
12.23	Modern knots	404
12.24	Kinky	404
12.25	Braided twist	405
12.26	Unmade hair	410
13.1	A drifter's consent	416
13.2	People in a celebratory mood	417
13.3	Showing consent through posture	418
13.4	(Native) wear and idealizing posture	418
13.5	Òṣun worshipers showing communality	420
13.6	Meat seller in an idealizing posture	421

13.7	Orange seller	422
13.8	Livelihood	422
13.9	Billboard and communicative power	423
13.10	Yorùbá market	428
13.11	Festivity and communal spirit	433
13.12	Township	433
13.13	Photo of township commemorating time	434
13.14	Celebratory gestures	435
13.15	Gestures and cultural symbolism	435
13.16	"A day at the office" manning the gates of the rich	436
13.17	Ibadan	437
13.18	Ibadan colonial architecture	437
13.19	Cocoa House	443
13.20	Màpó Hall	444
13.21	University of Ibadan entrance gate	445
13.22	Yorùbá colonial architecture (*Agboolé*)	446
13.23	Idealizing posture	447
13.24	Idealizing regalia and posture	448

NOTES ON LANGUAGE AND ORTHOGRAPHY

This book uses many Yorùbá words, explaining their meanings on the first mention, providing translations where necessary, and using them as key entry points to long analyses. As a tonal language, each syllable has a low, medium and high pitch, which affects the meanings of words. In recent orthography, sh has been replaced with a dot under the s (ṣ). Where dots are under e and o, they indicate shorter sounds. The overarching idea behind the design of orthography is the possibility of devising symbols (in this case, letters) to represent each significant sound of a language to ensure there is at least a one-to-one relation between sounds and the symbol that represents them – bearing in mind that humans started as speaking beings, and writing is a later development. Thus, to avoid the ambiguity resulting from the use of similar letters for different sounds of Yorùbá, particularly [ʃ, ɛ, ɔ] written as [ṣ, ẹ, ọ] and their relative: [s, e, o] written as [s, e, o]. Things become quickly complicated because there is a limited set of letters available in the Roman/Latin alphabet to be adopted. As a result, additional signs (technically, diacritics) above, below, beside, and before are being added to the alphabet. Meanwhile, convenience and familiarity are traded for esoteric symbols. From afar and to untrained eyes, [ṣ, ẹ, ọ] and [s, e, o] could be mistaken as being the same.

PREFACE

Decolonizing African Knowledge: Autoethnography and African Epistemologies demonstrates how autoethnography can enhance the study of Africa. Its fundamental features as a research tool provide channels to and for foregrounding and consolidating subaltern perspectives in the mainstream, that is, as central, especially outside the hegemony of Western methodologies and perspectives in the study of African cultures and knowledge forms. It also substantiates the work of African scholars decolonizing African knowledge and knowledge-producing centers by providing effective alternative strategies, methods, or methodologies.

The pervasiveness and absolute hegemony of the West and its philosophies in African countries – where a Western presence has become a metastatic cancer eating away at centuries-old traditions and the knowledge they hold – demands alternative, innovative, and sometimes far-reaching approaches to sustain African heritage and culture. The continuous Western infiltration, encroachment, and takeover of Africa, even after the institutions of slavery and colonialism have supposedly been halted, can be seen in the insurmountable presence and influence of Western capitalism and culture on the continent.

Western capitalism controls the direction and ethics of research, along with the knowledge, benefits, and profits gained from that research or the use to which such research and its findings are put. It provides the methodologies, principles, and philosophies that shape research on Africa. These allow research on Africa to be guided by Western modes and systems of thinking or rethinking phenomena, displacing them (African phenomena) outside of their natural, cultural scope. Sadly, Africa's position in the global matrix of power requires African researchers – whether Western trained or continental – to rely on these Western-derived methodologies and principles in their research engagement with African cultures. This perpetuates the conditions of coloniality that sustain the West's domineering presence in Africa. The condition of coloniality expresses itself in several ways and sustains several unequal equations or relational inequalities: it could be the objective researcher versus the voiceless African subject unable to shape the direction of discourse; the consideration of African culture as something only capable of producing data that researchers interpret from Eurocentric perspectives; the use of Western theories to examine African realities; or in claims of ethical concerns regarding researchers who also serve as subjects of research.

Knowledge fuels national progress and defines a nation's identity. The methods of producing such knowledge determine its relevance, uses, and outcomes. This makes it counterproductive to base the knowledge that defines Africa solely on outsiders' perspectives. Using Western concepts to generate knowledge about Africa can sabotage decolonial efforts because of their sometimes authoritarian, totalizing, and overly presumptuous conclusions about Africa, allowing for omissions, errors, sweeping generalizations, and provincial or prejudicial perspectives to form the foundation of African knowledge and knowledge about Africa. In this situation, that which is presented as African knowledge runs contrary to the realities, needs, and potential of African cultures.

Decolonizing African Knowledge: Autoethnography and African Epistemologies builds a connection between autoethnography and how Africa is and can be studied. The narratives it presents, which also foreground its argument, suggest that an insider's perspective can be merged with the rigor and principles of research to re-determine how African epistemologies are pushed to the center of global knowledge production. These perspectives can take any form, from autobiographical narratives to archived/archival and culturally relevant items. The book demonstrates that archival materials can serve as the basis for critical introspection on African culture. In doing this, individuality is expanded and retooled to reflect on the larger cultural framework.

This book presents an argument that cultural items, including sculptures, textiles, paintings, and photographs, can be transformed from archived materials into cultural vehicles, while also retaining their place as items within a personal collection. One implication of this book's argument on decolonizing African knowledge through autoethnography is that the experiences constituting an autobiography or life narrative can be reflected upon to critically interrogate the culture that shaped them. With the intent of emphasizing these experiences and the knowledge they represent as culturally significant, African epistemologies – serving as the bedrock of experiential knowledge – can be accentuated beyond the repressive allowances of Western-oriented research paradigms.

The book also serves as a litmus test for the decolonial power inherent in autoethnography, revealing how autoethnography can transform personal items into cultural vehicles, and how an archive can be approached, read, assessed, and accessed as a tool or prism for interrogating the larger culture. It focuses on Yorùbá culture, which also serves as an example of what autoethnography can do for Africa – its approach to Yorùbá culture, highlighting its knowledge forms and epistemic practices, without privileging Eurocentric perspectives at the ideological level or at the realm of the subject-object/research-researched dynamic. These encourage the centralizing of African knowledge and place it at the center of Africa and its knowledge matrix.

The conclusions, reached by merging personal experience with public knowledge while using the archive to reflect on aspects of folklore such as proverbs, hair making, sculpting, painting, singing, masquerading, festivals, burial ceremonies, and philosophical concepts and practices, reinforce the decoloniality of autoethnography. Through autoethnography, the personal learning of an archive is reworked into a tool for communal representation. This study critically blends personal and public realities, generic knowledge and private experience, the subjectivity of self-narratives and the objectivity of research, and academia's exclusivity and elitism with the accessibility of knowledge gained from folklore and pedagogical narratives. It recognizes that autoethnography is an essential tool that can emphasize and enhance African epistemologies, rivaling Eurocentric approaches while circumventing their faults.

Decolonizing African Knowledge: Autoethnography and African Epistemologies is different because it offers insights into the value of an insider's perspective, applied through any medium, when it is retooled into a critical paradigm in knowledge production or the understanding thereof. The approach it presents offers greater benefits in understanding African cultures than borrowing foreign paradigms or for an insider to rework these borrowed paradigms as templates for viewing their culture. It also takes readers on a journey that transforms personal reflection into communal inquiry, emphasizing both personal experience and belongings as parts of the public (communal) reality that defines them. The intersection of private and public knowledge in the book reveals that autoethnography can access an archive to examine a culture's foundational realities and knowledge base, emphasizing its ethos, thought system, epistemology, and philosophy in the process.

ACKNOWLEDGMENTS

My interest in knowledge decolonization dates back to the 1970s. During my university education, both at undergraduate and postgraduate levels, decolonization was the central theme. The challenge was how to replace the influence of the West on the curricular. Some regarded the adoption of Marxism as a decolonial project, treating Marx and his ideas as anti-Western. However, the real problem was how to draw from the indigenous in ideas, practices, and knowledge systems. The purpose of this book is to demonstrate that the indigenous is valuable if a systematic knowledge system can be undertaken.

To sustain various validations, conceptual and theoretical follow-up requires affirmation, additional work, and a search for new data. The validation work has been long, including my books on belief and spirituality as sources of epistemologies and various approaches to decolonize the academy. As "decoloniality" becomes a current trope, many concepts of the past, some dating back to those expounded on Negritude and Afrocentricity, were rescued and retooled for new understanding. This book also falls into this "rescue mission," but with a different approach: my lived realities merged with the life of the mind to undertake detailed research on the "Self" in the broader canvas of identity and people.

I wish to acknowledge the efforts of many scholars and friends who contributed to this work. For over a decade, Vik Bahl and I have discussed many of the ideas in this book. Some of them were even converted to verses as we looked for ways to focus them creatively. Members of the younger generation were also drawn into it to accomplish an interpretative framework. Notable among them are Tolulope Oke, Wale Ghazal, Ibrahim Odugbemi, Damilare Bello, and Kaosarat Aina. Hours of revisions could not have been possible without the hard work by Peter M. J. Gross and Adebukola Bassey. I would also like to thank, again, Damilare Bello of Duke University, who read the entire draft of this book and kept me sane through the difficult task of reducing the number of figures. Special thanks again to Tolulope Oke of the University of Bayreuth for his intelligent contributions to complicating the reading of the texts and stories, and for his generosity and kindness. In the final preparation of this manuscript for press, I must thank 'Tayo Keyede, my competent proofreader.

ACKNOWLEDGMENTS

The stories and objects that make this book possible are from diverse places and people. Thus, I am grateful to thousands of people for their work, creativity, stories, and ideas. From my introduction to wood carvings in the late 1950s to deeper engagements with paintings in my adult life, I have regarded objects in awe, precisely as I see wonders in words. Converting words and objects into "monographing" takes me back to moonlight stories in which humans and non-humans habit the intellectual space. I appreciate my three associates and friends in choices of objects: Z. Apata, a sculptor collector; Omo Lamidi Fakeye of Ilé Ifẹ̀, a prominent carver; and Moses Ogunleye, a first-rate artist. I am thankful to various institutions, notably my permanent base (the University of Texas at Austin), and various places where I delivered keynote addresses that supplied clarifications to many ideas in this book.

There is a unity of purpose in many African academies: the institutions are looking for the most effective way to achieve intellectual emancipation in order to empower their students to transform the continent. If this book helps to forward the quest for decolonization, the goal for which it was written has been more than fulfilled.

PART I

Introduction

1

Prologue: My Archive

As a collection, this archive is many things, a quality it demonstrates via its diverse manifestations. An archive as "schematics of self" can act as a "cognitive itinerary," providing insights into the formation of the self, the journey toward understanding the self within and without, and the methods of self-construction that involve navigating temporal, spatial, ideational, and ideological conduits toward establishing self-consciousness. An archive in this sense serves as a collection of items with representative power that speaks to the process of self-definition; it provides illumination on patterns of personal growth, which can be mapped for reexperiencing or interrogating the formation of the self, since the self is a progressive construct, continual in its self-redefinition. Manifesting in material form as a collection, the archive can disclose the interconnections between intellection as an activity or tool of self-construction, consciousness as a source of power, and choices or actions that define and individuate persons. An archive can also exist as a tribute to an individual's (intellectual) enterprise/industry; it can serve as a collection of materials that have past, present, and future significance, indicating touchstones that stand out in an enigmatic life, career, or that emphasize an ideology, idiosyncrasy, or proclivity. In this sense, the archive would be the material realization of a cognitive itinerary.

An archive's impact on liminal spaces, which human consciousness inhabits, is also pivotal to its significance as part of a matrix, a system. The human world is a composite system of relations where things, people, and events react to one another: each part works in tandem with the other to ensure effective functioning and the progress of nature and the species habituated within it. These relations afford human reality the luxury of continuity, even in the midst of ruptures and seeming discontinuities. An archive is part of this system, and there are myriad ways through which the archive can be conceived within this particular order. There are also several forms in which the archive can manifest that highlight this essence.

The archive's manner of composition also informs its value. As part of an organized system, the archive acts as signage, that is, as a systematic collection of signs with referents and significations. The significations can manifest in terms of any of the afore-listed realizations of the archive. Its referents can be specific moments or actions in human cultural history that are readable or can be historicized. Because the archive holds its constituents in a systemic relation, wherein the elements that comprise it interact systematically, reading, engaging, or exploring the archive yields knowledge that transposes it from "a mere assemblage of things" to "a complex system with an equally complex import." The transposition of an archive from a collection into a system is possible because of the complex levels of interaction within the archive itself or between the archive and the world external to it – the world within which it finds or achieves (greater) meaning. The nature of this interaction is based on the kind of knowledge the archive yields and also the kind of consciousness that interacts with it. The insight it provides and the interaction it allows – for instance, how accessible is the archive to intrusive reasoning? – determines what knowledge is to be gained from it. Equally important is the knowledge gained from exploring the significance of its composition as a system and that of its constitutive elements as independent (mini)systems.

Not all collections are systems, even if systems are collections of several parts, items, materials, etc. An archive provides knowledge that is conditioned by the relationship between its parts and between the parts and the referents residing within the world external to it, since all readable items including art and textiles are texts in their own right, and since archives wield referentiality. The archive can narrate the process of its being, stressing its significance as a "meta-schematics" to itself; narrate that of the materials that comprise it; and also narrate the generative force behind its creation, which in this case is the self. Two things must be noted here: conception and continuity. An archive is a conception; here that means a knowledge-scape conceived at some point in time and in some space, even if its quality, texture, and nature as a system are continually redefined. This means an archive is not static, regardless of being defined in and by space and time. Another way to see the archive in this sense is as an engineered knowledge cosmos – although in material form – generated (by the self) in the process of experiencing knowledge and thus fated to continuity, insofar as the generative center (the self) that transforms experiential knowledge into material forms or binds both persists.

I should, however, point out here that these positions are not definitely defined or fixed in their manner of relation: archive as knowledge source/cosmos and the self as a generative center. These roles can be reversed, and indeed this mutability is what shapes the relation, since both the self and the archive are constantly in a symbiotic relation in foregrounding their relevance, essence, usefulness, and continuity. As said earlier, the archive provides insight to the constantly evolving self, while, as will be shown, the self, by virtue of aiding the engineering of the archive, contributes to its essence and continuity, serving as a source to the archive's persistence and continuity in and across time.

However, this state of perpetuity does not detract from the archive's organicity as a system or its ability to yield knowledge of itself to others, or of others to third parties. What I mean here is that as an organized system it does not shut out possibilities of historicization. It means the archive opens up to external queries, queries that would aid its definition and contribute to its essence. In fact, yielding itself to historicization and (re)contextualization marks the dynamics and fluidity of the archive. The archive is thus fluid and organic.

The archive's process of conception, its state of perpetuity, and its positionality with the world it textualizes all define it and the knowledge it provides. Archives textualize the material space because they co-shape the human perception of things. More so, archives as part of cultural forces condition human reception, relatedness, or perception of things or phenomena, especially if they (archives) are located or discovered outside of the temporality within which they have been composed, or if their constituent parts date differently. If an archive's immanent parts date differently, this system of difference defines and contributes to its organicity as well as its relevance to the material world. Therefore, the archive is a sum of its constituent parts; hence, it cannot be treated independently of them or, at least, the diversity that defines it. An archive can be underscored by several forms of diversity, and temporality is only one of such. But in the case where a systemic difference occurs, the knowledge it provides is a mixture of the implication of this constitutive difference and its effects on the contextual world. Therefore, the knowledge an archive provides is multileveled with multiple implications. It becomes a blueprint, readable and applicable to several issues, so far as they relate to the ideology behind the archive's conception, the ideology conceived of by the self that has created it.

What then is the archive? The answer is simple without being reductive and complex without being mysterious. The archive is a narrative. To appreciate the archive as a source of information, it is vital to see the archive as a system-in-narration. The various manifestations of the archive all yield patterns that tell a story. The knowledge extracted from an archive after due exploration by a probing mind is a consequence of seeing patterns within these patterns. These patterns have corresponding referents in the outside world, which allows a logical interaction between the probing mind (third party) and the archive. This is possible because as a system and as a narrative the archive has an organizing principle, a nucleus to its circumference, a generative center that holds it together and transforms knowledge into experience and vice versa, an intelligence constituted in much the same way that the human as a living narrative has a nucleus, an intelligence that holds its parts in harmony. The interaction of the two nuclei (that of the archive and that of the probing mind as a living narrative) allows for exchanges that advance the transfer of knowledge. This knowledge can come from the probing mind relating parts of the archive to existing referents in the human world or worlds beyond it, or engaging the intelligence that has organized the archive, which can be within or without the archive.

The intelligence of the archive can exist outside it, but still be felt within it as its generative source, where it performs the function of a marshal, commandeering its various parts for cohesion and unity. The intelligence within the archive would, in this case, be a trace of the overarching intelligence, a sort of microcosmic force, which can be anything from the self, a cosmic intelligence, a super-computer, or any consciousness external to the archive, to cite a few possibilities. What I am essentially saying here is that the self that serves as the source of the archive, engineering it into a possibility, leaves a trace of itself within it, one organic to its composition. Therefore, the archive and everything about it can represent the self: its organicity, constituents, the patterns that define it, the implications of its internal relations, and its extratextual connotations. All these can inform on the inner landscape of the intelligence (self) that has created the archive, especially since archives wield referential power.

The archive therefore is a metaphor of the self. Its ability to represent the self and the processes of its definition underscores it as a narrative. An interpretive engagement with the archive leads to exploring the cognitive landscape of the self, as if the self were responding to an investigative force. In the case where the archive represents and narrates the self, it would be acting in the capacity of a trace of the self. Although the archive is a narrative, it is not the self, but a trace of the self. Being a trace, the archive leaves room for the narration of the self without being the self. The archive thus is a useful tool for connecting culture and self, private experiences and common knowledge, or introspection, cultural epistemologies, and personal perspectives – everything that defines the self as a sociocultural being. It tells a story of the self as it relates, works with, affects, or is affected by the larger culture. These qualities of the archive have defined its importance, particularly to me and my consideration of African knowledge forms and their place in the global world. As I entered the last phase of my academic career and began to ponder how best to use my remaining limited number of years, the possibilities the archive offers encouraged me to settle more for introspective work. The possibilities are vital to the introspective angle from which I approach the idea of bridging personal experience and cultural knowledge for revisiting African epistemologies.

Over the decades I have acquired tremendous experience as a scholar and researcher, teacher, and mentor, and I have equally served as a policy formulator and public intellectual. As I began to think of how best to cumulate the diversity of knowledge and experience into a set of writings, my mind became restless. I had already written two memoirs and was planning the third. I agonized on how to structure an interrogation of myself as archive in order to arrive at originality and value. I settled for two interrelated bodies of ideas and objects – the accumulation of my creative/literary and academic work as one part; and the cumulation of my extensive collections of sculptures, textiles, and paintings as the second. Both parts are archives that are both external and internal to me, an entry into an expansive library. Both have taken a lifetime to collect. The two archives speak to the African societies from which they emerge and to which they are addressed. Both reveal the path of history and all of its contradictions.

I am part of the contradictions, of growing up in colonial and postcolonial Nigeria. The visual objects speak to the contradictions of modernity. The literary works capture the anger and displeasure of modernity. In light of the foregoing, I consider my archive a narrative, a system-in-narration, a composition of patterns that tells a story, expressing all the afore-discussed possibilities. Comprising materials that hold value for me, it advances a theory that centers my lived approach toward decolonizing African cultural practices and knowledge form. The archive thus offers a narrative that not only textualizes this philosophy but also stresses my aesthetic choices in relation with my knowledge of the world and my cognitive itinerary in connection to my position within an epistemic space whose cultural vehicles continue to intimate me and to which I respond appropriately. The accounts this archive provides emphasize my position as a knowledge-scape; they present me as a matrix of possibility generating several layers of knowledge that find traction within a world outside of me.

This archive is thus an extension of me as a consciousness. In exhibiting cultural and personal significance, they advance a narrative of me and the experiences I have gathered over the years as the "intelligence" capable of organizing different elements into a system and an "organizing principle" generating patterns that cast private materials as cultural vehicles. This is buttressed by the fact that readers and viewers can respond to this archive, (re)negotiating the meaning of its composition as I have organized them and their knowledge of it as they have received it. This way, they create personal responses that interact with me as the "trace" within the archive, validating the evocative responses of an archive. This evocation is both of self and of culture.

Decolonizing African Knowledge: Autoethnography and African Epistemologies is, therefore, a product of ongoing interaction between me and the world, and between intelligence (self) and an archive as a collected system. I use my collection organized into an archive to explore personal and public perspectives in relation to the Yorùbá and the African world. This is the function of an archive, and mine is not different. The archive's revelatory power or connotative possibilities are revealed when the intelligence that organizes it engages it. Probing it for knowledge reveals several layers of connection between the self and the archive: there is, for instance, the layer of industry, where the archival or ethnographic effort is made manifest; the layer of epistemic significance, which relates how the archive serves as a cultural vehicle revealing cultural histories; and the layer of self-representation, which is the layer of the "cognitive itinerary" where the archive traces and embodies the self, symbolizing strategic intellectual effort toward the (re)definition of consciousness. The connotative possibilities of an archive can be the subject of debate since they can take several forms. But what is implicated when the archive is engaged by the intelligence that organized it, while it is also expected to speak to the larger cultural firmament within which both self and archive are positioned? One simple answer is that the archive operates on a dual level. The archive is a complex system with an equally complex import. While this rationale is straightforward, it does not answer the question of what happens when the archive is engaged by the intelligence that has created it and is responsible for its organicity. What is the result of my metacognition of my own archive?

A useful answer, which sets the tone for the chapters in this work and reveals the overriding premise, is that the archive as a trace of self not only narrates the self, but also reveals how the archive (as a network) intimates to the intelligence that has created it. What this means is that the archive, as a network with cultural and historical significance, demonstrates the intelligence that has created it as a matrix of possibility. The intelligence not only lives on in the archive, as a trace, but is projected as drawing cultural networks into close proximity through diverse cultural vehicles (that make the archive) in order to establish a convergent zone. This zone is the intersection between the self and culture; the self as an organizing principle and the created archive as an expression of this principle as well as a cultural vehicle and a source of knowledge in its own right; the archive as a narrative of the self and of culture; the archive as a trace of the self and a network of interacting cultural elements. Also, within this convergent zone (made possible by the archive as a trace of self and a network of cultural vehicles) is the intersection between conclusions of general scholarship and those of personal observation; general aesthetics or aesthetic appeal and personal knowledge of the archive's (and its parts') symbolism; and the intersection between what is intimate to the self and how it draws the culture into this private world of intimacy.

An instructive summary of this zone is that it creates room for the collusion of what is known to all and what is known to the self. This condition is brought about by two important things: the archive comprising personal materials that also are cultural vehicles; and the intelligence (self) also being the organizing principle, that is, the generating center of the archive, as well as the critical voice interrogating the archive. In other words, if the intelligence that serves as the powerhouse of the archive interrogates the archive, a trace of the self, the intelligence interrogates itself. Doing so, it emphasizes itself as a matrix of possibility or a knowledge source. Engaging the archive to establish the convergent zone depicts the self as an archive, while the endeavor becomes autoethnographic. The self is essentially an archive demonstrating its ability to generate another archive with personal and public significance. These are bounded by the merging of personal and public realms, which allow for personal and communal import.

PROLOGUE: MY ARCHIVE

The philosophy behind the book, to put it simply, adapts a familiar English expression: show me your books, show me your clothes, show me the art in your home, and I will show you who you are. This is possible because the self is a miniature of culture. Questions of "why" and "to what purpose" that address the self (and also implicate the culture) can be quickly answered by engaging the materials collected into an archive. A double channel of knowing is created: the self and the culture. The intelligence enters both simultaneously to establish a connection between the self as a generative center and the culture as the knowledge source, and vice versa, since the self can also serve as a source of knowledge and culture, a generative zone. In establishing this connection, experience is transformed into knowledge, personal items into cultural vehicles, and personal knowledge into public and vice versa.

Each chapter in this book operates on this principle. I demonstrate how personal objects as cultural vehicles tell my cultural history even as they intersect other histories. The chapters are autoethnographic because their premises are rooted in the convergent zone whence they observe the world and emphasize my position within it. Using my archive with its traces of the self to engage the world and its knowledge and to foreground African epistemologies allows me to demonstrate how autoethnographic approaches can transform experience into knowledge and derive from the convergent zone. To reveal this, the book is divided into two sections. Each focuses on a particular archive: the first section (Part II) contains six chapters that interrogate African culture through memoirs, existing scholarly works, and creative literature. The chapters approach the convergent zone by using personal narratives to explore African culture for a broader sociocultural significance. The second segment (Part III) differs slightly in its approach even though the premise remains the same. With five chapters focused on various archival materials – textiles, paintings, hair, sculpture, and photographs – the place of the archive as a trace of self is accentuated.

The larger context in the two archival categories that form the second part of this book confronts the Western encounters with Africa as well as two imposed competing models of development: capitalism and socialism. The encounters and models changed Africa, sometimes for good, sometimes for bad. As I am part of the changes, I had to document them, in minor and major tales, thereby constituting the primary archives of specific moments, as in the peasant rebellion of the 1960s captured in *Counting the Tiger's Teeth*. While each chapter focuses on a separate archive, this strategy gives the book an opportunity to closely examine the place of Africa and its cultures within a changing social climate initiated by Western capitalist forces from several perspectives toward generating useful and holistic conclusions.

Not only have we as a people had to accept many imposed cultures, we also had to rebel against them and their life-altering influences. I was part of both responses. But the tools of studying our experiences – the libraries, protocols, and ideas – were also foreign and largely imposed. I experienced this as well as part of my education system in Nigeria, from the elementary to the University of Ife where I acquired two degrees. Since the 1960s the humanities and social sciences have changed with the times, from a "dark continent" paradigm, to modernization theories, to Marxism, and to the current market-controlled liberal scholarship and so-called democracy. Thus, I have to accept and challenge epistemologies, and, as this book argues, make a case for alternative ways of thinking. If there is a core theme that this book demonstrates, it is to reinforce alternative ways of thinking based on African indigenous ways of knowing. This book provides a convergent zone, where alternative ways of thinking can materialize or be shaped to purpose.

From the introduction is revealed how autoethnography reinforces and is a product of this convergent zone. The subsequent chapters focus on several archival materials – autobiographies and essays, textiles, sculptures, paintings, photographs, and hair – to explore several aspects of the Yorùbá and African reality; and in their treatment of these subjects is reflected the strength of autoethnography in returning agency to African cultures, even if it investigates or researches it. The intricacy of this convergent zone is laid bare as each chapter implicates its decolonial leanings from several perspectives. The strength of autoethnography – in reestablishing/buttressing African epistemologies, foregrounding the transformation of experience in knowledge, and reinforcing the connection between the self, the archive, and the culture – is established from the book's introduction to its conclusion.

This book cannot be confined to one discipline. It is a work of History as of Philosophy; it is grounded in ideas associated with gods and goddesses as well as in sheer literary imagination. The book enhances the value of proverbs to the same pedestal as those of books. As the chapters range from folklore to academic work, they expand understandings around the limitations of disciplinary boundaries. While the book captures events in some chapters, it is not about these events but about the ideologies and epistemologies surrounding them. While the book references stories and tales, it is less about them than about meta-narratives and meta-theories, revealing the mega-ideas that shape societies. And those theories are largely non-Western, widely used in African communities as they draw from language and lifestyles. There is a major focus in this book on cultures, even when they speak to social hierarchies, modernity, ethnicity, and nationality.

There is cultural nationalism in basing the archives on the Yorùbá experience. Without a deep understanding of culturalism, the core of African indigenous knowledge systems would be lost. As deployed in this book, there is one advantage to culturalism: it reduces generalizations around Africa, thus offering challenges to some of my formulations as African culture becomes located in different people and places. There is yet one other advantage: one cannot be led astray, as an insider, by the failure to understand what one addresses.

Decolonizing African Knowledge: Autoethnography and African Epistemologies provides decolonial direction through the Yorùbá example. And this is very significant as there is not one single way to put decoloniality to work as a tool of decentralizing and distribution of agency. Its focus is on the Yorùbá space, past and present, and has implications on how Yorùbá epistemologies are presented and received, now and in the future. It also has implications for how the culture is studied as autonomous and historical, and as reflective of obtainable realities in Africa as a continent, without attempting to account for all of it. The connection between autoethnography and how Africa is studied is the thread that holds together the several levels of analyses and layers of meaning in the book. Autoethnography is an alternative and counter-hegemonic instrument and is useful to the African who has been branded the alternative to a Western standard; hence, it enhances the visibility of those branded as subaltern persons, centralizing their culture, institutions, and epistemic possessions away from Western hegemony. It draws attention to the importance of the rapport between individuality and communality, and how one affects the other. By doing this, it gains the cultural value it needs to be an evocative tool of decoloniality. As demonstrated in the chapters that make *Decolonizing African Knowledge: Autoethnography and African Epistemologies*, autoethnography rebrands the archive as a cultural vehicle to achieve cultural relevance since the archive returns the spotlight and value to African epistemologies.

OUTLINE OF THE BOOK

Part I: Introduction

Chapter 2: Autoethnography and Epistemic Liberation

This introductory chapter addresses the idea of autoethnography, examining its reliance on the objectivity of research and the subjectivity of autobiographical works in ethnographic efforts. It argues for the use and importance of autoethnography when researching indigenous epistemologies, drawing attention to autoethnography's relevance for decolonial studies. The discussion focuses on what autoethnography is, the arguments against it, the benefits, and ethnography's relation to existing research methodologies and patterns, particularly within countries located at the margins of global power. In its conceptual exploration of autoethnography as a research mode, the introduction argues for the book's approach toward centralizing African epistemologies. It also draws links between the theses of the chapters and the idea of autoethnography.

Part II: History, Fictions, and Factions

This book is an archival meta-narrative that reflects on my corpus as an ideological afterthought, considering the scope and concerns of my engagement with art and life as expressed in my writings, dealings, and experiences. The first part of this book focuses on the literary and historical dimensions of my textual narratives, highlighting the deep-seated ideologies within them. The recurring theme in this section is the *telos* present in textual narratives, regarded as "narrative politics" in different parts of the chapters.

The third chapter, "Narrative Politics and Cultural Ideologies," delves into the functional prism of a narrative by using *A Mouth Sweeter than Salt* as an ethno-autobiographical embodiment of cultural ideologies. By locating the personal within the communal, the memoir attempts a master narrative that can be described as narrative frames embedded in varying cultures, often unconsciously, to provide a culturally accepted communal guide for being a "good" member of that culture. The chapter investigates how the memoir contributes to the production of collective memory, providing a complementary–alternative approach to navigating the cluster of the past and the people, similar to myth, religion, literature, and history. Although *A Mouth Sweeter than Salt* is a negotiation and interpretation of my sociocultural beliefs, and my experiences in relation to my past, this chapter is a metanarrative that carefully guides readers through the reconstruction of the narrative's fragments of cultural ideologies – some of which might not be perceived by even the keenest of readers.

"Memory, Magic, Myth, and Metaphor" is an intersectional evaluation of the narrativity of memory and memory as a narrative. It also examines the purgatorial and historical dimensions of memory: "a walk on the fragile fragments of my memory." As in the previous chapter, this chapter extends the counter-alternative approach of narratives to past and culture, examining *Counting the Tiger's Teeth* as a viable cultural manifestation and sociohistorical documentation. It identifies the focalization of the *Ogun Àgbẹ̀kòyà* narrative, from personal and communal perspectives, as a representation of the absurd reality characterizing immediate postcolonial Nigeria; the country struggled to transition into modernity, and these struggles are sustained in the metaphors and symbols employed by the narrative. Surpassing a mere invocation of memory, this chapter establishes the narrative as a restitution of the past.

The next two chapters, "A Poetological Narration of the Nation" and "A Poetological Narration of the Self," examine the expression and manifestations of "self" and "nation" across different bodies of poetry. The concepts of "self" and "nation," as designated in these poetological narrations, may seem oppositional and discontinuous. However, there is an overlapping relation between the two concepts. The discussion in "A Poetological Narration of the Nation" is grounded in the idea that poetry, as a national narrative, and especially in postcolonial Africa, is an aggregate of sociocultural, political, and economic realities within a nation. The poet has a duty and desire to fulfill this sociocultural responsibility. As national narratives, the poems that this chapter engages with are characterized by significant embodiment and representations of society, including the diasporic as part of a nation. The chapter situates and equates the relevance and representation of African women within larger discourses of nation, nationality, nationalism, and nation building. It examines the conscious and unconscious functions of poetry in a nation's narration by examining the history, beliefs, and culture of a group of people with a shared sense of belonging.

"A Poetological Narration of the Self" pursues universalist-cum-collectivist interpretations of selected poems, extending and refracting from the personal and collective "self" respectively, as thorough invocations of emotions for understanding and creating an image of the self. The distillation of the emotions and thoughts provoked by the poem are re-recollected in this chapter. Through the prism of the universal self, the chapter highlights how emotions are quintessential to the survival of humanity and the universe in its entirety. Love, fear, despair, joy, disillusionment, and hope are portrayed as basic components of the human consciousness in understanding the self, the other, and the world. The discourse in this chapter highlights the poetological narrative of the self as a quest to sketch an identity and understanding of the self, established as the agency of consciousness prompting the existence of the self and others. This obtains a new, extended, and profound understanding of the self.

Chapter 7, "Satire and Society," explores the critical undertones of *A Mouth Sweeter than Salt* and *Counting the Tiger's Teeth* as reflective and refractive narratives commenting on society to encourage positive change. The chapter analyzes one of several narrative dimensions, engaging them as satire to reveal different vices that are latent in the society described by the memoirs – these flaws existed in the past but remain rampant in the present day. The societal ills include sociocultural follies, religious excesses, political menace, and environmental degradation. Their consequences, ranging from personal and previous shortcomings to present and collective vices, generate forces that push society away from development and morality. The environmental menace created by greed, recklessness, and careless acts continues to weaken nature's capacity to support life and human existence. These narratives ridicule the recounted shortcomings against this backdrop of deterioration and existing sociocultural standards in the hope of restoring proper civic conduct and fostering desired development.

The last chapter, "Narrative Politics and the Politics of Narrative," provides closure for the overarching frame of the book's first section. It shifts from literary narratives to several other textual narratives focused on society's history, sociopolitics, and cultural and economic reality. It describes the central aim of every narrative as the intent to persuade and achieve a desirable future for society, positioning them as conscious agents of human and societal development. This chapter establishes narratives as important and essential mechanisms through which humans order and stabilize reality as the constructs of their conscience and consciousness. It identifies relevant and common preoccupations across different narratives that span decades, presenting an overview of the politics of narrative. For example, *Narrating Violence in Nigeria* navigates the religious and political dimensions of violence, considering how it has impaired or enhanced Nigeria's development. It not only historicizes and intellectualizes discourse; it also provides the rationale for studying its causes, identifying its symptoms, highlighting its consequences, and proffering pragmatic solutions to harmonize and advance society.

Part III: Visual Cultures

This part uses archived images to argue for autoethnography in relation to African epistemologies. These chapters present another angle to autoethnography, allowing material collections to serve as cultural vehicles. This establishes a convergent zone between several concepts: self and culture; personal library, ethnographic work, and cultural knowledge; experiential and public knowledge; private and public realms; knowledge evoked from cultural materials and sourced from existing literature; and items belonging to public and personal archives. It also probes the space between that which is known to all and knowledge gained from observation.

Chapter 9, "Sculpture as an Archive," interrogates Yorùbá sculptural tradition using sculptures and carvings from my archive. It deploys the carvings as prisms through which several aspects of Yorùbá history and culture can be examined for extensive illumination. This chapter establishes that cultural items can be used to investigate a culture without undue subjectivity; also implied in the chapter is an unstated argument that using sculpture to address aspects of Yorùbá reality – by merging personal observation, experiential and academic knowledge, public/cultural knowledge, and perspectives from existing literature – is an effective strategy that applies autoethnography to oppose hegemonic, Eurocentric narratives of Yorùbá reality.

The chapter deploys sculpture to address not only Yorùbá reality but also scholarship on Yorùbá (and African) art, which foregrounds the function of sculptures as archival materials with cultural significance. It also addresses issues of the linguistic turn, authorship, and religious significance through the advocacy for, focus on, and use of Yorùbá epistemic concepts to appreciate the artistry and significance of sculptures. To properly engage sculptures as repositories of cultural knowledge, epistemic concepts and philosophical principles of indigenous tradition must be applied. The chapter buttresses this thesis by locating oversights caused by outsiders' perspectives within an insider–outsider dialectic, emphasizing its influence on the study of Yorùbá sculpture.

By identifying sculpted materials as tools for performing a critical appraisal of Yorùbá history, economics, politics, and artistic industry, Chapter 9 explores the methodologies of understanding, ideologies contained in, and epistemologies sustained by Yorùbá sculptures and sculptural tradition. The chapter discusses the idea of sculptures as agents of socioconsciousness, repositories of knowledge, cultural codes, and reflectors of Yorùbá spirituality, philosophy, and religion.

"Textiles as Texts," the following chapter, engages textiles as readable materials. It argues that Yorùbá textiles and sartorial tradition reflect the history, sociocultural economies, politics, and spiritualities of their culture. The presentation of textiles as text makes an argument for certain knowledge practices that define textiles as systems, especially ones that accommodate other mini-systems. These practices present a rich history of Yorùbá clothing, debating and correcting European misconceptions of Yorùbá garment origins and their dress tradition. This chapter also presents the Yorùbá cloth-weaver as a creator who allows intimate cultural values, as well as the configurations and ethos of society, to reflect through their created work.

Approaching textiles as text provides avenues for exploring their textuality, especially in their reflection of African epistemologies. In exploring the components of Yorùbá textiles, the chapter extracts the meanings invested in them, which have cultural and historical significance. These meanings retain, safeguard, and foreground histories that are an alternative to those created by Eurocentric scholarship. The readability of the texts is emphasized by the way that they reflect realities, philosophical concepts, and social codes when held in visual dialogue.

Chapter 10 reinforces the place of Yorùbá and African sartorial influences on Western designers, using different cloth types as primary data, and it reconsiders the European entry into the African cloth market. It also reexplores the theory that Africa has perpetually drawn creative influences from the West; this assumption is negated through a counter-narrative establishing how Yorùbá cloth types, tastes, and an established sartorial industry existed before European contact, influencing designers who sought to break into the African cloth market.

This chapter also emphasizes the readability of textiles by highlighting associations between different cloth types and existing cultural principles and folkloric practices. It not only imparts an understanding of a rich sartorial culture where clothes have designated functions and values, but it also explains how Yorùbá dresses serve as indexes that point to different junctures in time and space, as well as visions or ideas that have persisted throughout Yorùbá cultural history. Textiles embody cultural concepts and philosophies, reflecting cultural adherence or disobedience.

Chapter 11, "Canvas and the Archiving of Ethnic Reality," interrogates the rapport between Yorùbá painting and spirituality, cultural order and principles, and artistic practices. It provides a conceptual understanding of the canvas as a blank space upon which the collective Yorùbá unconscious is inscribed with brush strokes and vivid colors, tracing the functionality of Yorùbá art in a cyclical process of inspiration between the painter, the culture, and the artwork. The complementarity between Yorùbá painting and culture addresses how fundamental epistemic and philosophical concepts are realized in paintings. For example, Ọ̀nà (crossroad) in Yorùbá painting exists as an artistic expression and a culturally loaded concept related to epistemic concepts such as Ìpín (lot), Àyànmọ́ (destiny), and Kádàrá (fate), affecting how they are realized on the canvas with culturally coded patterns or symbols.

Examining painting as visual rhetoric provides channels for exploring its place and its networks in Yorùbá culture – it is a contrast to the exhibitive dynamics within which visual artwork exists in the West. Addressing these networks identifies the close-knit, dynamic interaction between Yorùbá culture and its artistic practices. In Yorùbá culture the mediumship of painting galvanizes the creation of networks for artistic patronage, which develop differently from those in the West. This chapter explores the importance of "the network of placement" for understanding patronage, and painting exhibition in Yorùbá culture.

Paintings are idealizing frames in Yorùbá culture; this chapter explores how paintings condition human behavior and succeed at redefining the ambassadorial qualities that the culture endorses. These engagements are supported by the link between the aesthetic qualities inherent in Yorùbá painting and their cultural values. The chapter engages the intelligibility that characterizes Yorùbá painting as visual rhetoric by examining cultural concepts and realities such as aesthetic of the cool, Orí (head/destiny), Àṣẹ (generative power), and communalism and kinship systems (Ẹbí, Ará, Mọlẹ́bí), using the archival images as examples. The examination is enriched by Yorùbá folklore, including proverbs, maxims, songs, and spirituality. Images from the archive support the exploration and allow the chapter to trace the circle that binds painting, painter, and culture together.

The subsequent chapter, "Yorùbá Hair Art and the Agency of Women," explores hair as art, power, and symbol. Focusing on women's hair, it addresses the hair's synedochical power, expressivity, and cultural symbolism. It also examines hair's metaphysical connotations in Yorùbá ontology and cosmology while addressing its proximity to Yorùbá spirituality. Yorùbá women are placed within this discourse, and the chapter discusses how the art of styling hair affects social perception, representation, and cultural expectations of women and the female identity. The art of the coiffeur in Yorùbá culture is a dedicated performance of identity; it narrates, instructs, educates, and holds people in visual dialogues.

Chapter 12 interrogates the styling of women's hair as an avenue for power shifts between the sexes as well as between the female subject and members of society. The workplace of the coiffeuse is a performative space where transformational power is exhibited – in the Yorùbá social sphere this is a fecund space for female solidarity, expressions of femininity, cultural pedagogy and reorientation, and a place to ventilate and learn as well as a space for excising mutually felt forms of oppression. It is germane to the structure of Yorùbá society as a space of both conformity and nonconformity, reaffirming orality and the efficacy of folkloric elements such as proverbs, songs, and panegyrics for cultural progress.

By focusing on the workplace of the *Onídìrí* (hairstylist) as a unit in the Yorùbá social sphere, the chapter considers the self-reflexivity and referential power of women's hair. Aside from foregrounding the symbolism of Yorùbá hairstyles and how they reveal accepted expressions of femininity, or their transgression, it also demonstrates how hair is an expression of self-fashioning for the Yorùbá woman. The chapter employs Yorùbá epistemic concepts to evaluate the function of women's hairstyles and their place in Yorùbá ontology and the culture's social space. It explains how these hairstyles reveal several Yorùbá philosophies on beauty, moderation, aestheticism, behavior, extravagance, artistry, tradition, authorship, civility, anti-aesthetics, and creation and rebirth, among others. The chapter also traces connections between Yorùbá hair and cultural beliefs on destiny, deity worship, and visual engagement or the act of seeing and being seen in Yorùbá culture. By evaluating women's hair as art, the chapter applies aesthetic principles associated with Yorùbá art, relying on images from the archive.

Chapter 13, "Photography and Ethnography," traces the connections between photography as a tool, an activity, and a producer of knowledge and culture. It reflects on the nature of photographs, especially in relation to African culture, its people, and black skin in general by engaging with photography as a colonial tool and activity, along with several photographs that provide physical representations of the camera's power. Aspects of photography are significant as processes and activities for encoding knowledge, and although they are nonmaterial they are integral to the way that photographic images and tools are received and used. The chapter also focuses on how racial politics, cultural practices, and knowledge – whether an insider's or an outsider's – influence perception of photographs and the impact of photographs on individuals.

This chapter traces the memory function of photographs, touching on the colonial imperatives sustained by cameras and the technology that aids their functionality. It also addresses the visibility and agency afforded by digital cameras, rescuing them from subaltern positions. It remains an open question whether digital cameras are completely autonomous from the colonial imperatives that are discoverable through the use and functionality of analog cameras. The gaze behind the digital camera, with its own cultural conditioning, controls what is produced. The camera lens that focuses on the subject is also conditioned by the human eye that directs it.

The chapter further addresses the possibilities that digital cameras offer to people as individuals, without sacrificing their position in a culture as members of a collective. It interrogates these possibilities because they do not erase the powerful relation between the camera lens and the human eye, despite the tools available to manipulate images during or after production. These explorations are carried out to foreground possibilities for the reception of photographs in a world where lenses, either human or machine, are conditioned by contextual knowledge.

Ultimately, this chapter explores how photographs can affect the remembrance of Yorùbá cultural history – the human eye that creates through the camera lens, or the eye that sees the finished product as a photograph, is a product of cultural conditioning. It examines photographs as major archives, exhuming history and establishing linkages. The discussions attempt to answer these questions: Do photographs represent certain sources of or advancements in knowledge? How are meaning and deduction, as aspects of seeing and gazing, implicated in, through, and by photographs? Do contextual realities extend the frame of photographs beyond that which is visible on the canvas? Images from the archive expand on this chapter's arguments.

Part IV: Conclusion

Chapter 14, "Self, Collective, and Collection," builds on the case made for autoethnography, concluding the thesis of the book by reflecting on the interconnection between the self, the collective culture, and the archive in the form of the collection. It presents the self as its own narrative, which can be understood via its actions, including the creation of an archive. It argues for a collection as a manifestation of cultural ideologies, especially in relation to the Yorùbá, who consider archives to be a means of defining selfhood. The chapter also makes arguments for the premises of the previous chapters by emphasizing their connection with the idea of autoethnography and their relation to one another, sustaining and reemphasizing African knowledge.

2

Autoethnography and Epistemic Liberation

"A nation's culture resides in the hearts and souls of its people."

-Gandhi

The relationship between knowledge and power is as old as civilization itself. Institutions support systems of knowledge that reinforce their power to rule.[1] The Pharaohs were central to the religion of ancient Egypt, and that religion reinforced their rule. Academia as a system is central to the power structure of the modern period – since the age of Enlightenment, it has become the center of knowledge that supports those who wield power in the global world. This originates, in part, from European colonization of the Global South, industrialization, and the projectile of (post)modernism. This historical process inflicted physical, economic, political, and institutional violence on colonized peoples.

The institutions that developed in the context of colonialism exist beyond liberation struggles and nation-state independence movements. They include global economic, political, and cultural patterns that disadvantage postcolonial nations, and these patterns represent the colonial matrix of power.[2] Knowledge is at the center of the colonial matrix of power. Western powers support academia as a system that maintains Eurocentricity.

Western universities are infused with colonial and Eurocentric perspectives. Their system of knowledge production, which originates from Enlightenment-era definitions of "knowledge," is the product of European epistemology. Globalization has spread this knowledge more widely as the standard and encouraged culturally inappropriate research. The Global South is estimated to produce less than 3 percent of academic articles published annually.[3] In Africa the percentage is only about 0.5 percent.[4] For instance, countries such as the

---

[1] Michel Foucault, *Power, Truth, Strategy* (Sydney: Feral Publications, 1979).
[2] Walter D. Mignolo, *The Darker Side of the Renaissance: Literacy, Territoriality, and Colonization* (Ann Arbor: University of Michigan Press, 1995).
[3] Peace A. Medie and Alice J. Kang, "Power, Knowledge and the Politics of Gender in the Global South," *European Journal of Politics and Gender* 1, no. 1–2 (2018): 37–53.
[4] Paul Zeleza and Garry Weare, *Rethinking Africa's Globalization*, vol. I: *The Intellectual Challenges* (Trenton: Africa World Press, 2003).

United States of America publish over 300,000 books every year. Postcolonial nations, such as El Salvador, Tanzania, and Oman, produce less than 500.[5] The social sciences have, arguably, the strongest cultural bias in research in psychology; 96 percent of studies are done on 12 percent of the world's population. Western, Educated, Industrialized, Rich, and Democratic (WEIRD) countries account for 12 percent of the population.[6] The term WEIRD acknowledges social sciences biases that stem from Eurocentric research. The global academic system amplifies WEIRD voices, drowning out the majority of the world.

Academia creates narratives that are represented as truth(s) through educational institutions. These narratives are the product of research. Research, as an academic activity, is implicated in a systemic process of "taking" data from subaltern cultures and "rebranding" them as Western. This academic culture was initiated by European modernity, which laid the groundwork for Western dominance. The ethics, procedures, and methods of this research produce narratives that favor the capitalist philosophies of the West. If these narratives are only created in Western nations, they do not represent a global truth. Western perspectives are influenced by economic and political motivations that perpetuate Eurocentric superiority and maintain the colonial matrix of power. These perspectives protect European self-identity – Western epistemology creates European frameworks for non-European issues.[7]

Women, minority groups, and the people of postcolonial nations have been made to represent what is called subaltern academia. This is not due to their population size, but to their lack of representation in academic literature. When studying the so-called subaltern, Western academics analyze research through the perspective of the West; they are unable to experience the perspective of this subaltern or create enough room for the subaltern's ascendance to power. This struggle for inclusion or independent representation within the matrix of power is what Denis Ekpo in his Post-Africanist[8] pursuit has totally condemned as self-deluding and obstructive to modernity, and which disregards the latent truth that Western ideologies and narratives of the

---

[5] Worldometers, "Book Statistics," New Book Titles Published. Accessed February 7, 2019, www.worldometers.info/books/.

[6] Joseph Henrich, Steven J. Heine, and Ara Norenzayan, "The Weirdest People in the World?" *Behavioral and Brain Sciences* 33 (2010): 61–135.

[7] Timothy Brennan, "Antonio Gramsci and Postcolonial Theory: 'Southernism,'" *Diaspora: A Journal of Transnational Studies* 10, no. 2 (2001): 143–187.

[8] See Denis Ekpo, "Towards a Post-Africanism: Contemporary African Thought and Postmodernism," *Textual Practice* 9, no. 1 (1995): 121–135; Denis Ekpo, "From Negritude to Post-Africanism," *Third Text* 24, no. 2 (2010): 177–187; Denis Ekpo, "Africa without Africanism: Post-Africanism vs Indigenous Knowledge Systems, Culture/Art," in *The Arts and Indigenous Knowledge Systems in a Modernized Africa*, ed. Rudi de Lange, Ingrid Stevens, Runette Kruger, and Mzo Sirayi (Newcastle upon Tyne: Cambridge Scholars Publishing, 2018), 1–28.

subaltern are forms of epistemic violence. They are so, for they are tangible forms of trauma inflicted on the ex-colonized when their story is told for them,[9] or are deliberately constructed and exploited by the West to fortify and maintain its place within the power matrix. However, his call for those forced into the category of the subaltern to literally prostrate before the purported Eurocentric ideologies to navigate modernity is itself more self-deluding. Kant defines human dignity, which separates humanity from animals, as the ability to reason. The subaltern's exclusion from academia denies these groups their membership in the genus of human beings.[10] It all adds up when we consider that one of the principal excuses behind the category of the "subaltern" used to describe and group ex-colonized cultures is the supposed lack of reasoning or the inability to think for themselves.

The solution to this is decoloniality: dismantling the colonial matrix of power. This is both a political and an epistemic process.[11] In academia, decoloniality requires the rejection of Eurocentric epistemologies and the acceptance of the Global South's epistemic perspectives. To reach epistemic liberation, subaltern academics must advocate for the legitimacy of subalternized epistemologies. Then they must put these epistemologies into practice. But these must first be preceded by a careful identification and rigorous conceptualization.

Epistemic liberation faces several challenges. Universities often respond to academic Eurocentricity by recruiting students from the Global South, and these students face a "sandwich problem." They internalize the Western epistemic perspective as truth and return home to view local problems through Western frameworks – they fail to integrate their education into their culture[12] and their culture into their education. This can create first- and second-order Eurocentrism. Finding ways to make research accessible to those in the Global South is also a challenge. Limiting factors include economics, politics, access to technology, and access to education. Bilingual papers may help make research more accessible to non-English speakers,[13] but this relies on Europeans to create the academic narrative and share it with the subaltern. Decoloniality advocates for the epistemic liberation of the subaltern. However, this literature

---

[9] Dennis Masaka, "The Prospects of Ending Epistemicide in Africa: Some Thoughts," *Journal of Black Studies* 49, no. 3 (2018): 284–301.
[10] Masaka, "The Prospects."
[11] Sabelo J. Ndlovu-Gatsheni, "Decoloniality as the Future of Africa: Decoloniality, Africa, Power, Knowledge, Being," *History Compass* 13, no. 10 (2015): 485–496.
[12] Birgit Brock-Utne, "Researching Language and Culture in Africa using an Autoethnographic Approach," *International Review of Education* 64, no. 6 (2018): 713–735.
[13] Yvonna S. Lincoln and Elsa M. González y González, "The Search for Emerging Decolonizing Methodologies in Qualitative Research: Further Strategies for Liberatory and Democratic Inquiry," *Qualitative Inquiry* 14, no. 5 (2008): 784–805.

is limited to the academic location of history or subaltern studies.[14] Subaltern academics still rely on publishing through Eurocentric epistemology for validation.

This chapter explores epistemology's role in the colonial matrix of power, specifically in relation to the field of ethnography. It deconstructs the researcher's role in ethnography, including the biases involved. It examines the merits of qualitative, narrative research and its congruence with indigenous epistemology. And it proposes the underutilized methodology of autoethnography as a tool for epistemic liberation. In doing so, it explores the epistemic foundations, criticism, and the decolonial value of autoethnography.

Defining Ethnography

Ethnography has its roots in nineteenth-century colonialism, when the study of non-Western cultures was fetishized as "orientalism" or understanding the ways of "backwardness,"[15] and the image and idea of Africa continues to be antithetically collapsed into an exotic and primitive frame. Ethnography provided ideological support for colonial efforts and the idea of the white man's burden. The Global South was perceived as helpless and hapless, so this Christ complex and "civilizing mission" attempted to convert its people to Christianity and teach them the ways of Western "civilization": the greatest deceit and irony of history, perhaps, was that the West had attempted to rescue the indigenous peoples it had endangered. Ethnography's foundational scholars were white men from the nineteenth and twentieth centuries, such as E. B. Tylor, Lewis H. Morgan, Franz Boas, and Bronislaw Malinowski. These scholars wrote about their extensive fieldwork in the Global South from the perspective of Western colonialism.

Malinowski established that his intent was to understand cultures from the perspective of the people he studied.[16] However, his research remains tainted by his assumptions that he studied people who were "backward," "less civilized," and "primordial." Researchers such as Alain Locke did not begin to explore the idea of cultural relativism until 1924. This concept began to deconstruct colonial terms, including "civilizing mission," to reveal their racist foundations. Cultural relativism in the social sciences marked a turn toward the acceptance of cultural and ideological differences.

The ideas of ethnography and cultural relativism have shaped the development of cultural anthropology. Although researchers in ethnography engage in extensive fieldwork studies to examine the perspective of the "other," they will

---

[14] Shome Raka and Radha S. Hegde, "Postcolonial Approaches to Communication: Charting the Terrain, Engaging the Intersections," *Communication Theory* 12, no. 3 (2002): 249–270.

[15] Edward W. Said, "Orientalism Reconsidered," *Race & Class* 27, no. 2 (1985): 1–15.

[16] Raymond Firth, ed., *Man and Culture: An Evaluation of the Work of Bronislaw Malinowski*, Malinowski Collected Works 10 (London: Routledge, 2002).

always be outsiders – they will never understand their subjects' perspective as if it were their own experience. This is seen in the mis- and underrepresentation of those epistemologies and their uniqueness as a cultural group.

Modern ethnography expands its scope beyond the study of the "other" to include academics researching their own cultures and the roles of culture in society. Modern ethnographers do not exclusively perform extensive fieldwork in foreign nations. They study various topics around culture, including human behavior, gender relations, minority relations, and societal patterns. An ethnographer was able to use data from traffic cameras to improve city parking communications.[17] The broad nature of ethnography translates to diversity in autoethnography, which explores not only the perspective of various cultures but also of subcultural groups.

The problematic nature of ethnography stems from Western academia's attempts to represent alternative cultures, to impose itself as the objective and universal viewpoint. Ethnography functions through the ethnographer's study of the "other," and all academic work is done through the identity of the researcher.[18] Ethnography is the intersection of two identities: the people studied and the self-identity of the researcher. The way that researchers view themselves, especially in relation to the subjects of their research, informs their analysis and conclusions. This identity is influenced by the transaction of gender, nationality, ethnicity, age, religion, self-image, and other factors. The neutrality of ethnography is a myth.

Many ethnographers correct for the biased nature of ethnography through a constructive approach where the researcher does not form theories prior to observation. The subject is handled in an exploratory manner, with the goal of collecting as much information as possible before evaluating it for patterns.[19] This approach creates less biased research, but it does not escape the researcher's identity that influences their perceptions. From start to finish, fieldwork ethnography is a result of the researcher's identity influencing the data.

Using the rainbow analogy: culture is similar to a rainbow that looks different depending on where the observer is standing. A person close to the rainbow will see a different shape and length than someone seeing it from far away, although they are viewing the same occurrence. Culture also appears differently depending on the position of the observer. An outsider's view of a culture may appear completely different from an insider's perspective.[20] The

---

[17] Ellen Isaacs, "Ethnography: Ellen Isaacs at TEDxBroadway," March 2013, TedxBroadway video, 12:02, www.youtube.com/watch?v=nV0jY5VgymI.

[18] Anthony Appiah, *The Ethics of Identity* (Princeton: Princeton University Press, 2005).

[19] Mayukh Dewan, "Understanding Ethnography: An 'Exotic' Ethnographer's Perspective," in *Asian Qualitative Research in Tourism*, ed. P. Mura and C. Khoo-Lattimore (Singapore: Springer, 2018), 185–203.

[20] Bruce LaBrack, "Disciplinary Approaches to Culture: Anthropology," in *The SAGE Encyclopedia of Intercultural Competence*, ed. Janet M. Bennett (Thousand Oaks, CA: Sage Publications, 2015), 245–248.

insider is not merely observing the culture and the patterns defining it, which connects to the premise of the research. Insider-researchers allow their identity as members to shape their approach to the observed phenomena.

Gary Alan Fine has focused his research on ethics and misrepresentations in ethnography. Fine asserts that ethnographic research must regulate the effect of the research on the community. This includes its effect on outsiders' perceptions of the community. Fine emphasizes the freedom that researchers have in ethnographic studies – their data is often paraphrased, and the ethnographer is vulnerable to myriad biases. In one representation of ethnographers Fine outlines the "candid" nature of their research: it is common practice for ethnographers to report narratives or data from events they did not witness. Much of the data is paraphrased or the result of hearsay or assumptions.

Another bias stems from the "chaste" nature of the ethnographers. When living in another culture, personal relationships influence data collection. They inevitably shape the community's perceptions of the researcher. Further bias results from the literary aspect of ethnographic research. Researchers can make their data as literary or factual as they like; the social nature of their research may lead them to exaggerate or include events and phrases that make the research more poetic.[21]

One distinction for ethnographers is whether they write realist or critical ethnography. Realist ethnography focuses on the researcher's view of reality from a neutral perspective. Critical ethnography focuses on minority or systematically oppressed groups, adopting a subaltern perspective. In this type of ethnography the researcher serves as a social advocate for underrepresented groups. The purpose of the research influences the conclusions of the ethnographer's fieldwork.

The attempts of Western researchers to perform realist ethnography on the "other" have resulted in the skewed literature of area studies. For example, Africana Studies should be focused on the perspective of the African diaspora, using African epistemic perspectives and advocating for contributions from African academics. However, its foundation rests on aid organizations, missionaries, and the imperial administrators of the nineteenth century. The field developed in Western universities, and African epistemic and philosophical perspectives did not enter the academic discussion until the 1980s. The field remains vulnerable to a desire for validation from Western academics; Eurocentric perspectives are still favored in publishing decisions.[22]

---

[21] Gary Alan Fine, "Ten Lies of Ethnography: Moral Dilemmas of Field Research," *Journal of Contemporary Ethnography* 22, no. 3 (1993): 267–294.

[22] Jeremiah O. Arowosegbe, "African Studies and the Bias of Eurocentricism," *Social Dynamics* 40, no. 2 (2014): 308–321.

Instead of confining African epistemology within a subsection of Africana Studies, every piece of knowledge produced within the field should take the African epistemic and philosophical perspective.[23] The only way to truly understand a culture or group of cultures is to analyze them from their own perspective. This chapter – and the entire book – is anchored on this premise. Chapters on textiles, painting, and women's hair, along with the memoirs, the poetry, and the photographs, all draw from this philosophy. Each chapter focuses on the Yorùbá people through representational materials.

The use of materials as touchstones is an approach to examine the onto-epistemology, worldview, folkloric practices, and life of the Yorùbá with an insider's critical perspective. The premises of these chapters converge at several ideological junctures, including the use of the indigenous perspective to explore the so-called subaltern reality. This approach complements the ethnographic approach on the one hand and, on the other, subverts the ethnographic misrepresentation that, as Fine argues, continues the unregulated effects of unethical research on the community.

When Yorùbá textiles – whose threads and fabrics are and can be read as metaphors of history or signifiers of cultural periods – are discussed as texts to explore and assert their readability, critical and realist ethnographic methods are combined. On the one hand, this approach channels historical and cultural materials for appropriate representation. On the other hand, it merges objective and personal perspectives for broader cultural representation. In reflecting on the Yorùbá textile industry and sartorial tradition, the sociocultural codes of belonging that define Yorùbá lives and culture are explored. The same concepts apply to the chapter on sculptural works, which allows for a broader appreciation of Yorùbá culture, epistemology, spirituality, and visual artistry revealed through the carvings. The Yorùbá people's collective consciousness is embodied and symbolized through the statuettes and effigies.

According to Ghandi, "A nation's culture lives in the hearts of its people." A responsible representation of culture must be made through the hearts and minds of the people studied. Autoethnography allows individuals to act as both researcher and subject, instead of restricting the researcher's role to that of an outsider. Autoethnographers have autonomy over their own story and what it represents for their culture. These chapters take this philosophy to a logical conclusion: the purpose of this endeavor is to critically and realistically explore an archive of memoirs, essays, artworks, photographs, textiles, and paintings to adequately represent a culture, merging existing conclusions with personal observation.

This exploration is possible because the researcher is part of a collective consciousness; their consciousness is an intelligence that can reflect and be

---

[23] Sureshi M. Jayawardene and Serie McDougal, "Francis Cress Welsing's Contributions to Africana Studies Epistemology," *Journal of Black Studies* 48, no. 1 (2017): 43–56.

reflected upon. The chapters herein unpack and creatively recombine the insider–outsider dichotomy of research, driven by the desire to serve as an interrogative voice that also casts illumination on itself and what it represents. The insider voice, besides being critical, is participatory. Through it, collective channels of thought and cultural wisdom that manifest through art forms such as canvas and sculpture can be duly appreciated and observed.

The Merits of Qualitative Research

Some scholars reject autoethnography because of the researcher's contradictory role as researcher and subject, although these chapters establish that neither is mutually exclusive. Autoethnographic researchers defy the Western epistemic value of neutrality in social sciences. This value of the "neutral researcher" represents separatism in research and the division of the humanities and sciences, or the separation of the mind and the heart in Western academia. In the West, science follows the empirical method. The researcher does not express interpretations of the research beyond that which can be proven through scientific inquiry. It is a Eurocentric view of knowledge as separate from personal experience, opinion, religion, or emotion.

A humanistic approach to social science requires qualitative research. Quantitative research is necessary in the physical sciences, where measurements are exact and nature responds often reliably, but research is more relative in the social sciences. Some researchers try to make social science research quantitative through coding, where they analyze interviews or behaviors and group them into categories. This reductionist approach simplifies the wide range of human experience into numbers. Although quantitative social science research can be useful, qualitative research adds a more complete picture of the human experience. A humanistic approach to research analyzes interviews or behavior from a narrative perspective that finds themes and showcases individual narratives.

Qualitative research is more appropriate to the social sciences because of its coherence with subaltern epistemologies. In many cultures the Western division between emotion and science does not exist. For example, African epistemologies commonly integrate religious themes with science.[24] They also value orations handed down from generations of experience and consider testimony as knowledge. The exploration of Yorùbá sculpture in Chapter 9, "Sculpture as an Archive," reveals that the Gbẹ̀nàgbẹ̀nà/Gbẹ̀gilére (woodcarver/ the artist) and the Gbẹ̀nugbẹ̀nu (the oral critic) act as living signifiers for the workings of indigenous epistemologies and cultural systems. Or the significance of Ìyá Lékuléja, as highlighted in *Counting the Tiger's Teeth* in Chapter 4,

---

[24] Stephen Ellis and Gerrie ter Haar, "Religion and Politics: Taking African Epistemologies Seriously," *Journal of Modern African Studies* 45, no. 3 (2007): 385–401.

"Memory, Magic, Myth, and Metaphor," as a representative of the ingenuity of traditional herbal knowledge.

When evaluating sculpture, the Yorùbá oral critic uses creative praise to critically appreciate beauty in the process of visually communing with the artwork and the artist. These oral renditions are not mere praise employed to appreciate delicate designs and skilled hands; they recognize and reflect the hours of work, industry, and mental fortitude required to create the sculptures. The criticism also considers the transformative power of the artist and the artwork. The testimony of the *Gbẹ̀nugbẹ̀nu* is respected for its knowledge within a specific field of art, and the knowledge required to perform this testimony is a product of genealogy and generational transfer.

The artworks themselves hold religious significance, even when they are subjected to scientific and methodical principles for the creation of art, such as measurement, luminosity, symmetry, height, and verisimilitude. Yorùbá art is holistic, and so is its criticism. The *Gbẹ̀nugbẹ̀nu*, as an oral aesthete with the critical power to make informed commentary, dovetails with the creative structures of African epistemologies. These holistic contributions touch on several aspects of the sculpture's world: its spiritual and moral connotations, historical and social importance, and creative significance. The critical "testimony" is a well-rounded approach supported by a need to sensitize other artisans or apprentices or to sanitize the society. This process reveals the holistic power of African epistemologies that can serve as critical modes of understanding. To appreciate this feature of African art, scholars such as Babalola Yai have advocated for a return to the use of African concepts and epistemologies to appreciate African cultural forms.

On a general note, African epistemologies are holistic, blending morality with the pursuit of science. African artisans, sculptors, painters, or hairstylists embody this symbiosis perfectly. They pursue excellence, experimentation, and innovation without neglecting the sociocultural implications of those choices and the existing tradition. Knowledge for the sake of knowledge is often considered unnecessary and futile. Afrocentric research typically privileges knowledge that improves lives within the community[25] because it centralizes issues and realities such as the aforementioned.

The global academic system validates knowledge based on the West's imposed epistemic foundations. The subalternized indigenous researcher must overcome this bias by actively reshaping epistemic foundations.[26] Many researchers advocate for methodological diversity to represent an

---

[25] Kiatezua Lubanzadio Luyaluka, "An Essay on Naturalized Epistemology of African Indigenous Knowledge," *Journal of Black Studies* 47, no. 6 (2016): 497–523.
[26] Mambo Ama Mazama, "Afrocentricity and African Spirituality," *Journal of Black Studies* 33, no. 2 (2002): 218–234.

Afrocentric perspective.[27] Afrocentric research uses the epistemology of African philosophies to theorize on data about Africa.[28]

However, researchers who present themselves as neutral often come off foreign and cold in Africa.[29] Afrocentricity rejects objectivity: the idea of the "neutral researcher" that originated in the West. Other elements of Afrocentricity in social science research are cultural centeredness, knowledge pluralism, and holistic thinking.[30] The ideal Afrocentric social science research is performed by a community member who can accurately understand and represent the culture, presenting it to the outside world in a way that is helpful to the community and appropriate for local philosophy. This researcher would practice methodological reflexiveness by considering how their personal life and position in the community affects their research. One of such frameworks for conducting Afrocentric research is autoethnography.

Introducing Autoethnography

Autoethnography defies the Eurocentric standard of conducting science from a neutral perspective; instead, the researcher's own narrative is used to explore cultural themes. Researchers embrace and analyze their biases, as opposed to ignoring them, as part of their work.[31] This autoethnographic research at the very least complements the deficiencies of and in traditional ethnographic fieldwork, while also serving as an alternative, especially with its emphasis or posturing as being heavily and perhaps more natural and humanistic than traditional ethnographic fieldwork, as pointed out already.

To understand autoethnography, we must break it into its parts. "Auto" requires the narrative to be a self-narrative. It must describe the author's own life, not the experience of anyone else or intentional research. "Ethno" requires the narrative to relate to larger themes about a culture or subgroup. The

---

[27] Shannon Morreira, "Steps towards Decolonial Higher Education in Southern Africa? Epistemic Disobedience in the Humanities," *Journal of Asian and African Studies* 52, no. 3 (2017): 287–301.

[28] Kenneth W. Stikkers, "An Outline of Methodological Afrocentrism, with Particular Application to the Thought of W. E. B. DuBois," *Journal of Speculative Philosophy* 22, no. 1 (2008): 40–49.

[29] Karanja Keita Carroll and DeReef F. Jamison, "African-Centered Psychology, Education and the Liberation of African Minds: Notes on the Psycho-Cultural Justification for Reparations," *Race, Gender & Class* 18, no. 1–2 (2011): 52–72.

[30] Lisa Schreiber, "Overcoming Methodological Elitism: Afrocentrism as a Prototypical Paradigm for Intercultural Research," *International Journal of Intercultural Relations* 24, no. 5 (2000): 651–671.

[31] Michelle Glowacki-Dudka, Marjorie Treff, and Irianti Usman, "Research for Social Change: Using Autoethnography to Foster Transformative Learning," *Adult Learning* 16, no. 3–4 (2005): 30–31.

narrative must contribute to the field of knowledge in order to be considered "Graphy."³²

Although there is much debate over what counts as autoethnography, there is a distinct difference between autoethnography and autobiography. Both describe the narrative experience of a singular person. Both can be emotionally gripping and culturally informative. An autobiography might provide insights on larger cultural themes, but autobiographies do not explicitly state the narrative's implications in the context of cultural research.

Olaudah Equiano wrote *The Interesting Life of Olaudah Equiano*, a narrative providing insight into the Atlantic slave trade and the problems of Africans enslaved in the Americas. The book provided a cultural commentary that motivated social change. However, Equiano did not write an explicit analysis of his experiences in relation to the larger culture or how it related to previous writings on the topic. An autoethnography must not only present a story; it must also bridge that story and its contributions to cultural understanding.

In contrast, this book's autoethnographic chapters explore an archive of collections in light of their relation to the Yorùbá sociocultural and epistemic firmament, reflecting the latter's cultural and religio-spiritual configuration. Autoethnography developed within the context of the 1980s, which was a time in academia when people began to lose their faith in master narratives, seeking more qualitative and humanistic data in research. Autoethnography functions not to discredit previous ethnographic literature nor the master narratives, but to offer new and complementary narrative perspectives.

Examples include the chapter on photography, which presents perspectives that do not reject existing positions on the subject, even if it takes a different approach to generating its conclusion. The chapter on Yorùbá women's hair contains commentary on the expressivity of these hairstyles, and not only because hair has been discussed in this light. It is also because I grew up within this tradition; my relationship with the subjects comes from a place that is simultaneously critical and personal. Likewise, my reflections on *Counting the Tiger's Teeth* establish the need for an alternative narrative that realigns history toward appropriate factuality and wider inclusiveness. Laurel Richardson describes autoethnography as a crystal offering new perspectives based on the positionality of the author. No single narrative perspective represents a complete truth, merely different perspectives on the same story. Autoethnography rejects master narratives to organize individual stories into larger cultural themes,³³ which is the premise of this book.

---

³² Satoshi Toyosaki, "Toward De/Postcolonial Autoethnography: Critical Relationality with the Academic Second Persona," *Cultural Studies ↔ Critical Methodologies* 18, no. 1 (2018): 32–42.

³³ L. Richardson, *Fields of Play: Constructing an Academic Life* (New Brunswick: Rutgers University Press, 1997).

Epistemic Foundations of Autoethnography

The epistemic foundation of Western science holds that there is a single truth to be revealed. The assumption is that any pursuit of this truth is beneficial to humankind, and Western epistemology is based on this binary of truth and untruth. In contrast, the epistemic foundations of autoethnography are based on the plurality of knowledge and humanism.

I have already explained the secularity of research and its incompatibility with subaltern epistemologies. Ultimately, secularity is not neutrality because subaltern epistemologies often include religious perspectives. This Western concept of secularity reflects a Western bias in research.[34] The West's attempts to remain secular extend far beyond religion: scientific articles disclose any conflicts of interest that may have affected the research, including personal biases, company affiliations, or personal relationships. With these acknowledgments, the author claims neutrality and asserts that any bias, even if it has been disclosed, has been removed from the final product.

Autoethnography embraces the context of research, and the author includes religious, personal, and cultural influences through their personal narrative. It encourages the synthesis of various facets of indigenous life, executing a reflexive investigation of culture. Therefore, the epistemic foundation of autoethnography is an investigation into the context of the research, biases and all.

Procedure is another epistemic foundation of Western science, operating under the assumption that the scientific method allows scientists to discover truth. Researchers are required to follow various procedures, including academic publishing requirements, IRB certification, and university guidelines. These procedures are deeply embedded in the academic system, to the point where any research that follows them is accepted as truth. Research that does not follow these procedures is typically rejected as pseudoscience. Autoethnography's lack of fixed, rigid, and preexisting procedure and standardization is epistemic disobedience – traditional research attempts to sort data into a framework of preexisting research, but autoethnography takes a constructivist approach that creates something new. The epistemic perspective of autoethnography is that procedure is not always rationality.[35]

The idea of a singular truth is also present in the social sciences. Western social sciences seek ultimate truths of human nature. Autoethnography assumes that human behavior is relative. Two theories explaining this assumption are cultural constructionism and symbolic interactionism. Social constructivism holds that human behavior is not standardized, and that it differs

---

[34] J. K. H. Tse, "Grounded Theologies: 'Religion' and the 'Secular' in Human Geography," *Progress in Human Geography* 38, no. 2 (2014): 201–220.

[35] T. A. Schwandt, "Farewell to Criteriology," *Qualitative Inquiry* 2, no. 1 (1996): 58–72.

between cultures. It rejects any standards or comparisons of morality, meaning, or behavior – each is considered to depend on preexisting cultural values.

Humans develop through their social interactions. Their knowledge and behavior changes in response to their physical and social environment, meaning that there can be no singular truth; knowledge is socially constructed by individual experiences within a culture. Autoethnography supports social constructivism by examining the truth of individuals in their social context.

Consider the prejudices structured into photographic tools that deny visibility to the black body, even when their functions are allegedly to improve it. This truth cannot be glossed over in the context of African postcolonialism, where matrixes of Western imperialism are sustained in overt and covert forms. By using select photographs as templates, the ethnographic impulse is sustained and relative truth in social constructivism is maintained for individual agency – that of the man whose black skin cannot be accommodated in the postproduction stages of photography, whether analog or digital. Any photographic representation is, at best, an afterthought of the tool's configuration. This is his truth, refutable when spread beyond his cultural domain.

Symbolic interactionism explains how groups socially construct knowledge. Symbols can take the form of rituals, items, words, people, or pictures that have meaning for individuals because of their cultural context. When ethnographers try to analyze another culture's symbols, they will never truly understand the meaning outside of their own cultural context. An ethnographer might see a Yorùbá religious mask as part of a play, which would miss the symbol's meaning as an embodiment of an ancestral spirit during those rituals. Autoethnography corrects for symbolic interactionism through the researcher's insight into the culture studied.

Another example is the potency of images and artwork, or even the exhibitive context within which photographs, paintings, or portraits come alive generally in the indigenous culture. To the West, exhibition is when works are set in a museum or capitalist-oriented public displays. The cultural transactions in the exhibitive milieus of native settings depart from those of the European world, and so does the ideology upholding them. The networked system of distribution and exhibition for paintings, sculpture, or photographs relies heavily on kinship and close-knit relational systems. The mix of the status symbol's value and the materialist orientation of the Yorùbá provide templates for art patronage that galvanize interest and initiate exhibitive procedures. Appreciation for these distributive networks rests on cultural awareness and aesthetic considerations informed by sociocultural and religio-spiritual consciousness.

Another epistemic foundation of autoethnography is its interdisciplinary flexibility, its ability to cross disciplines. Traditional Western epistemology separates science and the humanities. Scientists do not include poetry or commentary about their passion for research, and humanitarians rarely conduct scientific analysis of literary works. Autoethnography blurs the line between art and science.[36] It works from the epistemic foundation that literature, on its own, cannot provide the social commentary that contributes to knowledge about culture. Science alone is also considered too detached from the human experience to capture it in a relatable, practical way. In this way, autoethnography practices border thinking that stands in opposition to academic separatism.

Academic separatism divides the fields of the art and science and breaks them down further into categories. The arts break down into literature, history, visual art, and dance. The sciences are divided into physical and social sciences, and even further into sociology and psychology. Researchers in each academic field are expected to keep within the scope of their field of study, avoiding research that crosses disciplines. Complex subjects, such as globalization, culture, colonization, racism, and human behavior, are influenced by multiple disciplines. The ability of researchers to venture outside their field and consider problems from epistemic and disciplinary perspectives is called border thinking.

Border thinking recognizes the limitations and strengths of all academic disciplines. It encourages academics to look at every field as useful but limited. Researchers can decide how the different fields fit together to portray a more exhaustive truth. Through border thinking, the Western epistemic perspective is neither right nor wrong, it merely has limitations.[37] Autoethnography combines literary elements with the social sciences, practicing border thinking and allowing it to elicit emotion and retain relevance, while contributing to humanity's understanding of culture.

Autoethnography embraces pluriversalism of knowledge, an epistemic perspective asserting that no single knowledge system is complete. It is similar to border thinking in that it focuses on the limitations of various epistemic perspectives and fields of knowledge. Instead of seeking a singular answer, it advocates for the acceptance of multiple truths. Autoethnography utilizes individual experiences to invite researchers to express their own truth and accept the truth of others.

Autoethnography's focus on individual experience asserts that reality is ever-changing. Reality is seen not as a singular truth but as the result of humans' interaction with their environment. Autoethnography assumes that the researcher's positionality – their relationship to the research, which includes the beliefs that influence it – is a product of the researcher's lifelong learning and experiences. This allows autoethnography to understand culture

---

[36] Carolyn Ellis, Tony E. Adams, and Arthur P. Bochner, "Autoethnography: An Overview," *Historical Social Research/Historische Sozialforschung* 36, no. 4 (2011): 273–290.
[37] Walter D. Mignolo, *Local Histories/Global Designs: Coloniality, Subaltern Knowledges, and Border Thinking* (New York: Princeton University Press, 2000).

through first-person analysis and research reflexivity.[38] It accommodates the way that researchers' perceptions of reality can influence their actions and their interpretations of reality,[39] and in so doing proposes an adequate positionality to better understand a perception.

Finally, autoethnography is based on the epistemic foundation of humanism; it values social science research for its humanistic properties and its ability to enhance the human experience, as well as for its innate value.[40] Autoethnography can enhance the human experience by providing recognition to marginalized voices, which encourages peace and understanding and works against discrimination and ignorance. Autoethnography's literary nature is able to bring a human face to the social sciences and allows the sciences to advocate for social equality. It is also important because of the innate value of its literary and provocative nature. In contrast to typical ethnography, which attempts to be neutral, autoethnography engages readers through the emotional plight of others. There is value in the human connection that is formed by recognizing another person's perspective.

Diversity in Autoethnography

One of autoethnography's strengths is its extensive diversity; it is not a standardized process. Just as each autoethnographic essay is presented in ways best suited to its premise, researchers can present research in the way that best expresses their story. Although the approach in Chapter 11, "Canvas and the Archiving of Ethnic Reality," is autoethnographic, it differs from that of "Sculpture as an Archive" (Chapter 9) or "Satire and Society" (Chapter 7). The distinction lies in the degree to which the evocative is blended with the analytic. All are reflexive in their approach and focus, emphasizing larger cultural themes through critical evaluation of available data.

Images of humans, among other subjects, must be approached with a nuance that contrasts with the technical approach for stylized and abstract sculptures. A return to indigenous epistemologies and cultural concepts, in opposition to imperialist or Eurocentric paradigms, is as important as the exploration of pertinent contextual issues in the chapter on sculpture. When compared with the chapter on painting, one sees that the critical reflection on the significance of artwork as reflectors of a social framework takes primacy. While the reflexive mode in essays on my memoirs render them as meta-narratives, it foregrounds

---

[38] Jayne Pitard, "A Journey to the Centre of Self: Positioning the Researcher in Autoethnography," *Forum: Qualitative Social Research* 18, no. 3 (2017): 108–127.

[39] Kobi K. K. Kambon and Joseph A. Baldwin, *The African Personality in America: An African-Centered Framework* (Tallahassee: Nubian Nation Publications, 1992).

[40] P. K. Chepkuto and Stanley Kipsang, "The Social Sciences and Humanities in Africa: Which Way Forward?" *International Journal of Academic Research in Business and Social Sciences* 3, no. 12 (2013): 66–78.

the deep-seated knowledge in indigenous traditions that can only be harnessed through multiple layers of reflection and narrativity.[41] However, all perform the same functions, but the difference is to what degree.

The biggest debate in autoethnography is whether it should be analytic or evocative. Analytic autoethnography creates a narrative while focusing most of its research on an explanation of what that narrative means in a larger cultural context. Evocative autoethnography is typically more literary, leaving the reader feeling emotionally connected to the research – it can include an explanation of societal wrongs and advocacy for marginalized groups.[42] Some ethnographic research articles explain their narrative and quickly move to an extensive analysis, while others present narratives poetically, with little or no connection to their cultural implications. Autoethnography's immense diversity (along with an overuse of the term) has generated extensive research into what counts as autoethnographic writing. Most researchers agree that autoethnographic writing must balance engaging literary narrative with an explanation of wider cultural meaning.[43]

Another debate about ethnographic research concerns the validity of hard or soft data. The "-graphy" part of the research implies that the author will use hard data – letters or interviews from their own life – as samples for analysis. However, the epistemic foundations of autoethnography validate personal experience, accepting it as soft data and allowing for research that is primarily or entirely based on individual memory.[44]

The substantial diversity within autoethnography extends beyond its origins; individuals originally wrote about their own experiences growing up and discussed their thoughts on what it meant for their culture. Topics in autoethnography are now relevant for many fields of research. It is often used to explore ethnic groups, especially African American voices. In one research paper, self-titled as an autoethnographic work, a professor explores his experience teaching college students during a critical period in African American history, performing his analysis through the music of Prince – the author reflects on how popular music is an undervalued but effective pedagogical tool for young African Americans to relate with their historical struggles.[45]

---

[41] In this instance, the first layer is in experiencing the culture as a member of it, and harnessing them as a narrative constitutes the second level, while the third level is in unpacking and reassessing the core narrative at the different levels already established. At these different levels, different layers of meaning and understanding are attained.

[42] Ingo Winkler, "Doing Autoethnography: Facing Challenges, Taking Choices, Accepting Responsibilities," *Qualitative Inquiry* 24, no. 4 (2018): 236-247.

[43] Sarah Stahlke Wall, "Toward a Moderate Autoethnography," *International Journal of Qualitative Methods* 15, no. 1 (2016), https://doi.org/10.1177/1609406916674966.

[44] Winkler, "Doing Autoethnography."

[45] Zada Johnson, "Teaching Prince as Critical Pedagogy: An Autoethnography," *Journal of African American Studies* 21, no. 3 (2017): 337-352.

Another example is an autoethnographic work that examines an African American woman's childhood, discussing how her environment, which was shaped by ethnic and gender prejudice, shaped her development.[46] Gender studies is an unexpected but fitting use of autoethnography, allowing women to express their individual experiences and relate them back to the patriarchal culture surrounding them. In a TED talk Anita Sarkeesian explained how her YouTube series on gender equality in video games made her the target of a massive online hate campaign. Her presentation explained the facts of her experience while conveying her emotions throughout the ordeal, including the reading of individual hate messages. She then related her experience back to the culture of misogyny that she lived in, using her story to advocate for a culture of gender equality and female desexualization.[47] Other works titled as autoethnographies analyze topics that range from the culture of veganism[48] to LGBTQ rights.[49] Autoethnography has grown beyond its roots in distinct cultures, extending its influence into various subcultures and amplifying a large variety of silenced voices.

The immense variety within autoethnography has generated much debate about what counts as autoethnographic research. Critics dismiss autoethnographic articles as self-indulgent, focusing too much on the researcher and not enough on how their experience relates to the community at large. The crucial component of effective autoethnographic research is a conclusion that clearly establishes the meaning of the narrative, although the forms of ethnographic research know no boundaries. A dance autoethnography provides an example: researchers explored the social phenomena of teens who practiced self-harming, creating a dance that represented the voices of these individuals. Instead of discussing the research with self-harming teens, the article explored their experience of "dancing out their data" and how it related to the larger culture of academia and self-harm.[50]

Another example of a unique piece of autoethnographic research is that of a filmmaker who researched the male sex industry in Tunisia. Her narrative included the experience of creating and editing the film along with a discussion of her research process. This skirts the traditional boundaries of autoethnography,

---

[46] Nontokozo Mashiya, "Learning in Childhood: An Autoethnography of Girl Childrearing Practices and Identity Construction in Southern Africa," *Gender & Behaviour* 16, no. 1 (2018): 10739–1047.

[47] Anita Sarkeesian, "Anita Sarkeesian at TEDxWomen 2012," December 2012, TEDxTalks video, 10:29, www.youtube.com/watch?v=GZAxwsg9J9Q.

[48] Maria Marta Andreatta, "Being a Vegan: A Performative Autoethnography," *Cultural Studies ↔ Critical Methodologies* 15, no. 6 (2015): 477–486.

[49] Stacy Holman Jones, "Living Bodies of Thought: The 'Critical' in Critical Autoethnography," *Qualitative Inquiry* 22, no. 4 (2016): 228–237.

[50] Trish Van Katwyk and Yukari Seko, "Knowing through Improvisational Dance: A Collaborative Autoethnography," *Forum: Qualitative Social Research* 18, no. 2 (2017): 122–144.

because she was performing research, but the narrative extends beyond her research. Ultimately, it expresses reflexivity in the informal portion of her time in Tunisia and how it influenced her film editing.[51]

A development worker who reformed the educational system in Namibia found herself constantly debating her role as a white development worker in a postcolonial context.[52] Some researchers may not accept these examples as autoethnography, but they all have reflexivity of culture in common. All of the articles included how the experience affected the researcher and what could be learned about their culture.

Additionally, autoethnography takes on a wide range of forms. Some researchers continue to use the traditional structure of research papers, beginning with an introduction on the nature of autoethnographies, presenting their narrative as data, and ending with a full analysis and conclusion. Literary autoethnographies can be shorter, only connecting with culture at the end.[53] Many autoethnographies are structured as literary works, presenting the story in a chronological order that does not always include a brief introduction to the subject of autoethnography. These works combine their narrative with analysis that is performed throughout the text.[54]

Collaborative autoethnographies and exo-autoethnographies are special types of autoethnography. Collaborative ethnographies involve narratives from multiple people with similar experiences. The authors can reflect on their experiences together, discussing what they mean for the larger culture that they are part of. At Brown University, teaching assistants linked their individual narratives to express shared frustrations as African American women experiencing systemic disadvantage in academic publishing. In their stories of discrimination they were able to reflect on institutional biases and insufficient action from the university.[55] Collaborative autoethnography can lose some of its emotional power when it focuses on the experience of more than one person. However, it can show larger patterns by diminishing the individuality of narratives, explaining the cultural implications of their experiences.[56]

---

[51] Nicola Mai, "Mobile Orientations: An Autoethnography of Tunisian Professional Boyfriends," *Sexualities* 20, no. 4 (2017): 482–496.

[52] Stasja Koot, "Perpetuating Power through Autoethnography: My Research Unawareness and Memories of Paternalism among the Indigenous Hai//om in Namibia," *Critical Arts* 30, no. 6 (2016): 840–854.

[53] Hannah Rose Williams and Peter Joseph Gloviczki, "Storytelling across Generations: A Collaborative Autoethnography," *Humanity & Society* 42, no. 2 (2018): 255–257.

[54] Tasha R. Wyatt, "Knowing when to Step Forward, Back, or Out: An Autoethnography of a White Researcher in Two Post-Colonial Educational Contexts," *Power and Education* 10, no. 3 (2018): 301–314.

[55] Ileana Cortes Santiago, Nastaran Karimi, and Zaira R. Arvelo Alicea, "Neoliberalism and Higher Education: A Collective Autoethnography of Brown Women Teaching Assistants," *Gender and Education* 29, no. 1 (2017): 48–65.

[56] Winkler, "Doing Autoethnography."

Exo-autoethnography is an esoteric term describing the reflexive narrative research of an individual affected by an event that someone else experienced. It typically focuses on how another generation's experiences or trauma were passed down to their offspring to affect their lives. This type of autoethnography is useful for understanding the intergenerational effects of social phenomena. Autoethnography's qualitative nature leaves it open to interpretation. Researchers can apply the term whenever they use narrative to explore cultural themes through the larger perspective of the culture that they belong to.

Autoethnography and Epistemic Liberation

The colonial matrix of power shapes ethnography and the field of social sciences. However, the diversity of autoethnography allows it to be employed as a tool for epistemic disobedience, advocating for academic decoloniality, calling for epistemic diversity and acceptance of the plurality of knowledge. Any methodological approach to knowledge production embracing the subaltern philosophical perspective is a tool of decoloniality.

Autoethnography puts a special emphasis on the researcher's reflexivity – the researcher explains the biases of their perspective and their cultural relationship to the research, which often revolves around themes of coloniality and the colonial matrix of power. Through this the work analyzes the researcher and the system of knowledge within which they exist.[57] For example, the chapter on photography explores reproductions of coloniality through photographs and photographic technology to consider how these affect representations of the black body. It explores what it means to gaze through a colonial tool and the persistence of colonial infrastructure. Even a decolonial tool, such as the digital camera, can perpetuate coloniality with its ubiquity and representational power. Despite its radical properties, autoethnography exists within the global institution of academia; it will never truly overcome its colonial roots.[58]

Academia is a critical point for a decolonial intervention. It is privileged as "truth" in the global world order, and decolonial advocates must work within the system to make change. In literature the greatest challenge to decoloniality is its academic location within area studies or history. Autoethnography offers a pathway for decoloniality to expand and affect social sciences throughout the university. If coloniality advances a single narrative throughout the world, autoethnography

---

[57] Archana Pathak, "Musings on Postcolonial Autoethnography," in *Handbook of Autoethnography*, ed. Stacy Holman Jones, Tony E. Adams, and Carolyn Ellis (New York: Routledge, 2013), 595–608.
[58] Toyosaki, "Toward De/Postcolonial Autoethnography."

opposes it through personal accounts providing tangible contradictions of that narrative.[59]

The master narrative of colonialism is a product of the globalization of knowledge homogeneity. Also, the commoditization of knowledge and globalization work together, spreading the narrative of Western nations and silencing subalternized epistemologies. Autoethnography fights this process by resisting homogenization, exploring the relationship between colonizer and colonized and rejecting master narratives. However, autoethnography is not widely used within the social sciences; autoethnographic publishing is largely limited to the white majority.[60]

Autoethnography's relation to subaltern epistemologies makes it a tool of decoloniality. It is congruent with the epistemologies of Africa because it rejects secularity, neutrality, and Western narratives. Autoethnography offers an escape from the "sandwich problem" – in which Africans studying in the West put African problems in European frameworks – by presenting a methodology for non-Western academics to reject Western epistemology. The South African university that recognized the sandwich problem also acknowledged autoethnography's ability to support African values, such as *ujamaa*, through its focus on solidarity, personal experiences, and family. *Ujamaa* emphasizes the individual's role within the community, and autoethnography can represent a single person's story within the context of the community. This alignment encouraged the university to start a Master's program on the "narrative study of lives," focused on the analysis and production of narratives counteracting the master narratives pushed by the West.[61]

Criticism of Autoethnography

As an act of epistemic disobedience, autoethnography has faced heavy criticism. Dismissive scholars claim that it does not qualify as "real" research because it rejects rituals that have been formalized by the West. Many critics describe autoethnography as "self-indulgent" because of the researcher's reflexive role and the emotional nature of the narrative. Autoethnographies are not self-indulgent; they use personal stories to advocate for marginalized communities.[62] Even journals seeking subaltern epistemologies have different standards to qualify autoethnographies. A lack of standardization, which is the

---

[59] Mohan J. Dutta, "Autoethnography as Decolonization, Decolonizing Autoethnography: Resisting to Build our Homes," *Cultural Studies ↔ Critical Methodologies* 18, no. 1 (2018): 94–96.
[60] Devika Chawla and Ahmet Atay, "Introduction: Decolonizing Autoethnography," *Cultural Studies ↔ Critical Methodologies* 18, no. 1 (2018): 3–8.
[61] Brock-Utne, "Researching Language and Culture."
[62] Dewan, "Understanding Ethnography."

merit of methodology, can hurt individual researchers whose work fails to meet the requirements of specific journals.

Another critique of autoethnography is its lack of hard data, which leads some scholars to question its status as research and challenge it for being unreliable. Although autoethnography often relies on personal memory, it can also use hard data from diaries, photos, interviews, or letters. Advocates for autoethnography view the use of soft data, such as memories, as more humanistic research. Some have questioned the unclear ethical standards for the practice, which can involve publicizing personal stories and disclosing intimate details from the lives of others. Finally, the inconsistent use of the term autoethnography results in some "research articles" that are closer to autobiographies; their lack of cultural connection can confuse readers about the nature of autoethnography.[63]

Autoethnography currently faces a challenge in the demographics of scholars who practice it. The colonial matrix of power perpetuates the political, economic, and social advantaging of white European men, which puts racially and gender marginalized people at a disadvantage when trying to access educational and publishing resources for practicing this methodology. As a result, autoethnographies are typically written by a group's most privileged members. Autoethnographic literature still features many European perspectives on culture, instead of the subaltern voices it could amplify. The term autoethnography has also been misused to describe the reflexive accounts of researchers performing extensive fieldwork; such accounts are insightful for the nature of research, but they do not amplify the voices of those that they study.[64]

The primary reason why ethical standards have been questioned in autoethnography is because people have been included in personal narratives without consent; this can affect their lives and reveal personal details. Ethical guidelines maintained by the IRB and universities, which limit the amount of personal detail that a researcher can reveal, also significantly limit the ability of methodologies such as autoethnography to exist when they rely on personal narratives.[65] These restrictions often expand beyond personal details about people surrounding the researcher to include personal details from the researchers themselves. The ethical approval requirement for this research is designed to limit the potential for subjects to be harmed, but it can discourage the use of qualitative research methodologies and support colonial epistemology.

---

[63] Heewon Chang, *Autoethnography as Method* (Walnut Creek, CA: Left Coast Press, 2008).
[64] Annelies Moors, "On Autoethnography," *Ethnography* 18, no. 3 (2017): 387–389.
[65] Andrew Dickson and Kate Holland, "Hysterical Inquiry and Autoethnography: A Lacanian Alternative to Institutionalized Ethical Commandments," *Current Sociology* 65, no. 1 (2017): 133–148.

There is no standard evaluation system for autoethnographic research, but several researchers have shared their opinions about what qualifies as ethnographic research. Carolyn Ellis, who has written extensively about autoethnographic research and evaluates it for research journals, has named five criteria for successful autoethnographic research: (1) it must make a substantive contribution to the academic understanding of culture, which eliminates "self-indulgent" articles resembling autobiographies that do not reveal how their narratives relate to larger social structures; (2) the research must have aesthetic merit, telling a narrative in a literary way that is readable, interesting, and engaging; (3) the research must include reflexivity, where the researcher analyzes their role as both the analyzer and the analyzed; (4) it must be impactful, leaving the reader with an intellectual or emotional outcome that inspires curiosity, further research, or a call to action; and (5) the research must express a reality, conveying the lived experience of an individual to amplify subaltern voices.[66]

Ellis's outline of successful ethnographic articles is important for potential autoethnographers crafting successful research articles. More discussion is needed about guidelines and methodology for improving autoethnographic research, including embracing diversity, to encourage a rigorous development of the methodology.

Conclusion

This chapter has described Western epistemology's role in the colonial matrix of power and proposed autoethnography as a tool for decoloniality. Autoethnography is not a new field, but it has not reached its full potential. It can deconstruct the master narratives of coloniality through reflexivity, humanism, and individual narratives. However, it is challenged by overuse of the term, academic resistance, ethical review, and lack of accessibility for the marginalized. The field has expanded from anthropological ethnography to include other social sciences, offering challenges and opportunities for the growing field.

Autoethnographies focus on individual narratives and reject the notion of a single truth, which is a departure from Western epistemology. In this way, autoethnography embraces what researchers have called a constellation of knowledge. This constellation rejects a singular narrative truth that must be globally accepted, choosing instead to embrace the diversity of individual opinions, epistemologies, religions, and cultures.[67]

---

[66] Carolyn Ellis, *The Ethnographic I: A Methodological Novel about Autoethnography* (Walnut Creek, CA: AltaMira Press, 2004).

[67] Santos B. de Sousa, "General Introduction: Reinventing Social Emancipation: Toward New Manifestos," in *Democratizing Democracy: Beyond the Liberal Democratic Canon*, ed. Santos B. de Sousa (London: Verso, 2005), I, xvii–xxxiii.

The controversial issue of mental health offers insight into the different epistemologies involved. In the Western world extensive work is done on health from an individual perspective, and therapy and medicine are typically prescribed for individuals facing issues such as depression. In the Yorùbá culture, ailments such as depression may be seen as religious afflictions that require ceremony and community intervention. A constellation of knowledge holds that neither of these frameworks is right or wrong; they are different solutions to the same issue, and they can be either useful or harmful in their own ways.

Autoethnography allows individuals to express their perspectives on issues relating to their culture, adding to the global constellation of knowledge. One example is the critical take on the representation of women in Yorùbá sculpture – a Western audience might perceive the objectification or commodification of women. For the culture that created the artwork the representations depict ideas of fecundity and approachability, and submission and sacrifice. To surface this particular narrative one must tolerate cultural relativism. The latter takes central discussion in the analyses, with broader cultural implications.

Academic journals and universities often take a multicultural approach, inviting international scholars to contribute. This cosmopolitan approach to academia is ineffective at creating a multicultural view of knowledge. The institution of academia, through its economic and political processes, is biased against subaltern academics – a consideration of international entries means that the majority of papers will be written by European scholars. Cosmopolitanism does not actively advocate for the subaltern perspective, which leaves such voices underrepresented.[68] Another approach is "local cosmopolitanism," rooting the research of an area in its own epistemic perspective while acknowledging (and occasionally including) perspectives from other cultures, such as the West.[69]

Many scholars advocate for decoloniality in academia, but this movement has been limited to the academic specialization of postcolonial or area studies.[70] Decoloniality must be applied to every academic discipline; even in the field of decoloniality, minorities and women scholars are underpublished and undercited.[71] The underrepresentation of subaltern perspectives, especially in academic environments that advocate for them, displays the severity of their low participation. Although epistemic liberation has been accepted as

---

[68] Walter Mignolo, "Cosmopolitanism and the De-Colonial Option," *Studies in Philosophy and Education* 29, no. 2 (2010): 111–127.
[69] Mignolo, "Cosmopolitanism."
[70] Shome and Hegde, "Postcolonial Approaches to Communication."
[71] Mariana Ortega, "Decolonial Woes and Practices of Un-Knowing," *Journal of Speculative Philosophy* 31, no. 3 (2017): 504–516.

necessary for academia, it has failed to significantly increase the subaltern publication of academic articles.

It is important to understand the need for academic institutions to actively advocate for subaltern epistemic narratives. Autoethnography has grown as a field, but it requires greater encouragement from academia's institutions. It is designed to magnify the voices often institutionally silenced, which means that the people who would provide the most useful autoethnographies are those who are least likely to know about them, or who are unlikely to receive the education or publishers' approval to complete them. Universities must actively recruit and fund individuals from subaltern demographics, including women, religious minorities, international students, and ethnic minorities. Universities can encourage autoethnographic work from researchers who already practice subaltern epistemologies, creating collections of autoethnographies in books or at conferences. Active development of this methodology on the part of universities and scholars will allow autoethnography to play a critical role in the epistemic liberation of the subaltern.

PART II

History, Fictions, and Factions

3

Narrative Politics and Cultural Ideologies

Introduction: Narrative Politics

The term "narrative" has been adopted, in recent times, in various disciplines, as a more appealing medium of expression. The term used to be reserved and restricted to the fields of literature, history, anthropology, and the social sciences. However, new grammatical contexts have been opened for "narratives" by doctors, psychiatrists, psychologists, police interrogators, journalists, political chroniclers, politicians, lawyers, and others.[1]

The increasing adaptation and constant revisions of the term has pushed it to the verge of being semantically porous, overloaded with a burden of diverse meanings and functions. Roland Barthes regards it as "a prodigious variety of genres" when he asserts that it is "present in myth, legend, fable, tale, novella, epic, history, tragedy, drama, comedy, mime, painting ... cinema, comics, news item, conversation."[2] In comparison to terms such as *texts* and *stories*, which are equally applicable and adopted in literary, cultural, and historical discourses, its enquiry and analysis are intertwined with the intents of selves, identities, and social realities embedded in it.[3]

The suitability of narrative has become more appealing owing to its broadness as a universal medium of conveying human consciousness.[4] The term *story* is vitiated with stints of imagination, often held as untrue, and widely constrained to the confines of fiction. On the other hand, *text* barely does more than suggest a linguistic codification of a discourse or expression. Although its meaning is not static, the term *narrative* thrives above the limitations of its

---

[1] Ulf Palmenfelt, "Contemporary Uses of Narrative," *Elore* 16, no. 2 (2009): 1–12; J. L. Lucaites and C. M. Condit, "Reconstructing Narrative Theory: A Functional Perspective," *Journal of Communication* 35, no. 4 (1985): 90–108; Roland Barthes, "Introduction to the Structural Analysis of Narrative," in *Image, Music, Text*, ed. Roland Barthes, trans. S. Heath (New York: Hill & Wang, 1977), 79–124.
[2] Barthes, "Structural Analysis," 79.
[3] M. Hyvärinen, "Analyzing Narratives and Story-Telling," *Alasuutari: Social Research Methods* (2009): 447–460.
[4] Lucaites and Condit, "Reconstructing Narrative Theory," 90.

counterparts. Narratives are defined in relation with the functions they perform, which makes them a stretch of "an autonomous unit held together by a consistent inner logic of its own" or "a cultural form that selects and orders events into units of logical and chronological chains."[5]

Literature and history share a common point of convergence, which is reality. Both are undeniably based on premises of reality. Literature has been a tool for reflecting reality through imagination, while History is the documentation of reality through verifiable facts. In literature and history, often-cited points of discrepancy are concepts like imagination and fact. In literature, a writer relies more on his imagination to harness reality into a work of art; history makes use of facts to recount past reality.

These points of convergence and divergence do not hold much sway in the traditional African ideology of narratives and history, Àló and Ìtàn respectively. Ìtàn, which is history, engages the raconteur's imagination and creativity. In fact, the raconteur's aim is to achieve profoundness with his narrative, upholding a duty to provoke the listeners' imagination with his narrative prowess, relying on creativity so that that which is perceived to be real and imagined are seamlessly collapsed into one. Narrative seeks to achieve this same effect, blurring the contrast between reality and imagination.

This brings attention to the force embedded in the title of *A Mouth Sweeter than Salt*: rhetoric. It is the ability to collapse history or literature into a persuasive and fascinating expression. In this context, rhetoric is a confluence and summation of being a Mèsìògò first – all Mèsìògòs are defined by an adept use of language that transcends common vessels of expression to become a shield and a pellet, protecting oneself and disarming an enemy – and then an ardent historian. This is what Mary Louise Pratt conveys in relating the intention of the narrative writer: "His point is to produce in his hearers not only belief but also an imaginative and affective involvement in the state of affairs he is representing and an evaluative stance toward it. He intends them to share his wonder, amusement, terror, or admiration of the event."[6] Certain oral devices are employed to express such intent, what Peter Dickinson, in his "'Orality in Literacy': Listening to Indigenous Writing," describes as "oral features" operating "as powerful mnemonic devices within Indigenous texts, enabling their authors to talk without threat of censure about past traditions or injustices, and reminding their readers to listen to what is being advocated/ envisioned for the future."[7]

---

[5] Palmenfelt, "Contemporary Uses of Narrative," 12.
[6] Joseph Zalman Margolis, "Towards a Speech Act Theory of Literary Discourse by Mary Louise Pratt," *Journal of Aesthetics and Art Criticism* 36, no. 2 (1977): 225–228, at 226.
[7] Peter Dickinson, "'Orality in Literacy': Listening to Indigenous Writing," *Canadian Journal of Native Studies* 14, no. 2 (1994): 319–340, at 323.

These mnemonic devices, coupled with literary languages, possess the hermeneutic advantage of entertainment and aesthetic value over historical records. They render historical events and records with a more creative effect, to "not only make literary memoir more interesting to read, but actually heighten the author's ability to represent lived experience."[8] In paraphrasing Edward Barney, Ivor Goodson opined that manipulation is at the fore of narrative politics.[9] According to Goodson, appealing to the unconscious desires of people can persuade them to buy anything from soap powder to political policies. The key is crafting "the right kind of story." Against the postulations of new critics and the ideology of art for art's sake, every narrative contains an ideology at its core, a purpose steering it. It becomes ideologically deficient to confine narratives, or any other variant of art, solely to the premise of aesthetics.

History is neither as linear nor as monolithic as some older generations of historians might have us believe. Newer generations would argue that history "is fragmentary and always incomplete" and that "societies and cultures separated in time have differing values and beliefs."[10] Similar to the perception of a New Historicist, life narratives are not simple occurrences over a progression of a linear or monolithic time frame; they are embedded with intricacies and complexities, characterized by a back-and-forth switch in time and space. By further blurring the distinction between historical writing and literature, Hayden White posits in his "History as a Literary Artifact" that historical writers harmonize congeries of facts into a reasonable historical writing/text.[11] This procedure is what he refers to as employment, which he further identifies as that which R. G. Collingwood referred to as "the constructive imagination." *Ìtàn*, by virtue of orality, is neither linear nor monolithic in nature – the raconteur relies on his imagination and memory more often than not. The spontaneity that weighs in during performances achieves a grand historical aesthetic that is prone to constant change as it moves from one person to another, likewise, as the responses move from a group of audience to another.

Autobiography, a reflection on life through the self, is a genre that adapts imagination to reveal the reality of the past. It discovers a "truthful" honest metaphor that applies not only to the self, but also to the entire society. Memoirs, which are autobiographies, are narratives recounting a collective societal history with the narrator's personal experience; sociocultural

---

[8] J. J. Wallach, "Building a Bridge of Words: The Literary Autobiography as Historical Source Material," *Biography* 29, no. 3 (2006): 446–461, at 450.

[9] I. Goodson, "The Rise of the Life Narrative," *Teacher Education Quarterly* 33 (2006): 7–21, at 10, www.researchgate.net/publication/253187338_The_Rise_of_the_Life_Narrative.

[10] Hayden White, "The Fictions of Factual Representation," in *Tropics of Discourse: Essays in Cultural Criticism* (Baltimore: Johns Hopkins University Press, 1978), 121–134.

[11] Hayden White, "The Historical Text as Literary Artifact," in *Tropics of Discourse*, 81–100.

relationship and memory serve as a cynosure to the recounted narratives. Similar to this is the principle of collectivism, discussed later in this chapter, which is inherent in most indigenous African societies: by telling my story, I seek to relate my personal experiences, and also to reflect extensively on the society. It is what Carl Jung referred to as the collective consciousness, or collective memory, in form of a narrative,[12] that molded and still influences my consciousness from childhood.

"Ojú kan níí bímọ, igba ojú níí wòó" ("only an eye gives birth to a child, but two hundred eyes nurture him," where "two hundred" suggests an abundance or multitude). My life and experiences are not only a manifestation of my immediate society, but also a fragment of it. They are a construction and exhibition of identity, and in close relation to the cultural system in which they are conceived. My identity, and my narrative by extension, is an interaction between myself and my society. The product is an identity conception that could be identified as a sociological subject. Other forms of identification are the Enlightenment subject, which is an autonomous and independent identity, and the postmodern subject, which is characterized by unstable and fragmented identity.[13]

In relating this connection between society and myself, it is impossible to avoid relying on and drawing inferences from the lives of others, especially to indicate and substantiate the various cultural codes, historical events, and sociopolitical experiences that are at play. There is no absolute self; there is only the existence of self in relation to another self. The ideology of a singular self in the African context is as elusive as Christianity's concept of the Trinity. Perhaps such non-belief in the singular autonomy of the self marks Africans as postmodern, even before the world became "modern," at least in orientation.

Rather than the narrative of the self, autobiography is a narrative of personalized memory. It is a description of the world as it exists from one's perspective,[14] what Adetayo Alabi referred to as using personal experience to expatriate communal ethos.[15] In discussing narratives as social transactions, J. E. Davis aptly describes narrative as "powerful because it configures experience by selecting and plotting events within a temporal order that infuses this event with significance and exploits them for valued ends."[16]

---

[12] E. Zandberg, "The Right to Tell the (Right) Story: Journalism, Authority and Memory," *Media Culture Society* 32, no. 5 (2010): 5–24.

[13] S. Hall, "The Question of Cultural Identity," in *Modernity: An Introduction to Modern Societies*, ed. S. Hall, D. Held, D. Hubert, and K. Thompson (Malden: Blackwell Publishers, 1996), 595–634, at 597.

[14] Wallach, "Building a Bridge of Words."

[15] Adetayo Alabi, *Telling Our Stories: Continuities and Divergences in Black Autobiographies* (New York: Palgrave, 2005).

[16] J. E. Davis, "Narratives and Social Movements: The Power of Stories," in *Stories of Change: Narrative and Social Movements* (New York: State University of New York Press, 2002), 3–30, at 16.

History in Africa, unlike its manifestation in places such as America, is embedded in various manifestations of orality, such as proverbs, riddles, myths or legends, anecdotes, and songs. These manifestations become the deconstruction and codification of history itself: history has submerged its wholeness in fragments across its various manifestations. A Yorùbá proverb asserts that "Ìtàn ló dòwe" (it is history that transformed itself into proverb), and proverbs are regarded as the collective representation of a people's way of life.[17]

Ademola Dasylva, a poet and literary critic, concludes in his essay that *A Mouth Sweeter than Salt* "is more or less the first work that successfully combines orality in the true sense with contemporary history."[18] In the African community, tales, songs, and chants are the oral media through which collective memories are sustained, by storytellers or griots, and recounted from a generation to another. The oral medium serves as a bank for the preservation of ancient beliefs and experiences. The artists who reproduce tales, songs, chants, and other aspects of the oral tradition are viewed as the keepers of the people's ancient wisdoms and beliefs.[19] In so doing, "through his or her work of cultural historical transmission, the griot thereby serves the coexistent role of instigator, calling upon a form of social responsibility and connectivity across society."[20]

Slave narratives are considered the earliest written autobiographical narratives in Africa. These narratives are not written in Africa, or solely about Africa, but they established their importance by documenting the exodus of Africans into slavery in the Americas and Europe, as well as the brutality of the institution of slavery. As Ogude puts it, "the first Africans to write in English were all unwilling exiles and children of unwilling exiles. And they all wrote in response to a historical condition that denied them their humanity."[21] Their narratives contain gruesome accounts of slavery's horror and the terror experienced during their years in captivity; they were written by freed slaves or those who managed to escape.

These narratives, originally published in England in the eighteenth century, were deliberate creations that expressed and established their intellectual and moral universe. They were aimed at the abolitionist cause to preach religious

---

[17] E. Obiechina, "Narrative Proverbs in the African Novel," *Oral Tradition* 7, no. 2 (1992): 197–230.

[18] Ademola Dasylva, "The Archivist as Muse: Toyin Falọla's Experimentation with Alternative History in A Mouth Sweeter than Salt," in *Toyin Falola: The Man, the Mask, the Muse*, ed. Niyi Afolabi (Durham: Carolina Academic Press, 2010), 735–764.

[19] T. A. Hale, "Griottes: Female Voices from West Africa," *Research in African Literatures* 25, no. 3 (1994): 71–91.

[20] M. Krishnan, "The Storyteller Function in Contemporary Nigerian Narrative," *Journal of Commonwealth Literature* 49, no. 1 (2014): 29–45, at 30.

[21] S. E. Ogude, "African Literature and the Burden of History: Some Reflections," in *African Literature and African Historical Experiences*, ed. Chidi Ikonne, Emelia Oko, and Peter Onwudinjo (Ibadan: Heinemann Educational Books, Nigeria, 1991), 1–10, at 2.

redemption, as contained in the spiritual narratives, and to encourage progress. However, since the narratives tend to have a strong autobiographical motif, the abolitionist cause seems to be the most famous. These narratives became a path for navigating the historical experience of slavery and reconstructing the genealogy of the African American. Several of the freed slaves, from North America and the Caribbean, wrote the accounts of their lives. Popular examples of these narratives include: *The Interesting Narrative of the Life of Olaudah Equiano, Or Gustavus Vassa, The African* (1789); *Incedents in the Life of a Slave Girl* by Harriet Jacobs (1861); *My Bondage and My Freedom* by Frederick Douglass (1855); *The Life and Religious Experience of Jarena Lee* by Jarena Lee (1836); *Behind the Scenes* by Elizabeth Keckley; *Life of William Grimes, the Runaway Slave* (1852); and *Narrative of the Life of Henry Box Brown* (1849).

There was a subsequent surge in autobiographical writings from colonial masters recounting their stay and rule in Africa, followed by narratives from nationalist Africans during the attainment of independence in various nation-states. They gave accounts of the struggles that accompanied the attainment of freedom, highlighting their duties and contributions toward the cause and their nation-states at large. Life narratives became a point of observation for historical facts from Africans experiencing colonialism, which could potentially constitute a historical archive with an undertone of political liberalism.[22] Jomo Kenyatta's *Facing Mount Kenya* (1965), Oginga Odinga's *Not Yet Uhuru: The Autobiography of Oginga Odinga* (1967), Nelson Mandela's *Long Walk to Freedom* (1994), Kwame Nkrumah's *Ghana: The Autobiography of Kwame Nkrumah* (1957), and Nnamdi Azikiwe's *My Odyssey* (1970) are major representative works documenting the lives and roles of these authors in their various African countries' epic struggles for political independence and socio-economic development. Life writings by Africans are now mass produced, documenting the progression of their lives and societies. They are usually from a society's elites, those who have made a great mark in the society's development, and those who have the financial capability to fund the production of their writings. Life narratives, in Africa and beyond, have gained a prominence beyond historical documentation to be an inspirational mechanism, especially to motivate the younger generations.

Narrative is defined by setting and space. It has served multiple functions in different periods and places, applying its imitative, expressive, cultural, and historical properties. Perceptions of literary narratives are a reflection of norms

---

[22] E. Sankara, "History and the Production and Reception of Autobiography in Francophone Africa," *Canadian Review of Comparative Literature* 32, no. 3/4 (2005): 440–458; T. H. Ngwenya, "The Historical Dimension of South African Autobiography," *Alternation* 7, no. 1 (2000): 1–4.

and values, a revelation of cultural ethos.[23] Various means of human creativity are employed in a bid to sustain and preserve the sociocultural heritage and experiences of humanity, but literature has unarguably proved most effective for social and historical human experiences. To this end, it becomes a political device, burdened with the responsibility of sustaining the totality of humanity. There is no doubt that "literature is at one and the same time History's major bequest to mankind and the principal corrective of history."[24]

Narrating Collective Consciousness and Cultural Ideologies

> Words are not objects to be wasted. They represent the accumulated knowledge, cultural values, the vision of an entire people or peoples. We believe the proof of a thing or idea is in the doing. Doing requires some form of social interaction and thus, story is the most persuasive and sensible way to present the accumulated thoughts and values of a people.[25]

It is imperative to understand the ancient conception of narrative functions: the poetic function, the dialectic function, and the rhetoric function. To understand the cultural ideologies embedded in *A Mouth Sweeter than Salt* is to understand the dialectical function of a narrative and its role in upholding the sociopolitical and cultural consciousness of the people – the burden to discover, reveal, and present truth. The narrative function of the memoir, as aptly expressed by Lucaites and Condit, "is not to present a pleasurable tale for its own sake as with poetic narratives, but to illuminate the factual nature of the universe as a means of providing information for human use."[26] This part of the chapter attempts to reconstruct the narrative and extrapolate the cultural ideologies (un)consciously embedded in it.

Time as a Cultural Phenomenon

It is no coincidence that the first chapter of the narrative is titled "Time and Season." Time is an important concept that can mean Ìgbà (period) or Àkókò (moment) in Yorùbá culture. As in the narrative, time is a cultural phenomenon – it is described by the occurrence of certain events, occasions, or activities. Time can be marked by a change in the weather or climate, the

---

[23] Ogude, "African Literature and the Burden of History"; Arjun Dubey, "Literature and Society," *IOSR Journal of Humanities and Social Science (IOSR-JHSS)* 9, no. 6 (2013): 84–85; M. C. Albrecht, "The Relationship of Literature and Society," *American Journal of Sociology* 59, no. 5 (1954): 425–436.

[24] H. H. Okam, "The Novelist as Historian: Yambo Ouologuem's *Le Devior de Violence*," in *African Literature and African Historical Experiences*, ed. Chidi Ikonne, Emelia Oko, and Peter Onwudinjo (Ibadan: Heinemann Educational Books, Nigeria, 1991), 53–62, at 53.

[25] Lee Maracle, *Oratory: Coming to Theory* (North Vancouver: Gallerie Publications, 1990), 3.

[26] Lucaites and Condit, "Reconstructing Narrative Theory," 93.

harvest of a certain crop or farm product, the reign of a king or a famous warrior, or other events.

The understanding of time is a relative concept: time is being marked or described in methods that vary from one period to another as well as from region to region. Thus, time becomes a cultural product, understood and defined by the people's way of life and their conception of reality. Within the Yorùbá cultural concept of time framing, time before the advent of colonialism is not a linear progression of events, but fragments of events with a beginning and a closure. Time is conceived in relation to events, whether in the past, present, or future.[27] In the same vein, time is measured through celestial-cosmic cycles and terrestrial-cosmic cycles. Cosmic bodies, such as the sun and moon, divide the day into Àárọ̀ (morning), Ọ̀sán (afternoon), and Alẹ́ (night).

Ecological agents, such as human beings and monkeys, are adopted to codify the small units of time. Ìṣẹ́jù (a human blinking) and Ìṣẹ́jú-ààyá (blinking of the brown monkey) are roughly estimated to be minute and second respectively.[28] But the Yorùbá word for hour (Wákàtí) is a loan word from Arabic (waqt). This is an influence of Islam that came into Yorùbáland even before the advent of Christianity.

The opening chapter of *A Mouth Sweeter than Salt* presents a "curious mind" interested in knowing my mother's date of birth alongside a gentleman who inquired about my father's age. In both instances time is invoked by the description of other events occurring around the event in question. In the first instance "the information that my mother was born before the brother of her first cousin"[29] is the related event that describes my mother's date of birth. My father's date of birth is reckoned to be during the arrival of Ibadan warriors after the Yorùbá ended their warfare:[30] "on the day the Ibadan people heard the last war song."[31] Through these incidents time is made manifest as a presentation of events, or events are used as a description of time.

A notable downside to this conception of time is its lack of specificity, failing to provide an exact date within a time frame. This makes it difficult, if not impossible, to verify and establish the historical authenticity of events that took place in the distant past. Within the African community the relevance of time is in its functionality. The lack of specificity, or the understating of time by association, can also cause multiplicity and duplicity of dates accounting for events. For example:

---

[27] J. A. Ayodele, "Time in Yoruba Thoughts," in *African Philosophy: An Introduction*, ed. Richard Wright (Boston: University Press of America, 1984), 93–111.
[28] A. D. Fayemi, "Time in Yoruba Culture," *al-Hikmat* 36 (2016): 27–41.
[29] Toyin Falola, *A Mouth Sweeter than Salt: An African Memoir* (Ibadan: Bookcraft, 2013), 4.
[30] Falola, *A Mouth Sweeter than Salt*, 14.
[31] Falola, *A Mouth Sweeter than Salt*, 11.

Many were just victims of stories and events that gave birth not to them, but to dates. The story of the uncle might differ from that of the cousin, so that two new dates were possible. The outbreak of a flu epidemic could have been confused with that of a locust invasion so that dates had to be altered when confusion was cleared up.[32]

Dates, as in the specificity of time, became necessary during the shift to modernity; as such, dates "were arrived at by those stories [related events pertaining to the occurrence of an event within a time frame], and the public notary, after listening to a story or an event, could invent a date."[33] The conception of dates is a modern invention, unlike time, which bridges the gap between the past and the present: "Times and seasons were shifted and adjusted to accommodate dates and their documentation."[34]

The (Re)construction of Historical Events: The Formation and Expansion of Ibadan

With a life narrative it is expedient for its plot to be situated within a historical frame of real life. However, while I rely on my memory to project the events that are related, some events were selected purposefully – the hope is that by doing so, those events would be preserved. As I give a verifiable account of certain incidents, I am aware that those events would be understood not only within their context, but also from a different perspective. As a scholar of history, conscious attempts are made at (re)constructing historical events and providing readers with important and valid historical events to learn from, but they are devoid of tiresome historical accounts. This (re)construction of historical accounts requires keen attention from the reader who assembles them from their bits and fragments offered across the memoir.

In the early chapter of the narrative, while investigating my father's actual date of birth, I established that the "Yorùbá ended their long century of warfare,"[35] which took seventeen years,[36] and the British "imposed their first Resident, Captain Bower, in 1893."[37] I identified the cause of this war as a result of the political disorder among kings and chiefs of different Yorùbá cities, due to their failure to maintain order. Hence, thousands of people were displaced into new and bigger settlements such as Ògbómọ̀ṣọ́, Ibadan, and Ìjàyè.[38] However, the third chapter of the narrative reveals the specific war that caused the displacement of several Yorùbá people and the creation of these

---

[32] Falola, *A Mouth Sweeter than Salt*, 18.
[33] Falola, *A Mouth Sweeter than Salt*, 17.
[34] Falola, *A Mouth Sweeter than Salt*, 19.
[35] Falola, *A Mouth Sweeter than Salt*, 14.
[36] Falola, *A Mouth Sweeter than Salt*, 19.
[37] Falola, *A Mouth Sweeter than Salt*, 15.
[38] Falola, *A Mouth Sweeter than Salt*, 37.

new settlements: it was the war between Àfọ̀njá, the *Aàrẹ Ọ̀nà Kakaǹfò* (generalissimo) of the Old Ọ̀yọ́ Empire and its *Aláàfin* (emperor). With the support of the Fúlànì, an army was established that overran Ọ̀yọ́ and many other Yorùbáland settlements.[39]

Ibadan rapidly evolved from a war camp into one of the largest empires in Africa through its fierceness, restlessness, and numerous wars, "turning Ìbàdàn into a flourishing metropole."[40] It was characterized by street fights and conflicts, reflecting the instability of the era. There was no *Ọba* (king), as with most other Yorùbá cities. The traditional title known today as the Olúbàdàn was partly instigated by the colonial masters to foster peace within the city, as well as to gain control over the people:

> Ibadan was not planning on tradition; it was the British who forced them. Ibadan did not even want a king with a crown, like other Yoruba cities and kingdoms, with the powerful half man half god idling away at the palace with his harem. The British encouraged Ibadan to replace a warrior with a gentle king.[41]

In the third chapter I hinted at some of the factors contributing to the continual expansion of Ibadan after the death of its founders and the original settlers, which led to its heterogeneous nature. Ibadan did not belong to a particular Yorùbá group. It was originally a war camp, and soon developed into a city that continually embraced more people into it; like the bosom of the Lord, those who seek growth come into it. Hence the saying, "Ibadan, the town where the owner of the land does not prosper like the stranger."

A contributing factor to Ibadan's heterogeneous nature was its central location, which was a strategic position for the founding warriors to protect themselves from enemies and interact with neighboring cities. The Ìjẹ̀bú and Ẹ̀gbá came from the south to establish businesses; Igbo, Edo, Urhobo, Ibibio, and others came from the southwestern and eastern parts of the country; and the Hausa came from the northern part of the country. The mass production of cocoa, palm oil, and kernels attracted foreigners to Ibadan. Other neighboring cities brought goods and products to sell in Ibadan, establishing a central market. Thus, "With its history and central location, Ìbàdàn became one of the few colonial headquarters. Throughout the twentieth century, it remained a regional and state capital, a famous city."[42]

---

[39] Falola, *A Mouth Sweeter than Salt*, 111–112.
[40] Falola, *A Mouth Sweeter than Salt*, 63.
[41] Falola, *A Mouth Sweeter than Salt*, 62.
[42] Falola, *A Mouth Sweeter than Salt*, 133.

Greetings and Respect as Cultural Values

It is devastating that the customary significance attached to greetings, whether as cultural, ritual, or communicative gestures, has been reversed in recent times. Elaborate Yorùbá greetings are now associated with sycophancy, inferiority, and cultural excessiveness. However, greetings and salutations are valuable cultural traditions that characterize the Yorùbá people, especially the Ọ̀yọ́ and Ìbàdàn people. It is fascinating to note that a form of greeting metamorphosed into a name – the Ẹkú people, and a collective identity of the Yorùbá people – was coined by non-Yorùbá.[43] While *Yorùbá* is a more popular and widely accepted name referring to the Yorùbá people, *Ọmọlúàbí* ("the child given birth by the Lord of good conduct") is a more suitable cultural notion, capturing the heritage of the Yorùbá as a group of people with good conduct. Greeting is "one of the ways to test the commitments of youths to values, respect and love";[44] and it is a manifestation of *Ìwà pẹ̀lẹ́* (good conduct, gentility, or humility), which is the core value of *Ọmọlúàbí*.

Greetings are a tool for validating one's reverence for another person, especially elders. The Yorùbá language lacks words to express notions such as cousins, nephews, uncles, or nieces. As such, every elderly person is regarded as a father, mother, sister, or brother as the case may be;[45] strangers are not excluded. When the age of an individual is unknown, one is culturally obliged to address them with the aforementioned titles as an expression of respect and warm affection: to such strangers, "Ká rí ni lókèèrè ká ṣ'àríyá, ó yó ni ju oúnje lọ" (greeting a person cheerfully from a distance away is more satisfying than food).

> Seniority was valued in the older society when the events took place, and even long afterward. I knew not to disrespect those older than me, even when they were not members of my household. Within the compound, within the clan, within the village, everybody knew who was older, who died before whom, who married after whom.[46]

Greeting is a rite that establishes relationships between people, as well as the events and background surrounding the occasion. There is a greeting for morning, afternoon, and night; "The dry and wet seasons are marked by different greeting forms, again different from the harmattan period";[47] there are greetings for different occupations and occasions such as hunting, farming, or mourning; and festivals and celebrations also require different greetings. It would be disastrous to employ mourning greetings during a marriage

---

[43] Falola, *A Mouth Sweeter than Salt*, 41.
[44] Falola, *A Mouth Sweeter than Salt*, 34.
[45] Falola, *A Mouth Sweeter than Salt*, 211.
[46] Falola, *A Mouth Sweeter than Salt*, 19.
[47] Falola, *A Mouth Sweeter than Salt*, 32.

ceremony or to offer sympathy "to one who is rejoicing or joy . . . to one who is in sorrow," and "As events change, so do greetings."[48]

Greetings also vary by age, position, and occupation. Gestures and body postures, such as kneeling (for females), prostrating (for males), and bending the head characterize greeting. No one greets a king while standing – it is rude and offensive. It is a desecration. Kings are second-in-command to the gods, and by virtue they are to be greeted as such. It is important to understand these principles and elements, which I referred to as "Greeting Codes,"[49] to formulate a suitable greeting for a person during a specific time of the day, during an activity, or during an occasion.

It is not enough to understand these greeting codes alone; it is equally important to give adequate response to these greetings, or responses to the responses of a greeting. Some greetings are like conversations that go back and forth till they are blurred or evolved into a full and proper conversation. For example, "One wakes up in the morning to . . . greeting to welcome one to the day, asking about the night and the sleep, the state of the body, the physical alertness to start the day [and even prayers to accompany one throughout the day]. To each question, one must answer," and in turn greet, which would generate another cycle of responses.[50]

In the latter part of the first chapter an attempt is made to reveal formal education's corrosive effect, caused by modernity and multiculturalism. The cultural value of greeting and respect diminishes in fast-developing cosmopolitan cities like Lagos "that enables its citizens to escape greeting one another," compared to cities like Ibadan. Greetings degenerating into nuisance and wasted time show how this cultural value is displaced in society.[51]

Greetings within a community ensure respect, and they foster peace and unity among the people. The failure to utter a greeting, or a response to one, becomes a sign of conflict usually resolved by an observer, or an elder: "The observer can mediate, by asking the two to talk, to explain their problems, to pressure the one who refuses to talk to please state the reasons, whether trivial or substantial. Elders may be asked to mediate if the problem is bigger."[52] However, greetings do not always signify friendship, respect, or peace. Like every other thing, they can be manipulated to mean the opposite; proverbial expressions state that "Ìdọ̀bálẹ̀ kìí ṣe ìwà, ohun tí a ó jẹ ni à ń wá" (prostration is not an evidence of a good moral conduct, we are just looking for what to eat). The true intentions of greetings are concealed in their code and context, which can only be deciphered by the receiver's wisdom.

---

[48] Falola, *A Mouth Sweeter than Salt*, 32.
[49] Falola, *A Mouth Sweeter than Salt*, 32.
[50] Falola, *A Mouth Sweeter than Salt*, 33.
[51] Falola, *A Mouth Sweeter than Salt*, 34–35.
[52] Falola, *A Mouth Sweeter than Salt*, 40.

Names and Identity as a Cultural Ideology

The importance of names, and the process of naming a person, place, or other entity within the Yorùbá culture, cannot be overstated. Considerable efforts and justifications are involved in naming, and names transcend the common purpose of identification. They are symbolic, with condensed history and spiritual meaning. Names are not cherry-picked in the Yorùbá culture: "bí kò bá nídìí, obìnrin kìí jẹ́ Kúmólú" (if there is no reason, a female doesn't bear Kúmólú). For every name there is a story, a tangible purpose and reason behind it. The fate and destiny of a person can be shaped by their name; the religion or occupation of a family can be revealed in its name, and the circumstances surrounding the births of individuals can be highlighted in their names.

Among the numerous Yorùbá proverbs highlighting the importance of names are: "Orúkọ ń ro ni, àpèjá a máa rò ènìyàn" (a name influences the bearer, and an alias influences the bearer); "Orúkọ ọmọ ni ìjánu ọmọ" (a child's name is its reign); "Ilé làá wò, ká tó s'ọmọ l'órúkọ" (it is the house we consider before naming a child), etc. Names are cherished, and prevented from being tarnished at all cost. The biblical saying comes to mind: "A good name is more desirable than great riches; to be esteemed is better than silver and gold."

Names are crystallized history. Praise names are used to condense and trace the genealogy of a person or family: "To call me Isola is to move me quickly past the recent years, back to the nineteenth century, the beginning of time for my ancestors, and I mean the recent ones."[53] Abiodun, someone born during a major festival, is a name that embodies "the unity of time and season"[54] and names such as Oluwatoyin/Ọlọruntoyin (God is enough to be praised) or Oluwabusọla/Ọlọrunbusọla (God amplifies my status) signify the acknowledgment and significance of the Supreme Being (God) within the Yorùbá cultural belief. Names are totems, verbal symbols of the expressions, wishes, and aspirations of parents or relatives. In the memoir I recounted that my father gave us names that reflected some of his aspirations:

> As if to invite God to be on his side, his first two children had names of expectation: Olufemi (God loves me) was for his first daughter, an indication that he was going to do well in life. The name of his first son, Adewale (the crown is here), was of a superior order, indicating a preference for a male as well as for honour. Another son connected his present to the past, in the name of Akinlolu, a manifestation of courage and war.[55]

Meanwhile, names such as Igbẹkọyi (the bush has refused this one), Durojaye (stay to enjoy life), Kuti (he refused to die), Kosọkọ (there is no hoe to dig the grave), Ikudaisi (death spares this one), Igbosaanu (the bush is merciful),

---

[53] Falola, *A Mouth Sweeter than Salt*, 36.
[54] Falola, *A Mouth Sweeter than Salt*, 44.
[55] Falola, *A Mouth Sweeter than Salt*, 138.

Ikumapayi (death do not kill this one), Kokumọ (he is no longer dying), and others are traditional names given to children who are suspected to be *Àbíkú* (a child who dies after birth), presenting their survival as a victory over death.[56] These names thus transform from metaphor to magic to neutralize and sever the connection between the *Àbíkú* and their spiritual stronghold.

Hills and valleys are the prevalent topographic nature of the Ibadan landscape; they influence names given to places like Òkè Ajé, Ìsàlẹ̀ Ajé, Àpáta Gàǹgà, Òkebọ́là, Òkè-Àdó, Odò Ọnà, etc. Similarly, when "the vacant valleys and hills of Ìbàdàn were being occupied by churches, the hills and valleys were also being renamed – Òkè Àánú (The Hill of Mercy), Òkè Ìyanu (Miracle Hill), Ìsàlẹ̀ Àlàáfíà (Peace Valley)."[57] The same applies to the name of Ibadan itself, which means "by the boundary of the valley." These attributions highlight the romantic consciousness of the Yorùbá and how much they immerse themselves, culturally and spiritually, in the splendor of nature across time:

> These included Ilé-Olóòlù, Ilé-Ọmí, and Ilé-Ajé, all clans marked by cults and masquerades. There were clans and compounds defined by occupations, such as the one named Ilé-Aládìẹ to indicate its interest in poultry, Ilé-Elépo to show interest in palm oil, and so on. Each had its reservoir of history, its long cognomen, and its pride.[58]

Names, usually aliases, can be formed by occupation, or the name of one's house, one's complexion, and the names of one's children.[59] Such names lack specificity within a larger environment, but the bearers can easily be identified within a family or small community. One example is Ọmọ Bàbá Ọlọ́sanyìn (the son of an Ọsanyìn priest).[60] In the fourth chapter of the narrative I highlighted how the names of mothers and wives were generated within the family: "Ìyàwó Babalọla (if Babalọla was the husband's name)" and "when she produced her first child (whose name, say, was Bisọla), she would become Mama Bisọla or ìyá Bisọla"[61] while the names Màmá Pupa and Màmá Ẹlẹ́mu are associated with complexion (red) and occupation (*ẹmu* – palm wine) respectively, and Ìyá Lékulẹ́ja is the seller of assorted materials for native charms and medicine. Names are not a fixed mode of identification; as an individual evolves through time he or she acquires more names that define his or her presence.

---

[56] Falola, *A Mouth Sweeter than Salt*, 125.
[57] Falola, *A Mouth Sweeter than Salt*, 142–143.
[58] Falola, *A Mouth Sweeter than Salt*, 203.
[59] Falola, *A Mouth Sweeter than Salt*, 151.
[60] Falola, *A Mouth Sweeter than Salt*, 314.
[61] Falola, *A Mouth Sweeter than Salt*, 150.

Mèsìògò: Defining the City and its People

> A thousand words cannot fill a basket. As each drops into the basket, it disappears like water. The purpose of talking is to create effect.[62]

It is expedient to evaluate the narrative and its semantic implication in relation to the scope of this study. According to David Lodge, "The title of a novel is part of the text – the first part of it, in fact, that we encounter – and therefore has considerable power to attract and condition the reader's attention."[63] The title, *A Mouth Sweeter than Salt*, offers a distinct understanding of the narrative, the people, and the events. In the words of Marcela Salack, "As its title promises, *A Mouth Sweeter than Salt: An African Memoir* is an excursion into an unfamiliar world and the mysterious aphorisms and proverbs employed there."[64] The title is an ethnolinguistic embodiment of the narrative, offering an apt description of the linguistic prowess and philosophical bearing (*Mèsìògò*) of the Ibadan people; the narrative highlights the peculiarities of an Ibadan in relation to their rhetoric and some other oral features.

The general Yorùbá populace is referred to as the Ẹkú people, and Ibadan indigenes are referred to as *Mèsìògò*, an alias owing its etymology to the linguistic and behavioral peculiarities of the Ibadan people. *Mèsìògò* is "a system of thought and philosophy of life ... it is about understanding the codes of behavior in a highly stratified society" of Ibadan,[65] and "as the *Mèsìògò* speak, they intertwine proverbs with history, preventing the listener the clues to understanding the issues at stake or even suspending judgment."[66] The literal meaning of *Mèsìògò* denotes the creativity to give apt responses and avoid being foolish:

> The *Mèsìògò* must ponder the consequences of words and actions, the damage that *no* and *yes* may cause. The *Mèsìògò* will try to anticipate enemies, and how words will further empower them. If *yes* will weaken the enemies, the *Mèsìògò* will offer it. Living in a huge city, the largest in West Africa, the *Mèsìògò* are too brilliant to misread the intricacies of intrigue and conflicts into human relations, into the daily contacts between visitors and hosts. Human behaviours are not permanent, and the *Mèsìògò* relies on the fluidity of words to deal with the plastic beings.[67]

These peculiarities are present throughout the narrative, but the latter part of the second chapter[68] contains more instances of the *Mèsìògò* ideology

---

[62] Falola, *A Mouth Sweeter than Salt*, 92.
[63] David Lodge, *The Art of Fiction* (London: Vintage, 2011), 193.
[64] M. Salack, "An Unpredictable Sojourner," 2004, www.texasobserver.org/1751-an-unpredictable-sojourner-by-marcela-salack/.
[65] Falola, *A Mouth Sweeter than Salt*, 89.
[66] Falola, *A Mouth Sweeter than Salt*, 90.
[67] Falola, *A Mouth Sweeter than Salt*, 82.
[68] Falola, *A Mouth Sweeter than Salt*, 73–98.

portrayed and adopted by different people maneuvering to win arguments, escape severe punishment, mediate conflicts, persuade or pacify enemies, ridicule others, and be unpredictable or ambiguous.

Rhetoric is an important attribute for an Ìbàdàn. Any individual within the Yorùbá community known to have an elaborate and effective command of language, especially in greeting, insulting, praying, or cursing, is usually suspected to be an Ìbàdàn indigene – "Learning words, expanding vocabularies, and putting words together is one of the essentials of growing up in Ìbàdàn."[69] The saying that "Ìbàdàn is the place where the thief is justified over the owner" owes its origin to the importance of rhetoric among her indigenes.

One instance of rhetoric applied to escape punishment or win an argument is that of Ogunmọla, who has been accused of stealing an antelope. He twisted "the story from theft to bravery. He praised himself, reminded the chiefs of his contribution to the city, and made a closing remark, What is an antelope to me?" stressing that the carcass of the antelope cannot be compared to the many "corpses and wounded soldiers" he carried from battles.[70] To be a *Mèsìògò* is to understand how an expression or word is infused with ambiguous meaning; words such as "Kò burú" (no problem) and "Ó dára" (it is good) can be used to imply the opposite of their meaning, or to depict one's indifference to an issue.

> The *Mèsìògò* also use silence for effect. Single words such as *Kòburú* and *Bẹẹni* are used to create effects similar to that of silence, that is, talking without revealing anything. The *Mèsìògò* with the skill to talk can use many words and many sentences . . . Piling one proverb over another, the clever *Mèsìògò* exhaust the listeners.[71]

It becomes the listener's responsibility to decode the original meaning of such expressions using "a set of other circumstances to decipher the meaning."[72]

Taboos and Superstition as Products of Cultural Belief

Myths and superstitions are important conceptions in a culture's traditional belief system, guiding the actions and behaviors of its people. They are sometimes taken to be crude, underdeveloped attempts at explaining humanity's existence and universe, and deeply rooted in the culture. They are held to be true by some, despite seemingly not having any logical or verifiable source or reason; they are not necessarily the product of a primitive society, as they are prevalent in almost all cultures.[73] However, they are also established beliefs

---

[69] Falola, *A Mouth Sweeter than Salt*, 90.
[70] Falola, *A Mouth Sweeter than Salt*, 70.
[71] Falola, *A Mouth Sweeter than Salt*, 92.
[72] Falola, *A Mouth Sweeter than Salt*, 82.
[73] L. Holden, *Encyclopedia of Taboos* (Oxford: ABC CLIO Ltd., 2000); E. Durkheim, *Incest: The Nature and the Origin of the Taboo* (New York: Lyle Stuart, 1963).

that guide morality, ethics, and spiritual uprightness, preventing unfortunate or catastrophic events and inducing good fortune and luck.[74] For instance:

> But in waking up, one prays not to first see one's enemy or someone one dislikes ... If a day has a tale of bad news, a legitimate question would be, "Who did you see first this morning?" If it was a good person, the bad news is attributed to another evil agency; if it was a bad person, he or she must have been responsible for ruining the day for the innocent fellow.[75]

The essence of this superstitious belief, guarding against a bad day, encourages good spiritual and moral conduct to avoid being associated with another person's misfortune. Likewise, the Yorùbá believe madness cannot be cured "once a mad person reached the market place."[76] Superstition holds that markets are inhabited by supernatural forces and evil powers, which could possess the body of the mad person and intensify the strain of madness. But a possible logical explanation is that once a mad man has entered the market, madness and its shame become eternal in the conception of people who encountered him, including those who were told about it. There is also the possibility that the mad person will get lost in the market, reducing the chances that they will be ever found and cured. Taboos belong to this category as well.

Taboos are forbidden actions and behaviors within a culture. Some are considered sacred, but most are spurned to ensure morality and good ethics in all human endeavors. The breaking of taboos insinuates the disruption of harmony; there are taboos related to eating, sleeping, working, walking, talking, and whatever else one can imagine.

> In Ìyá Àgbà's opinion, no one in the household should break any Yorùbá taboo, even those that science had disproved. She was the taboo police, and one way to annoy her was to break a taboo or even query her. She repeated taboos before scolding or administering any punishment.[77]

Certain taboos, which are considered sacred, are observed more carefully than others. Examples include those related to deities, one's destiny, and clan or family taboos. Failure to abide by them can often result in irreversible disasters, endangering lives and a peaceful existence. It is a common belief among the Yorùbá that a witch dares not consume Èèpo Ọbọ (*Ficus platyphylla*), and that a dog that eats the intestine of a giant rat (Òkété) would run mad.

The worshipers of specific deities are forbidden to do certain things. For example, worshipers of Ọbàtálá cannot consume palm wine or get drunk; an

---

[74] O. C. Omooboola, "An Overview of Taboo and Superstition among the Yoruba of Southwest of Nigeria," *Mediterranean Journal of Social Sciences* 4, no. 2 (2013): 221–226; E. B. Idowu, *Olódùmarè: God in Yoruba Belief* (Ibadan: Longmans, 1962).
[75] Falola, *A Mouth Sweeter than Salt*, 33.
[76] Falola, *A Mouth Sweeter than Salt*, 201.
[77] Falola, *A Mouth Sweeter than Salt*, 280.

example of an ancestral taboo is related in the fourth chapter of the narrative: "We could eat a ram, and why we were not prevented from eating our totemic animal, as in the case of other clans, I do not know. What we could not eat was crocodile, and I refused to eat this during visits to South Africa and Australia."[78] Most times, during birth divination reveals more specific taboos for a person to ensure they have a happy life – this can include what to eat, whom to marry, what clothes to wear, where to live, and what occupation to take.

Generally, these taboos are meant to teach self-discipline on the individual level, to ensure peace and prosperity on the communal level, and to attain consciousness and perfection at the spiritual level. "When one reviews the Èèwọ̀ in totality, there is no doubt that the intention was to prevent common accidents, enforce basic rules of hygiene, ensure respect for elders and customs, prevent waste, promote spirituality, and provide an understanding of elementary science."[79] Thorpe reached the same conclusion when he identified the reasons for taboo: to avoid accident, respect elders and religion, teach moral values, explain things that are difficult to understand, guide against wastefulness, and ensure cleanliness.[80] However, the manipulative aspects of taboos, at the spiritual level, require discretion and caution. In a belief system grounded in the power of evil, one can be rendered vulnerable if one's taboos are made public; wicked people can manipulate taboos to defeat or humiliate their targets.

Collectivism as a Cultural Ideology

> They spoke the same language, and those who chose to have marks made on their faces received the same signs as those on my father's face. The taboos of Ile-Àgbò, the foods they must avoid, defined their identity ... All the members had one clan Oríkì.[81]

African communities have always been defined by collectivism: the common interest shared by the people, common heritage, and common cultural and spiritual beliefs. The identity and belief of an individual or family is shaped and closely intertwined with the larger society. Within the city of Ibadan, living structures are divided into Agboolé (compounds), which are gatherings of homes inhabited by a cluster of related families (Ìdílé). They are the descendants (Ìran) of a common ancestor, and the family is itself an extended one, which is the smallest unit of relation.[82]

---

[78] Falola, *A Mouth Sweeter than Salt*, 174.
[79] Falola, *A Mouth Sweeter than Salt*, 282.
[80] C. O. Thorpe, *Àwọn Èèwọ̀ Ilẹ̀ Yoruba* (Ibadan: Onibọn-Oje Press, 1972).
[81] Falola, *A Mouth Sweeter than Salt*, 173.
[82] Falola, *A Mouth Sweeter than Salt*, 172.

An instance of collectivism in the narrative is in the fourth chapter, where I reveal that it was considered rude even to say "your mother" when referring to the mother of your friend or relations in the household. The acceptable label was iyá-mi-ìrẹ, which means "our joint mother." The same was true of one's father; many people might not know their fathers' real names. Similar acts of a collective responsibility occur when a community, or the norms guiding it, decides on a course of action.

A child's cultural, spiritual, and moral upbringing in various Yorùbá communities is a typical example – the duty is a collective effort, not the sole responsibility of parents and immediate family. "Àgbà kìí wà l'ọ́jà, k'órí ọmọ tuntun wọ́" is a popular Yorùbá proverb, suggesting the role of an elder (and the community) in raising a child. Any member of the community could deal with an errant child. In the third chapter of the narrative I describe how the crowd that had gathered in front of my house, to witness my return from God-knows-where, prevented my parents from taking me inside. They "wanted to know my story," and "someone suggested that they should wash me, a purification rite," and they kept giving more advice to ensure my safety and well-being.[83] They own these rights, culturally, as they had not only partaken in my upbringing but had also shown great concern about my whereabouts.

> Compounds, neighborhoods, and villages were united in many social events. All religious ceremonies attracted people from various places and families. People came to the city for cult and masquerade events. Tragedy united everybody, as many suspended their activities when people died. Even when a relation died elsewhere, people flooded our house to sympathize.[84]
>
> I knew members of the clan who lived elsewhere, but this did not exclude them from claiming membership. I never lived at Ilé-Àgbò, even for one day, but I have remained a member since birth, and now in far away Austin I am called upon to pay dues for social events, to sponsor new members for titles, to pay funeral expenses, and to repair buildings. My connection to the city is ensured by my participation in the maintenance of Ilé-Àgbò.[85]

Religious festivals, as highlighted in "Seasonal Pleasures," are certainly important factors that ensure the unification of the people. "The Òkèèbàdàn festival was my earliest experience of the public display of loyalty to the city, and it has remained such a display ever since. It was a peaceful carnival, one that pushed people of all types into the streets in thousands."[86]

---

[83] Falola, *A Mouth Sweeter than Salt*, 122.
[84] Falola, *A Mouth Sweeter than Salt*, 277.
[85] Falola, *A Mouth Sweeter than Salt*, 176.
[86] Falola, *A Mouth Sweeter than Salt*, 384.

Cultural Ideologies about Spirituality

In OdeAje and many other parts of the city, many people, including the educated ones, did not see spirits as fantasies, the imaginative creations of fertile minds, but as events, objects, episodes, histories and reality.[87]

The Yorùbá cosmic belief consists of three worlds or universes: the world of the living, the world of the dead, and the world of the spirit or unborn. These three worlds are interrelated and interdependent – each cannot exist without the others. Events occurring in one are triggered or influenced by events in the others.

Aside from the events that (co-)occur in these worlds, the beings that occupy them are important. The world of the dead is occupied by the dead, who are usually referred to as ancestors (*Baba-ńlá, Egúngún*), sometimes acting as intermediaries between the living and the spirits. It was a common belief that spirits of the dead who had children do not rest because they are too busy looking after their children.[88] The place of the dead is remarkable within the Yorùbá cosmic belief. It is a common practice among the Yorùbá to pray and appease the dead, asking them for protection, provision, and guidance. The *Egúngún* worship and festival is one of those means through which the spirits of the dead are reincarnated, appeased, and celebrated:

> The spirit of the *Egúngún* was a positive one, most welcomed, and associated with all the good things of life. It was not that the dead corpses voluntarily chose to move from their scattered graves to revisit the earth. On the contrary, it was human beings who appealed to the dead to visit them. The flesh and bones of the dead were already rotten, and their souls were invisible. To overcome the problem that the dead were unable to be physically present, human beings chosen from among themselves the people to represent the dead. Once they put on the masks and garments that covered their entire bodies, following a ritual performance in a secluded grove known as *Ìgbàlẹ̀*, they were no longer humans but guests from heaven. The man in a mask, now a reincarnated soul, became more powerful than those who chose him in the first instance. We now had to beg the man in disguise to have mercy on us, to bless us, to forgive our transgressions.[89]

Humans, animals, plants, and certain other elements occupy the world of the living, the simplest world. The world of the spirit is largely occupied by beings whose existence is a mystery to humankind. Several spirits perform certain duties or behaviors, and they are known to cause certain events in the world of

---

[87] Falola, *A Mouth Sweeter than Salt*, 287.
[88] Falola, *A Mouth Sweeter than Salt*, 398.
[89] Falola, *A Mouth Sweeter than Salt*, 236.

the living. Examples mentioned in the narrative are Àbíkú, Iwin, Ẹbọra, Egbére, Emèrè, Àjẹ́, Òrìṣà Ìbejì, Olódùmarè, Èṣù, Ṣàngó, and Ọya.

The Emèrè (a child who can come and go at will) and Àbíkú (the one who is born to die) are examples of beings whose existence is both mystery and misery for mankind. "An Emèrè would accomplish so much within a short time in order to be loved and to attract praise"[90] but it would never live long enough to manifest its full potential. Unlike the Emèrè, which lives for years, the Àbíkú dies few days or weeks after being born. Their death in modern times has been ascribed to sickle-cell anemia, which doesn't solve the mystery of the signs and marks accompanying them in their reincarnation.[91]

Offerings and sacrifices are often presented to deities to protect an Àbíkú from death, or to prevent an Emèrè from reconvening with his spiritual friends, but only when such children are identified – usually by divination before their death or shortly after death. Some are strong-willed enough to return to their spiritual abode and friends, causing the offerings and sacrifices made on their behalf to be ineffective. In such cases the parents would mutilate the bodies of the deceased children to prevent them from reincarnating.

The Ìbejì, who bring their names, Taye/Taiwo and Kẹhinde, from heaven, are powerful children like the Àbíkú and Emèrè. Ordinarily, Taiwo is the first born and Kẹhinde the second, but the belief is contrary in Yorùbá culture. Kẹhinde (the one who came after) is believed to be the elder of the two: like a general, he commanded his twin to go have a taste of life first and return with his findings. Taiwo is a contraction of the expression "tọ́ ayé wò" which means "have a taste of the world." The deity of the twins, Òrìṣà Ìbejì, is worshiped to preserve and protect the twins, and to provide for the parents taking care of them.

> One could not visit Ibadan or any Yoruba city without seeing the mothers of twins singing and dancing in the streets and markets, like beggars, to seek donations but more to appease the spirit of the twins. Like Àbíkú, twins demanded sacrifices although they were not gods. If one of the two was angry that he was being treated with inequality or disrespect, he or she could reject the sacrifice and proceed to heaven. Even after this voluntary death, a wooden figure must be dedicated to the dead dressed like the other twin, who chose life, and propitiated in order to prevent anger that would lead to the death of the other one.[92]

Such spirits as Ẹbọra, Iwin, Àǹjànú, and Egbére occupy different strata in the Yorùbá cosmic belief system. They are usually feared, for they may be benevolent or malevolent. "Not all Iwin were evil: many actually led one onto the path of success and wealth; others simply gave advice or wisdom" or granted

---

[90] Falola, A Mouth Sweeter than Salt, 126.
[91] Falola, A Mouth Sweeter than Salt, 11, 124–127.
[92] Falola, A Mouth Sweeter than Salt, 127–128.

wishes,[93] and they are characterized by gruesome shapes and physical features. They are not direct descendants of the Supreme Being, and they do not wield enormous power, which means that they are not accorded the same respect as divinities and deities.

The divinities share distinct attributes of the Supreme Being, Olódùmarè. They are usually regarded as his ministers, and they are sometimes the personification of aspects such as the weather, events, emotions, or objects. For example, Ṣàngó is associated with thunder and lightning and intense anger; Ògún with iron and war; Òṣun and Yemọja with water; Ọya with wind and rivers; and Èṣù with discord and pluriversalism. The Yorùbá cultural and religious belief portrays Ṣàngó as the husband of Ọya and Òṣun as deity couples, which aids the explanation of natural happenings such as rain, thunder and lightning, and wind occurring together, which by extension is a metaphor for fertility.[94]

Olódùmarè ("the one that understands mystery") is unarguably regarded as the most powerful of the deities, and his role and function within the Yorùbá cosmology is clear. But Èṣù, another prominent divinity – so prominent that he wriggles his way into the narrative in several places[95] – is regarded as Olódùmarè's deputy and associated with mischief and discord. His importance lies in his task of conveying wishes and requests from human beings, as well as messages from other divinities to Olódùmarè, for whom he serves as an intermediary.

In comprehending and navigating the perimeters of the Yorùbá cosmic universe, spiritual concepts as Àyànmọ́, Kádàrá, and Orí become important. "Most statements about individuals were punctuated with words that placed emphasis on destiny – Àyànmọ́, Orí, Kádàrá – indicating the powerlessness of human beings to shape their future in the way they chose."[96] Kádàrá and Àyànmọ́ are profound spiritual Yorùbá beliefs, accounting for incidents happening to an individual over the course of their existence. They both suggest predestination, although they differ slightly in their conception and adoption. Àyànmọ́ emphasizes choices and wishes made by an individual in heaven before birth, and Kádàrá underscores the powerlessness of an individual in the face of events that have been preordained by Olódùmarè. Proverbial expressions as "Àkúnlẹ̀yàn làdáyébá, a dáyé tán ojú ń kán wa" (our destiny is preordained, we only become curious on arrival) and "Àyànmọ́ kò gbóògùn" (destiny has no remedy) affirm these ideas.

[93] Falola, A Mouth Sweeter than Salt, 287.
[94] Falola, A Mouth Sweeter than Salt, 184.
[95] Falola, A Mouth Sweeter than Salt, 22–28.
[96] Falola, A Mouth Sweeter than Salt, 267.

In the chapter entitled "Blood and Mouth" I narrate an instance where giving advice to an individual was problematic without having an idea of the recipient's destiny.[97] Decisions and actions must align with one's destiny.

> The yet unborn had a connection to God and other supernatural agencies who negotiated with its destiny. While one chose to be a king, the other could decide to be a king's messenger. At birth, the destiny was locked, and the person was unable to change most aspects of it. The trouble, as Alhaji and Baba Ọlọ́pàá always warned their children, was that a good destiny could change to bad, not because the gods were angry but because the children were bad. To ensure the actualization of one's Orí, one must not only work, one must also have a good character.[98]

Yorùbá proverbs, such as "Orí là bá bọ, ká fi Òrìṣà sílẹ̀" (it is one's head that ought to be worshiped and let the deities be) and "Òògùn ló ni ọjọ́ kan ìpọ́njú, orí ẹni ló ni ọjọ́ gbogbo" (charms are saviors in a day of torment, but only one's destiny saves one always) overrule the concepts of Kádàrá and Àyànmọ́, the potency of charms, and the prominence and dominance of divinities over man. However, Orí means destiny, and it can be argued to be Olódùmarè itself, justifying the supremacy of Orí over every other divinity.[99]

It is not enough to understand only the Yorùbá cosmic belief and its spiritual concepts; it is equally important to understand how this universe is traversed. Divination, offerings and sacrifices, prayers, magic, and charms are among the mediums used to maneuver spirituality and manipulate physical outcomes. At the birth of a child and other instances, oracles and divinities are consulted by diviners on behalf of the child's parents hoping to unravel the child's destiny and to seek spiritual intervention on matters regarding good living.[100] These diviners have garnered "esoteric knowledge and could predict the future. So deep was the belief in this capacity to know about the future and to prevent failure that many consulted a babaláwo [father of mysteries], even those who had accepted Islam and Christianity."[101] When divinities and spirits must be appeased, offerings and sacrifices are rendered.

The Òkè-Bàdàn, Ṣàngó, Ọya, Omi, and Egúngún festivals are popular venues for worshiping these divinities. They are also cultural events unifying the rich and the poor; the past, present, and future; and the physical and the spiritual to celebrate the heritage of Ibadan. "The belief was that the hill had offered protection to the earliest occupants, saving them from their enemies, offering shelter and protection. The carnival turned the hill into a god, worshipped as

---

[97] Falola, *A Mouth Sweeter than Salt*, 90.
[98] Falola, *A Mouth Sweeter than Salt*, 267.
[99] Falola, *A Mouth Sweeter than Salt*, 264.
[100] Falola, *A Mouth Sweeter than Salt*, 96.
[101] Falola, *A Mouth Sweeter than Salt*, 294.

the Òkè-Bàdàn (the hill of Ìbàdàn)."¹⁰² The Ibadan people come together to honor the hill, expressing gratitude in elaborate rites and rituals performed by the Abòkè. The vulgar songs characterizing the Òkè-Bàdàn festival are charged with spiritual, historical, social, and purgatorial effects: "Indeed, one of the great achievements of the carnival was to use songs to level the playing field, to allow the young and the poor to say whatever was on their mind, using sex and its symbolism as metaphors."¹⁰³ The vulgarity of the songs implies sex, and sex begets reproduction: the biological reproduction is a metaphor for expansion and growth in all spheres of life. The festival also becomes a vehicle for reflecting on Ibadan's history, "an opportunity to bring history to modern reality."¹⁰⁴

Conclusion: Literature as a Historical Artifact and a Cultural Archive

> History grows and develops from people's memories, and historians in the future will use these memoirs (carefully) to reconstruct it.¹⁰⁵

I had attempted a deliberate inversion of Hayden White's essay "The Historical Text as a Literary Artifact." A society's culture is an embodiment and the totality of a people's way of living, the fundamental principles one must be acquainted with or embrace to behave in a manner acceptable to its people. "Literature and art are normally ahead of other cultural carriers of ideology in providing us with new scripts, and define our personal narratives and life politics" and the "ideologies that we employ in structuring the way we tell our individual tales come from a wider culture."¹⁰⁶ I have stressed in several interviews that the ultimate purpose of documenting *A Mouth Sweeter than Salt* is to produce a platform on which history can stand; this memoir assumes the position of the proverbial Òwe, codified to contain a fragment of my people's collective consciousness. The memoir approaches what recent studies have referred to as a Master Narrative: stories embedded in a specific culture, providing illumination as well as instruction on how to be a "good" member of that culture. This narrative is more of a negotiation and an interpretation of my sociocultural beliefs, and my experience in relation to my past, than it is a reflection of it.

However, in documenting the narrative, I do not set it as an exclusive perspective for understanding the Mèsìògò in time and culture. It is by no means a substitute for systematic historical reconstruction, neither is it

---

[102] Falola, *A Mouth Sweeter than Salt*, 378.
[103] Falola, *A Mouth Sweeter than Salt*, 377.
[104] Falola, *A Mouth Sweeter than Salt*, 379.
[105] Paula S. Fass, "The Memoir Problem," *Reviews in American History* 34, no. 1 (2006): 107–123.
[106] Goodson, "The Rise of the Life Narrative," 8.

sufficient; but it is a cultural negotiation seeking a place in history,[107] an attempt at re-situating the history of a "society that was about to be destroyed by the activities of those that were changing too fast."[108] My life is only a tiny fragment of a whole, and my intent is to gather as many relics as I can to ensure their continuous survival against the defacing tenets of modernism, postmodernism, multiculturalism, trans-culturalism, cultural hegemony, and others. Like the biblical Noah, *A Mouth Sweeter than Salt* is my ark. It is an archive conserving the non-physical heritage of the *Mèsiògò*, and the Yorùbá in general, and one of the many ways of selectively referencing the past. It contributes to the production of collective memory and provides a complementary–alternative approach to navigate the cluster of the past and the people, just like myth, religion, literature, and history.

[107] Fass, "The Memoir Problem."
[108] Falola, *A Mouth Sweeter than Salt*, 236.

4

Memory, Magic, Myth, and Metaphor

Introduction: Memory as Narrative and History

The anticipation of an uncertain future, and the importance of having this ability to the survival of humans and their humanity, created and necessitated the need to understand the past. Our knowledge of the present is anchored to our understanding of the past. When events and information retrieved from the past are not attributed to supernatural inspiration or revelation – as it is with myths in cultural and religious narratives – they can be said to be regained from (a pool of) memory. Memory, collapsed into songs, poems, rituals, and myths, is one of the most fundamental human devices connecting the past to the present.

Everything known from the past is directly or indirectly sourced from the memories of witnesses, or from the forms in which those memories have been codified. These memories found their way through diverse methodologies into history, which is now widely regarded as the repository of the past. Events, philosophy, and cultural heritage have since time immemorial been preserved in and through memory; the totality of a people and their norms is absorbed into their social memory and transferred across generations through these expressive forms that can be taken to be material manifestations of memory. Tradition is itself an unconscious memory, describing that which is passed on from a generation to another. It is important that these memories are preserved, but of greater importance is the essence of the culture embodied by these memories, since this essence defines the society.

Memory is the retention of past events and experiences, a repertoire of acquired knowledge and information.[1] Memory is condensed and latent, but can be stretched and tooled to become a narrative when evoked and burdened with cognitive purposes and expressive intents. These narratives can be adapted into and taken as history. The invocation of facts and events is said

---

[1] R. Reiff, and M. Scheerer, *Memory and Hypnotic Age Regression* (New York: International Universities Press, 1959); and G. A. Miller, *Psychology: The Science of Mental Life* (New York: Harper & Row, 1962).

to be invoking declarative memory.[2] When they are specific, recurring, or made of very important experiences, they become episodic memory.

Episodic memory is based on our ability to recall certain events from the past, which allows us to relive, comprehend, and interact with them.[3] Remembrance is itself a component, a measurement, and a test of memory. For instance, in my narrative A Mouth Sweeter than Salt, my grandfather, Pásítọ̀, had taken me to Léku, the herbalist,[4] to fortify my cerebral cortex and hippocampus to prevent memory interference, forgetfulness, encoding, or retrieval failure. This would allow events to pass through the sensory stage to my short-term memory, settling in my long-term memory,[5] where it would later be accessible for retrieval.

If balanced diets, mnemonics, and eidetic images can enhance the memory, magic strengthens mine. As with science and technology, this comes with consequences. I had consciously attempted to repress traumatic events and experiences, such as the death of Pásítọ̀ during the counterattack launched by the police and military at Àkùfò, as narrated in Counting the Tiger's Teeth. According to Léku, these memories are impossible for me to forget, like emotional memories stored in the amygdala. They became a burden that I carry with me everywhere. Hence, to repress them would mean severing

---

[2] Declarative memory, in some studies (e.g., L. T. Robertson, "Memory and the Brain," Journal of Dental Education 66, no. 1 [2002]: 30–42), is described as explicit memory or conscious memory, which is responsible for housing facts, events, and experiences usually invoked consciously. Within the premises of literature, sociology, and humanities, declarative and explicit memories are autobiographical memory, defined as "an explicit memory of an event that occurred in a specific time and place in one's personal past" (K. Nelson and R. Fivush, "The Emergence of Autobiographical Memory: A Social Cultural Developmental Theory," Psychological Review 111, no. 2 [2004]: 468–511, at 486).

[3] E. Tulving, "Episodic and Semantic Memory," in Organization of Memory, ed. E. Tulving and W. Donaldson (New York: Academic Press, 1972), 381–403.

[4] Falola, A Mouth Sweeter than Salt, 456.

[5] In Psychology and Neuroscience studies, Atkinson and Shiffrin (R. Atkinson and R. Shiffrin, "Human Memory: A Proposed System and Its Control Processes," in The Psychology of Learning and Motivation: Advances in Research and Theory, II, ed. K. W. Spence [New York: Academic Press, 1968], 89–195) proposed that events and information only make it to long-term memory when they are of great importance, keep reoccurring, or are rehearsed. This was replaced by the concept of "working memory" from Baddeley and Hitch (A. Baddeley and G. Hitch, "Working Memory," in Recent Advances in Learning and Motivation, vol. VIII, ed. G. A. Bower [New York: Academic Press, 1974], 47–90). This only partially explains the events that have been deposited into my memory. Almost every event, experience, or piece of information makes it to my long-term memory without reoccurring or being of great importance. I have not sustained any injury to the head, and I am not looking forward to one, so old age remains the only test to measure the potency of Léku's Òògùn ìsọ̀yè (memory charm).

a crucial part of my personal identity.[6] Memory, either individual or collective, blurs into oblivion when it is neglected or discarded; it becomes a collective responsibility to safeguard memory through individual means.[7]

Similarly, the reader's ability to hold and process fragments of information provided in a narrative, assembling them into a coherent whole, is attributed to the retentive power of the memory in a term called a "situation model."[8] It is an attempt at reordering a narrative to negotiate a meaning. Situation model, like the working memory, "is the system that holds mental representations available for processing"[9] and its interaction with the long-term memory is equally important for the narrator. To meditate and travel back in time aids remembrance, and the span of memory becomes stretched and enlarged during invocation. This allows the narrator to beat his memory into a well-framed narrative.

It is equally important to identify memory's limitations in relation to history. Factors such as bias, misinformation, infallibility,[10] and the impossibility of rightly (in)validating memories – especially personal ones in the absence of multiple witnesses – often render memory unreliable as a genuine

---

[6] This is what Robertson referred to as a "fundamental process of being human" ("Memory and the Brain"). Memory influences our present and future activities, and the combination of memory and narrative is what James Olney (*Memory and Narrative: The Weave of Life-Writing* [Chicago: University of Chicago Press, 1998], 417) refers to as "the two major epiphenomena of consciousness – the dual defining conditions of our being human." As the dedication noted, *Counting the Tiger's Teeth* is homage to Pásító and the countless lives of heroes lost to the revolt.

[7] P. Nora, "Between Memory and History: Les Lieux de Mémoire," *Representations* no. 26 (1989): 7–24.

[8] The situation model describes the integration of accumulated information such as dates, events, characters, and information in a narrative to create a well-grounded mental representation. This is referred to as textbase representation (T. A. van Dijk and W. Kintsch, *Strategies of Discourse Comprehension* [New York: Academic Press, 1983]), reflecting the organization of the text elements as dictated by the text structure (M. Wolfe, "Memory for Narrative and Expository Text: Independent Influences of Semantic Associations and Text Organization," *Journal of Experimental Psychology* 31, no. 2 [2005]: 359–364, at 359). See T. Yarkoni, N. Speer, and J. Zacks, "Neural Substrates of Narrative Comprehension and Memory," *NeuroImage* 41 (2008): 1408–1425; and R. A. Zwaan, "Situation Models: The Mental Leap into Imagined Worlds," *Current Directions in Psychological Science* 8, no. 1 (1999): 15–18, at 15–17.

[9] K. Oberauer, C. Jarrold, S. Farrell, and S. Lewandowsky, "What Limits Working Memory Capacity?" *Psychological Bulletin* 142, no. 7 (2016): 758–799, at 758.

[10] Memory is validated by interaction, as "individuals always rely on other people's memories to confirm their own recollections and for them to endure over time" (M. Santos, "Memory and Narrative in Social Theory: The Contributions of Jacques Derrida and Walter Benjamin," *Time & Society* 10, no. 2/3 [2001]: 163–189, at 165). What is observed and accepted as truth would be a negotiation between reader and narrator, because the narrator constantly realigns past events and assigns meaning to them, imbuing the readers with different perceptions. This interaction makes truth in life narratives relative and unstable.

source of the past; it is prone to manipulation and interference from external factors or consequent memories. An individual or community is in a constant negotiation to ascertain validity of and produce meaning in memory, which can suggest infallibility. In other words, "output of human memory often differs – sometimes rather substantially – from the input. Remembering can fail not only because information is forgotten over time, but also because it is changed and distorted."[11] The role of memory is vital in the documentation of life narratives or autobiographies. However, it is also fragile, as memory becomes the standpoint on which life narratives are recast through retrospection and recall.

Memory Narrative as Alternative and Counter-History

> Memory and history, far from being synonymous, appear now to be in fundamental opposition.[12]

There have been several attempts to decentralize the status of history, both as a stronghold and as the only valid field of study and knowledge of the past.[13] Limiting factors have included historical errors, deliberate distortion, political manipulation, and the repression of past events, along with the overtly scientific approach of history toward past knowledge and knowledge of the past. Memory, unlike history, is a permanent and continually evolving product, created by a society that is shaped by it in turn, "open to the dialectic of remembering and forgetting, unconscious of its successive deformations" and "vulnerable to manipulation and appropriation, susceptible to being long dormant and periodically revived."[14]

Just as the postmodern Yorùbá proverb "Ònà kan kò wọjà" reminds us that no single path leads to the market, the same is true about the past. Its bank has become overflooded – what Nora[15] conceived as a demand for history that "has thus largely overflowed the circle of professional historians" – coupled with the delimitations and shortcomings of history.[16] The manifestation of history

---

[11] M. Freeman, *Rewriting the Self: History, Memory, Narrative* (London: Routledge, 2003), 119.

[12] Nora, "Between Memory and History," 8. In the past, a common knowledge is the conception of history as memory, and memory as history with the view that both are the same or interchangeable. This might not be totally erroneous, as an intricately interwoven relationship exists between them. There is no clear-cut demarcation between the two, but memory is a direct perception of the past by an individual or a community, with no restriction between it and their present. History is an account or record of the past; if history observes the past for documentation, memory is an essential and active participant in its occurrence.

[13] Santos, "Memory and Narrative in Social Theory."

[14] Nora, "Between Memory and History," 8.

[15] Nora, "Between Memory and History," 15.

[16] Nora, "Between Memory and History," 15.

within the Yorùbá culture and many African communities is quite different from Eurocentric historical methodologies. *Ìtàn*, which is the Yorùbá way of presenting historical narratives, is preserved in the collective consciousness, or the cultural memory, of the people for future retrieval and remembrance. When it is transferred from a generation to another, it becomes *Àrọ́bá*, which is the available memory of the past.[17]

These attempts have received labels that include historical turn, narrative turn, discursive revolution, cultural turn, and memory boom to designate alternative, independent, and counter-mechanisms for navigating the past. Postmodernism propelled history's needed decentralization to liberate multiple voices that have been silenced and relegated to the past. In lieu of the above, Santos avers that "intellectuals have embraced memory as the concept capable of doing what history can no longer do: build links between past and present."[18] This emergence promises to rework the boundaries of history, which had hitherto monopolized the production of a shared past by imposing an understanding of that past, regardless of the oppositions inherent in other alternatives that have been silenced.[19]

Memory is a core biological and cultural element of human survival. However, it is marginalized, barely understood, and accorded little relevance until there is a need to recall an occurrence – whether it was an instance that took place a few minutes ago or a complex body of knowledge acquired over an extended period of time. Memory entered the discourse of historiography as an essential oppositional and alternative route, as well as a force resistant to history, to studying the past. These attempts do not suggest that these other routes to history are new; they only emphasize the need to increase their relevance for the comprehension of the past. This elevation is what New Historicism upholds as the parallel reading of all texts. It is similar for postmodernism; these attempts show variations of methodologies for approaching the past. Memory and other devices have received the kind of accentuated relevance that Foucault refers to as the "insurrection of subjugated knowledge" (memory) already displaced by a more dominant field (history).[20] According to Medina:

> Subjugated knowledge[s] remain invisible to mainstream perspectives; they have a precarious subterranean existence that renders them

[17] An example in the narrative is when I wanted to know more about Ogundele, and had to consult *Ìtàn*, the collective memory of the people preserved and presented through conversations (Toyin Falola, *Counting the Tiger's Teeth: An African Teenager's Story* [Ann Arbor: University of Michigan Press, 2016], 15–16).
[18] Santos, "Memory and Narrative in Social Theory," 164.
[19] K. Klein, "On the Emergence of Memory in Historical Discourse," *Representations* 69 (2000): 127–150; and J. Medina, "Toward a Foucaultian Epistemology of Resistance: Counter-Memory, Epistemic Friction, and Guerrilla Pluralism," *Foucault Studies* 12 (2011): 9–35.
[20] M. Foucault, *Society Must Be Defended* (New York: Picador, 2003), 28.

unnoticed by most people and impossible to detect by those whose perspective has already internalized certain epistemic exclusions. And with the invisibility of subjugated knowledge[s], certain possibilities for resistance and subversion go unnoticed.[21]

Erll pursues a further argument, declaring that history itself is an embodiment of cultural memory through its medium of historiography.[22] History has always been an interdisciplinary field of study, relying on findings from various archives or other fields to form its narrative. It is dependent on memory, a methodology that Gvozden describes as prosthetic science constantly searching for a reliable means to reconstruct memory and validate the past.[23] Rusu's opinion, that "collective memory relies on history to legitimate itself and to emphasize the authenticity of its constitutive events,"[24] is not only erroneous but also impossible and contrary to logic – why should a collective memory,[25] which is a preceding variable to history, seek validation in history "which is conditioned by collective memory"?

The existing documentations of the Àgbẹ̀kọ̀yà Revolt, the central subject of *Counting the Tiger's Teeth*, is not capable of legitimizing my narrative. The "memoir is based on what I saw and heard, and what I suffered."[26] It is preposterous to seek a validation of my memory by referring to inaccurate historical records that seek to distort it. In this vein, Craig aptly notes:

> Historians are prolific contributors to the growing discourse on memory, but they are not the only occupants of the turf of memory studies. Cultural anthropologists, critics of art and literature, poets, novelists, and, inevitably, philosophers all have particular concepts of memory. Perhaps it is memory as a physical phenomenon, or as psychology; perhaps as a psychic place, or as a cultural space; perhaps as a political agenda or as a special social geography. But overall, and perhaps most tellingly, these conceptual differences highlight the complexity of memory, which is not a unitary thing.[27]

---

[21] Medina, "Toward a Foucaultian Epistemology of Resistance," 11.
[22] A. Erll, "Cultural Memory Studies: An Introduction," in *Cultural Memory Studies: An International and Interdisciplinary Handbook*, ed. A. Erll and A. Nünning (Berlin and New York: De Gruyter, 2008), 1–18.
[23] V. Gvozden, "Magical Realism and the Politics of Narrative: Historical Postmodernism in the Contemporary Serbian Novel," *World Literature Studies* 8 (2016): 64–75.
[24] M. Rusu, "History and Collective Memory: The Succeeding Incarnations of an Evolving Relationship," *Philobiblon* 18, no. 2 (2013): 260–282, at 264.
[25] This is not to dispute that there are false memories as a result of different psychological disorders, which can be negated by psychoanalysis or countered by history just as error-pruning checks the recounted memory of an individual in relation to others and vice versa, but the negation of a collective memory (not cultural memory nor collective history!) by history is highly improbable.
[26] Falola, *Counting the Tiger's Teeth*, xiv.
[27] B. Craig, "Selected Themes in the Literature on Memory and Their Pertinence to Archives," *The American Archivist* 65 (2002): 276–289, at 280.

The memory of an individual is enhanced and situated within the collective memory of a group of people, time, or activities. These memories are often shared and negotiated through conversations, folklores, rites, and rituals. The French sociologist Maurice Halbwachs argues in his *Collective Memory*[28] that it is impossible to separate an individual's memory from the collective. According to Halbwachs, there is no point of departure between the formation of recalled memory and the existence of a personal memory outside the collective.

Verovsek asserts that "Communal understandings of the past can even cause individuals to remember events they never actually witnessed. Although memory is experienced as coming from within, it can also be implanted from without."[29] These memories implanted from without are known as cultural memory, presenting us with the perception of what it feels or would have felt like to be present during an incident that took place in the past. "A cultural memory is a collective concept for all knowledge that directs behavior and experience in the interactive frame-work of a society and one that obtains through generations in repeated societal practice and initiation."[30] According to Rigney, cultural memory "is always vicarious in the sense that it involves memories of other people's lives that have been mediated by texts and images: inherited."[31]

Memories are defined by the sociocultural realities of an individual and a community, the bearers of these memories work as mediators. They cast their memories into narratives, oral or written, "as indispensable tools for shaping and giving meaning to the events of the past. So viewed, any reconstruction of a historical past results from an interpretative act a situated agent performs with a particular purpose,"[32] and the process of recalling and enlivening memory makes everyone their own historian. Thus, memory reconstruction affirms narrative as a representation of the "most basic and ubiquitous form of organization of human experience," providing tools for people to engage in the processes of remembering, forgetting, representing, and identifying.[33] However, it is important to note that the concept of cultural memory is transdisciplinary, like history. It can only be successful by the homogenization of the methodologies inherent in each discipline. In other words, "An even

---

[28] M. Halbwachs, *The Collective Memory* (New York: Harper & Row, 1980).

[29] P. Verovsek, "Memory, Narrative, and Rupture: The Power of the Past as a Resource for Political Change," *Memory Studies* 13, no. 2 (2020): 208–222, at 211.

[30] J. Assmann and J. Czaplicka, "Collective Memory and Cultural Identity," *New German Critique* 65 (1995): 125–133, at 126.

[31] A. Rigney, "Portable Monuments: Literature, Cultural Memory, and the Case of Jeanie Deans," *Poetics Today* 25, no. 2 (2004): 361–396, at 367.

[32] I. Luna and A. Rosa, "Memory, History and Narrative: Shifts of Meaning when (Re)constructing the Past," *Europe's Journal of Psychology* 8, no. 2 (2012): 300–310, at 301.

[33] M. Kuzmanic, "Collective Memory and Social Identity: A Social Psychological Exploration of the Memory of the Disintegration of the Former Yugoslavia," *Horizons of Psychology* 17, no. 2 (2008): 5–26.

more intensified dialogue among disciplines will help uncover the manifold intersections of memory and culture."[34]

It is impossible to narrate the totality of all that has taken place in the past exactly as it occurred – the plots of memory narrative are framed by their relevance.[35] An event can be relevant if it is vital to the comprehension of the present or a present discourse. The relevance of an event can also be determined in its relation to another, or an experience can be relevant if its occurrence is significant. Often, the purpose of a narrative is to relate an event or experience deemed relevant by the narrator. Memoirs are mostly credited as a reflection of an important event for the narrators, especially for events such as childhood experiences that have shaped their lives.

The definition of memory as an accumulation of events does not suggest that it is linear or monolithic. It is an accumulation of chunks of past experiences, which are also recalled in fragments and harnessed into a fine narrative "shaped through the superimposition of a theme and a narrative plot"[36] by the consciousness of narration. This superimposition of a theme and a narrative plot is what Hayden White regarded as the reasonable employment of historical narratives from congeries of fact.[37] Memories are disjointed by nature, interrupted by many narratives of events, and some events, like trauma,[38] cannot be fully comprehended in the moments of occurrence. Narratives are used as retrospective tools to invoke, relive, and relieve these experiences. The

---

[34] Erll, "Cultural Memory Studies," 3.
[35] It is important to highlight that, like recency, the relevance of an event applies to both recall and storage of memories. Studies have shown that most events make it to long-term memory due to their importance to the existence of their bearers.
[36] Luna and Rosa, "Memory, History and Narrative," 302.
[37] White, "The Historical Text as Literary Artifact."
[38] Traumatic events are not fully assimilated or experienced at the moment of occurrence, because of their enormous effect on the nervous system or psychology of an individual. The traumatized individual assumes a dual position of both the bearer and witness of such experiences; they are unable to process these experiences fully, but the creation of legible images of the past are made possible by the memories' haunting power (Santos, "Memory and Narrative in Social Theory"; N. Lotfi, "A Unique Approach of Memory Narrative Therapy in Diasporic Contexts: An Analysis of *The Bonesetter's Daughter* and *The Kitchen God's Wife* by Amy Tan," *Theory and Practice in Language Studies* 4, no. 9 [2014]: 1912–1917). In some instances, false memories are conjured or implanted to replace the lapses and gaps present in traumatic events (C. Laney and E. Loftus, "Traumatic Memories Are Not Necessarily Accurate Memories," *Canadian Journal of Psychiatry* 50, no. 13 [2005]: 823–828). There is a dialectical relationship between past experiences and narratives; as these narratives are used to shape the past experiences of the narrator, they equally shape the identity of the narrator (H. Hirsch, *Genocide and the Politics of Memory: Studying Death to Preserve Life* [Chapel Hill: University of North Carolina Press, 1995; P. Antze and M. Lambek, "Introduction," in *Tense Past: Cultural Essays in Trauma and Memory* [New York: Routledge, 1996]).

lack of specificity in the African conception of time is also a contributing factor to the disjointedness of time, events, and memory perceptions:[39]

> Experiences, impressions, and memory-traces may be revised at a later date to fit in with fresh circumstances or to fit in with a new stage of development. They may in that event be endowed not only with the new meaning but also with psychical effectiveness ... It is not lived experience in general which undergoes a deferred revision but, specifically, whatever it has been impossible in the first instance to incorporate fully into a meaningful context. The traumatic event is the epitome of all such unassimilated experience.[40]

The rupture in time's progression[41] is equally accountable for the disjointedness in the accruement of memory. In other words, "Memories are not static representations of past events but 'advancing stories' through which individuals and communities forge their sense of identity. Or, to put it differently: memories offer heavily edited versions of the self and its world."[42]

Collective memory is formed by the interaction of fragments of (individual) memory forming a cohesive, comprehensive whole. In *Counting the Tiger's Teeth* I narrated that "No one in those years could have seen everything. What I witnessed lacked coherence, and I did not understand how any one piece was connected to any bigger picture."[43] The Àgbẹ̀kọ̀yà Revolt is a collective memory, defined with a common goal but manifested at different places with different participants. Even in my location there were many separate activities, and no man can be in two places: "Seeing one meant missing another; listening to one conversation in the parlour meant you would not know what they were saying in the backyard. I had to focus and choose what was more interesting to me."[44] Hence, there is the need to merge the various memories into

---

[39] "While not associating absolute time and date with their tales and narratives – histories, memories, reflections, refractions – the farmers piled out one historical era on top of another, and it may take your understanding of a later era to make sense of the previous one. The year 1940 did not have to follow 1939, and 1970 could come well before 1895" (Falola, *Counting the Tiger's Teeth*, 151).

[40] J. Laplanche and J. Pontalis, *The Language of Psychoanalysis*, trans. Donald Nicholson Smith (London: Hogarth and Institute of Psychoanalysis, 1973), 111–112.

[41] Kuzmanic, "Collective Memory and Social Identity," a study of the 1990s disintegration of the former Yugoslavia federation, depicts how the historical rupture affected and modified the collective memory and identity of the people, culminating in a complex set of multiple, contesting memories with new identities.

[42] E. Caldicott and A. Fuchs, "Introduction," in *Cultural Memory: Essays on European Literature and History*, ed. E. Caldicott and A. Fuchs (New York: Peter Lang, 2003), 11–32, at 12–13.

[43] Falola, *Counting the Tiger's Teeth*, 50.

[44] Falola, *Counting the Tiger's Teeth*, 55.

a comprehensive whole – this again highlights the concept of relevance in memory making and reconstruction.

Narratives are structures through which memories are organized and conveyed, and "this ability to cast our experience in narrative terms has been referred to as narrative intelligence."[45] It is inherent in the human mind as a technological device for expressing and negotiating meaning. The presence of this ability to spin narrative is evident from childhood through the early process of accumulating cultural knowledge, constructing meaning from it and the environment.[46] Simply put, narratives are our understanding of the universe, how we make coherence of its chaos, how we negotiate the graspable and the improbable, and understand the past and present.

Memory narrative also has a therapeutic effect[47] that cannot be overlooked. In situations where an individual's memories are haunting, or burdened with trauma, shock, and depression, these narratives become a potent mechanism for navigating the past. While asserting the self and the identity of the self, narrators equally seek to expunge themselves of certain memories, hoping to repress them by writing them down. The rupture caused by traumatic experiences is mended through narration, which aids the process of autobiographical memory reconstruction and alleviates the psychological torment attached to those memories, a process that has "became an essential clinical tool to heal trauma."[48]

The word "memoir" is an English derivative of *memoria*, a Latin word meaning memory. Memory is the key component in life narratives, autobiographies, diaries, life histories, and others. All texts are equal by virtue,[49] and an undocumented past can be illuminated by texts considered to be inferior. This preference for other historical sources has birthed alternative and

---

[45] T. Anderson, "From Episodic Memory to Narrative in a Cognitive Architecture," in *6th Workshop on Computational Models of Narrative*, ed. Mark Finlayson, Ben Miller, and Remi Ronfard (Dagstuhl: Schloss Dagstuhl, 2015), 1–11, at 2.

[46] Q. Wang, Q. Song, and J. Koh, "Culture, Memory, and Narrative Self-Making," *Imagination, Cognition and Personality: Consciousness in Theory, Research, and Clinical Practice* 37, no. 2 (2017): 199–223.

[47] As with tragedy, memory narratives are purgatorial in nature. "Memory narratives could be considered the psychological solutions, to heal the victims of traumatic past incidents. Narrative therapy could be an inseparable part of memory narratives, in which recalling is the main narrative strategy to cure the past" (Lotfi, "A Unique Approach of Memory Narrative Therapy," 1912).

[48] K. Bušková, "The Role of Literature in Reconciling Trauma on Personal and Social Level," *Bohemica Litteraria* 16, no. 2 (2003): 83–91, at 85.

[49] Texts, like narratives, as used in this context refer to every medium of expression, reflection, and representation as all cultural products are regarded as a text by New Historicists. According to Nasrullah Mambrol, it is in this regard that Louis Montrose refers to the "textuality of history, the historicity of texts." (Nasrullah Mambrol, "The Textuality of History and the Historicity of Texts," Literariness, October 17, 2016, https://literariness.org/2016/10/17/the-textuality-of-history-and-the-historicity-of-texts/).

counter-narratives to history, which in their multitude seek to (in)validate, enhance, or correct an existing history – these efforts have been described as "a counterforce to manufactured and monolithic memory";[50] or in some cases, the production of history.[51] I recounted that at the onset of the rebellion "we lost over a hundred men, although only twelve, whose corpses were found in various places, were reported by the media the next day ... They claimed to have arrested only eleven, but we could not account for over fifty men."[52] During the attack at Àkùfò, toward the end of the rebellion, over a hundred and seventeen lives were lost to the counterattack that was launched by the alliance of army and police retaliating the Agodi and Ìyágànkú invasions. The media only reported the death of thirty.

According to Lowenthal, "Those who bring more of their past into their present thereby confirm their own identity and enrich the present with the past's amplified residues."[53] Just as I have stated in the preface to *Counting the Tiger's Teeth*, the "memoir is a contribution to that moment in history, a way of walking with ancestors, remembering the dead, reminding the living, converting orality into a permanent text and providing a small nugget about my own experience in life, as limited as it is." Its overall aim is to nullify certain records provided by the government, which "are dead wrong," to correct those that are "fabrications by state officials who were reporting what they knew nothing or little about," and to provide accounts where none existed.[54] Memory narratives have become a liberating tool, allowing individuals to think beyond restrictions imposed by various intuitions.[55] For the narrator and the reader it provides multiple facts to renegotiate existing knowledge.

---

[50] G. Hartman, *The Longest Shadow: In the Aftermath of the Holocaust* (Bloomington: Indiana University Press, 1996), 104.

[51] In most cases these alternative channels are the only true source for historical accounts of an event or experience, especially incidents that are considered to be less important or repressed for certain reasons. Thus, the "New generations, with no personal recollection of events can only experience the past indirectly. Their understanding of it will be shaped by community traditions and memories, nourished largely, it seems, by a growing buffet of popular historical books, films, and television programs" (Craig, "Selected Themes in the Literature on Memory," 279).

[52] Falola, *Counting the Tiger's Teeth*, 217. Similarly, when violence on both sides of the battle became intense "The government was frightened. It released figures announcing that in the span of three weeks, twenty people had been killed and fifty injured. This was false, very false. In December alone, our list of the dead was over a hundred, the injured approaching five hundred, and the missing over a hundred" (226).

[53] D. Lowenthal, *The Past Is a Foreign Country* (Cambridge: Cambridge University Press, 1985), 91.

[54] Falola, *Counting the Tiger's Teeth*, xiv. At the peak of the rebellion, history was fabricated. The real intention of the revolt was changed from demands for basic social amenities to conspiracy with Biafran forces to destabilize the Nigerian government and ensure Biafran victory in the civil war.

[55] Verovsek, "Memory, Narrative, and Rupture."

Language and the Invocation of Memory

The re-presentation of these events and experiences is made possible by language. The totality of an individual's past cannot be recounted or exactly related, but the use of an evocative language is an indispensable tool by which memory can be well illustrated. It is described as an imaginative thinking capable of rendering the continuity of our experience meaningful and intelligible.[56] According to Qi Wang et al., "the representational function of language and the inherent temporal-causal structures of narrative greatly increase the chances for memories to be formed and retained."[57] In this way, language becomes an indispensable tool for sustaining the working memory during the invocation of the past. In the same vein, Brockmeier describes language, in relation to life writing, as not only a representation and reflection of reality but also its creator.[58] An effective language becomes the sole medium of expression for the narrator to conjure up his past and engage the imagination of his audience or readers.

Memory, and its narrative through language, is a meaningful negotiation and reinterpretation of the past between the narrator and his audience. "Memory, therefore, which often has to do not merely with recounting the past but making sense of it . . . [is] an interpretative act [at] the end of which is an enlarged understanding of the self."[59] Accordingly, Craig gives a description of memory as a concept that transcends the functions of storage and retrieval; he refers to memory "as a mechanism that fixes items for later recall at will . . . This brings us to the idea of memory as a construction or a 'work in progress' and not as a thing received."[60]

Narrating the Absurd: The Narrative of Magic and Myth

Since ancient times the word "magic" has been associated with supernatural or illusory acts, capabilities, or events. Minimalist perceptions of magic range from things that seem out of place to rites that invoke metaphysical forces and conjure estranged reality. This simplification is echoed by Bailey when he describes magic thus: "In its rites, rituals, taboos, and attendant beliefs, magic might be said to comprise, or at least describe, a system for comprehending the entire world."[61] Magic can acquire a negative reputation when one culture inspects another's practices, especially when one culture is imposed on

---

[56] B. Misztal, *Theories of Social Remembering* (Philadelphia: Open University Press, 2003).
[57] Wang, Song, and Koh, "Culture, Memory, and Narrative Self-Making," 202.
[58] J. Brockmeier, "Autobiographical Time," *Narrative Inquiry* 10, no. 1 (2000): 51–73.
[59] Freeman, *Rewriting the Self*, 29.
[60] Craig, "Selected Themes in the Literature on Memory," 285.
[61] M. Bailey, "The Meanings of Magic," *Magic, Ritual, and Witchcraft* 1, no. 1 (2006): 1–23, at 1.

another, but magic has retained a foothold in almost every culture and society because "magic can mean anything that disregards empiricism," which may include "religious beliefs, superstitions, myths, legends"[62] and other occurrences.

In ancient times and societies magic was an essential means of survival in every culture. In the absence of appropriate scientific methods, people devised skills to tame nature for specific purposes, "particularly to aid the functioning, binding, and survival of a society."[63] For example, in *A Mouth Sweeter than Salt* I recounted how the Òkè-Bàdàn festival[64] is a cultural event commemorating the protective function of the hill for Ibadan city's earliest occupants, but more importantly, the sexually explicit songs characterizing the festival are rituals to invoke reproduction – socially and biologically.

The instability or variation of magic in each culture is also noteworthy. In cultures where magic has been embraced and validated it is deeply entrenched in that culture's core substance, perceived as a normal rite or tradition;[65] general examples are myths and superstitious beliefs, some of which are regarded as sacred – those that exist as part of a collective memory within a specific culture. Like its variants across cultures, religious perceptions interpret different manifestations of magic. In Christianity magic is considered illicit and ungodly – however, the expected outcomes of certain religious rites, which are no different from magic, are perceived as wonders and miracles. The source of miracles is embraced as divine, but magic is spurned and attributed to evil, diabolic means. The difference between magic and miracle thus seems to be the perceptions guided by the respective religious beliefs.

In *Counting the Tiger's Teeth* I reflected on the preachings of the emerging Pentecostal churches, exemplified in the character of Bùọ̀dá Gébú, which was targeted at traditionalists who believed in the potency of herbs (juju), charms, and magic despite the occurrence of similar manifestations of magical rites in Christianity and Islam. Imams write Quranic words on slate, washing them into water that is used by their clients/followers to solve physical and spiritual problems. A similar practice among the Christians is the transformation of ordinary water into "holy water" by prayers, hymns, and psalmic chants.[66] The cultural significance of charms and magic enables a parallel comparison of the Yorùbá *Ifá* divination system and the Christian Bible; like the *Ifá* divination system, the Bible "is a book full of powerful magic and charms; you just have to know the right verses to consult."[67]

---

[62] Gvozden, "Magical Realism and the Politics of Narrative," 70.
[63] M. Earl, ed., *Perspectives on Management* (Oxford: Oxford University Press, 1983), 128.
[64] Falola, *A Mouth Sweeter than Salt*, 376–393.
[65] At the onset of the rebellion, while Pásítọ̀ had refused the carrying of weapons, he did not oppose the use of charms and powerful magic to neutralize the enemy and for protection.
[66] Falola, *Counting the Tiger's Teeth*, 90.
[67] Falola, *Counting the Tiger's Teeth*, 155.

Stripping the words of their religious contexts, magic is *Idán* in Yorùbá, and miracle is *Iṣẹ́-ìyanu*. They describe unbelievable occurrences or supernatural acts, which are the expected outcomes of processes or rites. In both instances there is an inherent need or desire to transform reality or navigate the metaphysical to achieve a desired result. Stark opines that "It is the desire for control that motivates humans to develop skills, crafts, technologies, and ultimately, science. People do magic for the same reason."[68] However, science is open to observation, and its methods are physical and empirical. The processes of magic are concealed,[69] and they invoke the supernatural to manifest events that cannot be given a logical explanation.

Both science and magic are dominated by initiates or, if you prefer, experts who are properly trained. They are equipped with advanced or esoteric knowledge to perform scientific methods and magical rites, respectively – remember that "Ẹni mọ ojú Ògún, níí pa 'bì ní Ìrè" suggests that the rites of *Ògún* worship can only be performed by initiates.[70] Ìyá Lékùléjà is an example of an initiate who possessed such esoteric knowledge to perform magic and prepare herbs and charms. During preparations for the rebellion, when I was tasked with obtaining information and materials from Léku, I failed to locate her at Òde Ajé. Later I was brought to her at the village of Kúṣeélá, where she had joined forces with other herbal and charm makers:

> She was at centre stage, directing a large number of people to grind various herbs and mix them with other ingredients. These were for medicine, charms, and rituals. The wet ground plants and seeds were

---

[68] R. Stark, "Reconceptualising Religion, Magic and Science," *Review of Religious Research* 43, no. 2 (2001): 101–120, at 104.

[69] In *A Mouth Sweeter than Salt* I narrated how ominous feelings prevented me from revealing the esoteric knowledge I'd obtained from Léku through keen observation and her teachings during my stay with her at Òde Ajé. "By the time I could seek her permission to reveal her essence and quote her, she was long dead. And each time I feel like revealing the full essence, I am tormented by an overpowering feeling of awe and danger. The first time I mentioned a small part of her secret at a seminar at the Institute of African Studies at the University of Ibadan, I had a nightmare in which I was pursued by a tiger that would have killed me if I had not awakened in time. Most of my misfortunes, all my negative feelings, and my anticipation of troubles I attribute to a part of me that desires to unlock what I know about Leku" (Falola, *A Mouth Sweeter than Salt*, 291). Similarly, I recounted that the signs and symbols that I did not understand were used by the sixteen wives of the *Babaláwos* preparing charms and herbs to be used in the course of the uprising; "their signs and symbols were designed to invoke the forces of the cosmos, to attract spiritual energies to themselves so that they would become extra-human" (Falola, *A Mouth Sweeter than Salt*, 61).

[70] While I was an "active observer" of the methods and processes of making all sorts of charms, the comprehension of this complicated knowledge evades me, "both their processes and outcomes were vague, appearing disconnected." Thus, unlike science, the knowledge I obtained through the active observation is not enough to reproduce the charms with the same desired result (Falola, *Counting the Tiger's Teeth*, 43).

the visible components, but the most potent were the words, the incantations she chanted over those items which transformed ordinary leaves to something else.[71]

Frazer highlights the relationship between magic and science as similar where "the same causes will always produce the same result."[72] Perhaps the assertion made by Keith Roberts, that magic would someday be supplanted by science and a secular worldview,[73] explains the rise of Afrofuturism and other speculative concepts that seek to affirm the potency of African magic. These ideas use fantasy to evolve, or at least merge, black magic and myth with science to reenvision the African past and redefine its future. Magic, like science, has rules and organized methods with replicable outcomes; "Òògùn tí kò bá jẹ́, ewé rẹ̀ ló kù kan" is a Yorùbá saying that illustrates the organization behind the potency and replication of magic and charm.

> The successes of the rebellion, it was believed, were made possible by charms. Charms represent a belief system, and one cannot prove or disprove this belief with evidence of efficacy. You see what happens when a charm works, and when one fails to work, you say it is due to a badly executed charm.[74]

The replication of magic requires more than organized methods; the intense power of magic, and its potential for disaster (when not wielded properly or used for evil purposes[75]), makes it an esoteric knowledge possessed by few. Certain magical rites and rituals can only yield desired results when performed by initiates with suitable abilities.[76] Within a culture some magical rites are accepted, and in fact embraced as a norm, while others are prohibited as

---

[71] Falola, *Counting the Tiger's Teeth*, 43.
[72] J. Frazer, *The Golden Bough* (New York: Macmillan, 1950), 56.
[73] K. Roberts, *Religion in Sociological Perspective* (Belmont: Wadworth, 1995), 23.
[74] Falola, *Counting the Tiger's Teeth*, 231. The execution of charms and magic requires knowledge of the complex set of principles guiding their usage; "it was sad that some charms needed to rest in the evening or that the maintenance of potency required dialogue with unseen forces" (232), or that the efficacy of some can be neutralized by interactions with others, just like medication. It is general knowledge that each charm and magic has its *Eewo*, taboos, which must be strictly observed and adhered to.
[75] In *Counting the Tiger's Teeth*, while recounting the personality of one of the leaders of the revolt, I indicated that he was famous for a charm, *Ìsújú*, which made him invincible while confronting his enemy. "So potent was *Ìsújú* that the herbalists and diviners in the land agreed to make it only for distinguished hunters and warriors, to avoid its being used by thieves and armed robbers" (Falola, *Counting the Tiger's Teeth*, 219).
[76] My attempt to perform the "Club of Sixteen" rite that I had observed was futile, even after repeating the same incantations. I thought, perhaps, "Their incantations had been frozen in their language, tonality, and pronunciation, as if an adjustment or mispronunciation would prevent the charm or medicine from working" (Falola, *Counting the Tiger's Teeth*, 61). This suggests that magic requires a skill, demanding perfection in its performance, perhaps stemming from a metaphysical ability.

evil – the collective consciousness or cultural beliefs connected to the act's purpose, outcome, and process are the determining factors classifying magic as good or evil; it varies from a culture to another. This explains why Pásítọ̀ embraced the use of magic and charm during the revolt but objected to the use of weapons. Magic, myth, folklore, legends, and rituals, according to Faris and Zamora,[77] are collective practices binding communities together and keeping them invested in magical realism.

The Narrative as Magical Realism

> The ordinary is elusive, and one only gets hold of it via the extraordinary. What is always there is hard to explain, simply because it is always there. It does not ask for an explanation. It's normal, natural. Only what is different demands an explanation.[78]

More than fiction or illogical historic narratives, myths are deep meditations about life and existence; they are a group's collective consciousness. Like magic, the production of myth is necessitated by the human need to understand our existence and environment – myths are traditionally accepted as historical accounts of objects, occurrences, and beings.

Myths are used to express, to maintain solidarity and cohesion, to legitimize, to communicate unconscious wishes, mediate contradictions, to anchor the present to the past, and to anticipate the future.[79] They are cultural products limited to the boundary of a specific society and shaped by it.[80] In *Counting the Tiger's Teeth* I compared folklore, where Elephant was deceived, with the leader and the sociopolitical reality of post-independence Nigeria. The deceitful praise from other animals was similar to the endless promises made by political aspirants and government officials.[81]

In creative parlance, myths are often adopted into narratives for two broad reasons: first, for narrative purposes, to relate a cultural account of an event,

---

[77] L. Zamora and W. Faris, eds., *Magical Realism: Theory, History, Community* (Durham: Duke University Press, 1995).

[78] S. van der Geest, "How Can It Be!? Ethnography as Magical Realism and the Discovery of the Ordinary," *Medicine Anthropology Theory* 2, no. 2 (2015): 79–94, at 86.

[79] In the first chapter of *Counting the Tiger's Teeth* I had explained how the invocation of Ògún syncretizes our anger and bravery to embark on a rebellion. Ògún as a deity of war is an epitome of fairness and justness. The invocation of Ògún is also necessary to avert disastrous consequences if Ògún "chose to support the other side" (Falola, *Counting the Tiger's Teeth*, 26).

[80] P. Cohen, "Theories of Myth," *Man* 4, no. 3 (1969): 337–353; L. Bolman and T. Deal, *Modern Approaches to Understanding and Managing Organizations* (San Francisco: Jossey-Bass, 1984); R. Hirschheim and N. Newman, "Symbolism and Information Systems Development: Myth, Metaphor and Magic," *Information Systems Research* 2, no. 1 (1991): 29–62.

[81] Falola, *Counting the Tiger's Teeth*, 183–184.

phenomenon, or object; second, for cognitive purposes, adopting myths as constructive measures to evaluate current sociocultural and political realities. In the poem "If the gods must be," from Dasylva's *Songs of Ọdámọlúgbẹ̀*,[82] the poetic persona evaluates Nigerian postcolonial sociorealities as a consequence of the gods' negligence – they have instead committed themselves to pleasure. It is a reconstruction of Yorùbá myths, similar to the ritualized reconstruction of the road as infinite uncertainties plaguing postcolonial nations in Ben Okri's *The Famished Road*. In *Counting the Tiger's Teeth* I had attributed the Àgbẹ̀kọ̀yà Revolt's failure, at least in essence, to how we forgot to appease Èṣù at the onset of the war. Èṣù is the Yorùbá trickster god of mischief and confusion responsible for ferrying messages from humans to gods and to Olódùmarè.

According to Faris, the "combination of realistic and fantastical narrative, together with the inclusion of different cultural traditions, means magical realism reflects, in both its narrative mode and its cultural environment, the hybrid nature of much of postcolonial society."[83] This suggests that postcolonial writers adopt magical realism as a tool for recovering lost and repressed culture. In a more postmodern context it becomes an attempt at blending or deconstructing old culture, tradition, myth, belief, and religion in the new order of reality. In the words of Elleke Boehmer:

> Drawing on the special effects of magic realism, postcolonial writers in English are able to express their view of a world fissured, distorted, and made incredible by cultural displacement... They combine the supernatural with local legend and imagery derived from colonialist cultures to represent societies which have been repeatedly unsettled by invasion, occupation, and political corruption. Magic effects, therefore, are used to indict the follies of both empire and its aftermath.[84]

Magical realism contrasts reality with the fantastic or marvelous. A simple definition, according to Beverley Ormerod, is that "Magical realism is a literary technique that introduces unrealistic elements or incredible events, in a matter-of-fact way, into an apparently realistic narrative."[85] Magical realist narratives are reflections of exaggerated or heightened reality, making it unjust to confine them solely to the sphere of fiction and imaginative narratives. Describing *Counting the Tiger's Teeth* as a magical realist narrative would

---

[82] A. Dasylva, *Songs of Ọdámọlúgbẹ̀* (Ibadan: Kraftgriots, 2006).

[83] W. Faris, *Ordinary Enchantments: Magical Realism and the Remystification of Narrative* (Nashville: Vanderbilt University Press, 2004), 50.

[84] Elleke Boehmer, *Colonial and Postcolonial Literature* (Oxford: Oxford University Press, 1995), 235.

[85] B. Ormerod, "Magical Realism in Contemporary French Caribbean Literature: Ideology or Literary Diversion," *Australian Journal of French Studies* 34, no. 2 (1997): 216–226, at 216.

stretch the term's boundaries; magical realism is usually categorized as a genre that only applies to fictional forms of narrative. However, various descriptions, definitions, and elements have marked it as a mode of creative expression adopted in various narratives and regions. Rawdon Wilson opines that "magical realism can be, and indeed is, used to describe virtually any literary text in which binary oppositions, or antinomies, can be discovered."[86]

Initially, magical realism originated in the 1925 description of an avant-garde style of European painting by Franz Roh. The term was later adopted to describe a growing body of literary works that fused reality and fantasy in Latin America in the 1940s. Consequently, magical realism has evolved to comprise all works of any origin, time, or form, narrating reality in light of the magical.[87] Magical realism is not the narrative of the marvelous fused with reality, but the narrative of reality as marvelous; it seeks to overcome the limitations of ordinary realism trying to accurately depict reality.

The opening sentence in *Narcos*, the TV drama recounting barbaric crimes committed by the Colombian drug lord Pablo Escobar, states that "Magical realism is defined as what happens when a highly detailed, realistic setting is invaded by something too strange to believe." However, the perception of the magical as an estranged reality might be problematic – there is often a thin boundary between the real and the magical, "as readers become increasingly accustomed to the irreducible element of magic, their surprise and hesitation may disappear."[88] Likewise, narrating reality as magical doesn't suggest that the magical is an overtly estranged reality. In depicting realism as marvelous, Wandama compares magical realism with the reality of contemporary Nigerian society. According to him:

> A review of stories from *Newsline*, a presentation of the Nigerian Television Authority will convince any listener [that the concept of magical realism is Nigerian realism]. There were stories of a woman's body that did not decompose after almost thirty years in Lagos, the report about the bleeding image of the Virgin Mary in Benue State, the report of a youth corps member whose breast continued to swell uncontrollably until she died in Bauchi, or the report that people's private parts were disappearing and many more mysterious events.[89]

---

[86] R. Wilson, "Metamorphoses of Fictional Space: Magical Realism," in *Magical Realism: Theory, History, Community*, ed. L. Zamora and W. Faris (Durham: Duke University Press, 1995), 209–233, at 223.

[87] S. Slemon, "Magic Realism as Postcolonial Discourse," in *Magical Realism: Theory, History, Community*, ed. L. Zamora and W. Faris (Durham: Duke University Press, 1995), 9–24; M. H. Abrams, *A Glossary of Literary Terms* (Fort Worth: Brace Jovanovich, 1993); H. Kasikhan, "The Absence of 'Paucity' & 'Momentariness': Two New Components of Magical Realism in Günter Grass's The Tin Drum," *Journal of Teaching Language Skills* 4, no. 2 (2012): 155–169.

[88] Faris, *Ordinary Enchantments*, 49.

[89] W. Wandama, "Prospects of Studying Magical Realism in Nigerian Literature," *International Journal of Arts and Humanities* 5, no. 3 (2016): 1–12, at 2.

Commonplace Nigerian reality is similar to the plots and settings of magical realist narratives. Age has lost its role as the properly defining power and relevance within society, replaced by money in recent times. Human components are used in money rituals – they can involve used women's clothing, obtained by force or trickery; the theft of male reproductive organs; and even kidnapping – performed by greedy youths looking to accumulate unclean wealth and devious power. The horror experienced by someone who has lost their possessions is not due to the missing items; it is the fear that stolen property could be used in evil rituals.

Human rituals are performed for money, and men have died from *Mágùn* after sleeping with another man's wife; the woman must have crossed a charmed broom or thread at the suspicious husband's insistence.[90] In a society where supernatural forces are responsible for deaths, "even someone killed in a car accident might have been 'pushed' onto the road by the overpowering force of evil hands, or witches could have closed the person's eyes so that he or she would not see an oncoming vehicle."[91] In African society, incident involves more than what meets the eye.

The unbelievable postcolonial sociopolitical realities depicted in *Counting the Tiger's Teeth* have become normalized due to their frequent occurrence and accepted as commonplace. The evil has become good, and the good has become evil, which means that an attempt to reverse this status quo requires the provocation of the extraordinary. Magical realism within the African context is thus commonplace and cannot be seen in the context in which that term is used in the West or in its original context, as the perception of religion and culture in African communities includes the unreal and the metaphysical.

The onset of Nigerian film production – the industry that would become known as Nollywood – was marked by the projection of the complex African universe, which includes the living, the dead, and the spirits. *Kòtò Aiyé*, *Ìdè*, and *Ẹran Ìyá Òṣogbo* are movies written and directed by Alhaji Yekini Ajileye, whose works are characterized with magical realist projections. They depict goats that talk and animals capable of other human activities, as projected in *Ẹran Ìyá Oṣogbo*, and humans flying as birds at night to join their coven, as seen in *Kòtò Aiyé* and *Ìdè*. The actions may seem or may be unreal, but they are accepted as reality in many African communities.

The magic in magical realism merges with reality when the audience suspends its disbelief; the real becomes magical or the magical is seemingly indifferent to reality. Magical realism accounts for realism's inadequacies of language when projecting absurd realities and indescribable events – such as the Yorùbá belief in reincarnation, where spirits of the dead roam the

---

[90] Falola, *Counting the Tiger's Teeth*, 35.
[91] Falola, *Counting the Tiger's Teeth*, 205.

boundaries of heaven, making occasional visits to earth without being recognized. This dis-connection from reality is similar to the concept of defamiliarization, which describes the effort to transform the familiar into the unfamiliar and conversely. In the words of Faris and Zamora:

> The supernatural is not a simple or obvious matter, but it is an ordinary matter, an everyday occurrence-admitted, accepted, and integrated into the rationality and materiality of literary realism. Magic is no longer quixotic madness, but normative and normalizing.[92]

In *Ordinary Enchantments* Faris explains that the five building blocks of magical realism are (a) the irreducible element, which suggests actions and occurrences that are illogical or cannot be explained by the laws of the universe; (b) unsettling doubts, which indicate the reader's initial hesitation and eventual effort to synergize their perception of seemingly contradictory occurrences – the real and the imagined, and an often allegorical interpretation of the unreal; (c) the phenomenal world, which accounts for the presence of supernatural bodies or elements within the physical universe; (d) merging realms, which portray the interconnection or interrelation of multiple spheres, usually demonstrating the co-occurrence of the spiritual and physical worlds; and (e) the distortion of time, space, and identity, which accounts for the radical shift and disruption in the progression of the narrative time frame, setting, and identity of the narrators and the subjects of narration.[93]

Chanady summed up the merging realms as "two conflicting, but autonomously coherent, perspectives, one based on an 'enlightened' and rational view of reality and the other on the acceptance of the supernatural as part of everyday life." It creates a phenomenon world where "the supernatural is not presented as problematic," but rather "integrated within the norms of perception of the narrator and characters," while readers suspend their disbelief.

Hancock also offers brief defining markers of magical realism, which are more descriptive of the elements present in *Counting the Tiger's Teeth*:

> A few features can be identified: exaggerated comic effects: hyperbole treated as fact; a labyrinthine awareness of other books; the use of fantasy to cast doubt on the nature of reality; an absurd recreation of "history": a meta-fictional awareness of the process of fiction making; a reminder of the mysteriousness of the literary imagination at work: a collective sense of folkloric past.[94]

At the front burner of magical realism is the quest to capture reality, depicting it with maximum retention and "with little loss of meaning" during narrative

---

[92] Zamora and Faris, eds., *Magical Realism*, 3.
[93] Faris, *Ordinary Enchantments*.
[94] G. Hancock, "An Interview with Jack Hodgins," *Canadian Fiction Magazine* 32/33 (1980): 33–63, at 36.

construction through "the vitality of language expressed in images."[95] In conjuring a reality that is more than itself, magical realism supplements its use of magic, myth, and rituals with the magical use of language – as with the evocation of memory, language becomes an essential tool to show reality more truly with the marvelous aid of metaphor. The first chapter of the memoir imagines that the sacrificed dog, whose eyes are fixed on a machete lying on the ground, could reattach the two halves of its body and start cutting off human heads in revenge. This is a projection of magical realism; its possibility is anchored on the belief that dead people reincarnate, especially to seek revenge.[96]

> Spiritual and magical preparations were an integral part of the military. They cannot be separated from the behaviours of warriors, the preparation for war, or military actions... The religious and the military must be well combined so that we could see the enemies, as we hoped, but the enemies would not see us, as we believed.[97]

The presence of the phenomenon world, and the interrelation of the physical and metaphysical worlds, is established within the narrative by depicting the Yorùbá cosmic universe, which includes deities, spirits, metaphysical powers, and other forces, as well as by the essentiality of spirituality surrounding the subject of the narrative. The worship and invocation of Ògún is integrated into the narrative in several places to explain the courage and bravery of the rebellious farmers: "Ògún inspired acts of courage. Ògún gave them the courage to challenge the authority of chiefs, kings, politicians, and soldiers."[98] Yorùbá word relation, and meaning depiction through tonal expressions, highlights the semantic correlation of at least four lexical derivatives of the word ogun. It can refer to the Yorùbá mythic figure of war, it means war, it is the Yorùbá expression of sweat (Òógùn), and it can also mean magic or charms (Òògùn) – all of which depict vigor.

In *Counting the Tiger's Teeth* the invocation of Ògún at the onset of the war is an attempt to incite anger, terror, and bravery, which are his personified qualities, within the assembled soldiers. It is also "to send Ògún on an errand to terrorize the men that brought misery and agony."[99] The Yorùbá myth of creation describes Ògún establishing a path for the other gods, and he is known

---

[95] Hancock, "An Interview with Jack Hodgins," 41.
[96] Among the Yorubas, many war stories describe famous warriors who were beheaded in battle, only to reveal that their enormous magical power enabled them to reattach their heads and seek revenge on their enemies. The two most notable tales involve one warrior who mistakenly attaches a different head to his body, and another who had slain his own people, mistaking them for the enemy.
[97] Falola, *Counting the Tiger's Teeth*, 129.
[98] Falola, *Counting the Tiger's Teeth*, 126.
[99] Falola, *Counting the Tiger's Teeth*, 12.

for his creative and inventive skills as a smith – that is why Ògún, and not the furious Ṣàngó, is invoked to fix the anomalies plaguing his worshipers.

The manifestation of supernatural beings is noticeable in the message of Ogundele, an Ògún devotee. It was the collective worship of Ògún, and not Orí that had altered the people's mood "from soberness and silence to dancing and shouting, from calmness to rowdiness, from calm bearing to angry posturing."[100] The invocation of Ògún as a ritual is a manifestation of magic with the expected outcome of victory. A similar comparison is drawn between the character of Ọbafẹmi Awolọwọ and the deities Ògún and Ṣàngó. His defiance is likened to the fierceness and rebelliousness of Ṣàngó, the Yorùbá god of rain, fire, thunder, and lightning, while his reformative agenda is compared to the inventive skill of Ògún as the pathfinder who "had used his skills to clear paths in the forest and jungles so that humans had roads to read their game and farms."[101]

Narrating the Àgbẹ̀kọ̀yà Revolt

The Àgbẹ̀kọ̀yà Revolt (1968–1970) was a proletariat revolution and class struggle organized by peasant farmers in the Western Region of Nigeria. For a long time before the revolt there had been constant agitation by commoners and social groups to improve the country's standard of living. One example was the Ẹgbẹ́ Ìlọsíwájú (the progressive group), whose mission statement was to achieve "modernity and modernization: the need for roads, electricity, and pipe-borne water and the establishment of more schools, adult education centers, and much more."[102] The corrupt practices that had marred the democratic government, and its failure to address the repeated petitions, observations, appeals, and prayers of the public[103] led to the rise of the military government, which was facilitated by the naïveté of the military men.

Prior to the revolt, the fragmented Ẹgbẹ́ Àgbẹ̀kọ̀yà existed in different locations under different names and leaders. The Àgbẹ̀kọ̀yà group formed from an amalgamation of different peasant groups including the Ẹgbẹ́ Máiyégún, Ẹgbẹ́ Mẹ̀kúnnù Takú, Ògbóni Fraternity, Ẹgbẹ́ Ìlọsíwájú, and

---

[100] Falola, *Counting the Tiger's Teeth*, 14.
[101] Toyin Falola, *Ibadan: Foundation Growth and Change 1830–1960* (Ibadan: Bookcraft, 2012), 161. As a reformer, Ọbafẹmi Awolọwọ used the proceeds made from cocoa in pursuit of several pioneering achievements, including the founding of the first television station (Western Nigerian Television, WNTV) in Africa in 1959; the implementation of a free basic education scheme in what was the Western Region of the country; the naming of the Nigerian currency as Naira from the country's name, Nigeria; the founding of the University of Ife, which was renamed to honor him in 1987; construction of the first tallest building in Africa, located in Ibadan (formerly known as the house of farmers, Ilé Àwọn Àgbẹ̀, and now Cocoa House).
[102] Falola, *Counting the Tiger's Teeth*, 114.
[103] Falola, *Counting the Tiger's Teeth*, 180.

Ẹgbẹ́ Onímọ̀. The organization's central goal was the welfare of citizens, especially farmers: they formed the base of the economy, and their demands included a reduction of the tax rate from 8 pounds to 30 shillings, an end to forceful collection of tax, and an increase in the price of cocoa at a time when the productivity of the land was decreasing. They also asked for improved roads leading to villages and the removal of some traditional leaders and local government officials. Not only were farmers underpaid for their cocoa products and extorted through taxes, but sale proceeds received from foreign countries were also mismanaged and embezzled by corrupt government officials collaborating with traditional chiefs and rulers.

The uprising was undoubtedly the most well-organized protest against government decisions in Nigeria's history to date.[104] Through the Ògbóni Fraternity, plans and structures were concealed from outsiders, and members who betrayed the cause of the group suffered severe consequences. The methods, activities, and even the membership and leadership of the organization were sworn to secrecy "to prevent the infiltration of those who could not be trusted, to ensure that members spoke with one voice and that they were bonded on the basis of one philosophy."[105] Decoys were sent to negotiate with the government at different times, to conceal organization's true leadership: "Fake leaders were stationed in the city to write and send petitions to the government secretariat."[106]

The rebellion's military strategy merged the physical and spiritual to ensure victory; it was not wise to rely on the physical strength of the warriors and their weapons when charms and magic could render us invincible. Through the religious arm of the group, spiritual powers were summoned to assist the warriors in combat. Leaders of the revolt, such as Tafa, Abínúwáyé, and Àgékù-Ejò, "asides from having powerful charms, were actually very bright and strategically astute."[107] The attack plan was to lure and engage the police and army in dense bush, using confusing terrain to attack and kill state officials, and to retreat into the general populace when the battle became fierce. There were strict rules against raiding stores, taking food from vendors, and hassling noncombatants – the uprising was considered a socialist cause, and

---

[104] A. Ajayi, O. Familugba, and O. Oyewale, "Agbekoya Protest: It's Implication on Cocoa Production in Western Nigeria, 1960–1968," *International Journal of Development and Sustainability* 7, no. 3 (2018): 1169–1177; A. Ayeni-Akeke, "Collective Violence in Nigeria: Patterns and Significance," *Institute of African Studies Research Review* 4, no. 2 (1988): 28–49; T. Adeniran, "The Dynamics of Peasant Revolt: A Conceptual Analysis of the Agbekoya Parapo Uprising in the Western State of Nigeria," *Journal of Black Studies* 4, no. 4 (1974): 363–375.

[105] Falola, *Counting the Tiger's Teeth*, 123.

[106] Falola, *Counting the Tiger's Teeth*, 120.

[107] Falola, *Counting the Tiger's Teeth*, 221.

those acts would betray its philosophy. Further to the plan of the organization, seven signs must be witnessed before the rebellion could take place.[108]

However, before resorting to violent demonstrations, peaceful attempts were made by famers in the months of August, September, and October 1968 to compel the government to reach a peaceful agreement. "The famers began by following the established patterns of political behavior. They sent delegations to the chiefs and city managers to complain. They wrote petitions to the government ... These letters were many, but they were saying the same thing, which was all too obvious."[109] All were ignored; instead, the poor farmers received insults highlighting their illiteracy. "Ọmọdé bú ìrókò ó ń bojú w'ẹ̀yìn, òòjọ́ kọ́ l'olúwéré ń pa ni" (the repercussions for bad behavior do not come immediately).

The rebellion started with attacks replacing the traditional rulers and chiefs who had been representing the interests of the rich farmers and government officials who appointed them. The riot started at the grassroots, expanding like a spiral and garnering more momentum as it whirled: monarchs' houses and properties were destroyed, and government properties were damaged. The military government responded with more force to repress the group's activities.

The first encounter with military troops resulted in the death of more than a hundred members of the revolt. Curfews were imposed in towns and cities where the group's activities had the most impact. Following the Ayola Commission's failure to address the real societal issues prompting the rebellion, and the government's refusal to reduce the tax rate, more attacks were launched. The targets were traditional rulers who had connived with government officials to seize taxes from their people – when those individuals fled, their properties were damaged.

The fiercest attack led to the horrific death of the king of Ògbómọ̀ṣọ́, Ọba Ọlajide Ọlayode II, his wife, his child, and five of his chiefs: "The level of bitterness and anger directed at him was intense and so publicly expressed that his head and legs were displayed in different parts of the city."[110] This was followed by successful attacks on the Agodi prison and the Ìyágànkú police station, releasing members of the group who were serving jail terms and those who were still on trial. The government applied more force to repress the movement; the police and army were enthusiastic emissaries of death, and hundreds of people were forcibly detained. This culminated in the Anglican Church and governors of other states calling for the federal government's intervention.[111]

---

[108] Falola, *Counting the Tiger's Teeth*, 207.
[109] Falola, *Counting the Tiger's Teeth*, 199–200.
[110] Falola, *Counting the Tiger's Teeth*, 254.
[111] Falola, *Counting the Tiger's Teeth*, 291.

In the aftermath, hundreds of detained members of the revolt were released in different towns, tax raids were canceled, the flat tax rate was reduced, the activities of council workers were probed, and promises were made for a 50 percent increase in the price of cocoa purchased from farmers, to prevent the whirls of the revolt from spiraling into a full-blown civil war. The fierce struggle between the proletariat farmers and traditional and government authorities resulted in a heavy loss of life. Families were bereaved, and a new class of oppressors was created.

Some leaders of the revolt tarnished their image by joining with the government, neglecting their duty to negotiate on behalf of the group. At the end of the rebellion the group's leaders were in charge of obtaining taxes from the farmers who had comprised the core of the resistance. After their genuine expressions of anger and attempts to negotiate a better life, there was little significant change. Since then, the struggle and vision for true socialism have been blurred as the country rolls in a vicious cycle, replacing one group of corrupt leaders with another.

Metaphor as the Language of Magic and Myth

> The essence of metaphor is understanding and experiencing one kind of thing in the light of another.[112]

Language's essentiality to narrative is manifest in ordinary language's inability to portray reality's essence, due to "the frustrating inadequacies of language."[113] Magical realism surmounts this awkward barrier of representation and definition by using metaphor.[114] Magical realism, like hyperrealism and surrealism, seeks to represent life as more than it is. The thrusts of language in magical realism effectively transpose and blend the magical – features of the marvelous – with the real, using their evocative tendency to conceive mental images that perceive a true reality. Conjuring new realities, which is an essential characteristic of magical realism, is achieved through metaphor; every metaphor alters or modifies an existing reality. Metaphors do not conform to the rules of logic; they defy reason and make the impossible happen. This includes expressions of mythological thinking in magical realism.[115]

---

[112] G. Lakoff and M. Johnson, *Metaphors We Live by* (London: University of Chicago Press, 1980), 125.

[113] S. Simpkins, "Magical Strategies: The Supplement of Realism," *Twentieth Century Literature* 34, no. 2 (1988): 140–154, at 140.

[114] Simpkins, "Magical Strategies," 140; Craig, "Selected Themes in the Literature on Memory."

[115] W. Rueckert, "Metaphor and Reality: A Meditation on Man, Nature and Words," *KB Journal* 2, no. 2 (2006), https://kbjournal.org/rueckert; E. Korotchenko and V. Petrenko, "Metaphor as a Basic Mechanism of Art (Painting)," *Psychology in Russia: State of the Art* 1, no. 5 (2012): 532–567.

To paraphrase Lakoff and Johnson: metaphor highlights certain features while suppressing others.[116] This defamiliarization effect is adopted in magical realism to contrast two opposing views, beliefs, or existences to understand or highlight one's prominence. In the same vein, Strauss states that "metaphor interconnects what is similar and what is different in such a way that either of the two is manifest in the other: either the difference is shown in the similarity or the other way around"[117] in a clear and brief manner.

Unlike other figures of expression, metaphors are specific concepts. They are powerful comparative and contrastive literary devices, which "[do] not allow an object to belong to the class which it is actually a part of but tries to make it a part of the category to which it cannot be assigned on a rational basis. Metaphor is a challenge to nature."[118] Metaphors also forge a new reality by giving or adding new meaning to an entity, which is perhaps their most essential cognitive function. Metaphors are powerful tools advancing the evaluation, comprehension, and contextualization of human existence in relation to the environment.[119] By extension: "Metaphors create their own reality while attempting to explain some other reality ... Nothing is more real than the fact that we mediate every reality with our metaphors, an[d] often create realities more real and powerful than reality itself with them."[120] The expressive function of metaphors is appropriate because they "sanction actions, justify inferences, and help us set goals."[121] And like every other manifestation of culture, metaphors generate their usage and meanings from a specific context. A metaphor's true meaning can only be understood within the premises of the culture that created it, aided by personal experiences. Its meaning becomes unstable and indefinite when extracted to the context of another culture. Allegory as a symbolic representation of an idea, personification as the embodiment of abstract ideas within the premises of human capabilities, or vice versa, and other devices are extensions of metaphors as a representation.[122]

---

[116] Lakoff and Johnson, *Metaphors We Live by*.
[117] D. Strauss, "Metaphor: The Intertwinement of Thought and Language," *Koers* 76, no. 1 (2011): 11–31, at 23.
[118] N. D. Arutyunova, "Metaphor and Discourse," in *Theory of Metaphor* (Moscow: Progress, 1990), 5–33, at 17-18 [in Russian]. However, the further argument of Arutyunova is that "Metaphor is not a reduced comparison, as it was defined in the time of Aristotle, but reduced contrasting."
[119] M. Hyvärinen, "Foreword: Life Meets Narrative," in *Life and Narrative: The Risks and Responsibilities of Storying Experience*, ed. B. Schiff, A. E. McKim, and S. Patron (New York: Oxford University Press, 2017), ix–xxv.
[120] Rueckert, "Metaphor and Reality."
[121] Metaphor as a device for expression is what Lakoff and Johnson refer to as humans' "most important tools for trying to comprehend partially what we cannot comprehend totally: our feeling, aesthetic experiences and spiritual, moral practices and spiritual awareness" (*Metaphors We Live by*, 134).
[122] Arutyunova, "Metaphor and Discourse."

In the narrative, metaphor is the language of magic, myth, and memory. The title, *Counting the Tiger's Teeth*, is a metaphor for bravery, struggle, and liberation. The ritual and invocation of Ògún narrated in the memoir's first chapter foreshadows the ominous incidents to follow. Ògún is a deity of war and a personification of bravery; the tiny speckles of blood that splattered everywhere signify the devastating outcome of the revolt. In the narrative, Ògún is an ontological metaphor for bravery, Òkè-Bàdàn for unity, and Èṣù for discord or mischief. Close observation reveals an intricate connection between Ògún, the machete and other weapons of war, the sacrificed dog, and the rebels. If the blood from the dog appeases and incites Ògún, the people ready to wield the weapons are executing Ògún's duty with a similar fate of anguish or death.[123]

The connection reveals the dominance of the metaphysical over the ordinary. This fate of anguish and death stems from the inability to appease Ògún's thirst with the dog's blood, "and he was asking for more blood – my blood and that of others … If we could all contribute a drop, perhaps a teaspoonful, Ògún should be satisfied. Not so. Some had to give up all of their blood."[124] Similarly, a metaphoric evaluation of the dream[125] experienced in front of Léku's store, while awaiting her arrival, reveals a psychological manifestation of the anxiety and turbulence surrounding me ahead of the rebellion. The jungle of my dream was the turbulent reality, the dangerous animals represented the terror surrounding that reality, and the python's effortless gulp that consumed the squirrel symbolizes the intended rebellion's total repression by the establishment. The striking dash that he made at me also foretells my own tumultuous fate during, but especially after, the uprising.

Incantations and war songs are metaphors accompanied by magical powers to produce desired effects, and "The words communicated magical meanings, capable of turning ordinary-looking pouches of leather into power."[126]

> A dead dog does not bark
> A dead ram does not hook anymore
> Here we are
> Superior to dead dogs
> Superior to dead rams
> Ready for battle.[127]

---

[123] Further connecting the relationship between the sacrificed dog and the rebels, it is noted that, like Jesus, "The men gathered there were all martyrs unafraid to be crucified; even the blood they agreed to shed was not to wash away anyone's sin but to cleanse the world they disliked" (Falola, *Counting the Tiger's Teeth*, 6).
[124] Falola, *Counting the Tiger's Teeth*, 25.
[125] Falola, *Counting the Tiger's Teeth*, 34.
[126] Falola, *Counting the Tiger's Teeth*, 43.
[127] Falola, *Counting the Tiger's Teeth*, 14.

The song above, although neither an incantation nor a war song, contains metaphors expressing the powerlessness and defeat of anticipated enemies as represented by the dead dog and the dead ram. Incantations are drawn from observable facts and aligned with the present situation or the anticipated outcome.

Another manifestation of metaphor in the narrative is the use of Àrokò, a message with a hidden meaning that can only be understood by a group of people who share a common knowledge. The use of Àrokò can involve combinations of words and objects to conceal information.

> Àrokò delivered communication, and replies were offered also in a symbolic manner so that if you sent words and embers of fire to me to indicate trouble and warm, I could send a calabash full of waters to you to indicate that I had the means to quench your fire; or I could send you an additional firewood to say that we should keep fighting.[128]

Àrokò has technicalities that must be strictly observed; a lack of mutual intelligibility between sender and receiver can misconstrue the intended meanings of its messages. In all communication, words and objects are not randomly strung together – they must be properly combined and specific. The addition or subtraction of a word or object can alter the meaning of a message, and unintentional changes can garble the message that is received. For example, "add the red tail feather of a parrot to a string of six cowries, and you would be telling the person that he had outstayed his welcome; change the feather to that of a guinea fowl, and the message would change to that of goodwill."[129] The same applies to incantatory poems, where the substitution or insertion of an incorrect word would render the incantation impotent.

Metaphors are perfect and powerful tools of expression for their ability to transpose meaning, the ability to experience or express one concept in the light of another, without unnecessary clutters of expression. The word "locusts" and the idea of "locust invasions" (the title of one chapter) depict "the government of the day, and the members of the political class that ran it. The threesome was the military, the politicians and the city officials … With all their fingers infected with leprosy, anything they touch became contagious."[130] The locusts' destructive nature was merged with the corrupt practices of the government and its officials.

At the rebellion's peak, "Names of birds and animals were converted into signals and into Àrokò to spread messages. These names were changed as soon as numerous people understood them. The police acquired such names as leopard, tiger, and hawk, council officers were labeled as fox, vulture, bedbug

---

[128] Falola, *Counting the Tiger's Teeth*, 74.
[129] Falola, *Counting the Tiger's Teeth*, 75.
[130] Falola, *Counting the Tiger's Teeth*, 192.

and cockroach."[131] However, the most abundant expressions adopted in the narrative are proverbs. They are horses of expression, sufficient where words become scarce. Words and expressions are not punctuated with proverbs out of custom; they make them lucid.

Conclusion

> The dead shall rise again, and, when they do, they will repeat the fight. In that second battle of good and evil we will win.[132]

In this chapter I have not only addressed magic in its African context, especially through the Yorùbá example, but also engaged Western ideas surrounding myth and magic in a way that serves my approach to and reflection on the Yorùbá culture, and not in the commonplace ways those ideas displace local knowledge of indigenous realities. In addition, in *Counting the Tiger's Teeth*, beyond the intention of conveying my memory into narrative – rectifying the past's falsification through fabricated history by rendering my memory as an alternative narrative and counter-history – I invite readers to enter my world of mystery, where many paths lead to the same destination. Like the real and the fantastic, the boundaries between right and wrong are blurred, and the virtues of humanity are remnants of the past. I not only attempt to recount the past, I also seek to renegotiate my understanding of it. It is a cordial invitation for readers to suspend their disbelief, like Peter, and walk on the fragile fragments of my memory. Nothing has changed, "the more things changed, the more they remain the same."[133] *Counting the Tiger's Teeth* is my bearing of a repressed collective memory, a duty to the memory of fallen heroes and a cause, realigning a fabricated past so it be may be written of me that I didn't keep silent in the face of tyranny.

---

[131] Falola, *Counting the Tiger's Teeth*, 210.
[132] Falola, *Counting the Tiger's Teeth*, xvi.
[133] Falola, *Counting the Tiger's Teeth*, 295.

5

A Poetological Narration of the Nation

Introduction

The relation between poetry and the narrative of the nation is deep and has been in existence from the earliest of times across different regions. Among the most notable core focuses of poetry, apart from its ability to evoke strong emotions, is its narrative dynamics. Historical accounts are equally documented in poetry. Poetry, as in the example of classical epics, have been used predominantly as national and nationalistic narratives by navigating historical events, cultural beliefs, and sociopolitical realities that surround a group of people in order to create a common identity and evoke solidarity. The thesis of this discourse is to examine the poetic thrust of national narratives in *Etches on Fresh Waters*, *Scoundrels of Deferral*, *A Mouth Sweeter than Salt*, and *Counting the Tiger's Teeth*. Hence, nation and other related concepts are discursively highlighted.

A definition of "nation" is as elusive as understanding what "nation" is, especially in relation to similar concepts, such as state, nation-state, nationalism, and nationality. Viewing culture as the totality of knowledge and values shared by a group of people suggests the simple definition of a nation as a group of people within a defined political territory with common interests which may be cultural – and, by extension, common history, memories, religion, language, legal rights, and socio-economic components – and ultimately sharing a common national identity.[1]

A distinct approach, taken by Edensor,[2] is to view nation as a space in time where culture and everyday life operate and coexist. This is rather

---

[1] A. Smith, *National Identity* (London: Penguin, 1991); M. Guibernau, *Nationalisms: The Nation-State and Nationalism in the Twenty-First Century* (Cambridge: Polity, 1996); S. Wenk, "Gendered Representations of the Nation's Past and Future," in *Gendered Nations: Nationalisms and Gender Order in the Long Nineteenth Century*, ed. I. Blom, K. Hagemann, and C. Hall (Oxford: Berg, 2000), 63–81; S. Walby, "The Myth of the Nation-State: Theorizing Society and Polities in a Global Era," *Sociology* 37, no. 3 (2003): 529–546; A. Ahmed-Gamgum, "Nigeria at 100 Years: The Process and Challenges of Nation Building," *Public Policy and Administration Research* 4, no. 8 (2014): 114–139.
[2] T. Edensor, *National Identity, Popular Culture and Everyday Life* (Oxford: Berg, 2002).

a considerable shift, identifying a group of unique and sovereign people as a nation, the way people have always existed, and not using the term nation to define a group of people. "This nation consists of a people who are the source of individual identity, bearer of sovereignty, central object of loyalty and basis for collective solidarity."[3] The core of a nation is its people, individually and collectively affiliating themselves as nationals. The importance and expansive nature of this psychological and physical affiliation with a nation can be understood better within the proposition of Afropolitans, who consider themselves Africans of the world.

Apart from the broad definition describing a group of people within a geographical boundary as a nation,[4] there are further variegations of nations based on the specificity of the defining factors involved. Multiple nations can and do exist within a (bigger) single nation, which can be based on affiliations to specific cultures that define ethnic nations or specific ideologies that characterize political or religious nations. On the relevance of ethnics to the development of modern nations, Smith defines an ethnic group, a derivation of the Greek word *ethnos*, referring to a nation, as a "named human population with shared ancestry, myths, histories, cultures, having an association with a specific territory and a sense of solidarity."[5] This perception evolves into nation, and explains why and how the configuration of a nation is constituted by an ethnic group or dominated by one, which has prompted countless nations to disintegrate or certain ethnic groups to agitate for nationalization over the course of history. A forceful integration results in slow-paced nation building, and the development of the nation becomes hindered.[6] It is on this premise that Connor defines a nation as "a self-aware ethnic group."[7] That is, as a group of people with shared similarities and who are themselves conscious of their homogeneity.

However, a slight distinction that can be inferred between an ethnic group and a nation, which is useful for the focus of this chapter, is that an ethnic group can be a considerably smaller group in comparison to a nation, and it logically follows that a nation develops from an ethnic group by gaining a sense

---

[3] R. Utz, "Nations, Nation-Building, and Cultural Intervention: A Social Science Perspective," *Max Planck Yearbook of United Nations Law* 9 (2005): 615–647, at 622.

[4] In the context of this chapter, the notion of "nation" cuts across its political, geographical, and cultural variegations.

[5] A. Smith, *The Ethnic Origins of Nations* (Oxford: Blackwell, 1986), 32.

[6] In their studies drawing from the Nigerian experience, Onuoha and Ugwueze conclude that "states with ethnic and religious conscious political elite group will have more problems of nation-building than those with less ethnic and religious conscious political elites" (J. Onuoha and M. Ugwueze, "Political Scientists and Nation-Building: The Nigerian Experience," *International Journal of Social Science and Humanities Research* 2, no. 4 [2014]: 36–46, at 38).

[7] W. Connor, "A Nation is a Nation, is an Ethnic Group, is a . . .," *Ethnic and Racial Studies* 1, no. 4 (1978): 377–400, at 388.

of sociopolitical awareness. Nationalist scholars, such as Hobsbawm, hold the view that the notion of "nation" is a modern invention. Hobsbawm asserts that "the basic characteristic of the modern nation and everything connected with it is its modernity,"[8] which is its homogenized sense of sociopolitical awareness. Calhoun shares the same view when he opines that the conception of a collective existence was not inherent in every society, as it is in the case of modern nations.[9] In fact, he believes that both notions of nations and ethnic groups are "modern sets of categorical identities" invented by elites that are engaged in social and political struggles to keep their subjects constantly in check and under subordination. While this might be partly true, it is overstretched; the consciousness of belonging to a larger network of humans, not necessarily as a collective, is primary to survival.

Likewise, the importance of a nation's shared historical past cannot be ignored, as noted in Stalin's definition of a nation as a "historically constituted, stable community of people."[10] Beyond culture, a common history unifies people and establishes their roots in the past, their ancestry, memorable events, and a desirable future. A shared history has been a unifying entity in forcefully integrated nations because history has always been the agent for culture's consistency and harmonization. In Guibernau's view, "Antiquity is employed as a source of legitimacy for a nation and its culture. It binds individuals to a past stretching over their life spans and those of their present ancestors."[11] And the sense of nationality felt by individuals is often anchored in shared historical narratives. Such affiliations accentuate the loyalty of the nationals to the place that hosts the spirit of nationalism, as well as to each other.

A common ethnic and historical background defines a nation, while polity defines a state with "sufficient power and authority to command internal governance and external deference and to warrant being conceptualized as polities."[12] In contrast, Inac and Unal state that "nations are communities of people of the same descent, who are integrated geographically, in the form of settlements or neighborhoods, and culturally by their common language, customs, and traditions, but who are not yet politically integrated in the form of state organization."[13]

---

[8] E. Hobsbawm, *Nations and Nationalism since 1780: Programme, Myth, Reality* (New York: Cambridge University Press, 1990), 14.
[9] C. Calhoun, "Nationalism and Ethnicity," *Annual Review of Sociology* 19 (1993): 211–239, at 215.
[10] J. Stalin, "The Nation," in *Nationalism*, ed. J. Hutchinson and A. Smith (Oxford: Oxford University Press, 1994), 18–20, at 20.
[11] Guibernau, *Nationalisms*, 136.
[12] Walby, "The Myth of the Nation-State," 535.
[13] H. Inac and F. Unal, "The Construction of National Identity in Modern Times: Theoretical Perspective," *International Journal of Humanities and Social Science* 3, no. 11 (2013): 223–232, at 228.

The concept and definition of nation is quite unstable; the defining characteristics held by one group can offset those of another. While Nigeria problematically aspires to the category of nation, the entirety of the Yorùbá people can be referred to as a nation. Hence, the notion of nation, as depicted in this chapter, is expansive and shifts from one point of discourse to another as each occasion demands

Poetry as National Narratives

The interrelation between poetry and narratives can be examined from multiple perspectives. Poems from classical periods have long been regarded as narratives – on the one hand, epics and ballads, for example, have at their core the intent to tell a story. On the other hand, defining a narrative as a deliberate construction of events, or a cultural form ordered into "logical and chronological chains,"[14] allows poetry to be conceived as a narrative, as well as any other manifestation that expresses human consciousness.[15] In this sense, poetry becomes a creative mode of expression rather than just a genre of literature. A discourse could be written in prose, but poetry has a literariness that is not readily found in prose, and it "may be exploited for the additional modeling of narrative sequences, reinforcing, modifying, or counteracting the semantic plot-development."[16]

Therefore, as a narrative mode, poetry has its own profound way of expressing human consciousness. This point of convergence between poetry and narration is the existence of a sequence of events anchored on a specific setting and a time frame through a narrative voice.[17] In this case, the nation is the point of convergence as the works of poets are incorporated into the national narrative. Ahmed-Gamgum notes that the development of values, languages, history, culture, and other elements are at the core of nation building; these are deliberate and keenly directed efforts "that elucidate our history and culture, concretize and protect the present, and insure the future identity and independence of the nation."[18]

---

[14] Palmenfelt, "Contemporary Uses of Narrative," 12.
[15] Lucaites and Condit, "Reconstructing Narrative Theory," 90.
[16] P. Hühn, "Transgeneric Narratology: Application to Lyric Poetry," in *The Dynamics of Narrative Form: Studies in Anglo-American Narratology*, ed. John Pier (Berlin and New York: De Gruyter, 2004), 139–158, at 153.
[17] Narrativity is often perceived on the dimensions and interrelation of sequentiality and mediacy; all narratives have a given sequence of events with a beginning, a middle, and an end. They are related from a specific perspective that may distort the actual sequence of events, which is the thrust of the formalist's concepts of *fabula* and *sjuzet* that make the distinction between a plot and a story.
[18] Ahmed-Gamgum, "Nigeria at 100 Years," 115.

In all regions poetry performs the dialectic function of narrating a group's culture from a generation to another. This is evident in its oral manifestations, and by extension this includes the nations that embody those cultures. Like other art forms, poetry is a cultural manifestation bound to reflect and reproduce its culture; in the view of New Historicists, which also reflects my own beliefs, a work of art can only be properly understood when examined within the time and premises of its production. African narratives are deeply entrenched in the culture that produced them, and it is seemingly impossible to understand them outside of those cultures. Disintegrating an African literary narrative from the culture that produced it, as new critiques propose, denies the benefit that comes with using as prism the dialectic functions of socialization, entertainment, and moralization.

In Jameson's words, "all third-world texts are necessarily allegorical and in a very specific way they are to be read as ... national allegories."[19] By national allegories, he implies that African literary narratives are active political agents working against the colonial past and postcolonial realities; they have been referred to as "resistant literature"[20] challenging dominant, repressive forces. In Africa, and in post-colonial nations elsewhere, literary narratives that perform sociocultural functions are similarly politicized. The relationship between a nation and a culture is mutual and intricately linked – if a culture is a defining marker of a nation, a nation serves as a preserving body for the growth and continuation of a culture. This occurs through many agents, including art. In the words of Napoleon I in 1805:

> There cannot be a firmly established political state unless there is a teaching body with definitely recognized principles. If the child is not taught from infancy that he ought to be a republican or a monarchist, a Catholic or a free-thinker, the state will not constitute a nation; it will rest on uncertain and shifting foundations; and it will be constantly exposed to disorder and change.[21]

Poetry performs both the historical function of documenting culture, especially in cultures that are prone to eradication as a result of nationalism, and the pedagogical function of teaching it: "Peace, unity, progress and nations building may best be achieved under the pretext of historical awareness, which deals with the conscious of the events that happen around."[22] This aligns with

---

[19] F. Jameson, "Third-World Literature in the Era of Multinational Capitalism," *Social Text* 15 (1986): 65–88, at 69.

[20] Barbara Harlow, *Resistance Literature* (New York: Methuen, 1987).

[21] As quoted in F. Ramirez and J. Boli, "The Political Construction of Mass Schooling: European Origins and Worldwide Institutionalization," *Sociology of Education* 60 (1987): 2–17.

[22] K. Mohammed, "The Role of History, Historiography and Historian in Nation Building," *International Journal of Humanities and Social Science Invention* 2, no. 7 (2013): 50–57, at 50.

Mugambi's view[23] that true nationalism and effective nation building can only be achieved in Africa if practical socio-economic and political realities are engaged aggressively. According to him, "What African writers and scholars should do is deal with the issues that are afflicting our society such as violence, corruption and rising costs of basic needs, rather than waste time on the issue of 'Africanness'."[24] This intangible pursuit has been a central point of attack on idealistic poetry movements such as Negritude despite its enormous influence.

Anderson's perception of a nation as where a group of people live together as "an imagined community"[25] with the belief that they share a common origin highlights poetry's role in advancing the nationalist goal of a collective identity. Poetry and all literature, as cultural products, are valuable sources not only for the comprehension of a nation but also for the actualization of its goals. It becomes a national narrative in the creation of a collective identity, establishing culture and history through which the members of a nation can understand their common connection. In light of this, Anderson associates the development of the concept of nation with modernity – specifically, with the ascension of capitalism and the print industry.[26] He believes that the massive production of narratives plays a significant role in uniting the vast population through print media, which helps to create a collective memory that fosters nationalism.

As a cultural and literary narrative, poetry seeks to (re)negotiate the present by asserting the past and constructing a feasible future. On this premise, Bhabha argues that a nation is the construction of narratives.[27] More precisely, African poetical narratives, in their oral form, perform the collective, political function of documenting history. They reflect current realities with a view to sustaining development; hence, "in African societies art has traditionally been highly functional."[28] This explains the reverence accorded in African societies to bards, who are viewed as custodians of culture and history. This extends to the preoccupations of (modern) African literary output, whose focus is extensively expressed by Eileen Julien:

> African narrative and poetry, in the era immediately preceding and following formal declarations of independence, were born, for the most part, in protest against history and myths constructed in conjunction with

---

[23] M. Mugambi, "Forget Your Past, Thank Colonialism!" *The People, People's Digest*, January 23–29, 1998, 3.

[24] Mugambi, "Forget Your Past," 3.

[25] B. Anderson, *Imagined Communities: Reflections on the Origins and Spread of Nationalism* (London: Verso, 1983).

[26] Anderson, *Imagined Communities*.

[27] H. Bhabha, "DissemiNation: Time, Narrative, and the Margins of the Modern Nation," in *Nation and Narration*, ed. Homi Bhabha (New York: Routledge, 1990), 291–322, at 292.

[28] G. Mutiso, *Socio-Political Thought in African Literature* (New York: Barnes & Noble, 1974), 9.

the colonial enterprise. Writers struggled to correct false images, to rewrite fictionally and poetically the history of pre-colonial and colonial Africa, and to affirm African. The implicit or explicit urge to challenge the premises of colonialism was often realized.[29]

Poetry has always been a profound mode of constructing, narrating, and examining the African nation(s) at large. It has been a vital tool for reflecting and interacting with historical, cultural, and sociopolitical realities. It is on this premise that this chapter examines the function of poetry as a teaching body that facilitates the actualization of nation building, serving as a reflective prism through which a nation can be understood, as well as that of the role of a poet as a nation builder "in creating and proliferating a usable past among other members of the community."[30]

Salutation and Declaration: Setting the Pace for a Narrative

Many African traditional performances, as well as *Etches on Fresh Waters*,[31] include the salutation of gods, ancestors, spirits, elders, and persons young and old. An absence of salutation is a disregard for custom and existing order. The consequences of such disregard are believed to be difficulty and failure – sometimes the omission is believed to cause irrevocable disaster for the performer and his group. For example, *Counting the Tiger's Teeth* and *A Mouth Sweeter than Salt* are preceded by poetic homage to my father, James Adesina Falola, and Pásítọ̀, respectively.

In *Etches on Fresh Waters*, "Kèǹgbè Ọ̀rọ̀," "Ode to Mosáfẹ́jọ́," "Ode to Ìṣọ́lá" "Exhale: Ode to Morọ́láwò," "In Praise of Yánbíọlá," "Ọmọ India," "Ìṣọ́lá ògò" and "The Earth" include *Ìjúbà* (salutation) to the aforementioned: a libation and communion with the forebears. In "The Earth" homage is paid to Earth, the one who "feed and hunger / at the same time" for her incomprehensible vastness and kindness for sustaining lives "Which bursts forth / in their season."[32] As is typical of an oral performance, the poetic personae in "Kèǹgbè Ọ̀rọ̀" summons the readers to "Stretch out your calabashes / Come have a taste / Vintage wine from ancient vines." This summons declares his intent, which is to chastise the readers with truth. It is a serving of bitter leaf, a "Wonder leaf with Two ends / Sour at one / Sweet at the other,"[33] or "messages of debt and doom," as it is put in "The Singing Birds."[34]

---

[29] E. Julien, "African Literature," in *Africa*, ed. P. Martin and P. O'Meara (Bloomington: Indiana University Press, 1995), 295–312, at 297.
[30] Utz, "Nations, Nation-Building, and Cultural Intervention," 630–631.
[31] Toyin Falola and Aderonke Adesanya, *Etches on Fresh Waters* (Durham: Carolina Academic Press, 2008).
[32] Falola and Adesanya, "The Earth," in *Etches on Fresh Waters*, 97.
[33] Falola and Adesanya, "Kèǹgbè Ọ̀rọ̀," in *Etches on Fresh Waters*, 60.
[34] Falola and Adesanya, "The Singing Birds," in *Etches on Fresh Waters*, 63.

The juxtaposition of truth and bitter leaf is expressed through the Yorùbá proverbs that the truth is bitter and that the world detests it – Òtítọ́ korò and Ayékòótọ́ But they conclude that its aftermath is good, like the bitter leaf. The bitter end of the poem is the frank engagement of the spiritual and sociopolitical realities that ravaged Africa's postcolonial existence. These are maintained by "careless looters," "ignominious politicians," "daylight robbers," and others. Ayékòótọ́ is the Yorùbá name for parrots, "The Singing Birds,"[35] which are known and despised for echoing the truth. Poets, as custodians of art, have a duty to comment on sociocultural and political realities and, like Ayékòótọ́, they are despised for it. The forceful and savage imagery evoked counterbalances the highlighted cause; hence, the poetic persona reveals that the intent of the poem is to gag the readers with servings of truth to effect positive change, which is the sweet side of the bitter leaf, causing retrospection and repentance: "Songs, our weapons of war / to kill the cowards."[36]

These songs are revealed as the essence of a poet in "The Poet's Song,"[37] which "will come from / Mouths of truth that seeks no rewards / Enduring pain without any gain." Like Ayékòótọ́, poets are seen bearing songs of truth, expecting no personal gain but scorned for the virtue of upholding the truth. Similarly, the poem "Suspended in Space" echoes that "The world detests honesty / Tell the Truth and leave / Speakers of truth are the / World's enemies." This reemphasizes that the alleged liberation of truth is hatred with a mix of rejection and disaffection. Despite the difficulties that accompany declarations of truth, the poem states how inevitable they are: "Heaven hates untruth / Tell a lie and roast / In the heat of hell / The raging fire / Unextinguishable."[38] By placing truth and lies on the parallels of heaven and hell, the poem suggests truth's superiority over deceit, at least as a virtue.[39]

From general salutation to invocation, and then to self-declaration, the poems "Ode to Mosáfẹ́jọ́," "Ode to Ìṣọ̀lá," and "Ìṣọ̀lá Ògọ̀" declare praise for the performer, which is typical of an African oral performance – performers engage in extensive celebration of their identity, heritage, and achievement. This can be either to introduce themselves to the audience or for the sake of exalting themselves. In "Ode to Mosáfẹ́jọ́" the poetic persona draws a parallel

[35] Falola and Adesanya, "The Singing Birds," in Etches on Fresh Waters, 63.
[36] Falola and Adesanya, "The Singing Birds," in Etches on Fresh Waters, 63.
[37] Falola and Adesanya, "The Poet's Song," in Etches on Fresh Waters, 65.
[38] Falola and Adesanya, "Suspended in Space," in Etches on Fresh Waters, 111–112.
[39] "Wèrè ọrun" is an absurdist poem narrating the vague line between reality and perception: truth varies, that which is generally perceived to be the truth is altered by our perception, and the notion of truth can be distorted to be perceived as the imagined. The poem's narrator, who is assumed to be mad, accuses his accusers of madness, drawing parallels with factual observations of similarities between himself and others. His attempt to subvert their reality and project his own blurs the borders between the real and unreal. On the satirical level the poem suggests how accusers becoming the accused flips the notion of truth (Falola and Adesanya, "Wèrè ọrun," in Etches on Fresh Waters, 261–262).

between her personality and that of *Ifá* and *Odídẹ̀rẹ̀* (parrot). As a bard, she aspires to be as knowledgeable and wise as *Ifá*, and she aspires to be a bearer of tales like the parrot: "The tell tale rover / Ears on walls, eyes through the rafters."[40] However, while "Ode to Mosáfẹ̀jọ́" is a modest praise of one who is "Peaceful and reserved," "Ode to Ìṣọ̀lá"[41] is ebullient praise of a warriors' descendant; it is a panegyric swiftly sifting through my ancestral heritage, my city, my relationships, and my personality.

Narrating Culture

The cultural phase and the psychological phase are two of the four phases of nation building postulated by Greenfeld.[42] In a multicultural setting like Nigeria the cultural phase suggests the homogenization of different ethnic nations, imposing or elevating a single culture as the dominant one, which Gellner refers to as the "centrally sustained high cultures, pervading entire populations."[43] Over time this allows for eroding other cultures and psychologically harnessing people so that they identify with the nation by affiliation. These cultural and psychological concepts are often responsible for guiding an individual's identity difference and separation from others.[44]

In narrating the nation, the markers that are accumulated in the nation's cultures and traditions are exposed. The traditional marker that defines a Yorùbá, and some other African ethnic groups, is tribal marking. These were mainly adopted for identification, and later for the beautification of the face. This is echoed by the poetic persona in "ID Card,"[45] who believes "A permanent ID Card / Adorns my cheeks." He disregards the need to possess an ID card, because his tribal marks are unique and cannot be found anywhere else. The current generation condemns tribal marks as a defacement, but the poem projects them as unique identification and adornment for the face. Another marker is discussed in "Beads," which deals with the importance of beads in African culture. Although they are generally used as adornment, they are also a symbol of royalty and nobility: the poetic persona refers to them as an "index of nobility" and "emblems of honor."[46]

---

[40] Falola and Adesanya, "Ode to Mosafejo," in *Etches on Fresh Waters*, 69.
[41] Falola and Adesanya, "Ode to Isola," in *Etches on Fresh Waters*.
[42] L. Greenfeld, "The Emergence of Nationalism in England and France: A Study in the Sociology of National Identity," *Research in Political Sociology* 5 (1991): 333-370.
[43] E. Gellner, *Nations and Nationalism* (Oxford: Basil Blackwell, 1983), 53.
[44] Connor, "A Nation Is a Nation"; Anderson, *Imagined Communities*; Gellner, *Nations and Nationalism*.
[45] Falola and Adesanya, "ID Card," in *Etches on Fresh Waters*, 91.
[46] Falola and Adesanya, "Beads," in *Etches on Fresh Waters*, 87.

The Polemics of Culture: The Traditional and the Modern

> Learn our wordless language
> Decipher its grammar and meaning
> Expand its lexicon and force ... [47]

The poem "Mothers' Wisdom"[48] contrasts the polemics of African traditional knowledge with the acquisition of knowledge through Western education, religion, and school. The poem demonstrates a typical African traditional setting, where knowledge and wisdom are acquired and tested through various manifestations of culture as myths, legends, parables, rites and rituals, festivals, folktales, proverbs, riddles, and other pieces of lore passed from one generation to another, especially by raconteurs or elderly people – the ten aged women.

Usually, when riddles[49] precede a folktale, *Àlọ́* they are used to awaken the minds of the listeners. More importantly, the riddles are laced with puzzles to examine one's knowledge of a culture or to test one's consciousness about life. The chorus beckons the narrator in his dream, a state of unconsciousness, to "Go back to the village women / Seek the wisdom of the land / Listen to moonlight stories / Acquire the power, great power."

In the poem, culture is represented by "the village gate" – the village signifies a group of people living together with a common belief system, or culture. The knowledge of a culture is the gateway to understanding it, and riddles are one of many ways to engage with it. Contrasting the two systems for acquiring knowledge and wisdom is not done to establish one as supreme and the other as inferior; it is done rather to concretize both as necessities to survive the new challenges posed by modernity and westernization: "To make the old into new / The new into the familiar / The familiar into the new."[50] The poem

---

[47] Toyin Falola and Vivek Bahl, "The Oxygen of Culture," in *Scoundrels of Deferral: Poems to Redeem Reflection* (Durham: Carolina Academic Press, 2006), 203.

[48] Falola and Adesanya, "Mothers' Wisdom," in *Etches on Fresh Waters*, 55.

[49] Riddles are exemplified in the poem "Àlọ́ àpamọ̀," comprising seven riddles in the structure of an oral performance. Each riddle starts with a chorus, a call, and response, followed by a philosophical question and an answer (Falola and Adesanya, *Etches on Fresh Waters*, 195–196).

[50] The African traditional system has often been rejected by and is in continuous conflict against the depleting forces of transatlantic slavery, colonialism, Westernization, and postmodernism. The conflict has been the subject of countless literary works, especially during the neocolonial/postcolonial period. A prominent example is Okot p'Bitek's *Song of Lawino & Song of Ocol* (London: Heinemann, 1984); African indigenous languages have consistently been used against other languages imposed by the colonial masters (see Ngugi wa Thiong'o's *Decolonising the Mind: The Politics of Language in African Literature* [London: James Currey, 1986]). The most suitable resolutions have used the indigenous and the modern (Western) simultaneously, without elevating or imposing one over the other. "Hegemonic Culture" reveals how the emulation of Westernization has diminished our cultural identity, and "Route to Root" depicts an attempt at retracing and retrieving cultural values buried beneath imperialism and globalization (Falola and Bahl, *Scoundrels*

shows the importance of acquiring traditional knowledge, but it depicts the necessity of harnessing both systems of knowledge and wisdom, which the poetic persona refers to as "the calm after the storm." The same resolution is reached in "Hope for Wholeness,"[51] where the poetic persona concludes with the thirst for tradition to "Reclaim meanings / To generate resistance / Renewing minds / And forging new bodies."

The poem "Native Wisdom"[52] accentuates the importance of African traditional knowledge. Unlike "Mothers' Wisdom," it celebrates the supremacy of African native knowledge and wisdom, compared to European education that "saw nothing / ... told me nothing." The Western system of knowledge is represented by Westernization, *Òyìnbó*, and Christianity, *Ìgbàgbọ́*, symbolizing physical vision or extra visual aids that can be rendered useless by collision with external forces. The lens of African native wisdom is represented by the Yorùbá *Ifá* divination system, an epitome and embodiment of wisdom, knowledge, and understanding. The third stanza of the poem imitates an incantation, like the divining verses of *Ifá*, transposing his wish into proverbs, onomatopoeia, repetition, alliteration, metaphors, and invocation.

> *Yéèpàrìpà!*
> Barreness courts not
> The gourd which travels early to the stream
> *Wórówóró lálọ, dùgbẹ̀dùgbẹ̀ lábọ̀*
> Ifa, the lens of my ancestors
> Rescue me
> *Ojú inú*
> Knowledge I pine for
> *Là gẹẹ rẹgẹ, là gẹ̀ẹ̀rẹ̀gẹ̀*
> Clear the mist
> The water fetched at daybreak
> Always crystal clear[53]

The expression "Knowledge I pine for / *Làgẹẹrẹgẹ, là gẹ̀ẹ̀rẹ̀gẹ̀* / Clear the mist" resembles the chants ending the initial procession of *Ifá* divination, made by a diviner seeking access to concealed knowledge. A common expression that ends the divination chant is "Ọ̀yẹ̀ là. Táa bá fẹ́mọ lójú, aríran." "Ọ̀yẹ̀ là" literally translates as a request for understanding to be revealed just as blown air clears the clouded eyes of a child.

---

of Deferral, 77 and 83). It is important to acknowledge that Westernization and the long-lasting effects of colonialism in Africa cannot be reversed or erased; the need to overcome present challenges is more important than romanticizing the pains of the past (Mugambi, "Forget Your Past").

[51] Falola and Bahl, "Hope for Wholeness," in *Scoundrels of Deferral*, 151.
[52] Falola and Adesanya, "Native Wisdom," in *Etches on Fresh Waters*, 57.
[53] Falola and Adesanya, "Native Wisdom," in *Etches on Fresh Waters*, 57.

Ifá, arínúróde, òlùmọ̀ràn-ọkàn is a seer that sees the hidden and the obvious, knowing that which burdens the heart. This lens places an emphasis on spirituality, and inner meditation, which is *Ojú inú*; a Yorùbá proverb expresses the idea that *Ojú inú làgbànlò*, or inner meditation, aids the vision of an elder, and elders are wise due to their accumulation of experience. The lens of ancient wisdom lets the poetic persona proclaim a clear vision: "*Ifá, Arínúróde* / I can see! I can see!"

The poem "Slippery"[54] also emphasizes the importance of experience, patience, and wisdom acquired from the elderly, referred to as "The wisdom of grey hair," which "Is not bought with money / Or achieved by aggression" but through exercising patience. "The Oxygen of Culture"[55] describes traditional culture as a shelter of identity and growth. The relationship between culture and a group of people is mutual; culture defines and shapes a people, and the people preserve and redefine culture – as culture personified, the poetic persona states: "You must not forget us, / Trapped in your inner designs. / Be gentle when we do not see truth / Forgive us if we fail / Your heart and its longings." The poems highlight the importance and intricacy of culture in its traditional and modern forms.

Narrating Cultural Virtues

The non-material aspects of a culture are important to its understanding and continuous existence – as important as its material aspects. They embody the values and norms that are considered acceptable within the culture, holding a "very pervasive influence on the lives of the people of a particular culture."[56] Every society has codes to guide the conduct of its members, including strangers, ensuring and securing their physical, psychological, and sociocultural identities.[57] However, morality is important in African culture, and bards have a sociocultural duty to uphold the norms and mores that guide culture toward an acceptable way of living. Women and elders also contribute to these efforts, as in the proverbial saying "Àgbà kìí wà l'ọ́jà k'órí ọmọ tuntun ó wọ́"

The poem "Honor, Shame and Money"[58] is a parable illustrating and examining the relationship between honor, shame, and money in the present generation. Honor is a representation of virtues usually valued in all cultures and religions at different levels, and shame, which is a consequence of lacking honor, is to be avoided because of the damage it does to the reputation of a person, a family, a community, or a nation at large. Therefore, "To show the

---

[54] Falola and Adesanya, "Slippery," in *Etches on Fresh Waters*, 95.
[55] Falola and Bahl, "The Oxygen of Culture," in *Scoundrels of Deferral*, 203.
[56] G. Idang, "African Culture and Values," *Phronimon* 16, no. 2 (2015): 97–111, at 102.
[57] U. Etuk, *Religion and Cultural Identity* (Ibadan: Hope Publication, 2002); O. Antia, *Akwa Ibom Cultural Heritage: Its Incursion by Western Culture and Its Renaissance* (Uyo: Abbny Publishers, 2005).
[58] Falola and Adesanya, "Honor, Shame and Money," in *Etches on Fresh Waters*, 291.

extent of disapproval that followed the violation of values that should otherwise be held sacred, the penalty was sometimes very shameful, sometimes extreme."[59] The poem is steeped in the Yorùbá belief and custom of good conduct.

The Yorùbá people are originally and alternatively known as Ọmọlúàbí (Ọmọ tí Olú Ìwà bí), which translates as "the child begotten by the Lord of Good Conduct" – this is similar to the artistic reinvention attempted in the poem. The trio of Honor, Shame, and Money are begotten by Ìwà pẹ̀lẹ́ (gentleness)[60] and Ìwà rere (good will); their death signifies the eventual demise of honor and shame among humans. The restless pursuit of money, the root of all evil, further illustrates the surrender to shame and disregard for honor, lamenting the many heinous acts committed by humans.

This perspective is inverted with "In Search of Shame,"[61] which invokes shame as an examination of conscience. "Shame was watchful / Shame knew our heart," according to the poetic voice, meaning that the existence of shame instills honor and justifies the righteous, by "Repairing my torn ligaments of hope and innocence." In a similar manner, "Hawks Tale"[62] is a fable that denounces disobedience. It is illustrated by the story of a chick, like the proverbial dog, that refuses to heed the call of its mother, roaming carelessly "where eagles abound" despite severe warnings. This poem reemphasizes that disobedience precedes destruction.

The poem "The Goat Meat"[63] advocates moderation (Ìwọ̀ntunwọ̀sìn). Through the consumption of meat, the poem illustrates the consequences of greed and excess, depicted as "a protruding belly" which is not only unhealthy but also invites mockery from others. Moderation curtails greediness, covetousness, jealousy, thievery, and all manner of vices; it is a virtue at the foundation of good character. Like Silifa's torn dress, one's physical and moral wellness is threatened by excessiveness: "No one exhibits his/her wealth through the excessive consumption of salt."

---

[59] Idang, "African Culture and Values," 102.
[60] The virtue of gentleness, or humility, is the predominant preoccupation of "Humility"; the poetic persona meditates on his lack of humility and broaches the need for collectivism. The lack of humility prevents collectivism, which fosters peace and good relations – great achievements are not the sole effort of an individual, which is why he calls on others: "Come, let us join hands together." The poem advocates humility as the only true causal agent of greatness and national development: "Change through the small, the / daily efforts of duty. / Quiet gestures on a new path. / leaving the worn grooves / of ease and the destruction. / Fathom anew / Nourish identity / Sympathize with your faltering – Steady paces to a worthy end" (Falola and Bahl, "Honor, Shame and Money," in *Scoundrels of Deferral*, 291).
[61] Falola and Bahl, "In Search of Shame," in *Scoundrels of Deferral*, 4.
[62] Falola and Adesanya, "Hawks Tale," in *Etches on Fresh Waters*, 311.
[63] Falola and Adesanya, "The Goat Meat," in *Etches on Fresh Waters*, 115.

Similarly, "Ọ̀pọ̀lọ́ Àbénìyàn"[64] satirizes the notion of freedom and emphasizes the need for moderation, especially in the expression of unrestrained freedom. Ironically, the poetic persona asserts that "Everyone is free / To do whatever s/he likes," highlighting the consequence of such freedom by drawing a philosophical contrast between "the easy-going chameleon" that "stumbled into its death" and "the toad / who jumps up and down, saying: / 'It's my personal business, not yours'." In "Baba Mogbọ́tán"[65] a man believes himself to be the wisest, like the proverbial tortoise, and the poetic voice preaches caution. Baba Mogbọ́tán must exercise restraint to avoid trapping himself in his own web.

The ideal representation of women and cultural expectations of morality have been referred to as "a 'burden of representation', as they are regarded as the symbolic bearers of collectivity's identity and honor, both personally and collectively."[66] At the fore of "Tage Tage of Ibadan"[67] is the need to curtail the excesses of sexual immorality, addressing prostitution, which has been on the rise since the colonial period. The poem "Lust in Practice"[68] tells the tale of a lecturer and a doctor who are brothers and "owners of restless rods," indulging themselves in sexual acts with their students and patients by abusing their authority. Sexual immorality is considered a vice that "Mars his impressive credentials" and "Renders his noble practice / A puerile periled endeavor." Although the poem "Pota"[69] mainly satirizes the deplorable state of social facilities and insecurity in the country, describing the journey of a young lady embarking to Port Harcourt on roads, "Some Tarred, some full of pot-holes / Big enough to hide a lion"; the narrative voice notes that the lady's husband is afraid of losing his wife to "the young guys / Smart and bold / Who might be interested in the man's wife." This concern is coupled with Port Harcourt's infamous reputation for having a high rate of prostitution, evident through the constant repetition of the phrase "Port Harcourt!" in the poem.

Kindness and its communal effects are central preoccupations in "Hospitality."[70] A place where hospitality abounds is likened to "A space that nurtures / A place of growth / Offering relief and renewal / Attracting respect and honor." "Hospitality," like "Giving,"[71] provides comfort to the body, warmth to the soul, and healing to the spirit. The admonition for morality, and the virtues obtained in different cultures, transcends the node of

---

[64] Falola and Adesanya, "Ọ̀pọ̀lọ́ Àbénìyàn," in *Etches on Fresh Waters*, 309.
[65] Falola and Adesanya, "Baba Mogbọ́ntán," in *Etches on Fresh Waters*, 331–332.
[66] N. Yuval-Davis, "Nationalist Projects and Gender Relations," *Nar. umjet* 40, no. 1 (2003): 9–36, at 17.
[67] Falola and Adesanya, "Tage Tage of Ibadan," in *Etches on Fresh Waters*, 129.
[68] Falola and Adesanya, "Lust in Practice," in *Etches on Fresh Waters*, 119.
[69] Falola and Adesanya, "Pota," in *Etches on Fresh Waters*, 273.
[70] Falola and Bahl, "Hospitality," in *Scoundrels of Deferral*, 185.
[71] Falola and Bahl, "Giving," in *Scoundrels of Deferral*, 163.

individuality; it aims to achieve greatness at a collective level, which is a communal responsibility. "Whatever happens to the individual happens to the whole group, and whatever happens to the whole group happens to the individual,"[72] which is the African way of life. "From Isola's Grave"[73] advocates self-discipline while remarking on life's brevity. It puts vanity in the foreground, noting how all is led to ruin by the passage of time. A stanza of Pásítọ̀'s reconstructed poem and sermon about death reads:

> What is your *kakandu* [courage]
> What does it mean to be tall?
> What does it mean to be short?
> What does beauty amounts to?
> Remember the end
> We are all nothing.[74]

Virtues facilitate harmony and ensure communal growth while prompting the mind to remain aware that life is transient and man is mortal.

Narrating the Woman as a Nation

At the heart of nationalism and national development is the integrative and reproductive role of women, their image, and their activities. In reference to Dami Ajayi's *A Woman's Body Is a Country*,[75] the image of women is the map to understanding the soul of a nation – its whole essence – which Renan regards as the "spiritual principle."[76] A woman's role is vital for the existence of a nation, and a nation would be nonexistent without the contributions of women, whether biological, political, economic, or sociocultural.[77] This cultural reference to and of women is not in the objective manner in which it has

---

[72] John Mbiti, *African Religions and Philosophy* (New York: Praeger, 1969), 109.
[73] Falola and Adesanya, "From Isola's Grave," in *Etches on Fresh Waters*, 373.
[74] Falola, *A Mouth Sweeter than Salt*, 350.
[75] D. Ajayi, *A Woman's Body Is a Country* (Lagos: Ouida Books, 2017).
[76] E. Renan, "What Is a Nation?" in *Nationalism in Europe 1815 to the Present*, ed. S. Woolf (New York: Routledge, 1996), 48–60, at 57.
[77] N. Yuval-Davis, *Gender and Nation* (London: Sage, 1997) highlights the essentiality of women through various reproductive capacities. Biologically, women make nations possible by increasing their population through births. Women, especially mothers, are seen as cultural custodians, acting as the primary agents of socialization in families and society. According to Yuval-Davis, "The central importance of women's reproductive roles in ethnic and national discourses becomes apparent when one considers that one usually joins the collective by being born into it" (Yuval-Davis, "Nationalist Projects," 12). Women are entrusted with the cultural role of imparting morality, according to Mayer: "only pure and modest women can re-produce the pure nation; without purity in biological reproduction, the nation clearly cannot survive" (T. Mayer, ed., *Gender Ironies of Nationalism: Sexing the Nation* [London and New York: Routledge, 2000], 6). Women in different nations have contributed immensely to their nations' political development, especially as political activists.

come to be known in contemporary times. The image of a woman is often used to symbolize collectivity and progress in a nation, as with the Statue of Liberty and the personality of Moremi. Women regarded as figurative representations of nations are "subsumed symbolically into the national body politic as its boundary and metaphoric limit."[78]

The conception of nation as a gender is foregrounded in Anderson's definition of a nation,[79] as an imagined community, as individuals imagine that they belong to a specific gender group, or as ascribed by the culture. This leads to the cultural depiction of a nation as female, becoming evident in language. Wenk expresses her view of gender–nation relations within the significance of describing nations as "images or metaphors of gender."[80] This is evident in the works of Negritudinal poets[81] depicting Africa and her countries as women, adoring and worshiping them. More often, "Africa is depicted in pastoral images of nature and nurture, symbolized often as a woman in tropes that are both maternal and erotic."[82]

"The Gaze,"[83] "Any He,"[84] and "Mule No More"[85] are poems presenting the emotional ordeals of women and the difficulties of African sociocultural pressures on women expected to lift the burdens of others. "The Gaze" expresses the sexual betrayal of the poetic persona, who is a representation of women, by a partner described as "Lost in diabolical cravings / Awed by the lures / He turned a bee / He stung." The act of stinging like a bee implies a nonconsensual act leaving the poetic persona betrayed and sad: it is a state of being "Motionless / Speechless / Gazing at an empty sky."

"Mule No More" expresses how the female sex buckles under the weight of sociocultural responsibilities and anticipation, described as "Like morsels on dishes / . . . / In large doses / She bore the burden / Of brothers in need / And sisters alike." The quest for freedom from these duties confronts existing orders and relationships: "A NO? / Sister was stunned / Brother was bruised / By her new voice / And the way the family mule / Firmly planted her feet / On the threshold of freedom." Likewise, "Mortgaged"[86] expresses the objectification of

---

[78] A. McClintock, "Family Feuds: Gender, Nationalism and the Family," *Feminist Review* 44 (1993): 61–80, at 62.
[79] Anderson, *Imagined Communities*.
[80] Wenk, "Gendered Representations," 63.
[81] The reaffirmation of African culture, history, and values is at the forefront of preoccupations discussed by Negritudinal poets. The prominent Negritudinal poets include Léopold Sédar Senghor, Kwesi Brew, David Diop, Kofi Awoonor, Birago Diop, and others.
[82] T. Knipp, "English-Language Poetry," in *A History of Twentieth-Century African Literatures*, ed. O. Owomoyela (Lincoln: University of Nebraska Press, 1993), 105–137, at 108.
[83] Falola and Adesanya, "The Gaze," in *Etches on Fresh Waters*, 101.
[84] Falola and Adesanya, "Any He," in *Etches on Fresh Waters*, 157.
[85] Falola and Adesanya, "Mule No More," in *Etches on Fresh Waters*, 109.
[86] Falola and Adesanya, "Mortgaged," in *Etches on Fresh Waters*, 121.

women and their lack of control over important decisions relating to their existence.

> Father gave her away
> To the man of his vision
> She had no say
> She who must honor
> The Family name.

This type of relegation and the sociocultural place of women are captured in the refrain: "Warm the bed / Oil the body / Make babies / Argue not / Nod always," defining a woman only by her roles and responsibilities to men and society. Turner draws a similar comparison between the close association of a woman's body, her identity, and her existence. According to him, "to control women's bodies is to control their personalities and represents an act of authority over the body in the interests of the public order organized around male values what is rational."[87] "Mortgaged" captures the wave of feminism in Africa that is attempting to liberate women. They are likened to mules, struggling to break the shackles of tradition dictated by patriarchy and agitating for equal rights and responsibilities. In "Mortgaged," "Wife packed her trousseau / Her fledging child in tow / She bid farewell to servitude / And goodbye to mothers' song" in search of a better life. Similarly, the poetic persona in "No to Happiness"[88] resists remaining in a marital relationship with an abusive spouse who is "eager and quick to use his belt."

"Any He"[89] also focuses on the sociocultural relevance placed on the male figure in relation to the existence of a woman. The man is described as "The he to fertilize / The he to create / Fences of protection / The he to bring fortunes / The he to add to the number / For the lineage to expand," underscoring the relevance and place of women in the community. Unlike "Mortgaged," "Any He" emphasizes the overbearing attitude of the male figure that compares his woman to a "camel" and a "beast" to be mounted, continually seeking the submissiveness of the woman to assert his ego: "Tremble, Tremble / Like your seniors."

If the aforementioned poems depict the male figure's cultural elevation to become head of the house, "Àìbìkítà / (Ir)responsibility"[90] satirizes his inability to fulfill his sociocultural role. It highlights a man neglecting the responsibility to take care of his family: the man "Gave no money / For his household's upkeep / His salary he kept / For inanities and irrelevancies" and his neglect left his wife and family at the mercy of others, "a toy / In the hands of all and

---

[87] B. Turner, *The Body and Society: Explorations in Social Theory* (London: Sage, 1966), 197.
[88] Falola and Adesanya, "No to Happiness," in *Etches on Fresh Waters*, 173.
[89] Falola and Adesanya, "Any He," in *Etches on Fresh Waters*, 157.
[90] Falola and Adesanya, "Aibikita / (Ir)responsibility," in *Etches on Fresh Waters*, 187.

sundry." This underscores the sociocultural and political role of the man as a "guarantor of the family's and nation's well-being."[91] Roles switch in "Scavengers II,"[92] where the female figure is supreme in a society that accords more power and value to women, which is closer to an American or European society. The poem describes a vice-versa relationship between a woman and her irresponsible man, the latter's dependence on the former, and the man's ultimate eviction.

"Idunnu Oberekete"[93] offers a different interpretation by satirizing the laziness of a woman who accrues fat due to carelessness, bringing shame to her husband, *Oríyọmí*. "The Rear,"[94] "Hips,"[95] "Omoge to Pantele,"[96] and "Man, A Woman's Wrapper"[97] engage celebrating the physical and sociocultural attributes and relevance of women. "Omoge tó Pàntèlé" describes the emotional strength of a woman harnessing beauty amidst strain and praises her ability to endure difficulties:

> They look so attractive even with the load that they carry
> Although too much load puts one's neck at risk
> But ladies who can balance loads on their heads
> Turn such a head load into a thing of beauty.

"Man, A Woman's Wrapper" portrays a male figure, who is culturally perceived as superior, as subordinate. In fact, his existence is only made possible by his partner. At all stages, from birth to death, man is like a seedling nurtured by the care and love of a woman: "Wrapped in the womb / Wrapped on the back / Wrapped on the chest and / Wrapped in the earth." Similarly, "Mama"[98] describes the important role of a woman who sustains a family, a community, and a nation at large. This is evident in the woman's countless responsibilities listed in the first stanza:

> A life without rest
> The restlessness of work
> Feeding the babies
> Nursing the adults
> Managing wallets
> Resolving conflicts . . .

---

[91] V. Kesić, "Gender and Ethnic Identities in Transition," in *From Gender to Nation*, ed. E. Iveković and J. Mostov (Ravenna: Longo Editore Ravenna, 2001), 63–80, at 98.
[92] Falola and Adesanya, "Scavengers II," in *Etches on Fresh Waters*, 223–224.
[93] Falola and Adesanya, "Idunu Oberekete," in *Etches on Fresh Waters*, 315.
[94] Falola and Adesanya, "The Rear," in *Etches on Fresh Waters*, 237.
[95] Falola and Adesanya, "Hips," *Etches on Fresh Waters*, 239.
[96] Falola and Adesanya, "Omoge to Pantele," in *Etches on Fresh Waters*, 133–134.
[97] Falola and Adesanya, "Man, A Woman's Wrapper," in *Etches on Fresh Waters*, 145.
[98] Falola and Bahl, "Mama," in *Scoundrels of Deferral*, 179.

Like "Man, A Woman's Wrapper," "Mama" elevates, reverses, and combines the images of both the male and the female into that of the female, in recognition of the tireless efforts, responsibilities, and sacrifices made by women. Mama is described as both the Queen and the King, the center and periphery of a nation.

Narrating the Nation: The Historical and Economical

The title, preoccupation, and intention of the poem "Kèǹgbè Ọ̀rọ̀" (The Pregnant Gourd)"[99] is similar to Fela's "Basket Mouth." The poem sets the pace for the sociocultural and political discourses that follow in *Etches on Fresh Waters*. "The Vault"[100] traces the exploitation of Africa at different historical phases, from the infamous transatlantic slavery to post/neocolonialism, which "took their turn / In raiding her vault / They dipped, emptied and withdrew / Denuding her precious gems." The transatlantic slave trade significantly impaired Africa's progress, peace, and existence – the poem describes it as that which "Marred a flourishing era / A violent thrust."

The second raid, which is colonialism, comes with the deceit of education and Christianity.[101] This is described as a love offered "On fake templates / ... / On a plate of thorns" to empty the vault anew. The third phase is marked by the independence of African states, bringing the hope "To soar again / ... / From another age of pain." However, as seen in most independent African states, it is followed by "social dislocations and disillusionment"; this unanticipated reality "necessitated a change in poetic tradition, attention is thus shifted to the perennial socio-political and economic problems emanating from self-rule."[102] While the title depicts the continent as a depository of treasure, its semantic multiplicity also suggests the need for Africa to transcend the odds to attain its long-due progress. The poem suggests this with the clamor for rain to fill up the looted vault: "Raided to the last throe / Of unquenchable thirst!"

---

[99] Falola and Adesanya, "Kèǹgbè Ọ̀rọ̀ (The Pregnant Gourd)," in *Etches on Fresh Waters*, 59–60.

[100] Falola and Adesanya, "The Vault," in *Etches on Fresh Waters*, 211.

[101] The same subject of imperialism is well expounded in "Imperialism," which it describes as the act of strong states attacking the weak. The poem elaborates on the given reason Africa and other European colonies were colonized – a generous attempt to "redeem" the colonized from an impending doom they would bring upon themselves: "Civilize them / Their smell too odious / Their fate sealed in the / Contract of oblivion." The poem accuses colonialism of sowing discord, violence, and economic hardship afflicting the previously colonized nations; they are left with "Irritated eyes of bitterness / Tongues of venom" (Falola and Bahl, "Imperialism," in *Scoundrels of Deferral*, 71). One such outcome of the "Hatred sown / Germinating self-destruction / Hearty stalks of violence / Harvested with death" expressed in "Imperialism" is the Rwandan genocide against the Tutsi in 1994, which is the preoccupation of "Genocide" (Falola and Bahl, *Scoundrels of Deferral*, 73).

[102] H. Oripeloye, "The Development of Exilic Poetry in Anglophone West Africa," *Tydskrif vir Letterkunde* 52, no. 1 (2015): 155–167, at 157.

Metaphorically, "The Tree's Fall"[103] mocks the Nigerian government's gallant attempt to spearhead military missions in African countries in the wake of independence, attempting to address civil unrest in different parts of the continent. The poem describes the country, often regarded as the giant of Africa, as "The 'big brother' Africa / Who must fell our trees / In 'Ecomog' spirit / To fuel the fireplace / Of his indigent neighbors / While his homestead lacks / A common matchstick!" It is like a lamp illuminating the surroundings while its base remains dark. This poem and "The Grasshopper's Dance"[104] discuss how the failure of leadership is not due to external problems, but stems from the neglect of affairs at the supposed leader's home. Perhaps it is the strain that the position puts on the home; the strain "Saddens its leaves" but "Gladdens the infantry ants / Who hold impromptu conferences / On its sprawling length / And find a bridge / To their next meal."

"Trailers II"[105] is a survey of the precolonial/independent African states and the economic hardships ravaging them from the colonial period to the present. The structure and size of the family in the poem characterize the precolonial African period with bliss and bountifulness: "The more, the merrier!" As the poem recounts the family's reduction in the size, it depicts how the consequences of economic hardship affect the family as the smallest unit of the society/nation. In the second stanza, "The years of SAP" is a deliberate inversion of the Nigerian Structural Adjustment Program, adopted in 1986 during the military regime of General Ibrahim Babangida, indicating an adjustment to the narrated structure of the family and the country's economy.

The poem "The Strain Train (C. 1996)"[106] traces the political and economic history of Nigeria, focusing on the struggle and labor of the people while observing the leaders "who drank like camels / The toil of a nation" and plundered its natural resources. The poem traces the country's leadership from the time of "Women of substance / Men of valor" to the military government described as "the spoilers / Mutineers and usurpers / Harbingers of ills / Jackboots on legs." Eventually, it returns to the democratic government of dreamers and visionaries who "Came on the mainstream / To restore the train's steam," which only looted the coffers of the nation further and put additional strain on the citizens. This contrasts with "Leadership,"[107] discussing the fine qualities of leadership that should be emulated to attain a peaceful nation and sustainable development. The poem advocates humility, generosity, collectivism, affection, and dignity. Recognizing leadership as an opportunity to serve, the poem admonishes leaders to "Talk to the deaf / Make the lame walk / Fill hungry stomachs," satirically drawing a deliberate parallel

---

[103] Falola and Adesanya, "The Tree's Fall," in *Etches on Fresh Waters*, 205.
[104] Falola and Adesanya, "The Grasshopper's Dance," in *Etches on Fresh Waters*, 203.
[105] Falola and Adesanya, "Trailers II," in *Etches on Fresh Waters*, 287.
[106] Falola and Adesanya, "The Strain Train (C. 1996)," in *Etches on Fresh Waters*, 321.
[107] Falola and Bahl, "Leadership," in *Scoundrels of Deferral*, 167.

between the actions of Jesus, who performed those acts in the Bible, and African leaders, who have done the opposite in their own countries.

Cybercrime, armed robbery, and prostitution are some of the consequences of this unfavorable economic reality, which is the unsuitable situation that "Leadership" warns leaders to avoid. "Trailers III"[108] examines the vicious cycle of socio-economic hardship initiated by political leaders "who loot the state treasury" and shady businessmen who end up tormented by armed robbers. Exploited citizens are further terrorized by the "Unsolicited Landlord," and the vicious cycle continues when victims of exploitation enact jungle justice on apprehended or suspected armed robbers. "Trailer III" details how a misnomer at a level distorts the balance of existence and humanity at all levels. The last stanza of "Trickster-Monster"[109] depicts the chaotic and conflicting realities present in the nation:

> A phallic motherland
> Strong and lazy
> Able and feeble
> Rich and poor
> Masculine and weak
> Manifest and unmanifest
> Order and disorder
> Honest and dishonest
> Profit and loss
> Motherland, a trickster.

If the biblical account of a child requesting bread and receiving it offers assurance, "Bread and Bullet"[110] offers something other. The poem reflects both the expectation and the unfortunate reality of African countries where bullets, suggesting death, were given in place of bread, offering life. The poem reflects a typical African election, where innocent youths and thugs are manipulated to install a specific political candidate or party.

Narrating the Nation: The Sociocultural and the Political

"Yello Sisi"[111] responds to the alarming rate of bleaching among Africans of every age and gender. It depicts desperate African attempts to reinvent identities by altering physical appearance. The apportioning of status based on skin color originates from racism,[112] which associates black(ness) with everything

---

[108] Falola and Adesanya, "Trailers III," in *Etches on Fresh Waters*, 289.
[109] Falola and Adesanya, "Trickster-Monster," in *Etches on Fresh Waters*, 325.
[110] Falola and Bahl, "Bread and Bullet," in *Scoundrels of Deferral*, 89.
[111] Falola and Adesanya, "Yello Sisi," in *Etches on Fresh Waters*, 275.
[112] Racism shapes one race's perception of another based on skin color. In "Red and Black" the poetic persona narrates how racism through skin-color segregation is a colonialist invention to keep their subjects beneath them; from the name African to the more

inferior and bad. This creates a craving for any color other than black. The narrator laments:

> Yellow is in vogue in Italy
> Red in the Netherlands
> Lagos wants all colors
> Bodies are spare parts, sex objects
> In shameless company
> Betraying Mother Africa.

At the psychological level the discoloration of skin results in disillusionment and a personality in crisis: "A soul conquered by the body / A mind of concoction that / Vomits excreta of lies." Feelings of not belonging anywhere arise; the act of bleaching is a rejection of the black identity itself. The failure to achieve a true "white" skin through bleaching creams, which are a "Cancerous perfume of chemicals / Turning the face into yellow / the neck into orange / The fingers into green," leads to further rejection. Sales of lip-bleaching balm are common in the streets of Lagos. The pathetic sociocultural and economic realities plaguing most African states after independence are largely the result of mismanaged political affairs. This is in spite of government leaders who collectively clamored and struggled toward the eventual attainment of African independence;[113] the perceived inefficacy of democratic leaders led to military confiscation of power in most African states:

> Then came the spoilers
> Mutineers and usurpers
> Harbingers of ills
> Jackboots on legs
> Guns in hands
> Ensuring the rule
> Of bloodsucking vipers...[114]

Contrary to the goal of repairing the damage done by democratic leaders, military regimes are rife with more economic hardship, autocracy, and political instability; stiff criticism is meted out against the countless atrocities perpetrated by military authorities. "Lẹ́fú-Rete,"[115] like Fela's "Zombie," mocks the ignorance of military men who "Their left they know not / From their right/ Their right they know not / From their left." The poem projects

---

offensive name Nigger, imperialists seek to continually dominate black-skinned people (Falola and Bahl, *Scoundrels of Deferral*, 85).

[113] These leaders' struggles for the independence and advancement of African states is the recognized in "The Departed Comrades" whose guidance is invoked in order not to depart from the efforts of their labor (Falola and Bahl, *Scoundrels of Deferral*, 141).

[114] Falola and Adesanya, "The Strain Train," in *Etches on Fresh Waters*, 321–323.

[115] Falola and Adesanya, "Lẹ́fú-Rete," in *Etches on Fresh Waters*, 365.

them as caricatures who only take orders from their superiors – a conclusion about military rule is inferred from the phrase: "Where there is no right / what is left?"

Negligence, inefficiency, nepotism, and corruption characterize systems of governance in African countries. "Salutation to Work"[116] criticizes the negligence of leaders at different levels of government who were elected to serve the people. It depicts a leader abandoning his duty, engaging in all manner of frivolities and corrupt practices; he exploits his position as governor for selfish interests. A widespread video that surfaced online, showing the governor of a northern state in Nigeria smiling while tucking bales of dollar notes from contractors under his *Agbádá*, offers an example from real life. The poem states: "The governor needs one hour with the German / Contracts have to be reviewed – line by line for kickbacks, / They laugh loud and louder, to arrive at 35 percent."

"Ròfòrófò"[117] is a metaphor that describes the African political system and practice as a mud game, a deadly affair that mars the reputations of politicians and the political image of the continent. "Counter Violence"[118] reveals the trickery and violence accompanying African elections more explicitly. It shows how they are futile efforts that fail to represent the interest of the people, the masses who are "Too many to count."

"The Maradona of Politics"[119] reemphasizes the abuse of power by political leaders, examining their deceitful nature by comparing their dishonest tactics to those of Diego Maradona, an Argentinian footballer famous for his style and dribbling skills. The comparison of football and politics focuses on their shifting maneuvers, showing how the leaders deceitfully exploit followers with their "Beastly neck / Disfigured hands / Fast legs/ Blinded eyes."

Narrating Nature as an Embodiment of a Nation

Increasing dangers posed by climate change and natural disasters in different regions of the world have raised a clamor for a healthy and sustainable relationship between humans and their environment. An important agenda item from the United Nations Framework Convention on Climate Change is the concern for human activities that "have been substantially increasing the atmospheric concentrations of greenhouse gases, that these increases enhance the natural greenhouse effect, and that this will result on average in an additional warming of the Earth's surface and atmosphere and may adversely affect natural ecosystems and humankind."[120]

---

[116] Falola and Adesanya, "Salutation to Work," in *Etches on Fresh Waters*, 277.
[117] Falola and Adesanya, "Ròròrófò," in *Etches on Fresh Waters*, 337.
[118] Falola and Bahl, "Counter Violence," in *Scoundrels of Deferral*, 93.
[119] Falola and Bahl, "The Maradona of Politics," in *Scoundrels of Deferral*, 75.
[120] United Nations, "United Nations Framework Convention on Climate Change," May 9, 1992, https://treaties.un.org/Pages/ViewDetailsIII.aspx?src=TREATY&mtdsg_no=XXVII-7&chapter=27&Temp=mtdsg3&clang=_en, 1.

"The Tree's Fall"[121] emphasizes nature's importance for man's existence, along with the need to nurture it, not destroy it. In the poem the tree is a representative of nature, and its destruction is attributed to "Chief Woodcutter / For the careless swing / Of his thirsty blade." The act of felling trees is common in today's society; trees are felled for selfish reasons, with no plans to replace them.

In "Reincarnation"[122] the poetic persona adores and relishes the beauty of nature: "I desire the life / Of lush green leaves / The garment of fruitful trees / Flourishing in their season." Like a typical romantic poem, it highlights the tranquility that abounds in the presence of nature and in the coexistence of multiple manifestations of nature.

Conclusion: Narrating Home, the Migrants, and the Diaspora

> From Africa dispersed
> With hearts open to learn
> With minds and hands ready to work,
> We journeyed to escape constriction
> To make our mark
> To give our children opportunities
> To build the world anew.[123]

Arguably, the transatlantic slave trade is one of the most distorting events that ever happened to Africa and the people; it is the primary cause of the African people's dispersion and the diffusion of their culture. Since the forceful mass migration of Africans during transatlantic slavery, more Africans have emigrated to different parts of the world in search of greener pastures – this is on the rise recently, due to socio-economic difficulties and political instability ravaging post-independent African countries. This reality is noticeable in African literature's shifting motifs, moving from the reflection of Africa's dehumanizing realities to the sojourn and experience of Africans in foreign lands, which is being referred to as African migrant fiction. According to Oripeloye:

> The postcolonial era in Africa is indeed a time of economic recess as African leaders continue to plunder the resources of their respective countries to the chagrin of the masses. This has exacerbated the existential problems confronting the average person. A means of subverting this horrendous dysfunction has resulted in migration which eventually translates into exile.[124]

---

[121] Falola and Adesanya, "The Tree's Fall, in *Etches on Fresh Waters*," 205.
[122] Falola and Adesanya, "Reincarnation," in *Etches on Fresh Waters*, 219.
[123] Falola and Bahl, "Transnationalism," in *Scoundrels of Deferral*, 201.
[124] Oripeloye, "The Development of Exilic Poetry," 157.

This continuous movement is reflected in "From Slavery to Slavery,"[125] where the despairs and sorrows of transatlantic slavery abound today; they have manifested in the variegated, horrible post-independence realities. A modern myth, and perhaps a joke, explains the mass migration of Africans to Europe and the Americas as an attempt to reconnect with their ancestors – a subtle shift from the entitlement ideology of some African Americans who felt that they did not have to work because their forebears already did the work.

The poem "The Strain Train"[126] offers a reason for the "brain drain" in African countries, especially Nigeria, linking it with the "pipe drain" activities of political leaders. The "pipe" is a metonymy for the petroleum crude oil, which symbolizes the main driver of the nation's economy. Africans finding their way out of the continent, by the thousands, must engage in various acts to ensure survival; accordingly, Anyidoho observes that "Africans are not necessarily the world's most travelled people but it is hard to find any other people so ruthlessly flung across a hostile world, clearly against their will and choice."[127] This postcolonial menace is expressed in "Groom's Broom":[128]

> Twenty years ago
> When the proud nation
> Became a debtor nation
> Confused citizens
> Did anything to survive
> One went to Mecca
> Buying fake Teeth
> For Alhaji Balubalu
> One went to Merika
> To sell *satifikate*

This group of people lives outside the continent, carving new identities for themselves, but their existence and continuous movement outside the continent (re)shape it. One relationship is severed, disconnecting the continent from the migrants who hold the gloomy perception of Africa as a place for perpetual suffering. Africa is often set in contrast with these newly found abodes, such as the example of London in "Groom's Broom," which is "Dazzled by paved streets / Shining lights, fast cars" and "Coins, papers, banks / All money" everywhere. In the poem "The Atlantic Connection"[129] the narrator's fiancé, who just arrived from Europe, yearned to be "In the company of the civilized / Away from these mosquitoes / Pests and caricatures." Similarly, the narrator of

---

[125] Falola and Bahl, "From Slavery to Slavery," in *Scoundrels of Deferral*, 87.
[126] Falola and Adesanya, "The Strain Train," in *Etches on Fresh Waters*, 321–323.
[127] Kofi Anyidoho, "Ayi Kwei Armah and our Journey of the Mind," in *Literature and National Consciousness*, ed. E. Emenyonu (Ibadan: Heinemann, 1989), 108–117, at 108.
[128] Falola and Adesanya, "Groom's Broom," in *Etches on Fresh Waters*, 231.
[129] Falola and Adesanya, "The Atlantic Connection," in *Etches on Fresh Waters*, 251.

"Groom's Broom" considers himself superior to *Omo Campus*, because he has been "To the unreachable land / Protected by visas."

"Memory Lane"[130] expresses the nostalgia present in the migrant experience, seeking to reconnect the poetic persona with elements of the past or home: "She rides on the horse of memory / Gallops through planes and mounds of time." A similar sentiment is expressed in "Groom's Broom," where Africa is depicted as "The only homeland / With goods to offer."

> I come to touch the soil
> land of my birth
> I am here to feel
> Warmth and affection
> I want to see
> All that is glorious ...[131]

Africans, wherever they are, bear the (un)consciousness of Africa as the only home. It is that which can truly accommodate their identity, which explains the many attempts to create new identities in affiliation with Africa, which is the true homeland or origin. "Transnationalism"[132] states: "Our motherland is not forgotten – / She is who we are / She carries our heart / We carry our spirit / We hear her calls / Our lives and efforts answers her." This is also evident in "Red and Black,"[133] where the poetic voice laments the imperialist's imposition of names on his identity. They either refer to his homeland or skin color: "Call me names / Unmixed negroid / ... / Negroes of the Indians / Americans of the Africans / Natives of the Blacks." Similarly, "Children of the Diaspora"[134] expresses the bond shared by migrants with a common root, "tied to an unknown future." However, the poem also reflects on the socio-economic ordeals of those in diaspora, in a land where "the host is a shark / Ready to swallow," establishing the importance of fighting back against these oppressive forces.

This chapter, through poems in *Etches on Fresh Waters, Scoundrels of Deferral, A Mouth Sweeter than Salt*, and *Counting the Tiger's Teeth*, examines the conscious and unconscious functions of poetry in the narration of a nation by examining the history, beliefs, and culture of a group of people with a shared sense of belonging. This chapter not only reflects these commonalities as components of a nation, it also highlights their necessity in the development and sustenance of a nation – the poems are both a reflection and an evaluation of what a nation is. In achieving its aim, the chapter thus reinforces how culture and all that it encompasses can serve as the baseline for evaluating structures of collective identity and how they manifest along nationalist lines.

---

[130] Falola and Adesanya, "Memory Lane," in *Etches on Fresh Waters*, 107.
[131] Falola and Bahl, "Groom's Broom," in *Scoundrels of Deferral*, 231.
[132] Falola and Bahl, "Transnationalism," in *Scoundrels of Deferral*, 201.
[133] Falola and Bahl, "Red and Black," in *Scoundrels of Deferral*, 85.
[134] Falola and Bahl, "Children of the Diaspora," in *Scoundrels of Deferral*, 107.

6

A Poetological Narrative of the Self

Introduction: Defining and Understanding the Self

The self is a kind of aesthetic construct, recollected in and with the life of experience in narrative fashion.[1]

Multidisciplinary approaches to the study of the self have provided a holistic understanding that draws from psychology, literary studies, history, religious studies, and anthropology. Donald Polkinghorne posits that the "self" is a narrative of unconsciousness structured by constant development, instead of an existing substance or entity. Polkinghorne's theory holds that ultimate meaning can only be revealed when the self is observed in its entirety, and this process of comprehension is described as "the consciousness [to] interpret and give meaning to cues by identifying them as elements or parts of a structure,"[2] which is a narrative, with the purpose "to configure a person's life into a self and to provide personal identity in the self-narrative."[3] This idea of envisioning the self in its entirety in a way that makes it a narrative is common in Yorùbá cultural philosophy, and can be related to the psycho-cultural implication of visual dialogue, where the representation of a person as a specific image, in writing or imagistic art, requires attempts by people in understanding the subject's essence to engage it through continuous communication (visual, audio, tactile, etc.), thereby rendering the components of this essence as constituents of an illuminating narrative.[4]

This conception of the self as a narrative is comparable to what Strawson calls "psychological Narrativity thesis,"[5] where the self becomes a complex

---

[1] S. Crites, "Storytime: Recollecting the Past and Projecting the Future," in *Narrative Psychology: The Storied Nature of Human Conduct*, ed. T. R. Sarbin (New York: Praeger, 1986), 152–173, at 162.
[2] Donald Polkinghorne, "Narrative and Self-Concept," *Journal of Narrative and Life History* 1, no. 2–3 (1999): 135–153, at 135–136.
[3] Polkinghorne, "Narrative and Self-Concept," 146.
[4] Babatunde Lawal, "Àwòrán: Representing the Self and Its Metaphysical Other in Yoruba Art," *The Art Bulletin* 83, no. 3 (2001): 498–526.
[5] Galen Strawson, "Against Narrativity," *Ratio* 17, no. 4 (2004): 428–452, at 428.

spatio-temporal phenomenon unfolding in phases, time, and places. Narrative serves as an "anchor able to ground the self in the middle of instability,"[6] in any suitable form or genre. This does not suggest a disjuncture between the narrative of the self and the self as a narrative – it portrays the former as an actuating, substantiating agency of the latter.

The goal of a self-narrative is to understand the dynamics of the self as ever-changing and evolving; the self is always in a continuous state of becoming or actualization, acted upon by inner and external forces. Mark Freeman contends that "The self, insofar as it is poetically constructed, is perhaps most appropriately thought of neither as a 'thing' nor as a 'process' but as a work, always in progress, never finished."[7] This perception of the self, as a composite spatio-temporal phenomenon, is integrated by forms of communication like narratives that hold self-identity or self-consciousness within the multiplicity of time and experiences. This performs the synchronic and diachronic functions of maintaining "inner sameness and continuity."[8]

Paul Ricoeur identifies referentiality, communicability, and self-understanding as a narrative's mediational role for the existence of the self. According to him, "the mediation between man and the world is what we call referentiality; the mediation between men, communicability; the mediation between man and himself, self-understanding."[9] Self-narratives are important for communicating and understanding the existence of humans to themselves, to others, and to the world. Narrative's constructive significance to the consciousness and understanding of the self is foregrounded in Polkinghorne's concept of human existence in three realms. He writes:

> Human beings exist in three realms – the material realm, the organic realm, and the realm of meaning. The realm of meaning is structured according to linguistic forms, and one of the most important forms for creating meaning in human existence is the narrative. The narrative attends to the temporal dimension of human existence and configures events into a unity. The events become meaningful in relation to the theme or point of the narrative. Narratives organize events into wholes that have beginnings, middles and ends.[10]

---

[6] Aurelia Klimkiewicz, "Self-Translation as Broken Narrativity: Towards an Understanding of the Self's Multilingual Dialogue," in *Self-Translation: Brokering Originality in Hybrid Culture*, ed. Anthony Cordingley (London and New York: Bloomsbury, 2013), 189–201, at 194.

[7] Mark Freeman, "Culture, Narrative, and the Poetic Construction of Selfhood," *Journal of Constructivist Psychology* 12, no. 2 (2010): 99–116, at 112.

[8] E. H. Erikson, *Childhood and Society* (New York: Norton, 1963), 251.

[9] Paul Ricoeur, "Life in Quest of Narrative," in *On Paul Ricoeur: Narrative and Interpretation*, ed. David Wood (London: Routledge, 1991), 20–33, at 27.

[10] Donald Polkinghorne, *Narrative Knowing and the Human Sciences* (Albany: State University of New York Press, 1988), 183.

The existence of the self is realized through the agency of consciousness, the innate awareness that one exists within a larger frame of life, that is, the individual within the collective. Self-consciousness is how the self recognizes, understands, associates, and distinguishes itself from others, which is what Justus Buchler refers to as the order that constitutes a human being, invariably helping the self to define its own limits, and which can define the forum of primary belonging to other orders.[11]

Furman observes that poetry and narratives are vital "vehicles of social inquiry" and that they are "appropriate tools for exploring existential themes."[12] Self-awareness is not only possible in poetry – as narratives burdened with the poet's pursuit of self-understanding by baring his or her life out in narrative – it is also possible through this constructive process of self-discovery. Readers and audiences find themselves in the emotional truth rendered by the poet, and an individual "learns to view him or herself in a novel way."[13] This transcendental capacity of poetry or narrative transports readers to "a more authentic sense of life,"[14] and the "existentialist reminds us that man is not only a being who tries to know but a being who feels and acts."[15] This makes emotional behavior as significant as the cognitive process that renders meaning to the narrative of the self in "temporal [as well as spatial] events by identifying them as parts of a plot."[16]

The human consciousness prompts the reality of the self as an existing, acting, and continuously evolving phenomenon in its relation to others. Sartre,[17] in his constituents of the concept of "being," affirms the dynamics of the self and describes an individual's ability to rise above the ordinary state of objectivity or facticity to that of consciousness. Sartre's concept of the being – the being-as-itself, the being-for-itself, and the being-for-others – establishes human knowledge or consciousness as a "primary way in which we know something involves recognizing it as an instance or part of something. We order our experience by relating particulars to a conceptual whole."[18] This emphasizes the relational and systemic existence of the self as

---

[11] Justus Buchler, *The Main of Light: On the Concept of Poetry* (New York: Oxford University Press, 1974), 90.
[12] Richard Furman, "Poetry and Narrative as Qualitative Data: Explorations into Existential Theory," *Indo-Pacific Journal of Phenomenology* 7 (2007): 1–9, at 1.
[13] Furman, "Poetry and Narrative," 2. See also Goksen Aras, "Personality and Individual Differences: Literature in Psychology-Psychology in Literature," *Procedia – Social and Behavioral Sciences* 185 (2015): 250–257.
[14] Elinor Ochs and Lisa Capps, "Narrating the Self," *Annual Review of Anthropology* 25 (1996): 19–43, at 23.
[15] Margaret Chatterjee, *Philosophical Inquiries* (Delhi: Motilal Banarsidas, 1968), 213.
[16] Polkinghorne, "Narrative and Self-Concept," 136.
[17] Jean Paul Sartre, *Transcendence of the Ego*, trans. Forrest Williams and Robert Kirkpatrick (New York: Noonday Press, 1962).
[18] Polkinghorne, "Narrative and Self-Concept," 136.

either a phenomenon that is shaped and defined by other selves or as a representative or constituent of a larger self or selves.

The concept of the self, as adopted in this discourse, is universal rather than specific. The intention is to synergize and explore the collective experiences common to humankind by using the perspective of an indefinite self that serves as a representation of everyone. The concept of the self – unlike other concepts, such as "human," "soul," "man," and "person" – is neutral and devoid of religious, cultural, or gender affinity. Narrating the self is as much about the society and others as it is about the self, reflecting what could be said to be the comprehensive consciousness of an individual. This considers sociocultural, historical, emotional, and psychological dispositions, as well as political and economic dispositions, of the self in relation to others who are living and non-living, thereby exploring a narrator's existence in its entirety. As aptly inferred, "We come to know ourselves as we use narratives to apprehend experiences and navigate experiences with others."[19] To reconextualize Seamus Heaney, these narratives offer us a preconception of ourselves, a sort of guide to self-discovery; the recounted existence is described as "another truth to which we can have recourse, before which we can know ourselves in a more fully empowered way."[20]

Poetry and the Narration of Self

Poets are seen as profound navigators of the deepest human emotions and essence because they render themselves acutely sensitive and open to the energies, events, and experiences that surge around them. They unify these energies "given by the feelings coursing from the senses to the passions, struggling to say what words, when formally arranged, can say as the experience of the inner life makes itself articulate and available to others."[21] However, this expression can only be accessed and understood by readers who possess the same level of sensitivity as the poet. Wordsworth, in his summation of Aristotle's view of the function and nature of poetry, expresses this:

> Poetry is the most philosophical [profound] of all writing: it is so: its object is truth, not individual and local, but general [universal], and operative: not standing upon external testimony, but carried alive into the heart by passion, truth which is its own testimony, which gives strength and divinity to the tribunal to which it appeals, and receives them from the same tribunal. Poetry is the image of man and nature.[22]

---

[19] Ochs and Capps, "Narrating the Self," 21.
[20] Seamus Heaney, *The Redress of Poetry* (New York: Noonday Press, 1995), 8.
[21] Helen Vendler, *Soul Says: On Recent Poetry* (Cambridge, MA: Harvard University Press, 1995), 8.
[22] William Wordsworth, "Preface to Lyrical Ballads, with Pastoral and Other Poems (1802)," in *The Norton Anthology of Theory and Criticism*, ed. Vincent B. Leitch (New York: W. W. Norton & Company, 2001), 648–668, at 657.

Aside from the definitive tone of this assertion, it is evident that the introspective quality of poetry serves as a tool for self-realization, seeking to (re)construct the identity of the self through the evocative power of language. As a result, poetry effectively distills human emotions condensed through living. As a narrative, it becomes both the reflection and the interpretation of the self. Both *Etches on Fresh Waters*[23] and *Scoundrels of Deferral*[24] are poetological narratives seeking to distill and integrate the disjointed phases of the self; they document it, reflect it, and interrogate it to make a meaningful understanding. By virtue of poetry's universality, both narratives create a monovocality[25] of the human existence, expressing humanity's "collective unconscious" as a clustered perspective from which one can understand oneself and others.

On the interrelation between the self, narrative, and poetry, Freeman remarks that "through poeisis – through the process of re-creation, via the imagination – meaning is made to emerge as are new dimensions of selfhood. The self is thus rewritten and rebuilt in line with the power of language to name those aspects of experience that would otherwise remain silent."[26] Self-identity and consciousness arise as a corollary to self-negotiation during the narrative processes of self-construction and understanding that assemble multiple and partial selves.[27]

The self-negotiation process also occurs with readers who encounter these narratives and seek to (dis)integrate their existence into the one presented in the narrative, anticipating that the narrative "provides a resource for the display of the self and identity."[28] Vincent Leitch supports this view, stating that as "the reader passes [and parses] through the various perspectives offered by the text; and relates the different views and patterns to one another, he sets the work in motion, and so sets himself in motion, too."[29]

This discourse on the poetological narrative of the self is aligned with the quest to sketch an identity and understanding of the self: the sociocultural and physical attributes highlighted in praises and salutation, as well as essential existential thoughts and reality, are part of the agency of consciousness that

---

[23] Falola and Adesanya, *Etches on Fresh Waters*.
[24] Falola and Bahl, *Scoundrels of Deferral*.
[25] Monovocality is what Tunç refers to as "the expression of one voice or viewpoint that homogeneously speaks for all" (Tanfer Emin Tunç, "The Poetics of Self-Writing: Women and the National Body in the Works of Lucille Clifton," *Journal of Faculty of Letters* 26, no. 1 [2009]: 187–200, at 188. This concept is also similar to Bakhtin's Multivoicedness, which is the derivation of meaning or intent in a narrative as a result of an equal negotiation between the writer and the reader: Mikhail Bakhtin, *The Dialogic Imagination: Four Essays* [Austin: University of Texas Press, 1982]).
[26] Freeman, "Culture, Narrative, and the Poetic Construction of Selfhood," 115.
[27] Ochs and Capps, "Narrating the Self," 37.
[28] D. Schiffrin, "Narrative as Self-Portrait: Socio-Linguistic Constructions of Identity," *Language in Society* 25 (1996): 167–203, at 167.
[29] Vincent B. Leitch, ed., *The Norton Anthology of Theory and Criticism* (New York: W. W. Norton & Company, 2001), 1674.

prompts the existence of the self and others. These are charged toward obtaining a new, extended, and profound understanding of the self. The narratives become extensions of the self, a continuum that the self can retract from and progress into.

Narrating the Self

In Praise of the Self: Salutation and Adoration

Poems laced with self-appreciating lines eulogize the poetic persona, ancestors, and others to create an uplifting sense of greatness or to render a salutation. In "Kèǹgbè Ọrọ̀" (The Pregnant Gourd)"[30] the poetic persona describes himself as "emboldened" and "loaded," and his rendition is a "Vintage wine from ancient vines / I am practiced / To tease the tiger's tail." Before pronouncing his chastisement in the poem, he introduces himself, states his intention, and expresses his worth as a person and as a sociocultural critic.

"Ode to Ìṣọ́lá,"[31] as a panegyric and praise poem, explores the totality of a subject's existence, especially in relation to that subject's ancestry as one from Ibadan and descended from the line of warriors, "the Great warrior." Phrases such as "Ọkọ Lábísí," "Bàbá Dọlápọ̀," "Bàbá Bísọ́lá," and "Bàbá Tóyìn" depict him as a family man. Names such as *Fiki Baeli*, Ògúndìran, Afọlábí *Petogi*, and Mosáfẹ́jọ́ are close acquaintances, through whom he can be contacted or appeased. This definition of self-identity is expressed by Michael Bamberg as a "label attributed to the attempt to differentiate and integrate a sense of self along different social and personal dimensions."[32] As with all panegyrics, the poem creates images of greatness, bravery, and fierceness.

"In Praise of Yanbiọla"[33] is an adulation of Dr. Niyi Afolabi, whose personality is described as confident and elegant, "Yan yan Yanbiọla." He is described as overcoming the impossible and employing his creativity to solve challenges – the repetition of "yan" suggests persistence until triumph has been achieved, which is evident when the word collides and expands into "Yanbiọla":

> *Are*, he that pours water away
> On hearing the rumbling of the rain
> When the rain rumbles and refuses to fall
> *Yanbiọla* turns the Nile into a big pot
> To supply water to the city.
> If the rain so chooses
> Let it never fall again.

---

[30] Falola and Adesanya, "Kèǹgbè Ọrọ̀ (The Pregnant Gourd)," in *Etches on Fresh Waters*, 59.
[31] Falola and Adesanya, "Ode to Isọla," in *Etches on Fresh Waters*, 71.
[32] Michael Bamberg, "Who Am I? Narration and Its Contribution to Self and Identity," *Theory & Psychology* 21, no. 1 (2010): 1–22, at 4.
[33] Falola and Adesanya, "In Praise of Yanbiọla," in *Etches on Fresh Waters*, 71.

These adorations are not solely praise for these individuals and their greatness; they are exhortations of virtues that are worthy of emulation, appreciation of good gestures, and occasionally the condemnation of vices to encourage change. The subjects are exaggerated to highlight these observed features and render them noticeable for everyone, creating a distinctiveness as in "Ìṣọ́lá Àtàtà,"[34] where the narrator recounts the exceptional Ìṣọ́lá who "beautifies the black-eyed peas with his palm oil / And makes the (cooked) peas inviting even in the cooking pot."

"Ode to Ìṣọ́lá" and "In Praise of Yanbiọla" are steeped in the praise of their subjects, but they also admonish those subjects to tame their fierceness, cautioning them while praising their bravery. "Exhale: Ode to Morọ́láyọ̀"[35] attempts elaborate praise of its subject, remarking on her physical beauty, intelligence, and growth: "Flap flap flap / Flap your wings / The bird whose wings are fated / To soar high above your enemies." The repetition foregrounds certainty. As suggested in the first verse of the poem, it embodies the past, present, and future of the subject, extolling her and admonishing her to achieve greatness in her future:

> Don't be the butterfly
> Food for the common lizard
> Be the eagle
> The unicorn
> Oluwatosin, daughter of Ibadiaran
> You who swim
> And puts the fish to shame
> Your spirit distresses the hare.

"Ọmọ India"[36] offers an insightful view of Dr. Vivek Bahl, who is a guardian that is benevolent, supportive, and a good team player as "He watches at our war steps / ... / Ọmọ India, master of our moves." The poem veers off from a typical chant of praises to *Ìwúre*[37] in the third verse, further affirming the worthiness of the subject being celebrated.

"Ọmọge to Pàntètè"[38] is a celebration of beauty and resilience, honoring the strength to navigate the chaos that is life. In his adoration the poetic voice

---

[34] Falola and Adesanya, "Isọla Atàtà," in *Etches on Fresh Waters*, 85.
[35] Falola and Adesanya, "Exhale: Ode to Morolayo," in *Etches on Fresh* Waters, 73.
[36] Falola and Adesanya, "Ọmọ India," in *Etches on Fresh Waters*, 81.
[37] More profound than prayer (*Adura*), *Ìwúre* is laced in the cultural and spiritual belief of the Yorùbá people, marked by its exquisite use of language to invoke good wishes into reality. In the poem the narrator expresses himself thus: "If you are pursued by death / It will not catch up to you, / Eat Kola, the nut of life / The bitter kola that elongates life / May you live long / Eat sugarcane, / The sweetness of life / You will love a sweet life."
[38] Falola and Adesanya, "Ọmọge to Pàntètè," in *Etches on Fresh* Waters, 133.

declares: "They look so attractive even with the load that they carry / Although too much load puts one's neck at risk." The expression of a load well carried, to "Turn such a head load into a thing of beauty," is an idealized description of beauty's relativity and the resilience of the spirit as a beautiful thing; also idealized is living a good life amidst the enormous turmoil of existence in order to achieve coherence of the self. This defamiliarization deconstructs the boundary between beauty and chaos, supplanting the latter with the former.

The self seeks acknowledgment and craves affirmation, to be loved and cherished. It is common to adore one's self to evoke happiness, contentment, and self-confidence. An example of such self-adoration is expressed in "Beads,"[39] where the speaker celebrates herself, adoring the beauty of beads on her body. Her self-confidence, at its peak, is revealed in this expression:

> When they adorn my neck
> I change my gait
> I do the peacock stride
> If I have them around my wrists
> I wave my hands
> As one honored by a parade
> If they grace my hair
> My head and neck
> Reach out to the crowd
> If they encircle my waist
> Háà! Ójìgbìjìgbì!
> They simply tempt my arrogance
> And arrest even the eyes of kings

Similarly, "Màmá"[40] is a worship of the mother image, not only as the carrier of life, but also as one who nurtures it: "A life without rest / The restlessness of work / Feeding the babies / Nursing the adults / Managing wallets / Resolving conflicts." The appreciation of a mother's communal responsibilities is the focus of "Màmá," while "The Spirit of Ancestors"[41] is the salutation of elders and ancestors to acknowledge their presence in the affairs of the living. They are depicted as revered guardians who cure and counsel, and know and feel, who are able to "Restore us with rest and dream" that our spirits yearn for.

The poem "ID Card"[42] explores the celebration of a uniqueness that has been marred by the ideologies of modernism and Westernization. These forces subvert the true definition of culturally unique features, transforming them into something barbaric or primitive – the defiant subject of the poem declares pride in his identity, regardless of the negative opinions associated with it: "A

---

[39] Falola and Adesanya, "Beads," in *Etches on Fresh Waters*, 87.
[40] Falola and Bahl, "Màmá," in *Scoundrels of Deferral*, 179.
[41] Falola and Bahl, "The Spirit of Ancestors," in *Scoundrels of Deferral*, 197.
[42] Falola and Adesanya, "ID Card," in *Etches on Fresh Waters*, 91.

permanent ID / Adorns my cheeks / Where else can you find / A man like me / Whom your kind believes / Fought with a hyena." The poem advocates for the need to love oneself, embracing one's identity and looking beyond one's defects. It also suggests the futility of self-denial.

Interrogating the Self

>Did I see the whole picture?
>Can all questions be answered?
>Who deceived him me: him or her?
>Why did wisdom leave me?
>Did he change and forget to tell me?
>Did I lose what I never had?
>Did I jump from the frying pan into the fire?

Ochs and Capps caution that the attempt to seek coherence or self-understanding "does not always take the form of soothing narrative solutions to life's dilemma. Rather, narratives may illuminate life as we know it by raising challenging questions and exploring them from multiple angles by probing and forging connections between our unstable, situated selves."[43] The above excerpt is from "The Atlantic Divide,"[44] a poem that is riddled with the existential questions and challenges encountered in our day-to-day survival as humans.

In the second verse of "The Atlantic Divide" the poetic voice goes on to lament that "I worry about today / Spurred by calamity." Every part of the poem is streaked with distress and the consequences of choices that we make as human beings, or "To be forever worried / By things that we cannot control."[45] These occurrences, beyond the control of humans and their existence, is what the poetic voice in "My Cross"[46] expresses as "My body of contradictions / unable to resolve the / confounding of my mind." At the core of existentialism is the ability to create meaning from the mass of chaos surrounding one's existence. Paraphrasing Sartre, Furman remarks that "life has no inherent meaning and purpose other than what we ascribe to it through the process of being."[47] This drives the deliberate, continuous struggle of the self to create meaning and order from the dire, chaotic realities of life.

"Another Day"[48] interrogates the uncertainty of life and the necessity of hope. These uncertainties are laid bare in the introspections of the poetic persona, wondering "Happy day, / Where are you?" "What would be good to do?" "What have been the obstacles to doing all that would be good to do?" His

---

[43] Ochs and Capps, "Narrating the Self," 23.
[44] Falola and Adesanya, "The Atlantic Divide," in *Etches on Fresh Waters*, 255.
[45] Falola and Adesanya, "Honor, Shame and Money," in *Etches on Fresh Waters*, 292.
[46] Falola and Bahl, "My Cross," in *Scoundrels of Deferral*, 9.
[47] Furman, "Poetry and Narrative," 4.
[48] Falola and Bahl, "Another Day," in *Scoundrels of Deferral*, 9.

fundamental rhetorical inquisitions foreground the complexity and relativity of life. Human attempts to navigate these complexities have been likened to "brilliance" in several poems in *Scoundrels of Deferral*. Sometimes the search for closure is in vain, what Ochs and Capps describe as the "paradoxical position of creating coherence out of lived experiences while at the same reckoning with its impossibility."[49]

On the distinction between self-introspection and self-awareness, Krishnamurty notes that "Awareness is freedom, it brings freedom, it yields freedom, whereas introspection cultivates conflict, the process of self enclosure; therefore there is always frustration and fear in it."[50] Awareness evolves from introspection, and the latter can be likened to a quest in pursuit of liberation. In "Intellectualizing"[51] the human representative declares that survival requires "To practice the needs of living" by

> becoming an intellectual
> solving problematic
> answering cultural crises
> memorizing volumes
> divorcing the learned from the practical.

The centrality of discovering gender and sexuality in the formation of one's personality, especially in relation to societal roles and other expectations, is unfolded in "Sexuality 101," "Sexuality: First Steps," "Sexuality: Second Steps," and "Sexuality: The Multiplication."[52] In "Sexuality: First Steps" the narrator recounts the confinement, "the unending enchantment," and the rejection and betrayals that accompany recognition of and alignment with a particular gender or sex, "a turning point" to the path "To see and to be seen." The male voice in "Sexuality: Second Steps" expresses the difficulty of embracing a life expected of a man along with the cravings, "Reverent longing / Affectionate desire," to seek warmth in knowing the other and being known.

"Ode to Mosáfẹ́jọ́"[53] explores the intrinsic existence of humanity and the (in)stability of the mind, contrasting the opposing polarities that are germane to human existence and the innate wishes and desires that are frequently repressed in the subconscious. The narrator desires wisdom, to be "Ọpọ́n Ifá," although he understands the existential need to be on par with Èṣù – the latter has established themselves as central to life "with whom even gods

---

[49] Ochs and Capps, "Narrating the Self," 29.
[50] J. Krishnamurty, *The First and the Last Freedom* (Chennai: Krishnamurty Foundation India, 1954), 156.
[51] Falola and Bahl, "Intellectualizing," in *Scoundrels of Deferral*, 103.
[52] Falola and Bahl, "Sexuality 101," "Sexuality: First Steps," "Sexuality: Second Steps" and "Sexuality: The Multiplication," in *Scoundrels of Deferral*, 115, 117, 119, 120.
[53] Falola and Adesanya, "Ode to Mosafẹjọ," in *Etches on Fresh Waters*, 59.

must contend / And mortals grapple." This underscores the helpless nature of humans attempting to gratify their inner desires amidst the turbulent challenges of life, and it suggests the pysche's suppression of our desires, which is represented by Èṣù in the poem. It becomes inevitable that "To experience life as a meaningful whole, one must maintain and preserve the self against internal dissolution into its component parts."[54]

The importance of this stability is foregrounded in "Authority,"[55] where the narrator cautions that self-restraint is necessary:

> Tame Yourself
> Stabilize your household
> Measure achievements to offer calm
> Endure insults
> Acquire persistence
> And cultivate patience.

Contentment is necessary, which is how the self finds stability amidst the conflicting realities that confound it, the "complex multitudes of masks." The poetic persona states that "I have resolved to deny my desire / To avoid your endless deception." He later describes himself as "Peaceful and reserved," but the semantic implication of the narrator's name expresses reticence – it means to avoid the difficulties or controversies that arise from saying too much. "Power"[56] illustrates power's pervasive influence, in all its ramifications, affecting the thoughts and actions of those who wield it and those who desire or lose it. Descriptions such as "elixir," "intoxicant," "irritant," and "influenza" emphasize the vulnerability that accompanies the possession of power, making it necessary to apply it with caution and wit. Otherwise, it may consume and possess the one who wields it:

> The ultimate transformer
> Elixir and intoxicant!
> A well courted irritant
> Taunting tenant
> Smooth operator
> Deceptively innocuous
> Lethally promiscuous
> Infectious "influenza"
> Rapacious invader
> The virus in the brain of the fool

"Mothers' Wisdom"[57] expresses the innate nature of man in search of knowledge. The poetic persona declares that "Knowledge I pine for,"

---

[54] Polkinghorne, "Narrative and Self-Concept," 145.
[55] Falola and Bahl, "Authority," in *Scoundrels of Deferral*, 169.
[56] Falola and Adesanya, "Power," in *Etches on Fresh Waters*, 367.
[57] Falola and Adesanya, "Mothers' Wisdom," in *Etches on Fresh Waters*, 55.

highlighting the necessity of knowledge and its applications for human survival and well-being, which the poem refers to as "the calm after the storm," as our existence is "A dazzling puzzle to resolve." The Grammar School and the moonlight stories are symbols of wisdom and knowledge acquisition, which are "great power / To make the old into new" and to ensure personal and collective survival.

"Humility"[58] may be the work that is most reflective of the *Scoundrels of Deferral* collection: the mood is sober, the tone is gentle, and the intent is virtuous. The narrator's repentant voice is epiphanic, characterized by the realization of a divine/existential truth. The intention is to see humility, and the approach itself is humble: "Teach me to be humble / Do I think too much of myself, / or not enough of others?" In a lengthy reflection, expressing that "I have come to the limits of myself / ... / I relinquish my bold claims" the narrative voice desires inner peace, acknowledges his foibles, and craves redemption from them. "Humility" not only reflects the significance and struggle to obtain such a virtue, it also unravels one's relationship with others, including God.

Perseverance and Inspiring the Self

"Where is HE,"[59] on a surface level, strikes one as a romantic expression noting the absence or departure of a loved one. More symbolically, it expresses the worth of "hope" for humankind's existence – it is an unseen phenomenon that provides a continuous impetus to stay alive. The poetic persona refers to it as "what a teasing gift? / A smile playing around the lips / Resembling Sunset," and its importance for life is affirmed in the last verse, where she expresses that "I can still see the sun / Just a little sun / A Ray of hope ... / Then dusk!" Like the pain succeeding disengagement from a loved one, the narrator describes hope as a "vessel of life" and begs it to stay:

> Withdraw not from me
> Lest I pine away
> Like the vine without its root
> Lest I slosh about
> Like a lazy wind

A similar sentiment in "Waiting"[60] emphasizes the importance of perseverance and hope. It is the assurance of living a better life, which the narrator refers to as "the shimmer and glimmer / Of a bright new day," "the golden moon," and the "bright dawn." The ordeal of attaining that "bright dawn" is described in "Stray Cat"[61] as "the sting" that "stays on the tail of freedom,"

---

[58] Falola and Bahl, "Humility," in *Scoundrels of Deferral*, 160–161.
[59] Falola and Adesanya, "Where is HE," in *Etches on Fresh Waters*, 75.
[60] Falola and Adesanya, "Waiting," in *Etches on Fresh Waters*, 247.
[61] Falola and Adesanya, "Stray Cat," in *Etches on Fresh Waters*, 257.

establishing that the path to liberation is filled with pain. "The Traveler's Inn"[62] is a fundamental and metaphysical description of life as a journey, filled with trials encountered by human beings in their role as restless pilgrims. There often is the need for respite, hope, and other existential essentialities, but triumph is most important – it is relative to the ideological disposition or belief of an individual. The need for respite in life is likened to the biological urge for sex, expressed in the poem:

> Come traveler, come
> Come into my inn
> My gates are open
> Drive into my garage
> Or drive through it
> The rubbery gate
> A perfect fit
> For your longing frame.

Life is arduous, and its complexities and uncertainties are overwhelming, creating an irresistible need for comfort. "Fatigue"[63] captures the physical and psychological landscape of a mind in distress: weak legs that refuse to run, an aching body, "Damaging routines," "The overflow of thought," "Mind and heart separated / to blind the eye." Hope becomes a catalyst to alleviate the weariness of life, which the narrator regards as the expectation of the "New Promises" that can enliven him and cause the "pain to leave."

This constant thirst for respite helps to understand the voice in "Ponderous Rest,"[64] who declares himself "lazy" and intends to "sleep all day / The day after / Not to wake for days." The impossibility of this craving, and the threatening ramifications that this decision would have for his survival and that of others, lead him to rethink and declare that "I awake / Never to sleep again." At the heart of both decisions made by the poetic persona is the complexity surrounding human existence, reflected in what the consequence of his actions (and inaction) mean for his survival.

Human resilience is depicted in "Torture,"[65] where the narrator gives a collective affirmation that "You cannot defeat us." This is in spite of pain's tendency to "Drain the last drops of the persistent spirit" and break the brave.

---

[62] Falola and Adesanya, "The Traveler's Inn," in *Etches on Fresh Waters*, 77. The life-as-a-journey motif is also expressed in "Comfort Zone," which recounts the narrator's resolution to seek a better life and future, "Bidding farewell to harvests of sadness": "Comfort Zone," in *Scoundrels of Deferral*, 183. However, a poem such as "Homecoming" recounts the journey of a loner back to his provenance (which could be homeland, heaven, God, or death) seeking "warmth and affection" as it was before his turmoil-plagued existence: "Homecoming," in *Scoundrels of Deferral*, 187.
[63] Falola and Bahl, "Fatigue," in *Scoundrels of Deferral*, 23.
[64] Falola and Bahl, "Ponderous Rest," in *Scoundrels of Deferral*, 25.
[65] Falola and Bahl, "Torture," in *Scoundrels of Deferral*, 65.

The poetic persona demonstrates that only owning up to our ordeals can put us on the path to triumph: before the resolution; he declares, "I yield / Take even this / Take all you can."

"Silenced for Life,"[66] like "The Traveler's Inn," portrays life as a sojourn, focused on humanity's restless attempts to avoid the hardship and difficulties that accompany existence. The narrator recounts her attempts to escape her ordeals, "Journeying to the four corners / Never to reunite." The four corners are the cardinal points of the compass, symbolizing the whole of existence. However, her flight subjects her to further ordeals, extending her suffering: "I became a mosquito / Crushed to suffocation," and then arises a need "to ache for / A time to rest." At the end of her attempts to escape she reveals the truth about life's complexity and how there is no escape from its trials: "I run no more / My fate is sealed / The beginning and the end / Are nothing but the same."

Despite firm resolutions not to flee, continuity of life keeps resurfacing existential inquisitions, such as those posed in "All for You,"[67] as an attempt to validate the worthiness and navigate the muddle of existence. At every crossroad we are confronted with thoughts such as "Where is my destination?" "Is confusion my legacy?" "Will I remain exhausted?" "Has hope evaded me?" "Shall I give up?" and "Why must I be alone?" The human need for change, or perhaps assurance or growth, is highlighted in "The Chameleon,"[68] where the human representative is caught between waves of change and stability:

> Yesterday he sought change
> The predictability of change
> Reconciliation with the past
> A charged past
> A burning fire
> To quench optimism
> In the flame of hesitancy

"Departure"[69] captures the essence and inevitability of instability and the craving for change. An enduring human attempts the "Transient pursuit of dreams / With eyes wide open / Wobbling legs / Along unsteady paths of discovery," that depicts life as a journey. It shows how the hustle of humankind makes little sense and success from the abstractions of life, the "Diversified energies" that surround them. The same curiosity and pensiveness that characterizes humans completes them. In "Austin's July"[70] it is expressed as a "step

---

[66] Falola and Adesanya, "Silenced for Life," in *Etches on Fresh Waters*, 207.
[67] Falola and Bahl, "All for You," in *Scoundrels of Deferral*, 45.
[68] Falola and Bahl, "The Chameleon," in *Scoundrels of Deferral*, 51.
[69] Falola and Bahl, "Departure," in *Scoundrels of Deferral*, 55.
[70] Falola and Bahl, "Austin's July," in *Scoundrels of Deferral*, 61.

outside / To run inside," the catalyst for the attraction to things and people that ends up shaping a person, and vice versa.

"Climbing the Kilimanjaro"[71] narrates the odds of life as encountered by the mountain climber, revealing morals and tricks that are vital to surmounting the challenges posed by life: "keep good company / To be counted among them," "Risk failures / To build truths / From the foundations of errors," "Be lovable / Present the side of youth / A fire burns until / The last spark is quenched," "Imagination combined with expectations / Produced failure," "Never reveal weakness / For it turns into the other's strength." Life is not shown as a sojourn in "Climbing the Kilimanjaro," it is presented as a race whose layers are numerous and difficult to count – it is a test for the survival of the fittest. This life journey, or life as a journey, is what these poems transform "into sequences of events and evoke shifting and enduring perspectives on life experience."[72]

Space, Time and the Voidness of Self

"Suspended in Space,"[73] as suggested by the title, offers a deep reflection of existence. It captures the transience of life and its complexity, which is underlined in such antitheses as "Speakers of truth are the / World's enemies." The poem explores the spiritual dimensions of a journey to heaven after an earthly demise, emphasizing the importance of truth, as well as other virtues, as the only compass that can lead one to "the home." Descriptions of home and market, truth and lies, and eternity and death are used to contrast heaven and earth respectively. They highlight, or rather urge, the importance of upholding morals and virtues despite the turbulence that accompanies them. Heaven, which might equally be a symbol for peace and tranquility of the mind, is shown as the reward for standing steadfast. The poetic voice states: "To taste its offerings / Truth I must tell / To reach it at last." The brevity of life and the apparent impossibility of eternal existence on earth often prompt consciousness of death and that which exists afterwards, the vacuum that heaven has come to represent.

> He sees another life
> Where the angels will wake him
> The saints serve him breakfast
> Nuns kiss and ask for more
> Another life

The above rumination is from an old man in "Disincarnation,"[74] which considers what kind of life awaits after life on earth or death. The emotion that

---

[71] Falola and Adesanya, "Climbing the Kilimanjaro," in *Etches on Fresh Waters*, 303.
[72] Ochs and Capps, "Narrating the Self," 20.
[73] Falola and Adesanya, "Suspended in Space," in *Etches on Fresh Waters*, 111.
[74] Falola and Bahl, "Disincarnation," in *Scoundrels of Deferral*, 49.

heralds the realization of life's transience can be likened to Furman's concept of being "void," which he describes as "the experience when one is profoundly aware of the deep silence and emptiness of the existence of the universe that is often faced during meditation practices."[75]

The transience of time is explored further in "Ruined Time,"[76] which expresses the struggle – most frequently ending in failure – of humans to use their ever-fleeing time effectively by "Casual carelessness / Trifling neglect / only / A minor error / A mild postponement / Then / Anxiety and avoidance," and its inevitable loss from waiting " . . . too long / Doing the wrong thing first."

"From Isola's Grave"[77] issues a warning on life's vanity and the inevitability of death. The poetic voice addresses his child:

> Take a break to visit Isola's grave
> His flesh is no more – his
> bones have decayed
> So shall it be your turn
> When the body you now adorn
> Will disintegrate

Cautioning the Self: Virtue and Morals

"The Goat Meat"[78] is a timeless reminder to be wary of excess, as "No one exhibits his/her wealth through the excessive consumption of salt." Using the examples of Morufu and Silifa as archetypes, the poem illustrates the dangers awaiting those who are incapable of self-restraint, a dominant theme in Yorùbá culture. After Morufu greedily consumes extreme amounts of meat, including that which does not belong to him, he "ended up with a protruding belly / And people mocked him." Silifa's dress gets torn due to her "Excessive consumption of meat." The poem preaches Ìwọntunwọsìn, and cautions against overindulgence as something that is dangerous enough to shred the garment that makes us human. In a similar vein, "Anger"[79] calls for the moderation of "The red black blood / Pulsing through clenched eyes" to keep our fragile humanness intact, "To make a better day." Such a day lacks the consequence of yielding to anger.

"Ọpọlọ Àbénìyàn"[80] considers the need for caution in exercising freedom; there is a sting that "stays on the tail of freedom."[81] The poem emphasizes the

---

[75] Furman, "Poetry and Narrative," 5.
[76] Falola and Bahl, "Ruined Time," in *Scoundrels of Deferral*, 21.
[77] Falola and Adesanya, "From Isola's Grave," in *Etches on Fresh Waters*, 373.
[78] Falola and Adesanya, "The Goat Meat," in *Etches on Fresh Waters*, 115.
[79] Falola and Bahl, "Anger," in *Scoundrels of Deferral*, 159.
[80] Falola and Adesanya, "Ọpọlọ Àbénìyàn," in *Etches on Fresh Waters*, 309. Other poems on caution in this collection are "Hawks Tale," 311; "Baba Mogbọ́ntán," 331; and "Rọ̀rọ̀rọ́fọ́," 337.
[81] Falola and Adesanya, "Stray Cat," in *Etches on Fresh Waters*, 257.

cause-and-effect configuration of life, delivering repercussions for every action, reaction, or inaction.

> Honor looked at the world
> Full of disharmony and conflict
> Sorrow is the teacher they needed
> The sorrow of failure
> To open the eyes of success

The above excerpt is from "Honor, Shame and Money,"[82] which laments the growing disregard for virtue, represented by "Honor," "Ìwàpèlè and "Ìwàrere"; it portrays the "disharmony and conflict" that mark human existence as both the consequence for disregarding the virtues and, sometimes, necessary for success. "In Search of Shame"[83] foregrounds the fallibility of being human, depicting shame as a vital control mechanism or superego keeping humanity's folly in check. The poem describes it as "watchful / Shame knew our hearts / The judge and the accused, not far apart." Shame is presented as humanity's conscience, with "strong supple fingers / Repairing my torn ligaments of hope and innocence."

Narrating the Self and Emotions

In the work "Lost and Found,"[84] emotions, pain, and sorrow are highlighted as essentialities that constitute the existence of the self; they are gateways connecting memories, ancestors, and one's heart. Collectively, they are components of the mind's quest for consolation in others and things. In "Bitterleaf Love"[85] it is noted that "The rough and even edges / the sage enthused: Are the spice of life." in another poem, "Revengeless,"[86] the expression that "Pain is joy / Of a different order" connotes the ideology of emotion as significant – the interplay between negative and positive emotions is necessary to create balance.

The complexity of human emotions and their expression is further considered in "In Pain and Joy,"[87] where the poetic persona states that in the face of "Some disappointments, some triumphs," and other losses, pain, and joy,

---

[82] Falola and Adesanya, "Honor, Shame and Money," in *Etches on Fresh Waters*, 291.
[83] Falola and Bahl, "In Search of Shame," in *Scoundrels of Deferral*, 5.
[84] Falola and Adesanya, "Lost and Found," in *Etches on Fresh Waters*, 117. The poem "Pain" also expresses the unavoidable ordeals, the pain, that riddles human existence. At different periods in time one is bound to be "hit by pain / ... From errors of Yesteryears" and "struck by agony": Falola and Bahl, "Pain," in *Scoundrels of Deferral*, 53.
[85] Falola and Adesanya, "Bitterleaf Love," in *Etches on Fresh Waters*, 147.
[86] Falola and Adesanya, "Revengeless," in *Etches on Fresh Waters*, 243.
[87] Falola and Adesanya, "In Pain and Joy," in *Etches on Fresh Waters*, 191.

"Life endures." However, "The Last Days"[88] is a melancholic expression from a depressive narrator who is on the verge of ending his own life. He laments:

> I am a failure
> I am about to quit the world
> Let the champions inherit it
> Death is more valuable than life
> Life of pain, of bills, of worries.

His expression of grief captures the downside of human existence and its pressure to maintain stability amidst the chaos that surrounds the act of living. He regards these forces as the "thousand voices," and he declares that he lacks "the strength to resist."

This rush of emotions is normal, meant to wake the consciousness of the true self. Only the failure to manage these emotions results in "Displacements and deferrals / Illusions and Delusions / Blindness . . . " while "The regular flow of / emotions in a healthier life"[89] is cathartic. The integration of the self as a coherent, whole narrative can only be opposed by "temporal disorder, confusion, incoherence, chaos."[90] Like the voice of "Suspended in Space," the poetic voice in "Lost and Found" laments the vanity of life and the normalization of abnormality, where good virtues are "Judged by evil" and "Men's trust has vanished/ Truth is hard to swallow."

In *Scoundrels of Deferral*, the section *Transcending Agonies* explores human triumph over the struggles of survival, expressing hope and blissful eternity. The "Rhythms of Hope"[91] reverberate with elation for the arrival of a long-anticipated perfect day through a "Satisfied completion in the everyday." One is charged with vigor in "Futurity,"[92] which revitalizes the spirit of the broken-hearted through "The basis of hope / Sufficient to transform / The experience of the moment." The poetic persona expresses hope for a better future, exhorting everyone to:

> Repair the heart
> Stop its bleeding
> Insert courage
> Warm the mind
> Smile!

---

[88] Falola and Adesanya, "The Last Days," in *Etches on Fresh Waters*, 127.
[89] Falola and Bahl, "Catharsis," in *Scoundrels of Deferral*, 11.
[90] Polkinghorne, "Narrative and Self-Concept," 145.
[91] Falola and Bahl, "Rhythms of Hope," in *Scoundrels of Deferral*, 145. Poems such as "Souls Unchained" beam with hope; the beginning of every stanza is charged by the strong beseeching of the poetic persona, proclaiming, teaching, answering, concluding, inviting, and urging his listeners to seek liberation, and to "Resist the pressure / to conform . . . ": "Souls Unchained," in *Scoundrels of Deferral*, 171.
[92] Falola and Bahl, "Futurity," in *Scoundrels of Deferral*, 149.

> Clear the throat
> Utter the words
> About days ahead
> When the pains are gone
> With new rains
> To fertilize the land

Generosity's essentiality for human existence is presented in "Giving,"[93] which links human survival with the exchange of goodwill among humans. Such acts of bonded gifts include enthusiasm, hope, laughter, and peace. All of them are "bringing bliss / Watering the lawn of life."

Narrating the Self and Others

> The delicate urgency
> Of sympathy with others
> Witnessing
> Embodying
> And yet alone again
> Mourning loved ones[94]

Humans are social beings by nature, designed to coexist with others and with living and non-living entities. Humans depend on others for physical and psychological survival. In other words, "the development of self-awareness in all human beings is inextricably tied to an awareness of other people and things."[95] This is why "The delicate urgency / Of sympathy with others" and their existence is expressed in "Bereft"[96] as "Aggregated minds / communion of feelings" in life, which is the "the laboratory of complexities."

The poetic voice in "Wizards of the Day"[97] recognizes the vanity of his illusory self-reliance, realizing that "not everything rested / On my brilliance." The narrator craves a social life and coexistence with others, declaring: "Offer me solace / Read me a book sympathetically / I plead for feedback humbly /

---

[93] Falola and Bahl, "Giving," in *Scoundrels of Deferral*, 163. The same topicality is foregrounded in "Serving," which emphasizes the immense benefit of human interrelationship in alleviating burdens and pains, admonishing all to "Collaborate and connect / With one and many" to "Evacuate the cave of despair": "Serving," in *Scoundrels of Deferral*, 165.
[94] Falola and Bahl, "Catharsis," in *Scoundrels of Deferral*, 11.
[95] Ochs and Capps, "Narrating the Self," 30.
[96] Falola and Bahl, "Bereft," in *Scoundrels of Deferral*, 15.
[97] Falola and Bahl, "Wizards of the Day," in *Scoundrels of Deferral*, 33. Similarly, "ABD (All But Dissertation)" encapsulates the weariness of a battered academic who deserts brilliance and yearns for "affection, / a relationship," "the luxury of / long acquaintance," etc.: "ABD (All But Dissertation)," in *Scoundrels of Deferral*, 37; while "Sister's Band" expresses the sourness of desolation by beckoning: "My sister / Come with me / Distance is not so sweet": "Sister's Band," in *Scoundrels of Deferral*, 181.

I yearn for grace silently." Before his realization that he needs to exist interdependently with others, the narrator appears to be delusional, suffering a disruption caused by solace: "When I see rain / I call it sun / Feeling hot air / I stagger / The sun refuses to rise or set / Fate and hope turn sour ... " Death is an inevitable cause of desolation that claims loved ones, and the poetic persona in "Tragic to Yogic Life,"[98] explains that her numbness is because "Death has deprived me of my mother / My father, devoured by death." As a result, she waits for the cold hands of death to grip her as well.

The coexistence or interdependence of oneself and others helps create and reveal an individual's true essence and personality. It is a structuralist dimension for comprehending a phenomenon, setting it against another to reveal convergences and divergences and defining its uniqueness. This pace of polarity is set in "You, Me, and US,"[99] where the narrator emphatically declares the inevitability of human coexistence:

> You need me
> I seek you
> All of us
> A united audience
> for ourselves
> The We locked with Me.
> I seek more relations
> to comprehend myself
>   our identities
>   our experience
>   our purpose

The poetic persona explains the rationale for the coexistence of human beings and declares a selfless resolution – it ensures interdependence and coexistence with this expression: "I will be receptive to you / whether / you receive me / or not." The need for receptiveness among humans is also illustrated in "Hospitality,"[100] which expresses the love and peace fostered by "Offering relief and renewal" to people by "Weaving the fabric of life / Without expectation." It discusses how humans accommodate others in their homes and in their lives, literally and symbolically.

The self's inevitable coexistence may be understood better from the biological perspective of reproduction, where both male and female are required for the continuous existence of life. The inevitability of this coexistence is highlighted in "Sexuality: The Multiplication."[101] Similarly, the poetic voice in

---

[98] Falola and Bahl, "Tragic to Yogic Life," in *Scoundrels of Deferral*, 157.
[99] Falola and Bahl, "You, Me, and US," in *Scoundrels of Deferral*, 109. See also "You and Me," in *Scoundrels of Deferral*, 143.
[100] Falola and Bahl, "Hospitality," in *Scoundrels of Deferral*, 185.
[101] Falola and Bahl, "Sexuality: The Multiplication," 120.

"All for You"[102] crashes his existential reflection[103] into a clamor for solace, seeking a rationale for his loneliness and yearning. "Purchase a portion of my anguish, / press my faithfulness to your bosom/ as you travel of the promised land ... "; the narrator in "Pain"[104] also beckons for help, declaring:

> I suffocate
> I am choking
> Vanishing breath
> Help!
> My boat is sinking
> I am drowning
> I taste it
> Yes
> The brine of the
> Unknown.

"The Last Outreach"[105] expresses the heartbreak of unrequited love and the longing that one feels to be loved and cherished by another. The grief that follows the rejection of such gestures is described by the poetic voice as "the thorny pathways." The speaker observes that "I wonder / That which we cannot get / Interests us," philosophically querying the complexity of life – he holds unrequited love for a lady who is in turn a victim of domestic violence, suffering at the hands of the one she loves. This brings life's instability to the foreground, identifying the existence of the self within it.

"Shut Out"[106] conjures the imagery of a disconsolate lover who feels the devastation of unrequited love, like "In a cold room," while "Àpọ́n"[107] excavates the forlorn feeling that plagues the heart of a bachelor; he has been abandoned by his lover for falling short of standards and expectations. Unlike "Shut Out" and "The Last Outreach," "Never Again"[108] expresses a woman's longing as she laments the absence of her lover: *"But love, always remember / I am no French / So don't take a French leave / On me again!"* In "Bitterleaf Love" the poetic voice considers the deceptive love that is professed to her, which is "Sweet and sour / Life the bitterleaf."[109]

---

[102] Falola and Bahl, "All for You," 45.
[103] The poem "Souls Unchained" reflects on and proposes the act of self-reflection as a component of human existence when the narrator states in the second verse: "I teach: / Give yourself the benefit / of your self-doubt / Retain your fears / Reclaim your anxieties / Confront solemn questions / on your honorable journey": "Souls Unchained," 171.
[104] Falola and Bahl, "Pain," 53.
[105] Falola and Adesanya, "The Last Outreach," in *Etches on Fresh Waters*, 103.
[106] Falola and Adesanya, "Shut Out," in *Etches on Fresh Waters*, 185.
[107] Falola and Adesanya, "Àpọ́n," in *Etches on Fresh Waters*, 307.
[108] Falola and Adesanya, "Never Again," in *Etches on Fresh Waters*, 125.
[109] Falola and Adesanya, "Bitterleaf Love," 147.

In "Mule No More"[110] the rebelliousness of the self is shown defying limitations and oppressive conditions. The poem narrates the revolt of a woman whose benevolence is exploited – in essence, the poem highlights a breakdown caused by various manifestations of sociocultural pressures. These pressures weigh on the well-being of the self when it is isolated from interdependence and coexistence with others. Like a tender flower "That endures the buzz of bees," the subject of the poem is laden with responsibilities that soon overwhelm her, and she becomes a "maniac" to obtain her freedom. This poem emphasizes the self's need to create symbiotic relationships with others.

One such relationship subtly manifests in "Bar Rules,"[111] observing the communion of three men:

> Restless minds
> Consumed by insights
> Energized by revelations
> A celebration of rigor and pathos
> A forged community of
> Warmth and humor
> Ideas and idiocy united by bottles and noise

In the poem the bar is a microcosm of life. It offers an escape where troubled minds gather to seek solace in the presence of each other. "The bar is a home," away from (the troubles at) home, where the self seeks comfort and an alternate identity through social relationships.[112] The poem foregrounds the self's need to seek warmth and comfort in others to "Smile, stay happy."

In "The Resolute Lover"[113] a troubled husband attempts to seek solace in the enticement of a lady who has refused to be his. The narrator, wondering why his affection for the lady is not reciprocated, asks: "Is this why you say no? A no because you think I requested love / My emotions, my dreams, my desire are disconnected. / My desire comes first: to find ways to overcome my nagging wife and her allies."

These poems highlight the importance of others in overcoming challenges, especially when those challenges are psychological. This is emphasized in "A Conversation with Death,"[114] where the narrator laments the death of her lover. She did not appreciate his presence enough, and she asks whether she could have been responsible for his death: "I never said I loved him too much / Was that enough to kill him?" She reminisces on her lover's life and past, his

---

[110] Falola and Adesanya, "Mule No More," in *Etches on Fresh Waters*, 109.
[111] Falola and Adesanya, "Bar Rules," in *Etches on Fresh Waters*, 143.
[112] Theodore R. Sarbin, "The Poetics of the Identity," *Theory & Psychology* 7, no. 1 (1997): 68–82, at 68.
[113] Falola and Adesanya, "The Resolute Lover," in *Etches on Fresh Waters*, 183.
[114] Falola and Adesanya, "A Conversation with Death," in *Etches on Fresh Waters*, 193.

love for her, and possibly her regret for not loving him enough. "Is this a love story / Or the retelling of a dead past?" Her reminiscence is framed by the imminence of death, the transience of time, and the memory of the past and others.

"The Atlantic Connection"[115] advances the ideology of Carpe Diem in a romantic manner: "Darling, if we remember all our past / No times exists for new things." The statement indicates the transience of time and the need to enjoy the gloriousness of each day. As expressed by Polkinghorne, "Time has always confounded and vexed human understanding,"[116] which accounts for its immense value and the continuous need to utilize and understand it. This is also present in "Desert Love,"[117] where the narrator states: "Today is the day to celebrate / celebrate with joy and peace."

The poetic voice in "The Prisonhouse of Frozen Wisdom"[118] relishes the abundance of his desires: "Desires deferred is desire denied"; anger, love, and faith, which are all supposed as hindrances to human stability, are seen as the bars to his prison house. Instead of accepting them as constraints, he declares:

> I plan my escape!
> I test each bar
> I know their weakness
> I feel my strength
> I will grasp their worth,
>   Unmoor them into weapons ...

"Ìdùnú Ọbẹ̀rẹ̀kẹ̀tẹ̀,"[119] which describes conditions that can lead to isolation, tells the story of an obese woman who keeps accumulating fat through her own negligence. The fat is a metaphor for excess, driving people away from her or causing harm: "People are murmuring and complaining / Left and right, saying: / 'Excuse me! Don't you know you can fracture my bone with your weight?'" The poems "Treachery I" and "Treachery II"[120] explore the consequence of investing love and trust in others and the act of embracing "the bosom of a friend" as "a deadly thrust." It highlights the need for caution and discretion when associating with others, especially if such relationships are life dependent: "wisdom heals." The inseparable pairing of communion and departure after gathering with others is conveyed in "Lovelessness."[121] It examines the gradual dis-embrace of a close-knit group of people, due to

---

[115] Falola and Adesanya, "The Atlantic Connection," in *Etches on Fresh Waters*, 251.
[116] Polkinghorne, "Narrative and Self-Concept," 139.
[117] Falola and Bahl, "Desert Love," in *Scoundrels of Deferral*, 193.
[118] Falola and Bahl, "The Prisonhouse of Frozen Wisdom," in *Scoundrels of Deferral*, 7.
[119] Falola and Adesanya, "Ìdùnú Ọbẹ̀rẹ̀kẹ̀tẹ̀," in *Etches on Fresh Waters*, 315.
[120] Falola and Adesanya, "Treachery I" and "Treachery II," in *Etches on Fresh Waters*, 343 and 345.
[121] Falola and Bahl, "Lovelessness," in *Scoundrels of Deferral*, 47.

time and other reasons. One final individual is stuck with loneliness as a companion, and the narrator reflects on "Living with oneness / Wailing / Sobbing / Just as others cry."

"Kẹ́ Ẹ Pẹ́"[122] and "Ẹlẹ́sin Ẹlẹ́sin"[123] offer perspectives from people who possess pride, greed, and laziness, or whom others consider to be corrupt. The importance of these poems lies not in highlighting the views of others but in the ridiculous expression of those views, usually without the subject's knowledge, to avoid negative consequences. "Ẹlẹ́ṣın Ẹlẹ́ṣin" narrates the story of the "The village horse rider" who "Rides with impunity with vigor" and is praised by everyone when he emerges from afar:

> But let him turn his back and
> The praise singers jeer
> Stupid man
> Bigheaded fool!
> His horse rides in his brain.

The passage displays both ignorance from the subject of ridicule and hypocrisy on the part of the praise singers; it strikes a balance between the distasteful acts of both to show their interrelation and to underscore the righteousness of everyone.

There is another side to the relationships that exist between humans, which is foregrounded in "Ológúnẹrú,"[124] where the survival of many depends on a single person who is perceived as superior. That person is treated as a demi-god who possesses enough resources to subject others to his will. The poem highlights the increasing inhuman treatment among people and the prioritization of materialism over humanity. In examining the relationship between the "demi-god" and his subjects, the narrator states:

> Reticent
> Anguish assaults the retina
> Scare caresses their ghoulish frames
> Hanging on to strangulated breaths

The poem "Two Become One"[125] shows a more positive relationship, narrating the warmth and comfort attainable in the embrace of another, as in marriage. This relationship is the basis of the family, the smallest unit of the society, through which "The whole world flows." It is described as "Never too

---

[122] Falola and Adesanya, "Kẹ́ Ẹ Pẹ́," in *Etches on Fresh Waters*, 347.
[123] Falola and Adesanya, "Ẹlẹ́ṣın Ẹlẹ́ṣin," in *Etches on Fresh Waters*, 349.
[124] Falola and Adesanya, "Ológúnẹrú," in *Etches on Fresh Waters*, 371. The domination of one by another is most outrageous in colonialism. The poem "Imperialism" portrays the abject subjugation of a group of people by another just as "Big fish eat the small," relegating the colonized to filth, hunger, anger, and death by violence and destruction: Falola and Bahl, "Imperialism," in *Scoundrels of Deferral*, 71.
[125] Falola and Bahl, "Two Become One," in *Scoundrels of Deferral*, 173.

empty / Never too full, / Filled with gifts." In "The Spirit of Ancestors"[126] the revered duty of elders and ancestors is explored, considering how they engage in communal counseling and guidance to ensure the well-being of everyone.

"The Earth"[127] highlights the interdependency of the self and others, which includes non-living things. It shows the self as unable to exist solely on its own, establishing the need to maintain a peaceful coexistence with nature. Humans have struggled constantly with nature for years, especially against wildlife, which is "rooted in struggles among people over empowerment and access to resources or needs for survival."[128] Francine Madden has observed that this conflict between humans and nature is "increasing in both frequency and severity worldwide and will likely continue to escalate."[129] The poetic persona of "The Earth" engages in a celebration of nature, paying homage to its vitality, his own existence, and humanity in general by referring to Earth as "You who feed and hunger," which highlights nature's essentiality for life. The fierceness and wildness of nature is described by the narrator:

> No one dares you
> Who take back
> Everything taken from you
> The animate and the inanimate
> You gobble like the lion at repose
> Even the gods, you swallow

It identifies humanity's need to admit that nature is an extension of itself, and to treat it accordingly. A peaceful coexistence between humans and nature is what nature desires: "Worship me, it says / Today and tomorrow."[130] In response to suggestions that wildlife should be fenced off and kept separate from the hunting, encroaching, and poaching activities of men, Sarah Durant has cautioned that doing so would affect the "connectivity vital for the mobility of wildlife and people,"[131] offsetting the balance of nature and threatening human coexistence.

Since time immemorial nature has doubtlessly proved to be a significant companion and important element for human existence, "in the colour combination, structural stability, stimulating significant symbols, imagery, and the melodies of natural sound of music emanating from the animate world. Therefore, we could stimulate fantastic forms from nature, which,

---

[126] Falola and Bahl, "The Spirit of Ancestors," in *Scoundrels of Deferral*, 197.
[127] Falola and Adesanya, "The Earth," in *Etches on Fresh Waters*, 97.
[128] Francine Madden, "Creating Coexistence between Humans and Wildlife: Global Perspectives on Local Efforts to Address Human–Wildlife Conflict," *Human Dimensions of Wildlife* 9 (2004): 247–257, at 250.
[129] Madden, "Creating Coexistence," 249.
[130] Falola and Bahl, "Austin's July," in *Scoundrels of Deferral*, 61.
[131] Sarah Durant, "Fostering Coexistence between People and Nature," *ZSL Science Review* 17 (2016): 18–19, at 19.

subsequently, stimulate our creative capabilities."[132] In the ebullient spirit of romanticism, the poetic persona in "Austin's July"[133] rejoices in the abundance of nature: the thunder, the clouds, the brown grass, the rain, the dust, and the rainbows. Its companionship is fully welcomed: "I make one plea: / Rain, fall on me!"

In "Reincarnation"[134] the poetic voice is consumed by her immense passion for nature, narrating that "I desire the life / Of lush green leaves / The garment of fruitful leaves / Flourishing in their season." The vivid illustration of nature's life cycle, including birth, growth, and death, is similar to that of humans. And the expression about orphaned leaves, "Tossed about / To unknown destinations," highlights the travails of humans and their helplessness, especially in relation to the birth and death that are fundamental to their existence. Like the parable of the sower, "Reincarnation" emphasizes the relativity of human existence as dictated by fate/providence, time, and chance when it states:

> Some may kiss mother earth
> And fade therein
> Others may float on water
> To the envy of the swans
> The lucky ones on water
> Caress the waves
> Giving thought to no hurt
> On a journey in their own world.

Of all the examined poems, "Another Gathering"[135] offers the most extensive expression of togetherness and the existentiality of life. In the opening stanza it acknowledges the existence of human ordeals and the historical significance of sharing human resources to overcome challenges, and as a result "Today, our / faith has brought us to seek each other / anew ... " In the second stanza the narrator attempts to diagnose the collective struggle, the "old questions" that challenge the survival of the "gathering." A collective solution is sought, which the succeeding stanzas address as the "resolve to trust one another," first by understanding, respecting, and appreciating each other's efforts and existence. This must happen despite the differences, betrayals, and disappointments that arise among them. The narrator concludes his address with an affirmative expression of the strength, unity, peace, freedom, and liveliness that abounds in the "freedom of assembly."

---

[132] Imaah Ono, "The Natural and Human Environment in Nigeria: Their Implication for Architecture," *Journal of Applied Sciences and Environmental Management* 12, no. 2 (2008): 67–74, at 68.
[133] Falola and Bahl, "Austin's July," in *Scoundrels of Deferral*, 61.
[134] Falola and Adesanya, "Reincarnation," in *Etches on Fresh Waters*, 219.
[135] Falola and Bahl, "Another Gathering," in *Scoundrels of Deferral*, 205–208.

7

Satire and Society

Introduction

> The satirist sets himself certain standards and criticizes the society when and where it departs from these norms. He invites us to assume his standards and share the normal indignation which moves him to pour derision and ridicule on society's failings. He corrects through painful, sometimes malicious, laughter.[1]

The act of narrating a society is comparable to holding it against a mirror, which results in reflecting both the light and the darkness surrounding it. Rectifying anomalies in whatever form and manner present in this darkness, in the context of reflecting the society, is almost always in the interest of humanity and posterity, at least in the long run. Using satire to do this is one of the many ways this benefit of reflection can be achieved, which is the focus of this chapter. However, starting with or trying to navigate the origins and problematic technicalities of satire as a mode of reflection would be an undue diversion, lying on the far side of this discourse. More important is the relevance of satire in reflecting on the society as established in and by the two memoirs serving as and shaping the autoethnographic focus of this chapter.

Satire as a genre, device, technique, or other form is fluid and enhanced by a conscious artistic manipulation of its subject. From its usual depiction in prose, drama, and poetry, satire has been adopted into all possible art and media. In modern times it is a common device in television programs, advertorials, cartoons, movies, music, popular art, and memes that can be as short as a tweet.

In mosques and churches satire is included in sermons to admonish congregations to adhere to religious precepts and abstain from sins. At other times a person or a group of people in the congregation is chastised and told to desist from evil doings. One example is recounted in *A Mouth Sweeter than Salt*, where Pásítọ̀ angrily rebukes the acts of the wicked through a sermon,

---

[1] Ngugi wa Thiong'o, *Homecoming* (London: Heinemann Educational Books, 1972), 55.

proclaiming doom and eternal punishment on such people should they fail to repent. His sermonic attack was incited by a chief who had unjustly oppressed a member of the congregation.[2]

In contemporary times sheer ridicule and humor inadvertently pass for satire, but the general consensus is that satire, as a genre, artistic invention, or device, foremost highlights and ridicules a personal or societal folly. The intent is to provoke an important change: "Satire has usually been justified, by those who practice it as a corrective of human voice and folly."[3] Alternatively, "Satire is a writing technique for passing criticism using humor, irony or exaggeration."[4] Holman defines satire as "a literary manner which blends a critical attitude with humor and wit to the end that human institutions or humanity may be improved."[5] Likewise, Cohen defines satire as "the criticism of a person, human nature, events, movements or situations by the use of exaggeration, ridicule, sarcasm and irony in order to reduce the subject to absurdity."[6] These definitions indicate satire's purpose, highlighting, ridiculing, and correcting a (societal or personal) folly through literary elements such as humor, hyperbole, irony, or sarcasm.

Satire owes its "widely accepted" formation to the ancient Greek satyr plays and the Latin word *satura*. It developed further during the Enlightenment era of English history, which elevated reason and wit above emotions. However, every society and age is imbued with necessary corrective measures to rebuke and realign human foibles to an acceptable and established societal standard, which is the premise within which satire operates.

As a corrective tool, "satire cannot function without a standard against which readers can compare its subject."[7] That is, its agency is made operational by the norms guiding a people, which is their culture. Ridicule, irony, and humor are major corrective devices among various African communities that hold cultural codes, moral virtues, and spiritual uprightness in high esteem. The original name for the Yorùbá people is Ọmọlúàbí, which means "a child begotten by the Lord of good conduct." Bards and oral performers in traditional African communities provide entertainment and historical and cultural documentation – but, more importantly, they serve as a society's conscience, reflecting and refracting societal ills. Morality is often the end goal of tales,

---

[2] Falola, *A Mouth Sweeter than Salt*, 353–361.
[3] M. H. Abrams, *A Glossary of Literary Terms* (New York: Holt, Rinehart & Winston, 1981), 352.
[4] Dan Goldwasser and Xiao Zhang, "Understanding Satirical Articles Using Common-Sense," *Transactions of the Association for Computational Linguistics* 4 (2016): 537-549, at 537.
[5] Hugh Holman, *A Handbook of Literature* (Indianapolis: Odyssey Press, 1977), 472.
[6] B. B. Cohen, *Writing about Literature* (Chicago: Scott, Foresmann & Co., 1973), 195.
[7] Ruben Quintero, "Introduction: Understanding Satire," in *Companion to Satire*, ed. Ruben Quintero (Oxford: Blackwell, 2007), 1-11, at 3.

festivals, parables, proverbs, religion, panegyrics, and other cultural manifestations among Africans. In this context, the concerns of satire are beyond the satirist's personal dissatisfaction or anger; they are driven "with a sense of moral vocation and with a concern for the public interest."[8]

The interdependent or collective nature of Africans creates the necessary background for satire as a cultural phenomenon to thrive. Words, gestures, and other paralinguistic forms are potent corrective measures; a child's mother can send a warning with a look that is encoded with sociocultural meanings: "I could read gestures, and I understood perfectly the meanings of smiles and laughter and how laughter could communicate disagreement."[9] The use of irony, ambivalence, sarcasm, or rhetorical statements can conceal the dissonance in a speaker's request, while actions convey his true intention. An example of satire is evident during the Òkè-Bàdàn festival among the Ibadan people, where a day is set aside for the use of vulgarity, "using sex and its symbolism as metaphors,"[10] to ridicule both the high and low in the society, including the king, to effect positive change.

Songs of abuse are a common example of satire among the Yoruba, often expressed in an acrid temper and accompanied by fierce condemnation of behaviors or actions deemed unacceptable according to the prevailing social standards. In a typical traditional African setting, when murderers, thieves, witches, or other extreme violators of social conduct are apprehended, they are paraded (often naked) by community members, who chant songs of abuse. The offenders are escorted to the village square or town center, or the evil forest or the village border, where they are banished from the community. These songs undoubtedly shame the offenders, but they also explicitly reinforce the consciousness that community members must adhere to a code of conduct. Such songs are common corrective measures in households, where husbands condemn the acts of their wives and children to curtail their excesses. They are also rampant among rival wives in polygamous families to chastise one another. I recounted a subtle example of such songs in *A Mouth Sweeter than Salt*; the song chastising my father for investing his money in a car rather than a house, a clever attempt to ridicule his inability to prioritize. It goaded him into building "many houses rolled into one, such that from the front to the back, with an unused lot behind, it was almost the size of a city block."[11] The large house is not only my father's way of nullifying the claims of the ridicule but also his own clever attempt at exceeding their expectations as a counter-narrative; also, it demonstrates how satire can drive a desired change, deliberately or otherwise.

---

[8] Quintero, "Introduction," 1.
[9] Falola, *A Mouth Sweeter than Salt*, 272.
[10] Falola, *A Mouth Sweeter than Salt*, 377.
[11] Falola, *A Mouth Sweeter than Salt*, 139.

Satire in African literature was at its peak during the colonial and postcolonial periods. Its legacy makes it an obligation for poets, artists, critics, and other activists to highlight and condemn the ills and vices inherent in African nations' sociocultural and political systems: "To varying degrees, satire in the earliest forms of writing by Nigerian writers was grounded in the moral overtones and socio-political themes of anti-colonial struggles."[12] Every artist's duty is to act as society's conscience, holding it up against the beam of moral, sociopolitical, and cultural uprightness: "Over time, satire came to be seen as a useful yardstick for measuring the seriousness of the average Nigerian writer and assessing the depth of his commitment to progressive social, political and economic change."[13] As an artist, to be indifferent toward vices that threaten civility and hinder the betterment of humanity and society is to be an unconscionable party to such menace: there are no three sides to it; one can only be in support of or against it. A Yoruba proverb says that a thief has no other name.

> Today, as the new society has degenerated into a cultural morass, many of these commandments would sound hollow. "Thou must steal and flaunt the loot" is what people now subscribe to and mouth loudly. People no longer do what is just but what they desire. Service to the self has replaced service to the nation; loyalty to money counts far more than loyalty to God; family members are no longer relations but tenants living under the same roof; and fellowship is about transient alliances formed to seek fortune rather than to promote good virtues and values. The good leaders are all dead; the living ones are dangerous snakes with legs and wings; and their followers have taken ratting on others to the level of an art. Truth is getting leaner and leaner, and it may soon perish.[14]

To condemn and rebuke the evils threatening society's collective growth is everyone's responsibility, regardless of age, gender, class, or occupation. The Yorùbá people believe that raising a child is a communal effort,[15] likewise the development of the society. This justifies the drastic measures taken within the cultural norms to address violations, follies, and abnormalities threatening the community's sociocultural stability. *Counting the Tiger's Teeth* and *A Mouth Sweeter than Salt* document my past experiences within a society that has immensely contributed to molding it – to a large extent, the narratives

---

[12] Niyi Akingbe, "Speaking Denunciation: Satire as Confrontation Language in Contemporary Nigerian Poetry," *Afrika Focus* 27, no. 1 (2014): 47–67, at 51.
[13] Akingbe, "Speaking Denunciation," 54.
[14] Falola, *Counting the Tiger's Teeth*, 128–129.
[15] "Whether at Agbokojo or Ode Aje, elders did not need to seek the consent of any parent to discipline children, even the ones they did not know well. In taking up this role, the elders were not imposing their personal values on the young but enforcing collective values such as the commandments to be polite to all those senior to one in age, not to steal, and not to run away from school or errands. Thus, I saw Bàba Ayọ̀ as performing a role that society had created for him": Falola, *A Mouth Sweeter than Salt*, 262–263.

are a reflection of the society through my viewpoint, personal experiences, and collective memory. This reflection uncovers numerous vices inherent in that society during the time of the narratives, and they remain prevalent if not worse in the present day.

Counting the Tiger's Teeth and *A Mouth Sweeter than Salt* are autobiographical narratives that could pass for satire, amongst other things. Flaws are subtly highlighted and addressed, mostly as diversions, through humor, wit, sarcasm, irony, exaggeration, anecdote, fable, proverb, metaphor, pun, joke, scorn, mockery, ridicule, and other indigenous corrective methods. These satirical tools are abundant in both narratives, highlighting sociocultural and political vices: "Follies of this kind are protected by their trivial nature from the more serious philosophical inquiry, and would remain unheeded to lead men into excesses if satire did not expose their futility and make them a common laughing-stock."[16] The uses of elements that evoke laughter help the narratives correct social vices by repressing their intensity. There are many satirical devices, but humor, jokes, exaggeration, and sarcasm generate laughter, which distinguishes them from others.

> Readers of satire are expected to suspend disbelief, to play along with the game, but not ever to surrender sanity or sound judgment. And satirists may employ fiction for seeking truth but not establishing falsehood. The satirist, in seeking a re-formation of thought, expects readers to engage the satire by applying their reasoning, moral values, and taste to the subject.[17]

Although the authenticity of the narratives is unarguable, the humor is often generated by exaggeration, tilting the memoirs toward fiction and their subjects toward fabrication. The aim is to help readers, including the subjects of these satires, to look inwards without feeling overly ridiculed or condemned. The goal is for them to feel a sense of remorse that compels them to make amends, while they experience laughter and a feeling of pleasure concealing the bitterness that ridicule might have generated. Downplaying the identified follies with humor encourages others to avoid engaging in the same acts and becoming the subjects of such ridicule: "Such sanction for scorn or ridicule, however, does not mean that the satirist can lash out or laugh at just anything,"[18] "for where humor and the ridiculous are entirely lacking, there is no satire, but abuse."[19] The cognitive activities involved in the interpretation of humor help readers sustain their interest in the narratives, because "As soon as people realize that a message is funny, they will be motivated to concentrate

---

[16] Bradford Hill, "Ben Jonson's Theory and Use of Satire in Comedy" (MA thesis, Boston University, 1933), 12, https://hdl.handle.net/2144/8267.
[17] Quintero, "Introduction," 5.
[18] Quintero, "Introduction," 2.
[19] Samuel Marion Tucker, *Verse Satire in England before the Renaissance* (New York: Columbia University Press, 1903), 31.

and process its content because they eventually hope to be rewarded with a laugh."[20] It is both an incentive and a palliative that soothes the ridicule incurred by satire.

Follies manifest everywhere; it takes a satirist's ingenuity as an artist and critic to expose them with ridicule and effect a desired change. Although their means and devices can differ, the intent to drive positive change is a point of convergence between satirists, reformers, activists, and critics. On the similarity between satirists and reformers, Hill observes:

> The reformer and the satirist often seek the same end – that of destroying a thing by attacking it – but they use entirely different means. The reformer attacks the vices and follies of man by condemning vicious and silly practices; he appeals to the emotions and the moral sense of mankind. The satirist, on the other hand, is not usually interested from a moral point of view, but attacks vice largely because of its sheer folly; his method is wholly different, for he destroys the object of his satire by making it appear ridiculous and by literally laughing it to death. Satire thus becomes a means and not an end. The satirist seeks to destroy our weaknesses that we may add the more noble attributes of character; he destroys that we may rebuild. Unlike the reformer, he does not appeal to our emotions but rather to our intellect and to our reason.[21]

A proper evaluation of the narratives reveals attempts to criticize the numerous follies present in the society. More often than not, this requires keen attentiveness and observation from the readers, which allows them to scratch beneath the narratives' surface just as the satirist "perceives underneath the specious disguise of social conventions and nominal morality the native brutality and ignorance of mankind."[22] This chapter examines the satiric concerns evident in both narratives, from a range of vices that include socio-cultural follies, religious excesses, political menace, and environmental degradation.

Satirizing Western Education

> I was blunt in telling Moses that I could not help him but that he should tell his mother that he did not like school because his brains were porous: that for reasons unknown to him, messages that entered through the right ear ran out through the left ear; that when the teacher wrote notes on the blackboard, he was unable to read them; that his head and that of the fish were the same, full

---

[20] Mark Boukes, Hajo G. Boomgaarden, Marjolein Moorman, and Claes H. de Vreese, "At Odds: Laughing and Thinking? The Appreciation, Processing, and Persuasiveness of Political Satire," *Journal of Communication* 65 (2015): 721–744, at 726.
[21] Hill, "Ben Jonson's Theory and Use of Satire," 22–23.
[22] Allardyce Nicoll, *An Introduction to Dramatic Theory* (New York: Brentano's, 1924), 175.

of rubbish, useless inedible stuff. As easy as it is, he could not use the bottom of a bottle to write the letter zero on sand.[23]

The infamous transatlantic slave trade and colonialism brought Western education alongside Christianity and Western-influenced commerce. Since then it has been elevated as the standard for measuring intelligence and acquiring knowledge, to the detriment of other cultural methods and indigenous forms of creativity: "In those days, sports brought no money, and they lacked the prestige associated with being a school teacher or a clerk, not to talk of being a doctor or lawyer, the two occupations that people had begun to emphasize."[24]

The lack of a Western education quickly replaced the stigma of illiteracy to become synonymous with penury and stark ignorance. Western education, like race, gender, religion, and economics, became a criterion for classification that divided Africans among themselves. Educated Africans were elevated to superior positions relative to their uneducated peers. In light of this, I narrated that "The racist Europeans and the 'civilized Yoruba' began to behave alike. The racist Europeans had used all sorts of offensive words to describe Africans. In turn, the civilized Yoruba were using their advantages ... 'to turn others, because of their location outside the cities, into primitives, comparing them with monkeys, infantilizing their ideas, marginalizing their abodes.'"[25]

Because Western education was considered the only means to success and greatness, "Parents invested in their children to reap reward at a later age."[26] Education was the investment that yielded a job with the government or private establishments. This explains why Moses' mother cried and lamented the truancy of her son, "asking her son why he was not like me in secondary school, doing so well, and making my parents proud."[27] In virtually all African communities from the recent past to the present, Western education is the basis for evaluating one's accomplishments. A skilled artisan who lacked a Western education would be considered unskilled, leading to a loss of opportunity and lack of success. A passionate, professional sportsman without an education would not advance far in life because his lack of education would disqualify him from competing against educated ones: "So much emphasis was placed on hard work, defined mainly in terms of gaining Western education, that one had to sing about it every day."[28]

Less regard was accorded to people like Léku, who had an immense knowledge of traditional pharmacology without a "formal education." Her

---

[23] Falola, *Counting the Tiger's Teeth*, 40.
[24] Falola, *Counting the Tiger's Teeth*, 39.
[25] Falola, *A Mouth Sweeter than Salt*, 336.
[26] Falola, *Counting the Tiger's Teeth*, 39.
[27] Falola, *Counting the Tiger's Teeth*, 41.
[28] Falola, *A Mouth Sweeter than Salt*, 247.

"knowledge impressed even the most talented persons."[29] Overturning the importance of education at the expense of other channels for creativity, and correcting the erroneous claim that sports and other creative activities hindered the performance of children in school, I narrated that:

> The people who later distinguished themselves in music or soccer must have been victims of the satanic birds, which destroyed their mental capacity. Those who listened to their schoolteachers and obeyed all of their instructions did not become King Sunny Ade or Hakeem Olajuwon, the bad ones in those days who played too much, allowing the satanic birds to perch on their heads.[30]

Ironically, politics is the only arena on the continent where the under-or less educated triumph. In *A Mouth Sweeter than Salt*, subverting the importance of Western education, I narrated that "men of status and education regretted their decision to go to school, to become doctors and professors instead of joining the army to become state governors and diplomats who drive around the city in a convoy of cars with sirens to disturb all, to announce the presence of power."[31] I would be heeding Lárooyè's call if I had narrated that the army's misdemeanor is as a result of their lack of Western education.

The description of Moses performing poorly in school may be perceived as an exaggeration, but the goal is to acquaint readers with the absurdity circumscribing his reality. He is a child torn between his desire, the expectation of his parents, and a society that has given him little to hope for. He represents how the pre- and post-independence era is characterized by overemphasis on the acquisition of Western education over other skills, morals, and norms embedded in the cultural or indigenous educational system. The naivety and brash sincerity of my response to Moses highlights Western education's inadequacies in raising a child, and my humorous remark underscores the educational system's shortcomings in imparting true knowledge, building on "real facts and expectations, pushed to absurdity to express humorous insights about the situation."[32]

The same Western education that is elevated above every other thing is underfunded and ill-equipped, and the children of the masses are at the mercy of their incompetent, ignorant, and unmotivated teachers. The teachers are victims of the same inefficient educational system, and middle- and upper-class families enroll their children in private institutions that charge exorbitant fees. Some are even owned by churches and built from tithes and offerings made by the masses whose children are excluded.

---

[29] Falola, *A Mouth Sweeter than Salt*, 295.
[30] Falola, *A Mouth Sweeter than Salt*, 252.
[31] Falola, *A Mouth Sweeter than Salt*, 71.
[32] Goldwasser and Zhang, "Understanding Satirical Articles," 537.

Undermining the emphasis placed on Western education at the expense of an individual's creativity and ability, I narrated that Tafa Adeoye, who came to prominence as the head of the movement, was intelligent: "While he was unable to read or write in Yoruba or English, his memory was impressive."[33] And "Tafa and others, apart from having powerful charms, were actually very bright and strategically astute."[34] This challenges the misleading correlation drawn between the ability to read or write (literacy) and intelligence acquired through other means. I also highlight this during my inquisition of Ogundele's choice of occupation, working as a blacksmith and lacking Western education: "I wondered why he did not go to school, not even to an elementary school, so that he could make a living with a pen. After all, a pen was still an object of Ògún."[35]

Native wisdom and empiricism are depicted as superior to knowledge imparted by Western education. In *A Mouth Sweeter than Salt* I recounted:

> The king in power in the 1980s, King Asanike, a Muslim who did not go to a Western-style school, was one of the most astute Mèsìọgọ̀ of the twentieth century ... As he had not gone to school, those who did, like some members of my generation, mistook him for a dunce. Presenting the image of a dunce, he conquered the educated elite, confirming the adage that the wisdom of the educated is in their wrists and not in their heads.[36]

"To ridicule others and make them the target of buffoonery is comparatively easy but to mock at oneself jovially is most difficult thing in the world."[37] Unrestrained self-ridicule helps to highlight and conquer one's own foibles, which bolsters one's weaknesses and manipulates them to one's advantage. As with humor and comedy, self-ridicule dampens the acerbic feeling that trails harsh criticism and condemnation: "The ability to laugh at oneself reflects the inner strength, self-confidence and the capacity for self-criticism of an individual as well as a society. It makes a person more humane and a society more tolerant and balanced."[38] The ironic affirmation in *Counting the Tiger's Teeth* – addressing government claims that farmers are fools, lazy, and political tools used by opponents to disrupt national peace and development – is "a way of coping, staving off despair and attempting to come to terms with a world that lacked order and clarity."[39]

---

[33] Falola, *Counting the Tiger's Teeth*, 111.
[34] Falola, *Counting the Tiger's Teeth*, 221.
[35] Falola, *Counting the Tiger's Teeth*, 21.
[36] Falola, *Counting the Tiger's Teeth*, 83–84.
[37] Tazeen Gul and Tabassum Javed, "Humour and Satire in Urdu Literature," *The Dialogue* 7, no. 2 (2012): 178–185, at 180.
[38] Christina Oesterheld, "Humor and Satire: Precolonial, Colonial and Postcolonial," *The Annual of Urdu Studies* 26 (2011): 64–86, at 64.
[39] C. Bryant, "The Language of Resistance? Czech Jokes and Joke-Telling under Nazi Occupation, 1943–45," *Journal of Contemporary History* 41, no. 1 (2006): 133–151, at 149.

Humor and mockery are common formidable devices of resistance in humor studies.[40] While discussing the distinction between humorists and satirists, Adrienne Martín opined that "While satirists refuse to forgive or to see in themselves the 'vices' they castigate and instead remain at a critical distance, humorists use ironical distance to allow them to include themselves in the collective object of their humor."[41] This self-inclusion highlights and addresses a collective weakness without holding anyone superior to another. This implicitly indicates the frailty of the farmers' uprising strategy and the weaknesses inherent in the ideological bearing of members of the rebellion who are representatives of the common person.

A similar attack on the weakness of Western education, or its effect on cultural norms, is highlighted in *A Mouth Sweeter than Salt* through the mocking response given to the imaginary character attempting to learn my father's exact date of birth after providing his own: "Congratulations! I said congratulations, Mr. Alakowe. Fenmbuary eeeeteeni, nineteen fortisomuteen. Congratulations. We know those who sent you to school cannot ask us when we are born."[42] The response signals the inquirer's lack of culturally shaped mannerism, the codes which are learned at a tender age as part of being raised within the community,[43] despite the height of Western education he could have attained.

African cultural norms and values are summarily annihilated, or at least repressed, by Western education. In another instance I narrated:

> As the society ages in time but not in wisdom, elaborate greetings become a nuisance to a small number of the new generation, mainly products of formal school systems. An Economics teacher, when Economics was itself a new discipline in Africa, began to calculate the amount of time that was wasted on greeting and to regard it as a form of inefficiency.[44]

This is similar to schools banning the use of indigenous languages, commonly termed "vernacular," enacting severe punishments for anyone breaking the rules. The gradual death of these languages is the ultimate outcome of such rules, but they also repress the confidence and self-knowledge that children

---

[40] Simon Weaver, "The 'Other' Laughs Back: Humour and Resistance in Anti-Racist Comedy," *Sociology* 44, no. 1 (2010): 31–48, at 34.
[41] Adrienne Martín, "Humor and Violence in Cervantes," in *The Cambridge Companion to Cervantes*, ed. Anthony J. Cascardi (Cambridge: Cambridge University Press, 2002), 160–185, at 165.
[42] Falola, *A Mouth Sweeter than Salt*, 5.
[43] Falola, *A Mouth Sweeter than Salt*, 90. The proper understanding of history and tradition, greetings and panegyrics, the extensive use of indigenous words, idioms, proverbs, and cultural mores are examples of the essential cultural signals and codes that are deficient in Western education.
[44] Falola, *A Mouth Sweeter than Salt*, 34.

gain from expressing their culture, of which language is inclusive and a dominant vehicle.[45]

In a recent comment made by Ngugi wa Thiong'o, "The culture of teachers punishing their students for speaking their mother tongue must stop. In fact, we should encourage them to express themselves in their mother tongue."[46] In another instance of irony, average Nigerians know more about America than average Americans know about Nigeria, with the latter continuously mistaking countries in Africa for Africa as a whole and vice versa, despite their level of "education and exposure." Their ignorance and gullibility is evident in their credulity for tales of mysticism and absurdity from Africa, narratives aligning with their negative preconceptions of Africa.

> Ilà was something to be proud of, not hidden. As the Yoruba with marks traveled abroad, the story they spread was that they had had a long fight with a lion who made the marks in the struggle, turning them into heroes who became chiefs. Since their hosts believed that Africans lived only in dense jungles, at the top of trees, they could easily be fooled with such tales of successful encounters with lions, wrestling matches that tough human beings could win with their bare hands and even without the need to run ... No one at Ibadan would believe such a story![47]

At several instances in *Counting the Tiger's Teeth*, I had reiterated how members of the movement acquired "freedom" through their inability to read and write; they are content in their ignorance of government propaganda, which seems like less of a burden to bear. This is seen in the case of No Worries who turned down my offer to teach him how to read and write, because he believed that everything written in newspapers were lies. He thought that he already knew too much, and that there was little to gain from learning to read or write. Also, "Forgetting that many of our members could not read newspapers, the government launched a massive propaganda effort, using the media against us"[48] describes the communication gap between the masses and the government. The government's inability to adopt an effective channel for communication captures its overall inadequacy and the futility of many people's education.

---

[45] A common trend among elites is the extension of this regulation to their homes, where children are forbidden to communicate in indigenous languages. This is also becoming a fascination for middle- and lower-class members of society as well. The inability of these children to communicate fluently in either the elevated Western language or the condemned indigenous ones is shameful.
[46] Imende Benjamin Theokinda, "Let Pupils Speak Vernacular – Ngugi," *The Star*, February 7, 2019, www.the-star.co.ke/news/2019-02-07-let-pupils-speak-vernacular-ngugi/.
[47] Falola, *Counting the Tiger's Teeth*, 185–186.
[48] Falola, *Counting the Tiger's Teeth*, 258.

> I carried no instruments or weapons, other than the notebook and pen in my pocket. Pásítọ̀, my grandfather, was then opposed to the use of weapons; he avoided carrying a gun, and he did not allow me to put a knife in my pocket. Charms, yes!! Potent juju, yes!! Guns and clubs, no!! Pásítọ̀ was a warrior without weapons – his rebellious spirit was in his words, energy, his diplomacy, and his passion.[49]

Pásítọ̀, like Mahatma Gandhi and Martin Luther King, Jr., yearned for a peaceful reformation of the nation's economic and sociopolitical system to enhance the well-being of the marginalized and the masses. They were farmers, and Pásítọ̀'s ideology to actualize his goals did not include violence. Unfortunately, violence claimed his life at Akanran during the surprise attack by the state's security men, which was a cosmic irony. His ideology draws a powerful contrast between the outcome of violence and diplomacy in sociopolitical agitations.

Pásítọ̀'s ideology also compares the distinction between pen and notebooks, metaphors for diplomacy, and swords and knives, metaphors for war. It subtly elevates diplomacy and education over violence and war, further indicating the manifestation of intelligence and ideological supremacy without a Western education. He shows the need to balance various manifestations of Westernization, or at least their potential, with indigenous culture. Like the nursery lyric reminds us, education without farming is insufficient – so is farming without education.

Satirizing Religion and Spirituality

> Recited over and over again, and called many times thereafter, the prayer did not work. Maybe I did not shout it loudly enough, did not fast before I prayed, or did not kneel down in the middle of the night surrounded by twenty candles as the Aládúrà would do whenever they wanted a big favor from the Almighty. Being too casual with Jah was not always the best way to go.[50]

Alongside Western education and commerce, colonialism also brought Christianity, which to a large extent opposes existing African religions, spirituality, and culture. Ethnicity, economics, and religion have been the three primary sources of disunity in the continent. Christianity, Islam, and the African religions constantly battle for supremacy and validation to determine who serves the true God, which is why, "apart from common human weaknesses and follies, the all-too-powerful, arrogant or sanctimonious and self-righteous have always been favorite targets of humor, ridicule and satire. Often even the Divine is not spared."[51]

---

[49] Falola, *Counting the Tiger's Teeth*, 3.
[50] Falola, *Counting the Tiger's Teeth*, 156.
[51] Oesterheld, "Humor and Satire," 64.

One would be shocked to hear various religious leaders publicly claim they all serve the same God while constantly preaching enmity in their respective places of worship. In their home congregations they issue full-throated condemnations of other believers:

> If a travelling missionary preacher hawked his messages from house to house, he was careful to tread carefully in the compounds of Muslims. To tell the Muslims very early in the morning that Jesus was the son of God was to provoke them to anger...As if to provoke the Christians to anger, Muslims would tell them to their face that no one had died on the cross.[52]

This subtle enmity and discrimination between these religious groups are evident in the "forceful" conversion of Muslim children and "traditional worshippers" enrolling at schools founded by missionaries and churches, and vice versa:

> The Aládúrà schools did not generally admit Muslims, and, when they did admit them, they forced them to change their names to biblical ones, from Mudasiru to Emmanuel, such an offensive practice that it tore families apart. A boy could possess two names, Mohammed at home and David at school. The Bible was forced down the throat of Mohammed; when the poor student was about to leave school, he could be asked to say hello to Jezebel when he arrived home.[53]

Such religious hypocrisy has been a major detriment to national development and a continued cause of hatred and terrorism in the country.

Through the characterization of Bùọ̀dá Gébú and others, *Counting the Tiger's Teeth* repeatedly examines the flaws, intolerance, and hypocrisy of religions and their devotees. Bùọ̀dá Gébú's unstable temper and attitude toward other religions is typical of the way some Christians perceive other religions, and vice versa. The hatred is mutual: "Gabriel's words communicated love and hate, peace and anger, loyalty and scepticism . . . He was a friend and an enemy: He chose both on his own terms, displaying his temper to his enemies and offering exaggerated promises to his friend."[54] To a large extent, traditional African religions seemed to be a common enemy of Islam and Christianity; devotees demonized religious practices that did not align to their

---

[52] Falola, *Counting the Tiger's Teeth*, 90.
[53] Falola, *Counting the Tiger's Teeth*, 90. A recent case is the ban of hijab in some schools, including the privately owned ones. The use of hijab by female Muslim pupils at the International School Ibadan caused a recent uproar; their actions were against school codes. Another example is the state governments of Lagos and Osun ruling that female Muslim pupils can wear their hijabs to school, which generated unpleasant remarks from Christian bodies about Islamizing the government-owned schools (the governors of these states were Muslim). Traditional worshipers threatened school authorities, warning that their children would arrive at school armored in their religious apparel.
[54] Falola, *Counting the Tiger's Teeth*, 79.

own, condemning their practitioners to hell – the afterlife promised to "pagans" and idol worshipers.

> The Muslims joined the Christians to seek an end to the old cultural order. All forms of indigenous worship were to be attacked with extreme verbal warfare of a new kind. The Òrìṣà would be treated as enemies, far worse than witches and wizards, with stone and cudgels to kill all the gods and goddesses who the Muslims and Christians could recognize ... The Yoruba began to leave behind a major component of their past and their moral fabric.[55]

The life of Bùọ̀dá Gébú, as with most Christians in the continent, is in stark contrast to the doctrines and teachings of the Bible: "Bùọ̀dá Gébú was a man of confused faith without deeds, an impersonator who called himself an angel of light when he was actually an agent of darkness ... Bùọ̀dá Gébú was a man of God with a proud face and a lying tongue, with a heart full of wicked devices."[56] Christ taught humility and attributed his work to the glory of God, but Bùọ̀dá Gébú was "confident and arrogant. He proclaimed that no one could fight him, demolish him, destroy him, conquer him, or subdue him."[57] When Christ proclaims love as supreme to other laws, urging a peaceful coexistence with everyone, "Bùọ̀dá Gébú said that a man of God must not even go near this house [the house of the Olóriọdẹ], for it was full of demons and cursed spirits, not to talk of sleeping there."[58]

> No babaláwo in the land was more powerful than Bùọ̀dá Gébú, who claimed that he could cure leprosy, make the blind see, walk on the dirty Ogùnpa River, survive any raging fire, and be with the lion in the same cage at the University of Ibadan without coming to harm.[59]

The Bible teaches cautiousness and reverence, like Daniel, when observing religious rites and duties, unlike the Pharisees and Sadducees. However, "Moses' father said his morning prayer, very loudly, as if the God and Jesus that he prayed to had to be yelled at"[60] and "If ever there was a chorus, expect a volume that would be heard far away, as Pentecostalists in the city now shout halleluiah louder than the shout of 'goal' by spectators, players, and scorer in a soccer game."[61] A petition against the noise pollution that emitted every hour of the day from the blaring sound systems of churches and mosques was considered sacrilege, and a war against the heavens waged by forces of evil that must have possessed the petitioner. In fact, Muslims and Christians were

---

[55] Falola, *Counting the Tiger's Teeth*, 315.
[56] Falola, *Counting the Tiger's Teeth*, 108.
[57] Falola, *Counting the Tiger's Teeth*, 79.
[58] Falola, *Counting the Tiger's Teeth*, 100–101.
[59] Falola, *Counting the Tiger's Teeth*, 79.
[60] Falola, *Counting the Tiger's Teeth*, 42.
[61] Falola, *Counting the Tiger's Teeth*, 57.

scared of traditional worshipers and their gods; the traditional worshipers held their deities in more reverence than the Muslims and Christians hypocritically accorded to theirs. Hence, in *A Mouth Sweeter than Salt*, I narrated:

> Even those in my church were afraid of Ṣàngó. God lives in heaven, and He has not announced the day of judgment. Ṣàngó too, is no longer on earth, but in those days he made his presence felt so strongly that Muslims and Christians were afraid of him. They would easily swear on the Bible, even to tell a lie or cheat in a business transaction, but many were afraid of invoking the name of the ruthless god of thunder.[62]

Christianity became the anchor on which Bùọ̀dá Gébú and others tethered their pride and self-acclaimed righteousness and superiority. They looked down on others, those perceived as "pagans": "His natural height is about five feet two inches, but this was artificially elongated when he stood on a stool or climbed up to a pulpit. At the pulpit, he was taller than all around him. He became the tallest, which made him proud, really proud."[63] Bùọ̀dá Gébú's arrogance sets him in contrast to the divinity that he claimed to represent, and it set the stage for the people to reject him outright: "Léku ignored Bùọ̀dá Gébú and those like him, describing them as ignorant people with irrelevant education and useless knowledge. She did not hate Bùọ̀dá Gébú, rather she told people not to take him too seriously"[64] and "Pásítọ̀ referred to the Aládúrà as Àwọn oníyèyé, as clown and comedians"[65] neither to be taken seriously nor hated for their opposition, for they knew not what they are doing.

Léku and Pásítọ̀'s reaction to the likes of Bùọ̀dá Gébú and Alhaji Ajágbemọ́kèfèrí, who fiercely opposed their religious and spiritual beliefs, symbolizes true religious tolerance: the traditional worshipers "even attended church when invited. Similarly, they joined in Islamic celebrations, just as I did. The ethics of reciprocity probably gave Muslims and Christians no choice but to participate in Ṣàngó worship, at least in the main annual ceremony."[66]

While highlighting the weakness of the Western educational system, an attempt is made to resolve religious conflicts and highlight the hypocrisy pervading the religious environment. It was a common practice among Africans, regardless of their religion, to consult traditionalists/herbalists for solutions to their problems. That is why Moses' father had to visit Léku for a traditional remedy to reverse his dullness: "However, since Moses was no longer bad but terrible, no examination magic by Léku or any person in the land would work for him."[67] And "Christians, even some pastors, visited the

---

[62] Falola, *Counting the Tiger's Teeth*, 394–396.
[63] Falola, *Counting the Tiger's Teeth*, 79.
[64] Falola, *Counting the Tiger's Teeth*, 89.
[65] Falola, *Counting the Tiger's Teeth*, 91.
[66] Falola, *A Mouth Sweeter than Salt*, 392.
[67] Falola, *Counting the Tiger's Teeth*, 40.

babaláwo at night. At Adeoyo Hospital, when you were too slow to recover, the nurses and doctors would call your relatives aside to advise them to take you to an herbalist."[68] This resort to, or reliance on, herbalists and traditional diviners did not suggest that they were supreme, but it validated their belief and practice as genuine. The reconciliation of religious differences during the Òkè-Bàdàn festival indicates the harmonious nature of traditional African religion.

It is a shameful irony that Nigeria was once ranked with Ghana as the most religious nation in the world, and yet it was the most corrupt and impoverished country of the world. It is no coincidence, and little wonder, that Bùọdá Gébú fits perfectly into the same status quo, like most others: owing his landlord months of rent despite his religious persistence and the arrogant claims that his savior could do anything for him at his request. His display of unabashed arrogance renders him a subject of ridicule, and the comic irony of his haughtiness elicits mockery. As Milan Kundera explains, "We are laughing not because someone is being ridiculed, mocked, or even humiliated but because a reality is abruptly revealed as ambiguous, things lose their apparent meaning, the man before us is not what he thought himself to be."[69] When Bùọdá Gébú appeals to his landlord so that he can at least have his Bible:

> His Bible, the Ijebu landlord assured him, already belonged to someone else; a person like him already blessed who could use it for greater blessing. Since the Bible had been touched by a miserable poor man, it could also transfer poverty to the new owner; in that case, he would not hesitate to throw it into a gutter.[70]

This highlights the erroneous belief, often propagated by religious leaders, that all solutions can be found through religion instead of seeking empirical solutions. This also explains how Nigerians have remained calm and quiet despite the unimaginable economic hardship caused by their fantastically corrupt political leaders, as well as the extortion conducted by religious leaders. Religion has become a repressive mechanism of the government that instills fear and offers a mirage of hope. Religion, indeed, as the opium of the masses, is an efficient tool for concealing the suffering of the masses. A common expression among Nigerians is "e go better," a motivational mantra to keep pushing on.

The hospital is for the sick and the church for the sinners. Contrary to the messages of salvation, non-discrimination, and love that these religious bodies espouse, their sermons are punctuated with outright condemnation of supposed sinners in need of salvation. Meanwhile, religious leaders venerate themselves for being completely righteous, just like Bùọdá Gébú.

---

[68] Falola, *Counting the Tiger's Teeth*, 95.
[69] Milan Kundera, *The Curtain*, trans. Linda Asher (New York: HarperCollins, 2005), 109.
[70] Falola, *Counting the Tiger's Teeth*, 81.

> The society that produced these women who wasted their lives was also the society that paid the pastors and the Imams to crucify them in weekly sermons.
> "Just accept Jesus, the widow's husband," the pastor would proclaim and "your vaginas will no longer be a dustbin." But it was far more complicated than that: before the women could put food in their mouths, their vaginas must first be fed.[71]

I highlighted the hypocrisy of the society through religious deceit, and, more importantly, the need for a stable and solid economy as a solution to all manners of decadence in the Nigerian society.

> Years later, when the Aládúrà became known as the Pentecostalists, I counted forty-three of those churches on one long street at Ibadan. Yet I was only counting those on the roads, visible from the main streets, and not those behind them. Here and elsewhere, one could come across fascinating names such as Seven Seven Thunders of Jesus Church, High Tension Ministry, Jesus in the New Global Ministry, Trigger Happy Ministry (motto: always gunning down the devil) ... Run for Your Life Ministry, Jesus Heals Ministry, Face-to-Face Ministry ...[72]

There is an obvious progression in the number of churches on streets in Nigeria – every house seems to have a church. A renowned leader of a Christian denomination in Nigeria envisioned a church on every street and corner of the country, to afford a nearby place of worship for everyone. Regardless of this vision, the rapid increase in the number of churches is more often an attempt to defraud people of their hard-earned income: "As long as they remained committed to the church, giving it their time and money, their entrance to heaven was assured."[73] A distressing ideology among some sects is that contributions to the work of God on earth ensure glory and lodging in heaven, as promised by Christ. Someone who did not tithe and made meager offerings might get no crown, welcomed to a "face-me-I-face-you" apartment in heaven, while the rich who contributed immensely to numerous church projects through ill-gotten wealth have mansions and diamond-and-gold-studded crowns awaiting them in heaven.

> The babaláwo asked for palm oil, chicken, and goats for sacrifices; the oníyèyè said that that salvation was free because Jesus died on the cross for you and me. But on Sunday, we must contribute far more money than buying the palm oil and goats that the babaláwo demanded of us. And then once a month, we were told to pay a tithe, an amount that it would take ten years for the babaláwo to accumulate from our visits. The tithe grew in later years, to be supplemented by "seeds," a euphemism for more

---

[71] Falola, *Counting the Tiger's Teeth*, 313.
[72] Falola, *Counting the Tiger's Teeth*, 84.
[73] Falola, *Counting the Tiger's Teeth*, 85.

> cash. To obtain salvation, we must always sow seeds: special offering seed, first fruit seed, redemption seed ... mother's day seed, children day seed, olive oil seed and so on.[74]

Salvation becomes another possession, which can be earned by offering donations to the church and funding "the work of Christ." In my narrative, "We were always divided in the church – the pews in the front rows belonged to the rich. When a rich man died, his children took the best lot in the cemetery. Clergymen preaching sermons must be careful not to offend the church's biggest donors."[75] A complex near the University of Ibadan is occupied by three churches, two of which belong to the same denomination – one occupies the second floor, and the other the fourth floor. Every Sunday morning the three churches would have their stewards stationed on the ground floor to welcome congregants and direct new members to their gatherings. As absurd as it seems, it is a true and disturbing reality.

Ironically, the proliferation of these churches correlates with increasing social and moral decadence. If Christ and the Apostles sought to save the people, contemporary shepherds seek to extort their flock and lead them to the slaughterhouse: "As the number of small churches increased, so too did the number of those who anointed themselves as pastors and prophets, deceiving many by presenting themselves as devout and as servants of God."[76]

The importance of charms and magic is expressed in the course of the uprising, and at the same time the lack of society's social amenities is highlighted by asking readers to imagine an African society anchored on black magic, just by wishing it into existence, which is much easier than the numerous excuses tendered by the political government: "We could will development to happen, asking juju to supply electricity here and water there. The charm that glued the uniform of a police officer to his body could also be deployed to produce water in pipes as well as electricity from trees."[77] It signals the potential of African religion, culture, and spirituality whose revival has been the mission of Afrofuturism. It suggests the existence of a glorious Africa, with limitless possibilities, through the exploration of culture and primal science.

Highlighting Environmental Menace

> Refuse, dirt, and bad smells did not seem to disturb my people; from the heaps at the far back of the yard to the side alleys, today they are now stars in the façade of houses and even used to decorate the best streets in Ibadan. Instead of filling your cars with litter; you throw your trash on the streets as

---

[74] Falola, *Counting the Tiger's Teeth*, 92.
[75] Falola, *Counting the Tiger's Teeth*, 89.
[76] Falola, *Counting the Tiger's Teeth*, 86.
[77] Falola, *Counting the Tiger's Teeth*, 253.

you drive along. When you arrive home, the windows are heavily covered with blinds, so that you do not have to see the front yard where the garbage welcomes the guests.⁷⁸

A visit to Ibadan reveals a beautiful landscape with lofty hills and valleys, but it also reveals poor urban planning, faulty sanitation, and other environmental issues. However, the people's indifference to the stench and the unpleasant sight of this environmental menace is more disturbing. Blinds cover their windows and their consciences, along with the smoke released into the atmosphere by the overpopulated *Búkàs* everywhere in the city: "no one cared about this; it was the aroma that mattered."⁷⁹ What goes around definitely comes around, like the indignant palm tree from the proverb, throwing back whatever is thrown at it.

The consequence of carelessly dumping trash on the streets, in the gutters, and elsewhere, along with the environmental pollution, goes beyond the dirt that litters "the front yard where the garbage welcomes the guests." It also renders the area's inhabitants vulnerable to infections and diseases, including cholera, flu, and malaria: "As in Elépo, people were afflicted with guinea worm, and they nursed their painful sores for a long time."⁸⁰ Bad things happen to those who secretly dispose of dirt, a Yorùbá proverb warns.⁸¹ It is also an indictment of the government's failure to deal with environmental sanitization and proper health facilities, especially in rural communities: "There was no hospital at Akanran. In each election campaign since 1952, politicians had promised the village a hospital, or at the very least a dispensary, electricity, pipe-borne water, and a school. There were many promises. Nothing came of them."⁸²

It is a common practice to dump heaps of refuse at street corners in Ibadan, a practice that is rampant in other cities of the country. Uncompleted buildings are readily converted to dumpsites by neighborhood inhabitants, gutters make convenient incinerators, and walls and flowers in public places are watered with urine: "It was not necessary to have public toilets. Even the governor could stop his car and pee by the roadside."⁸³ Besides the ineffectiveness of environmental rules and agencies, there is a lack of appropriate public facilities and amenities to eradicate these environmental menaces. Where these facilities exist, they are poorly maintained by both the government and the people. In *A Mouth Sweeter than Salt*, while recounting the rules guiding our conduct as

---

[78] Falola, *Counting the Tiger's Teeth*, 57–58.
[79] Falola, *Counting the Tiger's Teeth*, 168.
[80] Falola, *Counting the Tiger's Teeth*, 105.
[81] Another metaphorical interpretation of the proverb is that bad things happen to those who betray a cause, relationship, or covenant, the *Ọ̀dàlẹ̀*.
[82] Falola, *Counting the Tiger's Teeth*, 102–103.
[83] Falola, *Counting the Tiger's Teeth*, 168.

primary school pupils, I commented that "some rules made perfect sense, but they were useless, like those on hygiene, which required us to wash our hands after using the toilet when no water was provided."[84] The damage of these environmental hazards has been normalized to the point where rebuking wrongdoers elicits insults and curses from them.

> The gutter was everywhere, in front of all the houses, as there was no hidden sewage pipe. Houses released their dirty water into the streets, from a gutter that passed along the frontage. If you dropped a Bible into it, there was no point in picking it up; it could not be washed clean as the stench in the gutter was like that of the pit. Both the backs and fronts of the modern houses smelled – feces at the back, urine at the front.[85]

Cleanliness is next to godliness: the stench and filth that the gutter inflicts on the Bible creates an imagery of darkness overpowering light. It is the image of an unpleasant pollution, defiling the moral uprightness of cleanliness, the prerequisite to holiness.

Walls, especially on uncompleted buildings, bear warnings. They are often heavy curses, written with charcoal and threatening crooks who would violate the cleanliness of such places: "Urinate here and die," "defecate here, ritualists need your feces," or "dump your refuses here and run mad" are popular examples. The friendlier ones only instruct violators to desist, and they are never heeded. Should someone find a bag of feces at the front door of one's shop, he or she would run to a pastor for fortification against the stench, which connotes rejection and loss.

> The hunchback woman was also said to have an incurable odor: Ògúndélé was advised to take her to the Ogùnpa River, which runs through the streets of Ibadan, to bathe her. This river travels slowly and has the color of dirt – it is one of the dirtiest of all rivers, not good enough even to wash dirty discarded metal. No one ever drank from the dirty Ogùnpa River, which was also a transmitter of countless diseases. People threw their thrash into it as we did at Agbokojo.[86]

It is a situational irony that the Ogùnpa River, which would easily pass for one of the dirtiest rivers in the country, is proffered as the solution to the odor problem of Ogundele's wife. It highlights the need to maintain good personal and environmental hygiene, along with the impossibility of quenching one stench with another. Hence, "The odor did not go away. Others in the compound believed it got worse, and they now said openly that the hunchback smelled like urine and feces dumped into the Ogùnpa River."[87]

[84] Falola, *A Mouth Sweeter than Salt*, 249.
[85] Falola, *Counting the Tiger's Teeth*, 81.
[86] Falola, *Counting the Tiger's Teeth*, 19.
[87] Falola, *Counting the Tiger's Teeth*, 3.

Ibadan, the largest city in West Africa, has poor urban planning: "Planning in the city has never been about beauty but about convenience."[88] Some houses in Bẹẹrẹ, and other less-developed neighborhoods in the city, are rumored to have drainage channels passing through their living rooms. This absence of proper sanitization and urban planning has caused floods that have claimed several lives and destroyed many properties in the city. During a return to my father's compound in 1988 I recounted in *A Mouth Sweeter than Salt* that "Half of it was no more, rebuilt as a one-storey building. In a series of floods, the Ogùnpa River decided to take some houses as a sacrifice to Yemọja, the goddess of the sea."[89] During the rainy season in Nigeria, countless public service announcements on TV and radio stations warn people about the dangers of careless waste disposal on the streets and in the gutters, but to no avail.

A popular folk song among natives and non-indigenes in Ibadan narrates the downpour of a rain that robs people of undergarments in their backyards. According to the song, the rain should not be rebuked; it is only sanitizing the city, an act that is commonly referred to as "environmental." The loss of these undergarments is symbolic of the lives, shelters, and properties lost to the floods caused by blocked drainage channels.

> A city once beautified by nature has become one of the ugliest, damaged by men who want to build cheap houses and corrupt officials who allow them to violate regulations to such an extent that you could even build an obstruction to stop the flow of water and extend your living room into the streets.[90]

In extreme cases, houses in Ibadan channel the waste from their restrooms directly into the public drainage system, causing very unpleasant environmental pollution. In those cases one would have to be an angel to refrain from muttering curses on the perpetrators of such evil.

Deforestation is another activity practiced by negligent people uninterested in cultivating a healthy and beautiful environment. The beautiful, tree-lined landscapes at the publicly funded tertiary institutions, for example, have been destroyed by their administrative heads. These people profit from the elimination of these trees, with little regard for their significance and no attempt to re-plant them. I recounted that "Fresh soil was brought from elsewhere to cover the spot and watered; three trees were planted. They grew, as I returned to this site some years later, but are now gone, as with most other trees that have now given way to houses that look poorer than trees."[91] The comparison between trees and houses indicates the environmental significance of the

---

[88] Falola, *Counting the Tiger's Teeth*, 168.
[89] Falola, *A Mouth Sweeter than Salt*, 145.
[90] Falola, *Counting the Tiger's Teeth*, 48.
[91] Falola, *Counting the Tiger's Teeth*, 48.

former and the poor planning of the latter. In this anthropocentric age the need to care for the environment cannot be overstated; earth is the only home known to and habitable by man, and our existence depends on our care for nature.

Satirizing Historical, Sociocultural, Political, and Economic Ills

My discovery is not like that of David Livingstone, who claimed to have discovered the Victoria falls when it was actually Africans who showed him the place, later named by the fellow citizens as one of *the* seven wonders of world. Neither was mine similar to that of the European explorer, Mungo Park, credited with having discovered the River Niger in the nineteenth century, a river that Africans had used for centuries to travel and fish, and one whose long banks had made many settlements flourish.[92]

In *A Mouth Sweeter than Salt*, while narrating how I was the first to "discover" my father's exact age and date of birth, I contrasted my discovery with those alleged by David Livingstone, Mungo Park, and other Europeans claiming discoveries or humanitarian acts contributing to the development of Africa. This diversion reorientates the world's perspective on African history, which has been erroneously presented by the colonialists – a neohistorical attempt at realigning the African story as it should be.

The historical example of Mary Mitchell Slessor, the Scottish Presbyterian missionary who acted to end the killing of twins in Nigeria, is quite misleading. The worship of twins is an ancient practice among the Yorùbá, which is why I reiterated, in comic disapproval, that "Mary Slessor had entered the elementary schoolbook as the pioneer medical worker in Nigeria who saved the lives of many twins destined to play for a while in the jungle."[93] Contrasting the European discoveries with my own downgrades their importance in comparison with true discovery, which "is actually used in its real sense of working hard and with luck being the first to know something."[94]

"In its long history of successful wars, Ibadan would take war booty but leave something for the defeated. Now when it was the turn of the British, they took everything, like the greedy merciless thief who carried the victim's chair and asked his victim to carry the entire house and walk behind him."[95] The magnitude, or, say, impossibility, of the thief's command commensurate with the havoc that colonialism wreaked on Africa. Similarly, contrasting the wartime attitudes of the British and the Ibadan warriors shows that colonialism, conquest, and its countless variations are common occurrences, even

---

[92] Falola, *A Mouth Sweeter than Salt*, 13.
[93] Falola, *A Mouth Sweeter than Salt*, 16.
[94] Falola, *A Mouth Sweeter than Salt*, 13.
[95] Falola, *A Mouth Sweeter than Salt*, 14.

among Africans, but it also emphasizes the colonizer's brutality and inhumanity.

A Yorùbá proverb asserts that the birth of a freeborn is no greater than that of a slave. In the long history of inter-ethnic warfare and slavery among African communities there has never been one ethnic group's brutal subjugation by another as witnessed during colonialism. Neither have humans been equated with animals, as the colonialists did with Africans, done to distance themselves from the impact of their actions. I derisively recounted this in *A Mouth Sweeter than Salt*, writing that "The white colonial officers had created their own zone, the Government Reservation Area. So that the natives would not come near, they created a large forest reserve as a buffer between them and the old city. I heard the story of animals living in a zoo, and the Government Reservation Area looked like one to me."[96]

Colonialism is more than a historical experience from Africa's past. Its evil manifestation distorted the African way of life and existence, running into neocolonialism, which is a period marked with greater menace and disillusionment that is worse than its predecessor. The political and military leaders of the post-independent/neocolonial government brought sociopolitical and economic instability through their intense corruption.

> When one offered a goat to a god, all that was left for the god was the blood. Even the powerful Ògún, the god of iron, would simply lick the blood and let you take the goat home to cook and entertain your friends. The government took the goat and the blood and asked you to clean up the blood, prepare the goat, cook the meals, smell the aroma, and leave.[97]

The people's relationship with the government was more demanding than their relationship with deities; the relationship was marked not only by abject domination but also by callousness and total disregard for the people's well-being.

> The drips of fluid from the intestines that were slit open, mixed with the blood and producing a range of colors, continued for some time. The odor was not as foul as I had expected, unlike the smell of discharges from human stomachs in latrines. I thought it might be that the smell of the men's bodies overpowered the odor of the dog.[98]

Contrary to expectation, the overpowering smell emanating from the men's bodies concealed the foul odor from the intestines of the sacrificial dog. This foregrounds the level of decadence among humans in the society, at both the sociopolitical and cultural and the physical levels. The "smell of discharges from human stomachs in latrines" corroborates this further. Likewise,

---

[96] Falola, *A Mouth Sweeter than Salt*, 136.
[97] Falola, *A Mouth Sweeter than Salt*, 433.
[98] Falola, *Counting the Tiger's Teeth*, 3.

comparing man and dog through smells subverts the superiority and morality of the former, revealing it to be inferior to the latter. The dog's sacrifice at the outset of Counting the Tiger's Teeth sets the tone for the imbalance, injustice, and marginalization narrated in the story and the futile attempt to correct them. Metaphorically, a keen reader would perceive the intent and meaning embedded in the extensive narration of the sacrifice in "Ògún's Gift."[99]

References made to the dog, the machete, the magicians, and Ògún are all metaphoric. The dog's inability to prevent its sacrifice, and its struggle for survival, makes it a representative of the masses, the farmers, who are at the mercy of the political leaders in government. The futility of the dog's death also foreshadows the failure and countless losses that will be sustained during the farmer's revolt, which further describes the vicious cycle that the masses are trapped in: "I imagined that the dog had the power to become whole and come back to life, but he did not do so on that fateful day."[100] Ògún, a vicious deity, represents the government, the political leaders, and the rich who profit from oppressing the masses: "I had heard all dogs being referred to as Ẹran Ògún (Ògún's meal), an indication that they are Ògún's favorite dish, his delicacy."[101] And the magicians who "had actually boasted that they could cut a dog in half and re-attach the two parts of its body" are synonymous with the acclaimed reformers and leaders making empty promises to reverse the misfortune of the masses: "The dog on his own could not return from heaven. Even the powerful juju men in the land could not undo his death. This dog was already consumed by Ògún."[102]

In worse scenarios, the magicians joined the oppressors to extort the masses through the art of deception. In A Mouth Sweeter than Salt I narrated a personal experience with one such con artist.[103] The impact of foreign intervention and exploitation in Africa is expressed through the havoc wreaked in Rwanda during the ethnic cleansing: "Africa had never had the machetes later used in Rwanda, those machetes that the Hutu imported in large quantities from China to slaughter their age-old ethnic rivals."[104] The machete became a tool of oppression, destruction, and division among the

---

[99] Falola, Counting the Tiger's Teeth, 1–27.
[100] Falola, Counting the Tiger's Teeth, 4.
[101] Falola, Counting the Tiger's Teeth, 3.
[102] Falola, Counting the Tiger's Teeth, 4.
[103] Falola, A Mouth Sweeter than Salt, 157–160.
[104] Falola, Counting the Tiger's Teeth, 5. Like the former colonialists, China and other Asian countries are fast occupying territories and influencing governance in Africa through their grants, funds, and empowerment offered to African countries as aid. This disguises their encroachment on African territories, exploiting her resources and making it a dumpsite for their inferior goods and projects. In a recent development, Mandarin is being included as compulsory subject/language in secondary schools in some regions of Africa.

masses, which is contrary to its traditional function of justice and path-finding in cultural beliefs:

> We disliked the Òyìnbó because they hated us, only keeping to the law of Moses that if you are slapped on the right side of the face, you should yield the left side to be slapped too. We thought that if we sent away the Òyìnbó, we would at least know the homes and addresses of the new leaders ... So we followed them when they asked for independence and for our support. We followed evil, and we reaped evil.[105]

Some leaders of the farmers' revolt, such as Tafa Adeoye and "No Baga," later worked alongside the government against their fellow farmers; their activities largely led to the collapse of the Àgbẹ̀kọ̀yà movement. Neocolonialism is a worse evil than colonialism – it is a fight against ourselves, brothers against brothers, a divided house. It is common for reformers to change sides after taking positions in government. A once-committed union leader in Nigeria became a political leader and threatened hail and storm on the masses, as though he was attempting to outdo the oppressive powers he once spoke against. Politics and the power accrued from governance is a locust corrupting anything it contacts: "The locusts I mentioned earlier were the government of the day and the members of the political class that ran it. The threesome was the military, the politicians, and the city officials."[106]

> Lunch over, they remembered work; more files to be read ... But many of them were already tired after their heavy lunch. Pounded yam and Ẹ̀bà have an excellent way of shutting down the body, asking the person to at least take a rest ... They did not want to rest: They wanted to work, but the relevant files were missing. Maybe they had mistakenly sent them to the Ministry of Finance. Well, there was always tomorrow, and it was better to work on those files when the head was "very cool" from a night's sleep. One man took his bag, and off he went; another took his bag and followed. They were supposed to close by 5 p.m., but by 3 p.m. half of them had already left for the day. Several files would be left open on the tables to give the impression that they were still around.[107]

Most of the blame for the menaces plaguing the nation gets heaped on the political leaders, but ignores the incompetence, irresponsibility, and corrupt practices of the workers in government-owned institutions and parastatals: "Government work was easy: Only fools worked methodically and with sweat. The wise ones knew that they must make more money than their salaries either from the government itself or from those who needed the government for one

---

[105] Falola, *Counting the Tiger's Teeth*, 176.
[106] Falola, *Counting the Tiger's Teeth*, 192.
[107] Falola, *Counting the Tiger's Teeth*, 170.

thing or the other: permits to build houses, to own stores, to register cars and businesses, and the like."[108]

It is a common misconception that one works very hard at executing the duties of a government worker, because it's an unending task, longer than one's life, and longer even than the lives of one's children; also, "Ọ̀gá tà, ọ̀gá ò tà, owó aláàárù á pé." I recounted the disposition of intermediaries, secretaries, and messengers, showing how the government and the famers differed in approaching their duties: "After the men at the secretariat had talked for two hours in the morning, they would take a break to drink tea and eat biscuits, read newspapers and relax. They were taking their second meal of the day at the same time that we were taking our first bite at Akanran."[109]

> The laborers were even talking of a "pension," the money you collect after you retire, when you can go back to your farm. As the farmers were told, these pensions were paid for as long as you lived, even when you were terribly ill or hit by any misfortune. Some were even warning their family members and children not to announce their death so that they could keep collecting the money. City officials, too, profited from the laborers, creating a long list of ghost workers.[110]

Another example of corruption, especially among government workers and administrative heads, was the falsification of age and the creation of ghost workers. The implementation of the Bank Verification Number in Nigeria revealed numerous bank accounts used to embezzle public funds and other anomalies. Some bank accounts cannot be claimed, due to the huge amount of money in them, which is usually owned by relatives of corrupt political leaders. Accounts filled with ill-gotten wealth have gone unclaimed, and numerous accounts for ghost workers and dead pensioners have been revealed.

Ghost working is a common practice, even among the National Youth Corps members allegedly serving their fatherland. In these cases, a member makes arrangements with the head of his or her assignment, continuing to receive a monthly allowance from the government, without performing any duties, for as long as an agreed percentage is shared with the assignment head and the local government inspector. Positions and offices in government-owned institutions are occupied by retired workers and dead people. In a similar instance, the appointment list for the Board of Government Agencies presented by the president contained the names of six dead people.[111]

---

[108] Falola, *Counting the Tiger's Teeth*, 91.
[109] Falola, *Counting the Tiger's Teeth*, 165.
[110] Falola, *Counting the Tiger's Teeth*, 197.
[111] Olakunle Olafioye and Ndubuisi Orji, "Number of Dead Persons Appointed by Nigerian President Buhari into Boards of Government Agencies has Increased to 8," *Sahara Reporters*, December 31, 2017, http://saharareporters.com/2017/12/31/number-of-dead-persons-appointed-by-nigerian-president-buhari-into-boards-of-government-agencies-has/.

In *A Mouth Sweeter than Salt* I recounted how different government policies had incentivized people to alter their age so that they could obtain benefits. Another policy was forced retirement for anyone who had worked for thirty years. "A Professor who had worked for thirty years and more complained that he was being asked to go in his early fifties or late forties, when he still had a lot to contribute to society. Could they have obtained their PhDs at the age of ten?"[112] The current deplorable state of African nations is a result of inefficient administrative systems in all sectors and the corrupt practices of the people and their political leaders.

***

> God is great
> But the rich man is not small either
> The very rich man, who has what God lacks
> The rich man has ten wives; God has none
> The rich man has fifty children, God has none.
> The rich man has five concubines, God has none.[113]

A comparison is drawn between the supremacy of God over man and the relationship between the rich and the poor. Money is indeed power, and those who possess it have power and authority over those below them. As a result, they are elevated to the position of demi-gods: "It was when it became uncountable that you became elevated to the level of a god, the *Igbákejì Olórun*, that is, the representative of God on earth ... After God, the next person is the rich man."[114] The ever-widening gap between rich and poor, and the elimination of the middle class, were the main causes of the farmers' revolt narrated in *Counting the Tiger's Teeth*: "In arranging the power hierarchies, you can put those who produced cocoa at the very bottom and those who managed the revenues at the very top."[115] Economic hardship stemmed from this imbalance, resulting in an unequal flow in the production and management of the nation's economy. I reflected on the economic hardship and its effects on standards of living of the people, commenting that "the rice and clothes of December now have to be purchased in November to prepare the way for battles with the powerful cults of credit cards that demand their sacrifices in January."[116]

The masses are at the mercies of the rich who exploit every opportunity to subdue the poor. One example is that of Jákòbù in *A Mouth Sweeter than Salt*, who was oppressed by a chief in the village. Hence, elsewhere, "The poor

---

[112] Falola, *A Mouth Sweeter than Salt*, 30.
[113] Falola, *Counting the Tiger's Teeth*, 158.
[114] Falola, *Counting the Tiger's Teeth*, 157.
[115] Falola, *Counting the Tiger's Teeth*, 163.
[116] Falola, *A Mouth Sweeter than Salt*, 415.

surrendered to the rich, voluntarily, willingly. They even agreed to become exploited tenants on cocoa farms. The rich man now carried a bag full of whips, although he had neither oxen nor goats but only poor fellowmen to use and control."[117]

An elaborate description of government worker orientation in "Cocoa Politics" reveals an ostensible difference between the corrupt political leaders, who misuse the state's finances, and the average government worker, who spends time plotting how to spend the yet-to-be-acquired wealth on luxuries, social excesses, and other vanities that their egos desire. They devote more time to making plans than to performing their job responsibilities. "They had all spent the money they were yet to make. Every week, they had a dream; they repeated their dreams each week. They needed the money from betting, as the profits made possible by cocoa were not enough to realize their ambitions."[118] A more contemporary saying, as if to absolve corrupt political leaders of their iniquities, holds that no one gets to the corridors of power without embezzling public funds: "Gbogbo wa lolè bílé bá dá."

***

Ex-convicts bear a terrible stigma, and they are subjected to miserable lives by Nigerian prisons, families, and the society at large ("An ẹlẹ́wọ̀n was always an ẹlẹ́wọ̀n, even after serving his sentence. It was a permanent condition of his definition of being, immutable, unchanging, fixed, and frozen in time"[119]). This often requires them to be relocated to a different part of the country, or even outside the country. In describing this condition, there is a subtle attempt at unifying religious differences, expressing the paramount importance of economic stability and opportunity: "Nigeria did not have or use identity cards or birth certificate, making it easier for an ẹlẹ́wọ̀n, if he liked, to change from Samson to Ibrahim, that is, from a Christian to a Muslim, or from Sulaimon to Jacob, from a Muslim to a Christian. All he need was to find a job in the informal economy and become part of the crowd."[120] This also highlights the inherent weakness of the country's security system, which has made several futile attempts to repress terrorism. This is further evident in the description of the farmers' attack on Agodi prison and the Ìyágànku police station.

My candid advice to Moses during our encounter was to "drop out of school and play soccer while I served as the referee to make sure he scored as many goals as possible."[121] Sports in Nigeria face greater challenges than the

---

[117] Falola, *Counting the Tiger's Teeth*, 158.
[118] Falola, *Counting the Tiger's Teeth*, 167.
[119] Falola, *Counting the Tiger's Teeth*, 279.
[120] Falola, *Counting the Tiger's Teeth*, 273.
[121] Falola, *Counting the Tiger's Teeth*, 40.

country's educational system, including low funding, lack of facilities, and favoritism: "The Nigerian Football Association introduced 'tribe' into everything they did, even the selection of players. Many blamed favoritism for the choice of players."[122] Favoritism was the criterion for making the national team, instead of an objective evaluation of the sportsman's passion, skill, and creativity. It led to the poor performance and rapid downfall of Nigerian sportsmen in the global rankings of various sports activities. The late, popular indigenous Nigerian rapper Dagrin lamented the government's negligence in an angry tone – his song titled "Democracy" laments the government's neglect of entertainment and sport activities apart from soccer. According to him, the soccer players are incompetent and play like crabs.

The contribution of thugs to the rebellion is important on multiple levels. It reveals the depravity of political leaders in their bid to attain political positions and hold themselves above the law. It remains a common practice to have thugs intimidate political opponents to win elections. It also reveals the extent to which political leaders remain unfaithful – I have narrated how they exploited the uprising for their own selfish gains, while the thugs joined the movement to seek revenge on political leaders who had neglected them after receiving assistance attaining various political posts. Their bravado had helped to secure members of the movement; the government security agents were terrified by their ruthlessness. Ejo and his boys could carry a steaming pot of soup from "Ìyá Alámàlà" (a food seller). "They were above the law, but they served useful functions – just because your son is bad does not entitle you to shoot him."[123] This brings to the fore the Yoruba ideology that there is good in evil, and vice versa. A "hard-headed child has its own glorious days."

Satirizing Food, Health, and Dietary Habits

Public health is challenged by the rise of diseases in present-day society. Besides poverty, ignorance, and other known contributors, a careful inspection of modern and ancient diets shows declining nutritional value over time. It is no coincidence that the life expectancy and health of village dwellers exceed those of city dwellers, although this is rapidly changing. As I narrated:

> All these good foods have disappeared from the current menu of the society, no longer made at all or desired, perhaps because there are now refrigerators or perhaps because a new generation has lost the knowledge of how to prepare them. Today, everything is fried, and even the rich and educated eat fried rice with fried chicken; fried fish and fried plantains, and chips are treated as delicates; and fried meat, put atop oil-soaked melon soup for consumption with heavy, starchy foods such as pounded

---

[122] Falola, *Counting the Tiger's Teeth*, 194.
[123] Falola, *Counting the Tiger's Teeth*, 228.

yam, is another favorite food. The rise of diabetes and obesity should be expected in the current dispensation. A previous generation was wise, much wiser, to have fed on grains, vegetables, fruits, and roasted food.[124]

Comparing the diets of the current and previous generations subverts the significance of Western education further, especially regarding the symptoms, causes, and cures for innumerable diseases. The technology that facilitated these discoveries does not necessarily improve the standard of living relative to those from previous generations. Metaphorically, the dietary changes alienate new generations from African culture, continuing the subjection of all that it represents as inferior: "There was nothing wrong with Yorùbá food, but the new elites in power were making bread and tea more important than corn and beans, turning the students' taste bud away from local foods and toward imported ones, preparing them for a future that would enslave them in the global economy."[125]

The unpleasant effects of dietary change is one of Westernization's numerous consequences: "Sauce and soup can be bitter, and I enjoy them better than those sweetened with cheese and sugar. Bitterness has its own pleasure that only a few can discover."[126] Traditional African communities understand the potency and significance of herbs and roots, relying on them for physical and spiritual fortification. A popular saying among the Yoruba explains that Òṣun healed and nurtured her children with herbs long before the arrival of medical practitioners. This expression highlights the communal significance accorded to traditional pharmacologists like Léku, whom I described in *A Mouth Sweeter than Salt*:

> To start with what was obvious, she was knowledgeable about all items used to cure diseases, that is, she was a trader in herbs and all ingredients for charms and medicine. Her knowledge of traditional pharmacology was deep. She had not gone to school and had memorized all the items. Even the smaller items, the visible dried leaves, and the wrapped ground leaves ran to over a thousand types. The bone pieces ran to another thousand. Even the various types of clay lamps were many. Léku could produce an object in a split second, pointing to where a customer should go and get it when she was not in the mood to get up.[127]

In "Cocoa Politics"[128] I relate cocoa's importance to the nation's economic development; regions and communities with higher cocoa production rates enjoy more social amenities than those with lower production rates or those that produce crops other than cocoa. In light of this, I highlighted elsewhere

---

[124] Falola, *Counting the Tiger's Teeth*, 115.
[125] Falola, *A Mouth Sweeter than Salt*, 249.
[126] Falola, *Counting the Tiger's Teeth*, 54.
[127] Falola, *A Mouth Sweeter than Salt*, 295.
[128] Falola, *A Mouth Sweeter than Salt*, 146–181.

the implications of the cocoa consumption by Westerners: "Just as we liked yam so much, especially with palm oil poured over it, so did these *Òyìnbó* people like cocoa, and, as we were told, added sugar to make it more delicious. There were two graves to be dug: the graves of those who were fighting for the tree and seeds; and the graves of those who drank cocoa powder and consumed the chocolate and sugar in excess."[129] The popular saying that sweet things kill expresses the Yoruba belief about sweetness, ordinarily and symbolically.

As with morality, etiquette, and other social conducts, the Yoruba people are cautious about food: its value, consumption, dangers and other cultural concerns. *Ojúkòkòrò/Ọ̀kánjúà* (greediness), *Wọ̀bìà* (gluttony), and *Àtẹnujẹ*, which "contains an element of greed, a careless desire to consume at the earliest opportunity,"[130] are vices associated with the consumption of food, and they are the subject of fierce ridicule among the Yoruba. Pásítọ̀, declining the food offered by Chief Ajibọla, and his subsequent lecture on *Àtẹnujẹ*, highlighted the cultural value placed on *Ìkóra-ẹni-níjanu* (self-restraint) as a virtue. "*Àtẹnujẹ* can kill, it destroys the body, he said."[131]

An *Ifá* corpus tells the story of a greedy fly that died trying to consume a heap of feces. These vices are as dreaded as thievery, and the above are often associated with *Olè*, a thief; a Yorùbá proverb declares that greediness is the deadliest infection – "Ọ̀kánjúwà, baba àrùn." A child with the tendency toward any of these vices is not spared. Every one of his shortcomings is linked to these sins, even when there is no correlation.

> There are too many disobedient students at school
> They hardly listen to their teachers
> When the teachers instruct in reading and writing
> It is then they think about food
> Let us eat and study
> Work is hard for them
> Play is their only passion
> Plantain and rice must not pass by
> They think only of food
> Let us eat and study.

This song is popular among nursery and primary school pupils to admonish them about hard work, but more importantly to discourage them from excessive food consumption. The popular refrain among parents is "Play is their only passion/ Plantain and rice must not pass by/ they think only of food/ Let us eat and study," because too much food is believed to affect the assimilation and concentration of a child. In later years the last line to the song has been

---

[129] Falola, *Counting the Tiger's Teeth*, 150–151.
[130] Falola, *A Mouth Sweeter than Salt*, 426.
[131] Falola, *A Mouth Sweeter than Salt*, 426.

replaced with "They eat, eat and eat, and score zero" to ridicule a child's poor performance or unwanted behavior.

> The big mamas thought that the small mamas were wasteful with money. Behind her back, Màmá Ade was accused of spending her husband's money on the best part of the cow – liver, tripe, intestines, and even the legs. The organs and the legs were the delicacies in those days. The lean beef was cheaper than the leg, far cheaper than the liver. To the big mamas, any wife spending her husband's money on cow organs did not mean well, wasting the money they ought to have saved to buy a piece of land and then build a house.[132]

Not only is excessive food consumption considered a vice, it is also considered folly to prioritize food consumption ahead of life's other necessities. Such people are said to be unconcerned about what they wear or how they look, so long as their stomach is filled. The utmost rule to a successful life, in Yoruba belief, is moderation, *Ìwòntunwòsín*.

Conclusion

> The world is crooked and only the just could make it straight.[133]

Literature's contribution to cultural sustenance, historical documentation, and national development cannot be overemphasized. As an artistic reflection of society, literature also refracts it – it is an imperative duty binding both the artist and his work to society. Societal reflection and refraction are satire's major concern, making it an indispensable device across ages and cultures; the work to correct societal ills is unending. *A Mouth Sweeter than Salt* and *Counting the Tiger's Teeth* reflect my personal experiences through a collective viewpoint, which further reflects the inherent vices present in the society, past and present, with the intent to document and inform readers of society's sociocultural and political realities. I reveal good and bad manifestations in and of society, but the intent is to effect positive change by bringing these foibles to the readers' consciousness, and to do so humorously. This reflection uncovers many vices inherent in society at the time of the narratives, which are still prevalent, and worsening, in the present time; they include sociocultural follies, religious excesses, political menace, and environmental degradation.

---

[132] Falola, *A Mouth Sweeter than Salt*, 163.
[133] Falola, *Counting the Tiger's Teeth*, 128.

8

Narrative Politics and the Politics of Narrative

Introduction

This chapter can only study some of the many intersections between narratives and politics; a *telos* guides the frame of every narrative as a catalyst driving their formation, development, and eventual resolution. The central aim of every narrative is to persuade, and this narrative's purpose, as well as that of the devices, is shaped by a narrative politics that mold and define the narrative's sustainability, relevance, and effectiveness.

Narrative as politics foregrounds the idea of a narrative as an agency in the substantiation of an idea or agenda. It is an approach to understanding the workings of past and present incidents, making sense of them to move toward a desirable future. In their latent manifestations, incidents are narratives themselves.

The implications of narrative can be best understood in the context of human lives, as well as with the implications of the politics driving it and the intersection between the two: politics and narrative. They are relevant because "man is in his actions and practice... essentially a story-telling animal."[1] Stories are ingrained in our biology, having existed for as long as human interaction has existed – they have been a means to communicate, to organize, to share common histories, and to form bonds. The totality of our existence is wrapped in narratives that have become significant for interpreting and understanding our realities at different levels.

As George Monbiot explained:

> We are creatures of narrative, and a string of facts and figures, however, important facts and figures are – and, you know, I'm an empiricist, I believe in facts and figures – but those facts and figures have no power to displace a persuasive story. The only thing that can replace a story is a story. You cannot take away someone's story without giving them a new one.[2]

---

[1] Philip Abbott, "Story-Telling and Political Theory," *Soundings: An Interdisciplinary Journal* 74, no. 3-4 (1991): 369-397, at 369.

[2] George Monbiot, "The New Political Story That Could Change Everything," filmed July 2018 in Edinburgh, TED video, 15:07, www.ted.com/talks/george_monbiot_the_new_political_story_that_could_change_everything#t-10426.

Humans exist in pursuit of a story or narrative to comprehend reality or to create one. Narratives thus are the vessel through which humans perceive, understand, and interpret their existence.

Politics, which is as fully ingrained in our society as any artificial construct could be, is a human narrative. From an anthropological standpoint politics is not a presupposed, inherent component of our biology like storytelling. Politics exists as a construct developed to create and sustain societies. Although it is not inherent in our biology, politics exists as an unyielding component of our modern world and as a narrative to maintain order and stability – life without politics is almost unimaginable.

From the New Historical viewpoint politics is an independent narrative that can be understood independently or in relation to other manifestations of human culture. However, a more personalized experience is created by combining the inherent narrative of stories with the constructed narratives of politics. Bringing the naturalistic component of narrative into the unnatural existence of politics allows for a more organic experience and understanding of our society and ourselves. To discuss this further, the concept of narrative politics must be examined.

In a discussion of narrative politics and their meaning, three questions must be answered to determine when collective action is needed, as well as how and why story-telling and personal narratives can drive collective action: How do individuals come together and act collectively in their common interest? Why is it that those promoting collective action frequently turn to stories? And why is storytelling so prominent when activists call for action, candidates solicit votes, generals rally troops, organizers seek new members, or coaches motivate their players?

The first question is answered in two words: *affinity* and *solidarity*. Individuals identify others with whom they share an affinity through organizing and narrating experiences. From this affinity, individuals identify what they need within their demographic. Solidarity is formed by establishing a common need, allowing a group to attain a common goal and bring desirable change. After identifying this goal, the group acts in its common interest by coordinating to achieve it. Narratives become the web that not only integrate these disparate experiences but also substantiate them. National narratives are steeped in this affinity to enhance development and foster solidarity and integration. The collective identity of the Yoruba, for example, originated from the deliberate, consistent narratives of the early nineteenth-century Yoruba intelligentsia as a way of attaining nationalism and integrating the Yoruba ex-slaves.[3]

Stories identify a shared affinity. A feeling of oneness and togetherness is fostered between persons when one is made to identify with the narrative of

---

[3] Toyin Falola, *Yoruba Gurus: Indigenous Production of Knowledge in Africa* (Trenton: Africa World Press Inc., 1999), 6–7.

another, and this cannot exist without the personal nature of storytelling. Storytelling also functions as a form of rhetorical argument focused on pathos, the emotions that define an individual. People feel that they can be part of something that appeals to their emotional or sympathetic side over their logical side. According to Monbiot, people have this remarkable capacity for togetherness, and by invoking that capacity, they can recover those exceptional aspects of their humanity – their altruism and cooperation.[4]

Using personal narratives to organize collective action creates an environment where individuals are driven by higher needs, rather than simply logical ones. The self becomes one with society and society accumulates narratives from the experiences of different selves, forming a complex but coherent master narrative. These harnessed narratives become a web of communality and create a continuum spiraling from the individual to the communal and vice versa. Higher calls to action (such as being called on behalf of a group) transcend the personal desires of individuals along with their weaknesses and constraints.

A consistent theme of stories exists within narrative politics – the most common type of story, and the story most typically associated with narrative politics, is the restoration story. According to Monbiot, this story follows a pattern: There is disorder in the land as a result of powerful and sinister forces working against the interests of humanity.[5] The hero revolts against this disorder to fight those powerful forces, overcoming them against all odds and restoring harmony to the land.[6] Humans strive for the happy ending, and when stories or narratives are framed within the restoration story – suggesting that they can join together and defeat an antagonist, ensuring that all will be well in the world – it motivates them to become allies and willing agents for the progress and success of the restoration narrative. Alternatively, as exemplified by Gus Casely-Hayford:

> When, in 1874, the British attacked the Ashanti, they overran Kumasi and captured the Asantehene. They knew that controlling territory and subjugating the head of state – it wasn't enough. They recognized that the emotional authority of state lay in its narrative and the symbols that represented it, like the Golden Stool. They understood that control of story was absolutely critical to truly controlling a people. And the Ashanti understood, too, and they never were to relinquish the precious Golden Stool, never to completely capitulate to the British. Narrative matters.[7]

---

[4] Monbiot, "The New Political Story."
[5] Monbiot, "The New Political Story."
[6] Monbiot, "The New Political Story."
[7] Gus Casely-Hayford, "The Powerful Stories that Shaped Africa," filmed August 2017 in Arusha, TED video, 19:54, www.ted.com/talks/gus_casely_hayford_the_powerful_stories_that_shaped_africa.

In the realm of politics, "narratives nearly always create an internal incommensurability with the [political] theory."[8] The political class often attempts to align political narratives and political theories with their own understanding and existence. This does not work, because "no matter how directly a story is related to a theory ... its impact can be challenged by the offering of another story."[9] Not only can the impact of a story be challenged by another story, but "the number of counter-stories is limitless."[10] And furthermore, "the story itself is subject to internal challenge ... historical reconstructions are subject to re-interpretations; fictional narratives are subject to alteration."[11]

The availability of counter-narratives and reinterpretations means that political stories cannot reliably provide stability or progress. This can be good; all things change, and so should stories. It can also present difficulties, because there is no way to completely rely on a story. The inadequacy of a single story does not indicate a need for counter- and alternate narratives, but it indicates the need for their intersection and consolidation in whichever way these stories are framed. As I stated in *Nationalism and African Intellectuals*,[12] the forefront of the liberation movement in Africa is a "nationalist historiography" seeking to subvert Euro-centered narratives of Africa and offering counter-discourses "for the achievement of Africa and the glories of the past in order to indicate possibilities for the future and combat racist views that Africans are incapable of managing themselves."[13]

Because of this, "each story seems to require a bridge to the theory which can be substituted with a counter-bridge based upon a reinterpretation of the proposed story or the introduction of another story."[14] Despite the variable nature of stories and their interpretations, "without the story we often cannot see the theory at all, at least not as the theorist hopes we will."[15] To examine how narrative politics work, we return to the notion of the restoration story. As Monbiot puts it:

> Political failure is at heart a failure of imagination. Without a restoration story that can tell us where we need to go, nothing is going to change, but with such a restoration story, almost everything can change. The story we need to tell is a story which will appeal to as wide a range of people as possible, crossing political fault lines. It should resonate with deep needs

---

[8] Abbott, "Story-Telling," 369.
[9] Abbott, "Story-Telling," 370.
[10] Abbott, "Story-Telling," 370.
[11] Abbott, "Story-Telling," 370.
[12] Toyin Falola, *Nationalism and African Intellectuals* (Rochester: University of Rochester Press, 2001).
[13] Falola, *Nationalism*, 224.
[14] Abbott, "Story-Telling," 391.
[15] Abbott, "Story-Telling, 394.

and desires. It should be simple and intelligible, and it should be grounded in reality.[16]

A restoration story that tells us where we need to go, and how we need to get there, inspiring collective action to accomplish shared goals, is a perfect illustration of narrative politics.

As with most political systems, narrative politics can be applied anywhere. However, its effectiveness in any given space is not guaranteed – it depends on how people receive it. With narrative politics in Africa there is an idea that "narratives of globalization ... rely on imperial systems of historical knowledge."[17] This perceived reliance on imperial systems of knowledge is monolithic and hegemonic, which hinders narrative politics and its ability to function effectively. However, existing outside of imperialist hierarchical standards, "minority literatures ... have the ability to function as sites of political value."[18] The existence of minority narratives alongside the pervasive implications of imperial systems of governance allows for a broader, more inclusive system within which narrative politics can be effective. The elevation of repressed narratives is an act of narrative politics that enables sociocultural and political emancipation.

Without "ideological distance, liberal narrative strengthening does not generally occur."[19] To manifest this ideological distance, there is a reliance on "the master narrative ... [which] develops a more holistic ideational account of forceful regime promotion by bringing together both elite-based and broader collective ideas."[20] Further, "master narratives tend to be the primary driver of policy"[21] because of their inclination toward the shared experiences of the collective.

In the discussion and sharing of narratives, it is necessary to understand the context within which narratives exist – "storytelling matters ... only when it matches up well with the right kind of event-driven political opportunity structure, notably external trauma for stories that strengthen the liberal narrative and internal trauma for those that strengthen the restraint narrative."[22] It is from this notion that "attention to cultural trauma allows us to understand why it is that similar kinds of stories keep strengthening and weakening over

---

[16] Monbiot, "The New Political Story."
[17] Peter Kalliney, "East African Literature and the Politics of Global Reading," *Research in African Literatures* 39, no. 1 (2008): 1–23, at 10.
[18] Kalliney, "East African Literature," 16.
[19] C. William Waldorf, "The Implications of Master Narrative Politics," in *To Shape Our World for Good: Master Narratives and Regime Change in U.S. Foreign Policy, 1900–2011* (Ithaca: Cornell University Press, 2019), 199–218, at 201.
[20] Waldorf, "The Implications of Master Narrative Politics," 203.
[21] Waldorf, "The Implications of Master Narrative Politics," 203.
[22] Waldorf, "The Implications of Master Narrative Politics," 205.

time."²³ The similarities among stories are rooted in the narrow context within which narrative politics are appropriate or effective.

The South West Africa People's Organisation (SWAPO) provides an example of narrative politics. SWAPO was a political party existing around the time of Namibian independence, in the late twentieth century. SWAPO won the Namibian election prior to the country gaining independence from Germany, and their victory in the 1989 UN-supervised election led to the SWAPO governing Namibia "with less than the two-thirds majority required to amend the constitution unilaterally."²⁴ Later in Namibia's history, "in 1994, SWAPO won an absolute majority in the National Assembly and has ruled alone since then, using this power base to vote through a controversial constitutional amendment in 1998 that would enable [President] Nujoma to seek re-election for a third term, on the grounds that his first term had been won in an election before independence."²⁵

SWAPO's position of power is relevant to narrative politics in Namibia, where "the centenary of 'the 20th century's first genocide' offered activists new opportunities to challenge their government's narrative of the nation ... targeting a key component of the ruling party's popular appeal."²⁶ The opportunity to challenge the government narrative arose from a perceived injustice that held the possibility of a restoration story. SWAPO had dominated Namibian government since independence, and it was displaying its power through "the building of memorials and the holding of commemorations around the country."²⁷ The restoration story is rooted in this perceived injustice, rewriting the narrative of the Namibian post-independence state. This opposed the "dominant current presentation of Namibian history [as] a Swapo-based narrative, in which Swapo is equated with liberation and support for Swapo with patriotism."²⁸ As Gus Casely-Hayford states:

> Just as in the nineteenth century, enslaved peoples of African descent in the Caribbean fought under threat of punishment, fought to practice their religions, to celebrate Carnival, to keep their history alive. Ordinary people were prepared to make great sacrifices, some even the ultimate sacrifice, for their history. And it was through control of narrative that some of the most devastating colonial campaigns were crystallized. It was through the dominance of one narrative over another that the worst manifestations of colonialism became palpable.²⁹

---

²³ Waldorf, "The Implications of Master Narrative Politics," 205.
²⁴ David Simon, "Namibian Elections: SWAPO Consolidates Its Hold on Power," *Review of African Political Economy* 27, no. 83 (2000): 113–115, at 113.
²⁵ Simon, "Namibian Elections."
²⁶ Elke Zuern, "Memorial Politics: Challenging the Dominant Party's Narrative in Namibia," *Journal of Modern African Studies* 50, no. 3 (2012): 493–518, at 494.
²⁷ Zuern, "Memorial Politics," 497.
²⁸ Zuern, "Memorial Politics," 497.
²⁹ Casely-Hayford, "Powerful Stories."

These narratives are the testaments of the past, expectations for the future, and the thesis of our numerous realities, whether they are appealing or appalling.

This chapter will attempt a master narrative, highlighting some of the African narratives I have curated and harnessed during my lengthy career as a passionate narrator. The political component has always been to advance a cause toward a desirable collective future. These narratives of people, cultures, places, and events matter to us: they are who we are.

Narrating the People

The people are the most important components of any narrative. Their narratives endear us to other humans, places, ideas, and the realities shaping our collective existence, and they are perceived as active agents of narrative development and resolution. Every person deserves to be narrated and celebrated, but narrative politics have marginalized some people – the domain of narrative is controlled by those who wield sociopolitical and economic power. These narratives are more than preservation mechanisms that immortalize and celebrate precious memories of people that are transitioning from one generation and moment to another, but are also orbits of power; these powers can be established, strengthened, and possibly rechanneled.

Before *In Praise of Greatness: The Poetics of Adulation* (2019), there was *Yoruba Gurus: Indigenous Production of Knowledge in Africa* (1999) exactly twenty years earlier, and there was *Nationalism and African Intellectuals* (2001). Although the need to narrate people exists, the base of narrative politics is composed of the unsung and less prominent, and history has become a device of the upper class. These people are a continuum of the collective, constantly engaged with and involved in activities that seek collective growth, making narratives about them into the narrative of the "people." *Nationalism and African Intellectuals* is not a narrative of the unsung per se, but it is a historical construction and theorization of these strands of individuals and the collective efforts of African intelligentsias – it reworks the development and continuity of ideologies from one period to another (precolonial, colonial, and modern) to further understand the development of Africa and its people.

The tremendous effort of early historical writers such as N. D. Oyerinde, J. D. E. Abiọla, and others who wrote on the Yoruba city-states of Ògbómọ̀ṣọ́ and Ileṣa are labeled in *Yoruba Gurus* as narrative politics "for the additional reason of responding to colonial reforms of local government, political re-organization, and resource allocation."[30] Oyerinde did this with *Ìwé Ìtàn Ogbomoṣo*[31] to spur modern development in Ogbomoṣo. The introduction to *Yoruba Gurus* charts a path for the foundation and development of

---

[30] Falola, *Yoruba Gurus*, 11.
[31] N. D. Oyerinde, *Ìwé Ìtàn Ogbomoṣo* (Jos: Niger Press, 1934).

writing – particularly in linguistics, history, and literature – and emphasis is placed on the contributions of people who have developed and added value to the comprehension of these subjects as they are (better) understood today. It is also true that:

> The conception of the Yoruba identity supplied by the chroniclers has been embraced by the academy ... To put this point in a different way – the chroniclers have defined who the Yoruba are, and the academics have accepted it; the chroniclers defined some key subjects of study, and the academics have followed their lead; the chroniclers have defined a modernization agenda which the academics have cleverly appropriated.[32]

Some academics have appropriated the knowledge produced by local, often uncelebrated and forgotten Yoruba intelligentsias. They claim credit for themselves without acknowledging the appropriate "local" sources, and "they regard themselves as superior ... Power and privilege have enabled them to criticize the chronicles and to berate some of them."[33] Joseph Odumosu's Ìwé Egbògi and Ìwé Ìwòsàn[34] are classics that detail the pharmacognosy knowledge of the Yoruba people. The failure to fully nativize academia and the educational sector of African society is largely responsible for these misattributions. These individuals are distinguished professionals in their chosen fields, regardless of their formal educational accomplishments, and the academy must engage with and fuse them (or at least those still living) into their respective knowledge bases. The knowledge they embody must be applied to achieve true socio-economic and political development.

Likewise, *Nationalism and African Intellectuals* is a narrative in pursuit of the image of intellectuals whose effort is "to reshape Africa."[35] A significant dimension to this historical framework is the emphasis on their collective actions and orientations, along with emphasis on the nationalistic and Pan-African reactions/reflections that preceded, accompanied, and succeeded them. In the spirit of nationalism and Pan-Africanism, Tom Mboya's sponsorship of several African citizens journeying to the United States for educational development was an effort "which became part of the African expression of nationalism."[36] From Ajayi Crowther and Surgeon Major James Africanus Beale Horton to Edward Wilmot Blyden and Bishop James Johnson, the African missionary and church personalities included many radical intellectuals who spurred and sustained the movement of nationalism and the eventual liberation of African states.

---

[32] Falola, *Yoruba Gurus*, 16.
[33] Falola, *Yoruba Gurus*, 16.
[34] Joseph Odumosu, *Ìwé Ìwọ̀sàn* (Liverpool: n.p., n.d.).
[35] Falola, *Nationalism*, xvii.
[36] Falola, *Nationalism*, 10.

Their ideologies transcended religion, addressing politics and other major facets of African society, creating the foundation for nationalist ideologies that included Léopold Sédar Senghor's Negritude, Amílcar Lopes Cabral's "African Marxism and Socialism," and the Pan-Africanism of W. E. B. Du Bois. Essays in the third part of *Nationalism and African Intellectuals*, titled Nationalism and the Academy, trace the significant impact of African academic intellectuals (re)configuring the African nationalist dream. It is impossible to overstate the interrelationship between the academic sphere and the economic, political, and sociocultural development of any society. One example is Kenneth Onwuka Dike's effort to rechannel the focus of historiography and truly capture and represent the African perspective. This orientation movement was later tagged the "Ibadan School of History" by "outsiders who wanted a descriptive category for the presentation of nationalist historiography."[37] The full significance of these vital contributions to national development is often omitted from national narratives.

The noticeable advancement made by the Yoruba community and beyond, especially in academics, is founded on the pioneering efforts of intelligentsias in the nineteenth century with the codification of language, narration of culture and tradition, and writing of literature. The pioneering effort of Theophilus Olabode Avoseh remains unbeatable, documenting the history of Ẹpẹ and Badagry. The chapter "Unsung Authors of the Modern Era: The Histories of Igbomina" in *Yoruba Gurus* is a deliberate attempt to spotlight the efforts of these early Yoruba historical chroniclers, especially in places that are discussed least in academic research and national history. The collective importance of this documentation is to "make progress and development, and ... join others to make demands or take concrete measures ... to achieve what they want ... The significance ... is that the work of history is at the same time a political manifesto, calling for change and stipulating or suggesting how this is to be achieved."[38] Writing about these people and their efforts reiterates the goals and thrusts of their narratives.

In Praise of Greatness may supersede the previous length of discourse, range of people narrated, and novelty of approach; it gives credence to traditional Yoruba poetics of adulation or narrating people. It is in people that we seek shelter, "Èniyàn laṣọ" and "Indeed, one of the hallmarks of true greatness is seeing and celebrating the greatness in others."[39] It is in the narrative of others that we unveil "new truths," and it is in narrating others that we gain true perception of ourselves in relation to others and to the entirety of life. This phenomenon is described by Epstein as the most assured destination for

---

[37] Falola, *Nationalism*, 228.
[38] Falola, *Yoruba Gurus*, 240.
[39] Toyin Falola, *In Praise of Greatness: The Poetics of African Adulation* (Durham: Carolina Academic Press, 2019), 15.

seeking answers.[40] In its full cultural splendor, it is a textual performance of Ìbà (homage), which itself precedes an oral performance. In this textualization it is both the gateway and the performance (the discourse) itself; this disrupts the boundary between the performativity of orality, literature, and technology as a carrier. The section "Heavenly Bodies" crystallizes and harnesses the significance of those who have passed on to the ancestral realm, exploring how they continue to shape our contemporary reality.

Beyond the poetics of adulation, *In Praise of Greatness* identifies the sociopolitical and economic conundrum of the spaces occupied by the narrated persona. In narrating the people as the focus of the narratives, I navigate the discourses and concerns that have shaped them, and vice versa. The narrative of Abimbola Adunni Adelakun is significant – it spotlights the sociopolitical and cultural contribution of a brilliant and courageous woman who belongs to a (younger) generation, suffering at the receiving end of a corrupt system controlled by gerontocrats. As a young but sound academic and creative writer, and as an active sociopolitical commentator, her life and career cuts across intersectional paradigms that are significant for understanding Nigerian society. While her "writing is expressive and engaging, and she focuses on bringing awareness on a vast range of issues,"[41] her narrative is heavily laden with the need for an equal and better society. In narrating Adelakun, I expose to the readers the rot that years of bad leadership, inequality, religious hypocrisy, and patriarchy have inflicted on our society. I also show how it can be revived through Adelakun: this is the ultimate politics of narrating people.

Narrating Places

Places are central to the development and understanding of a narrative, but unlike people they are relegated to the understructure of narratives. This explains why places in narratives lose their historical and cultural values, and consequently, in the interpretations of those narratives, in comparison to the people that inhabit them. This is not to suggest that places can be read or narrated independent of people or other sociocultural manifestations, but the argument is for the co-textualization of these codes as parallel and co-/intra-dependent. As a historian, the need, intent, and interest in unearthing narratives of places is not far-fetched – the need to narrate African places and culture in their countless manifestations is more urgent than ever.

The multiplicity of Nigeria's origination narratives is highlighted in the *History of Nigeria*, and this diversity poses difficulties, especially for the

---

[40] Joseph Epstein, "Why do we Read Biographies?" presentation, Hillsdale College, Hillsdale, MI, January 2016; Joseph Epstein, "'Why do we Read Biographies?' – Joseph Epstein," YouTube Video, 42:55, www.youtube.com/watch?v=IY_-S5_Lnbg.

[41] Falola, *In Praise of Greatness*, 380.

proper integration of the nation. It is noteworthy "that societies had existed for so long that tracing their beginning can be difficult; that societies had to cope with their environment and develop on the basis of their initiative; and that one group had to interact with others, as the migration stories point to important linkages."[42] While the "nationalist historiography" set to revert and correct the occidental perspective on the study of African history and the understanding of its culture, the plagues of post/modernism, "neo-westernization" and postcolonial disillusionment in contemporary times pose a far greater threat to this indigenous knowledge. Hence, the need to preserve them in narratives.

In *The History of Nigeria*, introductory chapters focus on the cultural formation and development of various ethnic groups and their kingdoms in Nigeria before colonial conquest and rule. They reveal the peculiarities that define each group and the socio-economic and political structures that aided their sustenance and expansion. An interdependent and diverse economy was built on agriculture, mining (gold, iron, tin, copper), manufacturing (leatherworks, textiles, ceramic, sculptures), and trade, all of which "relied on local resources, supplemented with raw materials obtained from regional trade."[43] Societies were further integrated by "religious, social, and cultural agencies such as age-grade associations, secret societies, marriage ties, and oracle practices."[44] The spiritual and religious inclination of precolonial Nigerian societies strengthened the political leadership system.

These historical precedents contrast with colonial and postcolonial Nigeria narrated in the subsequent text. The conquest and forceful integration of these diverse societies meant that "new possibilities and problems were created in all aspects of life, as Nigeria moved into the twentieth century, the so-called modern era."[45] The leadership problems afflicting the years of Nigerian independence are similar to those that beset precolonial kingdoms such as Mali, Ghana, Songhay, and Ọyọ, but they also "demonstrate the capability of Africans to create large states and manage them for a long time."[46]

The significance of places and cultures, and their intra-co-dependency on other codes, is manifested in their relevance in the process of deducting a holistic understanding of narratives about people. These narratives themselves are coded, and they explore spatial and cultural formations, as if in an ethnographic narrative, giving further credence to their relevance.

---

[42] Toyin Falola, *The History of Nigeria* (Westport: Greenwood Press, 1999), 18.
[43] Falola, *The History of Nigeria*, 25.
[44] Falola, *The History of Nigeria*, 27.
[45] Falola, *The History of Nigeria*, 65.
[46] Toyin Falola, *Key Events in African History: A Reference Guide* (Westport: Greenwood Press, 2002), 90–101.

My narratives about people, myself included,[47] are grounded in the communal development of such narrative personas and their interaction with communal codes and vice versa. Similar to what *In Praise of Greatness* set to do with narrating people, *Ibadan: Foundation Growth and Change 1830-1960*[48] concerns Ibadan and its culture (along with its people). For obvious reasons, the documentation of Ibadan is special to me, not only for my memoirs but also owing to the profoundness of Ibadan – it is the place Remi Raji describes as the Harlem of Africa.[49] "Both in its physical appearance, and the mentality, it is clear that Ibadan is traditional and modern, historic and contemporary."[50]

There are multiple, significant dimensions to my extensive narration of Ibadan.[51] In reconstructing Ibadan's historical narrative from oral and archival sources there is often the description and inclusion of other places whose existence is contingent to Ibadan's comprehensive narrative; the formation and expansion of Ibadan revolves around these other places. The book transcends the norm of mere historical narration to perform a careful and rigorous explication of events, people, ideas, and factors that shape the formation and development of Ibadan. *Ibadan: Foundation Growth and Change 1830-1960* recounts the city's existence from its earliest period into modernity, placing it in relation to the larger Yoruba and Nigerian society with a focus on its cultural, economic, and sociopolitical standing. For example, the chapter "Economic Expansion, Social Spaces and City Life 1920-1930" outlines the impact of colonial development programs – roads and rails aided agricultural production and distribution tremendously, further developing the city's economy.

Ibadan became a center of agriculture and commercial trading, and its output helped to sustain the colonial government. The economic expansion of Ibadan, which necessitated further geographical expansion and infrastructure, established Ibadan as a cosmopolitan city, comparable to Lagos. Ibadan quickly became a favorable destination not only for ethnic groups native to the country, but for Europeans, Syrians, and Lebanese. The foundation of Ibadan itself is characterized by modernity, and these rapid developments further spurred it into a modernity that created a new "cultural" class defined by

---

[47] As I have indicated elsewhere in this book, *A Mouth Sweeter than Salt* and *Counting the Tiger's Teeth* are ethno-autobiographic narratives that present larger sociocultural texts through my lens and experience; my narratives assume an archival state through which a collective reality can be alternatively or further understood.

[48] Toyin Falola, *Ibadan: Foundation Growth and Change 1830-1960* (Ibadan: Bookcraft, 2012).

[49] Remi Raji, "A Hilly Affair," in *Mesìọ̀gọ̀: A Celebration of a City, Its History and People*, ed. Dapo Adelugba, Remi Raji, Omowunmi Segun and Bankole Olayebi (Ibadan: Bookcraft Ltd., 2001), 72-75, at 73.

[50] Falola, *Ibadan*, 891.

[51] *Ibadan* has since been regarded as one of my major books.

economic privilege, literacy, and Westernization. This new cultural class sought distinction in speech, food, housing, dress, education, music, and politics: "The Ọ̀làjú in the township comprised 'successful and enlightened Africans' and over two hundred Europeans and Lebano-Syrians."[52]

The significant influence of Ibadan in colonial and postcolonial Nigeria is rooted in the military formation of the city and its subsequent expansionist warfare: the chapters "Warfare and Diplomacy" and "Chiefs, Wars and Wealth, 1850–1892" address the former, while chapters like "In Search of Freedom: The Adegoke Adelabu Era and Regional Politics, 1945–1960" explicate Ibadan's involvement in Nigeria's sociopolitical dimensions, focusing on Adelabu as central to this transition: "We found Adelabu behaving like Ogunmọla: displaying courage, physical endurance, and connections with powerful forces."[53] Ibadan remains a significant part of Nigeria's history even as the country continues to redefine its existence.

The historical navigation of a place is larger than a mere recounting of its "historical" narrative; it is a deep investigation of its workings and the infrastructure that cuts across the entirety of its existence. As *Ibadan* has demonstrated, the economic and sociopolitical dimensions of society are dependent on its past and formation, highlighting historical studies as a significant field for understanding not only the past but also the present and future. The narrative politics of history procure solutions and advancement for every possible phenomenon with an accountable past.

Narrating Culture(s)

> The definition and meaning of culture are broad: values, beliefs, texts about the beliefs and ideas, multiple daily practices, aesthetic forms, systems of communication (e.g., languages), institutions of society, a variety of experiences that capture Africans' way of life, a metaphor to express political ideas, and the basis of an ideology to bring about both political and economic change.[54]

Narrating people and places culminates in self-evidential narratives, and therefore is indispensable in appreciating the formation and operations of a narrative in understanding human histories and societies, especially over time. However, culture as a system is relatively often less self-evident and more crystallizing in a narrative. All the possible manifestations of culture are not often read independently or narrated as a code. As interpretive or suggestive cues for comprehension, one could do worse than reading or understanding places as the background upon which a narrative is set.

---

[52] Falola, *Ibadan*, 653.
[53] Falola, *Ibadan*, 653.
[54] Toyin Falola, *The Power of African Culture* (Rochester: University of Rochester Press, 2003), 1.

As a crystallizing agent, culture permeates the formation and exegesis of any narrative. My two memoirs, *A Mouth Sweeter than Salt* and *Counting the Tiger's Teeth*, along with my other poetry collections, embody culture as a crystallizing agent. However, *Culture and Customs of Nigeria*,[55] *The Power of African Culture*, *The African Diaspora: Slavery, Modernity and Globalization*,[56] and others embody culture as a narrative. In addition to their clarification, preservation, and celebration functions, they also advance unity and development for a related group of people. This creates a sense of belonging and existence, achieving the crystallizing effect.

Culture assumes a significant role as a prism in Africa and among her people. The richness, diversity, and continuous celebration of culture in its manifold expressions are a testament to this. Indeed, "Africans regard culture as essential to their lives and future development. Culture embodies their philosophy, worldview, behavior patterns, arts, and institutions."[57] *Culture and Customs of Nigeria* centers on "Religion and Worldview," "Literature and Media," "Art and Architecture/Housing," "Cuisine and Traditional Dress," "Gender Roles, Marriage, and Family," "Social Customs and Lifestyle," and "Music and Dance"; each aspect is discussed extensively within chapters that create a broad overview of the cultures and their dimensions in Nigerian society.

Food is a major representation of culture among Nigerians. Jollof rice, for example, has been used in many literary narratives to symbolize Nigeria and to foreground nostalgia among characters in the diaspora.[58] It is a national food that serves as a unifying socio-code, considered to be a staple food for most social gatherings and receiving wide acceptance among different ethnic groups, classes, and age cohorts. Despite the crosscultural reception, foods are major cultural symbols for ethnic groups, religious rites, and even age or class representation on certain occasions. The consumption of meat is rationed by age and class – the rich and the elderly take larger shares of whatever is being consumed. In naming ceremonies for twins, the preparation of beans (with plenty of palm oil) is considered a sacred rite among the Yoruba. Dishes such as bread, rice, cake, and salad have referenced different cultural and class signals in the wake of independence, spurred by colonialism and characterized by false impressions of civilization and modernity.

Soups are known as *owo* to the Urhobo, *banga* to the Itsekiri, *ẹfọ ẹlẹgúsí* to the Yoruba, *edikang ikong* to the Efik and Ibibio, and *miya makwa* to the Hausa. Starch dishes such as *ẹ̀bà*, *fùfú*, *iyán*, and *àmàlà*, popularly called *òkèlè*

---

[55] Toyin Falola, *Culture and Customs of Nigeria* (Westport: Greenwood Press, 2001).
[56] Toyin Falola, *The African Diaspora: Slavery, Modernity and Globalization* (Rochester: University of Rochester Press, 2013).
[57] Falola, *Culture and Customs*, x.
[58] Sarah Ladipo Manyika, *In Dependence* (Abuja: Cassava Republic, 2008).

or ọ̀wẹ "swallows," are common among the Yoruba.[59] Further distinction can be made to link specific "swallows" with different Yoruba sub-ethnic groups. For example, àmàlà láfún is common among the Egba, àmàlà iṣu/dúdú is prevalent with the Ibadan/Ọyọ, and the Ondo and Ekiti are known for their immense cravings for iyán. The slightly hard texture of ẹ̀bà, with red coloring provided by palm oil, is a distinct cuisine among the Igbo and Niger Delta residents, separate from that of the Yoruba. Among the Yoruba, the best gaàrí for drinking is reputed to come from Ijebu, one of the sub-ethnic groups and an ancestral home of the Yoruba – their gaàrí is distinguished by its well-grounded, clean grains that have a sharp, sour taste. Foods symbolically represent how the manifold ethnic groups of Nigeria have related, endured, and accommodated each other's differences. Cues can be taken from these foods and cuisines to foster stability, integration, and harmony in African societies.

Beyond their nutritional content, Africans value foods for their status as codes that communicate collective cultural meanings, including spiritual representation. Africans have used food to express logical facts and philosophical truths, foregrounding their deep moral understanding of life, their existence, and their environment. Among the Yoruba, proverbial sayings like "A kí ń fi ọla jiyọ̀," literally meaning that one's consumption of salt is not determined by one's acquisition of wealth, preach Ìwọ̀ntunwọ̀sìn (moderation) as a necessity for healthy living.

The corruption and mismanagement prevalent among contemporary African leaders constitute reckless acts of Jẹgúdújerá (nonreciprocal consumption) highlighting their deviation from African mores of restraint and contentment. Ìjẹkújẹ, Ìjẹ-wọ̀bìà, Àjẹranjú, Jẹunkóokú, and Àjẹpajúdé are related epistemic expressions and criticisms among the Yoruba that condemn greed. These suggest that "Development has to be grounded in culture – it should capture the essence of people's lives, profit from the creative and economic benefits unleashed by cultural production, and transform traditions and institutions that may create obstacles to progress." In other words, "Policies of change, in order to endure and be effective, must recognize the power of history, tradition, and cultural institutions."[60]

The *Power of African Cultures* reflects phases and tensions – slavery, Islamization, colonization, Christianization, politics, modernization, and industrialization – that have distorted the way that African cultures have evolved over time. In comparison, *The African Diaspora* presents alternative transitions, focusing on the existence of African cultures and identifying their manifestations among Africans in the diaspora, creating a continuum on which African cultures continue to exist in different dimensions. The power

---

[59] Falola, *Culture and Customs*, 98–103.
[60] Falola, *The Power of African Culture*, 51.

of African culture integrates the Africans in diaspora, not only contemporary ones but also those from the days of transatlantic slavery.

The transfer and negotiation of Yoruba culture is in manifestations of the Nago in Brazil and the Lucumi in Cuba. The survival of similar Yoruba religious practices among them "has exposed other aspects of culture: the use of language, food habits, expressive traditions, activities of diviners, priests, drummers, medicine and the like."[61] The resistance and resilience of plantation slaves were strengthened by culture through religious and spiritual rites. Despite the overwhelming suppression that characterizes slavery and colonization, the remanifestations of African religions affirm the power of culture. Afrofuturism, African futurism, and post-African Future are emerging ideologies that explore the dimensions of African culture in contemporary times.

The colonial phase of African history marks the modification and declension – or total repression, in some cases – of African cultures. Christian values were advanced to the detriment of existing traditional cultures. Polygamy and indigenous songs or festivals were regarded as pagan customs, and traditional languages were dismissed as vernacular, attributed to the illiterates or *Ará oko*. The purpose of narrating culture is for readers to "see their own cultures in different perspectives, understand the habits of Africans, and educate themselves about the customs and cultures of others" and that "they will come to respect the cultures of others and see them not as inferior or superior to theirs, but merely as different."[62]

Narrating Violence in Nigeria

Modern Nigeria is, to a large extent, the product of violence.[63] War, conflict, and hatred are substantial manifestations that arise from interactions between people. On a national level, conflict is unavoidable due to differences in opinion, as well as fear of alienation and domination. These occurrences are not only inevitable, but also important for the collective sociocultural, political, and economic development of any society. The resolution of conflict or its escalation into violence – or war on the extreme end – shapes the gradual and eventual integration of a society into a unified nation, forging the characteristics of tolerance and collectivism that typify nationalism.

Nigeria, as a multi-ethnic society, has experienced and survived different forms of conflicts, including political, ethno-religious, and military uprisings. "Violence has a political purpose: to dominate, to resist domination, to create

---

[61] Falola, *The African Diaspora*, 130.
[62] Falola, *Culture and Customs*, x.
[63] Toyin Falola, *Colonialism and Violence in Nigeria* (Indianapolis: Indiana University Press, 2009), 2.

conditions for negotiation, and to target people and objects that symbolize oppression."⁶⁴ For these reasons, the subject of violence occupies my historical and literary narratives.

Colonialism and Violence in Nigeria explores the causes, dimensions, and consequences of violence in Nigeria that arose from British colonization and rule. Protests and riots in different regions of the country escalated into violence. Initially, it was resistance against the establishment of a colonial authority over existing traditional political systems, witnessed in Benin, Ìjẹ̀bú, Ìlọrin, and Okrika. This resulted in the exile or execution of traditional rulers. Later there was resistance against specific policies of colonial rule, including the Ẹgba rebellion against taxation in the west in 1918, the anti-tax rebellion of rural Igbo women in Owerri and Calabar in 1929, and the subsequent formation of unions and political parties that included the Nigerian Union of Teachers (1931), the Nigerian Railway Workers Union (1932), the National Council of Nigeria and the Cameroons (1944), and others. These movements birthed nationalism in Nigeria and other African states: "Resistance and nationalism became two sides of the same coin. One side fought to protect the old order of traditions and pre-colonial nations and the other side fought to create a new order in an emerging nation-state."⁶⁵

In Nigeria most reoccurring conflicts are instigated by religious domination and partisanship, further heated by political and sociocultural divisions. However, religion is also considered to be a mechanism for integrating and developing the nation: "Indeed, religion has become so important in recent history that no analysis of modern Nigerian politics in the last quarter of the twentieth century can escape considering it."⁶⁶ These dimensions of conflict are examined in *Violence in Nigeria: The Crisis of Religious Politics and Secular Ideologies*. Despite claims of modernity and secularization, religion continues to play a significant role in the formation and progression of Nigeria's political system. Political ambitions and government policies are propagated via religion, which harnesses people through its ability to meet their physical and spiritual needs. This utmost significance of religion, and the spirituality attributed to sacredness, makes it most vulnerable to exploitation by the political class pursuing selfish agendas. It is exacerbated by political instability, diversity, poverty, and other factors.

Political tensions from the time of independence in 1960, along with enduring ethno-religious conflicts, have triggered several incidents of violence in Nigeria, from the 1980s to the present day. Countless lives have been lost, billions of dollars' worth of property have been damaged, and the democracy

---

⁶⁴ Falola, *Colonialism and Violence*, ix.
⁶⁵ Falola, *Colonialism and Violence*, 132.
⁶⁶ Toyin Falola, *Violence in Nigeria: The Crisis of Religious Politics and Secular Ideologies* (Rochester: University of Rochester Press, 1998), 2.

and the unity of the nation have been under constant threat. The Maitatsine riots in northern Nigeria in the early 1980s, instigated by the Islamic clergy Marwa (aka Maitatsine), "were the first large-scale religious disturbances in post-independence Nigeria."[67] They were fueled by Islamic fundamentalism, offering an alternative to the decadence and corruption that continued to afflict society in spite of the military dictatorship's efforts to cleanse it.

A study of the Maitatsine riots reveals society's inadequacies: high rates of unemployment and poverty due to economic mismanagement; weak security systems; the inefficiency or absence of traditional and local authorities in addressing violence or preventing it from spiraling out of control; and the exploitation of religion by political elites to cause rivalry, chaos, and disruptions to the system. The pattern of the Maitatsine riots continues in present-day Nigeria, showing that little has changed regarding the nation's inadequacies and the role of religion.

The trend of current political events in Nigeria is similar to the religious conflicts in the 1980s: the fear of Islamizing Nigeria through sharia law; the appointment of Muslims to government positions; the military and political domination of the Hausa-Fulani; and Christians as the victims of violence and terrorism enacted by Islamic extremists, which is met with Christian intolerance for Muslims and Islamic practices. On one hand, religious conflict in Nigeria is encouraged by Islamic fundamentalism, but on the other, the resistance of Christianity and firebrand Pentecostalism (Protestantism) decries Islamic domination and refuses to tolerate other religious or spiritual beliefs. "The first most brutal confrontation between Christians and Muslims occurred in Kaduna State ... in Kafanchan on Friday, 6 March 1987."[68] Subsequently, interreligious violence broke out in Zaria, Bauchi, Kano, Katsina, and Plateau states, leaving embers that have continued smoldering into the present.

Violence has been provoked by foundational, political, regional, or doctrinal differences within religions, such as anti-Sufi Islamic groups such as the Jama'at Izalat al-Bid'a wa Iqamat al-Sunna or the "Pentecostal" churches and those commonly referred to as Orthodoxicals (as in Anglican, Catholic). This dimension of religious violence is often repressed and quickly resolved, but it highlights the hypocrisy and tensions inherent within religion. Perhaps, due to civilization and the permanent consequences of physical violence, verbal assault has been used to maintain interreligious rivalries.[69] Hate speech has been hurled at opponents to declare one religion's superiority over another.

---

[67] Falola, *Violence in Nigeria*, 138.
[68] Falola, *Violence in Nigeria*, 179.
[69] This is similar to the verbal violence that characterizes the resistance to colonial rule (and now postcolonial dictatorship) by the political elites, through literature, press, and media (and now social media).

Stereotypes, misconceptions, and deliberate misinterpretation of holy books have been encouraged. Extremism and political propaganda are accompanied by simmering hatred and sermons delivered by clerics in churches and mosques that are interjected with (subtle) condemnation of other religions, promising that the souls of religious rivals would be cast into undying flame. Incessant proclamations of intolerance and hatred within these religions threatens the peace, integration, and growth of Nigerian society.

Nigerians seem to have lost all hope and interest in the existence of the nation, forgetting the trials and triumphs of early nationalists. But interreligious and other types of violence can be quelled, and hope can be restored. The narrative of violence doesn't seek to merely historicize it or intellectualize the discourse, but to study its causes, identify its symptoms, highlight its consequences, and proffer solutions for the harmonization and progress of society. Ultimately: "What can prevent the tension from degenerating to prolonged violence and the breakup of Nigeria is better political and economic management by a patriotic political class genuinely committed to change and the construction of a nation-state that is sensitive to the needs and concerns of a multi-religious, multiethnic society."[70]

Conclusion

The need for narrative is evident. Beyond recounting events, experiences, and people, along with reflecting sensibilities, there is a pressing desire to understand the present and enhance the future. My career and my existence have been dedicated to narrating, harnessing, and curating African narratives. Employing narrative as conscience-driven politics can highlight socioeconomic and political ills and proffer sustainable solutions. The politics of historical narrative, beyond establishing true historical incidents, can gear society toward collective development, returning us to the restoration stories that inspire change and growth.

---

[70] Falola, *Violence in Nigeria*, 303.

PART III

Visual Cultures

9

Sculpture as Archive

The Yorùbá are renowned for many accomplishments. Their religiosity is an approach to cosmic understanding, embedded in the fabric of reality and serving as a spiritual signpost to guide their existence through time and space. Their worldview is replete with instructive codes, culturally rich concepts, and pedagogical idioms framed from the ground up to advance their collective philosophy as diplomatic people with a rich mythico-traditional consciousness. Their artwork supports a judicious system of thought, in tune with their religiosity and serving as beacons of a flourishing culture – continually referencing, revering, and expressing devotion to the pantheon of spiritual deities (Òrìṣà) they consider themselves indebted to. These accomplishments substantiate the presence of a vibrant spatial and temporal consciousness, and an awareness of past, present, and future possibilities.

Yorùbá art, as a body of stylized and symbolic aesthetics, is an active and agentive institution that represents aspects of the sociocultural order that feeds into it. This assertion is supported by sculpture and sculptural tradition: Yorùbá history and culture can be perceived, interpreted, and understood from Yorùbá carvings as clearly as linguistic expressions or texts. Adesanya attests that the Yorùbá carving tradition is a plain and unambiguous manifestation of the tradition that gives it life and meaning.[1]

Yorùbá traditions of bronze, clay, stone and wood carving – which for ease of reference will be discussed simply as sculpture and carving traditions[2] – are products of many influences. Sculpture, like any art, is never performed in a vacuum. Instead, its soul and contours are formed within a "cultural

---

[1] Aderonke Adesanya, *Carving Wood, Making History: The Fakeye Family, Modernity, and Yoruba Woodcarving* (Trenton: Africa World Press, 2012), 106.

[2] Sculpture is mainly considered as a generic name for the art of sculpting images or other objects. A sculptor can employ bronze, wood, or stone as materials. Some sculptors in Yorùbáland, and Africa in general, have used clay to create images and statuettes. Artists in Ifẹ̀, a region in southwestern Nigeria that is dominated by and belongs to the Yorùbá race, are famous for their bronze heads. (See A. K. Quarcoo, "Yoruba Religious Carving: Pagan and Christian Sculpture in Nigeria and Dahomey by Kevin Carroll," *Journal of Religion in Africa* 4, no. 2 [1971]: 137–141.) For the purpose of this chapter, sculpture is interchangeably used with wood carving.

envelope."[3] This expression, highlighting the relationship between carving as an institution and culture as its foundation, describes the creative systems and thought processes that attend the creation of an image, supporting the tradition in general. The Yorùbá carver draws from his wealth of experience as a cultural participant, infusing his acquired knowledge into his creations.

Yorùbá sculptors manipulate natural elements into artistic objects. In proper and specific terms, they are regarded as Gbẹ̀nàgbẹ̀nà or Gbẹ́gilére,[4] which are referent-specific appellations. The terms signify the carver's creative capacity, producing objects for adornment/ornamental purposes, religious purposes, or utilitarian functions. Figures 9.1 and 9.2 exemplify the wide array of purposes and ideas that sculpted images can represent. Masks often serve religious purposes, while statuettes and posts, which are often elaborate with complex designs like Figures 9.1 and 9.2 carry ornamental, materialist, social, or religious-spiritual value.

The linguistic etymology of Gbẹ̀nàgbẹ̀nà/Gbẹ́gilére reveals the creative orientation of sculptural tradition among the Yorùbá. To Gbẹ́ (verb) is to create, specifically to carve. Igi is wood. Ère is an image. Gbẹ́gilére is a compound word that evokes active visual imagery: "to carve wood to image." It also translates as "to carve wood into image" or "image from wood," but these do not embody the same weight of signification as the first interpretation. These translations connote the wood carver's inventive prowess, conjuring aesthetically pleasing products out of a previous state. This transformative power means that society often expects the Gbẹ́gilére to Pa igi dà, to transform wood.[5]

This power framework is one of the main reasons the wood carver and his art, in the context of Yorùbá sculptural tradition, is the first ideological juncture in unlocking the rich meanings embedded within the firmament of Yorùbá artistry. This[6] is reflected in Adesanya's view that "the Yorùbá nurtured the tradition [of carving] with religious intensity as they required sacred images to connect with their many deities, prestige objects to celebrate their leadership, and utilitarian carvings for everyday use."[7] The Yorùbá passionately favor unbroken ties to history and culture, considering them essential to the Yorùbá identity, which demands[8] that a sculptor and his art are to be regarded as ambassadors.

---

[3] Olabiyi Babalola Yai, "Tradition and the Yoruba Artist," *African Arts* 3, no. 1 (1999): 32–35, at 34.

[4] See Adesanya, *Carving Wood*.

[5] Yai, "Tradition."

[6] The indispensability of the carver and his artistic offerings in understanding the ideologies behind their creation, the cultural principles activating the sculptures as totems and signs, and the metaphors they signify.

[7] Adesanya, *Carving Wood*, 1.

[8] This has been recorded as changing due to modernity and neocolonialism. See Adesanya, *Carving Wood*, 3 and Eva Meyerowitz's 1943 records on how the old Yorùbá aesthetic is degenerating (Eva R. Meyerowitz, "Wood-Carving in the Yoruba Country To-day," *Journal of the International African Institute* 14, no. 2 [1943]: 66–70), undermined by

Figure 9.1 Acrobatic dancers

many Western influences. The advent of modernity and the forceful incursion of the West and its philosophies into the African socio-sphere has had a drastic, negative impact on old Yorùbá notions of aesthetics and artistry.

Figure 9.2 *Egúngún Abale* mask

A sculptor's worth, which cannot be measured in Western currency, is judged first by the aesthetics of their creativity as embedded in the spiritual and sociocultural depth of their works, the quality of their patronage (by spiritual leaders, royalty, and elites of the society), and the number of homes graced by their artwork. Yorùbá carvers are evaluated by the wealth of ideas propagated through their art, the eminent personalities they celebrate, and the degree of inventiveness they achieve with their hands and imagination. One example of such inventiveness is well rendered in the idea of the "visual *Oríkì*" (invocative praise), in relation to Yorùbá art, propounded by Abiodun, which privileges a conceptual reading of visual art as power-laden items responsive (possessing the quality of *Ìlùtí*) to appropriate invocations – as a result of specific religio-aesthetic choices made by the artists in their construction – and capable of inducing the demonstration of spiritual power.[9]

These currencies are foreign to Western epistemologies and art critics, who may fail to grasp their use as transactional materials for fame and longevity.[10]

---

[9] Rowland Abiodun, "Ase: The Empowered Word Must Come to Pass," in *Yoruba Art and Language: Seeking the African in African Art* (Cambridge: Cambridge University Press, 2014), 53–87.

[10] T. J. H. Chappel, "A Woodcarving from Abeokuta," *African Arts* 15, no. 1 (1981): 38–43, at 40 discusses how the low-ranking trade generated little income. Meyerowitz, "Wood-Carving in the Yoruba Country To-day," reveals the decline of the art form in cities – like Ibadan – where it once flourished. There were few practitioners, engaged in other "seemingly worthwhile" trades.

Some Yorùbá artists are selected to live in royal courts, attending to the political and stature-specific desires of royalty, while some are given wives – as was the case with the father of Lamidi Fakeye, one of the most renowned woodcarvers in Yorùbá history.[11] The carver drives a medium through which the Yorùbá culture is reenergized through time and place.[12] The medium is the art itself, what David Doris considers to be the "visual guidepost of moral excellence"[13] and Abiodun postulates as the visual symbol of "an enigmatic and performative motive force"[14] otherwise called Àṣẹ.

Both the driver and the medium become agentive in social coordination because a carved image is a visual marker of an artist's stylistic and religio-cultural orientation. An artist is a social being, meaning that the artist is the sole living product of the various social processes that were witnessed, participated in, and contributed to. Through artistry and sculpture the carver becomes an agent of the prevalent social ethos, in the artist's immediate setting and for the entire Yorùbá race – there is an interrelation between the myths, religiosity, history, and philosophies of various Yorùbá groups,[15] culminating in a pan- Yorùbá

---

[11] Adesanya, Carving Wood, 1–2.
[12] Works such as Henry Louis Gates, Jr., *The Signifying Monkey: A Theory of African-American Literary Criticism* (Oxford: Oxford University Press, 1988) and Baba Raul Canizares, *Eshu-Eleggua Elegbara* (New York: Original Publications, 2000) have discussed the translocation, retention, and continued existence of African – especially Yorùbá – traditions, culture, and art in the New World and the Americas. Knowledge systems, such as the *Ifá* corpus, have been traced to diasporic Yorùbá formations in Brazil and Cuba. Òrìṣà (deities) like Èṣù (Ẹlégbárá), whose diasporic linguistic identity is *Eshu*, has also been identified in the New World. Canizares identifies the god as Esu Eleggua. Adesanya discusses the presence of a similar degree of cultural emphasis placed on *Ìbejì* (twins) by the Yorùbá in western Sudan and the presence of an *Ìbejì* (twins) cult in Brazil and among the Fon. These are only some of the Yorùbá traditions flourishing across geographical boundaries.
[13] David Doris's phrase is reminiscent of the premium placed on good morals and behavior, which is linguistically coded as Ọmọlúàbí. Individuals who lean toward acceptable codes of conduct, expected social behavior, and approved morals are engineered into arts. This enables them serve as signage, bearing semiotic material that precludes truancy, encourages morality, and threatens grave repercussions against acts of truancy. For more explanation on Yorùbá arts and aesthetics as symbols of repercussions for social transgressions see Davis Doris, "Symptoms and Strangeness in Yoruba Anti-Aesthetics," *African Arts* 38, no. 4 (2005): 24–31, at 24.
[14] Abiodun, "Ase," 57.
[15] Some of the Yorùbá groups, identified by Olatunji Ojo, as multiple Yorùbá ethnicities – despite their affinities – are Koko, Bunu, Èkìtì, Ìjẹ̀ṣà, Ìgbómìnà, Ijumu, Ìkálẹ̀, Ìlàjẹ, Oǹdó, Òwè, Òwò, Òwòrò, and Yagba in eastern Yorùbáland; Àwórì, Ẹ̀gbá, Ifẹ̀, Ìjẹ̀bú, Ọ̀yọ́ and Òwu in the center; and Ànà, Ànàgó, Ẹ̀gbádò, Ìdáìṣà, Ìṣà, Manigri, Kétu, Ọ̀họ́rí, and Ṣábẹ̀ in western Yorùbáland. Each group had its sub-units: Èkìtì was divided into sixteen chiefdoms; Ọ̀yọ́ consisted of the metropolitan, Ibọlọ, Ìbàràpá, and Epo districts; Ẹ̀gbá had Aké, Gbágura, and Òkeọnà divisions; and Ìlàje was carved into Ìkálẹ̀, Máhín, and Ùgbò chiefdoms. The argument is that up until the nineteenth century these ethnicities largely existed as independent groups before being fused together into what is now the Yorùbá race. See Olatunji Ojo, "'Heepa' (Hail) Òrìṣà: The Òrìṣà Factor in the Birth of Yoruba

consciousness. Cultural ideas, such as *Ọmọlúàbí*, *Ìrẹ̀lẹ̀* (humility), *Sùúrù* (patience), *Ìfarabalẹ̀* (calmness), *Inú-rere* (goodwill), *Akíkanjú* (bravery), *Ìtẹríba* (respect), *Ìsòtítọ́* (truthfulness), and *Ìwàpẹ̀lẹ̀* (gentility), among others[16] are common and essential to all Yorùbá groups.[17] Each group places a premium on them. *Ọmọlúàbí* is a concept that encodes much, if not all, of the Yorùbá people's philosophy and theories on character and morals. It is an organizing principle, or an epistemological construct that unveils reality as a simple concept.

The existence of these qualities in an individual, and their performance in relation to existing codes, creates methodical interaction of signs within a social system, leading to the individual's assessment as *Ọmọlúàbí*. There is a synchronization of contextual codes with personal codes, which may be the reason why Akinyemi considers the principles of Yorùbá traditional education to be founded upon the concept of *Ọmọlúàbí*.[18] The *Ọmọlúàbí* is the standard for an ideal being, a principle that organizes collective interaction and espouses the depersonalized state of excellence that others should aspire to. A sculptor's images (see Figure 9.3) suggest the philosophies within this organizing principle, engaging the society in a dialogic process to establish what is acceptable and to serve as the meeting point for this social interaction.

The term *Ọmọlúàbí* itself has undergone a blending of several linguistic categories. *Ọmọ* (child) + *tí* (that) + *olú* (lord) + *ìwà* (character) + *bí* (birthed). Olanipekun states that the terms translate as the "baby begotten by the chief [lord] of Ìwà,"[19] who happens to be the deity of character. Alternatively, it can be interpreted as *Ọmọ* (child) + *tí* (that) + *Olúwa* (Lord) + *bí* (birthed). The reason a child begotten by the Supreme Being should or would embody the best of good conduct is not far-fetched. Johnson considers the term to mean the summit of character;[20] this standard decides what is moral or immoral in Yorùbá societies. Akanbi and Jekayinfa emphasize the place of this concept in the Yorùbá value system:

Identity," *Journal of Religion in Africa* 39, no. 1 (2009): 30–59. See also Adesanya, *Carving Wood*; and Henry John Drewal, John Pemberton III, Rowland Abiodun, and Allen Wardwell, eds., *Yoruba: Nine Centuries of African Art and Thought* (New York: Center for African Art and Harry N. Abrams Inc., 1989), discussing the Western tendency to harmonize the group-specific art customs of Yorùbá ethnicities into a monolithic Yorùbá art tradition.

[16] Adesanya, *Carving Wood*; Olusola Olanipekun, "Omoluabi: Rethinking the Concept of Virtue in Yoruba Culture and Moral System," *Africology: The Journal of Pan African Studies* 10, no. 9 (2017): 217–231.

[17] Rowland Abiodun, "African Aesthetics," *Journal of Aesthetic Education* 34, no. 4 (2001): 15–23.

[18] Akintunde Akinyemi, *Orature and Yorùbá Riddles* (New York: Palgrave Macmillan Civic Education, Peace Building and the Nigerian Youths, 2015).

[19] Olanipekun, "Omoluabi," 219.

[20] Samuel Johnson, *The History of the Yorubas* (Lagos: CSS Bookshops, 1921).

Figure 9.3 *Ọ̀rúnmìlà Baba Ifá*

> The end of Yoruba traditional education is to make every individual "Omoluabi." To be "Omoluabi" is to be of good character. That is why the goal of Yoruba traditional education has always been to foster strong character in the individual and to prepare each person to become a useful member of the community.[21]

The concepts signified by these carvings, which are identifiers of morals, suggest a cyclical mode of inspiration. The wood carver is a creator-agent, the carving itself is a totemic text, and society is the envelope within which both find relevance. The Yorùbá consider a carved image symbolic in relation to this cyclical mode of inspiration as an open-ended process of contemplation.

---

[21] G. O. Akanbi and A. A. Jekayinfa, "Reviving the African Culture of 'Omoluabi' in the Yoruba Race as a Means of Adding Value to Education in Nigeria," *International Journal of Modern Education Research* 3, no. 3 (2016): 13–19, at 13.

The Yorùbá carving tradition is an archival system; the Yorùbá tend to their sculptures with religious devotion, and they are regarded as deeply spiritual. They express spiritual sentimentality in and through their arts. The Yorùbá pantheon is deeply revered, and their deities are worshiped with judiciousness. One of the unifying factors among the groups within the enclave of Yorùbá tradition is their pantheon. Their devotion to this pantheon establishes them as a highly spiritual and spirited people constantly communing with the otherworldly elements that surround them.

Polemics centered on the religiosity and spirituality of Yorùbá art have been engendered by notions like the ones above. Quarcoo[22] espouses the idea that Yorùbá art should not be made prey to a straitjacket taxonomy, where even abstract and naturalistic sculptures are labeled religious, collapsing an expansive tradition into a single whole. Quarcoo lends credence to this vulnerability in Yorùbá art theorizing and criticism, casting light on what he considers "the fallacy of labelling all 'African sculpture' as religion-orientated or motivated," refracting Carroll's emphasis on the "rudimentary pedagogic principle of reaching the unknown from the known,"[23] expanding the context of interpretation.[24] Although Yorùbá art can be abstract – stylized and

---

[22] Quarcoo, "Yoruba Religious Carving."
[23] Quarcoo, "Yoruba Religious Carving," 137.
[24] It is too insular to put all Yorùbá sculpture into one pigeonhole of "art with a religious background" or "art for religion." This argument, sustained by Quarcoo, has merits; it has already been recognized by recent art historians, anthropologists, and sociologists who examine society through art. One such scholar is Adesanya, who discusses the aesthetics and sociological functions of house posts, which are mainly for ornamental and other prestige-related purposes (Adesanya, *Carving Wood*). Meyerowitz ("Wood-Carving in the Yoruba Country To-day") identifies doors, stools, cups, kola-nut containers, knives, and many other objects as carvings created for utilitarian, everyday purposes. In an attempt to balance the extreme positions, Peter Osegi categorizes African art, and Yorùbá art by extension, on the basis of aesthetics, mode of pedagogy, function, and temporality, classifying artists into traditional, non-college-trained modern and college-trained modern sculptors/artists (Peter Osegi, "Contemporary African Art: The College-Trained Modernist," *Visual Art Research* 17, no. 2 [1991]: 56–59). Traditional artists are mostly responsible for the religious carvings employed by ritual cults and for ritual purposes; they are given strict parameters to follow. One example is recorded in Henry Drewal's "Art and the Perception of Women in Yoruba Culture," *Cahiers d'Études Africaines* 17, no. 68 (1977): 545–567, concerning Gèlèdé art, where the Ìyá Nlá mask is created with a specific type of wood, by specific sculptors following ritual-specific procedures, and only employed for the Gèlèdé performance. For this category of artists "creative inspiration and aesthetic consideration may be secondary to function" (Osegi, "Contemporary African Art," 56). Non-college-trained modern artists are more secular, creating most works for material purposes, while college-trained modern artists are mostly aesthetes, embodying the principle of art for art's sake. Osegi places the Òṣogbo school in the non-formal/college-trained modernists category of artists, separating it from other schools based on the nature of their foreign patrons – a continuation of the patron-influenced artistry specific to traditional artists. This group is argued to be first

naturalistic, and cult carvings exist[25] – the very religious nature of the Yorùbá, as a body of people with defined myths and philosophies, does not afford nonfunctional interpretations of art. This draws the problem of the insider–outsider dialectic to the center of discussion.

The direct and almost formulaic association of Yorùbá sculpture with religious contexts is a result of mythico-historical affiliations, the nature of the Yorùbá epistemic systems, the political character pervading their socio-sphere, and the nature of their festivities. It is almost impossible to miss the relation between spirituality and Yorùbá sculptures. The Yorùbá favor cult associations; there is the *Ifá* cult, the *Orò* cult, the *Ṣàngó* cult, and the *Ògbóni* cult.[26] According to Meyerowitz, "there exist many different forms of worship of the gods in human shape which make innumerable cult-objects and the decoration of temples and sacred shrines a necessity, while other cults demand the carving of masks. There are many masquerade performances in Yorubaland.[27] These Èfè/Gèlèdé and Egúngún cults demand masks for their performances."[28]

Masquerade performances, while diverse, are united by elements that include ideology and custom.[29] The ideology is the Yorùbá belief in the continued existence of life after death. It is the principle behind the continued invocation of and supplication performed for ancestral spirits (see Figure 9.4), keeping them invested in the activities of the living. Figures 9.5 and 9.6 are examples of masks with religious significance; other examples are Figures 9.7–9.13. Some of the masks are never carved without following ritualized procedures. The *Egúngún* is a generic popular term for the Yorùbá masquerade tradition, whether cloth, fiber, or masks are used – combinatorial specificities exist along the lines of sub-groups and ethnicities.[30]

The cult-specific procedures performed before and after creating these materials, especially the masks, involve the properties of their respective

and foremost about imagination and inspiration. As such, owing to the nature of their white patrons, they are particular about creating aesthetic experiences in their works. The informal school artists have been touted by many as the primary vehicle for keeping art in Africa alive and as the group that can lead Africa to an artistic renaissance (F. Willett, *African Art* [London: Thames & Hudson, 1971]). However, Odita warns that informal school artists, such as the Òṣogbo, remove traditional forms from their original contexts without adapting them to fit new contexts, obscuring traditional motifs and defeating the aforementioned purpose.

[25] See Adesanya, *Carving Wood*; Abiodun, "African Aesthetics"; Babatunde Lawal, "The Living Dead: Art and Immortality among the Yoruba of Nigeria," *Journal of the International African Institute* 47, no. 1 (1977): 50–61.
[26] Ojo, "Heepa."
[27] See Adesanya, *Carving Wood*, for extended exposition.
[28] Meyerowitz, "Wood-Carving in the Yoruba Country To-day," 66.
[29] "Custom" is used to mean that each falls under the cloth, fiber, or mask types of customs. Specificity in terms of artistry, origin, and end product now differs.
[30] See Adesanya *Carving Wood* for further elaboration on mask and fiber combination, and cloth and masks among the Ọyọ and Ijẹbu respectively.

Figure 9.4 Homage to *Ìyálọ̀jà*

cults. The *Egúngún* costume, or more appropriately, the cloth and the mask ensemble, is usually put together by a cultic representative. A herbalist, diviner, or priest oversees the necessary propitiatory or invocatory ritual to ensure the successful execution of the performance itself.[31] This is necessary because the rationale behind most *Egúngún* performances,[32] whether *Èfè/Gèlèdé, Agẹmọ, Èyọ̀*, or other second-burial practices,[33] is the invocation of ancestral spirits to celebrate their lives and to request their continued influence over the affairs of the living. Most *Egúngún* festivals are spiritualized ceremonies, signifying the religiosity and extraterrestrial and eschatological beliefs of the Yorùbá people. Lawal says that through the carved mask employed in this festival, "the soul of

---

[31] Adesanya, *Carving Wood*.
[32] The *Egúngún*, as explained above, can be group-specific, in which case it can be referred to as *Egúngún* cult, traceable to Ọ̀yọ́. As explained by Adesanya, it can also be employed as a generic name for all mask traditions.
[33] Because there are no ancestral markers – the point of masquerade traditions – in Ife, Henry Drewal makes a case for the tradition enacted for deceased hunters at Ife. Henry Drewal, "Arts and Ethos of the Ijebu," in *Yoruba: Nine Centuries of African Art and Thought*, ed. Drewal et al., 117–145.

Figure 9.5 Witchcraft mask I

a departed ancestor returns to earth in a physical form to inquire about the welfare of his living descendants."[34] The mask, created by a carver, is the ethereal screen or medium between the worlds of the living and the dead.

In the process of carving an Ìyá Ńlá mask for the Èfè/Gèlèdé performance, a wood carver is given a specific type of wood.[35] All the elders in the town, regardless of cult affiliations, must bring these pieces to the carver.[36] An elaborate sacrificial ceremony, to ensure success, must take place before work begins. A white goat, white cock, white pigeon (Eyelé), oil, kola, and one piece of white cloth with ten pounds (typical gifts of Òrìṣà funfun) are offered. After the mask's completion the elders immediately take it to the shrine, where a final application of charms endows it with spiritual force, making it the embodiment of Ìyánla.[37] In this context, Yorùbá carving cannot

[34] Lawal, "The Living Dead," 57.
[35] Drewal calls it Iroko, which is coincidentally a strong and sturdy tree that is famous for being the abode of witches.
[36] Drewal, "Arts and Ethos," 554.
[37] Drewal, "Arts and Ethos," 554.

Figure 9.6 Ọlọ́jọ́ festival mask I

be divorced from its spirituality, even if certain masquerade performances are meant for entertainment. Consequently, its reading has to pay attention to the process of each carving's assemblage: in the case of the masquerade and the mask, every material that goes into their preparation helps in forming a spiritually charged atmosphere that imbues the items with *Àṣẹ* of the proper deity or *Òrìṣà*, and also redefines them (raw materials) from mere physical items to the visual *Oríkì* that, when matched with appropriate verbal *Oríkì*, "activate, actualize, and direct socio-political, religious, and artistic processes and experiences."[38]

The abundance of sculptures in the temples of these gods results from a need to bridge the gap between the Yorùbá people and their *Òrìṣàs*. In their role as constituents of a shrine/system, they also aid in creating spiritualized aestheticized spaces. Put differently, their combination to differentiate deities makes them visual signifiers, what Abiodun appropriately calls visual *Oríkì*. They thus can emphasize the benevolence and power of these *Òrìṣà*, signaling the

[38] Abiodun, "Ase," 83.

Figure 9.7 Ọlọ́jọ́ festival mask II

importance of unwavering devotion on the part of worshipers. In this sense, images of the Òrìṣà[39] signify spiritual potency; in the case of carvings found in Èṣù shrines, they can be codes referencing the Òrìṣà's ethos and prowess. They can also host the presence of an Òrìṣà, like the anthropomorphic Èṣù statuettes (see Figures 9.14 and 9.15), especially after having verbal Oríkì (invocations) applied to them.

In a shrine, the spiritualized atmosphere created by associated cult images creates the ambience necessary to supplicate or invoke an Òrìṣà.

---

[39] Some ethnographic scholars and historians argue that Yorùbá Òrìṣàs are not anthropomorphized. However, Òrìṣà may be represented by tempered symbols signifying their essence or ethos, or dematerialized personage, like the thunderbolt in the case of Ṣàngó (god of thunder) or through cult-specific materials. See Lawal, "The Living Dead." In most cases, an Òrìṣà like Èṣù is anthropomorphized, but Olódùmarè (the creator) is never anthropomorphized because it is believed that no one is capable of knowing the extent of his power or the magnitude of his being.

Figure 9.8 Drummers mask

Even when taken outside its religious context, an Èṣù statuette still maintains its semiotic content. It serves as a code, signifying the absence of an Òrìṣà because it has not been activated through the system of relation (or related cult carvings and images) found in a shrine. As visual signs, carvings also index the Yorùbá pantheon – especially when considering other statutes that do not necessarily anthropomorphize Òrìṣàs but which may have worshipers, devotees, and other cult-specific instruments as their referents. This lends credence to the argument that Yorùbá sculpture is an archive.

The Yorùbá do not take their Òrìṣàs lightly, treating representations of their dematerialized states with respect, returning us to the popular prayer "Òrìṣàgbèmí." This tradition of deep reverence is group-specific but essential among the Yorùbá, especially pre-Western contact, precolonial Yorùbá. This could be the reason why Yorùbá people are said to possess many different Òrìṣàs. The peculiar thing about this is that not all the gods are directly represented in sculpture, which is considered anthropomorphic. Unlike

Figure 9.9 *Egúngún* mask

many other gods, Èṣù, the god of the crossroads, is anthropomorphized (see Figures 9.16–9.21).[40]

The ubiquitous Yorùbá tradition and belief in the spirituality of *Ìbejì* (twins)[41] further demonstrates the archival properties of sculptures. The Yorùbá belief that sculpture can hold the spirits of *Ìbejì* is expressed through *Ìbejì* figurines (see Figure 9.22). The carvings, which are always in pairs, are symbolic and indexical. They symbolize the Yorùbá faith in Òrìṣà *Ìbejì* as a deity to be revered, and they

---

[40] See Gates, *The Signifying Monkey*, and Adesanya, *Carving Wood*, for detailed descriptions of the personage and character of Èṣù. Then Canizares, *Eshu-Eleggua Elegbara*, for the mannerisms, narratives/*Odùs* about, and manifestations of, Èṣù.

[41] Adesanya, *Carving Wood*, and Lawal, "The Living Dead," both talk about *Ìbejì* extensively and how *Ìbejì* figurines are both symbolic and indexical.

Figure 9.10 Fiber ware and mask

are indexical because when one *Ìbejì* dies, it is believed that the dead twin's spirit can be housed in one of the statuettes. Lawal, proffering an explanation for this, posits that "Although they are physically double, twins are regarded as spiritually one; that is, sharing only one soul between them. Therefore, if one of them should die, a statuette is made to house its 'half soul'; otherwise, the other half in the surviving twin may want to 'leave' to join its partner."[42] The indexical relation is self-referential. The statuette symbolizes its own existence, housing a human soul the way the body does. It is fed and washed by the parents and treated like a normal being, serving as a spiritual and psychological mark of extreme personification. Psychologically, it communicates the existence of the departed twin to its surviving partner.

[42] Lawal, "The Living Dead," 56.

Figure 9.11 Metal mask

Figure 9.12 Wooden mask

Figure 9.13 Witchcraft mask II

Figure 9.14 *Èṣù Ologo*

Figure 9.15 Èṣù Oníkóndó

The sense of purpose with which Yorùbá revere their Òrìṣà, some of which make up Figures 9.23–9.28, connects to their roots as a people and their beliefs about their origin, which itself betray a mythic orientation. The history of the Yorùbá as a race is populated with mythic themes and leitmotifs, spiritualizing their historical accounts and affording them a mythico-historical origin that is coded into their sculptural arts. Smith,[43] assessing this relationship between myth and history, agrees that although religious rituals and mythic motifs may

[43] Robert S. Smith, *Kingdoms of the Yoruba* (London: University of Wisconsin Press, 1969).

Figure 9.16 Èṣù Rogodo

have regional peculiarities – and they are usually related to histories of the local kingdoms – they also contain many mutual elements. These elements range from language, which is the currency for corporeal and spiritual identity, to the themes of the myths and the core substance of the histories found in these Yorùbá regions.

Daniel McCall has explained that "all areas recognize the seniority and primacy of Ife as the oldest kingdom and as a kind of religious center."[44] This common focus, he says, "helps to some extent to hold in check fissiparous and centrifugal tendencies that otherwise would lead to greater cultural differentiation."[45] In other words, it is easier to comprehend how each Yorùbá region's history can be fused into a coherent narrative (if not a single

[44] Daniel McCall, "The Marvelous Chicken and Its Companion in Yoruba Art and Myth," *Paideuma* 24 (1978): 131–146, at 135.
[45] McCall, "The Marvelous Chicken," 135.

Figure 9.17 Èṣù Mẹ́ta I

one), despite peculiarities, and how they betray mythic characters: it is all embedded in their carvings.

The absence of statuettes denoting, symbolically or index-wise, the stature of *Olódùmarè*, the Supreme Being, is itself the presence of an ideological agenda. This vacancy in the sculptural representations of the Yorùbá pantheon and, by extension, in Yorùbá spiritual ontology, shows the instructive capacity of Yorùbá sculpture to signify the *Kòláfiwé* (uniqueness) and incomprehensible attributes ascribed to the deity. *Olódùmarè* is the creator, all powerful, who created the world. As creator, *Olódùmarè* is called *Atẹ́rẹ́rẹ́-kárí-ayé* (one who spreads over the earth) because of their expansiveness. In considering this indescribable quality, Lawal identifies the entity as the sum total of all existence.

Figure 9.18 Èṣù Ẹlẹ́gbárá I

The narrative of Odùduwà (see Figure 9.23), said to be the father of the Yorùbá people, has the deity land from the sky with a chain at Ilé Ifẹ̀.[46] It is encoded in a statuette of a woman holding a bowl shaped in the form of a chicken, or with a lid shaped in that manner. McCall argues, with substantial proof, that this is a theme in Yorùbá art – six versions exist in various museums

---

[46] Ilé Ifẹ̀, as mentioned above, is the ancestral home of the Yorùbá. McCall explains that the name derives from the incident of creation, where a bird, a fowl, spread (Fẹ̀) earth brought in a snail shell (Ìkarahun) by Odùduwà over the water on the surface of the earth, using its legs/talons to create solid ground for Odùduwà to land. Ilé means home. Ilé Ifẹ̀ translates as "home of the spread," referencing the original act of spreading, forming the earth, that occurred in the earliest origin of Yorùbá history.

Figure 9.19 Èṣù Mẹ́ta II

and regions.[47] Three such statuettes, contained in my collection, are shared below. In Figure 9.29 the woman is in a standing position, carrying the bowl with the bird-shaped lid in her hands. The statue in Figure 9.30 shows a woman genuflecting on her knees with the bowl and its lifted bird-lid touching the ground. Figure 9.31, which may show the most detailed one of the three, has the woman kneeling with a baby strapped to her back. Her hands hold a basket of fruit, perhaps for propitiation, while the bowl and its stylized lid are securely positioned on her head. The bird is usually a rooster, except in Figure 9.30, where the fanned or spread protrusion of its feathered tail suggests a duck.

Odùduwà is considered a deity – something of a deified ancestor, although this deity is also an Aráọ̀run (a celestial being), making the deity an Òrìṣà – sent by Olódùmarè to continue the creation of the earth, progressing from where Ọbàtálá failed. The bird symbolizes the chicken employed by Odùduwà to disperse sand and dirt over a world that was already filled with water, forming

---

[47] See McCall, "The Marvelous Chicken," for exposition on the iconography and iconology of the statuette and its regional variations, as well as their locations.

Figure 9.20 Èṣù Láàlú Ògiri Òkò

solid ground. Some scholars, such as McCall, have argued that *Odùduwà* is a female deity, goddess of the earth, represented by the female figure that kneels. Others have ascribed a male gender to the deity. McCall's position, although reminiscent of a handful of others like his, is suspect, however, because it charts a Yorùbá history linking them with the Asians. Aside from this controversy on the gender of *Odùduwà*, and McCall's genealogy to Asia, what is paramount is how the sculptured image signifies this historical narrative and its implication for symbolically affirming Yorùbá heritage and Yorùbáland. As such, the act of kneeling signifies communion with the earth. The female figure can also be seen as *Odùduwà* or a representation of a worshiper.

The statuette's significance to the creation story and the place of the woman are not a one-to-one correlation between a deity and the form taken by its signifiers. This would negate the vitality of symbolism. The recurring appearance of a female entity establishing this theme suggests functional variation in

Figure 9.21 Èṣù flautist

Yorùbá artistry and narration; it is the synthesis of individuality and collectivity expressed through belief and artistic tradition, enabled by the fluidity of symbolism. The visible representation of an argument, cast in the form of sculpture, does not invalidate the multiple narratives it can signify, or how it can depict the androgynous nature of Yorùbá gods on a context-by-context basis. It is also an instructive statement that corrects any presumptuous knowledge about the significations of Yorùbá carvings and image/statuettes, since what they signify culturally, spiritually, and historically is highly contextual and based on the network of meaning, images, and spirico-mythical signification in which they are placed and found.

Figure 9.22 Ère Ìbejì

Yorùbá people carve their history, which is related to their myths, into their sculptures; the sculptures are modes of cosmic comprehension. This is seen in the figures used in the cult associated with Ṣàngó, the god of thunder (Figure 9.24). Ṣàngó is another deified ancestor, a king of old Ọ̀yọ́, with the unnatural ability to wield thunderbolts and breathe fire. Ṣàngó was forced to abdicate his throne, and committed suicide as a result. He was elevated by his devotees to become an Òrìṣà. Persons from history are represented in sculptural forms found in Ṣàngó's shrine, such as Oya (Figure 9.25), a river goddess and Ṣàngó's wife, and Olúmọ̀mí, an old Ọ̀yọ́ princess.[48] In representing Ṣàngó's wives, Oya, Ọ̀ṣun (Figure 9.27), and Yemọja (see Figure 9.26) – all river goddesses – in Ṣàngó's shrine, the Yorùbá signify the place and prowess of these women whose waters succeeded in calming the fires of Ṣàngó after each of the many times he became enraged. Another example is Figure 9.32, which is a stylization of the Òrìṣà Ògún.

The importance of Yorùbá carving as a system of archiving Yorùbá reality is revealed by the industry, level of artistry, and spiritual consciousness put into

---

[48] See Adesanya, *Carving Wood*, 100–104.

Figure 9.23 *Odùduwà*

each piece of sculpture. Each work, through significations that find immediate referent in history or the present reality, is a language with an intelligible quality. Each one is a communicable idiom that can be understood by those within the culture from which it draws its influences and with whom it dialogues. Yorùbá sculptures reinforce the spiritual, mythical, artistic, sociocultural, and historical dimensions that support the Yorùbá as a race of people with unique histories. By communicating these dimensions, the sculptures demonstrate their archival propensities, historicizing and reporting on the ancient lives of Yorùbá people. This may be why Quarcoo submits that Yorùbá art illustrates Yorùbá history: the court, cults, festivities, and agrarian lifestyles, along with domestic lives, principles, and other aspects of everyday living seen in Figures 9.33–9.37.

Before making an iconology of the images that have prompted this chapter, we must examine some of the pertinent issues surrounding Yorùbá sculpture and iconography. This involves a critical survey of notions such as modernity

Figure 9.24 Oṣé Ṣàngó

in Yorùbá art and secularism versus religiosity. Yorùbá concepts and methodologies of understanding should also be discussed for two reasons: first, as a call to deviate from Western epistemological principles and embrace Yorùbá concepts in assessing Yorùbá art as nodes of aesthetical, religio-cultural, and secular/historical ideologies, accessing and unlocking the cultural codes embedded in them. The second reason is to present culturally coded Yorùbá concepts as epistemological frames.

Yorùbá Wood Carving and the Insider–Outsider Polemic

Much of Yorùbá tradition is subject to external terms of critical mode of inquiry, and principles of examination are from the alien and foreign perspective of Eurocentrism. Criticism of the Yorùbá carving tradition is no exception. The assertion that Yorùbá carving should not be appreciated with religio-mythical considerations is insular, promoting Western principles of art criticism that celebrate abstract and secular aestheticism over functionality.

Figure 9.25 Ọya (wife of Ṣàngó)

Kevin Carroll and other scholars have questioned the notion of spiritual symbolism as dominant in Yorùbá arts as asserted by African scholars. These concerns have been raised in response to the range of artistry and artistic influences expressed in such works, which include a broad variety of objects and even cooking utensils.[49] This may seem correct, but close examination reveals some problems: it glosses over the fact that spirituality itself is a source of inspiration for Yorùbá carvers – this position has been established by Osegi, Adesanya, Lawal, and many others. Lawal argues that "even in sculpture the

---

[49] See Quarcoo, "Yorùbá Religious Carving."

Figure 9.26 *Yemọja*

traditional carver begins with and emphasizes the head, the other parts of the human body being drastically abbreviated, as if to stress their physical and metaphysical subservience."[50]

This emphasis on the head is true of all Yorùbá art. In the second-burial practices that are dominant in Ife,[51] the head as a naturalistic art is attached to a wooden support. The ideology establishes an iconic relation between the dead and the effigies representing them. In such contexts, the emphasis placed on the head creates a final product that is always some sort of iconic image, bearing facial similarities with its referent, to enhance the ritual potency of the funerary activity. To paint a clearer picture of how the head functions in this context, Lawal explains:

> A good number of the naturalistic representations in Yorùbá art serve in a funerary context. For instance, a few days or weeks after the corpse has

[50] Babatunde Lawal, "The Significance of the Head in Yoruba Sculpture," *Journal of Anthropological Research* 41, no. 1 (1985): 91–103, at 94.
[51] See Drewal, "Arts and Ethos"; Lawal, "The Living Dead."

Figure 9.27 Òṣun

been interred, there is a second-burial ceremony. A naturalistic life-size effigy of the deceased is made; it is then dressed in the finest clothes of the deceased and paraded round the town, and finally buried like a corpse. The human surrogate is then led in a procession round the town. If the deceased was a chief, the human surrogate will be greeted and addressed like a chief. However, the human surrogate is not buried like the wooden effigy.[52]

In the case above, the head functions as an iconic image. With a full-bodied effigy, the head is enhanced to create an image that is an iconic diagram: a systematic arrangement of signs, none of which necessarily resembles the referent, but which mirror their referents' relationships in their relationship to each other. Every part of a statuette is a sign, with referents that are parts of the human body – as a full statuette, it becomes a system or relation of signs.

In the cases where the head is extremely big or disproportionate to every other body part, as in many stylized and abstract Yorùbá sculptures, it mirrors

[52] Lawal, "The Living Dead," 52.

Figure 9.28 Ògún

the metaphysical and spiritual emphasis placed on the head as the most vital part of the body. In other words, each statuette performs an active and vibrant spiritual evangelization.[53] The emphasis that the Yorùbá place on *Orí* and its metaphysical connotations engenders the maxim "Òrìṣà wo là bá bọ bí kò ṣe órí" (which deity should we worship if not the head?). Even a simple image,

---

[53] It is believed that the *Orí* (head) has two parts: *Oríinú* (internal) and *Orí òde* (external). *Oríinú* is molded by *Ajala Alámọ̀*, the deity in charge of molding heads. It contains *Àṣẹ*, the essence of power breathed into man by *Olódùmarè*. *Oríinú* emphasizes the individualistic destiny of man, charging a person's destiny and inspiring the phrase "Oríburúkú òṣeéyàn" (a bad head/destiny is not to be chosen). In Yorùbá cosmology a person chooses their head/destiny before coming to earth – after *Ọbàtálá* molds a body and *Olódùmarè* breathes life into it, each creature selects the *Orí* for their time on the planet. In the case of repeated misfortunes, an individual is asked "Irú orí wo lo yàn" (what kind of head did you choose?) This *Orí*, *Oríinú*, is a metaphysical codification of destiny. See Lawal, "Significance."

Figure 9.29 *Ajere Ifá (Olúkòso)*

seeming to evoke the unique biological bond between mother and child, is depicted only with a carving of heads to signify the primacy of *Orí* in Yorùbá ontology. A careful examination of Figure 9.37, with Yorùbá philosophy in mind, will reveal that the essences uniting both beings are contained in the head. Other body parts are not included.

Claims like Carroll's reject what Quarcoo describes as the "effective evangelization"[54] of Yorùbá sculptures. For a participant in the culture, even when that participant is an outsider with minimal substantive interaction with its arts, cognitive transfer is at play during the appreciation or decoding of the motifs and themes loaded into the images. This transfer is only possible for non-insular minds. By unpacking various semantic materials deduced from Yorùbá sculptural arts, they are nudged toward recognizing religious elements or the presence of a spiritual consciousness.

[54] Quarcoo, "Yoruba Religious Carving," 138.

Figure 9.30 *Ajere Ifá (Olúmeye)*

Claims that undermine the religious symbolism of Yorùbá art are attempts to institute a non-functional appreciation of artwork, contravening the principles of holistic criticism. This explains the continued advocacy for a return to – or the use of – African indigenous concepts and discourses, in African languages, to investigate African cultural features. For Yai, "this will help us best perform our duties as *Gbẹ̀nugbẹ̀nu*."[55] He argues that critical commentaries in English can be made, and homage can still be paid to African artists, provided that indigenous concepts are revisited and checked against African-language art criticism. A failure to do so leads to intransitive discourses; such

---

[55] Yai ("Tradition") explains *Gbẹ̀nugbẹ̀nu* in terms of a Yorùbá appreciator of art, an aesthete explained as a critic who uses the power of rhetoric, which is both critical and steeped in cultural oratorical strategies, to evaluate the worth, beauty, and functionality of a work of art and its creator.

Figure 9.31 *Arugbá Ṣàngó*

discourses fail to highlight the cultural agents and processes that led to creation, resulting in a side-stepping of relevant history.

The corollary of this is the "pro-motion of dubious universals and all brands of what the French theorist, Roland Barthes, called 'white mythology.'"[56] This is not to say that Yorùbá sculpture cannot be secular, which would be as insular as the charges being refuted. The premise of the argument is to assert that functionally, and in terms of thought, ideology, and aesthetics, Yorùbá sculptural art is very symbolic of spirituality. Blinkered Yorùbá art criticism, and other challenges such as the difficulties of naming and authorship, can be

---

[56] Yai, "Tradition," 32.

Figure 9.32 *Ògún Lákáayé*

avoided by comprehending African and Yorùbá art within the linguistic and cultural contexts that give it life.

Yorùbá art has been criticized on nomenclatural principles. Those who hold Eurocentric biases and use Western theoretical categories in biased ways regard Yorùbá wood-carving tradition, and African art as a whole, as having authorship issues. It is not novel for African art to be addressed as anonymous by those who are external to its cultural practices. With this in mind, and advocating for a return to indigenously constructed critical concepts of understanding in African art criticism, Yai asks whether anonymous is a linguistic concept or whether it is indigenous to the traditions that are accused of having anonymous arts in their sculptural repertoire. The answer to this query is a categorical no.

The submission that anonymous is an indigenous concept in Yorùbá artistry, and the epistemic firmament of the Yorùbá, divorces it from the cultural

Figure 9.33 City drummers

peculiarities that birthed it. It reveals the narrow worldview and limited scholarship practiced by those who would not investigate this phenomenon, hurrying to agree that authorial self-naming of artwork is an absent tradition. The argument supporting this lopsided appreciation of African art history is the idea that the sculptor's identity is not a significant part of the work as it is perceived by the West and its art tradition.[57]

---

[57] Yai, "Tradition"; Abiodun, "African Aesthetics."

Figure 9.34 *Fúrá* seller (contemporary art figure)

The question to be asked is whether African artistry must conform to Western models. To approach the subject of nomenclature differently, one must wonder whether the anonymous tag, applied to African art, translates as the anonymity of African artists. Such conclusions, however indicated by such Western positions on African art, display the West's hegemonic superimposition over Africa in general. In defending African art against the charges of anonymity, Yai argues in favor of cultural specificity; notions of universality are covert colonial instruments. Yai submits that each culture has its own way of relating art forms to agents,[58] which is a truth that could not be stated better.

Abiodun declares that such conclusive positions of Western or Eurocentric art historians, ethnographic scholars, and critics are dubious. In his refutation, Abiodun asserts that "there is no doubt that establishing the authorship of a work of art, or associating specific forms with names, is important for the

[58] Yai, "Tradition," 33.

Figure 9.35 Contemporary art figure

Yoruba."[59] In African ontological space, naming is principal. A great amount of value is placed on names and the art of naming, or even authoring a creation – but discretion is of utmost importance. Yorùbá place a premium on discreetness and diplomacy. Even the discussion of art and its subsequent criticism is not without culture-specific strategies and diplomatic approaches. The art of naming itself is ritualized, and names are never uttered without taking precautions.[60] Abiodun explains one of the central reasons why the Yorùbá may not publicly or openly associate specific art forms with the names of their authors:

---

[59] Abiodun, "African Aesthetics," 18.
[60] For example, it is considered ill luck to speak a person's name when certain sacrifices are made.

Figure 9.36 Contemporary art figure

> Names given at birth are closely linked to and identified with the essence of one's personality and destiny (called oriinu, inner spiritual head), which in Yoruba religious belief determines [a] person's success or failure in this world and directs his or her actions. Though the act of calling out a person's given names generally functions to differentiate individuals, in the Yoruba religious thought system it is also believed to have the ability to arouse or summon to the surface a person's spiritual essence and cause him or her to act according to the meaning of those given names or in some other way desired by the caller.[61]

---

[61] Abiodun, "African Aesthetics," 18.

Figure 9.37 Mother and child motif

The naming system in many art traditions is culture specific, with its own rationalizations. Yorùbá artists, to avoid malicious interference, may avoid associating their real names to their work. They can use initials or stylize their work with specific embellishments that can signal their authorship. These embellishments are understood within the immediate context of creation, and even outside of it. Patrons, other aesthetes, *Gbẹ́nugbẹ́nu*, or members of society can ascribe correct authorship to specific works of art due to their familiarity with authorial patterns.

The authorship of specific artworks is decoded by *Gbẹ́nugbẹ́nu* – they have been described as oral aesthetes, persons with the critical intelligence to appreciate beauty, or oral critics because many pre-Western traditions of Yorùbá and African artistry are conducted orally. The absence of insignia or names on an art form does not indicate the assessor's ignorance of the sculptor's identity. When referring to Yorùbá art, and the art of naming, the unavailability of scribal evidence does not signify total absence.

Carvings for religious purposes automatically exclude author-specific signatures or inscriptions, due to the nature of their commission. Such carvings, commissioned by priests, herbalists, or other cult personalities, are integrated

Figure 9.38 Motherhood abstract figure

into a network of cult symbols. To aid their metamorphosis from works of art to religious totems, they must divest all secular signs and significations, whether physical or ideological.

The failure or negligence involved in omitting these factors from theories about Yorùbá art and artistry shows the foreign nature of alien concepts, such as anonymous artist and anonymity, along with their attendant meanings. To quote Yai, they are "colonial inventions, lacking descriptive and analytical relevance. Part of a vast terminological arsenal used by the West in its discourse about other cultures, they derive their truth value from uncritical repetition by generations of art critics, not from empirically and rationally established links with African cultural practices."[62] As Abiodun succinctly explains, such Eurocentric critics thought "the artifacts and the supporting traditional thought systems belonged to the Africans but that the interpretation and theorization of African art must always be theirs (that is, the early Western researchers)."[63]

---

[62] Yai, "Tradition," 38.
[63] Abiodun, "African Aesthetics," 18.

Hegemonic ideology underscores the nature of most (cultural) contact between the metropole, represented by Eurocentric scholars, and the postcolony. For a culture that founds its epistemological pride on the alleged superiority of the written word – one that derives its value judgments from logocentric positions – any contact with a phonocentric culture is perceived as an encounter with a culture devoid of structured knowledge systems. Critics who employ such terms as "anonymous" and "anonymous artists" in their assessments of Yorùbá art display their failure to grapple with the challenges of naming traditions outside their own social customs. This cognitive shortcoming may have fed the assumption that authorship is unimportant to the Yorùbá.

Such conceptions and their attendant supremacist impulses motivate the anti-aesthetic classifications of cultural and sculptural concepts, such as juju, fetish, and idol, when analyzing Yorùbá art and culture. Yorùbá sculptures portrayed in this light reflect the orientation of scholars who undertake such engagements – although the nature of their work requires them to take critical, objective, and unbiased postures, they reveal colonial subjectivity coming from the metropole in much of the theorizing on African art. It could be argued that these categories of understanding, however misinformed they may be, are scholars' attempts to emphasize the secularism of Yorùbá art, decentralizing the religiosity that is considered mainstream in Yorùbá art scholarship. This requires dubious intellectual manipulation, because there is no clear relationship between establishing a system of signification's secularity and demonizing it; any attempt to establish one will terminate in false conjectures.

There is also the matter of modernity in Yorùbá wood carving. Yorùbá artists, schematized by Osegi as belonging to either traditionalist or modernist groups comprising college-trained and non-college-trained artists, are not to be seen as members of a single class. Okeke's classification[64] does not treat African sculpture and its artists – as well as Yorùbá sculpture by implication – as a single monolithic tradition. They are sorted into traditionalist, transitional, and modern groups.

Modernity, meaning the themes of everyday life in the modern century, is well represented in Yorùbá sculpture. Yorùbá artists are products of their environment; it gives them their inspiration, and they produce works that mirror it. The so-called traditional artists have deviated from old Yorùbá lives to produce more than religious totems. And college-trained artists, who embrace the modernist spirit of nonconformity, defy the customary religious aesthetics of traditional artists.

---

[64] See Uche Okeke, "The Story of the Contemporary Art of Nigeria's Eastern States," *Ikoro: Bulletin of the Institute of African Studies, University of Nigeria, Nsukka* 1, no. 2 (1971): 35–46.

In explaining the non-college-trained artists, Osegi comments on the "tourist trade" artists. After leaving rural settings for the cities, they sculpt, carve, and mold images and objects that are remakes of traditional themes; their works are polished and sanded to look attractive. Because they are driven by profit, they can lack aesthetic originality. These artists are also called survivalists or souvenir artists.[65]

College-trained modern artists have received their training in institutions styled after Western artistic traditions. According to Okeke they constitute the major art establishments of the continent. They work for aesthetic purposes, producing more than local themes alone. They are also influenced by world themes and Western opinions. As a result, they have been accused of alienating themselves from traditional themes and established aesthetic values. For many college-trained modernists, drawing from African art traditions or using traditional themes can be seen as backpedaling.[66] As Osegi notes, this does not seem to prompt uproar because "academic art considerations and technical prowess have been confused with the progress and modernity that altered cultural traditions."[67] This summarizes the futile struggles of traditional practitioners and artists in an increasingly modern world. Any departures from classical approaches are seen as progress. However, the themes and traditions of contemporary modernity are also reflected in the works of Yorùbá carvers.

Traditional themes have been carved in modern styles. Figures 9.38–9.41 are a reinvention of the mother–child motif common among canonical Yorùbá sculpture; so also is Figure 9.37. Figures 9.39and 9.40, showing subjects with raised hands with objects cradled between them, are references to the Yorùbá emphasis on submission and postural diplomacy. The kneeling posture of the images, reinforcing acceptable Yorùbá behavior in the presence of spiritual deities, reinforces the *Arúgbá* theme. The indistinct features of the carved representations shown in Figure 9.9 embody fluidity and the absence of explicit visibility (*Ìfarahàn*). It contrasts sharply with the graphic and sharp styles of traditional artists that accentuate features. Fluidity has always been a feature of modernism.

Linguistic Return in Yorùbá Art Theorizing

It is impossible to overemphasize the argument for a return to traditional Yorùbá linguistic concepts in the appraisal of Yorùbá art. The use of foreign concepts, premised on and generated from Western philosophy, is inadequate for the unique requirements of African art; such activity can only lead to insular theorizing and counterintuitive approaches. Yorùbá art reflects

---

[65] Osegi, "Contemporary African Art," 56.
[66] Okeke, "Story of Contemporary Art."
[67] Osegi, "Contemporary African Art," 57.

SCULPTURE AS ARCHIVE 249

Figure 9.39 Motherhood abstract figure

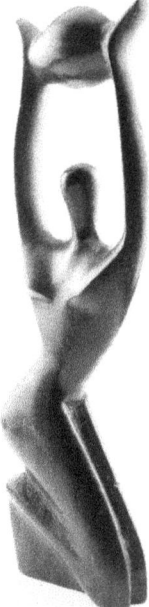

Figure 9.40 Motherhood abstract figure

Figure 9.41 Motherhood abstract figure

a diversity of thought, and knowledge of this diversity and the systems that disperse this knowledge is essential – subjecting it to foreign scrutiny will not yield its vital meanings, assuming it yields anything worthwhile.

A Yorùbá approach favors the insider's view over that of the outsider. This belief is expressed in the idiom "Kò s'ẹni tó mọ èdè àyàn, bí ẹni tó mú ọpá rẹ dání," asserting that no one knows the language of the drum better than he who beats it. A linguistic return is necessary for Yorùbá art history and criticism.

Scholars have identified several aesthetic principles and cultural frames for examining Yorùbá art. Robert Thompson, commenting on the nature of art criticism in Yorùbáland, has drawn from the richness of Yorùbá aesthetic responses to wood art. In generating a schema of analytic procedure, essential to the Yorùbá carving tradition, he observed that there is a direct relation between the activities of artists and emotional ideas; their art becomes expressions of emotion.[68] Thompson, concluding that African critics and aesthetes measure the

---

[68] Robert Farris Thompson, *African Art in Motion* (Berkeley: University of California Press, 1974).

quality of works in words, subtly advocates for a firm and rich familiarity with native aesthetic criteria. According to Adesanya, concepts such as *Ìbárajọ* (relative mimesis), *Ìfìjọrahàn* (relative visibility), *Ìtànṣán* (relative luminosity), *Gígùn* (straightness), *Ìbádọ́gba* (compositional balance), and *Àwọ̀mọ́-ọ̀dọ̀* (ephebism)[69] are germane to a robust understanding of Yorùbá sculpture and wood carving.

Other scholars, including Yai and Lawal, lend weight to the place of Yorùbá language and meta-language in discourse on Yorùbá carving. To Yai, even the concept of *Àṣà*, which translates as tradition, is germane to carving. Sculptures reveal an artist's personal ideology, deviating from the accepted norms – such as those of the college- and non-college-trained artist – and exhibiting style, effectively managing to *Dáṣà/Dáàṣà*, or create a tradition. *Dá*, as a linguistic item, is a verb that means to create. It also means to deviate or depart. The wealth of theoretical possibilities embedded in Yorùbá linguistic categories enables a meta-language through application.

In expounding on the word *Àṣà*, and how its etymology affects and induces a well-rounded critical commentary on Yorùbá carving tradition, Yai asserts that the noun *Àṣà* is derived from the verb *Ṣà*, "which means to select, to discern, to discriminate. When it refers to a human society, *Àṣà* is the set of behaviors, deeds, and habits that characterize it after it has been subjected to a historical process of deliberate choice."[70] For Yai, *Àṣà* can aptly be described as a tradition that is linked with novelty, informed by preceding phases in the process. Abiodun, whose concepts of visual and verbal *Oríkì* are also very germane methods, describes it (*Àṣà*) as "any set of ways, approaches, or practices that characterize a person's behavior or mode of work of a group of people or a period."[71] Going by this conceptualization, *Àṣà* can either mean style or tradition.

Àṣà is not constrained, and it reinvigorates itself with compatible advancements in history. For that reason, *Àṣà* is never static or dormant. Like any tradition, *Àṣà* can be individual or societal, held by groups, cities, villages, lineages, or even nations. It can intersect at certain levels. But when new elements are added, and they are not based on an understanding of earlier elements in the process, the Yorùbá mark this oddity with the concept of *Àṣà* – it is a word with exactly the same syllables, but using low tones or tones that signify low tonality.[72] The oddity is perceived as a break from tradition, entailing what is stated above as *Dáàṣà*. It creates a distinct tradition within the broader envelope of a mother tradition. Of course, this is obtainable in Yorùbá carving tradition.

Recognizing the dynamics, theoretical concepts, and rich episteme embedded in Yorùbá linguistic categories establish the need to return to a much more culturally oriented, inward-looking appreciation of Yorùbá art. By unlocking

---

[69] Adesanya, *Carving Wood*, 23.
[70] Yai, "Tradition," 34.
[71] Abiodun, "African Aesthetics," 17.
[72] Abiodun, "African Aesthetics," 17.

the codes embedded in sculptures, such as those that inspired this chapter, the place of Yorùbá meta-language – and its rich semantic properties as a bearer of cultural idioms, content, and symbols of ideologies – will be evident for assessing Yorùbá art.

Orí as Frame and Motif in Yorùbá Sculpture

Yorùbá place a premium on individuality, especially in connection with destiny and existentiality, and it is encoded in their sculpture. This is accented by the culture-specific philosophy of individuality that serves as the foundation for Yorùbá beliefs and pedagogic systems. Yorùbá ideology holds that there are no two persons with the same Orí, or head. This reveals a pivotal aspect of Yorùbá ontology: the direct relationship between Orí and individuality. Orí is individuality's central point.[73] In identifying Orí as the prominent focus around which human affairs are organized, the Yorùbá ascribe it the status of a deity. Profound sayings such as "Òrìṣà wo là bá bọ, bíkòṣe orí ẹni" (which deity might we worship if not one's head?) and "Kò sí Òrìṣà tíí dá ni í gbè léyìn orí ẹni" (no deity saves one better than one's head) are rife among the Yorùbá. These statements instruct and codify perceptions about Orí, promoting a direct relationship between Orí and its Òrìṣà (deified) status.

Any examination of a statuette, whether cursory or detailed, reveals the Yorùbá preoccupation with this essential part of the body. It is often stressed, and also decoded, through intra-relational carving. Parts of the sculpture are consciously disproportionate in relation to other body parts, either enlarged or reduced. The head is frequently larger than other parts of the body. This preoccupation is seen through stylized images created for such thematic purposes, through abstract images, and in naturalistic images. They have all been identified as ways of depicting Orí in Yorùbá sculpture.

Although the Yorùbá recognize the head's physiological and biological importance as the domain of vital organs and the center of consciousness, they place greater value on its metaphysical importance as the locus point of individuality. This fixation with the head is reflected in Lawal's submission that it is the "biggest and the most elaborately finished part of Yoruba figure sculpture."[74] By focusing on the head in the naturalistic images of second-burial performances, where the head alone is sculpted, the Yorùbá signify the head's vitality and essentiality in relation to the body on a physical level. Through a conscious thematic evangelization, the sculpture becomes a system of signification and an organizing ideological frame. Figure 9.41 is a stylized representation of a full human being, with only the shape of the Orí (head) fully

---

[73] Abiodun, "African Aesthetics," 15.
[74] Lawal, "Significance."

Figure 9.42 Ifẹ̀ head (wooden)

defined; other parts have been merged into a uniform indistinctness. Figure 9.42 can be seen to be fitted with *Ojú* (eyes), *Imú* (nose), *Ẹnu* (mouth), and *Etí* (ears), and so are Figure 9.43 and Figure 9.44, made from clay and bronze, respectively.

On a metaphysical level, the Yorùbá accord ontological functions to the head's features: the eyes are a source of light, or lamps that individuals use to navigate their journey or existence;[75] the nose is a window to ventilate the soul; the mouth is a source of nourishment for body and soul;[76] and the ears detect sound. Bulging foreheads – or *Ọpọ́n*, which translates as seat – represent the presence of *Àṣẹ*, *Olódùmarè*'s essence and the power that he used to create the universe. This power is released into each individual at their creation. *Àṣẹ* is best described as a generative force, capable of bringing things into existence,

---

[75] The Yorùbá believe that life on earth is a journey, and that every person will return home one day, which accounts for the Yorùbá belief in life after death.

[76] The mouth and its features (tongue and lips) functioning as a single unit is an instrumental force in human existence. It is held that there is *Àṣẹ* (power of utterance) that can make or mar an individual through the mouth. Metaphorically, the mouth that makes utterances instigating or attracting curses becomes a means of nourishment or decay for the soul.

254 VISUAL CULTURES

Figure 9.43 Terracotta head

Figure 9.44 Ifẹ̀ head (bronze)

Figure 9.45 Asante art

and its power and essence is self-contained. A mask, like the one in Figure 9.43, or a complete statuette, as depicted in Figure 9.45, may show an unusually large head to demonstrate how beliefs could be codified through sculptural art. Humans embody the essence of *Olódùmarè*, and *Oríinú* is the seat of *Àṣẹ* in their sculpture. A robust, round head signifies the expansive presence and nature of *Àṣẹ* in a person.

Because *Olódùmarè*'s *Èémí* (breath) and *Àṣẹ* (divine power) enter the body through the head and reside there, sculptors emphasize the head during the process of sculpting. A child is born head first, and other parts of the body are said to follow the head to earth, so Yorùbá sculptors begin with the head and shape other parts of the body to emphasize it.[77] This follows the mythic belief that *Ọbàtálá*, in reiterating the primacy of *Orí*, creates humans by molding the head first. The relational incongruence and absence of combinatorial uniformity (*Dídọ̀gba*) of the head with other body parts encodes the physical, philosophical, and spiritual primacy of the head. Sculpture reinvigorates the popular myth of creation, and in a hierarchy of body parts the head is king.

[77] Lawal "The Living Dead."

Figure 9.46 Contemporary art

Olódùmarè breathes into the divine clay molded by *Ọbàtálá*. After this, the humans being formed proceed to *Ajala Alámọ̀*, the one that molds *Oríinú* (the inner head). There, they select a pre-molded *Orí* that already contains *Olódùmarè*'s *Àṣẹ*. This selection underscores their *Ìpín* (lot), and their will culminates in their destiny (*Àyànmọ́*). The temporal sequence of the narrative establishes that the *Oríinú*, the metaphysical component of *Orí*, is originally molded separately, by a different celestial artist – the molding of *Orí* is an important task that requires the utmost delicacy. Such importance is replicated through the process of carving and through carved statuettes. *Orí*, in its entirety, is a guiding principle in Yorùbá sculpture.

The *Orí* under discussion is the *Oríinú*, or inner head. The *Orí ìta/òde*, the outside head or the one that is visible, conceals the *Oríinú*. The prominence that *Orí* commands in Yorùbá sculpture and over other body parts is an index of a metaphysical consciousness, the signifier of a rich mythico-spiritual collective awareness as part of Yorùbá culture. *Orí* acts as a system of signification, and its existence in any sculpted form acts as a subtle mode of cultural crusade.

Yorùbá spirituality is present in their assessment of artistic representations of body parts. The distinction of one *Orí* from another, in terms of one's destiny on earth, means that each *Oríinú* is intrinsically different. *Oríburúkú* (an unfortunate head) guarantees an unfortunate life unless appeasements are made. The Yorùbá saying "Orí là ń bọ" (we make appeasement to one's head), is pertinent for understanding how *Orí* is central to the Yorùbá philosophy for existentialist matters. A bad *Orí* is also part of the axiom "Oríburúkú kò gbọṣẹ," a bad head cannot be cleansed with soap. A bad *Orí* can be spiritually medicated by making appeasement to it, which is why *Orí* is often regarded as *Ẹlẹ́dàá ẹni* (one's creator).

The semantic implications of Yorùbá sayings establish the primacy of *Orì* (*Oríinú*) symbolizing the predetermined destiny of a person's life. It is clear that in Yorùbá sculpture the head is no ordinary body part; it symbolizes various ideological peculiarities, and it indexes history. The physical and metaphysical aspects of *Orí* signify much more than personal destiny.[78] Another ontological issue exists in the way that the head is seen as *Ẹlẹ́dàá ẹni*. The category of *Ẹlẹ́dàá* (creator) is reserved for *Olódùmarè*, the divine creator. In Yorùbá cultural space the status of the *Orí* – considered an *Ẹlẹ́dàá* – signifies that it is an aspect or component of *Olódùmarè*. This is supported by the idea that *Orí* contains the essence of *Olódùmarè*. To reference Alade's and Lawal's position, *Olódùmarè* is the head-source (*Orísun*) of the universe, just as both the outer and the inner *Orí* of an individual constitute the personal life-source. *Orí ẹni*, acting as a miniaturized aspect of the broader essence, becomes the source of a person's origin. From this perspective, *Orí* is appreciated in the light of an *Òrìṣà*. This is why it is mostly considered from its metaphysical dimensions in Yorùbá art.[79]

Although aspects of *Orí* and the metaphysical realm of reality are portrayed through head carvings, the physical aspect of *Orí* is not ignored. Rather than being the sole indicator of a spiritualized consciousness, carvings of *Orí* also suggest philosophy about the essentiality of other facial features. Figures 9.46 and 9.47 are wood carvings of heads absent body parts. The presence of all facial features supports the thesis that Yorùbá do not consider the head for its metaphysical attributes alone; they employ it as a means of sensitization, educating on the implication of the absence of other parts. In other words, *Orí òde* becomes useless or less functional on its own.

The Yorùbá also reference *Ojú inú*. This signifies the metaphysical in the physical, connoting that every physical feature, like those in Figures 9.46 and 9.47, is an index of its metaphysicality. As signs, they are self-referential. The length (*Gígùn*) of the topmost parts of the heads in Figures 9.46 and 9.47 shows a stylized rendition of ideologies specific to human ontology for the Yorùbá. In

---

[78] Lawal, "The Living Dead"; Adesanya, *Carving Wood*.
[79] M. Alade, "Ori, Ipin ati Kadara, Apa Kini," *Olokun* 10 (1972): 8–10; Lawal, "The Living Dead," 52, for the *Odù*, *Ifá* narratives, and other myths that accentuate the relationship between *Orí* and *Olódùmarè*.

Figure 9.47 Contemporary art

Figure 9.48 Beaded *Oṣé Ṣàngó*

Figure 9.49 Kòríkòtò Òrìṣà Èwe I

Figure 9.46 the smoothness (Dídán) of the protrusion signifies the Yorùbá ideology that the head contains both the Ọpọlọ, the exit point of Olódùmarè's Èémí, and his Àṣẹ. In Figure 9.47 the vein-like markings that reach upward can represent the veins of any Ọpọlọ (brain) that is situated in the head; the rectangular projection can represent the brain seated appropriately at the topmost part of the head.

Naturalistic images are used by the Yorùbá to signal the essentialism of Orí in their social and religio-cultural order. These images are created for functional purposes, especially ceremonial functions in second-burial events. Although idealized, they are also very realistic, as is common with Ifẹ̀ terracotta and bronze heads. This is often done to enhance the believability required for such occasions. Because only a facial resemblance is needed, the head is often the only part that is carefully carved. Other body parts are adorned with fitted garments. These images give prominence to the Yorùbá people's preoccupation with identity. In Yorùbá sculpture Orí becomes a mode of relating cultural emphasis on identity, individuality, and destiny.

Stylized conceptions of Orí in Yorùbá sculpture are mostly graphic portrayals of their spiritual consciousness and myths. Yorùbá conceive of their Òrìṣà as capable of performing human functions and possessing human attributes. They can replicate human forms, although those forms would be dematerialized and noncorporeal. The dematerialized forms of the Òrìṣàs, which include deified ancestors, can be housed in the stylized representations of some sculptures. Masks, created with wood, clay, or bronze, are examples of these stylized images. The matching of a dematerialized ancestor or Òrìṣà with a stylized image is fully expressed in the masquerade festival, where performers act as ancestors to reconnect with the living. In these cases the mask becomes a screen between ancestor and descendants, bridging the worlds of the living and the spiritual. A mask, which is a stylized representation of Orí – in this case, that of a dematerialized Òrìṣà – is a vehicle for interdimensional transference that furthers a whole tradition: see Figures 9.2 and 9.4. Representations of dematerialized ancestors and Òrìṣà can also be full-bodied statuettes. In such cases the statuette is reconfigured to create an obvious incongruity among body parts, and human physicality is stylized to reflect supernatural essence. The heads of such images are rendered in a primordial state, which Lawal calls an embryo:[80] the eyes, ears, mouth, and other facial figures are distended and enlarged to symbolize celestial essence. This approach makes the figures depersonified, and they lose their distinctive human qualities to become spiritualized subjects. Many cult statuettes and figurines are created in this form. The distention of the head's features give prominence to the generative power (Àṣẹ) said to reside in each Orí, signifying the presence of the supernatural. Unlike simple statuettes, these types of figurines cannot be tied down or said to be icons of any Òrìṣà (except in the case of Èṣù). They are said to symbolically embody the Òrìṣàs, believed to be capable of hosting the invoked essence of Òrìṣàs. By being dematerialized, and by tempering absolute identity through stylization, their representational identity emerges.

Figure 9.46 offers an example: the head extends into a pointed apex, and in Figure 9.47 includes a visible protrusion. In Figure 9.48 the wide and rectangular beaded projection of the head suggests that it should be schematized as a figurine from Ṣàngó's cult. This is also true of Figure 9.24, an Oṣé Sàngó. The specific structure of the heads shown in these images identifies the cult that they belong to. Figure 9.14 can, through the stylization of the head, be seen as belonging to the Èṣù cult. This reaffirms the place of Orí as a compass or marker for identity – in this case, spiritual identity – in Yorùbá sculpture. Other cult-specific images are used on staffs employed during cult performances.

Giving the Òrìṣà stylized faces, represented through carvings and cult-specific symbols, enhances the accessibility of the Òrìṣà and, by extension, the spiritual world. It enables supplication and propitiation, enhancing their effectiveness, and Orí performs the function of effectuation. By furnishing these symbols with faces that markedly separate the Òrìṣà, Orí becomes a mode

[80] Lawal, "The Living Dead," 56.

of access. A critical survey of the place, function, and signification of Orí in Yorùbá sculpture shows how it transcends artwork into subject matter. It becomes a plane for discourse and a framing principle that organizes a people's ideology.

Sculptures as Idiomatic Expressions and Agents of Social Consciousness

For the Yorùbá, sculptures have always been instruments of mobility, vehicles of signification, dialogical planes, and a decodable language with intelligible components. Their role as a decodable language is the reason why the concept of Ẹwà (beauty) is functional to the Yorùbá. Ẹwà, and its converse, Burẹ̀wà (ugliness), are metaphoric, or polysemic in utilitarian terms.

In the Yorùbá socio-sphere, Ẹwà is not solely an aesthetic phenomenon. It is an expression of Ìwà, which accounts for the saying "Ìwàlẹ̀wà" (character is beauty). The attributes of something are its beauty, and the characteristics of a person affect their beauty. An individual who is perceived as possessing awful traits – such as Olè jíjà (stealing), Ìwà ipáǹle (despicable behavior), Àìgbọ̀ràn (stubbornness), or Ìbínú (anger) – is an Òbùrẹ́wà ènìyàn, an ugly person. This process of identification contextually repurposes the concept of Ẹwà, and it is how Yorùbá understand the concept of Ẹwà.

Statuettes like those in Figure 9.49 embody attributes such as Ìtànsán, Ìfijọrahàn, Ìbádọ́gba, and Àwòmọ́-ọ̀dọ́. They summarize the ideal attributes of youthfulness for the Yorùbá, and are pertinent to the appreciation of artwork as an embodiment of visually stimulating aesthetics. To the Yorùbá these statuettes embody communicable features. An image's intelligible codes signify the emphasis that society has placed on beauty. A brilliant, beautiful, and well-crafted statuette immediately commands approbation, drawing attention to itself, its contextual significance, and its possibilities as a sign or a narrative code.

Carvings instruct on the necessity of care by signaling the care that went into their production. Artwork that is patronized for its beauty engenders further preoccupation, yielding it to continuous appraisal from either the Gbẹ̀nàgbẹ̀nà or the public. This reveals the critical need to unlock a work of art's multifaceted aspects and the layered meanings embedded in it. The fixation with a sculpture's obvious utilitarian beauty connotes the Yorùbá conceptualization of Ẹwà, which symbolically narrates how a person's attributes invite praise, goodwill, and other benefits. Consequently, a statuette becomes a meta-language that expands on the potential semantics of another (Ẹwà), and it draws attention to its own linguistic and sociolinguistic peculiarities. As a sign, an iconic diagram, or a symbol, it signifies the function of Ẹwà in relation to humans – an idea of human appreciative prowess in a sociocultural network.

By being a meta-language that places premium on Ẹwà, sculpture indirectly proscribes Burẹ̀wà, that which is undesirable. This is done through

Figure 9.50 Homage

a binary system of linguistic operation. The positive reaffirmation of Ẹwà, embodying its principles, contains the presence of Burẹ̀wà's absence. This absence is effectively a condemnation of Burẹ̀wà. In the process of attaining or instigating the socio-relevance of Ẹwà, artworks weave and reweave it into society's fabric and reject or outlaw Burẹ̀wà, displacing it to the margins of normative culture. This reveals how it is a vehicle of social engineering and behavioral retooling.

An image is only effective at sensitization to the extent that it has been collectively recoded and ascribed the status of a symbol. In figurines, each contortion and the placement of body parts are specific and have significance. Figure 9.50 is a perfect example of the meanings that exist in a network of images: the angles at which these images manifest contribute to social dialogues. Through the juxtaposition of a standing woman, clothed in elderly attire, and a young woman, identifiable by her adolescent dress, the sacred rites of passage are manifested. Adulthood (Àgbàlagbà) is contrasted with youth (Ọ̀dọ́). The vertical posturing, minus genuflection, shows deference and affords an elevated status to Àgbàlagbà in the Yorùbá social order. Yorùbá people do not tolerate insolence to adults or the elderly, and this is wired into the concept of Ìtẹríba and Ìrẹ̀lẹ̀ – two principles of Ọmọlúàbí.

The image portrays *Ìtẹríba*, but that is only a start. The mother, as can be assumed through the angles of relational posturing and proximity between the figures, confers blessings on the child. This frames the belief that blessings come from respecting one's parents or elders. For the Yorùbá, blessings flow from positions of higher authority to those of lesser authority, which is shown in the image. Genuflection and posturing are ways to portray *Ìwà* among the Yorùbá. The placement of a gourd-like object on the head references the spiritual primacy of *Orí*, as the receiver and seat of power, and its influence over a person's destiny. A rite of passage in Yorùbáland often bears powerful spiritual implications for a person's destiny, and a gourd, bowl, box, or *Igbá* (calabash) is often present.

The image, showing the older figure on her feet and the younger figure on her knees, becomes an enforcement mechanism for social control and a vehicle for social choreography. It highlights the benevolence, calmness, and authority to be expected from elders, and it shows the rewards that youth can expect for obedience and respect. Aged people are cautioned with "Àgbàlagbà kò gbọdọ̀ ṣe láńgbáláńgbá" (an elder must not behave anyhow). The image becomes a self-idealizing mirror, signifying acceptable postures in which members of the two cultural categories should desire to see themselves.

Yorùbá carvings are instructive and reflective. Images like these reactivate succinct proverbs like "Ọmọ tó bá ṣí'pá ni ìyá rẹ̀ ń gbé" (the child who puts forth his hands is hoisted by the mother). The statement metaphorically connects to the sculpture, and culture-specific statements finding expression in Yorùbá sculpture are transformed from abstract images to idiomatic expressions. An interpretation of this sculpture would also place an emphasis on time; only time separates *Ọ̀dọ́* from *Àgbàlagbà*.

Figures 9.50, 9.51, and 9.52 signify similar values and the agency of carvings in a socio-sphere. They symbolize the premium placed on unity, communality, respect, hierarchies, and reverence for positions of authority. In a family context, the man is considered the household's *Orí*. He must be revered, just as the Yorùbá believe all *Orí* should be pacified and worshiped. By doing this, a transfer of *Àṣẹ* forces a rapid actuality of desires – benefits are reaped – as is shown in the placement of the male's hand on the head of the female, signifying a transfer of blessings or generative power. In Yorùbá ontological space, power often flows from top to bottom.

In the figures, social hierarchy is also reaffirmed; the male image is defamiliarized to eliminate any relation to a specific referent. In Figure 9.52 communality and togetherness are emphasized as currencies for progress, shown in the postures of the two figures and the item cradled or supported in their hands. A gourd or calabash has a principal connotation and place in Yorùbá culture, symbolizing power or a container in which powerful things are kept. As such, the essence of a community is only secured when it is safeguarded by all component parts, which is suggested by the image. Both carvings have male

Figure 9.51 Contemporary art Ia

Figure 9.52 Contemporary art Ib

and female figures, but the placement of hands is a substantial difference. In Yorùbá epistemology Ọwọ́ (hand) is seen as a powerful mechanism for tuning one's destiny.

SCULPTURE AS ARCHIVE 265

The carvings in Figures 9.53 and 9.54 depict the concept of time. Two Yorùbá proverbs are relevant: "Arìngbẹ̀rẹ̀ kò ní kojá ilé" (the slow walker will not travel past his home) and "Bó pẹ́, bó yá akólòlò á pe baba" (sooner or later, the stutterer will pronounce father). These statements emphasize the role of destiny in relation to time. They are invoked by two animals, a snail and a tortoise, which are two of the slowest creatures on earth. Although the tortoise is slow for its size, it still arrives at its destination. In animal folktales the tortoise is considered one of the craftiest animals, although some believe that it is second to the snail – "Gbogbo ọgbọ́n tí ahún gbọ́n, èyìn ni ó ń tọ ìgbín" (all the wisdom of the tortoise trails after the snail).

These two creatures, embodying both wisdom and slowness, reflect that being fast does not guarantee success or indicate the most successful. These two will achieve their goals eventually, especially when considering folktales that highlight their craftiness. They point to the notion that slow and steady can win the race, or that destiny can be delayed, but it can never be avoided. These beliefs about destiny (Àyànmọ́) or one's lot in life (Ìpín) are held so strongly by the Yorùbá that the appearance of a snail or tortoise emphasizes their inevitability. The two sculptures exist as epistemological frames that

Figure 9.53 Contemporary art Ic

Figure 9.54 Contemporary art Id

encode and reactivate indigenous beliefs for society's remembrance, consumption, and use. Their symbolism of the import of time is comparable to that of an hourglass. Both images are metaphoric expressions of time and destiny's inevitability in the same capacity as the proverbs mentioned previously.

Sculptures reflect and instruct on the social order and several aspects of Yorùbá life. Images such as Figures 9.32 and 9.55 are visual and thematic renderings of Yorùbá social life. The royal figure is seated on a horse, and the individual who acts as *Akígbe* (praiser) is announcing his arrival. Royalty tower above others, and this is reflected in the size of the royally adorned figure on the horse, of greater stature than the figure perched behind him. By placing the second figure behind, the sculpture instructs on royalty's position and that of others in society. Images provide visual reminders of Yorùbá industry and their folkloric life before European colonization. These images are visual codes, created to appeal and instruct on the benefits of upholding tradition. Tilling the land, being a warrior, performing household chores, cultivating crops, and involvement in court activities and governance as chiefs or members of society are idealized roles for individuals. The sculpted images draw several possibilities into the ensuing visual dialogues, and their ultimate pedagogical relevance as well as the sensitization of the polity.

In Yorùbáland, while carvings act as agents of social consciousness they also act as social coordinators. Through their existence, and through ownership of them, they assist in social ordering and organization through the emphasis that the Yorùbá place on acquiring beautiful and ornamental objects. The acquisition of an exquisite carving or sculpture displays an individual's social standing and wealth. The number of house posts possessed by an individual, and their

Figure 9.55 Black warrior

increasingly elaborate designs, reflects that individual's rank in society. The presence of different categories of sculpture in a home indicates that a person is materially powerful enough to acquire them. These images not only carry prestige, they engender competition among artists and patrons.

Artistic competition leads to self-aggrandizement, not only among patrons of these expensive creations, but also among the artists who create them. Artists strive to prove their intellect and skill through the work they create. Patrons commission posts, figurines, and utilitarian carvings that are also exotic to showcase their class and material superiority. As a result, any carving, whether expensive and exotic or otherwise, symbolizes something beyond itself: it becomes an agent that reorganizes social elements into classes. The kinds of carvings found in the king's palace are different from those found in the Balógun's home or that of an ordinary citizen. Thus, sculptures become mementos of power.

Yorùbá sculptors, especially postcolonial ones, incorporate modernist themes and influences into their depiction of life and social order. From sculptures rendering still images found in Western formal education to abstract images emphasizing the importance of music and its intricate relationship with the human soul, we see a wide range of modernist influences. Sculptures show men and women in colorful, Western-influenced attires, and these elements can be found in other expressionist carvings of humans with elongated or indistinct features. These sculptures serve as indicators of history and shifts in tradition (Àṣà). Sculptures also record the daily activities and features of Yorùbá people, such as carvings of drummers plying their art, or hunters, animals feeding their young, and other animals including lizards, crocodiles, and elephants.

Sculpture as Index

The strong interrelation between the epistemes that inform the subject of this chapter means that much of what is discussed here has also been considered elsewhere. This section emphasizes the king's crown and the bird symbols around it, along with some cult-specific carvings that could have been included in discussions of Orí and women in Yorùbá culture.

A king's crown is an index of hierarchy and power – in Yorùbá philosophy an exquisite, potent crown signifies the properties of the king's Orí. This signifier of royalty separates the king from the public as an embodiment of spiritual authority, which is why the king is considered "Aláṣẹ èkejì òrìṣà" (second after the gods). The king is believed to be a representative of the Òrìṣà on earth, wielding maximum power that is only checked by the judicial authority held by specific spiritual cults and groups: Ògbóni and Ọ̀yọ́mèsì. The king is often called the "guardian of moral reality, secular and sacred authority."[81]

Immense power is invested in the king, supplied by spiritual forces through sacred rituals that involve having his head incised or sacralized to allow this metaphysical power to be absorbed. As a result, his face is hidden from the public. He is no longer considered to be an ordinary human, and the quality of his Orí determines the fate of society. The crown is considered an Ìbòrí (head covering)[82] and adorned with various designs and beads. The beads, along with a stylized mask in some cases, hide the king's face from the public to validate the idea that he is a representative of the community's ancestors. By reaching toward communally held ideologies and recasting them through imagery, the crown becomes an index of politico-spiritual power and hierarchy along with its ornaments, beads, and its mask. They also index the process of spiritual fortification and the presence of ancestral essence.

---

[81] Adesanya, *Carving Wood*, 40.
[82] Lawal, "The Living Dead."

The bird-shaped symbols and images attached to the crown symbolize the presence of the powers of Àjẹ́ (witches), supporting the crowning and continued reign of the king. The Àjẹ́ are powerful women, each seen as a "possessor of uncanny powers."[83] These women are revered, feared, and diplomatically engaged by the Yorùbá. They are called *Ayé* (the surreal), *Ẹyẹ* (bird), *Àgbà* (the elders), *Ìyá* (mother), *Ẹ̀rù-jẹ̀jẹ̀* (fear), or *Atapájorí* (one who consumes the head from the hands) in recognition of their metaphysical power. The bird imagery is a graphic rendering of their relationship with birds; they are believed to hold nocturnal meetings, when the Àjẹ́'s soul journeys from the physical realm into the spiritual one by taking the form of a bird. The flight, levitation, swiftness, elegance, and almost omniscient attributes of birds are also accorded to them. The transformative and generative (*Àṣẹ*) power of the Àjẹ́ is said to be contained in a calabash or bowl. The genuflecting representation of the birds in Figure 9.56, with their beaks fastened to or pecking the crown, is a symbol of such birds releasing powers

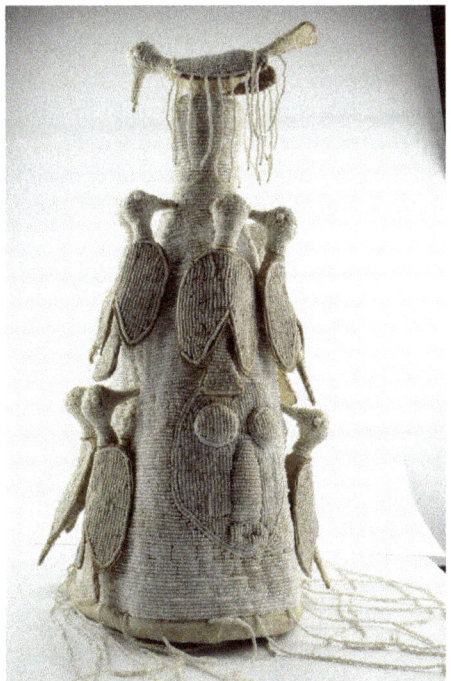

Figure 9.56 Beaded crown (contemporary)

[83] Adesanya, *Carving Wood*, 37.

into the *Adé* (crown). The king is never allowed to see the inside of the crown, because it contains the power of the *Àjẹ́* that consolidates the king's supremacy.

The bowl is a symbol of power in Yorùbáland, signaling highly spiritual and potent power. In several Yorùbá cults the bowl is presented as one of the objects used for cult-specific ritual purposes. In *Ifá*'s cult many figurines and images portray a woman holding a bowl, sometimes on her head or in her hands, and the receptacle has spiritual and utilitarian functions. As an *Agere*, an *Ifá* storage bowl, it stores important items. The bowl is mostly circular, resting on a base of sculpted human or animal forms. It is normally carved out of wood or ivory,[84] holding the sixteen sacred palm-kernel nuts used for divination, and it depicts the wealth of the *Ifá* priest or Babalawo. The *Agere* bowls carved from ivory are deeper and wider than wooden ones.

The subjects of *Agere* bowls are usually based on the desires of clients seeking *Ifá* priests for divination, becoming frames through which human desires can be understood. The *Agere* itself is an iconic symbol of the cosmic universe, and the act of divination (within it) is tantamount to navigating it. The image of a kneeling female spotlights the importance of submission (*Ìtẹríba*) and strategic posturing toward higher authorities. The image symbolizes the efficacy of *Ẹbẹ̀* (supplication) in relating to the *Òrìṣà* – a proper diplomatic approach can ensure a deity's speedy consent to supplication. By serving as a mediumistic symbol the image acts a framing mirror to instruct potential beneficiaries seeking to avoid the wrath of the gods and win favors. *Agere* bowls do not always have lids, but the lids often bear stylized faces meant to represent *Èṣù*. See Figure 9.57. These sculpted trays for divination show abstract representations of *Èṣù*'s face.

Due to the hermeneutic relationship between *Ifá* and *Èṣù*, some of these receptacles include carvings of heads. The heads are said to represent *Èṣù*, who is said to have taught *Ifá* how to interpret the *Odù* corpus, a system of divination specific to the *Òrìṣà* that connects the earthly world to the celestial. This knowledge makes *Èṣù* instrumental for the process of divination. As an *Òrìṣà*, *Ifá* is said to have been present at the time of human creation. *Èṣù* also attends each person's selection of *Orí*, making *Èṣù* familiar with everyone's *Ìpín* (destiny), and that is why he is often consulted at desperate times for advice regarding one's destiny. *Èṣù* is sometimes depicted as holding a bowl storing the *Àṣẹ* of *Olódùmarè*.

Èṣù, the *Òrìṣà* of the crossroads, symbolizes harmony and contradictions – especially in humans. The potency and universality of this antithetical essence in humans is why the Yorùbá believe that there is a bit of *Èṣù* in everyone. This idea explains the good and bad forces contending for supremacy in humans and their moral systems. For instance, there is a story about how *Èṣù* tricked *Ọbàtálá* (see Figure 9.59) and the latter was accused of stealing *Ṣàngó*'s horse.

---

[84] Adesanya, *Carving Wood*, 92.

Figure 9.57 *Ifá* divination tray

Ọbàtálá was imprisoned for seven years because of this. Many disasters struck Yorùbáland during this time until the truth was finally revealed and Ọbàtálá was set free, restoring peace to the land.[85] The negative force represented by Èṣù, the trickster Òrìṣà, is not comparable to that of Lucifer or Satan in the Christian religion. The mischief of *Èṣù* represents ambivalence, antithesis, and contradiction.

Choice is a major component of their reality. It is involved during an individual's creation and over the course of their existence. *Èṣù* participates in the latter. A crossroad is disconcerting. It is a confusing ontological space that every individual encounter, which the Yorùbá call "Ìkóríta mẹ́ta tó ń dààmú àlejò."[86] *Èṣù* signifies confusion, unpredictability, and duality. This includes binary notions such as good and bad, benevolent and malevolent, dull and witty, and calm and restive. These all indicate the presence of *Èṣù*, and all are found in his ethos and essence. This notion of duality is shown in statuettes created to profile this trickster god, such as those in Figures 9.14–9.19 and Figure 9.58.

---

[85] Omofolabo Ajayi, *Yoruba Dance: The Semiotics of Movement and Body Attitude in a Nigerian Culture* (Trenton: Africa World Press, 1998).

[86] Adesanya, *Carving Wood*, 62.

Figure 9.58 *Èṣù Ẹlẹ́gbárá II*

In some images *Èṣù* possesses both male and female genitalia. It is a symbolic rendering of the cooperation needed between the sexes to engender vitality, progress, and (re)production. *Èṣù* is regarded as the emblem of sexual vitality, libidinous energy, and productivity. Avatars of *Èṣù* are often shown with projections on their heads if they are male, or headdresses if they are female, and they are interpretable as phallic signifiers. The phallic projections – interpreted as phallic for their sturdiness and contouring – on the headdresses of female statuettes symbolize the mediatory nature of *Èṣù* between the sexes.

Another indexical feature specific to an *Èṣù* avatar or images of his worshipers is the style of hair: it is often woven or shaped into a phallus. Projections that are not phallic are styled to reflect either sharp objects or cudgels, used to pummel detractors who refuse to pay the tribute that he demands as the facilitator between the *Òrìṣà* and human supplicants. Sometimes he holds a cudgel, like the one visible in Figure 9.15, or a calabash. The prominence of

Figure 9.59 *Jagunjagun* (Ọbàtálá)

these projections supports the mythical belief that Èṣù does not carry burdens. As signs, they signify parts of the creation story that narrate Èṣù's mischief and his refusal to carry burdens, unique among the Òrìṣà. As the deputy divinity to Olódùmarè, Èṣù punishes those who have violated divine and communal laws,[87] and thus is responsible for peace and order, and vice versa.

The styles of the projections substantiate Èṣù's mischievous persona and provocative nature. The saying "Ohun ọwọ́ mi ò tó, ma fi gọ̀gọ̀ fàá,"[88] meaning

---

[87] This mythico-religious attribute of Èṣù perhaps explains why he is conflated with the biblical Satan.
[88] Adesanya, *Carving Wood*, 71.

to reach for the actualization of desires through any means, is suggested by Èṣù's Gògò-shaped head projection. The Gògò is employed by the Yorùbá to retrieve items that are out of reach, and in artwork it is a figurative reexpression of ambition and excessive ambition. Those who exhibit such behavior reveal that they possess the ethos and essence of Èṣù. It is clear that the Yorùbá, as indicated by the statuettes that profile this trickster Òrìṣà, believe there is a bit of the god in everyone.

Having extensions on a statuette's head forming specific shapes is not unique to Èṣù's cult. It is a general feature of cult figures, signifying spirituality in humans and the presence of spiritual embodiment. The presence of Àṣẹ in an individual's Orí, and the spiritual possession of humans during rituals and cult ceremonies, is reflected in Yorùbá artwork showing human heads carved with extended shapes, symbolizing spiritual mounting by celestial beings. This makes them indexical. The Yorùbá believed humans to be wives of the Òríṣà, which is why women and the feminine ideal are central to Yorùbá knowledge systems.

Women in Yorùbá Sculpture

Female representations are common in Yorùbá sculptural tradition. They center on ideas of female sexuality, personhood, and being (see Figures 9.60 and 9.61). The trait of Ìrójú (perseverance/patience), the ability to keep secrets and refrain from divulging them through speech or acts, is valuable for keeping a person's essence (Oríinú) secure. By divulging personal details or making Àṣẹ-laden evil utterances, the Oríinú can become vulnerable to malevolent forces. This discretion is considered unique to the female sex. The popular saying "Ọwọ́ èrò lobìnrin ní" (referring to the fecundity of women) is another example of the temperance valued in an ideal woman. To display these attributes in in Yorùbá sculpture, women are presented with cool and calm exteriors. In an ironic circle of influence, this becomes an index of strength alongside the tempered persona associated with women. The paradox is that softness is strength.

This softness – which indicates concealed strength, not weakness – manifests itself in many ways to reflect Yorùbá beliefs. Yorùbá sculptors often provoke consideration of these attitudes and behaviors by carving and presenting images of women with children clinging to them or strapped to their backs, as in Figures 9.62 and 9.63.

Depictions of the maternal bond are highly symbolic. Figures 9.61 and 9.63 present women in propitiatory modes; they are lifting heavy bowls on their heads, while sustaining the weight of another human being. These strong visual metaphors serve as testaments to the strength of women in Yorùbá culture. The character of a woman's Oríinú will never allow her to abandon her

Figure 9.60 *Arugbá Ṣàngó* I

children in any context, unless her senses have taken leave of her – if something has changed in the composition of her *Oríinú*.

A woman's capacity for self-sacrifice is presented in carvings of kneeling females, signifying the appropriateness of a woman as the ideal supplicant to any *Òrìṣà*. The industry of women and their resilient spirit are reflected through carvings that show them catering for their children while engaging in folkloric activities; they are sculpted with hoes, bowls, and baskets that depict their industriousness and the strength of motherhood. The mother toils to ensure survival, caring for herself and another, which is an unending sacrifice often depicted by Yorùbá carvers.

A kneeling woman in Yorùbá sculpture is a visual code for the potency of *Ẹ̀bẹ̀* or *Ìwúre* (supplication) to unlock the benevolence of deities. She is always in a propitiatory mode, cradling a basket of fruit or a huge basin, which is a visual signifier of the power of appeasement and humility. In her genuflecting

Figure 9.61 Kneeling figure (contemporary)

mode, accompanied by other visual signs, such as children, baskets of fruit, farming implements, and bowls, carvings portray the woman as a force of supplication (see Figures 9.64, 9.65, 9.66, and 9.67). It is one of Ẹbọ (sacrifice) and Ẹ̀bẹ̀ (supplication). The principle of Ẹbọ surfaces the sacrificial nature of women in any discourse on their physical posture. By manifesting the principle of Ẹ̀bẹ̀, her genteel and submissive nature becomes an instructive code to unlock other codes.

When the visual components of images are examined from both Ẹ̀bẹ̀ and Ẹbọ epistemic frames, the woman gains primacy, relevance, and ideological luminosity within the boundaries of Yorùbá cultural discourse. By performing supplication on behalf of society, herself, her children, and by birthing and caring for children, she contributes to the cycle of life. These activities avert disaster and populate the earth through productivity at home and in the field. These are reasons why Yorùbá people seek the mercies of deities.

Figure 9.62 *Arugbá Ṣàngó* II

Women being shown semi-nude is another visual code signaling the Yorùbá and the efficacy of total submission and commitment, or the efficacy in assuming a mien of absolute meekness, and being in the position of request and of zero contention – these are interpretable as total surrender of one's will, spirit, soul, and body to the whims and caprices of the gods. To the Yorùbá this is the zenith of propitiation and submission. The gods are benevolent to those who show this behavior; it is a significant attribute of the Ọmọlúàbí.

Conclusion

The entirety of Yorùbá sculpture is a system of archiving Yorùbá reality. An assessment of Yorùbá sculpture along ideological, ontological, methodological, and epistemological lines reveals how sculpture can be one and many things at

Figure 9.63 *Ìyá Ìbejì* (mother of twins)

the same time. It provides visual content for social coordination; serves as a religious totem, historical artifact, and medium for accessing the spiritual plane; and exists as a codification of the people's way of life. Yorùbá sculpture can be read from historical, sociocultural, stylistic, and mythico-religious angles to reveal layers and multiplicity of meanings, acting as an archive. Like all archives it serves as a frame, an envelope, an idealizing mirror, and a perspective that guides the Yorùbá people and promotes their tradition.

Figure 9.64 *Igbá Ọpẹ*

Figure 9.65 *Kòríkòtò Òrìṣà Èwe II*

Figure 9.66 *Kòríkòtò Òrìṣà Èwe III*

SCULPTURE AS ARCHIVE 281

Figure 9.67 *Onílù* (drummer)

10

Textiles as Texts

I have always held the notion that to fully recognize, appreciate, and gain entry into the expansive and rich firmament of Yorùbá art, which includes textiles, is to proceed from the premise of its readability, which ultimately requires an engagement with textiles or dress or cloth as an intelligence, a system of knowledge, a science, and a structure of interpretable signs – that is, a text. To me, the idea or proposition of textiles, Yorùbá textiles, used as a generic term to accommodate youth cloth and dress, to be precise, as texts is never an exercise in conjectural scholarship. This claim achieves utmost agency when interrogation is executed from African-centered positions. More so, the magnitude of the assertion is furthered by the abundant presence of requisite qualities and materials that can sustain engagements that attempt to read Yorùbá life off its textiles. It is in these (briefly extrapolated) senses that Yorùbá textiles fulfill the conditions of a text, which M. H. Abrams describes as the manifestation of a social institution,[1] which in this case would be sartorial. Proceeding accordingly from what is best an inferred logic, a creator, who is the cloth-weaver,[2] would be the intermediary who and within whom the elements, aesthetics, and codes of preexisting sartorial traditions to be found in the particular text are precipitated. This way, the artist's mediumship as an agency for cultural/stylo-aesthetic birth and rebirth is accentuated. Through functionality, the created – that is, the text – becomes impersonal.

Another way to view Yorùbá textiles in terms of its textuality is the text as a work paradigm, or what we can call an artifact. This emphasizes the personal ties engendered between the creator and the created before, during, and after the process of creation. That is why as a creative work, text-as-work underscores the salience of "process" as a fundamental constituent in the universe of a text. "How?" you may ask. The reply is simple. The text is a product of the creator's design, while its meanings are contoured by the creator's intention

---

[1] See Abrams, *Glossary*.

[2] A cloth-weaver is a creator by virtue of his reliance on preexisting aesthetics and cognitively transferred stylo-artistic sensibilities and by working within a framework of artistry within which and with which he brings to life a whole living material (a material that existed not simply by being but through its utility and functionality).

and intentional use of the aesthetics of the mother tradition.[3] Consequently, the creator or, for ease of reference, the weaver retains their primal position in the hierarchical domain of a creative work, which a textile is.

The vital continuity between both conceptualizations discussed so far is the readability of Yorùbá textiles. As a generally held idea,[4] a text is anything than can be read and subjected to analytic investigations. Marcel Danesi explains it as composite phenomena[5] because its constituent parts are interpreted in concert as parts of an integrative system. At this juncture, the necessary question should be: Can Yorùbá textiles be seen in the light of a text? The paramount answer makes recourse back to readability as pivotal in ascertaining the textual status of anything – that and interpretation. Yorùbá textiles, examined holistically, are fit for the designation of text by possessing interpretational possibilities. This premise is influenced by the simple fact that any successful interrogation of Yorùbá textiles is affected by a process or processes of reading – what Abrams calls a "lecture"[6] – that expose levels of familiarity with the inherent codes and, thus, invest the textiles themselves, as well as their aesthetics and codes, with contextual values otherwise referred to as messages.

Of course, any such "familiarity" is a function of prior exposures to the nature and functioning of the system(s) within which particular texts exist and from which they draw their potency or aesthetics as nodes of messages. By virtue of a text possessing and dispensing such powers of cultural (re)direction, (re)memory, and reestablishment, through its messages, the reader/interrogator invests the text itself with what could be designated as inherent meanings and references to an outer world. These meanings are only possible manifestations of the message every text embodies, for message is not the same as meaning. Relating the foregoing to Yorùbá textiles, it is clear that not only are they readable, they fulfill one other mandatory function of texts: intelligibility.

The language of Yorùbá textiles is intelligible. It is couched in patterns, colors, threads, designs, imprinted images, contextual codes, metaphors, and stylo-artistic conventions that when visualized are rendered as visual signs and which, drawing from Danesi's argument, when combined, form a text. These codes manifest the dialogic potentials of Yorùbá textiles which, when activated

---

[3] See Abrams, *Glossary*, 317, for distinctions between personal and impersonal texts. Furthermore, although a creator's intention is paramount in the critical uncovering of a work's substance, contextual codes, and artistic offerings, that is, its meanings, to solely base interpretation on such a node of understanding would lead to cases of intentional fallacy – which is the attribution of a deciphered code or meaning to and as the author's intent.

[4] Terrence Hawkes, *Structuralism and Semiotics* (New York: Methuen, 1977). Also see Marcel Danesi, *Messages, Signs, and Meaning* (Ontario: Canadian Scholars' Press Inc., 2004).

[5] Danesi, *Messages*, 32.

[6] Abrams, *Glossary*, 317.

in a visual encounter, engage and hold the critical gaze and interest of any interrogator.[7] Decoded meanings are results of such visual dialogues. Unpacked meanings, varied and sometimes disagreeing,[8] depending on contexts, are then, as posited by Abrams, "naturalized in the activity of reading."[9] My choice of the excerpted phrase has an agenda: to show that by virtue of the shared conventions between weaver and the woven (impressed by one; manifested by the other) textiles and their codes are made to embody or represent reality, or, at the very least, an illusion of it.

Putting all these into consideration, a textile is an integrative system of thought framed as signs and whose import (hence intelligibility) is predicated on conventions, ideologies, and codes common to members of a particular society. More so, even Yorùbá's aesthetic consideration, manifesting as subjective or critical reading, of a Yorùbá dress as an emblem or adornment is indexical of a patterned social process and philosophy, one whose essence is aptly reflected in the following proverb: "Aṣọ là ńkí, kí a tó kí ènìyàn" (we praise/appreciate a person's dress before them). Abiodun, who also employs the same maxim in his chapter on Yoruba cloth, uses it to establish how Yorùbá textiles can be seen within the Yorùbá social space as performing the "agency of regeneration," whose power of renewing/effecting subjecthood is manifest in how it "oftentimes takes precedence over one's physical attractiveness or deformity."[10] Therefore, to channel from Abrams' argument, "by being brought into accord with modes of discourse and cultural stereotypes that are so familiar and habitual as to seem natural,"[11] the seeming vagueness of a textile's language is rendered accessible, so much so that each aesthetic or textual unit of meaning is related to and is deemed a representation of extratextual units such as the society, human, actions, etc. To render the foregoing in a more simplified form, Yorùbá textiles form a text constituted with codes whose messages can be parsed for the extraction of meanings. If Yorùbá textiles were to be a text, then its sartorial tradition would necessarily transcend a random assemblage of designs, aesthetics, conventions, and threads/fabrics into a system.

---

[7] "Interrogator" as used is here is expansive. It could range from a simple cloth user or an appreciator of dress to a researcher.
[8] This is because a message can have one meaning, and several messages can have the same meaning as is very evident in Yorùbá textiles and art generally. There are instances of the same textile depicting the same thing.
[9] Abrams, *Glossary*, 317.
[10] Rowland Abiodun, "We Greet Aso before we Greet its Wearer," in *Yoruba Art and Language: Seeking the African in African Art* (Cambridge: Cambridge University Press, 2014), 142–177, at 162.
[11] Abrams, *Glossary*, 316.

While it is no longer doubtful that Yorùbá textiles are and can be read as a text, it is essential to emphasize that in proffering its messages to be parsed into culture-specific meanings, it serves as a veritable system that accounts for and accentuates the history, economics, culture, and social peculiarities of the setting that powers its institution. Like any art, Yorùbá textiles are reflective of the culture of their people.[12] This functional peculiarity of Yorùbá textiles is a corollary of their status as craft and art.[13] As art, it shows stylistic conventions – that is, Àṣà (tradition) – idiosyncratic stylistic peculiarities, aesthetics, artistic signs and designs, and elements, or what Banjoko describes as aesthetic peculiarities and stylistic forms[14] and which also culminates into a form of visual Oríkì, given the ability of the constitutive elements of a dress and cloth ensemble to redefine and charge the significations of such cloth along spiritual and religious lines. All these form a complete system that raises the appeal of Yorùbá dress, rendering it highly relevant to Yorùbá society. As craft, it reveals the process, economics, and history of its making. As such, Yorùbá textiles or dress are multifaceted in their existence, and cannot be pigeonholed on the basis of artistry or craftsmanship.

As craft, and by self-referencing the histories and conditions of their making, Yorùbá textiles fulfill the major mandate of Yorùbá art: serving as a mirror of Yorùbá culture and history. In reference to this imaginal function in particular, Yorùbá textiles excel. How? The history of Yorùbá textiles, especially Yorùbá sartorial culture in general, however sketchy or vague it might be in terms of its precolonial provenance, is tied to innovations, continuities, or disjunctures obtainable in Yorùbá tradition and history. The strength of any relationship between cloth and culture is further accented in the history of the presence of European countries in what is now the southwestern region of Nigeria (inhabited by the Yorùbá) and how it affected the sartorial tradition of

---

[12] Thessy Akinbileje, "Symbolic Values of Clothing and Textiles Art in Traditional and Contemporary Africa," *International Journal of Development and Sustainability* 3, no. 4 (2014): 626–641, at 627.

[13] Although it should be noted, and as championed by studies such as Jan Vansina, *Art History in Africa: An Introduction to Method* (London and New York: Longman, 1984), Yorùbá textiles are not accorded the same status in Yorùbá stylo-artistic tradition or scholarship like sculpture by certain art historians and ethnologists. This is also very visible in the lack of substantial and substantive study of and on the history of precolonial Yorùbá textile and sartorial tradition (Bukola Oyeniyi, *Dress in the Making of African Identity: A Social and Cultural History of the Yoruba People* [New York: Cambria Press, 2015]; Dani Lyndersay, *Nigerian Dress, the Body Honoured: The Costume Arts of Traditional Nigerian Dress from Early History to Independence* [Lagos: Centre for Black and African Arts and Culture, 2011]). See also Akinbileje, "Symbolic Values" for how Yorùbá textiles are sometimes seen as more craft – or lesser and minor art – than art, and the consequences of such lopsided conclusions. Of course, such views betray colonial impetuses, or are championed from parochial and Eurocentric positions, as they tend to emphasize the functionality of Yorùbá dress over artistry.

[14] C. H. Banjoko, *Visual Art Made Easy* (Lagos: Movic Publication Co., 2009), 84.

that region.[15] Steiner's position on this presents for critical observation a time frame in Yorùbá history where there existed a significant culture contact between Europeans and Yorùbá people, and where each affected the other's economy. To shed more light on this is to quote Steiner: "The textile trade between Europe and Africa in the 19th and early 20th centuries was a back and forth process in which European textile producers responded to African desires, and in which African consumers reacted to European stylistic and commercial proffers."[16] This quotation reveals a significant period in Yorùbá history necessitated and underscored by the sartorial tradition of one culture, as well as its vibrant economy. The implication of this historical foregrounding is that it negates the much-believed idea held by European scholars that African cultures are affected by the West and that the former are often the receiving cultures. By proposing a different narrative, accurate too, Yorùbá textiles – that is, the dyed and woven fabrics – reveal a historical account that subverts the colonial account and establishes precolonial Yorùbá as an abode of aesthetic and stylistic peculiarities influencing European designers. Furthermore, Yorùbá textiles, in their capacities as historical texts, push the narrative of African and, by extension, Yorùbá cultures as vibrant economies for European markets and civilization.

On a temporal basis, the historical provenance of dress (*Aṣọ*) and the tradition of dressing (*Àṣà ìmúra*) in Yorùbáland itself, as ancient Yorùbá features, are also reflected by the dresses themselves, although this time through sculptures. Several sculptures, stone figures, and figurative expressions, with what Oyeniyi calls "their minimalist humanism and realism" dated as far back as AD 800–1000, including *Ìdènà* and *Oreluere* from *Ore* groove in Ilé Ifẹ̀, and terracotta heads with brass and bronze sculptures dated AD 1000–1400, all attest to the existence of the use of dress in Yorùbáland at such ancient times.[17] Some of these stone, brass, or terracotta images, despite a wide gap between them in terms of temporality and geography, have similarities and motifs that further entrench this claim: headgear, crowns, and coronets, beads and other materials of adornment are visible indications.

The power of such visual images in serving as cultural ambassadors and historical self-witnesses is underscored by Oyeniyi. He claims that the ancientness of these Yorùbá arts and the fact that, although they existed at different times, their similarities border on dressing and dress types is a strong and credible testifier to the position that Yorùbá dress, however narrowly or broadly conceptualized, existed before the arts were made. This position is

---

[15] See C. B. Steiner, "Another Image of Africa: Toward an Ethnohistory of European Cloth Marketed in West Africa, 1873–1960," *Ethnohistory* 32, no. 2 (1985): 91–110. See also Oyeniyi, *Dress in the Making*.
[16] Steiner, "Another Image," 91.
[17] Oyeniyi, *Dress in the Making*, 35.

logical since an artwork is expected to reflect the social and historical conditions that have influenced its creation – influenced the artist who channels such influences into what is created. Yorùbá artists make use of sociocultural and historical materials. More so, artists do not create in a vacuum. All these buttress the place of Yorùbá cloth and textile in serving as reinventers, reconstructors, and indicators of Yorùbá history, and especially as instruments of counter-Western and counter-hegemonic discourses that seek to cast a despicable image of the Yorùbá: one of such positions is the claim of the absence of dress in Yorùbáland, and that Yorùbá people walked about naked and unclothed. This is false, as there was a range of different forms of Yorùbá dress in use even then. Young boys wore *Bàǹtẹ̀* (a sort of triangle-shaped pants) for play time, while girls used a kind of apron (*Tòbí*). Other dress forms used by young children, and also by women, are *Yẹrì* and *Ìlábírù* – the former drawn up to cover the chest, the latter worn as undergarment. There are also several others categorized as *Aṣọ iṣeré* (play), *Aṣọ imúroko* (work/farm), and *Aṣọ ijáde* (outing/festivities).

In addition, in the same historical strength, Yorùbá cloth subverts colonial interpretations of Africa and Yorùbáland as a vast spread of creative emptiness and a void filled only with blabber and dark uselessness. This functionality of Yorùbá dress affords it the prestigious status of an anticolonial historical text, considering the fact that "the image of Africa which emerges from the woven threads, fast dyes, and printed fabrics differs from the image put forth in the writings of 19th-and-20th century explorers, missionaries, colonial administrators, and amateur anthropologists."[18] For, as scholars such as Beoku-Betts,[19] Curtin,[20] and Hopkins[21] put it, while colonial writings mostly offered the popular visual images/imageries of a dark continent populated with thoughtless humans and gerrymandering stick figures, African textiles presented far more subtle but rich interpretations of the ontology and stylistic richness of African life. It is this stylo-artistic richness that serves as impetus or drive for the creative capacities of European weavers and designers who sought to penetrate African cloth markets.

The details of this particular timescape in the Yorùbá historical timeline are not only readable in Yorùbá textiles, but the very presence of some of these old fabrics in present-day Yorùbáland attests to these historical details embedded in them. As such, they serve as template for intra-textual considerations. Some of those textiles such as tie-and-dye fabrics had their patterns remade in prints

---

[18] Steiner, "Another Image," 92.
[19] Josephine Beoku-Betts, "Western Perceptions of African Women in the 19th and Early 20th Centuries," *Africana Research Bulletin* 6, no. 4 (1976): 86–113.
[20] Phillip D. Curtin, *The Image of Africa: British Ideas and Action, 1780–1850* (Madison: University of Wisconsin Press, 1964).
[21] A. G. Hopkins, *An Economic History of West Africa* (New York: Columbia University Press, 1973).

otherwise called African prints.²² These African prints and their presence in Yorùbáland signifies the borrowing, adaptation, and adoption that existed in early Yorùbá (art) history. The implication of this is the revelation and reemphasizing of the presence of Europeans on African soil at some point. Yorùbá textiles, thus, become a meta-historical document. It is no wonder then that Yorùbá dress is referred to by Oyeniyi as a fertile space where cultural ambassadors and external participants can critically dialogue with Yorùbá culture and history, just as I have chosen to do in this chapter. These, however, as contained knowledge, are unlocked by and mostly through a conscious and informed interrogation, an approach I am conscious of. Drawing on the established propositions, I believe that as a system of artistic intelligence, highlighting the back-and-forth processes of artistic influence and inspiration, borrowing, adoption, and temporality in Yorùbá space, Yorùbá textiles reinvent themselves as a meta-historical text: a historical text that sheds light on its and other related histories. Also, extending on Abiodun's methodological conception of *Oríkì*, I hold the view that it is their (dress) function as visual *Oríkì* that effectuates their ability to evoke and reflect adequately portions of history when held in an informed visual dialogue. To clarify, as a form of *Oríkì* existing visually to stimulate referents (spiritual entities, notional/ideational abstractions, as well as living persons), Yorùbá dress would expressly center the dyadic relation between *Ìwà* and *Ẹwà*. This means that its *Ẹwà* (artistic and stylo-aesthetic beauty) enables a reading of its *Ìwà* (composition) and that of its wearer or owner, who is a product of history. Ultimately, to further clarify, this conception best exemplifies how the dress archive relates to me and my understanding of Yorùbá history. Thus, by self-relating the history of the sartorial tradition to which it belongs, Yorùbá dress as visual *Oríkì* allows for evocative commentaries on the history of the Yorùbá in general, while also drawing the latter into a conversation on its artifice and functionality.

The way textiles perform the aforementioned is simple and aptly captured by Oyeniyi, who argues that Yorùbá dress "offers a space through which the sociocultural and political history of the Yorùbá people and Yorùbáland can be studied."²³ For example, in tracing the provenance of Yorùbá dress one discovers that in Yorùbá history, from the earliest times, and as supported by the *Ifá* corpus,

---

²² See Steiner, "Another Image," 99. Artistic borrowing flowed from the bottom up – if world hierarchical power structuring were to be used, with African tribes and their markets below and European cultures above. Steiner gives vivid and iconographic details of how artistic borrowings ensued, how this history of borrowing is impressed and can be read on modern dresses such as *Àǹkárá* prints and other African prints; and how the resist methods employed by Africans in their tie-and-dye/indigo dyeing procedures were copied on technical basis by European designers. This is evident in similarities between patterns on locally made and imported dresses.

²³ Oyeniyi, *Dress in the Making*, 6.

the Òkànràn méjì and Òyèkú méjì,²⁴ that men have always worn Ṣòkòtò (trousers) and Bùbá (tops) while women wore Ìró (wrappers) tied around their bodies. In the same Odù (loosely translated as verse), the provenance of bosom covering for women is given. It is revealed that such cloth was introduced at a time to avoid and preclude unsolicited and uncouth gazing at female breasts,²⁵ signifying a particular temporal trajectory in Yoruba history.

Tracing the history of cloth in Yorùbáland leads to the conclusion on and identification of the industry of Yorùbá sub-ethnicities such as Ìjẹ̀bú, Ọ̀wọ̀, and Òṣogbo, who are well respected as good cloth-weavers pre-European contact. Oyeniyi argues that the Ìjẹ̀bú exported high-quality and durable textiles to Benin, which were brought home to several looms manufactories. He also comments on the texture of these materials as very fine.²⁶ Òṣogbo and Ìséyin are popular places heralded as the home of Yorùbá weavers.

In Ṣakí, Kìṣí, Ìgbẹ́tì, and Ìgbòho, cloth-making thrived before colonialism.²⁷ That Kíjìpá is regarded as the first Yorùbá cloth is not without reason. Regardless of whether it is traced to Òyó, where it is called Kókó cloth because Àkókó women made it, or to Ẹ̀gbá and Ìjẹ̀bu, where it is called Egbedí, or Aṣọ Ila, or to Ìgbómìnà, from where it is rumored to have emanated and which is believed to be the home of cloth production among the Yorùbá,²⁸ Kíjìpá as a Yorùbá cloth does not fail to portray the historical ethnic units of

---

²⁴ See Oyeniyi, Dress in the Making and Lyndersay, Nigerian Dress. Òkànràn méjì and Òyèkú méjì are two Ifá corpuses that explain the provinciality and historicity of Yorùbá dress. The Ifá corpus is regarded as the Yorùbá science of divination, handed to Òrúnmìlà, the Ẹlẹ́rìí ìpín, upon the creation of the universe. References to items and materials as well as events that can be dated to more recent times can be found in the Ifá corpus. This is the dynamism and spiritual potency of that system of divination in Yorùbá cosmology and to Yorùbá ontology. As such, the Ifá corpus to some extent can be said to explain/spotlight Yorùbá sartorial history. See Oyeniyi, Dress in the Making, for more details. Although, in relation to the Òyèkú méjì and Òkànràn méjì, Oyeniyi calls into question the veracity of the Odù, which also relates the history of Ṣàngó, who at the time of Òrúnmìlà's composition of the entire corpus had not existed. While this seems to point at a time continuum or temporal incongruence, such a position only follows in line of the kinds of scholarship that take African epistemological systems at face value and seek to understand them as they would Western knowledge mediums. The Ifá corpus is a spiritual-empowered, driven, composed, and functional system of divination and knowledge, not a modern computing system; as such, it is open to mysteries that transcend human comprehension and conception of logic and temporal coherence. On this note, Western theoretical principles should be applied judiciously in excavating knowledge from Yorùbá knowledge and divinatory systems that are rooted in Yorùbá epistemic culture.
²⁵ See Oyeniyi, Dress in the Making, 37.
²⁶ Oyeniyi, Dress in the Making. See also Deji Ogunremi and Biodun Adediran, eds., Culture and Society in Yorubaland (Ibadan: Rex Charles Publications, 1986), 6.
²⁷ Oyeniyi, Dress in the Making.
²⁸ The absence of consensus on the origin of Yorùbá cloth production, or of a written orthographic document to support any region's claim, and the proliferation and appearances of the earliest cloth, which in this case would be Kíjìpá, in many Yorùbá ethnicities during the first wave of researches into the subject matter undermines the veracity as well as authenticity of scholarship that identifies one particular tribe as the home place of Kíjìpá. As such, any claim identifying one is circumstantial at best.

Yorùbáland. Its very existence is a testament to a dynamic Yorùbá history, with various sub-ethnicities that share enough extreme cultural, mythico-spiritual, epistemological, and philosophical affinities to be grouped under a pan-Yorùbá taxonomy and consciousness. The vital import of this historical fact is not tied to *Kíjìpá*'s place of origin. It lies in its ability to shed light on ethnicities mentioned above, even as they existed independently, as having the same type of textile as the first cloth produced in Yorùbá history. It then cements the established notion that although the nomenclature "Yorùbá" might be a relative new cultural designation, Yorùbáness, the spirit/essence that unites the people, is not.

In addition to the historicity of *Kíjìpá*, which itself is a form of bark cloth, early Muslim and European traders accounted for the presence of nonwoven bark cloths as the earliest cloths in sub-Saharan Africa. Other materials are goats' wool, raffia, and cotton.[29] Although the "when" of Yorùbá use of bark cloths cannot be accurately determined for lack of materials and uniformity of sources already identified, some sources[30] identify the use of wool and cotton cloths by elites and rulers in sub-Saharan Africa, while the common people wore bark cloth (*Kíjìpá*) around the twelfth and thirteenth centuries.

Furthermore, changes in dress styles, color, production, and the types of material employed – woven (*Òfì*) or imported (*Àǹkárá*) or enhanced dyes *Kàmpálà* –are indicators of changes in Yorùbá history. Lyndersay accentuates this when she submits that political situations, economic health of the country, new imports, and availability of materials are temporal signifiers of changes and shifts in Yorùbá *Àsà aṣọ* (cloth culture/tradition). According to her, for instance, implying oral history as her source, there have been times in Yorùbá history where there was a ban on the use of shoes, boots, socks, gloves, wide-brimmed hats, and umbrellas by everyone except the king and his chiefs.[31]

In the case above, dress and dressing signify times in history and the prevalent spirit/practice/ethos of a period. Such practices were in place because "Ostentatious court dress was considered imperative for high-ranking chiefs in the eastern Yoruba kingdom of Ọ̀wọ̀."[32] In cementing this assertion, Lyndersay asserts that Oshogboye, the Ọlọ́wọ̀, the sixteenth ruler of Ọ̀wọ̀, introduced the dress. Various Yorùbá textiles and the overarching Yorùbá sartorial culture could reflect precolonial Yorùbá history, transitions in terms of dress designs, patterns and styles, and the changes in *Àsà aṣọ* (dress tradition)

---

[29] See Elisha P. Renne, *Cloth that Does Not Die: The Meaning of Cloth in Bunu Social Life* (Seattle: University of Washington Press, 1995), 102.

[30] Peter Adler, *African Majesty: The Textile Art of the Ashanti and Ewe* (New York: Thames & Hudson, 1995). See also Stanley B. Alpern, "What Africans Got for their Slaves: A Master List of European Trade Goods," *History in Africa* 22 (2005): 5–43.

[31] Lyndersay, *Nigerian Dress*, 296.

[32] Susan Vogel, ed., *For Spirits and Kings: African Art from the Paul and Ruth Tishman Collection* (New York: Cosmopolitan Museum of Arts, 1981), 133.

and Àṣà ìmúra (tradition/culture of dressing) by their very existence. They also signify the presence of historical factors such as Christianity and Islam and colonialism as well as postcolonial history and historical conditions.[33]

To cite a vital example, in relation to the post-independence period in Yorùbá history, Oyeniyi argues that, "much unlike the pre-colonial period, the use of indigenous dress, including African wax prints, was slightly greater than during the colonial period."[34] Therefore, by pointing to such historical shifts and moments in Yorùbá history, indigenous garments signify a period of cultural renaissance. This is because, as posited by Oyeniyi, "the independence and post-independence periods however recorded marginal increases in the number of indigenous dress users, as more than half of Yorùbá population used Yorùbá indigenous dress."[35]

Yet, again, the introduction of foreign/hybrid suits, such as the conductor suit, which was most fashionable during the post-independence period, led to a decline in the production and availability of male indigenous dress, a gross decline compared to independence period. In relation to women, the use of

---

[33] See Lyndersay, *Nigerian Dress*, and Oyeniyi, *Dress in the Making* for influences of these historical stages on Yorùbá cloth and textiles and how in an ironic turn they reflect these influences. Oyeniyi identified them as internal factors and external influences, among which are the interactions with Islamic/Arabic and Christian/European influences. Adeyemi B. Oyeniyi, "Dress and Identity in Yoruba Land, 1880-1980" (Ph.D. thesis, Leiden University, 2012), http://hdl.handle.net/1887/20143, also comments on Yorùbá dress and contemporary Yorùbá history.

[34] Oyeniyi, *Dress in the Making*, 260. More so, and as explained above, African wax prints had found their way into Yorùbáland from European weavers who had studied Yorùbá fashion styles and were disposed to producing for African/Yorùbá markets; such dress became domesticated over time. Steiner, "Another Image," dates the introduction of such wax prints into Africa between the nineteenth and twentieth centuries, although European fabrics themselves had been sold in West Africa since the fifteenth century; he also identifies two main types: wax prints (wax batiks) and non-wax prints (fancy or roller prints). Oyeniyi, *Dress in the Making* (170-171) further expounds on the presence and indigenization of these once "garish and crude ..." cloths. He identifies cost, African tastes, profit, cultural renaissance, and affordability – on the part of both the Yorùbá consumer and European producer – as reasons why some of these prints, like the Àǹkárá, remained, were accepted, and turned or were regarded as classic or traditional African cloth. Furthermore, to expound on the foregoing, Ruth Nielsen, "The History and Development of Wax-Printed Textiles Intended for West Africa and Zaire," in *The Fabrics of Culture*, ed. Justine M. Cordwell and Ronald A. Schwarz (The Hague: Mouton, 1979), 467-498, advances eight types of inspirational sources used in designing both wax and non-wax prints for the African market: (1) Indian cottons; (2) Javanese batiks; (3) European prints; (4) African indigenous cloth; (5) traditional African objects and symbols; (6) historical events, current events, political figures and ideas; (7) natural forms; and (8) geometrical designs. That these prints were specially designed for African markets and produced using African motifs, symbols, styles, designs, and woven around current events, ideas and political figures in the continent explain how they were easily adopted and domesticated overtime, despite other foreign elements.

[35] Oyeniyi, "Dress and Identity," 260-261.

female indigenous dress rose during post-independence period. Oyeniyi explains this as a result of an improved work condition for the females and as a result of women's increasing realization of their self-worth.

Hence, it is obvious that by being relatively absent or present, in varying degrees, over time Yorùbá fabrics function as compasses, pointing to historical conditions, like modernism and globalization, which are offshoots of independence and colonialism that are themselves historical periods. That historical details like these can be unearthed from Yorùbá fabrics buttresses the above position, which encompasses the thesis of this chapter: that Yorùbá garments are "mute and unintended witnesses to the events and circumstances that produced them."[36]

Summarily, it should not be disputed that Yorùbá textiles are a vital component of Yorùbá reality. The same way they serve as a transparent device through which Yorùbá past can be revisited, they also allow for a revisit of the socio-economic realities of Yorùbá history. The history of Yorùbá textiles is not without its economic implications, especially when tastes and market trends, popular rituals and fashion, availability of raw material and finished products are factored in.

One of the marketing values of Yorùbá textiles is their design. Yorùbá weavers are artistic in their creations. Artistry remains one of the pillars of Yorùbá craftsmanship. Artistry births beauty. Beauty to the Yorùbá is the sum of many things; hence, the saying "Ìwàlẹ̀wà" (character is beauty) is foremost among indigenous Yorùbá commentaries on social life. To underscore the importance of artistry, Steiner explains how Yorùbá (African) conceptions of creativity and design in relation to cloth serves as major sources of inspiration to European weavers and textile designers who sought to satisfy African tastes and produce for African markets. In other words, African textile tastes and stylo-artistic preferences served as major impetuses for cloth and fabrics produced and shipped down to Africa from Europe.[37] This cross-sectional /transnational and transcontinental inspiration between African clientele/ market and European designers was so evident that Christopher Steiner submits that: "Manchester textile producers took special interest in satisfying the aesthetic and practical demands of their West African clientele. It was a period in which Manchester printers were able to conquer the West African textile market by producing quality cloth of special colors and patterns suited to West African tastes and desires."[38] Taking into cognizance the enormity and significance of the cloth trade engendered between both parties, it is enough to assert that Yorùbá textiles impacted heavily on the economy of Yorùbáland.

---

[36] Oyeniyi, *Dress in the Making*, 36.
[37] See previous paragraphs and Steiner, "Another Image," for further clarification and explanation.
[38] Steiner, "Another Image," 91.

By being a cultural participant – being the material transacted – bearing the signatures of the stylistic tastes of one party and the artistic and reinventing prowess of another, and by existing through time to redirect the astute reader-interrogator who seeks to comprehend Yorùbá historio-economic details, Yorùbá textiles become self-reflexive.

The argument above rests on the premise that by influencing Yorùbá markets through the attraction of foreign interests and capital, which in turn influence their proliferation as fabrics – through use and (re)design and, hence, their participation in the economic history – the textiles attest to their inherent powers as instigators and vital denominators of Yorùbá socio-economic life. They also exist as testaments of/to themselves. Yorùbá textiles perform two functions: as socio-economic participants and as signifiers of economic history. This way, the dual tenets of New Historicism – the textuality of history and the historicity of text – are contained and realized in a single material, Yorùbá fabrics, which are, as explained already, texts.[39] The ways through which Yorùbá textiles participate and reflect Yorùbá economics are tied to the marketability of the cloths themselves. The marketability of Yorùbá cloths are anchored on many major conditions: style, taste, fashion, quality and pricing, affordability, time, accessibility, and fullness and length.

Quality has always been a major feature of Yorùbá fabrics because the average Yorùbá cloth is as functional as it is symbolic – the very reason that the functionality of a cloth in protecting the individual from the environment and its elements is crucial to the Yorùbá people. The ability of a cloth in withstanding such environmental elements and protecting the people is of utmost importance in determining its durability. The essentiality of these factors is that Yorùbá men and women often employ cotton cloths or *Òfì* to protect their bodies from cold. In recognition of the functional role of textiles to Yorùbá, or Africans in general, with regard to durability and quality, Governor Alfred Moloney, after a visit to Senegambia, issued warnings to European weavers that reemphasized quality, substantiality, and durability as essential factors that should be considered by home manufacturers should they aim at replacing the native weaving industry. According to Marion Johnson, the governor buttressed his point on the consequence of exporting shoddy goods when he wrote, "African cloths are now exposed for sale in every market

---

[39] New Historicism concerns itself with texts as historical documents. Historicizing a text and textualizing history is New Historicism's way of activating a text for its historical content and archiving history, respectively. This is very applicable to Yorùbá fabrics because of their self-reflexivity. While New Historicism requires the placement side by side and on an equal footing of both literary texts and historical documents to reactivate, reinvent, and properly understand history, it is as if Yorùbá textiles perform both functions simultaneously and as such become self-contained, a holistic medium or vehicle in understanding culture. See Peter Barry, *Beginning Theory: An Introduction to Literary and Cultural Theory* (Manchester: Manchester University Press, 2006).

place beside the European goods, and are not unlikely in time to beat them out of the markets on the coast."[40] One other very important reason for such a premium on durability by Yorùbá people was the humidity of the region. Dust, mud, and hot temperatures that induce perspiration necessitated constant washing, and only durable cloth can survive constant washing without fading.

Consequently, emphasis on durability and quality of textiles by Yorùbá led to a reorientation of European weavers that sought to cater for Yorùbá needs and maintain a strong presence in Yorùbá markets. The corollary was a competitive market that involved the African, British, and French – competitive but also vital/relevant.[41] Effects of the nature of Yorùbá textiles (their durability and quality) became causes of other effects – a case of an effect becoming a cause and producing the same effect. The insistence on durability and quality of textiles effected the production and introduction of European-produced textiles that were patterned after African wears and tastes, and were eventually domesticated by Africans as a result of their embrace of those aforementioned qualities.[42] In what eventually I consider a chain-link, the presence of alternatives in Yorùbá textile market, caused by the specificities of Yorùbá textiles and the European desire to break into this market, eventually led to other economic details such as pricing, style, fashion, and issues of accessibilities and production time.

The strong presence of European weavers in West African markets, like the Yorùbá, and their wax prints, which replaced the Indian cotton cloth, turned around the composition and nature of Yorùbá markets and economy. Competition and opportunity cost became appropriate terms through which Yorùbá textile markets and the economy in general can be understood. The wax prints were patronized owing to their relative cheapness compared to the

---

[40] See Marion Johnson, "Cotton Imperialism in West Africa," *African Affairs* 73, no. 291 (1974): 178–187, at 182.

[41] This type of market presented various options for the African consumer who is able to pick among alternatives – a commercial condition through which wax prints became indigenized. One such print is the *Àǹkárá*, which as a popular Indonesian cloth is called Ankara Mohair. Brought to West Africa by European merchants, the designs of the prints reflected the designs, color, and quality of West African weavers and textile industry, and grew in use during a period of cultural reinterest in Yorùbá/African dress in Yorùbáland, and other parts of West Africa. The introduction of these prints, patterned after African taste and styles, after a period of observation, what Oyeniyi explains as the sponsoring of European cloth merchants and craftsmen to visit and observe the West African indigenous cloth-making tradition, led to the sidelining of Indian cotton cloths, and production of prints that were cheap, colorful, although inferior, symbolic of renewed nationalist sentiment, and affordable. Affordability was a vital reason for the warm welcome of these prints, because, and according to Oyeniyi (*Dress in the Making*, 171), one who could not buy *Sányán* or *Àlàárì* could buy *Àǹkárá*, which could be made into various styles that reflected Yorùbá consciousness.

[42] See notes 33 and 41 above.

indigenous cloths such as the Àdìrẹ (tie and dye), after which they were patterned in terms of aesthetics, color, patterns, and designs. Although these cloths were initially considered garish looking and inferior, the availability of raw materials and the accessibility of these cloths compared to locally produced Àdìrẹ, which took a longer period of time to produce, improved the popularity of such prints among the Yorùbá. However, the imported Euro-African textiles brought about an increase in tariffs. Some of these European cloths, especially the Manchester cotton which preceded the prints, came at costly prices to the average West African, who could not afford such cloths that would signify a change in status. The consequence of this was a boom in local cotton manufacture. As such, the sometimes cheap, sometimes costly prices of hybridized prints as a result of changes in transportation tariffs and policies, the availability of these prints, the emphasis on quality and durability of indigenous cloths, and nationalist sentiments all contributed to a constantly dynamic Yorùbá economy.[43] This impact of the tariffs on local textile economy is better captured by M. Levecque:

> Since the increased price of textiles, which render our fabrics almost inaccessible to the natives of the interior, the latter have taken to cultivating cotton once again; a task which they neglected while they were able to purchase inexpensive textiles in our shops. Around the villages today, we notice numerous fields of cotton, and the weaver's loom has reappeared in many marketplaces. Indigenous cloth, which [for a time] was considered too expensive, has come into favor once again, and business is now idle in the shops of our merchants who are well stocked with imported European goods.[44]

That afore-discussed is why I submit that the Yorùbá cloth and textile industry not only served as a bridge through which Yorùbá taste, textile styles, and designs were introduced to the world, or through which European markets merged with African, leading to a dynamic local economy, but also became a vehicle of employment. Yorùbá textile production and sartorial industry became a platform through which families and individuals were occupied and employed, and through which Yorùbá emphasis on heritage and notions of unity and social units like Ìdílé[45] (generation/lineage) were kept. In addition, any examination of Yorùbá dress and textiles, sartorial tradition, and textile industry on historical and economic grounds would eventually spotlight

---

[43] See Steiner, "Another Image," for more on the back-and-forth mode of influence.
[44] Quoted in Steiner, "Another Image," 96.
[45] In Yorùbá ontology and social system, Ìdílé as a social unit comprises those who can trace their lineage to a single or common ancestor. In simple terms it is a (patri)-lineage. It transcends generations.

Yoruba sub-ethnic diversity and heritage. This means that each garment is a historical/geo-cultural index.

The history and commerce of Yorùbá textiles has implicated and impacted the popularity of several Yorùbá regions. Ìṣẹ́yin, a town northwest of Ibadan city in Ọ̀yọ̀ state in Nigeria is very popular – in fact, known – for its production of hand-woven cloth. The town is famous for its cloth woven on narrow horizontal looms by males, which is the town's major craft. As Jennifer Bray puts it, "there are 670 compounds in the town and the total population, which is probably now approaching 60,000, includes 28,000 tax-payers."[46] According to the tax returns, there are about 540 full-time weavers, who are members of 188 compounds. This means that about 55 percent of the town's taxable population is engaged in indigenous cloth-making.[47]

These statistics provided by Bray, in plain terms, accentuate Yorùbá dress, its cloth industry, and its sartorial tradition, as not only a means toward the generation of a town's source of income or a means of revenue, but as compasses. As compasses, Yorùbá fabrics readily identify a town's specific constitution from another – in Ìṣẹ́yin there are both male and female weavers. More so, they also distinguish a Yorùbá town from another. For instance, Ìṣẹ́yin is particularly known as the home of cloth weaving, while Abẹ́òkúta, another Yorùbá region, is popular as the home of *Àdìrẹ*. Yet again, the popularities of the various markets where these cloths are sold are also a function of the indexical nature of Yorùbá textiles.

To cite an example, markets for *Àdìrẹ* are Ìtokù (in Abẹ́òkúta), Akéréle (in Lagos), Gbági and Òjé (in Ibadan), Ọjà-Ọba (in Ìlọ́rin), Powerline (in Òṣogbo), Ẹ̀rẹ̀kẹ̀san (in Àkúrẹ́).[48] All these are places popular for the textiles and cloths marketed there. For woven cloths, such as *Òfì*, Lagos and Ibadan, especially Òjé market in Ibadan, which Bray submits is the largest market in Nigeria and the most important in the western region,[49] are major places where they are sold. In addition to such structured markets, there are systems in place that show that Yorùbá sartorial tradition is an industry, a commercial venture.

In Ìṣẹ́yin, the extended family (*Mọ̀lẹ̀bí*) united mostly in an *Agbo ilé*, which is a physical site (more like an extensive compound) housing several individual homes of kindred or *Ẹbí* (family members) or relations from the same *Ìdílé* in a closely knit physical structure, is the unit of production for cloth weaving and dyeing. Training, place of work, and sometimes, when Ìjẹ̀bú buyers whom Ìṣẹ́yin people are said to produce for at certain periods of the year come buying, retailing occurs inside the *Agbo ilé*. This structure serves as the major reason

---

[46] See Jennifer M. Bray, "The Organization of Traditional Weaving in Iseyin, Nigeria," *Journal of the International African Institute* 38, no. 3 (1968): 270–280, at 270.
[47] Bray, "Traditional Weaving."
[48] Oyeniyi, "Dress and Identity," 270.
[49] Bray, "Traditional Weaving."

cloth weaving in Ìsẹ́yìn is mostly a family heritage and business, with several families performing the same sartorial task. Established weavers train members of the same Ìdílé, especially those in the same Agbo ilé. Thus, those trained, when established, do not set up themselves or their own establishments outside this extended family unit, but contribute to it. Each continues to work as one of the weavers in the compound. In the case of Ìsẹ́yìn, though, and most Yorùbá communities, except Ọ̀wọ̀ and Kàbà,[50] the men are believed to weave for business purposes, on narrow horizontal looms, while women weave on broad looms for household purposes.

Ìsẹ́yìn has been presented as an example to highlight the benefits of Yorùbá sartorial culture to the Yorùbá economy because of its detailed structure, popularity, and essentiality to the Yorùbá clothing industry and tradition. It is obvious at this point that this industry is premised on Yorùbá social structure, and is reflective of how the Yorùbá economy rests on structured societal units (like the Ìdílé and Agbo ilé) which in turn contribute immensely to the group's economy. In quoting Bray, the systematic nature of cloth enterprise in Yorùbáland through the Ìdílé structure is reflected thus:

> When a boy becomes a "perfect weaver," it is customary for his father to provide him with a loom and the basic tools of the trade, but this responsibility does not extend to the purchase of cotton thread, silk, and dyes. Young men must therefore obtain initial capital elsewhere. There is no class of professional moneylenders in Iseyin, but a system of entrepreneur weavers is in operation.[51]

At this juncture then, it is undeniable that Yorùbá textiles are never just cloths but referential texts – texts that are as self-reflexive as they are pods of historical, economic, and contextual details, carrying within their visual designs, threads, dyes, even styles and aesthetics, historical accounts, cultural, and then economic messages that can be unlocked as codes of meaning. As such, however hard they may be or pose themselves to be read as texts – which would not be more complex than any intricately composed or difficult text – Yorùbá cloths, when studied within the context of Yoruba culture, eventually yield rich cultural and sociohistorical meanings that buttress their claims to be texts. Owing to this undeniable reality of Yorùbá textiles as archival mediums and visual sources of intelligence, I, in an effort to expose how the textiles that

---

[50] In Ọ̀wọ̀ it is believed that men did not weave, while in Kàbà, among the Bunu people, men's weaving was minimal. See Aretha Oluwakemi Asakitikpi, "Functions of Hand Woven Textiles among Yoruba Women in Southwestern Nigeria," *Nordic Journal of African Studies* 16, no. 1 (2007): 101–115. Although in places like Ìlọ́rin and Ìjẹ̀bú, and generally, wherever men's weaving is minimal, women's weaving is prominent. And as such, cloths produced are not solely used for household purposes alone, but for also religious and socio-functional purposes.

[51] Bray, "Traditional Weaving," 273. See also Bray for extensive explanation on the structure and system of cloth-making in Ìsẹ́yìn.

have defined me as a cultural agent as well as a medium through which they attain their fullest realizations as nodes of rich meanings, examine several personal Yorùbá textiles and fabrics to establish a synthesis between my knowledge of their significations, their capacity to embody and embed Yorùbá ideologies, concepts, philosophies, and their potentialities to exist as symbols and frames through which Yorùbá ontology and culture can be understood.

Textiles as Expressions of Yorùbá Visions

Yorùbá textiles are physical or visual expressions of Yorùbá philosophies and sociocultural realities, in that their very existence is symptomatic of socio-dialogic processes. Putting it differently, the textiles are representations of Yorùbá social structure, in both literal and non-literal senses, that engage social adherents in visual dialogues rich in (nonverbal/mental) indigenous discourse practices, and through which they come alive as visual codes. Hence, through relational functionality – that is, on a contextual and context-specific basis – Yorùbá textiles express, symbolize, and also serve as physical signifiers of sociocultural beliefs, structure, ethos, and other pillars of the Yorùbá social firmament. As such, they can be seen as frames through which the scaffolds of the society are rendered visible or as nodes of cultural notions, nuances, and postures, or as vehicles of signification and transitions. In accentuating the symbolic and signifying capacities of Yorùbá textiles, Oyeniyi submits that "dress offers itself as a canvas upon which innumerable codes-kin relations, sociopolitical status, group affiliations, and gender are written."[52]

As an idealizing mirror, a vehicle of signification, and a pod of social meaning, Yorùbá textiles lean inwardly to shore up external meanings. This is because, by virtue of being, of existing as a fabric, any Yorùbá textile performs the function of a code, a reflector of the Ọmọlúàbí principle – that corpus of Yorùbá people's take on the ideal being, what Oyeniyi calls a master code and describes as permeating all uses of dress.[53] The Yorùbá consider dressing, as an act (Ìwọṣọ), and dressing, as style or culture (Ìmúra), a way of rending one's civility and a conscious attempt at keying into the generally upheld ideal state of the Ọmọlúàbí. Ìmúra is a process and a vehicle through which individuality is conceived within the permissions of a broader social

---

[52] Oyeniyi, Dress in the Making, 6.
[53] Ọmọlúàbí is a moral and ethical requirement that relates to everyone in the society, be it old, young, male or female. It is also a confluence of principles that dignify the Yoruba: Ọ̀rọ̀ sisọ (speech), Ìtẹríba (respect) Inú rere (good heart), Otitọ (truthfulness), Ìwà (good character), Akíkanjú (bravery), Iṣẹ́ (hard work), Ọpọlọ pípè (intelligence), and Ìmúra/ Ìwọaṣọ (dressing well) among others.

collective, or personal identity is conceived and as well maintained within the collective one.

Bùbá (top) and Sòkòtò (trousers) can be seen as an act of social distancing – of separating the civilized self (Ẹni tó lajú) or (Ọ̀làjú) from the uncultured self (Ará oko). This idea is best represented in the proverb that says "Àìfini peni, àìfèèniyàn pèèyàn, ló ń mú ara-oko sán bàǹtẹ́ wọ̀lú" (it is crass incivility that makes a country bumpkin enter the city in his Bàǹtẹ́).[54] Bàǹtẹ́ is a kind of clothing worn to cover the private parts and is tied in a triangular pattern. It is mostly used by those who the Yoruba call Ará oko[55] – those who live on their farms inside the bushes and forests and as such are withdrawn or separated from urban(e) traditions.

Consequently, to dress well is seen as a counteracting action or a binary opposing force to being an Ará oko who is not an Ọ̀làjú (a civilized person). "Là" means to open; "Ojú" is eyes. Ọ̀làjú, a blending and contraction, is thus opening of the eyes, an expression which when activated on a metaphoric level means to be open to innovations, and the tenet or principle of dressing well (Ìmúra) is seen in statements like "A fẹ́ là wọ́n lójú" (we want to civilize them – bumpkins or the bucolic persons).

Dressing well is so prevalent among the Yorùbá that they often say "Kí a dára díẹ̀, ká tó ṣ'àwúre ni àwúre fi ń jẹ́" (to dress well or look well before conferring/ pronouncing blessings expedites the activation or actuality of such pronouncements). This is why any social activity that demands the flow of Àṣẹ or power-laden pronouncements from someone in a position of authority to a beneficiary is often attended by well-dressed persons, and demands that the participants look good. Any opposition to such ideological visions, in terms of looking the part, engenders sayings like "Ọ̀bùn ṣìọ̀ṣìọ̀, ni yóò ru ẹrù afínjú wọlé,"[56] which means "a dirty person would serve the beautiful." This owes to the Yorùbá idea that anyone who places or pays inadequate attention to his Ìmúra and appearance is a dirty or filthy fellow (Ọ̀bùn) – although there is always an accompanying emphasis on moderation.

---

[54] Oyeniyi, Dress in the Making, 22.
[55] The Yoruba people have three different farm types: Oko Etílé, Oko Ẹgàn, and Oko Igbó, all of which are differentiated by the distance between the farms and the homes of the farmers. The first two are relatively close to home, with the first being established just outside a town's outskirts and the other in the distant but open savanna. The third is usually in the forest, and because of the distance between such forests and the homes of those who cultivate such farms, homes are usually built beside them, to enable the farmers live for as long as they want to farm there. Yoruba people hold the belief that the longer one stays on such farms, the more removed one becomes from the codes of civility found in the towns, and as such from civilization. Hence, such Oko Igbó farmers turned and remained bucolic. As such, Ará, which means person, is combined with Oko to designate the absence of civilization, and presence of bucolic people.
[56] Oyeniyi, Dress in the Making, 20.

It is obvious that dressing well is a significant part of the Yorùbá cultural sphere. To dress well is to present one's self to be appreciated by the public and to be an idealizing mirror through which others temper the sharp contours of individuality in order to find acceptance within the broader collective identity – the identity of civilized people. The aesthetic of the cool thus becomes paramount in appreciating such functional relevance of Yorùbá cloth in tempering and eliminating the wildness that comes from incivility. The calm and presentable veneer afforded an individual through dress exalts the personality of such a person into an ideal one worthy of emulation by others. For instance, in Figures 10.1 and 10.2 there are ranges of Yorùbá textile clothing that when worn denote a full dress sense or Ọmọlúàbí emphasis on Ìmúra appreciated by the Yorùbá. These figures show Dànṣíkí (a short flowing gown). Each image boasts a complete dress set: the Dànṣíkí are accompanied with Ṣòkòtò sooro (long trousers) and Fìlà (caps). Each garment of the whole Dànṣíkí ensemble is cut from the same stock or made from the same loom/thread. Furthermore, the design of each piece varies from image to image to signify the rich and expansive creative tastes and stylo-artistic flourish of Yorùbá cloth-weavers and designers.

Figures 10.3, 10.4, and 10.5 are examples of the Agbádá dress ensemble (a long flowing gown). The Agbádá (Figure 10.5), which is a large gown made of locally hand-woven cloth is worn by traditional Yoruba noblemen

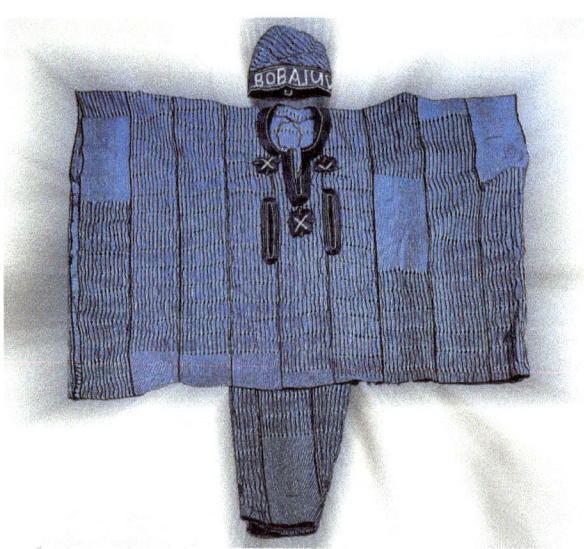

Figure 10.1 Dànṣíkí

Figure 10.2 *Dànṣíkí*

and royalty,[57] is appreciated for its complete and ensemble sense. It has the *Bùbá* (top – see Figure 10.5 – worn underneath the *Agbádá* and on the *Ṣòkòtò*), *Ṣòkòtò* (Figure 10.5), *Fìlà* (on top; Figure. 10.5), and the *Agbádá* (the longer version of the *Agbádá* – flowing gown). Anyone who puts on an *Agbádá*, especially one that has rich embroidery and design, as such in Figures 10.4 and 10.5, and does not disuse or misuse any of its components, is accorded great respect. Initially it was worn by the high and mighty in the society, and as such was a visual insignia of royalty and power, serving in the capacity of a social divider. But the fluidity of modernism as a sensibility has collapsed any such boundaries reflected by and engineered by the use of *Agbádá*.

Still, despite Western modernism and overwhelming sartorial influences from the West's fashion culture, the *Agbádá* in the Yorùbá socio-sphere retains

[57] Oyeniyi, "Dress and Identity," 278.

Figure 10.3 *Agbádá*

Figure 10.4 *Bùbá* and *Ṣòkòtò*

Figure 10.5 *Agbádá* and *Fìlà*

its significance and reflects Yorùbá essentialist visions of honor and prestige. In any gathering, the *Agbádá* signals civility, prestige, class, and a taste for fashion (*Ìmúra*), and as such produces more reverence and appraisal than the other aforementioned garments. In addition, there is the presence of beads when such clothes are worn, which indicates a rich appreciation of adornments by the Yorùbá people. By being associated with a certain class and by, as consequence, identifying the degree of eminence and the type of personality of each wearer, Yoruba dress, such as the *Agbádá*, reflects the notional content and semantic ranges of the idiomatic expression "Adé orí la fi ń mọba, ìlèkè la fi ń mọ ìjòyè," which means that it is the cloth and clothing items we use in distinguishing people: chiefs and royalty, amongst others. Figures 10.3 and 10.4 are other *Agbádá* designs. The expansive nature of the *Agbádá* and the intricate design on the neck–chest regions of each *Agbádá* image further shore up the exotic and classy position of the *Agbádá* among Yoruba dress types. Like in Figures 10.2, 10.4, and 10.5, we can see clearly the other dress parts (*Bùbá*, *Ṣòkòtò*, and *Fìlà*) that complete the *Agbádá* ensemble. Owing to the cost of weaving, making, and design, it is not common to find lower-class or middle-class persons wearing *Agbádá*, especially heavily embroidered and, consequently, expensive ones.

Furthermore, when observed, especially considering Figures 10.6, 10.7, and 10.8, the difference between the *Dàńṣíkí* in terms of width and size is revealed. This is a testament to the ranges of Yorùbá sartorial styles. Both *Bùbá* and *Ṣòkòtò* (see Figure 10.9) are embroidered with beautiful and colorful threads. The design and colorful *Aṣọ òkè* material enhances the artistry of the final product. The garment in Figure 10.10 is not *Dàńṣiki* but *Bùbá* (with obvious and extended arms) and *Ṣòkòtò* with its matching *Fìlà*. Figure 10.11 is simpler compared to the rest, and as such less elaborate, which means less costly. Figure 10.12 is also an example of a short *Dàńṣíkí*. These clothes could be worn by anybody in the society. Anyone who wears cloths of such design and make

Figure 10.6 *Agbádá Yẹbẹ* I

Figure 10.7 *Agbádá Yẹbẹ* II

would not belong to the same category as those who wear heavily embroidered *Agbádá*, for obvious economic reasons.

To further comment on how dress reflects Yoruba social atmosphere, *Dàṅṣíkí* or *Gbáriyè*, especially the longer ones, when worn by members of the middle and lower class, are mostly in response to a significant event: naming ceremonies, work freedom ceremonies, and other social events. As such, Figure 10.8 belongs to the category of clothes considered *Aṣọ lílò nílé* (home clothes) or casual clothes as opposed to *Aṣọ ìmúròde* (outing clothes). Figure 10.13 is an example of *Ṣòkòtò Kẹ̀nbẹ̀* types that are often large and expansive and worn under *Dàṅṣíkí or Gbáriyè*. Figure 10.14 is also a *Dàṅṣíkí* type made from an *Aṣọ òkè* material, but with *Kẹ̀nbẹ̀* trousers.

The same specificity is also extractable from precolonial female wardrobe culture. A young woman mostly wears a wrapper (*Ìró*), but a married woman, to portray her transition, wears both *Bùbá* and *Ìró*. This very structured attitude to dress by the Yoruba testifies to how the ability to dress well is not only functional in *Ọmọlúàbí* terms but also considered one of the factors

Figure 10.8 *Agbádá* (Five Knives)

Figure 10.9 *Bùbá/Ṣòkòtò/Fìlà* (Five Knives)

TEXTILES AS TEXTS 307

Figure 10.10 *Bùbá* and *Ṣòkòtò* type I

Figure 10.11 *Bùbá* and *Ṣòkòtò* type II

308 VISUAL CULTURES

Figure 10.12 Short-sleeve *Dànṣíkí*

Figure 10.13 *Dànṣíkí* type (*Gbáriyè*)

Figure 10.14 Ṣòkòtò Kẹ̀nbẹ̀

underscoring the process of choosing wives for sons by family members (parents). Other than the physical act of dressing, which signifies a tolerance for civility and moderation (*Ìwọ̀ntunwọ̀sìn*),[58] the emphasis on the ability to dress well carries the metaphor of wellness, well-being, and deportment. Dress, how one is dressed, is believed to enhance the body's reality. More so, by virtue of dressing, individual members are believed to be ambassadors of the family. Putting all these into perspective, Yorùbá textiles show their ability to engage onlookers, members of the society, and other interrogators, in a cultural visual dialogue, for it is through this dialogue, through exchange of meanings, that signification is established.

---

[58] Yorùbá people place a big emphasis on moderation. Excessiveness in anything is frowned upon. Excessive dressing, especially by females, is frowned upon. Such person is called *Onífààrí*. Hence, the proverb "*Fáàrí àṣejù oko olówó níí rán wọn lọ*" (excessive dressing leads to bankruptcy). See Oyeniyi, *Dress in the Making*, 100.

Figure 10.15 Aṣọ ẹbí

Family (Ẹbí) is vital to the Yorùbá social structure. It is the smallest unit of the society – a closely knit one, somewhat like a collective of blood relations – and as such each member of that unit is seen as an ambassador, and must not contravene the ethos or tarnish the image of said Ẹbí. Members of Ẹbí refer to themselves as Mọ̀lẹ́bí to reflect the emphasis on familial bond which ties and exalts the Ẹbí unit above most social/cultural units in Yorùbá social system. The Ẹbí is considered both governing system – for its unifying principles[59] that hold members in submission to its authority – and a unit of social interaction. The underlying ideology is unity. It creatively rehashes and draws from the celestial pantheonic relations between Yorùbá deities and Òrìṣà founded on notions of kinship, while also retaining the political influences of such cosmological ordering in relation to Yorùbá ontology and social-cultural hierarchy. The political hierarchy in Yorùbá cosmology, with Olódùmarè being the head, and the Òrìṣà following one another according to divine potentials, is reflected in the Ẹbí system. Furthermore, the ancestral link to Ilé Ifẹ̀ as well as to Odùduwà is also manifested in the guiding principles of the Ẹbí.

In addition to textiles emphasizing Yorùbá notions of kinship, prestige, and royalty and signifying the Yorùbá kin system and social hierarchy, they also function as occupation and gender compasses. The kind of cloth worn, for

[59] Obedience and relationship to the overarching Ẹbí principle is not enforced forcefully, but engendered through a common acceptance of the authority of the organizing principle: relation and unity by blood.

example, by a farmer is different from that of a hunter, and that worn by a man is different from that of a woman. In a social order they act as visual signposts, aiding and communicating identity without the input of verbal communication. Strict notions of masculinity and femininity in Yorùbáland are espoused and maintained through strict principles on the act of *Ìmúra*. For instance, a man cannot wear or use any of the female attire, which mainly consists of *Ọ̀já*, *Ìpèlé*, *Ìborùn*, *Bùbá*, *Gèlè*, and *Ìró* (as seen in Figures 10.17 and 10.18). Likewise, a woman cannot wear *Ṣòkòtò* or (male) *Bùbá* or *Agbádá*.[60] It is almost a taboo to see a man wear a *Gèlè* (headdress).

Figure 10.16 Hunter. Source: Courtesy of Michael Efionayi.

[60] It should be noted that there are exceptions in the use of *Agbádá* and *Ṣòkòtò*, as a result of the influx of modernism (Western modern culture) and Western civilization. Women now sew clothes in the *Agbádá* style – which mandates the use of *Ṣòkòtò* (this is often purposive, and not the norm). Yet, even if such instances are considered, the truth is women's clothing types are and can only be made to resemble Yorùbá male styles (*Agbádá*); they seldom wear male *Agbádá* or any other male garment.

Figure 10.17 Woman's clothing ensemble. Source: Courtesy of Michael Efionayi.

Figure 10.18 Yèye Falola

Figure 10.19 Dress with beads on *Abetí ajá* (a type of *Fìlà*)

Principles of *Ìdílè*, *Mòlẹ́bí*,[61] and *Ará* that are predicated on and underscored by a pervading and prevailing sense of unity thus become applicable and are manifested through dressing. At a social function, *Mòlẹ́bí* or members of the same *Ìdílé* wear the same attire to separate them from others and well-wishers. This is called *Aṣọ ẹbí*. This entails the use of the same textile which may come in different designs in the same social gathering by members of the same family. The use of *Aṣọ ẹbí* textiles to signify the political and cultural implication of the *Ẹbí* system, which mirrors the strong affiliations between the different Yorùbá sub-ethnicities, is a visually aided communication of support, unity, and familial love.

Aṣọ ẹbí is different from *Aṣọ ẹgbẹ́jọdá*. *Aṣọ ẹbí* is limited to members of the family, while the other can be used by well-wishers, friends, and co-workers to signify a cohesive unit of supporting friends or to portray Yorùbá ideology on

---

[61] To simplify: *Ìdílé* is the basic socio-economic and political unit, with members possessing common deities, observing common taboos, farming on common or contiguous land, and answering to the same descriptive or eponymous name. Group identity derives from this. Many *Ìdílés*, when combined, form a town. The oldest male from the family of those who founded the town is regarded as head of the town. More so, to underscore the importance of *Ìdílé*, anyone who seeks to be a true member/son of the town must be identified with an *Ìdílé*, and the said *Ìdílé* must be able to trace its ancestry to Ilé Ifẹ̀ and Odùduwà. *Ẹbí*, on the other hand, is considered a commonwealth of blood relations. See Oyeniyi, "Dress and Identity" and Oyeniyi, *Dress in the Making* for further exposition. Although it is a closed unit, a migrant could be incorporated into the *Ẹbí*, and could form his own *Ẹbí*, but he cannot head the *Ìdílé*. In Oyeniyi's words, only autochthonous *Ẹbí* members can.

the nature and effect of communality. This way, individual identity is integrated into group identity. A good example of how Aṣọ ẹbí signifies unity is the marriage ceremony, which to the Yorùbá is not merely the unification of the newlyweds but also of their families. By wearing the same cloth, the two families espouse love and solidarity and identify as members of the same newly co-joined unit. This is why in Yorùbá tradition, couples cannot single-handedly end their marriages. Family members often have to wade in and adjudge marital squabbles and lend in their voices.

The Aṣọ ẹbí is so much structured as a means of identification and symbol of unification in Yorùbáland that during marriage ceremonies, and sometimes during other public functions, couples wear matching traditional outfits, mostly Aṣọ ẹbí, separate from the other members of the Ẹbí and those gathered. Unification in Yorùbá marriage ceremony thus begins from the use of Aṣọ ẹbí by both bride and groom, and continues with the use of Aṣọ ẹbí during social functions attended later on in the marriage. This is powerful symbolism, emphasizing the matrimonial bond, love, and unification. It is also a status symbol – a nonverbal and visual indicator of marital status.

The pivotal place of cloth/dress in signifying the unity between humans is also encoded in the saying "Ènìyàn laṣọ mi" (Humans are my clothes), which, literally, means humans (both of the Ẹbí and Ará – friends/acquaintances) are clothes. On a connotative level, it means humans are pillars of support. On a spiritually metaphoric level, it reveals the belief that clothes are gifts of Olódùmarè to cover the soul. Clothes are seen as coverings. In relation to notions of Ẹbí and Ará, anyone without Ẹbí or Ará is considered alone, exposed, and naked in Yorùbá ontology. Now, during public ceremonies, what signifies the value of an individual is the presence of those who support them, and this is visually represented by those who have employed a single cloth in depicting their presence and solidarity in support of the celebrant.

In summary then, Aṣọ ẹbí and Aṣọ ẹgbẹ́jọdá as well as those of the couples, in the case of marriage, are mediums through which Yorùbá people codify their emphasis on family, unity, support, loyalty, communality, ancestry, and household ambassadorship. In addition, Aṣọ ẹbí and Aṣọ ẹgbẹ́jọdá are indicators of representational identity. As a compass, they clearly indicate which family is being represented. Hence, misdeeds and misdemeanor by a single individual wearing a particular Aṣọ transcend personal lines to become blights and cast ignominy on the Ẹbí represented. Aṣọ ẹbí thus becomes an idealizing frame as well as a moralizing one. Visually, it precludes errancy by extracting the liberalizing powers of individuation through blurring the sharp contours of personal identity and situating an individual in a frame of a representational identity. The individual, by simply wearing an Aṣọ ẹbí, becomes more than themselves. Figure 10.15 is an example of Aṣọ ẹbí and Aṣọ ẹgbẹ́jọdá. In such functions there can be as many as twenty different groups wearing the same cloth sewn in different Bùbá and Ṣòkòtò/Ìró/skirt types.

In summary, it is apparent that Yorùbá textiles as texts work on interpretive and connotative levels. They are visual codes and frames which when activated through *Ìmúra* (dressing) and sociofunctional contexts proffer messages that can be unlocked into various and rich meanings by Yorùbá-conscious interrogators – that is, knowledge seekers who are rooted in Yorùbá epistemology – meanings that reveal the sociocultural ideologies, notions, and realities of the Yorùbá.

Textiles as Indexes

Textiles in Yorùbáland are an embodiment of power, and as such self-reflect their potency as power-contained/wielding material while also cementing whatever claims to power the owner/wearer makes. This way, textiles act as signs, that is, as indexes of power. This trait is most visible with regard to royalty and spirituality in Yorùbá religio-cultural space. At a particular point in Yorùbá history, *Aṣọ òkè*, with its many fabric varieties, made into *Agbádá*, *Bùbá*, and *Sòkòtò* as exemplified in several instances above, was one of the insignia of the kings and chiefs in the traditional period. The presence of such clothes signified the presence of court authority (with regard to chiefs) and royal power, and demanded reverence from members of the society. The various types of *Aṣọ òkè*, *Òfì*, *Sányán*, and *Àlàárì* were considered favorites and royal dresses. Akinbileje recalls that the Olúbàdàn of Ibadan (a notable Yorùbá king) once forbade his chiefs from wearing *Aṣọ òkè*, demonstrating the importance of clothing as an indicator of social status.[62] As a consequence of a royal move, *Aṣọ òkè* became a political insignia, an emblem of political/royal power.[63] This way, Yorùbá textiles act in the capacity of and serve as fabrics of culture and life, in both literal and non-literal senses. In addition, they are definers of social role.

In addition, textiles and garments with exquisite designs, some of which are also known as *Iṣẹ́ tínkó*, are employed to beautify clothes. Owing to the highly ornamental nature as well as the exoticness of these designs as tactile and visual signs, these embroideries become metaphors. Their costliness automatically excludes the proletariat who cannot afford cloths that display them; more so, by being sewn into dresses used predominantly in a social capacity, they betray the complementary union that exists between Yorùbá functions and Yorùbá dress in the signification of power. For instance, an occasion where heavily embroidered *Agbádá*, *Bùbá*, and *Sòkòtò* are used

---

[62] Akinbileje, "Symbolic Values," 628.
[63] Although, with the advent of modernity and cultural fluidity, *Agbádá*, with its heavy embroidery work, is now available to those who can afford it, and as such still indexes power, even if not royal but aristocratic or bourgeois power. More so, the *Agbádá* style can now be made from various materials apart from *Aṣọ òkè*.

automatically redefines the nature of those who are to attend. And it is a given fact in Yorùbá societies that the way one dresses is the way one would be addressed. Garments on such occasions are defining metaphors and indexes.

Some of the names of these designs and embroideries[64] placed at different places/points of a dress are: *Òsùpá*, placed on the front of a fully embroidered gown (*Agbádá* or flowing *Bùbá*) as seen in Figure 10.14; *Ìda*, the embroidery on the front of *Agbádá* as seen in Fig. 10.2; *Àjùfù*, the decoration around the neck; *Ìbo olóríkan*, placed at the leg of trousers or cap, as visible in the third cap in Figure 10.26; *Alaagba*, also placed in the front of *Agbádá*; *Ìbòrí olórímèjì*, placed or woven around the pocket of *Gbáriyè* (a kind of *Bùbá*), which is an embroidery used for the legs of trousers or caps and sometimes placed in front of *Agbádá*; *Ìbo álejó*, also used for trousers and occasionally caps, as seen in Figure 10.5; *paco*, placed in front of *Gbáriyè* as seen in Figure 10.7, and sometimes atop caps, as seen in the second and fourth caps in Figure 10.26 and *Ìbòrí olórímèjì*, also placed at the legs of trousers.

The range of artistry and stylistic ingenuity with which Yorùbá cloth-weavers and designers attend their textiles and garments is inexhaustible. By investing clothing with such visually appealing designs, they empower their art – textiles – and the sartorial tradition with visual and economic power, drawing patronage from the high and mighty of the society and, as vehicles of commercial relations, facilitating commerce and, by extension, aiding economic growth. This is because a poor person, even in twenty-first-century Yorùbáland, cannot afford to embroider traditional wear. Other designs peculiar to Yorùbá cloth embroidery work can be seen in Figures 10.3, 10.4, 10.8, and 10.7.

Yorùbá dress as index or as indexing the creative enterprise of Yorùbá cloth-weavers and their sartorial ingenuity/artistry is not limited to woven fabrics alone but applies also to *Àdìrẹ* (tie and dye). Compared to woven *Aṣọ òkè*, *Àdìrẹ* was mostly a woman's craft, which means that the mere presence or sighting of an *Àdìrẹ* garment is a testament to the industry of the Yorùbá women cloth-weavers. *Àdìrẹ* could be *Àdìrẹ ẹlẹkọ*, *Àdìrẹ alábẹrẹ*, or *Àdìrẹ oníko*. *Àdìrẹ ẹlẹkọ* requires tying and dyeing with corn pap or starch. This process involves cloth printed using the resist technique with a paste such as corn pap or cassava.[65] The others involve the use of resist techniques which entails using stitched thread or raffia. *Aró*, indigo dye, is often used to dye these cloths. The cloth, like *Aṣọ òkè*, is used by both men and women, and can be combined with *Bùbá* of a different and lighter cloth by women or used as wrappers for sleeping by men.

Àdìrẹ cloths are visually laden with themes and motifs that hold members of the society in dialogic conversations. Designs reflect geometric signs and shapes, while others point to animal or flora motifs, such as frogs, trees, lizards, butterflies,

---

[64] See Lyndersay, *Nigerian Dress*, 306–307.
[65] Lyndersay, *Nigerian Dress*, 338.

fishes, and snakes. Lyndersay admits that sometimes human characters – eminent ones like the Ọba, or cultural icons such as drummers, are often imprinted on Àdìrẹ to charge and activate them as socioculturally conscious readable texts.

To summarize the above paragraph, Àdìrẹ cloth, despite having diminished in use as a result of the presence of Kàmpàlà, which itself has given way to other African prints, and Aṣọ òkè, references a whole sartorial tradition, the industry of women, and the creative enterprise of traditional cloth-makers as cultural ambassadors. The motifs themselves are signs, whose significations are both inward (self-reflexive) and outward (pointing toward the contextual meanings running undercurrent). The fabrics in Figures 10.20–10.24 are all Àdìrẹ cloths with various designs and motifs that fall under the purview of what has been discussed so far.

Furthermore, Àdìrẹ as signs do not only refer to themselves as creative products, or reference the human labor, gender culture, and historical details that have gone into their production as a signage or system of signifying symbols, but also index the myths that surround the sartorial culture of the Yorùbá, and the arts in general. Any culturally informed interrogator would approach Àdìrẹ with a consciousness of the presence and power of the patron saints of Yorùbá arts. The dress-making process as well as the reality and use of the garment as finished product signify a rich mythological culture that ties with Yorùbá cloths as indexical signs. Àdìrẹ, famous as the major craft in Abẹ́òkúta, the home of Àdìrẹ, and Òṣogbo, is believed to be controlled by Òrìṣà Ọ̀ṣun, Ìyá-Mọ̀pó, and Ọbalúfọ̀n. As posited by Oyeniyi, the two goddesses and one deity are the forces behind the dexterous craftsmanship in Yoruba sartorial culture and industry.[66]

More so, the famous appellation accorded to Òṣogbo, "Òṣogbo ilú aró, Òròki Àsálà," is historic as it demonstrates the mythico-historical foundations of Àdìrẹ in Òṣogbo. Òṣogbo is considered the birthplace of Àdìrẹ for many reasons: a traveler, Lárọ̀ọ́yè by name, is believed to have settled close to the Osun River, where they felled trees to make room for dwellings. Ọ̀ṣun, the river goddess, cried out and decried this practice, promising to reward them with abundance and protection should they halt their acts. On their complying, Ọ̀ṣun blessed them, and they worshiped her. She eventually introduced the tie-and-dye skill to the women, who as a result of trade relations spread it to other towns.

In another account, Ìyá Mọ̀pó is considered the patron saint of all female crafts. She is believed to embody the totemic features of Ìyámowo, Ìyálóde, and Naná Ìbùkún. She is the owner of the indigo dye, Aró, and also a weaver of cloth and hair, and a potter. Ọbalùfọ̀n, worshiped at Ilé Ifẹ̀ as a divinity, as well as Idò-Ọ̀ṣun near Òṣogbo, Isesa, Igbókìtì, Igbó Ọya, Ìjẹ̀bú, and Ṣàgámù, is also a potter and weaver like Ìyá Mọ̀po. The three divinities are believed to be patrons of tie and dye, bronze casting, weaving, and pottery making. Their worship is common among various production centers of Àdìrẹ and Aṣọ òkẹ̀. There are

---

[66] Oyeniyi, *Dress in the Making*, 220.

Figure 10.20 Àdìrẹ type I

other deities and Òrìṣà associated with garment production like Olókun, Ṣàngó, Ògún, and Oya.[67] The Àdìrẹ images provide examples of Àdìrẹ cloths that cover a range of stylistic and inventive designs. As seen in the examples of Àdìrẹ used

---

[67] Oyeniyi, *Dress in the Making*, 222.

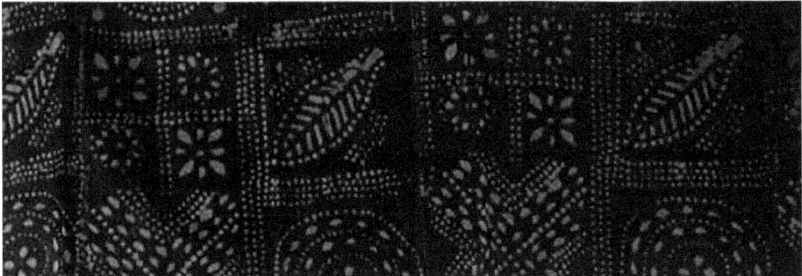

Figure 10.21 Àdìrẹ type II

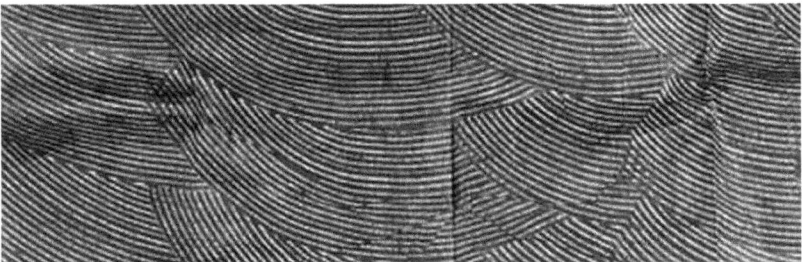

Figure 10.22 Àdìrẹ type III

in this chapter, Àdìrẹ materials can be made into garments for both male and female wears, and they are often colorful and appealing.

Consequently, factoring in the mythic relationship Yorùbá establish between their dress and their pantheon, it is impossible to comprehend and appreciate Yorùbá textiles outside the context of their spirituality. Inasmuch as there is a strong reference to deity worship in centers of production and a mythic history embedded in the fabrics of these textiles, the presence of any textile signifies the presence of a higher essence. Then, the sense in which textiles are indexes of spiritual potency is all the more manifested. Hence, Yorùbá dress can be said to mark spiritual power, presence, and space.[68] More so, aside from representing deities and patrons, and their powers, they serve as mythological codes, signs referring to and explaining history.

The emphasis on the spirituality of cloths and its ability to index a person's spiritual essence is reflected in the belief that garments are individual gifts from

---

[68] Religious votaries, herbalists and diviners, and other merchants of spiritual power rely very much on their cloths, which are often imbued with potent spiritual powers. As such, the presence of these cloths signifies the presence of the power of whichever Òrìṣà has given power to the wearer.

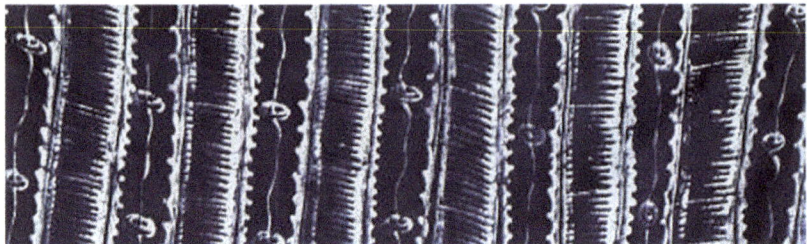

Figure 10.23 Àdìrẹ type IV

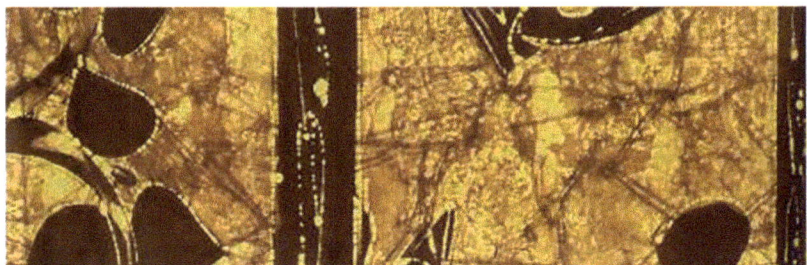

Figure 10.24 Àdìrẹ type V

God[69] and in the practice of burning old cloths rather than giving them to others, especially those who are not members of the Ẹbí. This is done to prevent the machinations of evildoers who would seek to inflict harm on the benevolent through the gifted cloths. More so, that cloths are often used in rituals to appease and propitiate the divinities emphasizes the spiritual potency of Yorùbá cloths. Sometimes expensive garments are required and offered for use in ritual performances, at the specification of Ifá, to either court the benevolence of the Òrìṣà and deities or as honorifics.

More so, that Yorùbá dress serves as an emblem of spiritual forces is strongly portrayed by the color and make of certain textiles. For instance, the Ìtagbẹ́, particular to the Ògbóni of Ìjẹ̀bú, is a cult-specific garment used by Ògbóni or Òsùgbó members.[70] According to Asakitikpi, the cloth, which is woven by women, is a symbol of political power and is heavily reflective of Yorùbá mythology. To quote her directly:

> [Ìtagbé] was a covenant between Ọ̀rúnmìlà and a woman called Poroyẹn when the former fell into a deep pit and could not come out. After seven

---

[69] Oyeniyi, *Dress in the Making*.
[70] Oyeniyi, *Dress in the Making*; Asakitikpi, "Functions of Textiles."

days and nights without any food or water he began to sing and this attracted Poroyẹn to the side of the pit. She offered to get him out of the pit only if he would marry her. Ọrúnmìlà agreed and she used her wrapper (which is similar in form to Ọ̀já) to pull him out. Ọrúnmìlà kept his promise, and married Poroyẹn who eventually bore him a son. She is said to have used the wrapper, which she used to pull Ọrúnmìlà out of the pit to strap her baby on her back.[71]

The cloth, aside from ushering to the fore the mythic history charging its cultural relevance, also testifies to the industry of weaving – a testament that seeks to negate the Eurocentric hypothesis about men's weaving being art and women's weaving being craft, and that also refutes the claim that women only wove for household purposes. It is woven on a broadloom used by women. It is never woven to the end, and the loose strands are tied into seven knots. *Ìtagbé* is spiritual in its implications because on it are woven various symbols with meanings known only to its wearers who are *Òṣùgbó* members. More so, prayers are woven on the *Ìtagbé* in modern times, which therefore could, as such, be considered visual equivalents of prayers. This is a vital representation of how power is inherent in a garment – that and the fact that as highly personalized symbols of status they can be offered to deities as symbols of gratitude or prayers.[72] There are several other cloths such as *Ebolo, Girijo, Ashigbo*, and *Ago*, among many others, woven by women, especially Ọ̀wọ̀ women, that also possess spiritual connotations and demand spiritually conscious obeisance or ritual empowerment/consecration (*Rírò*) during their production and before use. Cleanliness and purity of heart are some of the requirements for weavers before certain Yoruba garments are woven. Another example that supports textiles as spiritual indexes is *Ṣàngó sọ̀wọ̀* cloth, made from *Kíjìpá*. It could either be *Aṣọ-Ọ̀wọ̀, Ẹ̀wù Ọ̀wọ̀, Yẹ̀rì Ọ̀wọ̀*, or *Ṣòkòtò Ọ̀wọ̀*. A sleeveless tunic which has resuscitating properties, it is dyed purple and consecrated.[73]

Strips of traditional *Aṣọ òkè* cloth have been employed in modern times by Christians to symbolize spirituality. These can be seen investments such as chasubles, albs, and altar cloths[74] – for the latter, some use *Àdìrẹ*, especially for altar cloths and as items of dress. In fact, Yorùbá textiles and dress work on several levels of connotation. The colors of Yorùbá

---

[71] Asakitikpi, "Functions of Textiles," 109–110.
[72] See L. Aronson, "Ijebu Yoruba Aso-Olona: A Contextual and Historical Overview," *African Arts* 25, no. 3 (1992): 52–62.
[73] See Tola Olaoye, "Iwa: Symbolism and Significance in Sango Ritual Textiles," in *Yoruba Religious Textiles: Essays in Honor of Cornelius Adepegba*, ed. E. P. Renne and B. Agbaje-Williams (Ibadan: Book Builders, 2005), 129–155.
[74] See Renne and Agbaje-Williams, "Introduction," in Renne and Agbaje-Williams, eds., *Yoruba Religious Textiles*, 1–21.

textiles themselves have metaphoric meanings as they can signify Ìwà, that is, portray the character of deities ascribed to them. For instance, white cloths – Aṣọ funfun or Aṣọ àlà – signify Olódùmarè and his holiness or is used to mark the abode of spiritual forces, while red cloths –Aṣọ pupa – signifies the Ìwà of Ṣàngó, who is notorious for his hot-temperedness. The uses of such cloths also transcend the context of traditional religions into modern Yorùbá religions such as Christianity and Islam. The spiritual potency or significations of Yorùbá cloths cannot be exhausted in any one single chapter[75] because not only are they functional as metaphoric signs in religious contexts such as shrines, sanctuaries, altars, ritual sacrifices, masquerade festivals and costuming, traditional, Christian and Islamic rituals, and not only are their qualities as cloths – like absorbency – self-reflexive of their capacity to contain spiritually concocted dyes and symbols, and thus reflect the circumstances of creation and use and the power inherent in them, but they also reflect the spiritual power associated with cloth users.

In addition, underlying the spiritual signifying potentialities of Yorùbá textiles is the philosophy of the deathlessness and immortality of cloths. This comes from the idea that even during masquerade festivals such as Agẹmọ, Èyò, and Gẹ̀lẹ̀dẹ̀, among many others, textiles of Yorùbá origin (domesticated or indigenous) are assembled creatively to form a masquerade cloth ensemble which serves as a screen, a frame ushering into contact but separating the ancestral spirits from human relations or the world of the living. The cloth, an ensemble of layers, strips, and shreds of various cloth materials, is reflective of what Abiodun terms the Yorùbá association of shreds with longevity and deathlessness.[76] This is because the cloth of a masquerade self-testifies by symbolically unveiling its transformation from ordinary cloth to a fabric of immortality worn only by ancestral spirits. Furthermore, the aesthetic of deathlessness that frames the Yorùbá religious thought system in relation to textiles is borne of the idea that cloths don't die. This belief is buttressed by the fact that cloths only wear to shreds.[77] They don't die. To cement this perception of their cloth, Yorùbá compare the deathlessness of their cloth to the immortality of their Supreme Being, Olódùmarè.

---

[75] Renne and Agbaje-Williams, "Introduction," for a more rounded perspective on Yoruba textiles and religious symbolism.
[76] Abiodun, "We Greet Aso."
[77] Abiodun, "We Greet Aso," xi.

Textiles as Repositories of Cultural Meanings and Functional Values

While it is at this point undeniable that Yorùbá textiles constitute a readable text, that is, the very sign of Yorùbá reality, be it economic, historical, cultural, political, religious, or mythic in composition, it is also irrefutable that it is a repository of many more meanings that are both functional as well as ideological. It has been revealed earlier how dress symbolizes the *Ìwà* of deities with which it is associated. In the same vein, Yorùbá cloth symbolizes the *Ẹwà* (beauty) of persons – considering *Ìwà* and *Ẹwà* in tandem. The saying "Aṣọ là ń kí, kí á tó kí ènìyàn" provides enough justification. It espouses the Yorùbá belief that a cloth is worthy of appraisal before the individual who wears it, which of course makes recourse to the popular maxim that appearance makes a lasting impression.

This emphasis on the appearance of an individual dress composition reflects Yorùbá people's fascination with *Ojú ọnà* (eye for design). Anyone who reveals themselves as embodying this trait projects the possession of a high sense of aesthetic awareness, which contributes to the person's *Ẹwà* and *Ìwà*, for to have a good sense of dress and to be able to beautify the self with dress is to exhibit one of the *Ọmọlúàbí* principles, which is *Ìmúra*. In that case, choosing beautiful *Àdìrẹ* colors, using the *Aṣọ ẹbí*, or any of the *Aṣọ òkè*, is operating within the permits of the *Ọmọlúàbí* frame, and likewise exhibiting the richness of one's *Ìwà*. Furthermore, the type of *Aṣọ òkè* one buys or wears, or even possesses, has its own symbolism. *Sányán*, for example, hand spun into silk threads which give it a natural beige color, washed and soaked in corn starch, is considered the king of cloths as a result of its expensiveness. Associated with kings and chiefs, it is considered *Baba aṣọ* (king of cloths). *Ẹtù*, dyed in indigo blue dye and sun-dried repeatedly, is of lesser quality and used for social purposes. *Àlàárì*, made originally from *Sányán* dyed in camwood solution but now machine spun, is worn by kings and chiefs to welcome visitors. The exquisite natures of *Aṣọ òkè* types are revealed through their use. According to Asakitikpi, "*Sányán* and *Ẹtù* are used for official functions or ceremonies (for example, harvest festivals, weddings, installation of chiefs)."[78] Folk music also testifies to the prestige each cloth has through specified use and which rubs off on the wearer:

> Kíjìpá aṣọ ọlẹ́, òfì aṣọ àgbà / Àgbà tí kò rówó ròfì, kó ra kíjìpá / Nítorí pé sányán ni baba aṣọ, Ẹtù ni baba ẹ̀wù /Àlàárì ló tẹ̀lé e. The translation: Kijipa, a lazy man's cloth, Òfì, an elder's cloth / A poor elder who is incapable of buying Òfì should Kíjìpá/ As sányán is the best of cloth, Ẹtù is the father of garments / While *Àlàárì* is the next in rank.[79]

---

[78] Asakitikpi, "Functions of Textiles," 104.
[79] Oyeniyi, *Dress in the Making*, 74.

It is hard to attempt a discussion of Yorùbá cloths without remarking on their highly functional domestic uses. A cloth like Òjá, worn and used by women, is used in securing a baby. It is a sort of sash used to tie a baby to a woman's back due to its toughness and strength. The Ìborùn is also very useful as it helps in shielding both a woman and a nursing mother and child from environmental elements like sun or rain. It has the function of a shawl, which is revealed in its linguistic word: Ìbo (covering) + ọrùn (neck) = Ìbo ọrùn/Ìborùn. Òfì, an Aṣọ òkè type, which is thick, is sometimes used as Ìborùn as well as a wrapper during cold times. An Òṣùká, which is also part of the female dress, is often employed to ease the carriage of heavy things of the head. It is a cloth folded or packed in a circular form and placed on the head to cushion the effect of the weight of heavy luggage.

A woman's wardrobe is highly significant and functional in symbolizing various cultural values. In a woman's wardrobe there are several sets of Òjá, Ìpèlé, Ìborún, Ìró, Gèlè, and Bùbá. Some of these cloths are handed down through the maternal line, and because these Yorùbá Aṣọ òkè cloths are very durable, it is often no surprise that some cloth-sets survive for generations. Such cloths become heirlooms, signifying the continuance of a sacred tradition. They also act as mementoes, signs of a treasured heritage unifying a matriarchal line. Merely feeling the texture of such cloths or seeing them evokes memories and meanings. Furthermore, when a young bride leaves for her husband's home she is often given a set (or many sets) of complete female wear, as part of the Ẹrù ìyàwó (bride's luggage) that she takes to her husband's house and which not only signifies but certifies her transition from a young woman (Òdọmọbìnrin) or spinster to woman/bride/wife (Obìnrin/Ìyàwó). The cloths, in these instances, point away from themselves to reveal their symbolic and functional values. Figures 10.13 and 10.17 are examples of female dresses. While Figure 10.17 shows a woman with Ìró, she is also clothed in Bùbà, Gèlè, and Ìpèlé, slung across her shoulder – all of which are matching to create a visually appealing ensemble, such as those in Figure 10.13. In the figure we see a simply dressed woman with Ìró, Bùbá, and Gèlè. This figure presents the full range of female dress ensemble. With the Ìró, Bùbá, Gèlè, Òjá, and Ìpèlé present, the beauty of the dress and the ensemble, the more appreciated the individual is.

An Ọmọlúàbí persona through dressing is not fully expressed when one does not don Fìlà (a cap) whenever Yorùbá dress is used. As such, it is hard to be taken seriously, especially as a man dressed in native attire, when the Fìlà is absent. Yorùbá use various types and designs of Fìlà, but any worn at any point in time and on any occasion must match (as is in the case of examples above) the material and color of the other cloth types. Figure 10.26 shows various caps detailing and portraying the

Figure 10.25 Various types of women's cloth

design, artistry, and emphasis Yorùbá place on *Fìlà*. Apart from those, another style of cap dominant among the Yorùbá is the *Abetí ajá*, seen in Figure 10.14. The *Fìlà* is also designed to enhance the beauty of the garment. One who does not wear a *Fìlà* is not considered a fully dressed person. Consequently, a person whose dress is complete, with appropriate designs and colors, is appreciated for his looks, and then respected as an *Ọmọlúàbí*. This is because, to the Yoruba, "Ìrínisí ni ìṣenilójọ̀," which means that one's appearance determines one's reception. In addition, in Yorùbá ontology, a young man differs in diverse ways from a woman, likewise the married man from the unmarried, and as such the respect accorded each by virtue of his standing and growth in stature and experiences differs. This difference is expressed through caps too. A married man wears his cap with the folded part to the right, while the unmarried man wears his to the left. This way, in a social gathering a cap becomes a compass and an instrument of taxonomy.

I cannot conclude this careful exploration of dresses as cultural pathways within which my participatory and experiential understanding centers me as an agent without reiterating that the only way the dress, the weaver/designer, and the wearer can assume any symbolic agency on cultural terms is if all of them – including the tradition/institution they embody – are seen as evocative

Figure 10.26 *Fìlà*

texts, or as readable visual *Oríkì*. When this is achieved, the interconnections between possession and the possessed (myself and my dress, that is), through which a person can be fully understood as an active system of both personal meaning and cultural symbolism, are made increasingly visible and rendered comprehensible.

11

Canvas and the Archiving of Ethnic Reality

Introduction: Yorùbá Painting and Yorùbá Culture

Yorùbá people are tremendously creative, as a group and as individuals – this has been established by studies of Yorùbá history, religion, commerce, artistry, and social life.[1] These studies have identified a robust cultural and aesthetic awareness shared by the Yorùbá, defining them as a people of specific artistic tastes, aesthetic traditions, and artistic institutions. The artistic components are interconnected with their sociocultural reality. Nothing stands in isolation; to the Yorùbá, everything is connected.

This crisscrossing influence might have been at the fore of David Joselit's mind when he argued that "When you say art, then everything possible belongs to it."[2] Yorùbá art exhibits this attitude, drawing materials and influences from highly developed institutions in society. It develops and sustains its manner and matter, or its form and content, by lending itself to Yorùbá reality – it becomes a frame, system, or method of understanding. This emphasizes its role as a force for social organization, control, and sensitization.

In a self-reflexive sense, Yorùbá art portrays the cultural systems and processes that have fed it from ideation to materialization. This fact is essential, serving as a compelling factor to shift Yorùbá art from the domain of folk art to a global precinct. Braide[3] holds the view that the Yorùbá people, through their

---

[1] See Renne and Agbaje-Williams, eds., *Yoruba Religious Textiles*. See also Lyndersay, *Nigerian Dress*; Abiodun, "African Aesthetics"; and Adesanya, *Carving Wood*; Doris, "Symptoms and Strangeness"; L. J. Kaman, "Conceptual Patterns in Yoruba Culture," paper presented at the Ninth International Congress of Anthropological and Ethnological Sciences, 1973, repr. in *Language and Thought*, ed. W. C. McCormack and S. A. Wurm (The Hague: Mouton, 1977), 359–389; and O. O. Braide, "Stylistic Features of Contemporary Adire in Nigerian Textile Practice," *Journal of Humanities, Social Science, and Creative Arts* 11, no. 1 and 2 (2016): 104–116. Each of these research papers, some essays, some books, and other books of essays comment analytically on various aspects of Yorùbá sociocultural space to reveal patterns of artistry and a well-developed aesthetic awareness.
[2] David Joselit, "Painting Beside Itself," *October* 130, no. 10 (2009): 125–134, at 126.
[3] Braide, "Stylistic Features."

art, have contributed immensely to world culture.⁴ Art has brought Yorùbá culture to the world stage, where it is studied, appreciated, and imbibed.

Yorùbá life – the entirety of the Yorùbá social sphere and cultural firmament – is a living organism whose soul is Yorùbá culture and whose contours are its various arts. The relationship between art and culture follows the structure presented in the mythic tale of *Ìyá-Mòpó*, an *Òrìṣà*, a potter, and a weaver of hair, cotton, and cloth, according to folklore and scholarship.⁵ She is owner of the indigo dye and patron of women's trade, childbearing, and birth, molding shapes around preexisting spaces. To *Ìyá-Mòpó* all bodies are pots and form is a later addition, which means that a form is a product of creative discretion; it can take any shape.

The philosophy of *Ìyá-Mòpó* is expressed in Yorùbá cosmology, where the potter's wheel, represented by the navel (*Ìdodo*), is a fixed point. The female potter encircles it with her body, preserving the idea of form.⁶ One can say that Yorùbá culture is the navel around which the arts are formed, along with the contours, affording it the definite and fluid forms with which the world engages. Although these contours are fluid in various art expressions, their fluidity enshrines the constancy of their contouring functions. The defining features of Yorùbá art are changeability in constancy and constancy of changeability, both due to Yorùbá art's chief utilitarian function. Regardless of form, it reflects Yorùbá life in all its diversity. To quote Justine Cordwell, "Form can change constantly, but the Yorùbá patterns remain constant."⁷ Cordwell's statement underscores the proposition that the use to which a thing such as art is put bests the form itself, especially in Africa.

Yorùbá painting can and should be seen as functional – only in its functionality does it affect the culture that is originally instrumental to its status as art. The implication is simple but potent: locked in a painting's functionality are undercurrents upholding it and serving as ideological and artistic scaffolds. For this reason, a cyclic affective process between painting and culture creates an open-ended process of complementation between culture and art. Ikoro⁸

---

⁴ An example of this is how Yorùbá (and much of West African) art influenced Pablo Picasso and his Paris School. Stylized arts of African people served as nodes of artistic influence for European painters who incorporated it in their art, shifting from European naturalist traditions to three dimensionality and Expressionism. African art has been identified as a major source of influence for Picasso's Cubism. See Catherine Bernard, "Patterns of Change: The Work of Loïs Mailou Jones' Technology in the Arts" (Pittsburgh: Carnegie Mellon University, 2012), www.anyonecanflyfoundation.org/library/Bernard_on_Mailou_Jones.essay.html.

⁵ See Oyeniyi, *Dress in the Making*.

⁶ Oyeniyi, *Dress in the Making*.

⁷ Justine M. Cordwell, "The Arts and Aesthetics of the Yoruba," *African Arts* 16, no. 2 (1983): 56–100, at 56.

⁸ E. A. Ikoro, "Painting and Society in Modern Nigeria," *International Journal of Arts and Humanities* 3, no. 11 (2015): 87–93.

agrees that in this process the complementarity of painting and society is open-ended. He states:

> The interface between painting (and indeed all art) and society is arguably as old as both phenomena-art and society. One had always influenced the other and vice versa. All art is inspired by life and society on the one hand. On the other hand, throughout human history, art and artists have made significant contributions to the development of the societies in which they have existed.[9]

Ikoro is not alone; Vye[10] and Abodunrin[11] also share the position that painting, and visual artists in general, participate in the growth and sustenance of culture. In addition to providing visual gratification and creative inspiration, paintings engender and sustain dialogues and critical commentaries that are germane to the existence and advancement of culture and tradition, serving as a tempered means of protest, acculturation, sensitization, and criticism.

Another example of the symbiotic unity and cyclic mode of inspiration between culture and art is the way mythological, historical, diurnal, and aesthetic aspects of Yorùbá reality are reflected in Yorùbá paintings, ensuring the appreciation of culture. Abodunrin's discussion of this notion states that these aspects of culture exist as themes and motifs defining painting as both art and cultural symbol – themes and motifs in paintings are results of sociocultural processes and shifts. These processes are also historical[12] and open-ended; not only do paintings generally reproduce life and pass judgment on its phenomena,[13] but the icons with which they manifest their artistic nature also make statements of their own.

Yorùbá painting is the convergence of aesthetic tradition and sociocultural framework. It is the canvas[14] upon which aesthetics and social content interact, reaccentuating the complementarity of artwork and culture. If we agree that paintings, through their themes, are products of culturally and socially configured processes and shifts, and that they narrate and are self-reflexive, then we must accept that they narrate these processes. The processes are as artistic as they are social and historical.

The visual artist also contributes to the reflection of artistic aesthetics in painting, which is possible because shifts and continuities manifest within the artist as a cultural participant. The Yorùbá code this as Àṣà and Dá àṣà,

---

[9] Ikoro, "Painting and Society," 87.
[10] Alana Vye, "The Role of Visual Artists in Society," Work, Demand Media, http://work.chron.com/role-visual-artists-society-22517.html.
[11] See Johnson A. Abodunrin, "Thematic Concerns in 21st Century Paintings in Nigerian Art Schools," Scholars Journals of Arts, Humanities and Social Sciences 3, no. 3B (2015): 681–691.
[12] Vansina, Art History in Africa.
[13] Abodunrin, "Thematic Concerns," 681.
[14] By this, I refer to painting.

underscoring tradition and the act of creating a divergent style within it. The fluidity with which the Yorùbá painter navigates an individual style, within the permits of the broader tradition, to create something different – without deviating from it to the point of alienation – informs Cordwell's position: in relation to Yorùbá stylo-artistic sphere, "nothing was adapted that could not be used in an old pattern, but with greater efficiency or meaning."[15]

Yorùbá aesthetic tradition, especially in painting, is anchored in contextual and formalist territory. Principles such as Onaism, formed from the word Ọnà, and other philosophical concepts, like Ọmọlúàbì, are structured on canvases[16] that form aesthetic bases for such works. The word Ọnà is polysemic and polymorphic, but its derivative forms all link to artistry and its interrelatedness with cultural concepts. The word Ọnà, in Yorùbá linguistic repertoire, means arts and aesthetics. Because of the morphological peculiarities of Yorùbá lexemes, the aesthetic wideness of Ọnà can accommodate words such as Ojú-ọnà (critical eyes/design consciousness), Gbẹnàgbẹnà (sculptor), Oníṣẹ-ọnà (one who makes pattern/design), and Oníṣọnà (designer).

Ọnà is art, aesthetics, design, style, and all these combined. It reflects these in its manifestations as various types of art: fine art, applied art, visual art, and even liberal art. Ọnà itself manifests in verbal artistry, in Ojú-ọnà, which is an orthographic coding of the possession of critical sensibilities and consciousness to identify and appreciate art; this concept is otherwise known as aesthetic appreciation. If Ọnà can be dynamic in art such as carving, weaving, sculpting, and painting, then the term would mean art, stylo-sensibility, and aesthetics in the creative context. I am inclined to agree with Godwin Ogheneruemu Irivwieri, who holds that Ọnà as both art and aesthetics refers to decoration, pattern, ornament, embellishment, design, composition, form, and plant and animal motifs – all of which are basic to art and painting to be specific.[17]

As an artistic concept, Onaism has its focus on recharging Yorùbá arts with Yorùbá-centric motifs and forms. As a form of reviving the indigenous, its impulse as an aesthetic concept lies in experimentation with local[18] resources, designs, and forms. In the words of Irivwieri, it is characterized by the use of "significant symbols charged with related motifs to give verbal luminosity in such a manner that there is scarcely any surface of the picture plane without action."[19]

Understanding Ọnà in the artistic and aesthetic sense, and how local symbols manifest through it, boosts our understanding of how it functions as a rich, unified Yorùbá essentialist aesthetic. Linguistic and philosophic concepts of

---

[15] Cordwell, "Arts and Aesthetics," 56.
[16] The words canvas and painting are used interchangeably in this chapter.
[17] Godwin Irivwieri, "Onaism: An Artistic Model of Yoruba Civilization in Nigeria," *An International Multi-Disciplinary Journal, Ethiopia* 4, no. 3a (2010): 234–246, at 236.
[18] Local is not meant as a derogatory term, or as a less advanced form in comparison to a more sophisticated alternative. It is used to refer to specific, native indigenous forms.
[19] Irivwieri, "Onaism," 236.

Yorùbá epistemology and thought on art, such as *Àrà* (artistic wonder/skill), *dárà* (style/performance of artistic skill), *Ẹwà* (beauty), and *Sùúrù* (patience)[20] are so intrinsic to *Ọnà* that they form ideologically related features. On a non-metaphoric level, *Ọnà* can mean way,[21] or to contextualize it in artistic terms, style. This accentuates how *Ọnà* can signify artistic deviation within a broader tradition – by implication, revealing the permissions granted to stylo-artistic individuation in the Yorùbá art-sphere.

Ọnà can also be a philosophical encoding of Yorùbá attitudes toward journeys, roads, and pathways. These are essential to art, because a painter's corpus, along with the painter's life, is a journey. Yorùbá believe that any vocation or choice in life is a manifestation of one's *Ìpín* (lot/choice in life) and *Àyànmọ́* (destiny); their actualization mirrors the unfolding of a journey. *Ọnà*, in such terms, exposes the Yorùbá fixation with crossroads and choices as sacrosanct themes in human affairs. To them, a major life choice is comparable to a crossroad.

To Moyọ Okediji, *Ọnà* is "a Yorùbá bi-syllabic term that is loaded with metaphysical, poetic, and factual condiments."[22] Figures 11.1 and 11.2 are pictorial representations of this conceptualization of *Ọnà* and its sacrosanct position in the Yorùbá existential framework. At the heart of the images are roads, bounded on each side by humans at various states in their journeys, patient enough to tread their chosen paths without hindering others. The roads run deep, cutting through the hearts of cities in a way that suggests life is an unending trek. Bound to this concept are virtues such as patience and order that are vital to Yorùbá society.

By embodying a range of motifs that are culturally rich and symbolic, including geometric patterns and images of people, as can be seen in Figures 11.3, 11.4, and 11.5, Onaism serves as a rich and vibrant aesthetic. It espouses philosophical concepts such as *Sùúrù*, *Àrà*, *Ìwà*, and *Ẹwà*, especially

---

[20] These reveal how the aesthetic fuses with the sociocultural. All these principles are germane to artistry; every art student is expected to utilize them in varying circumstances. Concepts such as beauty and patience, in an ironic turn, are virtues that every individual must have to succeed and be an *Ọmọlúàbí* worthy of emulation. An *Ọmọlúàbí*'s life is an ideal, and they are represented in paintings as idealized figures with tempered identities, making them relevant to the generic. These identities perpetuate a collective idea in form and composition, espousing ideas that reemphasize or signify the (visual) state of the form as an aesthetic that can be generated across other art platforms. The painted image of a sitting man with a calm demeanor and composed form, for example, espouses the aesthetic of the cool. The idea of this aesthetic and its physical form manifest in various other paintings through other images. The images are no longer those of individual people. Having transcended, they become representations that reveal how concepts become aesthetics manifested for social sensitization across many arts.

[21] Gbenga Orimoloye, "Foreword," in *Ona: Exhibition of Paintings/Drawings by Gbenga Orimoloye* (Lagos: Terra Kulture, 2021), www.orimoloye.com/wp-content/uploads/2016/08/ona_2012.pdf.

[22] Orimoloye, *Ona*, 2.

Figure 11.1 Path to the Town. Source: Courtesy of Kole Owokunle

Figure 11.2 Soweto

through the postures, along with their accompanying connotations, represented in Figures 11.5, 11.6, and 11.7. By incorporating a campaign for a return to indigenous materials and designs as its philosophical undercurrent,

Figure 11.3 *Yemọja*. Source: Courtesy of Moses Ogunleye

Onaism betrays the convergence of aesthetic tradition and cultural awareness in the process of actualizing itself on canvas.

Yorùbá paintings not only render visions of daily life through their subjects or associated symbols, they also narrate and visualize aspects of spirituality and mysticism that are characteristic of the Yorùbá. Some of these aspects have been identified in other images; Figure 11.3 contributes to the Yorùbá representation of spiritual existence by depicting a *Yemọja* avatar. *Yemọja* is a water deity, considered to be the mother of the *Ọnà* and the patron of childbearing. She is believed to be a mermaid, half woman and half fish, as is apparent in the painting. Her dual nature is also reflected in her name (*Ìye* – mother + *Ọmọ* – child + *Ẹja* – fish).

Socially informed principles such as *Ọmọlúàbì* also form aesthetic bases for Yorùbá painting. Several naturalistic postures and framings reflect individuals

Figure 11.4 Ọ̀ṣun I. Source: Courtesy of Moses Ogunleye

performing attitudes that exhibit collective notions of appropriateness. Epistemologically, these performances become idealistic, rendering the personal in a generic form. A cool exterior, stooping women, the use of complete garments, dressing well (*Agbádá*: Figure 11.8), symmetrical alignment of body parts in a composed posture (Figures 11.9 and 11.10) – all these are collective frames embodied by individuals, perpetuated through their effort to fit into those frames and to be seen manifesting appropriate identity and proper conduct. These postural forms transmute to aesthetics, revealing the utility of artistic conventions with vibrant cultural implications.

Stooping, for example, is a cultural act of reverence and propitiation of superior authority (royalty, elder, ancestor, or Òrìṣà). It is well documented in Yorùbá visual art as an aesthetic and as a codification of permissions on behavior and character. As an aesthetic it is well rendered across various types of visual arts – paintings, sculpture, photography, and others – to visually appeal to people with *Ojú-ọnà*, who can see artwork as an icon and as a piece of art. Stephen Sprague

Figure 11.5 Ọ̀ṣun II. Source: Courtesy of Moses Ogunleye

explained how specific body contouring and exterior appearance, captured in painting, can be performances of cultural notions and visually coded artistry:

> Yoruba culture placed great emphasis on tradition, proper conduct, and the identity and maintenance of one's proper social position in society. Early British portraits and Yoruba traditional formal portraits visually codify these commonly held values by the dignified manner in which the subjects pose … There are distinctions, however; Yoruba traditional formal portrait is meant to memorialize the subject in terms of how well the individual has embodied traditional Yoruba ideals and fulfilled his given traditional position in Yoruba society.[23]

---

[23] Stephen Sprague, "How I See the Yoruba See Themselves," *Studies in Visual Communication* 5, no. 1 (1978): 9–28, at 9.

Figure 11.6 *Obìnrin omi*. Source: Courtesy of Moses Ogunleye

Although concepts like these can be collected under terms such as "aesthetic of the cool,"[24] Yorùbá art aesthetics such as *Ìfarahàn* manifest in paintings with rich cultural significations.

Ìfarahàn is visibility, and it aesthetically informs paintings where subjects are produced with visually identifiable peculiarities fitting and coinciding with the collective frame. Through *Ìfarahàn* subjects are identifiable and appreciable within the domain of their culture. Clothing, background, and color contribute to the aesthetic fabric of *Ìfarahàn* and how it implicates the merging

---

[24] Robert Farris Thompson, "An Aesthetic of the Cool," *African Arts* 7, no. 1 (1973): 40–91.

Figure 11.7 *Ètùtù*. Source: Courtesy of Tosin Adesanya

Figure 11.8 *Ìmúra*. Source: Courtesy of Tosin Adesanya

Figure 11.9 Yèye Bisi Falola. Source: Courtesy of Segun Ajiboye

of individual identity with ranges of socially permitted exhibitions of identity, behavior, respect, and class. *Ìfarahàn* also covers cultural items, along with motifs that are visually expressed as background and foreground materials in paintings. Not only do they connote metaphorical cultural meanings, they also serve as visual indices of associative power and status.

Material properties, ranging from colors to textures, express nonverbal communication in Yorùbáland, establishing an individual's stature or *Ìwà* (character). Items and concepts are signifiers that work in a system of relation that holds specific meanings. These meanings are incorporated, through their signifiers, into visual arts as aesthetics. From there, they propagate meanings that are at once symbolic and recognizable – Yorùbá paintings are products of aesthetic considerations and cultural awareness.

Yorùbá painting exists within a network that encompasses a well-developed system of critical appreciation, a defined linguistic conceptual framework, and a robust system of distribution. The distribution explains the noteworthy levels of patronage that depend on healthy appreciation for beauty, relying on the Yorùbá penchant for material acquisition. To them, it is a vibrant system of symbolism.

Figure 11.10 Ọ̀jọ̀gbọ́n Toyin Falola. Source: Courtesy of Segun Ajiboye

Cordwell argues that the Yorùbá can become obsessed with accumulating wealth and prestige through the acquisition of material possessions.[25] The position is a reach, construed from an alien ideological perspective developed by an outsider relative to the culture under discussion, but it contains a truth: painting is favored by the Yorùbá for its mediumistic capacity and the potency of its symbolism. Creation, appreciation, and acquisition of paintings stem from this motive. One might argue that painting has always been associated with distribution and exhibition networks in Yorùbáland.[26]

Patronage in Yorùbáland is a mode of exhibition. In the Yorùbá sociosphere, symbolic status is ascribed to painting, and art in general. A painting is hung in a home to make it visually appealing, and the entire home setting, including the color of walls and the ambience of the immediate setting – parlor, kitchen, or bedroom – is crucial to the art's interpretation. It is not enough to hang a painting and appreciate it outside the context of its placement. The placement itself is important. The sitting room, parlor, and study

[25] Cordwell, "Arts and Aesthetics."
[26] Joselit, "Painting."

are all separate levels of private space; the presence of specific paintings in these spaces indicates an individual's intimacy with the idea, person, motifs, or color represented in the painting. Displaying paintings in shops or public spaces is a show of endorsement for the notions, beliefs, and ideas espoused by such works. These contexts, even personal ones, provide modes of exhibition and endorsement without verbal accompaniments or formalized structures.

There is also the matter of status in relation to Yorùbá painting. Claims of stature are implicated within painting frames, and persons of greater economic power and social standing will have more and larger paintings displayed. Many such paintings may also be ornately designed.[27] Such exhibitions are also modes of commercialism that contribute to the network, moving the painting along the chain of relation between painter, consumer, and critic (*Gbẹ́nugbẹ́nu*).[28] As Joselit asserts, it is not enough for the Yorùbá to hang paintings and call them art: "that would be dreadful. The whole network is important."[29] Themes with social relevance and aesthetic or traditional appeal are maintained and furthered, and allowances are made for creative, idiosyncratic remakes and revisions of tradition.

Artwork garners publicity through its presence in specific parts of the social space, which invites structured critical commentaries and appraisal. These are opportunities for new and continued patronage, which are vehicles through which cultural participants are proselytized. Theme and style can be remade creatively by other artists, leading to and sustaining the evangelization of themes and aiding cultural pedagogy.

The network in which paintings thrive is possible because paintings speak to power and emotions. The surface reflectivity of Yorùbá paintings acts to trigger social thought and the collective unconscious. By signifying codes that are imbued with social meaning, the canvas becomes a product of systematic revision and reproduction of collective thought and wisdom. Themes and motifs contained and reflected in paintings have social relevance, resonating with cultural exigency in ways that allow the medium to be a plane for sociocultural rallying. Much of Yorùbá painting, regardless of the painter's stylistic ideology, falls into this category based on the sociocultural utility of art.

The majority of artistic expressions in Nigerian painting reflect Abodunrin's viewpoint, which is firmly rooted in the people's sociocultural and political existence, regardless of the artists' residence or creative manipulation of subject matter, medium, and technique.[30] The premise is better understood

---

[27] Sprague, "How I See the Yoruba."
[28] One who verbally and creatively exercises the creative ranges of Yorùbá rhetoric for art appreciation, critiquing a work of visual art to commend its beauty and purpose, as well as the creator's ingenuity. This is highly contextualized; the mode and form are deeply rooted in Yorùbá oral culture and folkloric expressions.
[29] Joselit, "Painting," 125.
[30] Johnson Abodunrin, "Taxonomy of Painting Styles in Nigeria," *Africology: Journal of Pan-African Studies* 10, no. 3 (2017): 234–247.

in the sociocultural context of Yorùbáland, where art is often engaged on indigenous terms and with indigenous tools, valued for its ability to store and visually activate cultural thought, nuance, ethos, myths, and ideologies. Art serves in these capacities as cultural memory.

Accentuating this position, especially in contrast to Western and Asian painting traditions, Abodunrin asserts that "Nigerian paintings are those that portray issues relating to the environment and draws inspiration of style and technique from traditional art forms found in textiles, sculpture, weaving and architecture embedded in Nigerian society."[31] Any visual encounter with a Yorùbá image is immersive; it immediately exposes the individual to various levels of awareness that have cultural implications. A sense of power, emerging from the agency of awareness and the knowledge of a particular thing, ethos, or aspect of Yorùbá reality is exchanged between viewer and canvas. This knowledge, on the part of the viewer, is processed through interpretation, which further charges various parts of a painting's surface. Such knowledge, when exercised over members of the same social order, displays the functionality of Yorùbá painting grounded in Yorùbá life.

How does this power manifest? One example is the way that an encounter with a visual and aesthetically influenced composition is a sensitizing experience in Yorùbá social life. The viewer, born in a social atmosphere where possession of beauty and its accumulation in material form is considered a manifestation of one's Ìwà (character), grows up attributing social significance to the aesthetic object itself. By purchasing such objects to signify Ìwà, the viewer activates the representational power of the object, visually asserting dominance over those whom the viewer has risen above – people who were previously in the same social circle. The act of purchase has conferred the proceeds of visual appreciation. When beautiful artwork is praised for its artistry and composition, as in oratorical instances of Yorùbá appreciation, the creator and owner are often the beneficiaries. The art attests to the buyer's sense of good taste (Ojú inú) and economic prowess, which contribute to an individual's Ìwà. The artwork is a leveler across social categories.

In practical terms, viewing a painting in single or multiple dialogic experiences shifts the cognition and awareness of the viewer. The buyer, already educated on the possibilities of power through art, continues purchasing artworks that reinforce a position of power. This is why Cordwell states that the desire to possess power, in order to exercise hegemony over another person in a social situation, has generated many occurrences of inventive aesthetic behavior among the Yorùbá.[32]

Functional or aesthetic consideration of Yorùbá art can be summarized by the idea that Yorùbá painting speaks to power. To charge the canvas with

---

[31] Abodunrin, "Taxonomy of Painting Styles," 235.
[32] Cordwell, "Arts and Aesthetics."

Yorùbá-centric motifs, aesthetics features,[33] imageries, and themes[34] is to increase a painting's level of appeal for culturally oriented individuals who appreciate its agency. The motifs, themes, and artistic styles are chiefly responsible for the appeal and popularity of painting in Yorùbáland, despite the momentous shift from traditional to modern in style, materials, and medium. Even through the advent of colonialism and the changes that it brought, Yorùbá painting did not alter its nucleus of functional and evocative power.

Power, not emotion, charges the creation and acceptance of painting in a Yorùbá social matrix. This also manifests in the inclusion of specific mythic and historical themes on a canvas; painting is itself a manifestation of this principle. For example, it is believed that the more celebrated an ancestor is, the more the relevance they accrue in the afterlife.[35] This relevance increases the devotee's popularity with the ancestor. In this sense, painting is no longer a status symbol or signifying plane, but an instrument of proselytizing and campaign. Paintings of deities or dematerialized Òrìṣà, as well as those performing masquerades, exemplify this position best: they celebrate and campaign for the potency and might of such mythic figures, visually narrating the dominance of those figures in Yorùbá social hierarchies of Ìdílé (lineage), Ẹbí (family), and Agbo ilé (conglomeration of houses/extended compound), as well as the hierarchy of Ìlú[36] (town) and the lives of those who populate these structures.

The Yorùbá believe that the spiritual realm controls the physical, which accounts for the numerous methods devised to propitiate and revere spiritual beings – painting is one of them. This reflects the functionality of Yorùbá wall paintings, from which painting grew onto mediums such as canvases.

---

[33] Aesthetic traditions and aesthetic qualities such as Jíjọra (relative mimesis), Ìfarahàn (relative visibility), Dídán (relative luminosity), Gígùn (straightness), Mímọ̀sà (skill), Ìdọ́gba (compositional balance), and Ọ̀dọ̀ (ephebism) manifest in Yorùbá painting. See Thompson, *African Art in Motion*, for further discussion.

[34] Studies such as Ikoro, "Painting and Society"; Abodunrin, "Thematic Concerns"; and Abodunrin, "Taxonomy of Painting Styles" have shed light on Yorùbá themes reflected in Yorùbá paintings and how modern Yorùbá painting styles, such as naturalism, symbolism, abstraction, and realism, all manifest the Yorùbá epistemic take and positions on life. Some of these styles, such as Expressionism, Impressionism, and Cubism, have foreign provenance, especially in terms of their final codification as systematic approaches to artistry, but they have been domesticated in the Nigerian Yorùbá painting tradition because of their heavy similarities to indigenous art concepts and beliefs, which make them fit in modern-day classification of Yorùbá – Nigerian – painting tradition, as schematized by Abodunrin, "Taxonomy of Painting Styles." Even Cubism is Picasso's fusion of West African artistic and European painting styles.

[35] Adesanya, *Carving Wood*; Thompson, "An Aesthetic of the Cool."

[36] Cultural idioms, heavy with spiritual connotations, such as "Aláṣẹ ìkejì òrìṣà" (second authority after the gods/deities), are often used to praise the king (Ọba). It is believed that only the gods and spiritual beings, like the Àjẹ́, have authority surpassing the king who heads the Ìlú.

Paintings were spiritualized through context and use and via processes of creation. Shrine paintings have been defined by a pedagogic principle: proselytizing and instructing the Yorùbá about the potency of spirituality, showing the benefits of revering and fearing heavenly beings to harness their powers and have them intercede in human affairs, obliterating malevolent forces or fate. For taxonomic purposes these can be collapsed into an aesthetic of power.

Such paintings were made to evoke fear and trembling, inducing absolute reverence and increasing the value of worship through the inclusion of fear-inducing images and shapes. Grotesque and contorted figures, along with repulsive color combinations, form functional sets of horrifying motifs. Some of these motifs are the contorted shapes of animals, such as lizards (*aláṅgbá*), snakes (*ejò*), chameleons (*ògà*), tortoises (*ìjàpá*), and birds (*ẹyẹ*). Color types and lines of different width, thicknesses, and shapes form part of the motifs. Figures 11.11 and 11.12 are paintings influenced by such shrine aesthetics. They are all symbolic, with their own metaphoric contents.

Figure 11.11 *Sisí Èkó*. Source: Courtesy of Victor Ekpuk

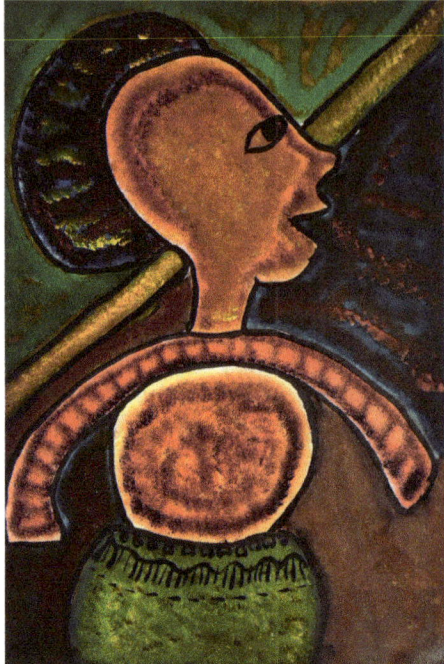

Figure 11.12 *Iwin*. Source: Courtesy of Moses Ogunleye

The animal motifs and colors have meanings that could be traced to the deities in certain Yorùbá myths. To Aremu et al, "Animal motifs are apparent because they have from the earliest times been favorite motifs in Yoruba visual and verbal arts."[37] Yorùbá culture, as an embodiment of several aspects of Yorùbá reality, has always been a veritable source of inspiration for Yorùbá art. In whatever time, and regardless of artistic tradition, these motifs remain potent as cultural symbols. They are scattered within the categories of flora, fauna, and the natural in modern-styled Yorùbá paintings.

The intense emotionality that arises from coming into contact with such motifs, rendered within these shrine contexts, is a sign of the presence of power differentials: the trembling subject is terrorized by the dematerialized essence, or the rendered state of the mystical being, because his power/essence is less than that of the spiritual being. This is especially true in the spiritual hierarchy of Yorùbá humans and their Òrìṣà. It is also symptomatic of a popular saying, "man fears what he doesn't comprehend."

[37] P. S. O. Aremu et al., "Re-Defining Wall Painting of the Yoruba of South-West Nigeria for Cultural Tourism," *WIT Transactions on Ecology and the Environment* 161 (2012): 343–352, at 347, www.researchgate.net/publication/268191803.

The Òrìṣà are spiritual phenomena whose essence cannot be totally understood or comprehended; even their states of rendition are dematerialized and abstracted. Fear of such incomprehensible subjects is a manifestation of deference to superior power. Shrine paintings in Yorùbáland conform to "the act of honoring, soothing and cooling the gods and likewise influenc[ing] their decisions to favor man in his incessant struggle on earth."[38] This same impulse is active in the modern framed and canvas-based paintings of the Yorùbá. Within and underlying the active surface of every painting are structural possibilities of power; it is for this reason that Yorùbá paintings are functional. They serve as storehouses for the collective unconscious, rendering and informing on cultural life. As frames, they render emotions (as aesthetic considerations), beliefs, and communally held ideologies.

By being objects of contemplation, Yorùbá paintings begin to visualize the networks within which they exist. For the attentive interpreter, seeing is relative, and perception even more so. The paintings illustrate the passages of social thought and wisdom that run through them, as well as levels of illumination that activate the various parts of their surfaces. The artist, as a creator and as an embodiment of aesthetic traditions, is emphasized to display the shifts in cultural knowledge that have been invested into and manifested through the painting. The artist's agency is validated through their work. Through the artist, and through those with whom the artwork engages in visual dialogues, the painting exchanges codes and contextual meanings, attaining the apex of its signifying power and becoming both an object and product of social processes and consciousness.

When I see paintings as crystallizations of interwoven cultural processes, I envision their collectors as those who are implicated in a multi-tier web of associations. Such persons become the midpoint of evocation, the canvas upon which derivable meanings are etched; or better yet, the canvas around which those meanings are intertwined, like the roots of a yam tuber buried in the soul of the earth, growing out and around a raised support system. If then, as rightly asserted by Joselit, the network is important in appreciating the status of painting as art, then I assume that, by possessing these paintings, I belong to this network. I belong not only as a channel through which cultural and private meanings interact, but also as a knowledge system, an intelligence through which personal meaning and cultural symbolism are fused and interrogated for their rich connotations.

The Canvas as an Idealizing Frame

Moralist criticism, a term associated with Northrop Frye, tries to sum up the Yorùbá people's approach to life and its various representative media.

[38] Aremu et al., "Re-Defining Wall Painting," 343.

The concept of Ọmọlúàbí seems to have agency through virtually all aesthetics and art of the Yorùbá. The Yorùbá are didactic people, with intricate knowledge systems and structured channels through which those systems manifest in the lives of men and women, young and old, and rich and poor. Everyone is held to this ideal standard. In this light, certain requirements are expected from individual members, because a person is a nation. (By this, I refer to the Yorùbá belief that each individual represents an Ìdílé.)

An individual in a social context is no longer the man or woman that he or she physically represents. They become an index, an ambassador, or the proxy of the commonwealth of families that compose the Ìdílé and Ẹbí. Certain character and behavioral manifestations, which must conform to acceptable standards, are expected of such individuals. Any contravention leads to an instance of marginality: the individual is cast as Ènìyàn bíburẹ̀wà (someone with unpleasant character), viewed as a manifestation of poor upbringing – such an assumption reflects poorly on an entire family. Yorùbá people are highly diplomatic, and verbal criticism of unacceptable behavior might be couched in popular queries such as: "Ilé wo lo ti wà" (from which family did you come?); "Ọmọ tani ẹ́" (whose son are you?); or "Ṣé ìwà lo hù yẹn" (is that a good thing you have done?).

Such queries are strategic, revealing the Yorùbá preoccupation with the home as the focal point of society. A delinquent individual is believed to have inherited their delinquent nature or to hail from a poor (morally bankrupt) background. Sayings like "Òwú ìyá gbọ̀n lọmọ ó ran" (the thread spun by the mother does a child weave) reflect this attitude. Through their dexterous manipulation of linguistic categories, bending syntax to suit social use through oratorical and discursive strategies, Yorùbá people engage offenders in a linguistic mirror that invokes a state of reflection and soberness. Instead of declaring that an offender has committed a serious offense or disgraced their lineage, they apply rhetorical questions that provoke deep and soulful reflection. These Yorùbá processes of social and cultural retooling are manifested in their paintings.

The Yorùbá frown at extravagance, viewed as excessive, Afẹ̀ or Fáàrí. Ìwọ̀ntunwọ̀nsì, which is moderation in appearance, posture, choice of words, behavior, and action, is the sign of an Ọmọlúàbí. In pictures it is represented by a cool and tempered posture. Ìjánu (verbal discipline, learning how and when to speak, or the cautious withholding of speech) or Ẹnu tútù (having a cool mouth, or possessing a reassuring, composed rhetorical style) and Ìfarabalẹ̀ (composure/inner-outer equilibrium) are appreciated by the Yorùbá. They can manifest in individual situations or within a collective. The ability to comport oneself in extreme situations – manifesting traits of social stability, inner balance, and unwavering concentration during intense moments of provocation – is an exercise of control that the Yorùbá highly respect. It is not hard to find photographic paintings and other forms of painting that depict people in composed states.

Figures 11.8, 11.9, 11.10, 11.13, 11.14, and 11.15 are examples. Fig. 11.13 depicts a seated person whose right hand, spread and resting on the body, protrudes from a colorful garment. This body composure is so prevalent in Yorùbá photographic presentations that it has been described as the "aesthetic of the cool."[39] The cool is a metaphoric code for all acceptable visual manifestations of behavioral moderation and socially endorsed Ìwà. Thompson explains it as "the purifying means by which worlds are taken out of contingency and raised to the level of aspiration."[40] The possibility of instigating and encouraging aspiration to achievable standards is how the canvas enables social awareness and functions as cultural coordinator.

Figure 11.13 Isola Ológbojò. Source: Courtesy of Moses Ogunleye.

---

[39] Thompson, "An Aesthetic of the Cool."
[40] Thompson, "An Aesthetic of the Cool," 41.

Figure 11.14 Dolapo Falola. Source: Courtesy of Moses Ogunleye.

The various manifestations of a cool and calm persona, as seen in the six figures referenced, all fit as parts of an aesthetic. By being recast as an idealizing posture and theme, sensitizing the populace to the premium of coolness, and removing traces of individuality, they enable the complete transformation from a portrait of an individual to a collective pedagogic frame.

A critical look at the images suggests that the subjects are at peace, exhibiting different levels of smiles or tempered laughter. It is not unbridled, full-blown laughter, which could be interpreted as excessive, inappropriate, or charged with ulterior motives. The subjects are at peace with themselves, exuding inner equilibrium within the borders of their frames. A sensitizing impulse radiates from the surface of these images, placing a premium on control. The Yorùbá believe that one should be cheerful regardless of one's situation – the idiom "Tì kó bá sí lójú, kìí kán sí àyà" (if it isn't in the face, it doesn't weigh on the mind) supports the ideological postures on display in the images.

Instead of an ostentatious or forceful display of wealth and prestige, the Yorùbá diplomatically allow physical possession, carriage, posture, and composition to speak on their behalf. This is significant in Yorùbá culture, and it is manifested in the paintings. The subjects in Figures 11.8, 11.9, and 11.13 are ornately dressed figures; their appearances reveal their social stature. This show of status is matched with gracefulness, tempering the severe manifestation of wealth and exemplifying diplomacy and moderation; it allows inanimate materials to perform the necessary act of signifying. Owing to the

Figure 11.15 *Ìmọ̀*. Source: Courtesy of Ronke Adesanya.

celebratory tone and attitude with which Yorùbá attend such instances of physical composure and bodily composition – with body parts aligned in relaxed, symmetrical positions, with a gentle parting of the lips to reveal moments of delight and inner peace that banish frustration and other forms of inner discontentment – Yorùbá subjects in visual arts, such as those featured, are presented within a framework tempering absolute identity to achieve compatibility with a collective agenda.

David Doris explains this behavior as an individual opting to associate the self with lasting traits of excellence that exceed particularities of uniqueness.[41] Fig. 11.16, which is also a photographic portrait, seems to deviate from the aesthetic of the cool, if one considers the overly relaxed, blithe, and nonchalant posture of the subject. His hands are folded atop his chair, he exhibits a cheery

[41] Doris, "Symptoms and Strangeness."

Figure 11.16 Ọ̀jọ̀gbọ́n Isola. Source: Courtesy of Segun Ajiboye

smile, and his body settles in an almost sprawling manner that appears to be anything but moderate. It creates a surface illusion; this extends the aesthetic to accommodate the fluidity of Yorùbá forms, but the idea establishes that there is constancy in changeability. To quote Cordwell again, "Forms can change, but patterns remain the same."[42] Despite the apparent happy-go-lucky-attitude of the subject, his expression still resides within the aesthetic of *Ìwọ̀ntunwọ̀sì* and *Afẹ̀* (liveliness), which are key components of *Ìwà* and expected from every *Ọmọlúàbí*.

Within the collective framework, it can be said that the discrete identity of the person is mediated by a sense of shared identity. By choosing to be recognized in a set of conventionalizing sociocultural features, the subjects in the images embody the self and the other. The self is a person of specific social status, with a unique and acceptable *Ìwà*. The other is the collective identity or collective *Ìwà* of a class of persons who are wealthy, respectable, calm, introverted, or simply *Ọmọlúàbí*. The beads, caps, *Fìlà*, and colorful flowing gowns (*Agbádá*) worn by these subjects testify to their aspirations of being seen within the context of being an *Ọmọlúàbí*, properly dressed and equally ambassadorial.

Drawing significance from the illustrative images along cultural lines, paintings in the Yorùbá cultural sphere perform best as guides for ethical excellence, sensitizing the people, sanitizing the social order, and retooling wayward *Ìwà* for social compatibility. We can say that Yorùbá paintings are idealizing

---

[42] Cordwell, "Arts and Aesthetics," 56.

frames; the power to provoke a return to acceptable conduct lies not only within the metaphoric interior of the canvas as the non-visible core of the images, but also in the channels of dialogue performed during the visual processes of interpretation and appreciation. Endorsed visions and acceptable ways of being become a standard that many can aspire toward.

The functional aspect of paintings as sensitizing tools is further manifested extra textually and even intra-textually, especially in the case of Figure 11.13, where the idealized subject is surrounded by several human figures. Their heads are raised, as if in reverence to the centralized image. Respect, admiration, awe, and veneration can be interpreted within and from the surrounding faces, which have been obscured by the angle of their heads. All of them are textural, miniaturized representations of visual dialogic processes, showing admiration and respect for beauty in the Yorùbá social sphere.

In a related sense, Yorùbá paintings perform dual duties of validating and sanctioning as idealizing frames. By endorsing acceptable ways of being, composure, and moderation, they inherently sanction any manifestation of contravening opposites. Opposing forces and binaries continually jostle for relevance within such paintings and on their surface. This triggers eruptions at the level of ideology and beneath the surface of the paintings – they are almost imperceptible outside the context of that which is endorsed, but that which is embraced wholly during the dialogic process will decenter and overwhelm any contrary message. This may be why Wole Soyinka describes Yorùbá classical art as an expression that is utterly devoid of conflict on its surface. Its deft, luminous peace is blinding to darker powers.[43]

Paradoxically, the presence of behavioral sanction is contained within behavioral endorsement; it is the presence of an absence. Through functionality, and because the visual dialogue is an open-ended process, these absences rise to the surface of the canvas. The dialogue, which is open to several levels of interpretation anchored on cultural values and knowledge systems that are themselves dynamic, activates these absences in the process of viewing to make them present. A painting that accommodates and endorses proper dress, composure, and symbolic-but-restrained displays of wealth alongside a collected self is also a painting that admonishes against flamboyance. Such paintings, like Figures 11.13–11.15, can be seen either as endorsements of cultural notions or sanctions of contravening ones.

The calm demeanor and graceful exterior of Figures 11.8, 11.9, 11.10, 11.13, 11.14, and 11.15 accentuate the Yorùbá preoccupation with beauty and aesthetically pleasing objects. If the cool exteriors of these images draw attention to themselves at first glance, the dialogic process is sustained by the levels of

---

[43] Wole Soyinka, "The Fourth Stage: Through the Mysteries of Ogun to the Origin of Yoruba Tragedy," in *African Philosophy: An Anthology*, ed. Emmanuel Chukwudi Eze (Oxford: Blackwell, 1998), 438–446, at 444.

Figure 11.17 Toyin Falola Jr. Source: Courtesy of Segun Ajiboye

beauty identified within. Simplicity, not ordinariness, is a measure of beauty – for the Yorùbá, beauty is not measured in terms of ornaments, flamboyant clothing, or rich embroidery (Figure 11.13 is notably different from Figures 11.8 and 11.14 in terms of simplicity and colorfulness, and Figure 11.9 differs from Figure 11.17, even though they are both representations of female figures, while all of them remain aesthetically pleasing). Beauty is measured by how persons define their selves within the permissions of a broadly defined cultural project like the Ọmọlúàbí.

It is hard for a simply dressed individual, or one projected by a painting, to be ordinary. Their simplicity finds expression within the concept of Ọmọlúàbí, as well as within parts of the collective frame suited for it. Varying levels of beauty are emphasized because they manifest the specificities of a person's individuation. Ìwà is Ẹwà as Ẹwà is Ìwà. This consideration of beauty in relation to painting informs Doris's statement that the beautiful object is a moral and "visual guidepost of moral excellence."[44] Doris writes that "beautiful [objects] ... proffer in form the attributes and rewards of good behavior."[45]

---

[44] Doris, "Symptoms and Strangeness," 24.
[45] Doris, "Symptoms and Strangeness," 24.

To the Yorùbá, the levels of patience and attention to detail required to conjure an attractive, visually stimulating image with paints, brush, and colors indicate a person's levels of tolerance and creativity. The reward for these is patronage and effusive appreciation. It means goodwill and benefits for those who create the painting and for the individual who chooses to behave in a similar manner. The Yorùbá people are known for their praise rhetoric and effusive panegyrics – this is a huge benefit and endorsement in its own right.

Paintings exist as activists, reinvigorating cultural support for artistry. They proclaim the richness of an ethnicity's creative repertoire and advocate for themselves beyond the glossy surface of the canvas. They self-reflexively advocate their own usefulness, their own Ìwà, the same way a person communicates Ìwà through their appearance.

Painting as Visual Rhetoric

Rhetoric can refer to the formal properties of art (artful words, rendered intelligibly for defined purposes), the aesthetics comprising its elements, or the substance and content it purports to communicate. Rhetoric can refer to content or medium, manner or matter. In an expansive sense, rhetoric is not limited to the domain of words, rendered in speech or writing alone – such limitations would reignite the phonocentricism and logocentricism debate.

Rhetoric includes the multiple manifestations and possibilities of language. Art of any kind is a text,[46] governed by the rules of its own language. Artwork can only be interpreted due to the presence of mutual intelligibility between the painter, as the source of a message, and the viewer, who receives it. Mutual intelligibility only occurs when art is encoded, structured, and invested with readable properties, like any language. These properties can be engaged and unlocked by a cultural participant, an informed observer, or both.

The language of all Yorùbá art, including painting, is intelligible because it is couched in familiar patterns, colors, motifs, brush strokes, designs, painting styles, images, contextual codes, metaphors, and stylo-artistic conventions. When visualized independently or together, they are rendered as decodable visual signs. The signs embody the dialogic potential of Yorùbá paintings, and they are activated in visual encounters that engage the critical interest of a participant-interrogator/viewer in communicative processes.

Visual rhetoric differs significantly from the verbal in terms of the dialogic process, but they are both enabled by four components: infinitely generative structure, convention, content, and scaffold – convention encompasses that which is categorized under content and scaffold. Dominic Baker-Smith has written that "the relationship between the visual and the verbal arts has been

---

[46] Abrams, *Glossary*. See also Umberto Eco, *A Theory of Semiotics* (Bloomington: Indiana University Press, 1976).

founded for the greater part of its history on a common concern with communicating: that is, with providing a socially based set of conventions for conveying ideas or images."[47] Words and speech, as art, can be enabled by a langue that is the organizing principle structuring language and speech formation. They can exist as parole, the different manifestations of words at speech and written levels. Yorùbá painting also has its own langue and different paroles, which manifest through the various paintings communicating similar and dissimilar themes and styles, as well as those that are conventionalized. Baker-Smith summarizes the concept with the idea that "a great deal of the activity which the arts shared in common might be summarized under the heading of narration, of telling a story and telling it vividly."[48]

An excerpt reflects the three vital components of rhetoric: telling an idea (communicable content), narration (the process of telling it), and telling it vividly (the elements employed in communicating the idea). Each of these three elements is essential to Yorùbá painting. Visual rhetoric is not only about patterns, design, style, or aesthetics; it is also about how images reflect, communicate, and change meaning and culture. This engenders visual literacy: knowing and responding to ideas communicated by images. Yorùbá painting is a visual rhetoric because it communicates and narrates Yorùbá life. By chronicling Yorùbá communal reality,[49] it functions as a visual record of their ethos, myths, history, and philosophies.

Yorùbá paintings communicate ideas and themes that are rooted in their culture and knowledge systems. The Yorùbá are highly communal people, apparent in their kinship structures, such as the Ẹbí and Ìdílé systems. These influences are reflected in their myths and the kinship system of their hierarchical Pantheon. The concept of Àjùmọ̀ṣe, connoting a sense of togetherness in philosophy and action, further exemplifies this. It is reflected in Figures 11.18 and 11.19, and even 11.20. Communalism in every sphere of life is crucial for the Yorùbá, which is why the "I" is always seen in ambassadorial terms, representing the collective. Figure 11.21 depicts women engaging in joint tasks, serving as pictorial campaigns for the division of labor and a collective ideology where many hands make light work.

Figure 11.18 is a rendering of different subjects in postures of protest. Male, female, young, and old are represented. Both sexes hoist weapons, from sticks to guns – there are even drummers adding rhythm and sustaining the agency of the occasion. Melody is food for the soul, as stated in the maxim "Orin ladùn ọkàn." This sense of togetherness is projected by an image that is not only

---

[47] D. Baker-Smith, "Literature and the Visual Arts," in *Encyclopedia of Literature and Criticism*, ed. Martin Coyle, Peter Garside, Malcolm Kelsall, and John Peck (London: Routledge, 1990), 991–1003, at 998.
[48] Baker-Smith, "Literature and the Visual Arts," 998.
[49] Ikoro, "Painting and Society."

Fig 11.18 *Àgbẹ́kòyà*. Source: Courtesy of Moses Ogunleye

Figure 11.19 *Èyò*

instrumental in the growth of society, but also educates with several layers of meaning. The history of the Yorùbá is dotted with protests, either against dictatorial rule or the abuse of power by chiefs. On another level of meaning,

Figure 11.20 *Ògún* I. Source: Courtesy of Adeniyi Dagunduro

Figure 11.21 *Ọmọdé mẹta ń ṣ'iṣẹ́*. Source: Courtesy of Ronke Adesanya

enabled by the polysemic nature of paintings and texts, the painting is an instance of celebration or the performance of some communal rite, especially when considering the horn and calabash held by the center figure. Either interpretation would suffice; the underlying ideology is one of communalism.

Figures 11.19, 11.20, and 11.22 are better examples of the agency of collectivity, oiling the machinery of the society for growth and prosperity. In Figure 11.22 the concept of *Àjùmọ̀ṣe* (doing it together) is well rendered: one figure hits a drum carried by the other. It is a metaphor for the spirit of social cohesion, especially when considering that social order is only possible in the presence of alliance and unity. This is further emphasized by the ritual context

Figure 11.22 *Ọdún*

Figure 11.23 *Fúrá*. Source: Courtesy of Olusegun Ade

that the image signifies. The apparel and items, and even the placement of the drum, are signs of spirituality and ritual. The *Aru-ìlù* and *Arugbá* themes, which are portrayed in Figure 11.23, showing two women hoisting large calabashes on their heads, are well represented in canonical Yorùbá visual arts. The Yorùbá believe strongly in the concepts of Ẹ̀bẹ̀ (supplication) and Ẹbọ (sacrifice).

The choice to carry loads, such as the drum of Figure 11.22 or the calabashes in Figure 11.23, can be seen in a ritual context where the individual assumes a sacrificial role to benefit every other member of society, and also for the benefit of society itself. In ritual spaces the drum is often seen as a symbol of spirituality. The beating of the drum can either be seen as a placatory measure, softening the hostile influence of malevolent spiritual forces, or as propitiatory measures to gain entry into the realm of spiritual forces and win their favor. This theme of spirituality is well communicated in Figure 11.19, an Èyò festival, which involves a masquerade of spiritual entities or ancestors who circulate amidst their living relatives. This painting, communicating the Àjùmòṣe theme in a spiritual context, also comments on the mythological realties of the Yorùbá.

The Èyò festival, like any other masquerade festival, is an occasion for the Eko Yorùbá to celebrate the spirits of their ancestors. The mask and the white garment are icons, seen as mediums that enable the spirits of the dead to manifest in the world of the living. The intensity of celebration for a spirit or deity will dictate how well it is recognized in the spirit realm;[50] it signifies the power of the entity and shows that it would be well invested in the affairs of those who celebrate it. The rationale behind most Egúngún performances,[51] whether Èfè/Gèlèdè, Agemo, or Èyò, involves the following motives: the invocation of ancestral spirits, a celebration of their lives, and a request for their continued participation in the affairs of the living. Most Egúngún festivals are spiritualized ceremonies in which the entire society participates. They signify the religiosity and eschatological beliefs of the Yorùbá people, providing an opportunity to celebrate their departed ancestors.

The presentation of music is a cultural mainstay among the Yorùbá, which explains the motif of drums as a cultural sign of rituality. Music, through drums, allows humans to enter a hostile spiritual realm, feeding the human soul with merriment. The Yorùbá have several types of drum, each with its own mythic history[52] and significance. The Ìpèsè drum ensemble is associated with Òrúnmìlà, Àgéré with hunters, Gbèdu with the Ogbóni, Àgbà Obalùfòn with Obalùfòn, the Ìgbìn ensemble with Òrìṣà-oko, and Bàtá is the drum of Ṣàngó. Dùndún is the ultimate speech surrogate, recognized for its excellent communicative properties and

---

[50] A general Yorùbá belief, as submitted by Cordwell, "is that the ostentatious display of materials elevates the status of that spirit in the other world" ("Arts and Aesthetics," 59).

[51] The Egúngún as a name of a masquerade festival can be tribe specific, in which case it would refer to the Egúngún cult traceable to Oyo. Also, as explained by Adesanya (see Carving Wood), it can be employed as a generic name for all mask traditions to which the Èyò, belongs.

[52] Idinguda and Òkànràn òbàrà méjì verses of the Ifá corpus detail the mythic provenances and narratives of these drums. See Sesan Azeez, "Gender Dialectics of Yoruba Drum Poetry," Rupkatha Journal on Interdisciplinary Studies on Humanities 5, no. 2 (2013): 168–177, at 168, 177.

used as the favored drum of Ọ̀yọ́.[53] Others include *Ìyá ìlù*, *Gángan*, *Omele akọ*, *Omole abo*, and *Kongà*. Each drum has a robust origin story that is implicated in visual renderings on the drums. This reinforces the symbolism in Figure 11.24 and its connection with rituality and spirituality.

Drumming itself is an art that is highly celebrated for its musicality and its effective communicatory features. It is not unusual to find well-dressed *Àyàn* (drummers), as depicted in Figure 11.24. They perform independently at

Figure 11.24 *Onílù*. Source: Courtesy of Moses Ogunleye

[53] *Dùndún*, and indeed much of Yorùbá drum as an ensemble and as individual types, is not solely seen as a musical instrument, but also in political and social terms. As put by Azeez, "The popularity of *Dùndún* drum is also made possible because it can easily approximate human speech" (Azeez, "Gender Dialectics," 170).

public occasions, celebrating eminent patrons. They are performing artists (called *Eléré*, from the word eré for performance), and the material that they use is language. Olujubu argues that "through their command of language they form grand conceptions that stimulate powerful and inspired emotions. These they achieve by the proper formation of figures of thought and speech, and through the creation of noble diction by clever choice of words. The total effect of all these techniques is beauty, sublimity, and grandeur of language."[54]

The Yorùbá drums, especially the *Dùndún*[55] and *Gángan* used for these occasions, are appreciated for their ability to mimic human speech. Through the poetry they produce, the figures of thought and speech can be appreciated in relation to drumming and drummers. Yorùbá drumming and drum poetry is a well-developed art, using aesthetic features of tonality, repetition, harmony, and other stylistic effects to produce rhythm. Apart from the musicality, the drums are also well-designed aesthetic objects – considering the emphasis that the Yorùbá place on beauty, and how Ẹwà evinces Ìwà, drums are understandably the recipients of elaborate designs like the one seen in Figure 11.24. Figure 11.24 can provoke several discussions, establishing the richness of Yorùbá paintings as visual rhetoric.

Yorùbá paintings also chronicle aspects of daily life, including chores, farm work, and the roles and duties of women, as seen in Figure 11.21, and men, seen in Figure 11.20. Figure 11.20 shows men collectively killing and smoking game. The image shows how collectivity is highly valued in the Yorùbá social order, emphasizing proverbs such as "Àgbájọ ọwọ́ la fi ń sòyà" (the bunched fingers/fisted fingers is used in striking the chest). The symbolism of selflessness and togetherness is evoked in the image of men engaging in a joint task to sustain the stomach, considering that "Okun inú la fi ń gbé ti ìta" (strength starts from a filled belly). The symbolism connects with that of Figure 11.21, showing that togetherness in Yorùbá sociocultural space is integrated into the foundations of life, such as what to eat and how to go about it. It renders a philosophy in images: "Àjọjẹ ló layé" (sharing progresses the world).

Figures 11.21 and 11.25 also depict social roles, portraying women in various activities specific to the Yorùbá social framework. Although women are in charge of cooking[56] and buying at the market, the duties of fishing,

---

[54] Oludare Olajubu, "Yoruba Verbal Artists and their Works," *The Journal of American Folklore* 91, no. 360 (1978): 676.

[55] See Figure 11.24. Some scholars classify *Gángan* as a type of *Dùndún*.

[56] In Yorùbáland the expression "sisí ń se'bẹ̀" (lady in the kitchen) is used to playfully recognize the woman for her culinary skill, while the saying "Ọlọ́bẹ̀ ló l'ọkọ" (she who owns the soup owns the husband) praises the role of excellent culinary skills in the home and their importance as something that every woman should possess. The saying is as instructive as it is as meditative, and Figure 11.25, of a beautifully adorned woman efficiently carrying out her duties and maintaining her visual appeal, is equally instructive.

Figure 11.25 *Ìdí Ìlẹ̀kẹ̀*. Source: Courtesy of Adeniyi Dagunduro

hunting, and farming are those of the men, represented in Figure 11.20. Even ordinary moments in Yorùbá life are captured in paintings, as can be seen in Figures 11.26 and 11.27. Figure 11.26 reveals a typical *Adúgbò* (neighborhood) setting, with single-story buildings and the exposed balconies typical of Yorùbá architecture. Figure 11.27 captures an early morning setting with people visiting a vendor to read newspapers and pondering the ups and downs of life. Before the advent of the internet, this happened often in Yorùbá cities.

Yorùbá painted images can serve as records, visually relaying the importance and nature of different aspects of Yorùbá social structure, but they also capture simple existential details of life, including a day at the market (Figure 11.28). The focus can shift from the mundane to the spectacular, such as the painting of an *Olú Awo* (chief priest) in white apparel (Figure 11.29), mostly likely departing from his palace; this interpretation is suggested by the composition of the painting.

Figure 11.30 is a portrait of a *Ṣàngó* worshiper, indicated by the dress, plaited hairstyles, and the *Oṣé Ṣàngó* (wands) held in the hands of the painted image. *Ṣàngó* is an ancestral figure, originally one of the kings of old Ọyọ who was deified. The cult of *Ṣàngó* perpetuates his ritualized celebration; his power and persona are often rendered in abstract statuettes like those held by the painted subject. Figure 11.31 also shows a *Ṣàngó* worshiper, but the image goes beyond

Figure 11.26 Pópó Ibadan. Source: Courtesy of Den Light

Figure 11.27 Àdánwò. Source: Courtesy of Oye Ajayi

a visual narration of Yorùbá mystical life. The image captures the highly engaging, ostentatious, and consuming nature of performances during the Ṣàngó festival – it can be read from the subject's histrionics, body contortion, and dramatic posture, as well as from the presence of a drummer providing the necessary rhythm. In most cases the level of performative energy displayed by a subject is a result of a deity successfully mounting and possessing the subjects.

Figure 11.32 is a portrait of Ọbàtálá, another major deity. In Fig. 11.32 the figure stands tall in the midst of numerous other, dwarfed figures looking up to him. This is highly symbolic of Ọbàtálá's place in Yorùbá ontology and cosmology, where he is said to be the divine creative artist. Ọbàtálá as a deity is integral in the creation of humans, as he is responsible for shaping their forms. Figure 11.32 also reminds of a creative rendition of the deity Ọbàtálá, the patron of creativity and the god who molds the human form.

Ọrúnmìlà's presence is evoked by Figure 11.29, because the Olú Awo is priest of Ifá, otherwise known as Ọrúnmìlà. Ọrúnmìlà in Yorùbá cosmological belief is often depicted by associated symbols such as Àgéré Ifá and Ọpọ́n Ifá, as well as other cult calabashes. Ọrúnmìlà in Yorùbá epistemology and cosmology is said to be the Ẹlẹ́rìí (witness) Ìpín (lot), the one who is witness to every individual whenever they choose (Ìpín) their destiny (Àyànmọ̀) before coming to earth. This is why Ọrúnmìlà is

Figure 11.28 Ọjà Bódìjà. Source: Courtesy of Ekeolu Kazeem

Figure 11.29 *Olú Awo*. Source: Courtesy of Adeniyi Dagunduro

often propitiated and sought as the source of knowledge and a solution whenever an individual is at the crossroad of his or her life. Ọ̀rúnmìlà, to whom the *Ifá* corpus, the Yorùbá science of divination and encyclopedia of all knowledge, is credited, is a veritable source for solutions. This knowledge of Yorùbá mythology is well coded into the painting where humankind sees the presence of an *Ifá* priest, who represents Ọ̀rúnmìlà whom he serves and to whom he reports, as the presence of possibility, solution, knowledge, etc. The priest is the mediator between individuals and Ọ̀rúnmìlà, who himself is the mediator between humans and other Òrìṣà.

Èṣù, the trickster figure, is close to the divination process. Èṣù is said to have taught the system of divination to Ọ̀rúnmìlà and to be instrumental to the process itself. It is represented by avatars and symbols. One of Èṣù's avatars always holds a cudgel used to pummel those who refuse to

Figure 11.30 Ṣàngó I. Source: Courtesy of Moses Ogunleye

pay their dues or pay homage during the divination process. The protrusion on the head of Èṣù avatars is a symbolic codification of the deity's refusal and inability to carry a load at the creation of the world, unlike other Òrìṣà. It also indicates Èṣù's libidinous nature and the deity's duality, as well as its gender-neutral personality. Because Èṣù embodies and engenders confusion and contradicting forces as lord of the crossroads, Èṣù is often depicted as having both male and female genitalia. Another important deity evoked through representation is Ògún, the god of iron, well signified by Figure 11.33, with the hand-held iron instruments.

In continuance of the trickster god, any who seek to find their path at the crossroad of life must seek Òrúnmìlà for direction, but they must pay dues to Èṣù first. Èṣù can be cunning, creating problems and then offering to broker solutions for them, appearing to be the ultimate force controlling demand and supply. Èṣù is also symbolized by and believed to be present wherever a stone is worshiped. Palm oil is constantly poured on such stones as acts of devotion and reverence.

Figure 11.31 Ṣàngó II. Source: Courtesy of Adeniyi Dagunduro

Aesthetics of Yorùbá Painting and Symbolism

Yorùbá art aesthetics, which are culturally influenced, manifest in more than paint. They also have cultural symbolism, being deeply rooted in a tradition that is culturally informed. Aesthetics like *Jíjọra/Ìjọra* (relative mimesis), *Ìfarahàn* (relative visibility), *Dídán* (relative luminosity), *Ìdọ́gba* (compositional balance), and *Ọ̀dọ́* (ephebism)[57] are germane to a robust understanding of Yorùbá cultural philosophy and epistemic visions through canvas art. These aesthetics are mostly used to appreciate sculpted forms, but they also find relevance in Yorùbá paintings.

Ephebe, connoting youth (*Ọ̀dọ́*) and vitality (*Okun*), is crucial to Yorùbáland as a sociocultural space, represented in canonical Yorùbá visual arts. This

[57] Adesanya, *Carving Wood*, 23.

Figure 11.32 Ọbàtálá. Source: Courtesy of Moses Ogunleye

emphasis on vitality, vigor, and strength stems from the Yorùbá requirements of strength (*Agbára*) and bravery (*Akíkanjú*) for prospective *Ọmọlúàbì*. Because these features are found in youths, their youthfulness is a desirable condition, set up as an ideal frame and encoded as one of the ladders to relevance in Yorùbá society. This does not sanction or devalue aging or being old. Even in old age, elders are expected to be vital and strong in mental acuity and frame of mind as well as smart in their physical composure. Ephebism is a measure of beauty in young and old individuals, reflected in painted Yorùbá subjects as an aesthetically pleasing and symbolic plane of meaning.

Figures 11.8, 11.9, 11.10, and 11.14 reflect ephebism. The subjects are projected with a strong frame of mind, reflected by a calm exterior (only an internally cool individual, having advanced beyond all preoccupations, can present an externally visible equilibrium). Vitality is specifically manifested in Figures 11.23 and 11.24, especially in the postural contortion of the subjects to

Figure 11.33 *Ògún* II. Source: Courtesy of Moses Ogunleye

present a visual narration of the process of playing the *Dùndún* – such activity requires energetic movements and physical skill. Figure 11.31 presents a drummer and a young priestess engaged in a vigorous ritual dance.

Figures 11.23 and 11.25 are also examples of the premium that the Yorùbá place on vitality, showing how ephebism as a Yorùbá art aesthetic is displayed in painting. The continuous appearance of half-clothed men and women, as seen in Figures 11. 5 and 11.6, symbolizes the beauty and strength of youth, especially in Figure 11.20, where a subject is presented hacking game. Pictorial peculiarities abound – the specific rendering of vitality differs from image to image – but a critical survey of the paintings yields an aesthetic of youthfulness, or, better still, ephebism. These images are symbolic renderings of the primal place of liveliness, vivacity, vitality, and strength in the social expectations that the Yorùbá people hold for themselves and others, which becomes a ubiquitous principle in the aesthetics of their visual art. Ephebism also encompasses beauty, productivity, and fertility, which are prime features of youthfulness. This accounts for the repeated use of visually appealing female figures and subjects that strap babies to their backs, hold, or carry babies and young ones in their arms. Figures 11.4, 11.6, and 11.9 emphasize beauty as a signifier of ephebism.

Dídán (luminosity) and Ìfarahàn (visibility) are also essential to Yorùbá painting. The rationale behind Ìfarahàn is the visibility of the individual, which fits with the idea of an idealizing frame that painters create to identify their subjects. Painting subjects in canonical postures reflects the cultural identity serving as the framework for the posture, and the subject is seen and appreciated within the frame of the collective. In this way, the individual rises above the noisy multitudes to attain a highly celebrated pedestal, and individual and collective identities are made visible to viewers.

Luminosity, which is the presence of visual brilliance, glossing, and clarity, also holds cultural symbolism and is represented in Yorùbá painting. Bright colors accentuate the defining qualities of the painted subjects and their associated symbols, allowing easy identification and beautification. Their use is linked with the emphasis that Yorùbá people place on identity. Identity is crucial to the Yorùbá, and it is shown in different ways. They do this through tribal marks, as seen in Figure 11.34, or the body designs and markings in Figure 11.6 or through the glossy surface of items, especially masks. The use of bright colors and shinning surfaces, as seen in Figures 11.4, 11.5, 11.6, 11.7, and 11.10, is also an attempt to aid visibility, beautification, and identification. These are all aspects or consequences of the aesthetic of Dídán.

Ìjọra/Jíjọra, considered to be relative mimesis or imitation, is a significant aesthetic aspect of Yorùbá painting. It serves as the basis of the art itself; at the core of any art is its imitation of something else. In Yorùbá painting, Ìjọra takes several forms as Yorùbá painters attempt to capture life and represent it in artistic ways. The logic behind these representations contains its own cultural orientation. At the core of artistic styles, or painting styles, is a drive to capture life and the cultural values that shape it.

The different painting styles identified by Abodunrin,[58] such as symbolism, stylization, abstraction, Cubism, naturalization, Expressionism, realism, and Impressionism, can be informed by different aspects of Yorùbá epistemology. For example, the Yorùbá believe that it is impossible to fully comprehend the Òrìṣà or to render them artistically – the Òrìṣà are not corporeal, and accurate representations would require a concise knowledge of the unknowable. In their full glory, Yorùbá Òrìṣà defy total rendition, requiring stylized images to capture their dematerialized states. This belief manifests in paintings and human representation; by dematerializing the corporeal, absolute identity is tempered through stylization, and representational identity emerges or is accentuated for pedagogic or philosophic reasons.

In painting, stylization itself is "a decorative generalization of figure and objects by means of various conventional techniques which include the

[58] Abodunrin, "Taxonomy of Painting Styles."

simplification of line, form, and relations of space and color."[59] Figures 11.18 and 11.23 are examples, along with several others used in this chapter. There are too many Yorùbá images of stylized representation of a mounting process; it is believed that Òrìṣà worshipers can be mounted or possessed during celebrations or ritual performances. A distended head or limb signifies the presence of Àṣẹ (power) or the essence of an Òrìṣà.

Symbolism as an aesthetic tradition is anchored on the pedagogic and epistemic peculiarities of Yorùbá culture and life. The need to instruct through art manifests in this aesthetic tradition, and several aspects of Yorùbá life are rendered through symbolic items, materials, and subjects. Symbolism is often a means of resuscitating and maintaining traditions: the subjects are made to resemble their originals, or constructed in a way that symbolizes ideas that are easily deciphered. Figures 11.7, 11.19, and 11.33 are examples of totemic items presented in painting, through symbolism, as signification-laden subjects. Images made under the naturalistic aesthetic tradition perform similar functions.

Other aesthetic traditions influenced by cultural consideration are Expressionism and Cubism. Cubism fragments and reduces objects into geometric forms, while Expressionism tends to project emotion onto canvases. Expressionism explores emotion-filled themes to examine fear, horror, and grotesque images. Paintings made in this tradition are jagged, violent, and distorted to evoke specific feelings in the mind of the viewer. Images discussed in the context of Yorùbá shrine painting and their influences on Yorùbá canvas painting fall into these categories. The value of such images is to instill spiritual fear and trembling in cultural participants or the participant-viewer.

Cubism itself manifests the dematerializing principles adhered to by Yorùbá art/culture practitioners. Figure 11.34 is an example of a Cubist paintings, containing geometric shapes patterned together. Spirituality and the power of the indefinable realm of the celestial is represented though Cubist images, and Picasso himself, a pioneer of the movement, was influenced by the abstract, geometric, and stylized sculptures of West African traditions, including those of the Yorùbá. These sculptures have high spiritual symbolism and utility.

Realistic and naturalistic paintings, operating on the aesthetic demands of realism, reflect the Yorùbá fixation on beauty. They also serve as cultural ambassadors, reflecting the idea that Yorùbá art must be grounded in its cultural reality.

---

[59] Abodunrin, "Taxonomy of Painting Styles," 238.

Figure 11.34 After market. Source: Courtesy of Rasaki Adetunji

Conclusion

On the surface of the canvas, the aesthetic and the cultural congeal into a thing that is visually pleasing and symbolically instructive. Within the core of a painting, pathways and connections that are rich in cultural substance and stylo-artistic materials can only be appreciated through a human conduit, and that conduit can only attempt to give voice to these various layers of nuance. In an attempt to serve as that voice and consciousness through which channels of thought and cultural wisdom manifest on the canvas to be appreciated and observed, I have presented these materials and commented on how they stand in relation to me as frames of ideologies and symbols of a structured epistemic system.

12

Yorùbá Hair Art and the Agency of Women

Introduction: Hair as Art and Symbol

The premise of the human body as a site creates a singular impression of interdisciplinary harmony, despite the extensive and divergent subject matter covered by scores of disciplines in the social sciences and humanities. It serves as an ideological springboard for scholarly explorations into the human condition and its relationship with its environment, which is an ever-expanding, ever-growing framework within which human (in)significance is well rendered. Anthropology, literature, psychology, social science, science, and history, among other disciplines, do not fail to explore, investigate, or reconstruct the entwined interaction of the human body and the natural phenomena surrounding it. They uncover ways that the latter provides the former with workable materials, and vice versa. In the same vein, they highlight the character of a union that is best considered symbiotic or a fluid process of complementation.

This fluid process can be seen in the way the human body serves as a channel through which humans act on their environment. The body itself reacts to environmental stimuli. These stimuli react consequentially to the human body and its actions. This cycle is useful for the continued, proper functioning of the environment, which comprises the society, landscape, natural environment, culture, institution, and humans together.[1] The human body, and even its seemingly[2] minute and unimportant details, such as hair, become agentive and crucial to the understanding of the entire human framework – skeleton, tissue,

---

[1] See William Slaymaker, "Echoing the Other(s): The Call of Global Green and Black African Responses," in *African Literature: Anthology of Theory and Criticism*, ed. Tejumola Olaniyan and Ato Quayson (Malden: Blackwell, 2007), 683-697. See also Kate Rigby, "Ecocriticism," in *Introducing Criticism at the 21st Century*, ed. Julian Wolfreys (Edinburgh: Edinburgh University Press, 2002), 151-178.

[2] I use the term "seemingly" because the hair, when examined from some sort of hierarchy, seems to be the least significant. In some cultures it is often shaved off. During certain medical procedures, such as surgery, it is considered an impediment to be removed.

and flesh – as a site where cultural, notional, natural, and physical forces interact.

In light of this premise, the idea of hair – the slender and tender outgrowths or "mass of fine flexible protein strands that grow from follicles"[3] – transcending itself becomes pressing. The performativity of human hair along symbolic, agentive, and expressive lines acquires requisite and urgent transparency. Hair grows from and occupies pivotal spaces in the body, such as the head, armpits, face, and nether regions, which reinforces its status as a powerful symbol. By performing what Angela Rosenthal describes as "mediating between the natural and the cultural,"[4] human hair acquires centrality in the discourse of the body, connected to that which encompasses it. The natural and the cultural are rich metaphors of the environment and humans, respectively, which once again highlight the centrality of hair's role as medium.

The expressivity of hair is highlighted by its mediating, performative role. In the case of the traditional Yorùbá, hair actively signifies gender: it is impossible to see a man with *Kojúṣọkọ* or, as it is known today, all-front, on his head. Men can plait hair, as can be seen with Ṣàngó worshipers. But merely considering the idea of men adopting that hairstyle is a travesty, considering that the *Kojúṣọkọ* (a combination of *Kojú* – face + *ṣọkọ* – your husband) already establishes the male gaze as central, indexing the viewer for whom the hair is made to be appreciated, externalizing them symbolically and physically. Only women make this hair, and the semantic possibilities of the lexical item hint that the subject adorning herself with this style is not just a woman, but a married one. Whom would she face with the hairstyle, if not her husband?

The narrativity and expressivity of hair take up essential space in this discussion. Cultural injunctions, processes, and ideologies underpin the act of *Dirí/Dídì* (plaiting/braiding/weaving/styling hair); they are centralized and communicated via the visual dialogue between a viewer-participant[5] and the subject-carrier's body. This type of hair expresses marital fidelity, an ideological policy that is sacrosanct and culturally useful. The term *Kojúṣọkọ* is a linguistic coding of a subtle but fierce persuasion,[6] reminder, and instruction on the necessity of a pure, undistracted, and genuine relationship with one's *Olówó orí* (one who pays the bride price). The woman must center everything on her man, removing herself from wayward and useless preoccupations.

The construct expresses an unequivocal declaration of fidelity on the part of the woman, signaling devotion, commitment, and self-willed and self-sustained abiding fusion with her husband; she denounces promiscuity and

---

[3] Microsoft, "Hair," Microsoft® Encarta® (Redmond: Microsoft Corporation, 2009).
[4] A. Rosenthal, "Raising Hair," *Eighteenth-Century Studies* 38, no. 1 (2004): 1–16, at 2.
[5] I have used this to mean a viewer who also participates or is a member of a culture.
[6] The name itself is somewhat jocular in implication, reminding us of the sometimes Èfẹ̀ (hilarious) and unusual approaches of the Yorùbá toward pertinent and instructive issues.

wanton frivolities. Through her hair, the woman tells everyone that she has chosen to *Kọ ojú sí ọkọ* and everything that could attach to it, such as family and home. Her *Kọ ojú sí ọkọ* prevents errant acts of seeing the unseeable, potentially triggering misbehavior (*Ìwàkíwà*), for the Yorùbá believe that "Tí kò bá kán sójú, kò le kán sáyà." The mind ponders what has been seen, which is the sense behind the maxim. With *Kojúsọkọ* the hair not only narrates, it also expresses choice, discipline, and cultural ethos.

This level of expressivity is due to the hair's constant attachment to and extrusion from the human body and its extensively symbolic potentiality. The performance of hair as a narrative medium, or as a symbolic plane, can be seen in its clear indication of points of interception and interaction. The cultural, involving man-made beliefs, orientations, and institutions, interacts with natural elements, such as landscape, flora, atmosphere, and fauna. This convergence and departure between natural and cultural[7] is potently manifested in hair's narrativity. A fitting example is the *Onílé gogoro* hairstyle, or the modern variant seen in Figure 12.1, emulating the human desire to reach for greater heights – and the Yorùbá architectural expression of this ambition, such as duplexes and tall structures – through tall, ornately styled, and long weaves. The image's import reaches within the body and without. In view of this connectivity, Rosenthal argues that hair, human or not, whether it is natural,

Figure 12.1 *Onílé gogoro*

---

[7] In this context, cultural is contrasted with natural, indicating things that are made and conceptualized by humans, either in thought or manifested physically. They have been ritualized, or normalized into conventionalized standards, which can be loosely termed *Àṣà* (tradition/culture) in Yorùbá.

synthetic, or otherwise, always communicates. She says: "Emerging from the flesh and thus both of, and without the body – at once corporeal and a mere lifeless extension."[8]

Rosenthal scores a critical point by reemphasizing the communicatory potency of the hair, but she addresses the complementarity of hair and body in an insular fashion. Biology and human ontology establish that hair grows while it is still attached to the flesh, and it only withers when detached by means of willful or accidental cutting. However, this Western conception is not universal.

A claim flourishes within Yorùbá ontology and spirituality to counter Rosenthal. Hair works on metaphoric and context-specific synecdochic levels to communicate effectively. Even when detached, the hair works as an index that signals toward a living referent, betraying its active state even in metaphor. In synecdochic terms, a lock of hair that has been cut, or even a single strand, is seen as representative of the owner or the body from which it has been detached. It can be an instrument for malevolent, spiritually activated and Àṣẹ-laden injunctions or machinations. Attached hair grows and beautifies or disfigures the body, but it also works as an identifier for spiritual, cultural, ethnic, gender, and physical status.

It is a cultural injustice to conceive of hair as "a mere lifeless extension" when detached from the body; it is a rich and vibrant spiritual compass and communicative medium. Within the Yorùbá cultural space, hair is symbolic on many levels, rendering itself as a device. In the words of Angela Rosenthal, "It is for this reason not surprising that the growing, grooming, cutting, shaving or losing of hair – on the body and head – were often associated with transformative life experiences, with rites and rituals, and with the marking of cultural difference."[9] Spiritual practices in Yorùbá cultural spaces warrant specific plaiting of hairstyles or cutting or weaving; this practice varies from naming and cult festivities to mourning, pageantry, and celebrations.

Hair narrates, communicates, speaks, and conveys like any other part of the body. It is essential to examine how this narration is performed, the mechanics of its performance, and the nature of that which is communicated or symbolized, as well as the significance of the symbols. Hair, as part of the body, is a site for cultural production, agency, and staging, and a gendered agent itself. All this occurs with the hair of Yorùbá women.

An excursive examination of hair as agentive, in relation to Yorùbá women, does not translate as an exercise in reducing the woman or the sum of her worth to a single body part. Neither does it suggest that her objectification is a fertile ground for the engendering or importation of gendered perceptions in interrogating her agency. Instead, it marks an attempt to trigger the agency of

---

[8] Rosenthal, "Raising Hair," 1.
[9] Rosenthal, "Raising Hair," 2.

a central piece of her physiognomy, provoking progressive and continued discussions on her dynamic reality. This traces the active interconnectivity and synthesis of self, body, image, and beauty: the body is the physical framing of the self, what the Yorùbá call *Ará*, housing perceptible features such as *Ojú* (eyes), *Orí ìta/òde* (head),[10] *Imú* (nose), *Ẹnu* (mouth), *Apá* (hand), and *Etí* (ears). The self is an inner entity, housing and operating the psychic components – the id, ego, and super-ego – that are responsible for the outer physical image seen and identified, either for its physical beauty or the beauty of its character (*Ìwà*). The sum of these is significant because it emphasizes the human as a cultural and social being, navigating feelings of exclusiveness and inclusion, along with tides of power, prestige, and relevance that delineate the self from the other, the generic identity, in a defined sociocultural construct. The identity of a woman in the Yorùbá cultural sphere is predicated on a host of factors that are both internal and external. These factors are tied to her hair.

The Yorùbá, like many traditional and modern cultures, place a premium on hair;[11] this premium is reflected in the Yorùbá description of humans as the species that grows hair on the head (*Ọmọ adáríhunrun*). Hair becomes an index that carves out space for what Miller terms the "visuality of physiognomy."[12] It accentuates the importance of a body's feature, or spotlights the body in general, to the point where it becomes an adequate subject for discursive interrogation on character and being. The hair serves as a compass, pointing to the nature of individuation while manifesting contours of the collective.

Because individuation seeks to set the self apart from the overbearing presence of the species, it is easier for hair to act as ethnic agent, growing with time and changing with the growth of the subject. Hair is one of the most efficacious signifiers of identity because it is as malleable as identity, which is never static. The same impulse is present in Kobena Mercer's explanation why the hair receives a great amount of time and energy: "In the complexity of [the] social code, hair functions as a key 'ethnic signifier' because, compared with bodily shape or facial features, it can be changed more easily by cultural practices."[13] Its malleability is echoed by Miller, who compares it to

---

[10] The visible *Orí ìta/òde* (outer head) is different from the *Orí inú* (the inner head). The *Orí inú* is pivotal in Yorùbá human ontology and cosmogony. See Adesanya, *Carving Wood*; Lawal, "Significance"; S. A. Folaranmi and A. N. Umoru-Oke, "Orí (Head) as an Expression of Yoruba Aesthetic Philosophy," *Mediterranean Journal of Social Sciences* 4, no. 9 (2018): 59–70.

[11] See T. R. Miller, "Hair in African Art and Culture," *American Anthropologist* 103, no. 1 (2001): 182–188.

[12] Miller, "'Hair in African Art and Culture,'" 187.

[13] Kobena Mercer, "Black Hair/Style Politics," in *Out There: Marginalization and Contemporary Cultures*, ed. Russell Ferguson, Martha Gever, Trinh T. Minh-ha, and Cornel West (New York: New Museum of Contemporary Art, 1990), 247–264, at 248.

skin – the most agentive feature of the human body in race and identity matters – agreeing that it adapts itself to human creativity in a multiple of expressive appearances.[14] He argues that:

> Because it is both naturalized as an inherited biological signifier of binary racial difference and cultural-ized as an unfixed and potentially destabilizing sign of group identity, hair is widely seen as a bodily indicator of cultural self-identification, political ideology, and social status. It is second perhaps only to skin color as a socially defined determinant.[15]

It is no wonder that women's hair and hairstyles signify cultural shifts and changes in the spirit of the times, indexing traditional modes of living and transitioning to modern ways. Traditional *Dídì* hairstyles have returned – like *Pàtẹ̀wọ́*, which has its weaves starting from the side and meeting in the middle, now known as Mohawk (Figure 12.2), and *Ṣába*, woven individually with weaves of equal length, restyled into the modern zip (Figure 12.3). This is also true of traditional *Dídì àdìmọ́lẹ̀* without attachments and the Ghana weavings, usually with synthetic hair attachments. They not only project the fluidity of hair as an index across temporal lines, they also show its malleability as a cultural and historical signifier.

Figure 12.2 *Pàtẹ̀wọ́* (modern Mohawk)

---

[14] Miller, "Hair in African Art and Culture," 182.
[15] Miller, "Hair in African Art and Culture," 182.

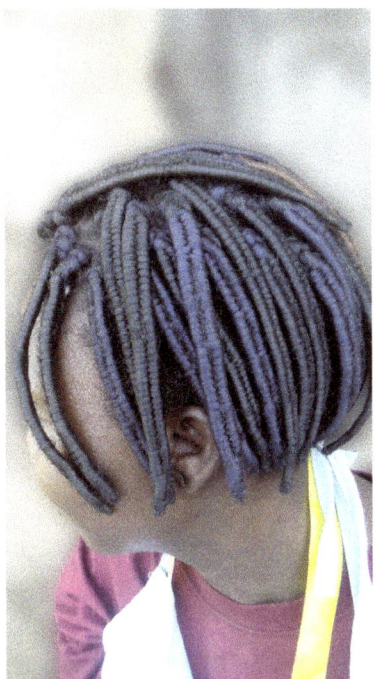

Figure 12.3 Ṣába (modern zip)

By serving as a cultural and biological signifier, hair achieves the full status of both compass and sign, especially when its fluid, unfixed nature is considered. A sign is an arbitrary thing of effective evocative power[16] whose meaning is conventionally agreed upon. The semantic import, or the identity hair generates, is conventionalized on cultural and biological levels. Traditional Yorùbá hairstyles, such as *Koroba* (Figure 12.4), *Ṣùkú àdìmọ́lẹ̀* (Figure 12.5), and *Ṣùkú ọlọ́gẹ̀dẹ̀* (Figure 12.6), are indexes of femininity and the female gender. But their ability to signal is based on hair's inherent capacity to be representative, wielding meaning outside of itself. Hairstyles are signs that cultural participants have invested with meaning, relating them to specific referents: women.

In addition to their role as biological signifiers indexing humans – consider that there are also animals with hair – hairstyles are culturally charged toward the generation and reconstruction of identity. Women's hair symbolizes shifts and changes in tradition. For example, the traditional hairstyle of *Pàtẹ́wọ́*,

---

[16] See Barry, *Beginning Theory*; and F. Saussure, *A Course in General Linguistics* (New York: McGraw-Hill Book Company, 1916).

Figure 12.4 *Korobá*

Figure 12.5 *Ṣùkú àdìmọ́lẹ̀*

Figure 12.6 Ṣùkú ọlọ́gẹ̀dẹ̀

a kind of *Dídì*[17] whose strands are woven from the sides of the head to terminate at the center, has been slightly remade and termed Mohawk to mirror modern sensibilities. The style itself expresses the modern Yorùbá woman, not the traditional one, calling attention to the absence of a one-to-one relationship between the sign, the hair, and the signified.

Hair can symbolize age or social category; traditionally, older and married women often wear hairstyles that proceed from the front down to the nape of the neck (Figure 12.7), or from the sides to gather at the top. Married women also had styles where the hair started from the forehead and back and terminated at the middle (Figure 12.8. Unmarried women tended to wear hairstyles where braids flowed or were laid from right to left and vice versa, like the modernized *Òjòkòpetí* (Figure 12.9). In the distant past, hairstyles like *Ṣùkú* – which now can be braided or woven, depending on stylistic choice,[18] starting from any point on the head and ending up in a protrusion either at the center or at the back of the head – were worn by eminent persons in society. Most of these hairstyles are now expressed in

---

[17] In Yorùbá traditional hair styling the *Onídìrí* (hairstylist) either plaits (*ba*), braids/weaves (*dì*), or uses thread or ribbon (*kó*) to form different styles. *Irun bíba* refers to braiding that is done in preparation for *Dídì* or *Kíkó*. *Irun kíkó* is done with the use of thread, while *Irun dídì* is braiding without thread.

[18] B. E. Adiji, B. I. Oladunmiye, and T. I. Ibiwoye, "Visual Documentation of Traditional Nigerian Hair Styles and Designs as a Means of Expressing Social and Cultural Heritage through Photography," *Global Journal of Arts, Humanities and Social Sciences* 3, no. 6 (2015): 25–33.

Figure 12.7 All-back

Figure 12.8 *Dídì*

modern forms, especially in woven and braided forms. However, they show structural and stylistic fidelity to the traditional forms that inspired them.

In addition to representing time and gender, women's hairstyles point to one crucial factor: identity is both an external and internal construct. This

Figure 12.9 *Òjòkòpetí* (modernized)

philosophy is echoed in the words of Paulette Caldwell, who, reflects that "I want to know my hair again, the way I knew it before I knew that my hair is me, before I lost the right to me, before I knew that the burden of beauty-or lack of it – for an entire race of people could be tied up with my hair and me."[19]

Caldwell speaks of a knowledge that is not to be conceived solely in the literal sense. It should be approached as the confession of a craving: the return to a state of useful unknowingness, of being unaware. This unawareness is not symptomatic of total or partial physical ignorance or a state of unfeeling. It denotes the lack of knowledge sufficient to comprehend the hair's signifying power. It is an ignorance of the mediumship of that assemblage of fine protein strands, and the unawareness of hair's potency as signage, a flexible system capable of generating, encoding, receiving, symbolizing, and suspending meanings that are contextually crafted and based on the hair's own fluid nature.

Caldwell's desired state of blissful ignorance is useful because of the absence of power's instability and the burden arising from the tension of its fluctuations. This state does not redefine or repackage hair as a vehicle for power acquisition and disempowerment, or for self-devaluation and its converse, or to move toward a state of othering, alterity, or marginality. It does not attempt to position hair as the gateway to a bourgeoisie ideal or an escape from

[19] P. M. Caldwell, "A Hair Piece: Perspectives on the Intersection of Race and Gender," in *Critical Race Theory: The Cutting Edge*, ed. Richard Delgado and Jean Stefancic (Philadelphia: Temple University Press, 2000), 275–285, at 275.

a proletariat reality; it does not color hair as an emblem of racialized or gendered reality. It presents hair the way a child experiences oxygen before encountering it in biology or chemistry class. Outside of this useful safe zone, the hair becomes a burden – like any symbol, not so much by itself, but by the conventionalized codes that it is made to embody.

Yorùbá hair is symbolic, expressing an institutionalized ethos that delineates gender from race, class from group, private identity from the collective, and accepted notions of being from instances of cultural deviation. When hair is read appropriately by a skilled participant-viewer, it displays principles of social life, artistry, and religiosity. On a cultural-specific physiognomic level it spotlights the *Ìwà* (character) and moral fiber of the individual. A woman's hair undone signifies dangerous behavior, emotional discontent, and an inner state of distress or disengagement. It could be a show of dissent, a claim to power through the rejection of the standard, surrender to noncorporeal forces, or an exercise of a troubled *Orí* (essence).[20] Disheveled hair is also the symbolic revelation of an anti-aesthetic, going against the principle of *Ìmúra*; this principle is one of the core components of an *Ọmọlúàbí*, the Yorùbá ideal of being and of beauty. Unruly and disheveled hair connotes an *Ará oko* (a bush person), someone who identifies with the bucolic in principle and practice, or someone who has departed from the essence of order and who is no longer in touch with him- or herself. These people are seen as having zero social stability, being unable to conform to the dictates of the ideal, show a mastery of self, or maintain social balance.[21] To borrow Robert Farris Thompson's conceptualization of coolness, these people exhibit "uncoolness," showing that they are not cool.[22]

On another plane of meaning, a shiny, well-oiled, and carefully crafted hairstyle is a testament to the artistry behind its creation and to itself as a cultural symbol, affirming the benefits of conformity. These painstakingly done hairstyles are crafts and arts, drawing attention to the vibrancy of a cultural institution, the presence of well-developed stylo-artistic sensibilities, and the mix of aesthetics and social symbolism. Adiji et al. consider these to be the basis of their attractiveness. Yorùbá hairstyles are attractive "because of their powerful emotional content and beautiful, abstract design principles."[23] Adiji et al., mentioning the essentials of line, shape, texture and pattern, posit that these textured features are aspects of design.

---

[20] In Yorùbáland, where *Ojú ẹwà* corresponds with one's essence and beauty is paramount, undone, unruly, or disheveled hair is a travesty. It is something to be found on the heads of *Were* (mad persons) and those whose heads have *Kan àbùkù* (met downfall), or whose *Orí* or *Ẹlẹ́da* (essence) has been manipulated and wrecked by extraterrestrial forces.

[21] See Thompson, "An Aesthetic of the Cool," for more on the concept of transcendental balance in relation to the state of coolness.

[22] Thompson, "An Aesthetic of the Cool."

[23] Adiji et al., "Visual Documentation," 24.

The Yorùbá attitude toward hair is a corollary of the Yorùbá people's conscious inhabitation and existence within a state of expressive liminality. The result of this condition is that the average Yorùbá functions in synchronization with the core of their cultural being-ness, religiosity, essence, myths, philosophies, and other principal aspects of Yorùbá reality. One can hypothesize that the Yorùbá have uncovered the indissoluble link between hair and identity, marshaling this to good use. This explains why many Yorùbá women view hair as affecting, symbolic, and an inseparable part of their identity.[24]

Hair's affecting quality is embodied in its ability to emote a state of being. It can convey a desire, a craving, or identification with a position occupied in the social hierarchy. Among the women in traditional Yorùbá lands, spinsters (Ọdọ́mọbìnrin) wear their Dídí (plaited hair) differently, while married women also favor a specific hairstyle. Examples of the former are Ṣùkú ọlọ́gẹ̀dẹ̀ or Àdìmọ́lẹ̀, also known as sleeping Dídì with Ṣùkú. Examples of the latter are all-back, which can include the Kòlẹ́sẹ̀. Figures 12.5 and 12.6 are good examples. The hair functions as a compass, identifying the referent in a system of related entities and accentuating the class to which she belongs.

Hair also symbolizes the acceptance of assigned social roles and the presence of power differentials: it indexes choice on the part of the self in rejecting or embracing externally assigned social roles. Hair symbolizes more than power struggle, beyond the notions of inclusion and exclusion.[25] In Yorùbáland, hair also signifies age, ethnic identity, social rank, religiosity and cult affiliations, political status, and power and prestige.[26] All these are interpretable from hair as aspects of symbolism, owing to its inherent capacity to hold a viewer in dialogue. This stems from its nature as Àwòrán (image), that which we look at (Àwò) and remember/recall (Ránti), or that makes us remember.[27]

As a woman gains greater ability to beautify her hair, she attracts more people of commensurate character – those with whom she shares a set of social and attitudinal codes, those who appreciate beauty, those who are able to afford beauty, eminent persons with impeccable character, and morally vindicated people who labor to further beauty's campaign. Permissions within the Yorùbá culture allow beauty and its observance, or association with it, to be a measure of character and to signify wealth or prestige. Beautifying the hair becomes a self-reflexive act; the hair creates a powerful validating aura around the person. It also penetrates inward, highlighting the fabric of the individual's moral being, and blazing outwards as a representational insignia within

---

[24] See T. A. Johnson and T. Bankhead, "Hair It Is: Examining the Experiences of Black Women with Natural Hair," *Open Journal of Social Sciences* 2 (2014): 86–100.
[25] See Mercer, "Black Hair/Style"; Caldwell, "A Hair Piece"; Rosenthal, "Raising Hair."
[26] Tracy Owens Patton, "Hey Girl, Am I More than my Hair? African American Women and their Struggles with Beauty, Body Image, and Hair," *NWSA Journal* 18, no. 2 (2006): 24–51.
[27] Lawal, "Àwòrán."

a defined social network, attracting like-minded people of the same sensibilities and shared philosophies while occluding those with contrary Ìwà.

The hairstyles of Yorùbá women serve as an entry point to the domain of the norm; in fulfilling emotive potentialities, these hairstyles allow bearers to express and maintain expressive connections with femininity. Yorùbá women emote through styled hair, especially within the bounds permitted by the broader tradition, signaling the content of their inner being and channeling their feminine essence in an outward-facing, efficacious manner. Expectations of femininity are often manifested in a woman's ability to maneuver cultural prescriptions of identity to a satisfying end, especially one heavily bordered by defined social ethos. The Yorùbá woman must find expression in the collective. However, the permissions she exploits are expressed in terms of styles (Àṣà) and flavor (Àjásà/Járá[28]) or the Àrà – style – that must conform with socially construed standards of beauty.[29]

Modern Yorùbá hairstyling involves mixes of styles that demonstrate artistry and artistic choice or dexterity (Àrà): Figure 12.10 is a mix of weaving with Pàtẹ́wọ́; Figure 12.11 is a mix of Ṣùkú and all-front, resembling the frontal part of Ìpàkọ́ ẹlẹ́dẹ̀/Kọkojúsọ́kọ; Figure 12.12 is a blend of Dídì and Bíba hairmaking styles (a part is weaved); Figure 12.13 is a combination of Dídì – that is, weaved hair – and braided (attached) part. One thing common to all these styles is that regardless of innovation, they resemble older forms mixed with contemporary hairstyles.

Apart from measuring standards through styles, they also manifest through cutaneous treatments and hair adornments used to beautify or strengthen Yorùbá hair.[30] A woman's hair and its styling signify her embrace of feminine wisdom and power. It becomes her "Ojú ẹwà, tí kò gbọdọ̀ gúnlẹ̀,"[31] a powerful statement instructive on the sacredness of a person's essence.

Ojú here is manifold in meaning. It could mean eyes, face, presence, and index – all of these indicate visibility and visual-narrative potency as an

---

[28] Àjásà as used here is an aesthetic term, denoting the extra flavor introduced to increase the appeal of an art, as well as to infuse idiosyncratic or personally constructed artistic expression or style or signature.

[29] Patton, "Hey Girl"; Caldwell, "A Hair Piece."

[30] Adekunle George, Adebola Ogunbiyi, and Olaniyi Daramola, "Cutaneous Adornment in the Yoruba of South-Western Nigeria – Past and Present," *International Society of Dermatology* 45, no. 1 (2006): 23–27.

[31] Ojú ẹwà translates as the face of beauty. Yorùbá are careful to guard their source of success, which means that the statement is often metaphorical. It means the face or source (as Ojú here means several things that connotes presence and index) must not be soiled or hit against the earth, which is the Gúnlẹ̀ part of the idiom. Whatever is dashed against or dragged through the earth has been cheapened and devalued, showing the power of that prescriptive statement: Ojú (face) + Ẹwà (beauty) Gún (hit) Ilẹ̀ (earth). On a more urgent level, the Ilẹ̀ and the act of hitting are metaphors for activities or acts (either by the self or the other) that have detrimental effects on a person's essence as an individual.

Figure 12.10 *Pàtẹ́wọ́*

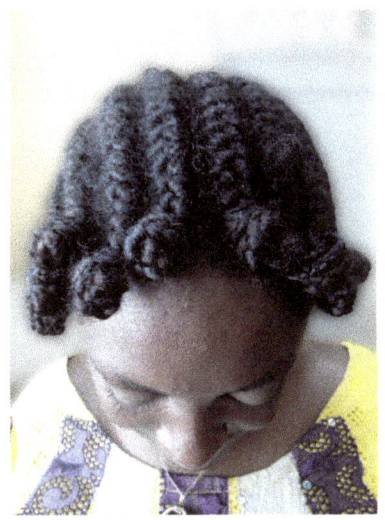

Figure 12.11 *Ṣùkú* (Made with all-front)

essential communicative trait.³² In relation to humans, especially in Yorùbá ontology, *Ojú ẹwà* means the presence, face, eyes, and index of a person's beauty. Any part of the body that is well-shaped, visually appealing, or capable

---

³² David Doris, "The Unfunctioning Baby and Other Spectacular Departures from the Human in Yoruba Visual Culture," *RES: Anthropology and Aesthetics* 49/50 (2006): 115–138.

Figure 12.12 *Dídì* (weaving) and *Bíba* (braiding)

Figure 12.13 *Dídì* (weaving with attachments)

of performing inspiring feats would be the symbol or, more appropriately, the source of a person's beauty. It is that which attracts others and makes the person phenomenal. It signifies a person's dynamic character, serving as the source of a larger-than-life personality. (To the Yorùbá, anything can be a person's *Ojú ẹwà*, including things that are external to the person.) For

Yorùbá women, the hair is part of the index and face of her beauty. It symbolizes the presence of an affecting feature, resituating the entire body as a site of visual appeal and enticing viewers who hold its gaze, commune with it, or dialogue with it. In this sense, hair can be said to have eyes, or even a face (one that possesses eyes and mouth – two powerful vehicles of communication) calling out to passersby and intending for communicants to view it, and also to relate it to its host. This reflects the Yorùbá belief that "Ohun gbogbo ló lójú" (everything has eyes). It also references the popular idiom that "Ojú l'ọ̀rọ́ wà" (the eyes are where the matter lies).

The hair of Yorùbá women, having been styled, oiled, and braided or woven by an experienced and skilled Onídìrí (hairstylist/coiffeuse) into any of the numerous, beautiful traditional hairstyles, becomes a presence. It is the eye or the face of a woman's beauty, seeing others and being seen by others. This binary situation is what David Doris calls the "double exchange of mutual gazes, one exterior and the other interior."[33] According to him, this exchange allows person and community to exist. It means that seeing is a requirement for existing, which is an existential fact. Likewise, the ability to project oneself – or a part of oneself – to be seen is a prerequisite for entering into the exchange of mutual gazes that enables the proper functioning of the universe. What ensues in the brief or lasting instance of each visual encounter is what Doris describes as efficacy residing in communication. This efficacy holds the world together; after all, the world is only the product of the interrelationships of its peoples. More so, as Doris argues, "a person is a person because he sees and is seen by others."[34]

For these reasons, a woman's hair can and should be considered as an Àwòrán (image) and Ojúbọ (face or site of worship/reverence/sacrifice). As an image or Àwòrán, it is something to be viewed. It communicates, and through its communication the visual participants remember, which is what Àwòrán means linguistically: Àwò (what is to be looked at) Ránti (to remember). The symbolic power of the hair is potent in its capacity as Àwòrán, not only underscoring the shared frame of reference between subject and viewer enabling intelligible communication, but also pushing associated knowledge like myths, ethos, historical narratives, and other sociocultural elements to the surface of the dialogue.

By introducing the knowledge of social categories into the dialogue through the act of remembrance, the hair validates itself and helps the viewer navigate the required social process of identification necessary for social interaction. A wife is seen as a wife, and a spinster as a spinster, and potential bachelors or interested suitors can act accordingly. In the same vein, royalty and prestige are identifiable, as well as commonality. Hair wields and dispenses immense

---

[33] Doris, "The Unfunctioning Baby," 125.
[34] Doris, "The Unfunctioning Baby," 125.

power in its symbolism. As Doris rightly said, "like any of the Àwòrán that constitute the canon of Yoruba "art," [it] prompt[s] one to look and remember that, indeed, a person is a person because he sees and is seen by others."[35] Yorùbá hairstyles heighten the significance of the viewer's recognition and interpretation of women; they also indicate the signifying or communicatory capacity of hair as an index of power. Some scholarship on Yorùbá art[36] uses Àwòrán to refer to any naturalistic or stylized two- or three-dimensional representation. However, I see that conceptualization as rigid and exclusionary, collapsing its expansive sense and shifting its nucleus – its quality of referring to the visual and artistic entity stimulating recall or memory – to the margin.

Hair as *Ojúbọ* calls attention to the outcome of the visual exchange binary. *Ojúbọ*, a compounding and syncopation of face (*Ojú*) + i (functionally expressing the preposition "of"), and sacrifice (*Ẹbọ*), draws from the Yorùbá conceptualization of *Ojú* as eyes, presence, index, and face to shore up its meaning. "Face" could be presence, which could also mean place or site of sacrifice. Hair can relate to *Ojúbọ* because *Ojúbọ* is the place of labor,[37] especially where the supplicant (the *Agbẹ ẹbọ/Agbẹ́bọ*) performs the act of *Ẹbọ rírú* that renders them morally transparent to divinity, community, and to the self. This labor indexes the power differential between the supplicant and the supplicated: each of the three categories of recipient is greater than the supplicant: the self,[38] the *Òrìṣà*, or the community.

The sacrifice here is self-judgment, and it is transparent to all. The act is consciously perpetuated, presenting the individual in an idealizing light. Doris has argued that it demands conformity with socially prescribed ideals of surrendering and giving. Hairstyling can be seen in this same light; it is an act of labor, surrender, and sacrifice. Sometimes, the length of time it takes even the most skilled *Onídìrí* to complete an elaborate hairdo can span days. The final product conforms to societal standards of beauty, serving as symbols of appropriateness and furthering the norm, which betrays the sacrificial impulse in Yorùbá hair making. Styling hair can be an act of surrender because the hair projects the individual into the public space, where the sharp contours of the self – those that define and accentuate individuation, and which the Yorùbá pride themselves on and conceptualize as the effectuation of *Orí* – are blurred to fit the collective identity and to further prescriptive, instructive, and idealizing ethos. The goal is to depersonalize the person, making her conform

---

[35] Doris, "The Unfunctioning Baby," 125.
[36] Lawal, "Àwòrán"; Doris, "The Unfunctioning Baby."
[37] Doris, "The Unfunctioning Baby."
[38] The self here is the inner man, the aspect of the essence of *Olódùmarè* every Yorùbá carries, and which is made in his image, especially from the divine clay. It is not the external body.

so that there is an embrace of generic identity. This is a labor of self-sacrifice for the community.

The subject may also be examined through spirituality. Some Yorùbá cults, such as the Ṣàngó cult, permit only one hairstyle.[39] Certain cults, such as the Ọsun, permit specific types of hairstyles and adornment. Priests often shave their hair, while priestesses style it in specified ways. *Dádas* do not cut their locked hair, which identifies them as special humans, and royalty must style their hair in a specific way. The act of wearing a particular hairstyle in a spiritual setting is a surrender and a labor, even a sacrifice, on the part of priests and priestesses serving as intermediaries between Òrìṣà and the people – especially in the case of Ọsun priestesses, also known as *Ìyá Ọsun*. During Ṣàngó cult performances, worshipers are often mounted by the deity; the hair, which must be appropriately styled into an Oṣù, becomes a vehicle or an entry point for Ṣàngó. There is also the generic identity tempering the personal, meaning that *Ìyá Ọsun* or *Àwò* is no longer seen as a man or woman but as cult priest or priestess.

While styling the hair is an act of sacrifice and surrender to a greater power – to channel from Doris's argument on the *Ojúbọ* – hair is the site of labor, judgment, and reward, where power sees and is seen, and through which one sees oneself as if one were being seen by powerful others. The judgment is the dialogue engendered by the hair, provoking the binary exchange into existence and accommodating instances of judgment on the extent of conformity, ingenuity, beauty, and consideration of these effects on the subject's *Ìwà*. The rewards are many: a good hairstyle draws social and monetary rewards for its wearer and even for the *Onídìrí* (coiffeuse) who styled it. The *Onídìrí* experiences increased patronage and goodwill, both of which are valuable currency for the Yorùbá.

A carefully crafted hairstyle changes the quality of a person's interpersonal space. Because the Yorùbá are natural aesthetes, and because *Ìwà* signifies *Ẹwà* (and vice versa), and because materiality communicates power and prestige, there is no limit to the benefits that can accrue from having a beautiful, well-made hairstyle. This means that a Yorùbá woman's hair is both *Àwòrán* and *Ojúbọ*, a great symbol of power. If the Yorùbá woman's hair can be an *Àwòrán*, which Babatunde Lawal describes as "mnemonic in nature, identifying a work of art as a construct specially crafted to appeal to the eyes, relate a representation to its subject, and at the same time convey messages that may have aesthetic, social, political, or spiritual import,"[40] it is also art. More so, if a Yorùbá woman's hair is *Àwòrán*, it is art by extension. As art, it works within a tradition of artists, styles, conventions, and institutions, all of which are anchored on a strong mythic system and cosmological view for the Yorùbá.

---

[39] Adesanya, *Carving Wood*.
[40] Lawal, "Àwòrán," 498.

By being art and having its own support system, Yorùbá hair thrives as part of an institution, demanding the Onídìrí's fidelity to collective notions of creativity applied to beauty and aesthetics. This fidelity does not translate into the absence of individual taste, or the total hegemony of established tradition above individual talents and taste. Hair is a symbol of identity that signifies the power and agency of individuation, and for the Yorùbá this cannot be totally overwhelmed by the generic. Apart from the expansive space allotted to expressions of individual talent and style – which is seen as the ability to Dá àṣà, or deviate stylistically from the norm without being at variance with it – the points of convergence are accentuated over points of departure from established tradition, navigating a balance between artistic expression and the present past. This position is echoed by Thomas Stearns Eliot's own position about artists; in this case the Onídìrí must be responsible for transforming raw materials into emblems or symbols. To Eliot, the artist, must "develop or procure the consciousness of the past and that he should continue to develop this consciousness throughout his career."[41]

Eliot postulates that the agent of change, the Onídìrí, should divest herself of any insularity or idiosyncrasy that halts her search for relevance from the place of deviancy, especially that which is without meaningful connection to the source. This source, which Eliot describes as the present past, is valuable for providing both inspiration and heritage for the conscious present; it also serves as a launch pad for artistic ingenuity. In consideration of these priceless affordances, Eliot advocates that the artist should continually surrender him- or herself to something more valuable,[42] which is the past tradition embodied and manifested by the conscious present.

Eliot's take on artistry, tradition, and the artist is pivotal to the cultural reality of the Onídìrí, the Yorùbá hair artist, and the Yorùbá hair tradition for women. In the traditional Yorùbá setting the Onídìrí works within the permissions of the larger culture, where her agency is unrivaled. This is typical of Yorùbá artists; in African traditional society they were not just hands for the society and the Òrìṣà that inspired them. Onídìrí exhibited creativity that amounted to individuality in style that made them recognized and identifiable.[43] This relationship that Eliot speaks of, between past and present, is reflected in the modern Yorùbá hairstyles identified above. They rely heavily on old forms while remaking them. An example is Figure 12.14, which is the modern all-back Obama – a style that is patterned, with significant variation, after the Dídì all-back traditional style. Another example is Figure 12.15, which is basket weaving, a modern style that involves weaving attachments into hair. In this sense the Onídìrí is a medium where past and present interact and are synthesized. As the platform upon which

---

[41] T. S. Eliot, "Tradition and the Individual Talent," *Perspecta* 19(1982): 36–42.
[42] Eliot, "Tradition and the Individual Talent."
[43] Folaranmi and Umoru-Oke, "Orí."

Figure 12.14 All-back *Obama* patterned with modern *Dídì*

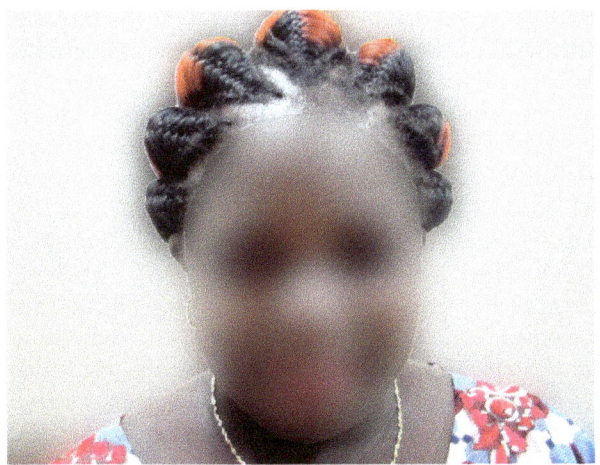

Figure 12.15 Basket weaving

influences are enacted, she is responsible for the interaction of social consciousness and artistry; she and her art are aspects of social history, myth, and culture.

The art of creating an image, of *Yíya àwòrán* or *Ọnà yíyà*,[44] or of plaiting hair and beautifying the *Orí*, draws immensely from the wealth of Yorùbá

---

[44] Ona is art; for clarification see Lawal, "Àwòrán"; see also Oludare Olajubu, "Yoruba Verbal Artists and their Works," *Journal of American Folklore* 91, no. 360 (1978):

cosmology and cosmogony. Ọbàtálá is the grand patron of the arts,[45] molding humans from divine clay. It is believed that he molds the head first, attending to it with unequaled care. This is said to be the rationale behind visual artists, especially sculptors, attending to the head first[46] when creating commissioned or non-commissioned sculptures.

The Onídìrí is a sculptor of sorts. She weaves, braids, plaits, or carves hair into various positions that, depending on the style involved, she might bind with rubber to form a pronounced shape. This transformation is nothing short of sculpting. By concerning herself with the head, she not only follows in the footsteps of Ọbàtálá – the divine artist of creativity and patron of the arts – she also performs hair making and hairstyling as artistic practices, establishing that hair itself is an art. This emphasizes the usual synthesis common to Yorùbá art: the intersection of the sociocultural and the mythico-spiritual. The Onídìrí is an aspect of Ọbàtálá, who is the prototypic Oníyàyà.

In addition to this strand of cosmological implication in the documentary value of art, the Onídìrí uses instruments such as Kóòmù/Ìyarun (Figure 12.16), Ìlarun (a special type of hair-making instrument shaped like a trident that is used to part hair), and other items involving the creative enterprise of Ògún, the Òrìṣà associated with iron tools and weapons. According to mythology, this Òrìṣà is said to put finishing touches on humans formed by Ọbàtálá, clarifying and delineating principal features, especially the face.[47] The divinely sculpted human manifests this prowess of creation by creating patterns within a pattern, finding credence in the expression Ọnà yíyà, which means finding or creating art or artistic style. By working with natural human hair to create art, the Yorùbá woman engages with a significant part of a divine entity – all humans are products of divine acts – manifesting the creative impulse gifted to her during creation through Èémí and Àṣẹ breathed into every human by Olódùmarè.

The point of convergence between art and hair, affording artistic and creative agency to the woman working as Onídìrí, does not terminate with this connection to Yorùbá cosmology. The processes that define an artist or the creation of an artist also manifest in the life of a budding Onídìrí. Established principles of art mandate and determine the extent to which apprentices can attain the status of artists working within the established parameters of Yorùbá art, and these principles are relevant to the hair-making tradition. Principles like Ìmọ̀ (sufficient knowledge), Ìmọ̀ọ́ṣe (proficiency), and Ojúọná, which can be said to be design consciousness, are required of any Onídìrí; they are pivotal

---

675–690; and Gbenga Orimoloye, Ona: Exhibitions of Drawings and Paintings by Gbenga Orimoloye (Lagos: Terra Kulture, 2012).

[45] Lawal, "Àwòrán"; see also Lawal, "Significance."
[46] Adesanya, Carving Wood.
[47] Lawal, "Àwòrán."

to the success of any visual artist. It is *Ojú ọnà*, the ability to process from memory or to project styles when sighting potential art in its natural form, that is germane to the success of an artist. It enables difference, stylo-artistic innovation, and the ability of the artist to *Dá àṣà* and perform what Eliot described as being grounded in the present past without stagnating in it. Through *Ojú ọnà* the artist is able to channel from historical art traditions and infuse his or her own style into the subject, creating something novel. In an insightful commentary on *Ojú ọnà*'s pivotal place in creativity, Lawal submits that:

> *Ojú ọnà* can be defined as ... the visual cognition that enables an artist to select and process images from daily experience into schemata or templates (determined by the Yorùbá style), which are then stored in pictorial memory, to be retrieved and modified when needed to express an idea. As a result, a well-trained artist does not need a life model or a preparatory sketch to represent a particular subject.[48]

Lawal's position underscores the essentiality of visuality and visualizing for the process of hair making, and all visual arts. In affecting the level of an apprentice's *Ojú ọnà*, the apprentice keeps watching, self-instructing, and memorizing the style and the processes of artistic ingenuity that birth those styles. With this knowledge, she can carve out her own style within the already established that she has familiarized herself with, using adequate and informed observation. Hair as art is premised on principles, mythic histories, concepts, and symbolism, presenting itself as *Àwòrán* – however, it also projects the centrality of *Ìwòran*, the act of looking, which is germane to the process of creating and receiving Yorùbá canonical art.

The process of hair making reflects its artistry. The *Onídìrí* uses techniques that have been equated with sculpting: *Lílà*, separating the hair (Figures 12.16 and 12.17) into blocks of strands, or relatively equal clusters, to reveal mass and volume (see Figure 12.17) with the *Ìlarun*; *Ọnà-lílà*, further accentuating the paths of division into recognizable forms and maintaining the idea of form (Figure 12.18); and *Dídi irun*, which this is the actual plaiting. Depending on the subject's choice, the plait could be braided, woven without attachment, or woven with a type of black elastic thread (see Figure 12.19) or ribbon (see Figure 12.20). There is also the aesthetic of *Dídán*, which involves using materials such as *Àdí-àgbọn*, butter, oil, lime, *Osùn*, clay, synthetics, human hair, or even "extensions of human hair from spouses or relatives and vegetable fibres"[49] to heighten the finished hair's luminosity and brilliance, attracting people with its appeal and artistry. Hair self-reveals its own artistry and artistic

---

[48] Lawal, "Àwòrán," 500.
[49] Roy Sieber and Frank Herreman, "Hair in African Art and Culture," *African Arts* 33, no. 3 (2000): 54–96, at 60.

396 VISUAL CULTURES

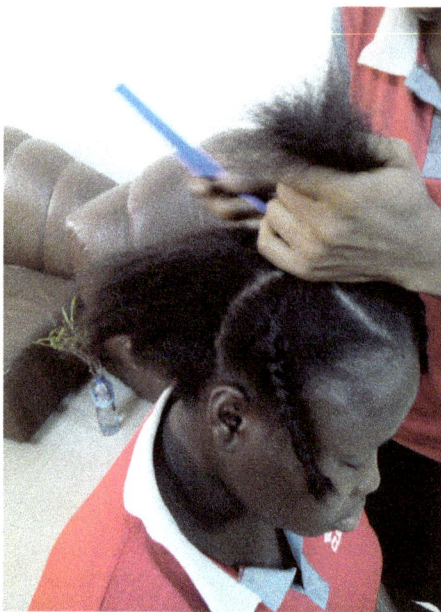

Figure 12.16 *Kóòmù/Ìyarun* (comb)

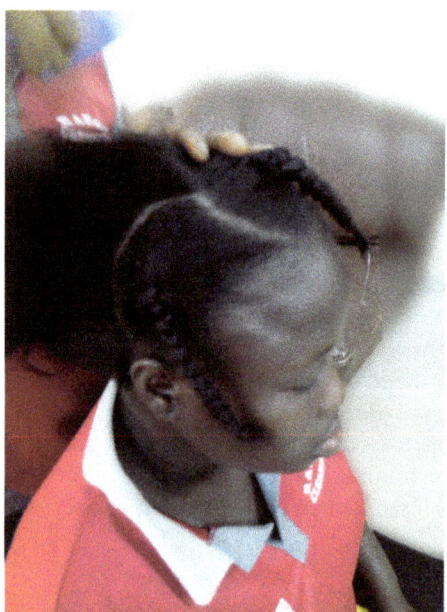

Figure 12.17 The process of hair making

YORÙBÁ HAIR ART AND THE AGENCY OF WOMEN 397

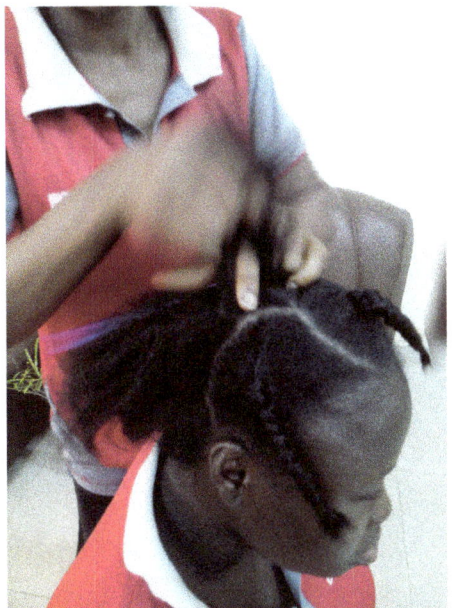

Figure 12.18 Hair-making process

Figure 12.19 *Kíkó* with black thread

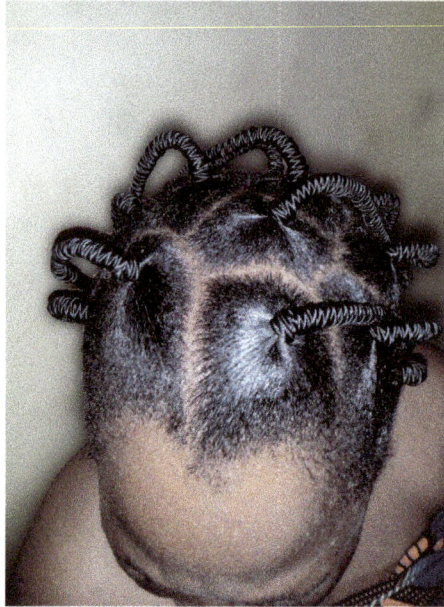

Figure 12.20 *Kíkó* with black ribbon

processes like any artwork, showing the map to its essence through defined, oiled, and accentuated patterns and through the act of *Ìwòran*.

Other aesthetics of canonical Yorùbá art, like *Ìdọ́gba* (balance of composition), *Gígún* (aspect ratio/length), and *Jíjọra* (relative mimesis),[50] are also present in the stylo-creative arsenal of an *Onídìrí*. Hairstyles like *Onílé gogoro*, Ghana weaving, braids, *Obama*, *Ṣùkú*, and *Pàtẹ́wọ́* thrive on the principles of *Gígún*; the length of braids and weaves depends on how they fit a particular hairstyle in the canon. Hairstyles like zip, a modern remake of traditional *Ṣába* hairstyle (Figure 12.3), demands equal length for its parts; its full name is Zip Equal Length. Each end of the braids must achieve balance and stylistic equilibrium, especially in relation to hair styles like zip, *Pàtẹ́wọ́*, *Ìpàkọ́ ẹlẹ́dẹ*, or *Kòlẹ́sẹ̀* (see e.g.Figure 12.21) – in fact, with any traditional or modern Yorùbá hairstyle. The regularity in length enables the ends of the hair, called *Ẹsẹ̀ irun*, to be tied together. In the case of *Ṣùkú* or doughnut hairstyles (Figure 12.22), this ensures that no part comes off to create the visual effect of disorderliness.

The plaited hair is almost always long, especially in the case of the *Ṣùkú*, braided or weaved so that it can be packed upwards. The braids of any

---

[50] Adesanya, *Carving Wood*; Lawal, "Àwòrán"; Cordwell, "Arts and Aesthetics."

Figure 12.21 *Kòlẹ́sẹ̀*

Figure 12.22 Doughnut (*Ṣùkú*)

hairstyle must *Dógba* (be balanced) in size and length, to add to finesse, symmetry, and appeal. The braids or weaves might be small or big, but they must be identical. This means the *Onídìrí*'s eyes and hands are measures of balance, used to achieve the measurements demanded by each hairstyle. These aesthetics reveal that the *Onídìrí*, and Yorùbá women coiffeuses and hairstylists, work with the aesthetics of the visual creative canon like many other *Oníṣẹ́-ọnà*. They are also part of the creative tradition, emphasizing that hairstyling/making is itself an institution and art, with instances of orthodoxy and artistic deviation.

Ojú ọnà and Jíjọra hold principal positions in Yorùbá hairstyling aesthetics, especially in relation to the Onídìrí and the plaited hair. The Onídìrí artist conjures styles from memory that have been seen and studied before: they are the Irun she must have Wòó (seen) as Àwòrán (image) or Ọ̀nà (art) through Ìwòran (the act of seeing) as an apprentice or during her professional life. When working to make the same hair, the artist recalls the details of that particular style and recreates it, adding Járá or reinventing some parts for personal artistic purposes. This is how traditions are furthered and how Àṣà is created within Àṣà. The Onídìrí is at liberty to Dá àṣà (create a style) within a tradition that is always open ended and permanently opened to influences from earlier phases in the process. This implies that tradition, Àṣà, "is the set of behaviors, deeds, and habits that characterize the setting within which it thrives after it has been subjected to a historical process of deliberate choice."[51] Departure from this tradition innovates on patterns to create an overlap between individual Àṣà and societal Àṣà. This avoids the opposite, which is also termed Àṣà (a homographic word, pronounced with mid-tones on both syllables instead of the low tones used for its opposite). Àṣà here marks a futile, unwelcomed, unproductive, and deviant attempt to break away from Àṣà (tradition). Yai describes it as a hopeless endeavor to break away from Yorùbá tradition *ex nihilo*.[52]

Yorùbá hairstyles employ principles of art and design, courtesy of the brilliant Onídìrí, involving curves, zigzags, horizontals, perpendiculars, and straight lines.[53] Any contrary arguments, arising from mythological, historical, spiritual, or artistic considerations, cannot deny the status of hair as art and woman as artist. This presents a pertinent query: if hair is art, what networks ensure its visibility and continue its tradition? Some of them have been addressed previously, but I would shed more light on this in the consciously crafted section that follows.

Hair Making as Social Activity

The domain of hair, as made art, is public. It is made for public consumption, appreciation, use, and appeal. Knowledge of the public space's dynamics and functional structure is also instrumental to its creation. The Onídìrí and the subject perform as societal beings in the heart of the public space, where women generally navigate the tides and tensions of public life. The salon, which is the home of the coiffeuse or Onídìrí, naturally doubles as a place of

---

[51] Yai, "Tradition," 34.
[52] Yai, "Tradition."
[53] Adiji et al., "Visual Documentation," 24.

creation and exhibition. In fact, it functions as an interconnecting space, supporting the fluidity of tradition and serving as the home of patronage, artistic influence, entrepreneurship, apprenticeship, and the place of power shifts.

Hair can be a symbol of power, and symbolic power rests mainly on recognition and conventionality. For symbolic power to establish its dominance in visual dialogue, the parties involved must demonstrate their decoding capacities. They must operate from mutually intelligible positions, which can only be possible if they share similar frames of sociocultural references. For example, both the man and the woman must adhere to and imbibe the Yorùbá philosophy that the *Ilé Onídìrí*, the hairdresser's home/shop, is a space of exhibition and power shifts.

The power of transformation, via the *Onídìrí*'s shop, is total in the Yorùbá sphere; the transformation itself is complete. A woman enters with unmade hair – the signifier of an unattractive, disempowered state – and she is beautified by a fellow woman who shares her cultural position as a member of the same gender category. When a transformed woman exits, she is immediately exposed to the power of the public gaze, where she is assessed based on her appearance. This assessment begins with the head, which is very important to the Yorùbá. The head is the totem of individuation that is deified as *Orí*, and the *Orí* is reified as one's totality. An *Onídìrí*'s shop is a space of transformational power, altering the woman from object to subject and from the generic to the individual, helping her to accentuate her profile and her individuality. A woman whose hair is styled with *Kojúsókọ* has not only beautified herself, but also visually amplified her marital status. A spinster (*Ọmọge*) exhibits her spinsterhood through the hair she carries. The beauty, quality, and materiality of a woman's hair becomes accessible to the evaluator, the *Gbẹ́nagbẹ́na*, or the general appreciator of beauty, who can be any Yorùbá residing in the public space as a social agent.

The interaction of the material and the public gaze, with the public space serving as the performative space, amplifies the agency of the *Onídìrí* and the woman-subject, according it requisite urgency. The exhibited hair becomes the transactional link between the subject and the public gaze. Observers, who engage in the act of *Ìwòran*, can offer praise to the woman that is transferrable as goodwill and potential patronage to the *Onídìrí*. The instrumentality of the hair is rendered through its beauty, symbolism, and artistry – its materiality. Praises accorded the hair by ordinary or professional praise singers, women and men, and even by old and young, are currency in the Yorùbá social network. In the Yorùbá traditional setting the *Onídìrí*'s shop could be her backyard, front yard, room, or other space, but it becomes a social unit on its own. It becomes an abode of immense significance, and the act of styling hair becomes a transformational activity. Any visit to an *Onídìrí*'s shop affords a visual encounter with an array of hairstyles that are done, about to be done, or in the process of being done, which renders the visual setting as an art studio where artworks exist in various stages of completion. In this space, patronage and exhibition are performed.

Even the carriage of the hair, as required by nature, is itself a testament to its existence. Throughout the duration of its existence, the hair continually self-reflects and signifies. Contained in its self-reflection is also the presence of the *Onídìrí*, whose imprint is seen in the patterns and movements of each braid and weave that culminate in a finished product seen as a particular style. The hair is a powerful signal on many levels, reemphatically stating the importance of the *Onídìrí*, as a wielder of creative/transformational power, and the subject-carrier, as a source of visual appeal. Salons are enclaves of transformation, and they serve as outlets for solidarity and power resistance or accommodation.

During the creative process, women sing songs or deploy rhetoric either as validation of the beautification process or as testaments to the gender's monopoly on hair beautification, the efficacy of the (finished) hair as a potent instrument of persuasion, the suitability of the female body or gender for intense and immense beauty, or as a forceful but diplomatic censure, rejection, and disapproval of institutionalized male hegemony. Within the social unit, and through the rhetoric of censorship or rejection exercised via folk songs and other oracular and narrativized strategies, they navigate power, which Weitz describes as "the ability to obtain desired goals through controlling or influencing others."[54] In relation to the spatial context of hair making, this could not be more true. One of the major rationales behind the desire to transform one's hair, and behind the styling of hair by a Yorùbá woman, is the desire to acquire or redirect attention either to her beauty or to her person. Hairstyling is underpinned by the need to drive or influence the perception of others in some way, and by extension their acts and attitudes.

The dynamics of power that women brew in the *Onídìrí*'s shop are visible in the control of these attitudinal and perceptional responses. As Weitz contends, power is transacted within a given context, and not absolute; it wanes and waxes as relationships evolve.[55] Women find strength in numbers, settling into and exiting the physical space, waiting turns and passing time with banter exchanged through narratives bearing the burden of personal experiences. This strength is reinforced by the power of shared experiences and shared frames of reference that invoke an affecting level of mutual understanding. When such occasions arise, the realities of the female gender are made skeletal, or lucent. This is followed by that which sociologists consider to be an informal and covert form of resistance. The word "unorganized" does not suffice to characterize this form of activism in the Yorùbá sociocultural sphere.

---

[54] Rose Weitz, "Women and their Hair: Seeking Power through Resistance and Accommodation," *Gender and Society* 15, no. 5 (2001): 667–686, at 668.

[55] Weitz, "Women and their Hair."

As Weitz suggests, it is hard to comprehend the fluid nature of power, accommodation, and opposition in the lives of Yorùbá women without a robust understanding of the nature of their world. Their daily bodily discipline of femininity needs to be understood. Yorùbá beauty, whether innate, acquired, or hereditary, is material – the material is power. The discipline of femininity through hairstyling furthers a strategic aim to resituate women in the center of power plays that occur in any of the Yorùbá social units: Ilé (house), Ìdílé (lineage), Agboolé (extended compound), Ọjà (market), Ìlú (town), and Àwùjọ (public) in general. The discipline of femininity is also executed through acts of accommodation[56] by the women.

A woman choosing to style her hair in an appropriate fashion accepts the power that comes from being associated with the orthodox, the generic, and the institutionalized. This choice reflects Yorùbá attitudes toward the actuality of unity through numbers: "Ènìyàn laṣọ mi" (human beings are my clothes/pillars). That proverb is well rendered on a metaphorical level. Humans as clothes establish that humans hide their nakedness, which is true even in a non-metaphoric, physical plane of interpretation. Identities and individuals are easily shielded in a crowd. There is also strength in numbers, which is an idea that the proverb invokes.

By choosing to be seen in the generic, the Yorùbá woman channels the strength, wisdom, and power of old – power that is institutionalized. Traditional hairstyles like puffs or modern variants like twists (see Fig. 12.23) are made by young girls trying to stretch their hair; Àdìmọ́lẹ̀, Pàtẹ́wọ́, and Kíkó are also traditional hairstyles for Yorùbá women before the advent of relaxing chemicals, rollers, and hair straighteners that result in styles such as kinky (Figure 12.24) and curled braids (Figure 12.25). In this way, women make strategic decisions to embrace or accept mainstream ideas of attractiveness. As Weitz argued, the ideas of attractiveness are fissured along the social channels of class. Ṣùkú are often linked with royalty, while Àdìmọ́lẹ̀ kọ̀lẹ́sẹ̀ are often seen as standard hairstyles for maidens. Conventionalized beauty, or ideals of beauty, are considered a route to power for women, even with the Yorùbá.[57]

---

[56] Emphasis must be made here that equating beauty with the material is not the same as the debased associative reading in millennial culture that relates the objectification of women and sexist stereotyping to the material or immaterial. The Yorùbá sociocultural context supersedes these presuppositions – to the Yorùbá, the material is an extension of character/Ìwà, as it reveals choices and preferences. These exhibitions of individuality have been reified and deified as Orí, an Òrìṣà that must be sought, propitiated, and revered. To the Yorùbá, the material is not an end or a means to an end alone; it is a totem, an expressive symbol that must be read with appropriate social cues and codes.

[57] Deborah A. Sullivan, *Cosmetic Surgery: The Cutting Edge of Commercial Medicine in America* (New Brunswick: Rutgers University Press, 2001).

Figure 12.23 Modern knots

Figure 12.24 Kinky

A woman who decides to transcend class or cultural lines with her choice of hairstyle is not merely flouting established order, and neither is she choosing to be disempowered; she is channeling the power that derives from unorthodoxy or resistance to the established. Cutting hair, shaving heads, or wearing male hairstyles outside of spiritualized or contextualized edicts or allowances are unorthodox ways to engender power. Women, especially modern-day Yorùbá women, recognize that the power acquired through acceptance of traditional

Figure 12.25 Braided twist

styles is often slow and painstaking, demanding time and energy. The Yorùbá, responding to such styles and the person wearing the hairstyle, would say "Ńṣe ni ó ń dá àṣà" (she is creating/exhibiting/performing her style). This act, once again, redirects to the essentiality of individuation in social matters.

This *Àṣà* (personal style) might be dismissed as *Àṣàkáṣà*, which is considered erring and uselessly deviant. In these instances, power is denied and the act might be punished. But the attempts show that dissent through hair can be an active and radical tool of female agency. Choosing to transgress social, spiritual, gender-based, and class-specific divisions embraces the feminist impulse to overturn an established order that is hegemonic and stifling. Although Weitz argues that social power acquired through conformity is considered delicate, bittersweet, and limited, in the Yorùbá sociocultural sphere it can also be assured and expansive. Contrary to modern culture, hair is never linked solely to femininity or notions of attractiveness; it is highly symbolic of social order, historical details, lineage architecture, spirituality, mythology, class, gender, ethnicity, and many other things. It is hard to deny the power that works through hair.

Solidarity and unity are created, acquired, and maintained within the social space of the shop. Only when acceptance is established can unity thrive and engender a collective scrutiny of the situation. Appropriate verbal responses are developed via feminine sanctions, transfer of feminine wisdom, and the deployment of permissible abuse rhetoric, non-transgressing songs of ridicule, and other forms of oratorical sanctions placed on oppressive systems to ascribe power and agency to women. Through the social unit of the shop, and the collective power of hairstyles, the hair becomes an agentive female/feminist tool of social ordering and reordering. To extract the agency of the Yorùbá woman's hair from the controversy of femininity and its relation to beauty and female objectification, Yorùbá hair must be examined as expressive, interrogating the relationship between hair and Yorùbá principles of beauty.

Hair and Yorùbá Principles of Beauty

The idiom "Ìwàlẹ̀wà," which means "character is beauty," shows how the Yorùbá place a premium on beauty (Ẹ̀wà) as one of the central principles of a person's moral philosophy. This statement is laden with rich meanings implicating Ìwà as more than an expression of innate character; it is the sum of one's appeal. This emphasis on character as the measure of all men and women led to the conceptualization of the Ọmọlúàbí principle, the apex of morality that any Yorùbá can aspire to. The Ọmọlúàbí is the fusion of the outwardly acceptable (expression) and the internally celebratory (innate) to create an ideal generic image. Character is germane to the social fabric of the Yorùbá cultural framework, and anything exhibiting character is turned into a metaphor of self and seen as an expression of character. In such cases, physical exhibitions of temperament are transposed or conceived of as tradable currencies that increase one's appeal. We have discussed how coiffures embody and signify the characters of the wearers, but tracing the relationship of a woman's hair to the creative capacities and character of her coiffeuse, the Onídìrí, can be discussed further.

The concept of Ìwọ̀ntúnwọ̀nsì blends the phrases Ìwọ̀ntún and Ìwọ̀nsì ("equalizing to the right and the left"), showing how humans can exhibit a state of equilibrium or of balance. To the Yorùbá it is an essential expression of moderation and social/personal stability – all are expressions of inward coolness. Only an internal cool and a balanced personality can transcend beyond preoccupation to exude a state of morality conforming to the level of social constancy expected of individuals. In Yorùbá social contexts, hairstyles are prime reflectors of appropriate behavioral constitution. Properly done hair that conforms with aesthetic principles signifies the outward conduct and inner personality of the Onídìrí, as well as that of the subject-carrier.

As creative art, hairstyling is delicate and demanding. To divest oneself of preoccupation and attend to the matter of styling is to exhibit a concentration level reflecting a person's character. Celebrated ideals, such as Ìlùtí, Ìfarabalẹ̀, Ìmojúmọra, and Títọ́ – and also Ojú inú, which Folaranmi and Umoru-Oke describe as an "acquired attribute that is derivable only through cultural experience and interaction with the elders"[58] because it directs creatives on appropriateness of style to context – are expressive characteristics that beautify

---

[58] Folaranmi and Umoru-Oke, "Orí," 62.

an individual as an Ọmọlúàbí, the opposite of Èniyàn bíburẹ́wà; they can all be revealed through hair. Ìlùtí, as put by Folaranmi and Umoru-Oke, refers to efficacy from the place of obedience and understanding. Ìlùtí, which literally means good hearing, means to possess responsive skills informed by knowledge.

Ìfarabalẹ̀, on the other hand, refers to calmness of body, soul, and mind so that one can imbibe, learn, and execute the task at hand perfectly. It involves the possession and application of a non-impulsive, calculated, and restful temperament. Ìmojúmọra is vital, ensuring the artist's ability to know when to expunge or inculcate foreign materials. It underscores authorial signatures and the ability to navigate the borders of intertextuality, excessive borrowing and influences, stylo-artistic sensibilities, and originality. Like Ojú-inú, it depends on a critical eye and one's informed artistic taste.

Another quality is Títọ́, which is described as "enduring, unfading qualities and reality, as well as genuineness and steadfastness."[59] According to Abiodun, Títọ́ enforces the durability of artistic material and style, discouraging transient innovations, fads, and ephemeral beauty.[60] Títọ́ is affected by the quality of one's Ojú-inú, which Abiodun describes as "insightfulness,"[61] helping to create durable styles and to identify appropriate and authentic hair-making materials, such as synthetic black thread. These are all manifestations of a mind that is in a state of equilibrium, composed, and synchronized with itself and the public. Títọ́ and Ìfarabalẹ̀ rely on Sùúrù (patience) and Ìwàpẹ̀lẹ́ (gentility) – without them, an apprentice would be unable to master or apply herself to the work at hand, leading to superficial knowledge and second-rate designs.

The key idea linking these concepts is the intersection of ethico-cultural orientation and individual character though art. The qualities required of the Onídìrí must be part of her character framework. By giving a voice to them through art, the Onídìrí projects society's ideals, and in Yorùbá traditional thought, Abiodun explains, they "embody the highest and most desirable attributes of Ìwà."[62] When these ideals are projected onto or reflected by the exterior of hair art, it references the Onídìrí by signaling backwards or inwards to the interior surface, where the present absence of the coiffeuse exists – to borrow Deconstruction terminology. The absence of the physical Onídìrí is marked by the presence of her artistic signature, making the Onídìrí into an Àrẹwà. She is someone worthy of adulation and to be emulated, not for her physical beauty but for her ability to possess, showcase, and exhibit ideal traits and create something lasting and beautiful from them. These traits are

---

[59] Folaranmi and Umoru-Oke, "Orí," 69.
[60] Rowland Abiodun, "African Art Studies: The State of the Discipline" (paper presented at a symposium organized by the National Museum of African Art, Smithsonian Institution, Washington, DC, September 16, 1987), 81.
[61] Abiodun, "African Aesthetics."
[62] Abiodun, "African Aesthetics," 21.

currency and behavioral principles that appeal to society; anyone who possesses them becomes a favorite.

A philosophical principle such as *Ìwọ̀ntunwọ̀nsìn* affects the idea of inner beauty manifested outwardly, as expression of character in the form of physical adornment. Folaranmi and Oke explain that "All these cultural norms, formulas, conventions and rules in an African environment inform the preference and ideals of beauty in traditional African artistic forms."[63] One of the preferences and ideals of beauty is moderation. Moderation or balance, existing in an obvious state of social equilibrium, is pivotal for the Yorùbá as an ethical requirement. Whatever is done should be in accordance with moderation; such balance projects a mind that is in harmony with itself and its environment.

A woman styling her hair, wielding it, or carrying it, must strive to avoid needless extravagance and refrain from creating a spectacle that would attract negative criticism. The *Onídìrí* must select from appropriate canonical hairstyles that are suitable for the subject, and when she infuses her style through the application of *Ojú-inú* and *Títọ́*, she must preclude instances of ephemeral or extravagantly made hair. Hair is symbolic and totemic in Yorùbá culture, affording the woman social power, and so it must never exist within ephemeral bounds. It must transcend the mundane to become something significant. Its artistry, however beautifully achieved, must never detract from its symbolism, especially to the extent that it becomes a distraction. This explains why the Yorùbá believe that undone or poorly done hair signifies a state of inner turbulence, or an *Ará oko*[64] – unless the state of hair is itself significant and symbolic.

Undone hair can serve in the capacity of anti-aesthetics, which David Doris explains as objects that "enunciate the symptoms of pathology, the 'conflict and irruption' that cannot be accommodated within the idealizing frame – that is, the 'deft, luminous' ideological surface"[65] of the canonical/traditional hairstyles. Attention can be drawn to its disheveled state as symbolic planes of conflicting meanings, which can differ from established meanings or assume significance that contests standard notions of beauty. These meanings, and the appropriate coiffures, reside within the margins of culture.

---

[63] Folaranmi and Oke, "Orí," 60.
[64] An *Ará oko* is a bucolic person removed from modernity or society's general sociocultural temper. The name derives from the three farm types formerly maintained by the Yorùbá people: *Oko Etílé, Oko Etí ilú*, and *Oko Igbó*. The *Oko Igbó* (forest) was usually far from town, requiring days of travel and an extended stay at the worksite. As months passed, workers lost touch with the latest developments in city life. The division of town and country is based on differences in behavior and taste. See Oyeniyi, *Dress in the Making*.
[65] Davis Doris, "Symptoms and Strangeness," 25.

Among women, cut hair is usually associated with widows, while disheveled hair could signify a mad woman or a woman in mourning.[66] These hairstyles are not manifestations of beauty, but their beauty-opposing and repudiating states manifest the symbolic power of their anti-aesthetic nature. They warn visual participants, who hold their gaze (as explained earlier, they are Àwòrán who have Ojú [eyes]), about the nature and extent of calamity and misfortune. They may even draw narratives to the fore that explains the unpleasant state of the individual, emphasizing causation as instructive mechanisms for sensitization. The adept Yorùbá instantly rejects this with a prayer, "Kí Ọlórun má jẹ́ kí n ríbi" (may God not allow me to see evil). This prayerful rejection of evil manifests the Ojú of such anti-aesthetic hairstyles; their Àwòrán state is expressed along with their marginality as art. Their anti-aesthetic natures, rendered in their undesirability, are also made apparent.

Apart from unmade hair serving in anti-aesthetic capacities, it also renders and refers to the symbolic cycle of birth and rebirth. In Yorùbá ontology and cosmology, life is believed to have come from chaos. Olódùmarè spoke the world into existence, mandating the Òrìṣà to create the earth in a space that was previously void and filled with water. Beautiful hair is a finished product created from something more unrefined and chaotic – the unmade hair. Proceeding from the metaphor of the phoenix rising from ashes, well-styled hair is a beautiful thing that has grown and received life from the disheveled hair. In this context, the unmade hair is neither anti-aesthetic nor a signifier of a troubled state; it is the first stage of creation for a thing that will be aesthetically pleasing.

Disheveled, unmade hair can manifest semantically with several meanings, and an adequately done hairstyle can express the nature of a woman's Ìwà. An overstyled and overdone hairstyle also mirrors a type of Ìwà, one that might be troubled or be unfamiliar with the demands of moderation. Figures 12.16 and 12.17 are examples of the process of beautification. Made hair emerges from a previous state of chaos (Figure 12.26).

The opposite of Ìwọ̀ntunwọ̀nsì would be Fáàrí – unbalanced extravagance. Although the Yorùbá appreciate art and artistry, they frown at beauty and aesthetics that are not functional. An expression existing only for its own sake, flaunting its ephemerality, is useless. (This uselessness is not beneficial in the sense of Yorùbá anti-aesthetic Ààlè;[67] its symbolic power stems from the association of things that have been divested of their initial state of usefulness to become useful on another plane of significance.) The unyielding reproof of Fáàrí is reinforced through folk rhetoric: "Fáàrí àṣejù, oko olówó ló ń rán wọn lọ" (excessive dressing leads to bankruptcy).[68] The Yorùbá consider coiffures

---

[66] Miller, "Hair in African Art and Culture"; Adiji et al., "Visual Documentation."
[67] Doris, "Symptoms and Strangeness."
[68] Oyeniyi, Dress in the Making, 100.

Figure 12.26 Unmade hair

as part of a person's outfit, which is why they consider women who cut or shave their hair as *Aláìláfínjú*, *Ọbùn*, or unfashionable.

It was not traditional for women, regardless of age or status, to leave their hair unstyled.[69] In fact, it was uncommon for women not to weave or plait their hair; they started at an early age. To claim her Yorùbáness, a woman must either *Ba irun* (plait) or *Di irun* (weave) her hair. The style can either be one of the modern Yorùbá hairstyles, described by Oyeniyi as having displaced older Yorùbá hairstyles in the modern cities, or one of the precolonial hairstyles, which still exist in rural places.

Hair is a fundamental requirement of Yorùbá femininity, making it a starting point for the examination of a Yorùbá woman's character. If a woman conforms, and does not shave or cut her hair, she is identified as having a non-deviant character. This presents her as trouble-free and obedient, which are two of the behavioral expressions expected of the ideal Yorùbá. If she styles her hair according to her spiritually affiliated cult's standards, she exhibits an acceptably reverential posture. If she styles her hair to project an identity, she presents herself as the ambassador of her home, lineage, ancestry, and the female sex, projecting her sexuality and sense of appropriateness and appeal. The way a woman wears her hair speaks volumes about who she is.

The judgment does not rest solely on the woman wearing the hairstyle. The process of hair making involves both the *Onídìrí* and the subject who requested the hairstyle. Certain styles, and hairstyling in general, take time and resources

[69] Oyeniyi, *Dress in the Making*, 100.

to execute,[70] but neglecting one's duties to beautify one's hair is considered irresponsible. Conversely, spending adequate time and resources to beautify the hair displays the woman's inner character. The love for beautiful things and the desire to acquire them (through the material) is not a sin to the Yorùbá,[71] if it is done on reputable grounds and within permitted boundaries. In those cases, the time and resources involved display the important characteristic of *Ojú inú*, differentiating someone with a taste for beautiful things from another who is not. The difference lies in balance; the woman who would be an *Ọmọlúàbí* must find a balance between her desire to spend time and resources on her hair and the impulses that lead to excessive materialism or extravagance.

Orí and the Hair as Synecdoche

Expressions such as "Òrìṣà wo là bá bọ bí kò ṣe orí" (which deity might we worship if not the head?) are prevalent within Yorùbá thought and philosophy. This is because *Orí*, as both essence and body part, is considered sacred by the Yorùbá in human ontology. The head, the *Orí*, receives primacy on ontological and cosmological grounds; it is believed to embody the *Àṣẹ* of *Olódùmarè*, the generative power breathed into individuals upon creation,[72] that with which humans become creators themselves who will and work things into being. It is also believed to be the first part sculpted by the divine artist *Obàtálá*[73] as humans were molded with divine clay. It houses vital parts of the body like the eyes, nose, and ears, and it is the part through which *Òrìṣàs* mount humans during cult festivities.

The *Orí* has such preeminence in Yorùbá human ontology, merging the spiritual and the physical, that it can be called the seat of individuality, or what Doris describes as "the complex conception of personhood ... or the site of one's destiny."[74] As Yai conceives it, it is the result of premium individuality deified.[75] The head is the site of one's destiny in Yorùbá thought, based on the cosmological principles that order human creation and birth; after creation a human must select from a series of pre-molded *Orí* made by *Ajala Alámọ* to accompany them on earth. The selection itself is *Àyànmọ́*, or chosen destiny. The chosen *Orí* determines one's *Ìpín* (lot) on earth. This narrative serves as the impetus for certain folkloric expressions that deify the head:

---

[70] Folaranmi and Umoru-Oke, "Orí"; Doris, "Symptoms and Strangeness"; Weitz, "Women and their Hair."
[71] Sprague, "How I See the Yoruba."
[72] Lawal, "Significance"; Adesanya, *Carving Wood.*
[73] Lawal, "Significance."
[74] Doris, "Symptoms and Strangeness," 25.
[75] Yai, "Tradition."

> *Tí mo bá lówó*
> *Orí ni màá yìn,*
> *Orí mi, ìwọ ni,*
> *Tí mo bá lọ́mọ láyé,*
> *Orí ni màá yìn,*
> *Orí mi, ìwọ ni,*
> *Gbogbo ohun rere*
> *Tí mo bá ní láyé,*
> *Orí mi ni màá yìn,*
> *Orí mi ìwọ ni,*
> *Orí mo yìn ọ́*

The *Orí* is considered one's personal deity, or one's *Ẹlẹ́dàá*, because it is an intermediary between a person and their *Òrìṣa*, serving in the capacity of protector. It is also an aspect of *Olódùmarè*, *Ẹlẹ́dàá ẹni* (one's creator). For these reasons, the *Orí* is worshiped and deified. The highly spiritual Yorùbá perform elaborate rites and rituals to worship, invoke, and propitiate celestial or extraterrestrial forces – these principles apply to *Irun* (hair), which is an extension of the *Orí*.

Extensive beautification of the hair, through elaborate but not extravagant coiffures, draws attention to one's head (*Orí òde*/outer head, which is different from *Orí inú*, the inner head that is celebrated). By transforming hair into an aesthetically and visually pleasing object, the woman celebrates, worships, and propitiates her *Orí*. The praises and panegyrics that well-made hair can provoke from well-wishers and members of the community, who are aesthetes themselves, fuel the head – what the Yorùbá term *Orí ń wú*. These *Oríkìs*, panegyrics, or praises, directed at the subject-carrier and the hairstyle, fill the head. The head is incited and provoked into physical demonstrations; the process of the *Oríkì* influencing the head is noncorporeal, but it can be gauged by the physical responses of the recipient. In these cases, the woman with the well-made hair has successfully made her *Orí* the beneficiary of praises and adulation. Because there is a systematic structure of reciprocity between deities and subjects, between the propitiator and the propitiated, the *Orí* in turn blesses the individual.

Hair making is a means to various ends. Badly made or disheveled hair can receive malicious verbal spite, such as "*Ọbùn ṣìọ̀ṣìọ̀*," or comparison with *Ìwọ̀fà*s, the slaves who are generally unkempt and uncared for. Each individual has *Àṣẹ*, the generative power that can will into being, and one must always keep one's head in an appealing aesthetic state to avoid bad utterances that might distress the spiritual head (*Orí inú*) as a result of the state of the physical one (*Orí ìta/òde*). Arguably, Yorùbá women generally avoid having their hair left without adornment in order to avoid such a malicious fate, which is why considerable time is spent making it aesthetically attractive.[76]

The proximate distance between Àṣẹ, in the form of negative verbal utterances, and one's destiny, in the form of one's Orí, is so close that the Yorùbá's generally pray "Kí orí mi má gbàbọ̀dè" (may my head not be a victim of malevolent powers), "Kí orí mi má sùn" (may my head not sleep), or "Ẹlẹ́dàá, má jẹ́ kí wọ́n gba ibi orí mú mi" (God, do not let them catch me by my head). A lock of hair might be employed to charm or ruin a person's destiny. In this sense, hair is vital as a synecdochic object. In Yorùbá spiritual ontology a lock of hair represents an individual, and negative Àṣẹ, or evil utterances and acts, can be used on it to destroy the individual. Hair is cautiously guarded, and parents who are aware of such practices often advise that people avoid sharing hair instruments, even at the hairstylist place (Ilé onídìrí).

In the spiritual realm the hair is a signature, an index of identity, and a representative of the body. Although it might serve as physical adornment, it is also the protector of the head, the seat of transformational power. Hair encloses the head, and because it grows directly from it, hair indexes the head; it is one of the easiest ways to attack the Orí, which can affect the whole being. These realities mean that the hair on a woman's head is guarded on all fronts, as an aesthetic material, a social signifier, symbolic power, means of protest and representation, of identity, and as a spiritual synecdoche.

Conclusion

Hair works differently than other visual arts, where there is an extended, secondary, external, and indirect transfer of benefits from viewer to art and to recipient/creator. In other visual arts the artistic presence in the work is signified by the artist's physical absence. With hair, the distance is closed between recipient (carrier and creator) and art. One can immediately perceive the effects of the patronage or the benefits of engagement, because the body is the site/domain of engagement/manifestation in relation to hair as art and symbolic power. The Onídìrí (creator) is the second party whose presence is represented by her absence.

It can be argued that other visual arts have a double level of significance – signifying themselves and their creators – but a woman's hair has three levels of significance: it signifies the body as the site of existence, the Onídìrí, and itself. Yorùbá women's hair is styled and made as a creation, an art, that carries incontestable gender imprints and cultural messages. It is capable of powerful symbolism, acting as both cultural art and an image, implicating all that are involved in its creation and as active participants in its functionality.

---

[76] Folaranmi and Umoru-Oke, "Orí."

13

Photography and Ethnography

Introduction

Photographs are representations, although the contestable nature of the photographic medium leaves the specifics of the representations up for debate. Photographic images are influenced by politics surrounding their engineering and utility, the kinds of subjects they capture, and the culture within which their agency is felt. Aside from the object represented in the photograph – the concretized representation – the dominant factors shaping the receptivity/understanding of photographs, along with the photographic tools and their utility, are often defined by things that are not concrete but still bound within the frame of the photographic material.

This chapter engages my photographs to reflect on the nature of photography itself, teasing out the dynamics of photography's non-material aspects, which are extremely significant for approaches to and the reception of photographic images and the photographic tool itself. Invisible aspects, such as knowledge, politics, and culture, are fueled and propelled by the visible and unseen textures of photographs, and each is implicated in the other. I attempt to answer these questions: Do photographs represent certain sources, and how? How do photographs advance knowledge? How are meaning and deduction as aspects of seeing and gazing implicated in and by photographs? What place do the invisible aspects of photography have in framing meaning? And to what extent do contextual realities extend the frame of photographs, beyond what is visible on the canvas?

On Photograph(y)

Photographs, whether digital or analog, encapsulate a world of possible meanings, significations, and implications. Apart from the concrete objects displayed within the image, what else can be observed? This is an open-ended question, because it involves the act of seeing or the conditionings that permit the process or modes of envisioning along with the instrument or vehicle with which the envisioning is performed. It is not enough to ask what can be seen in a photograph beyond the obvious; within that question is an entire world of complications.

A photograph is a social contract and a physical mnemonic mechanism. It is a souvenir[1] and a product of changing cultures and climates. Its materiality contains the conditions of its social contract and construction. If photographs are social constructions, it is because the ways of understanding them or the processes from which they are created have been socially driven. Howard Becker exhibits this type of interpretive posturing when engaging three forms of photography, and he is not far from the truth. He writes that with photographs, "Their meaning arises from the organizations they are used in, out of the joint action of all the people involved in those organizations, and so varies from time to time and place to place."[2] This is especially relevant when focusing on the value and functionality of photographs as utilizable constructions with culturally relevant essences. The creation process that supports the act of making photographs, from taking the shot and reproducing the image, along with the process of interpretation that defines their composition, are all social processes with social beings involved.

A photograph's uses – whose instructing principles are premised on socially defined modes or logic of conduct – shape the types and nature of approaches to understanding photographs. Becker identifies three categories of photographs to make his point: photojournalism, visual sociology, and documentary photography,[3] which are socially driven contexts of engagement attempting to ascribe specific essences to photographic materials. To a large extent, pictures themselves dictate how they should be engaged, even though lines of demarcation are often blurred in the disciplines or processes of interpretation.

As with any endeavor, the subject of inquiry conditions the tools and logic of engagement to a certain extent. Otherwise, photographs might as well be explained as something like calligraphy, which lacks those crucial defining boundaries. It stands to reason that photographs would enable taxonomic endeavors for proper engagement, betraying their agentive fiber in the process. We can talk about the performance of photography in a network, eliciting responses through their reflection of the reality that underlines their construction. In spite of everything, the nature of the photograph determines how and where it should be categorized. Jorella Andrews articulates this performativity of photographs by referring to them as inorganic powerful agents or actors.[4] However, the reference to photography's agentive function is too complex to

---

[1] Anselm Haverkampf, "The Memory of Pictures: Roland Barthes and Augustine on Photography," *Comparative Literature* 45, no. 3 (1993): 258–279.
[2] Howard S. Becker, "Visual Sociology, Documentary Photography, and Photojournalism: It's (Almost) All a Matter of Context," *Visual Sociology* 10, no. 1–2 (1995): 5–14, at 5.
[3] Becker, "Visual Sociology."
[4] Jorella Andrews, "The Photographic Stare," *Philosophy of Photography* 2, no. 1 (2011): 41–56.

accommodate a simple analysis – we must return to a primary detail about the nature of photographs.

A photograph is a social contract because its pixelated assemblage contains evidence or signifiers of the social negotiations defining the performative connections between accepted modes of seeing and of being seen. A single photo is the product of the object's simplicity or overtly demonstrated acceptance to be stared at or displayed in a frame by an equally consenting second party. Figures 13.1 and 13. 2 portray this sort of consent. The presence of consent – the natural first juncture of art appreciation, by nature of its importance to any mutual activity – can be deduced from a photograph through the posture of its subject. Through consent, the photographed object becomes the subject of the photograph.

Figure 13.1 recalls familiar situations where subjects are identified and persuaded to be photographed – the implicit coercion enabling the activity can be inferred from the subjects represented – although sociocultural dynamics also influence these assumptions. That is the point of the photographs and this chapter: to show how images assist in comprehension. It is highly unlikely

Figure 13.1 A drifter's consent

Figure 13.2 People in a celebratory mood

that a drifter would aspire to have his image taken in that context, especially when considering the socio-economic realities presented in the image.

It is likely that the subjects' consent is the driving force behind Figure 13.2, considering the celebratory mood indicated by bottles of drinks, even though both subjects appear to be members of the proletariat class. Regardless of who has done the persuasion or what motivations are involved – the promise of financial reward, the desire to be the center of attention and subject of someone else's gaze, or to have one's image and reality replayed – a form of contract exists in any photographic activity.

Figures 13.3 and 13.4 show various subjects in idealizing or preparatory poses. The attitudes indicated by their physical stances are communicating whether the photographic act is a mutual engagement or a stolen act. The subject in Figure 13.3, positioned in a marketplace that serves as a backdrop of urban commercialism, stares straight into the camera with his wares about him. He assertively owns and portrays his desire to the object of focus, which is an interpretation suggested by the image itself.

Photographs are products of agreements and physical manifestations of processes of social exchange. These processes occur between the object of attention and the photographer, or the camera, as a representation and extension of the human gaze interacting with the object of attention. On a deeper level, the photograph is also a concretization of a dialogue between the lens and the body stamped into being by the "click." Consequently, birthed by the click,

Figure 13.3 Showing consent through posture

Figure 13.4 (Native) wear and idealizing posture

shutter, or snapshot (depending on the type of camera used and the time of the photo), the pre-shot orientations of the individuals are allowed to mix and traverse boundaries that would otherwise have been impassable. A subject ready to be photographed presents the self as expected, especially within accepted definitions of picture-friendly positions.

A photograph is the product of a mutually inclusive agreement, one that must border on either the erection and sustenance of cohered sensibilities and tolerated differences or the recognition of points of cultural or ideological intersection. These circumstances ensure that a photograph bears signatures from the process of acknowledgment, capitulation, compromise, compulsion, theft, othering, and other such conditions. Contracts can be hegemonic, in which case consent might be absent and the photographic agreement might be coerced or fraudulent. Living subjects can be defrauded through ignorance or deliberate misrepresentation, and bodies can be forced into photographic positions by conditions beyond their control. (Many examples can be found in pictures from the colonial archives.)

A photograph is a social contract because underlying contractual possibilities align to create a single, socially essential product: replication of that which can never be repeated experientially or existentially.[5] The contract is time-bound, but the product is time-binding even in stillness or aborted transition. The captured incident or image does not outgrow the moment or immediacy that defines it, even if the desire is to have it continue its relevance across time whenever it is introduced into visual dialogue or discourse. This accommodates its ability to shift time. All the images previously discussed have been trapped in their own universe: the drifter will forever appear in that same moment and in the same pose, even after moving on to other things. However, the image ushers this time-past into the present moment, breaking the chain of chronology within the mind.

Unlike much of what defines humans or their world, a photograph persists without transitioning beyond itself. A picture is often considered the representation of an absence, or something that does not exist in the real world – the real world is continually in transition, and it does not repeat itself. The photograph repeats forever in a state of perpetuity.

This explains why a photograph is a souvenir; its mnemonic quality stimulates memory to perceive the past, or as Barthes puts it, to welcome the return of the dead[6] – "dead" referring to those moments eternally frozen in time but reproduced for as long as the photograph exists. These moments are either personal, as with Figures 13.1 and 13.4, or communal, as seen in Figure 13.5. They may also have broad-spectrum relevance to a group of individuals, like Figure 13.5.

The defining feature of a photograph is the preservation of moments that hold some significance, especially through time. For this reason, the photograph is often accused of undermining or deposing memory, the natural

---

[5] Roland Barthes, *Camera Lucida*, trans. Richard Howard (London: Vintage Books, 2000), 4.
[6] Barthes, *Camera Lucida*.

Figure 13.5 Ọ̀ṣun worshipers showing communality

mechanism of daily life. Photographs are often held to be the most "real" representation of that which exists and the most congenial method of remembrance.[7] Haverkampf points out that photographs might as well have replaced the contents of memory, or life itself.[8] This seems extreme, but it carries significant weight when photographs are seen less in a memorializing light and more as a tool for forming identity and as a pivotal mode of communication, which is a point made emphatically by Jose van Dijck.[9]

A man who poses for pictures with his wares, for example, wants to be identified with his trade. As seen in Figures 13.6, 13.7, and 13.8, the subjects display their professions or sources of income, showing how photography is a means for communicating as well as contouring identity. We do not need to ask these subjects what they are doing – some are caught mid-action, while others hold informative poses showing how they spend their days. However, this does not remove the memorabilia-like quality that has been attributed to photographs since the nineteenth and twentieth centuries, when photographs became a social force. Photography is no longer an end; it has become a means for shaping knowledge and information. The foregoing appeals to van Dijck's position,

---

[7] Haverkampf, "The Memory of Pictures," 264.
[8] Haverkampf, "The Memory of Pictures," 258.
[9] Jose van Dijck, "Digital Photography: Communication, Identity, Memory," *Visual Communication* 7 (2008): 57–76.

Figure 13.6 Meat seller in an idealizing posture

especially to the extent that photographs are products of changing cultures and climate.

Digital photographs have transcended their previously narrow role as methods of preserving or retrieving memory; they have become communicative tools due to their place and functionality within social networks. Photographs already have an inherent communicatory virtue (as seen in Figures 13.6 and 13.7), whether they function as keepsakes or as evidence of biographical details. They communicate something about the past that is worth recalling, or they safeguard something from the present to convey it into the future.

It was generally held that analog photography, or photographs in the analog age, chiefly recommended themselves as an efficient means of recalling and verifying the past.[10] The duty of recall is very much fitted to the specifics of mental imagery, using the imagination through the production of mental images. Mental images have been relied on through the ages as agents of memory, acting as "mentally stored visual representations."[11] The forte of photographs is their ability to link a material presence with images that are remembered or projected, allowing for their verification. Mental imagery facilitates memory in similar

---

[10] C. M. Stuhlmiller, "Narrative Picturing: Ushering Experiential Recall," *Nursing Inquiry* 3 (1996): 183–184; see also Susan Sontag, *On Photography* (New York: Delta, 1973).

[11] Haverkampf, "The Memory of Pictures," 258.

Figure 13.7 Orange seller

Figure 13.8 Livelihood

ways, conjuring metaphoric equivalence between the agency of the mental image and memory – remembering is essentially imagination, projection, and remembrance.[12] The process of recalling through a photographic picture allows for the concretization of part of the process, affecting the entire activity and making it more reliable than the mental image.

The concrete imagery delivered by photographic images, combined with their ease of shareability within a network, has contributed to a significant shift in the way that pictures are currently used. The use of photographs for identity construction and communication is not new, but these activities have been enhanced by increasing technological advancement, the expanded globality of the world, and the need to bridge the digital and expressive worlds through varied methods of communication. Billboards, for example, are photography used for large-scale communication that enables brand and identity building.

Photography often blends the functions of identity and communication. Figure 13.9 illustrates how photography, especially digital photography, can serve as a communicatory vessel. In addition to this combination of the two functions, photography works to communicate an identity construct for anything, on any scale, from concrete to abstract.

The shift in photographic functionality has been fueled by digital cameras and sophisticated mobile phones – it is not enough to have pictures for the sake of remembering; they have become an active component of networking in

Figure 13.9 Billboard and communicative power

---

[12] Van Dijck, "Digital Photography."

postmodern social culture. These functions are less relevant to sustain photography's use as a memory tool. In contrast, the use of photographs in the analog age accommodated identity formation and communication as subordinate to the primary goal of aiding recall.[13] This convention of the analog age makes its photographs distinct from those of the digital era, which are for identity building and communication; it is a consequence of the technology and media that improve connectivity and bind the world together. In Figure 13.9 Maltina has used photography to market its brand and communicate its product on a large scale with the aid of technology. Remembrance is a secondary function, and several works have made intellectual investments in making this distinction. Reality itself tries to instruct us on what is commonplace.

The digitized atmosphere of the twenty-first century and the import of the global village are constructed just as McLuhan declares: the medium is the message.[14] The photograph's entirety is often revealed by and in itself, evidenced by its materiality. Figure 13.5 for instance allows viewers to make near-accurate guesses as to why it exists as a picture and what it represents. Such declarations would seem to have exhausted all there is to know, especially were the picture to perform the function of spurring us to imagine or project mentally. Even if it were to remind us of a previous instance in time, or something previously known or experienced, it is nonetheless communicating something.[15] When McLuhan declares that the medium is the message, his emphasis is on how media itself affects and effectuates levels of interaction, ensuring the collapse of boundaries to enable interactivity in an unprecedented way. His classification of "old" media as hot or cool identifies photography as hot – it enhances the senses in ways that do not require much effort from viewers trying to understand the content.[16]

Photography's place in the digital era has been a transition that other forms of media, such as films and radio, have not replicated. A one-way channel of

---

[13] Sontag, *On Photography*.
[14] M. McLuhan, *The Medium Is the Message: An Inventory of Effects* (New York: Bantam Books, 1967).
[15] It is reductive to delineate the function of analog or digital photographs based on their provocations upon the imagination, spurring the intellect to invoke or project something through their materiality – their ability to be seen and felt – considering van Dijck's argument that all three processes are bound together in the process of remembering. It is not enough to say that Figure 13.8 has a trader selling tomatoes. For all we know, she could be helping her friend, the other woman, who appears to be suckling a child. Our perception of the workings of the Yorùbá socio-economic sphere is not enough to foster assumptions about the image. We cannot totally exhaust the photograph, regardless of how familiar we are with that reality or how it informs us of previous – but disremembered – knowledge. If the memory function of analog pictures is most potent when they are retrieved from an album or shoebox, it is the same with images retrieved from online cloud storage platforms like Dropbox or Google Drive.
[16] McLuhan, *The Medium is the Message*.

communication had constrained the use of photographs, along with other old media, to serve as memorabilia. This changed due to the use of photographs in digital communication, especially in real time, which is two-way or multiple ways. Within digital network spaces, pictures now perform as or are regarded as messages, applied as letters in a uniquely structured interactive exchange.[17] As van Dijck describes it, pictures assume a language function, becoming a new currency for social interaction and employed to convey messages and dialogue, or to express or show effect.[18] These qualities are not enough to exhaust the offerings or semantic possibilities that a photograph has to offer, since images offer up several meanings based on context, and context is a flexible and fluid thing.

The ease of sharing and real-time effect of responses to photographs through other photographs, along with the use of digital cameras for live communication, are transitions imposed on photography by the currents of technological and sociocultural transformation. Technological advancements in photography and its related tools have brought cloud-based computer storage, easier deletion, powerful resources for manipulating images, instant editing, global distribution, and rapid assessment for perfect self-idealization and representation, along with the individuation of the photographic experience. As cultural and individualized performances,[19] current photographs are products of the realization that digital-image technology offers opportunities for peer-group building, bonding, and communication, as well as self-identification, representation, and other self-beneficial performative rituals. These realities support McLuhan's explanation of media transforming human experience – recollection, imagination, or communication – through the affordances of photography.

Modern digital photography is more than the image that is presented. The material form assessed by humans is influenced by a host of cultural factors, whether personal, technological, or other, and they are conditioned by dominant cultural practices; the understanding of a photograph naturally extends beyond the material form we can see and touch. The type of photography, the instrument used, the goal of the photographic performance, the type of performance and its context, the context of interpretation, the gazer, the poser, and everything else in these categories are all essential and constrained

---

[17] Olivier Liechti and Tadao Ichikawa, "A Digital Photography Framework Enabling Affective Awareness in Home Communication," *Personal and Ubiquitous Computing* 4, no. 1 (2000): 232–239.

[18] Van Dijck, "Digital Photography."

[19] Photographs in the present age, especially in social media, are seen less as modes of sharing family bonds, or in the context of family or related kinship structures, than as components of individual and individual-related social structures such as peer groups and social contexts like parties or movies. Social media and digital cameras have allowed the motives behind photography to become inward and individualized.

within the photograph. These particulars are essential to any attempt to engage the essence of a photograph, because their presence can be felt, even implicitly for an unknowing observer, on the surface and around the material. In Figure 13.5, for example, what is seen that is visible and what is seen that is not? What has led to the visible product, and what sort of transformations has the photograph undergone, and to what end? What knowledge is perpetuated by eliding, editorial choices, or increasing or shortening the framing?

If photographs are combinations of these possibilities – the concretization of defining particulars that exist beyond the frame of a photograph in material form – how do they affect the relevance, acceptance, and materiality of photographs? Context is principal in appreciating photography, and the aforementioned particulars can be accessed by centering our gaze beyond that which is visibly represented on the canvas, although we cannot isolate the material form from its extratextual properties. The importance lies in teasing out possible implications of those photographic realities existing beyond the photograph, understanding how their possibilities affect the essence of the photographic picture.

Modes of Seeing: The Lens

The orthographic and etymological peculiarities of the word perceptibility (distinguishability, visibility, reflectivity/reflectiveness, and prominence, as well as other fitting synonyms) suggest that a picture's perceptibility depends largely on perception and the medium used to actualize, configure, and activate that perception. Perceptibility and perception are related on the basis of derivation, but they hold distinct meanings: perceptibility is the reception of a photograph and the impression it can make as a result of its uniqueness, inimitability, or similarity in terms of aesthetics and focus, which relies extensively on the vision that births and/or receives it. In photography, perception and the conduit for actualizing this perception are bound together in the lens. The lens can either be technological or biological – the camera's photographic lens and the human's ocular lens are responsible for the perceptibility of the photograph and the perception with which it is received.

That the lens of the camera is structured like that of a human, functioning in similar ways, signifies the unique position that both lenses occupy in relation to the photograph. The lens of the camera inverts the subject-image, which is eventually reversed by the camera's mirror, a metaphoric keyhole that instrumentalizes perception for agency. This follows the pattern of the human eye, which inverts an image on the retina to be reversed by the brain. A camera's lens functions in parallel terms with a human eye, producing recognizable everyday images[20] and betraying a transference of the visions of both gazers: one

---

[20] Nicholas Foster, "Photography and The Gaze: The Ethics of Vision Inverted," *Parallax* 12, no. 2 (2008): 78–92.

performing the duty of capturing the subject-image and the other interrogating or coming into visual contact with the photograph. As Levinas argues, "the intention of one who contemplates an image is said to go directly through the image, as through a window, into the world"[21] (and straight at the subject-viewer).

Levinas might not have been referring to photography (he was concerned with the painted image), but his assessment of engaging with an image is fitting. The act of photographing and the end result of viewing a photograph's details both involve imagistic illustration. What is the intention behind photographing a man wheeling his wares around, as seen in Figure 13.7, or one who is caught looking askance while on the job? Photography requires a significant degree of visual interaction with a subject, and it occurs in the eyes. No matter what intention is behind this engagement, which will become concretized as a photograph, it is visually defined in the execution of the photographer and the reception of the viewer.

Because both photographer and viewer contemplate their subjects, the visualization involved in the photographic task of capturing an image transfers perceptions, intentions, and the conditioning that powers those activities. The eyes that perform the visualization, or from where visualizing is initiated and through the lens of the camera, set the envisioned photograph in focus. They eliminate the surrounding visual noise, allowing the concretization of these strategic actions and processes for the viewer, who must receive and attempt to interpret what has been obtained. If the task is to render or present economic vitality, mercantile bustle, or the industrial activities of specific people, Figure 13.10 has succeeded in presenting, relating, communicating, and engaging with viewers. The original photographic intent is presented visually when there is a kinetic communication between biological and technological lenses at both ends of the dialogic spectrum.

The human eyes discern an image, the camera lens captures the image, and they commune with the eyes of the viewer attempting to retrieve visions from both forms of "eyes" within the physical material of the photograph. The viewer of a photograph is engaged in the act of envisioning, continuing, and completing the visual dialogue. The photograph and its image are engaged by photographer, photographed, and viewer. They use whichever lens is implicated in the act of staring, which is correctly considered to produce various forms of social, political, cultural, and ethical estrangement.[22] Staring is fundamentally political: it is often an expression of solidarity, commitment, confrontation, attestation, or objectification.

---

[21] Emmanuel Levinas, "Reality and its Shadow" in *The Levinas Reader*, ed. and trans. Sean Hand (Oxford: Blackwell, 1989), 129–143, at 132.
[22] Andrews, "The Photographic Stare."

Figure 13.10 Yorùbá market

Viewing, or the prolonged contemplation of a photographic image, is fueled by a base feeling similar to that which underscores the photographic act – a photographer choosing to commit a source of contemplation to a fixed state. The natural progression is for the photograph to instruct, shaping engagement as if it had pushed itself into a conversation with the eyes of a viewer staring with their own eyes. This recalls the concept of the photographic stare, which reiterates the perceptual and perceptive possibilities of engaging with a photograph. The stare of the photograph is implicit, but its effect and affect are felt potently, experienced or revealed in human actors. By being visually literate and holding the gaze of a photograph, viewers are embedded in the world of the photograph and engaging it in a visual dialogue. Viewers are orientated, reorientated, or misorientated through this activity.

Viewing a photograph and taking delivery of its offerings is the natural progression from the act of photographing an object, only this time the viewer is a different sort of visual communicant. What is it about the photographic process – from the human eye selecting and framing the object, through the shutter fixing the object in a state of perpetual stasis, to viewing an end product as photographed material – and the photograph's mutual stare that informs the dynamics of photographically relating to reality?

In photography, technological and biological lenses are bound in a system of close interaction, informing and feeding one another in a symbiotic process of envisioning. The camera's lens performs photographic work, defining the scope of envisioning and registering a concretized shadow of reality in ways that the biologic lens cannot.[23] The camera acts as a technological extension of the biological lens, while the biological lens provides visionary direction, impetus, and a functional template for both lenses to follow. The technological lens is implicated in the postural currents that fuel a photographic performance on the part of the photographer. The biologic lens, which the camera relies on, is conditioned by cultural and social postures.

The eyes of the viewer are conditioned by these pre-contact engagements between camera lens and human lens. What is seen are the products of a complete system of visioning. If we are to question, interrogate, appreciate, or familiarize ourselves with an image depicting women in white, or the display of a masquerade engaged in ritual practices, it is because a dialogic process has brought that specific reality into existence. Whatever knowledge we arrive at would not be beyond the provisions of this reality.

The technological lens relies on the postures of the photographer as performed visually, and it duplicates those postures virtually and materially. The biological lens, by being a part of the body, is affected by sociocultural ethos, ideals, notions, and sanctions – the camera lens must produce these forms of affect in concrete form. These visualization tools are defined by contextual norms, reproducing these effects in reinforced ways.

The pervasive use of the camera during colonialism effected greatly its current reference as a colonialist and hegemonic tool for the West, producing a vista of viewing in which the Caucasian or Eurocentric male is the alpha gazer. Being implicated in colonial history influences the reading of the tool as perpetuating hegemonic modes of engagement, beyond ideological or corporeal performance, into the realm of visuality. During the colonial period it was employed to project the colonized other as an exotic body or subject-object. The colonial archives are replete with images that can be investigated for these approaches.

Many tomes have discussed the Western cultural exoticization of the African. A popular starting point is the relationship between the advancement of the photographic tool and the industrial and colonial expansion of the nineteenth and twentieth centuries.[24] The history of photography and its nuances are often implicated in the social and cultural atmosphere of those periods. The age of the colonial enterprise coincided with that of photography, and its functionality is primal in the place of seeing, gazing, and envisioning. It

---

[23] The human lens captures reality once, only storing it in the brain as a mental image. The digital lens captures the same reality for physical reproduction, which coincides with Barthes' argument, explained earlier, that the photograph repeats that which cannot be repeated existentially (see Barthes, *Camera Lucida*, 4).

[24] Werner Mraz, "Albums as Archives," *History of Photography* 2, no. 2 (1978): 176–178. See also David Bate, "Photography and the Colonial Vision," *Third Text* 7, no. 22 (1993): 81–91.

is easy to find traces of the regnant philosophy of colonialism powering photographic activity, the photographic material (especially in the archives), and the tools themselves. Online archives of Yorùbá colonial photographs display ways of seeing and positioning through images.

The present photographic lens not only betrays cultural conditioning, transferring the photographer's postural peculiarities – and by extension, those of the pervading social-cultural ethos from which the photographer draws – it is also a tool built from that legacy. The lens perpetuates and conditions racial behavior in relation to colonial legacy. Cameras calibrate light, and because light skin is frequently a benchmark for the calibration of colors, the black skin is done injustice in representation. Not only can this calibration set the black skin against a white yardstick (especially during the early days of analog cameras), the black skin is often misrepresented in low or poor artificial lighting conditions.[25] This problem persists with digital cameras, as can be seen in unedited photographs like Figure13.7, where the subject's face is almost obscured.

Bias persists in digital and analog photography, seen in the use of the Shirley card,[26] dual skin-tone color balancing and image-stabilization features. A biased algorithm manages the camera screen, affecting the image when the camera is poised for a snapshot and in print afterwards. It is a consequence of the non-white legacy's tertiary status in global technology. The incorporation of dual-tones was an afterthought, suggesting that African or black skin in general was never on the agenda during photography's inception – it is a strong indication of the biases present in those centuries that have been brought into the universe of digital cameras. These alterations frequently need to be color corrected after the fact, using editing software, or neutralized with digital enhancers to bring black skin out from the background.

Misrepresentation through the lens feeds into a larger pool of coloniality. The conditions of coloniality are orchestrations, performances, and devised methods of daily living that maintain and promote colonialist power structures: subject–object, oppressor–oppressed, and seen–unseen. The oversight that enabled the digital anomaly producing contrast problems, and the persistent difficulties in correcting it, are a result of the imperialist gaze through which the African is accessed by Western eyes. The camera perpetuates these hegemonic transactions by producing a reinforced and material form of

---

[25] See Sarah Lewis, "The Racial Bias Built into Photography," *New York Times*, April 25, 2019, www.nytimes.com/2019/04/25/lens/sarah-lewis-racial-bias-photography.html for more on how photography and the art of digital imaging "others" represses, and misrepresents, non-white skins in a colonialist and imperialist fashion.

[26] The Shirley card, the image of a white woman, was used by analog photographers and developers to calibrate color for their images. This controversial method eventually led to more accommodating procedures, and four Shirley cards were created: black, white, Asian, and Latino.

misrepresentation and envisioning. The technological and biological lenses both advance specific brands of knowledge. They mislead, reinforce, and produce set worlds from which the viewer must choose. No matter what semantic possibilities exist, the viewer is incapable of choosing any beyond those offered by the photograph.

The Western viewpoint that makes the African invisible to Western eyes is particularized by the camera that also refuses to see black skin. The fact that black skin must be held in contrast to white for relevance – a benchmark created by hegemonic imagining – is a major feature of the world created by the camera and its lens. The idea that the African must be enhanced to be seen follows the West's messianic approach to trade with black skin. These modes of seeing, produced by the camera, show how the biological and technological lenses are never completely independent. The viewer sees what the photographer has seen, or what the viewer is meant to see through the camera, which can include subjects that have been rendered invisible. The ranges, ethical boundaries, and philosophies of engagement, which include exoticization, fascination, ethnography, documentary, counter-hegemonic representation, political intervention, archival purposes, and voyeurism, are transmitted from the eyes of the photographer to those of the viewer; their vision is already constrained before beginning the process of knowledge acquisition.

Dwelling, however, solely on the condition of coloniality expressed by both lenses is to miss this chapter's point completely: the photographer can also project their own private vision, modified by context. The knowledge that a photographer encodes through an image is defined by that photographer's way of seeing the world. Stephen Sprague has noted that Yorùbá photography prizes posed portraits and portraitures of single individuals or groups above pictures that feature landscape, architecture, or ordinary items.[27] Postmodernism has blurred the neat categorization of strategies and preoccupations in art globally, but some reservations persist in today's African art.

What are we Seeing?

A photograph ultimately pushes a brand of knowledge. Whether this knowledge is misleading or not relies on the presence of mind of the viewers. It is hard to read a photograph for and by itself. It is harder to read a photograph without proper context. If a photograph is a concretization of the photographer's vision or brand of knowledge, and the interpretation of the viewer is important, then the photographic image is the canvas where gazes make contact. In this case, what are we seeing when we see a photograph?

A photograph has no single meaning; numerous semantic possibilities exist even within its dominant message. However, photographs contribute to our

[27] Sprague, "How I See the Yoruba."

understanding of concepts and phenomena in ways that are only possible for some media. One example is the level of material connection with the event or reality depicted. A photographic image is a representation of the power of the visual and the visualized, meaning that contemplation of a photographic image is at the very least double-sided – the act of contemplation becomes a process. The photograph is a transparent concretization of reality: its materiality is evinced by the features of physicality, substantiality, solidity, and the general principles that define matter, and its ability to enable contemplation of a specific referent that exists outside the photograph in the past or present, validating its oxymoronic qualities.

Viewing a photograph connects the viewer to the image in a pseudo-telekinetic sense. Levinas argues that the intention, which involves the mental acuity of the viewer, goes through an image as if through a pothole into the world it represents, connecting with an object.[28] In this case, viewing a photograph develops an invisible mental rapport beyond the image with the object represented. In most cases that object has ceased to exist, leaving an absence that cannot be recovered. This absence renders the image as a mere representation of the world, which evokes feelings upon interrogation. The realities captured in Figure 13.11 have ceased to exist, and each now reveals a scene of collectivity or collective action that is trapped in time. These events have been isolated by the unstoppable passage of time, and all that remains is their absence in the world. In these cases, the images are not only reflections of things that no longer exist, but insights into their previous existence.

As Barthes reveals in *Camera Lucida*, the photograph carries its own referent in a manner that makes sign and referent hard to separate, even when both exist in parallel worlds – world of the living, which is fluid and continuous, and the world of the photograph, which is static and futureless. For reflections of events, such as those in Figures 13.12 and 13.13, we view a world that once was and still is, but they are different. The worlds captured in pictures do not exist with the same particulars that defined them, even when landmarks and other environmental details remain where the shots were taken. If the images are representations of that which no longer exists, what are we seeing and what knowledge can be drawn from such images to represent an absence?

Levinas argues that the image is a shadow of the world. However, an absence – for a photographic image captures an aspect of temporality that can never be retrieved – offers no knowledge of the world.[29] The image offers knowledge of the world, even in its representational state, or what Levinas calls the "Meanwhile." His term signifies the stasis within which an image is grounded, from where it gains its essence. Every image persists only as it has

---

[28] Levinas, "Reality and its Shadow," 134.
[29] Levinas, "Reality and its Shadow."

Figure 13.11 Festivity and communal spirit

Figure 13.12 Township

been, surviving without a future for as long as it remains. But even this quality of the image offers insight; it has its own story to tell.

Figure 13.13 Photo of township commemorating time

Figures 13.1, 13.2, 13.3, and 13.4 are forever trapped in their poses, just as Figures 13.11 and 13.12 are forever frozen in their realities, at those times and in those places. In Fig. 13.14 the subjects will forever hold hands and smile, facing the camera, while that event is irrevocably lost to time. Nevertheless, they tell us something and offer an understanding of the world. We can ascribe implicit acceptance to Figure 13. 14. The subject is obviously involved in a public ritual, engaging in accepted conduct while awaiting an award, citation, or recognition. He is indirectly signaling his readiness to be photographed, especially through his posture. We might not understand the events playing out in Fig. 13.15, unless there are other images to aid us in arriving at an accurate conclusion, but we are privy to another type of knowledge provided by the action of the subjects: genuflection.

We can assume that the subjects of Figure 13.15 are cultured, or culturally conscious, and that participants in that image are acknowledging power dynamics. By persisting without change, photographs offer an opportunity to comprehend life's details, and these opportunities would otherwise be lost in the whirlpool of rapid continuity that is the human reality. By stopping time, photographs present viewers with a chance to deduce that which could not be reproduced in the presence of human reality's moorings – the exact time, action, place, atmospheric conditions, and other factors. Photographs are mechanically induced pauses or force-stops required to make meaning of the swift flow of events holding up human reality.

Figure 13.14 Celebratory gestures

Figure 13.15 Gestures and cultural symbolism

Whenever contact is made with an image, we see lasting absences and the paused unfolding of time. The audience can take a slice of reality and expose it to scrutiny, viewing the complexity of life without missing its details. This

Figure 13.16 "A day at the office" manning the gates of the rich

possibility, presented by photographs, enables a factual perception of images, delivering a fitting understanding of representational reality. Figure 13.11 provides knowledge that cannot be obtained when reality is a flurry of ongoing activity. In the photograph, showing the collective butchering of an animal, the viewer can identify faces and participants without losing essential details. With such a large audience, one can assume that it is some sort of festival, jointly celebrated and communally engaged. The converse can also be assumed: that this is spectatorship, and the audience is less involved. They could merely be voyeuristically observing the plight of a soon-to-be-butchered cow. This is the inherent contradiction in photographs and the kinds of knowledge they permit.

In Figure 13.10, when we see a woman sleeping at a stall, while tomatoes wait to be sold, are we seeing a tired woman or a slothful one? What essential aspect of the market structure, developed in ancient times, has made its way into the urban era to be revealed when such images make their way into public memory? What is readily assumed about the security officer in Figure 13.16? And what of the broad-based urban city captured in Figures 13.17 and 13.18, where most of the houses in the background are old, giving off a contradictory sense of a metropolis?

Seeing the Invisible: Politics of Seeing

Photographs are byproducts of intentions, like most images – if not all of them. They are essential drivers of knowledge distribution, maintenance, and

Figure 13.17 Ibadan

Figure 13.18 Ibadan colonial architecture

perpetuation. The principle of causation demands that a viewer's contact with a specific photograph meets with certain brands of knowledge. A viewer encountering a photograph comes into contact with the intention of the original creator and the intention of the represented subjects' reality. In this case, the medium acts true to its nature and promote specific types of visions.

A viewer's relationship with a photograph is conditioned by extratextual details. The components that a viewer chooses to see or gloss over are a function of their familiarity with the world in the image. Human vision, with all its glory and possibility, has its blind spots – one cannot see in all directions at once. The conclusions made in the aftermath of a photographic encounter are products of how we have been conditioned to see. An African, or a Yorùbá man, would see maternal instincts at play in Figure 13.8, thanks to his upbringing. Two women are busy sorting tomatoes and peppers (*Atarodo*) for sale in a basket (*Apèrè*). This type of organized reality is not alien to the African, especially one who is exposed to the inner workings of the *Agbo ilé* (communal household). Activities in this environment are often jointly executed, even when one is only cracking jokes to keep the atmosphere entertaining for the other performing the task.

A foreign pair of eyes might see two hungry-looking kids in dirty clothes – a familiar image of Africa peddled by Western news sources. The African child with the protruding belly in Figure 13.8 would be considered lost, staring straight at the camera. The shirtless child in Figure 13.10, presumably running errands, is a familiar trope within Western circles. It immediately elicits responses that confirm the knowledge of Africa as a place of lost hope, sucking the life out of its younglings. But the vision performing this analysis is completely detached, reinforcing old and provincial or reductive knowledge.

A picture is an active and constructive agent,[30] presenting whole worlds for viewers that help shape visions and affiliations between events and individuals or persons and circumstances. It is often the case that the agency of interpretation arises from the human agent, remaining so for the duration of the photographic engagement. A picture might be intended to provoke certain affects, but its success depends on the modes of seeing that the viewer can access and rely on. It depends on the level of identification with the forms of knowledge revolving around the universe of an image, allowing the viewer to look beyond the images to see the epistemologies and ethos that brought the image into play. Western vision might interpret Figure 13.6, the meat seller, as an unhealthy and unsanitary abattoir, while others could see an industry that thrives despite a defeated economy and a negligent government.

The overarching idea is not whether one photographic interpretation can trump others, or which is more accurate to the source – an interpretation can be affected by attempts to identify and affiliate with a represented reality, or it can attempt to understand that reality. Photographs do not necessarily require intimacy or a state of remove before pictographic knowledge can be ethically uncovered, but it is necessary to have an objective understanding of the limits,

---

[30] Andrews, "The Photographic Stare."

realities, relationships, and possibilities provided. Identification with a photograph requires assumptions that might be reductive, involving "high degrees of insensitivity and lack of self-awareness,"[31] since one cannot be what one is not. It is better to apply what Haraway calls "passionate detachment."[32] Such detachment enables the kind of understanding that does not attempt to assume the position of the subject, accommodating the worlds of others in our own during the uncovering of knowledge. It is an approach that avoids the fostering of alien and unrelated knowledge on a photograph.

To see well is to see together from a balanced viewpoint, without identifying with the object. Andrews explains this as trying not to be "someone or somewhere else, but to be and take responsibility for who and where we are now, in relation to those others [in relation to how, and what, we see]."[33] Haraway summarizes: "One cannot 'be' either a cell or molecule – or a woman, colonized person, laborer, and so on – if one intends to see and see from these positions critically."[34] If we see as we should, what ensures what we see upon contact with an image: the need to identify with their subjects and the realities, or to critically understand the realities of those images without betrayal?

This requires a conscious activation of passionate detachment. Even for so-called culturally identified insiders who perform the viewing task, the exact world of the photograph is still alien, although the degree of alienation differs from that of cultural outsiders. To appreciate the realities of the children and ethically deduce knowledge from Figures 13.8 and 13.10, we must step away from the province of preconceived knowledge to assume a critical stance that is fed equally by familiar epistemologies and the pictographic specificities. It would be hard to make conclusions about Figures 13.17 and 13.18 without stepping away from prescriptive knowledge – we must remove the knowledge of what an urban city "should" be like in our engagement with the image.

The ideas of what something should be and what it is, determining how pictorial representations are received, are products of existing knowledge. What should a good market be like? What should a city look like, especially its inner city? Figures 13.17 and 13.8 are examples of reality defying knowledge, confirming or expanding it. If pictures can expand, shrink, reaffirm, or contradict knowledge, what is the benefit of performing pictorial deductions or seeing photographs entirely through predetermined epistemologies?

Gazing can be an immersive activity, defined by a system of power relations. Interpretation, which is a frequent result of such activity, is defined by this structure of power. The kinds of knowledge extricable or derivable from ethical

---

[31] Andrews, "The Photographic Stare," 51.
[32] Donna Haraway, "Situated Knowledges: The Science Question in Feminism and the Privilege of Partial Perspective," *Feminist Studies* 14, no. 3 (1988): 575–599.
[33] Andrews, "The Photographic Stare," 51.
[34] Haraway, "Situated Knowledges," 585.

interpretation depend on the ethics involved in the act of staring, or how biased our approach is to a photograph. Engaging an image manifests visible, preconceived notions that can be overtly political. A photograph requires us to stare at it, while it metaphorically stares back by holding our gazes. The viewer, just like the photographer, engages the subject by staring at an image in longstanding practice drawn along objectifying, invasive, voyeuristic, and violent lines. Staring can also be a passive activity, in which the viewer engages with the subject uncritically. This can be problematic for ethically teasing out possible knowledge, since an uncritical engagement is prey to knee-jerk ideological impulses and conjectures that do the photograph no benefits.

The inequality that comes with gazing might be tempered by the dynamics of staring – there is an ethical benefit attached to staring, if viewers can access absorbing levels of prolonged and immersive visual engagement. According to Andrews, staring can bring about high levels of "absorption, concentration, and attentiveness."[35] Prolonged visual dialogue can incite and transmit affecting and unsettling stimuli, disturbing the foundational knowledge and ideologically cohered precinct serving as the basis for the viewer's engagement with the image. By disturbing the dynamics of power, the viewer and the viewer's world of perception can be realigned with the subject. To quote Andrews, "as [viewers] slip into and are stilled by the temporalities of the stare, [they] become aware of [their] capacity to be acted upon and altered, a capacity that [they] can only intelligently embrace or resist to the degree that [they are] conscious of it."[36]

A photograph provides the knowledge that worlds, notions, and ideas can be significantly altered. Based on our reception of the world that the photograph provides, it releases information and knowledge about itself just as much as about the viewers: their biases, prejudices, extent of ethicality, aggression, receptivity, and power dynamics. We do not visually encounter all this knowledge, but enough of these realities are bound within the borders of a photograph to question accountability and differences in viewing orientations. After being made aware through photographic stimuli, the first juncture of knowledge is how essential it is to see faithfully.

Seeing faithfully requires an extensive and immersive degree of fidelity to accommodate the various scenic and indexical provisions made by the visual details of the photograph when approached through different perspectives. This requires a balance between photographic realities that are jettisoned and those that are made primal. Tensions abound, and visual glossing is likely to occur. As Haraway argues,[37] these signify the place of power; even though objective awareness seeks to strike out unfaithful visual engagement and

[35] Andrews, "The Photographic Stare," 45.
[36] Andrews, "The Photographic Stare," 45.
[37] Haraway, "Situated Knowledges," 585.

accommodate the conflicting visual possibilities, the processes of accommodating, rejecting, and harmonizing the semantic possibilities in a photographic encounter are occurrences of power actualizing itself. Still, there is accountability, and there is nuance.

We might choose to see Figures 13.6 and 13.10 holistically, without privileging one possible meaning or reality over others. We might also choose to reconcile the various possible meanings to arrive at a midpoint that could move us closer to the worlds of the images. Gazing photographically does not eliminate the dynamics of power, but it addresses what it means to stare, to inhabit the worlds of our visual targets, and to be accountable for whatever positions we assume toward reorientation, unlearning, or relearning. To Andrews, the photographic stare is about meaning and being.[38] Consequently, a photographic stare puts us in situations where contextual laws hold less influence and instability abounds. This instability can cause the kinds of disruptions that travel along visual pathways to instigate ethical engagement, allowing for instructive and objective knowledge regardless of how subjective the modes of seeing from lens or eye can be. There is no passive vision, since viewing tools are active perceptual systems that draw their essence from established modes of envisioning,[39] but vision can be critical and constructive. Photographs goad us into questioning our own visual patterns, critically coming to terms with seeing or redefining the mainstays of our perceptual experience. By staring at photographs, we inadvertently gaze upon ourselves and stare at ways in which we visualize.

Seeing the Invisible: The Narratives

Visually engaging a picture involves more than attempting to interpret its hidden meanings or communicate a specific identity with it. A photograph brings its own historical basis to the fore of visual dialogue. It can serve as a form of personal record or autobiographical recall, due to the modern cultural approach to photography, but it is still a means of communal reflection. Regardless of the photographic tool or its digital or analog configurations, the longstanding function of the camera has been to serve as a means of remembering, and these functions of memory and historical encoding are not the sole preserve of analog pictures. Perceptual possibilities, and the human mind that powers vision, are constructed as a network of interacting media and gazes, drawing associated knowledge into the mix to be preyed upon by memory, for storage or recall.

Photographs are often seen as "visual resources in the micro cultures of everyday life,"[40] especially in the digital age of visual redirection – any image

---

[38] Andrews, "The Photographic Stare," 49.
[39] Haraway, "Situated Knowledges."
[40] Ron Burnett, *How Images Think* (Cambridge, MA: MIT Press, 2004), 62.

can be manipulated, even before public consumption. Photographs are visual resources because they are integral to the functioning of social networks, where visual communication serves purposes that include identity formation and peer bonding. As van Djick argues, this function does not remove memory from the value of photographs. We must look further inward. The malleable world of digital interaction has increased photography's use in shaping appearances and tailoring relationships, but memory, which has always served to unite the individual and the collective, is integral to those uses.

A photograph, which is fundamentally a sign, carries its own referent. This means that in the network of interaction, where the photograph moves along a visual path, the referent held within its canvas is often evoked – covertly or overtly, implicitly or explicitly – in every optical dialogue into which it enters. The ease of sharing images, facilitated by digital networks and platforms, increases the totemic and commemorative function of photographs. The more a photograph moves within a social network, the more it enters the realm of distributed storage. In van Djick's words, "personal 'live' pictures distributed via the internet may remain ... for life, turning up in unforeseen contexts, reframed and repurposed."[41]

Distributed storage is the province of the internet. Its numerous media and hyper-interactivity maintain the condition of longevity by keeping pictures in circulation. As long as such pictures remain in circulation, the conditions that birthed them and the subjects represented in them are kept alive in public and collective memories. Distributed digital storage spaces, known as cloud services, store photographs for extended periods, keeping collective histories for as long as possible without moisture, rust, or decay destroying the images and their associated memories.

The internet and digital media have allowed the photograph to integrate the individual with collective cultural memory; the process of sharing involves individuals who keep the collective's history and culture alive. Images such as Figures 13.19 and 13.20 are poignant because of the narratives they evoke. They are socioculturally rich images, and their entry into the social sphere via ocular exchange enables an unearthing, remembrance, or recall of the cultural histories surrounding their subjects.

Photographs not only point toward themselves or the history of their subjects, but also the contextual realities surrounding them at the point of their entry into reality – the photographic history of an object is not the same as that of the existence of its referent, even though both histories can be bound and reflected within the frame of the photograph. The subject of Figure 13.19 is the 105-meter-high Cocoa House in Ibadan, built in 1965, which was once the tallest building in tropical Africa. Cocoa House was built from the proceeds of

---

[41] Van Dijck, "Digital Photography," 69.

Figure 13.19 Cocoa House

commodities such as cocoa, timber, and rubber, showing that the Yorùbá who lived in the region were highly industrious, foresighted, and organized people.

Similar approaches can glean cultural knowledge from other images. One represents the palace of the Olúbàdàn of Ibadan, with its royal ambience, and the other depicts the University of Ibadan (Figure 13.21), the oldest university in the country. Contact with these images evokes cultural memories that have receded into the archives of collective memory: by evoking them, the photographs reinforce their historical significance, reestablishing the knowledge

Figure 13.20 Màpó Hall

associated with their history and reaffirming how much knowledge can be gained through extensive visual association.

Figure 13.20 is Màpó Hall, a design constructed under the colonial regime by Robert Jones. The project was completed in four years, costing over 20,000 euros (about $23,000 now), and it is popular for the seven columns that are said to represent the seven hills upon which the city of Ibadan is built. The hall evokes memories of the colonial era and the influence of the British, especially because it was modeled after St. George's Hall in Liverpool. The hall is also associated with other important historical details, including the 1955 convention of the NCNC (National Council of Nigeria and the Cameroons), where Nnamdi Azikiwe gave his presidential speech. The hall is also the location where the state's ex-governor, Ajimobi Abiola, crowned twenty-four kings in an unprecedented cultural and historic event.

These narratives are historical and collective. They have cultural implications, and they are sealed within the photographs, to be excavated when they enter the public domain or the hands of an individual whose consciousness is awakened by the collective memory. The memories are not represented inside the images, but we see them because we are reminded of them. The mind is ultimately challenged, upon visual engagement, to draw those antecedent narratives to the fore. They surround or make up the world of the image, providing and confirming knowledge to be retained in the collective consciousness, distributed storage, and public and or digitized spaces without losing relevance, import, or affect.

Figure 13.21 University of Ibadan entrance gate

An image does not need to address its subject in historical terms, but it may espouse historically significant cultural sentiments. Figure 13.22 is a visible rendering of both early-modern Yorùbá architecture and, by implication, the household dynamics (*Agbo ilé*) specific to the Yorùbá kin and familial structures. It informs us of the close-knit ties characterizing Yorùbá societies; they (such kind of structures) are still present in modern-day Yorùbá townships.

Fig. 13.22 not only representative of Yorùbá architectural peculiarities; it also provides additional details to patient viewers. Houses in pre-colonial, colonial, and even early post-colonial Yorùbá territory bore influences of these periods, revealing an ethos and cultural worldview that values communal living and togetherness. Homes were closely built because of the pervading philosophy of the *Ẹbí* (family) and *Agbo ilé* (household/group of homes) systems, suggesting that people bound by familial and communal ties could literally, physically, and figuratively live in harmony. Colonial- and Euro-influenced architecture did not immediately jettison such structures. Instead, the kinship system and the *Agbo ilé/Ẹbí* pattern of living were merged with Euro-American styles of architectural design to build modern homes that can accommodate extended or complex family structures.

Images can remind viewers of the early impluvia house types, which were common among the pre-European Yorùbá, and how the Yorùbá graduated into more modern and complex house structures over time. The incorporation of balustrades, corrugated-iron sheets, concrete blocks, welded metal, and

Figure 13.22 Yorùbá colonial architecture (*Agboolé*)

ceramic tiles were a result of influences from other European housing styles and the return of Africans from the diaspora.[42]

It is possible to hypothesize which photographs were staged by photographers – regardless of the photographed subject's desire – and which ones involve power dynamics centered on the subject's desire. Figure 13.23 supports the latter interpretation; the subject is in stasis, directing his gaze at the camera's lens, and his sitting posture is well within the range of expected poses for such kinds of imagery and photographic virtue signaling. The knowledge of consent is implicit in such acts, relying on the regenerative capacity of the camera in generating identities. In these kinds of images, the subject controls the knowledge that is reproduced for public, visual consumption. A firm grip is maintained on the projected identity, especially when subjects position themselves within a broader photographic tradition.

In Fig. 13.23 the subject's identity is tempered by a larger collective identity: the broad positioning in a chair, with visible hands strategically spread out beside the body, involves conspicuous posturing and clothing that bear traces of earlier Yorùbá body contouring in photographs. In this tradition, an individual fills out the frame of the photograph to be seen easily.

---

[42] See Bayo Amole and Stephen Folaranmi, "Architecture: Indigenous," in *Culture and Customs of the Yorùbá*, ed. Toyin Falola and Akintunde Akinyemi (Austin: Pan-African University Press, 2017), 171–202, for more details on Yorùbá architecture.

Figure 13.23 Idealizing posture

Figure 13.24, unlike Figure 13.23, shows a subject in motion. It reveals either the subject's implicit acceptance of being photographed at any point or the primacy of the photographer's discretion and a desire to capture the subject as deemed fit. The images reveal contractual possibilities involving the desire to be seen and to be the one serving as midwife to such visibility, with agency and control shifting between subject and photographer.

Emphasis on human and group photography is a functional reaction to a cultural heritage in which togetherness and social bonding is the default mode of being. In this value system, ambassadorial composition and posturing reflect how well one conforms to accepted notions and modes of being and of being seen. Humans are emphasized over material things, and the latter must serve the former, not the other way around. A single photograph might show humans in certain postures or idealizing frames, as in Figures 13.23 and 13.24, which owes to the culturally conditioned mode of seeing the human as a representative figure and how humans are the measure of things.

Figure 13.24 Idealizing regalia and posture

The Mediumistic

Photographs are mediumistic because they represent something; what they represent is often the domain of interpretation and meaning, which are political provinces. They are often carriers of embedded knowledge requiring a host of perceptive possibilities to unlock. Photographs and photographic tools can advance a cause or issue propaganda. By representing a visual object and potentially acknowledging the presence of other invisible subjects – forms or categories of knowledge – photographs embody overt and covert, or intended and unintended, agendas.

Can photographs mislead? They are instruments whose gaze, like any other perceptual tool or means of seeing, is structured along permitted and established pathways of seeing. The knowledge to be deduced from a photograph is at once driven by a programmed logic, casting it as media capable of misleading, reinforcing, or instructing on existing knowledge. Photographs do not mislead by themselves; they depict their subjects with relative accuracy. They become misleading when they are subjected to corrections, or when they are approached with insufficient knowledge or when the invisible realities within them are missed completely – which is the point of this chapter: to avoid missing the unseen details that are always present.

Correcting or manipulating photographic images is not a modern concept. Analog images have always been subjected to corrective procedures, but deletion and editing has been made easier by digital culture. Eliminating details to correct situated knowledge can lead to a loss of important information, especially in ways that make images misleading. This process robs the image of its own referent: the image has been manipulated in ways that significantly move it beyond the referent it indexes, cutting the cord that hems a picture and its natural extraphotographic object. When images are manipulated, a gap is created that hampers the transfer of accurate information from photographic object to viewer. Sufficient and appropriate knowledge falls into this gap, to be lost irretrievably. For the unknowing observer this gap is inexistent, and the viewer is misled in their intervention. The informed observer may detect the deceit and draw appropriate conclusions.

Photographs are mediums that can be affected in transformational ways, and this property must affect the way we receive them and the facts they provide. They advance brands of knowledge by remaining vessels that are capable of being affirmed or misread, shared on a large-scale network, and holding public memory and private recollection together through time.

Conclusion

Once again, do photographs represent certain sources, and how? Do photographs advance knowledge? How are meaning and deduction, as aspects of seeing and gazing, implicated in and by photographs? What place do the invisible aspects of photography hold in framing meaning? And to what extent do contextual realities extend the frame of photographs, beyond that which is visible on the canvas, to increase their affective qualities? These are bound within the borders of a photograph and included in the very act of holding a picture in visual dialogue. Knowledge is forever locked within images; the kinds of knowledge involved and how such knowledge is received depends on a host of factors. These factors exist invisibly within the pictographic material, including the culture of reception and the cultural configuring behind the techno-scientific build of the camera and its lens. They also involve the dominant ideology behind the gaze and its politics, historical and cultural details, the nuances of approach and visual engagement, and the creation, use, and functioning of the camera itself. Without them, the knowledge within photographs might be lost, even when it is present. Ultimately, the question of what (apart from a photograph's visible subjects) exists beyond or within the image has its ready answer: a host of possibilities and knowledge.

PART IV

Conclusion

14

Self, Collective, and Collection

Introduction

The idea of the individual within a collective, used to represent the workings of the system, has always found traction within African epistemology – it is reflected by cultural principles rich in epistemic considerations. Popular cultural concepts, such as *ubuntu* or the *Ọmọlúàbí*, are sophisticated conceptualizations of the individual's place in a larger matrix.[1] The matrix is that of the collective, providing habituated spaces for expressing, engineering, or choreographing individuality and the individual spirit that finds and defines its relevance within or against the collective. When the Yorùbá speak of the *Ọmọlúàbí*, it is often to reflect on the ambassadorial qualities of a specific individual or self-carrying the permissions and/or sanctions of culture within his or her person. The self becomes a text, and is judged as a narrative[2] because it excels when examined as a progressive entity whose value is ensconced in a structure; it must be viewed holistically to tease out the significance of its being.

Structures that support individuals can be inward (structure of self) or outward (structure of feeling), with each representing or affecting the other as forces of sociality. As a representational force, the "narrating self" embodies the behavioral moral codes authorized by the community, reflecting the (unspoken) general consensus on what is tolerable, enforceable, or forbidden by the community. If *Ọmọlúàbí* is defined as a progeny of the "Lord of character," or the sublime of virtues, or transcendent excellence of character (*Olú ìwà*), it is because of its metaphoric and denotative take on the admirable qualities expected of a Yorùbá person. One who bears that label must exude and espouse, in character and in action, the distinguishing features that set the *Ọmọlúàbí* apart, or underscore the sociocultural import of the concept.

---

[1] *Ubuntu* speaks to the "collective" (the social, like the *ujamaa* in Swahili), while *Ọmọlúàbí* speaks to the human character that locates the individual in the larger web or social framework.

[2] Polkinghorne, "Narrative and Self-Concept," 135–136.

Generally, it reflects the structure of feeling that conditions the Yorùbá cultural space and differentiates it from others.

The actions, conduct, and even posture of an individual reflect on and allow for reflections on the internal dynamics sustaining society. In maintaining the image and affective mechanics of society, the individual acts as a reflecting, consolidating, or refracting agentive force – depending on the context of agency – and as a portal of intelligence, presenting a consciousness through which readings of the foregrounding culture can be made. The self as a narrative, like all narratives, provides details through specific cues. The psychological Narrativity thesis[3] conceptualizes how the self, as an entity, progressively grows into a complex spatio-temporal phenomenon that unfolds in phases, time, and places. This transformation is a product of the malleability of the self in response to external stimuli and control. Forces of cultural configuration do apply their reconstructive agencies on the self, either to conform or transgress in response. Examining the lives of a group of people illustrates these processes, which in turn narrate the cultural workings of the space they inhabit.

Not only is an individual's identity tempered within the collective, the collective is reflected through the individual to show its state or degree of temperance. The extent to which an individual transgresses or conforms determines the extent to which they embody the culture or whether they can be seen as its emissary. Associations such as these display the self's conscious choice to visually echo the processes of self-construction beyond self-particularizing details. Reading non-particularizing markers of the self establishes a closer connection with features that are culture specific, and the self becomes a referential object for the culture that defines or shapes it. As David Doris argues, such connections exemplify an individual as self-identifying with traits that exceed defining features of uniqueness.[4]

Society shapes the individual through its mores and institutions,[5] along with the guiding notions of belonging or non-belonging that influence the construction of identity premised on the unique configuration of spaces as determined by their cultural anchors.[6] This makes it hard to miss the pivotal influences of culture on the individual, and vice versa. To cite another popular concept, the same applies to the *Ubuntu* philosophy encouraging or perpetuating the principles of communalism. It is undeniable that the culture of a specific setting can be read from the actions, character, possessions, choices, idiosyncrasies, ideologies, and intellect of an individual. Cultural space – embodying factors that include socio-economic institutions, geographical

---

[3] Strawson, "Against Narrativity," 428.
[4] Doris, "Symptoms and Strangeness."
[5] Etuk, *Religion and Cultural Identity*.
[6] Tim Cresswell, *Place: A Short Introduction* (Oxford: Oxford University Press, 2004).

boundaries, mores, practices, and historical foundations – impacts the individuals that inhabit it. Through their life stories and actions, individuals attest to the cultural and other conditions as forces that shape individuality. They show lasting imprints of the collective consciousness or culture from which their individuality has been molded, taking part in an unending process of cyclical influence.

The process is cyclical because individuals shape their society. The cultural space is a signifier of the coalition and interaction of energies, individual consciousnesses, and networks of characters. The sharp contours of individuated identity are tempered in a collective frame that is modeled after the mixture of several consciousnesses. A space is a space only to the extent that it exudes the beliefs and philosophy of its people.

Cultural space, as an index or signifier, is not a fixed entity. It is a product of the interaction between the perception and reality of its inhabitants,[7] continually shifting and being redefined. Individual perceptions are melted, refined, and shaped in the cauldron of reality to conform with a generic pattern that consolidates differences into a harmonized whole. With this understanding of the relationship between culture or the collective and the self, we can appreciate the expression "people are their space and a place is its people."[8]

"Rootedness" fuels a solid comprehension of one's place in the order of things. It is the quality of having a secured place from which campaigns of appreciation, criticism, or interaction with the world can be mounted. Edward Relph calls this a secured point where the spiritual, psychological, and physical are mixed to define an individual's approach to grappling with reality/existence.[9] As individuals contribute to the development of their space or culture, the culture provides a vantage point from which individuals can define themselves against the world and are distinguished from others. It also provides channels, via the space of social practice, that can be used to identify with the world or appropriate it without losing the self. People and their cultures are locked in an infinite embrace, undergoing a continuous process of mutual influence.

Individuals, and the physical possessions that contribute to their individuality, co-shape perceptions of culture as much as culture co-shapes the perceptions of individuals – specifically, the perceptions of others. Notions of belonging and nonbelonging heavily influence collectivity and cultural progress, and spaces are socially constructed by human action and inaction.[10]

---

[7] Edward Relph, "A Pragmatic Sense of Place," *Environmental and Architectural Phenomenology* 20, no. 3 (2009): 24–31.
[8] David Seamon and Jacob Sowers, "Place and Placelessness (1976): Edward Relph," in *Key Texts in Human Geography*, ed. Phil Hubbard, Rob Kitchin, and Gill Valentine (London: Sage, 2008), 43–52.
[9] Seamon and Sowers, "Place and Placelessness."
[10] Cresswell, *Place*.

Culturally coded principles of being and sociality owe their formation to the human cognitive ability that institutionalizes practices and choices, and they are foundational to the notions of belonging and exclusion. Each signifies sociocultural acceptance or rejection. The affective power of cultural acceptance or expulsion is demonstrated in the lasting effects of familiarity: the more that an individual identifies with the features of a particular culture, the stronger their sense of belonging. As these individuals are accepted for their familiarity with the culture, the space is increasingly reflected or portrayed as welcoming, which is one way of establishing mutual influence between a culture and its people.

The Yorùbá are not Yorùbá because their culture existed from time immemorial. The success of the Yorùbá project, uniting once-independent nations and empires into a Yorùbá identity, relied on the extent to which nationalists could establish connections along folkloric lines – although in some quarters this is seen as the continuance of the colonialist enterprise. Nationalists relied on similar and shared histories, mythologies, and folklore that were already in existence; the revision and reconstruction of histories and heritage became a means to an end that enabled affective connections among the many sub-ethnic groups. Their methods engendered the (hard) encoding of shared features into a generic identity that serves as the benchmark.

People belong to a specific space because they identify with its mores, institutions, and shared realities. The attributes that distinguish that space from others allow the social processes of belonging and nonbelonging to be negotiated by members and nonmembers – they are the defining realities of the space engineered by its inhabitants. Established cultural and behavioral codes, and the extent to which individuals absorb, embody, and manifest them, contribute to the process of differentiation that sets cultures apart. Cultural differentiation depends on the categorization of members as belonging and nonbelonging, which means that a cultural space, or the essential features of a place, will manifest in the lives of its members. These individuals, or their selves, can act as microscopes through which the culture is explored, accessed, and appreciated. The psychological constitution of the self confirms its position.

According to psychoanalysts and Western psychoanalytical theorists, the self is a psychological construct that combines psychical apparatuses of the id, ego, and superego. In a setting like Yorùbá culture and worldview, reality is both tangible or physical and intangible or spiritual. Similarly, the self is psycho-spiritual – spiritual elements not only have direct bearing on the world of the physical, they control it. Western terms define this as magic or the magical, which can be a generic explanation for anything ethereal or exceeding the physically explicable.[11]

---

[11] Gvozden, "Magical Realism and the Politics of Narrative."

The Yorùbá concept of *Orí* (inner head/the soul or essence) is seen as connected to the spiritual realm, manifesting generative powers comparable to the force that created the earth. Considering the constructive capabilities of the human race, and the progress that humans have brought into existence, it is not a far-fetched idea. To the Yorùbá, this *Orí* is the wellspring of individuality;[12] cultural programs and mores that celebrate or advance the philosophy of individuality and individuation recognize the dynamic interaction of supernatural powers and biological/physical processes of being. The sayings "Òrìṣà wo là bá mọ́ọ bọ bí kò ṣe Orí ẹni" (which deity might we worship if not one's head) and "Kò sí Òrìṣà tíí dá níí gbè léyìn orí ẹni" (no deity saves one better than one's head) reflect this reality.

In cultural settings where magic is construed as an otherworldly invocative and evocative power, such realities are discursively flattened or simplistically approached by scientific minds. But that which separates Yorùbá magic (jùjú, generative or invocative power, *Idán*) from Western miracles or "technological wizardry" is the place of provinciality typical to addressing matters of what defies material realities and laws – these subjects are explored in the narrative *Counting the Tiger's Teeth*.

It is held that the *Orí* is a miniaturized form of an original creator – complete with its spiritual connotations, strength, and potency. The *Orí* is the point of entry through which deities and spiritual entities mount individuals, spurring them to actions and incredible feats that would otherwise be impossible. It is the locus of existence and the powerhouse of being. If I narrate, as in *Counting the Tiger's Teeth*, that magic strengthens my memory, it is because the ethereal forces of the Yorùbá world go beyond the simplistic binaries of metaphysical and corporeal, or mythic and realistic, that Western imagination erroneously assumes and imposes through Eurocentric theories.

The influence of the spiritual world on the physical goes beyond empiricist strategies or the objective approaches of Western science. Even when the process is veiled from uninitiated eyes, the results are physically observable. Cultural, religious, and cultic ceremonies are anchored in magical spaces that are simultaneously physical and ethereal. The space of the ritual blurs the distinction between physical and spiritual; the architectonics of its reality are better appreciated by a mind that can accept the shifting possibilities that result from the material world colliding with the ethereal and numinous. The process of enacting festivals, and their manifestations in the lives of participants through songs, chants, and other folkloric activities, are inexplicable to objectivist minds. These events would not yield much to objectivist procedures or critical inquiry. Just as Western technological magic requires a specialist to decode its mysteries, so traditional magic and its spiritual influences require

---

[12] Ojo, "'Heepa'"; Yai, "Tradition."

practitioners or initiates to comprehend its dynamism – it is more than the wild fancy of an illiterate mind.

Spiritual influence can manifest physically, shaping our perception of individual actions as physical. However, the Western explanation for human action is a process of chemical reactions between the brain, body, and heart that provides blood and oxygen. For the Yorùbá it is a complex interaction of spiritual influences and psychological processes. An individual exhibiting a fight-or-flight response is manifesting the character of his or her *Orí*, in whichever way it was configured before birth. An individual whose actions appear insane is said to experience spiritual interference through his or her *Orí*. The collision of the id's desires and the superego's watchdog, leading to transgressions such as dancing naked, is explained as a failure of the *Orí* to protect itself and the individual.

Several things can affect the individual or the *Orí*, which is the key point. The Yorùbá are material-conscious people. Their relationship with material possessions carries many connotations: spiritual, physical, economic, historical, status based, mythological, or totemic. The Yorùbá's passionate approach to material acquisition provides a strong and vibrant system of symbolism. Some claim that the Yorùbá can be obsessed with accumulating wealth through material acquisition.[13] The truth of this is subjective, with room for nuanced opinions, but the Yorùbá consciousness and its drive to acquire and signify through possessions is undeniable.

The unique configuration of the Yorùbá social system and its art tradition connect the possession of art, beauty, and associated materials with an individual's *Ìwà* (character), or self. In the Yorùbá sociocultural semiosphere, the signification of a person's character or virtue occurs when goodwill is transferred through visual symbolism: possessions draw their owners into a visual discourse between third-party appraisers and the object. Positive appraisals of the possessions reflect well on their owners. When clothes are praised for durability, or their aesthetic or financial value, it makes indirect reference to the owner's sense of dressing (*Ìmúra*) or sophisticated tastes (*Ojú inú*) or *Ojú ọnà*, that is, to possess a right mind for aesthetics, or have the correct artistic sensibility, to indicate social standing and economic power. The same applies to artwork.

Indirect references have direct impact on the owners, who obtain, retain, or feel the impact of the praises on their psyche (*Orí*). It is a process that rewards the id through agents of the supergo. The *Orí* can receive stimulus through several means, including psycho-spiritual means, materials with socio-religious import, or mythico-religious invocations through aesthetic objects, depending on context (through praise chants/*Oríkì*, also). The *Orí* is ultimately

---

[13] See Cordwell, "Arts and Aesthetics."

the recipient of magical, material, or oratorical transactions between bodies or between bodies and forces.

In a more physical sense, these transactions aid and propel the uniqueness of self, to the extent that the individual allows such engagements to direct their mode of self-fashioning. The more that an individual attributes worth to possessions, as evaluated by others, the more that individual is conditioned to define the self through material things and the ensuing public dialogue. This motive drives every approach to self-growth and the fashioning of identities. Ìwà (character) underscores individuality and the self – a strong cultural awareness links the materials, serving as that culture's insignia or housing the culture's consciousness, and the owner, serving as the consciousness or intelligence organizing and retaining the connection. The culture itself is enlivened through the collective that includes the materials and their collector.

Influences can move beyond the physical or psychological; possessions can confer spiritual sanctions onto the individuals that possess them. A person's Ìwà (character) can be altered spiritually to manifest a specific Ìwà (trait), reconstructing their entire personality (Ìwà). The effigy of a person can receive powerful and malicious incantations or invocations that alter that person's psychological formation – physical manifestations can compel the individual to behave in strange ways. This sort of spiritual intervention can also be performed on other material possessions, such as clothing, furniture, hair, or other personal belongings.

In the Yorùbá realm, the Orí can be attacked spiritually or physically, and psychic attacks can leave psychic evidence pointing to the perpetrator in the same way that physical acts leave physical traces. The psychological composition of an individual, which drives their manners and behavior, is subject to several levels of influence that rely on access gained through their possessions. The possessions have become a means of approaching the person and appraising the culture to which both belong.

These are all manifestations of psychological perceptions and postures toward human affairs. What do they say about a culture that celebrates the collection or creation of beautiful art as one of its core values? Aesthetic behavior, demonstrating a specific kind of psychological behavior, is anchored in the psychological desire to apply social power through representation. What more powerful manifestation of self exists? The cultural sanctions that permit such modes of representation and self-construction impact the development of the self's psyche. They reflect the superego's place in inhibiting or enabling the desires of the id. The superego embodies many sociocultural forces that seek to recondition members of a culture. The consciousness that arises from knowing the potency and representative power in something like an art collection is a manifestation of the influence of social structures on an individual's self-formation.

This is not hegemonic social power-seeking domination or repression. Magic can have lasting liberatory or purgatory effects, and aesthetic behavior at either a personal or collective level can liberate, inform, sensitize, or sanitize. Through "informing," an individual's possessions or the aesthetic judgment to acquire those possessions can speak to the configuration of a culture as much as the culture can speak for the peculiarities of the self. The material possessions provide opportunities for evaluation that are similar to those of the individual and their actions (or simply the self).

By "sensitizing," the observable patterns in the process of coming to terms with the aesthetic behavior of cultural ambassadors can reframe existing opinions or deepen previous understandings of cultural realities. The same process is applicable to art's sanitary capacities; the patterns and networks that are read from or experienced through contact with a system of art ownership can expunge Eurocentric notions that have pervaded the reception and taxonomy of indigenous life. Aesthetic behaviors, and the art that enables them, all speak for the culture within which they draw life and meaning. Therein lies the liberatory affect and effect of art and the aesthetic behavior engendered by indigenous art tradition: ferreting out its various possibilities allows cultural knowledge, indigenous epistemologies, mores, ideologies, and methodologies to receive primacy and be freed from their Eurocentric bonds.

Critical cultural exploration can take many forms, and either individuals or the self can serve as the intelligence through which a culture and its structures are appraised. By shifting indigenous epistemologies to the center, and by decentering colonial legacies of knowledge formation, retention, and dispersal, it is possible for decolonial approaches to continually reinvent themselves – the hegemonic force situated within the postcolony and its centers of knowledge production undergo the same reinventive processes. The thesis of this specific exploration coincides with the nucleus of this entire book: the central concept recentralizes African knowledge, epistemology, ideology, and methodologies of knowing. This is done by exploring the relationship between the self as the intelligence, the collective (ideology, epistemology, and culture) as the source and referent, and the collection (items) as signifiers and representational material forces. Exploring the relationship of these three entities will resituate, emphasize, and foreground African knowledge, while decentralizing European ways of interrogating it.

We can foreground the relationship between the self and the society by emphasizing connections between the self's material properties and the culture feeding them. It shows a reading of culture that is clinical, methodical, and critical, performed through critical research and analysis of self-owned artworks or material properties – these are located within the cultural system that the individual belongs to. Although this approach is autoethnographic, it moves the culture closer to the center, coming from the same ideological impulse that holds decolonialism as an imperative enterprise against the colonial matrix of power threatening indigenous knowledge and life. The chapters in this book perform exactly this duty, exploring how personal narratives and works of art (which themselves are visual metaphors and narratives) are mouthpieces for culture. They also show how the intelligence that critically probes these items need not come from outside the tripartite structure of self, collection, and collective. A foreign voice is not necessary to mount a worthwhile enterprise, shifting the culture along appropriate agentive mediums toward the center.

What lies between the self, collective, and collection that has made such a project significant and worthwhile? What connections exist within the realm of the three to encourage a critical observation of indigenous life beyond the provisions of colonial or Eurocentric pedagogy and education? How can the self, serving as an intelligence through which material possessions and intellectual works actualize their signifying potentials, be appraised in the light of signifying properties that have evocative and potent social mandates? How does this activity, seeking the culture within the self and the materials that define it, contribute to research patterns that advance the Africanization of knowledge? In what ways is it important to situate the self as a voice of critical reasoning so that narratives can be assessed as important, vital, and welcomed in the general intellectual struggle against Eurocentrism?

This book addresses these questions directly and indirectly, from its introductory chapters to its conclusion. It is the direct focus of this chapter, casting a holistic, broader lens over these issues to foreground the salient factors that revolve around the matter at hand. It begins by interrogating how the narratives of the self, as the critical intelligence probing and illuminating through autoethnographic endeavor, counteracts hegemonic disruption and refraction of African knowledge. This is done by reemphasizing the representations of African epistemology and ideologies.

Counteracting Distortions and Refractions

Decolonial activity is a solution to Eurocentrism and as a means to de-Westernize African knowledge, epistemology, culture, and knowledge dynamics. One method involves Africanizing research or decolonizing African research methodologies, which can take several forms. It could be the integration or involvement of native or indigenous epistemology into the research process, or it could involve dialogue that accommodates the perspectives of the researched as part of the research process, beyond having them serve as mere sources of data.[14] The absence of these dynamics often results in outsiders performing research by collecting indigenous reality into documentable forms, and having it called research, without sufficient

---

[14] Linda T. Smith, *Decolonizing Methodologies: Research and Indigenous Peoples* (London: Zed Books, 2012).

dialogue and allowing for misinterpretation, generalization, or sweeping conclusions that objectify and sideline the producers of knowledge.

Research is invasive; it is an intellectual endeavor backed by capitalism, and its Eurocentric heritage is continually evoked in its essence. Western capitalist forces provide funds and grants to aid the acquisition of data from subaltern sources – it motivates adventurers to fulfill specific intellectual mandates favoring Western centers of knowledge production to the detriment of the subaltern sources of knowledge. Coloniality's proximity to research, or the colonial matrix of power's influence on research as an instituted practice, is revealed in the promotion of Enlightenment or Westocentric ideals. John Overton touches on this in his submission recognizing research as an activity that embraces a history driven by commerce that trades the subaltern.[15] Careers have been made, and status has been gained, through the misrepresentations accruing from such capitalism-based research.[16]

Rectifying this dynamic is a defining tenet of decolonial studies, and the activity can take several forms. It can blur the Western-imposed divide between researcher and the researched – this divide is justified as part of the ethics of research, but it ultimately reduces the agency of the indigenous as both researcher and researched.[17] The connotations and applications of words like ethics and objectivity are implicated in the Western imperialist approach to researching the subaltern world. Research applications hold indigenous people at the disadvantaged end of the process, especially when colonial standards of contact determine rules of research engagement that "determine the nature or evidence of harm in research with Indigenous people."[18] Ethics protocols in research and the institutional thinking behind them make it almost impossible to identify as both indigenous researcher and the researched;[19] the colonialist impulse within research ensures that it is conducted using power categories that certify or maintain traditional binaries. One must either be a researcher or the researched.

The clear-cut divisions of researched and researcher, or foreigner and indigenous, enable the extraction of knowledge solely for the benefit of Western centers of knowledge and those funded by the West. Not only is knowledge extracted from indigenous spaces under the West's revisionist and

---

[15] John Overton, "Decolonizing Methodologies: Research and Indigenous Peoples," *Development in Practice* 23, no. 4 (2013): 598–599.
[16] Overton, "Decolonizing Methodologies."
[17] See Madeline Whetung and Sarah Wakefield, "Colonial Conventions: Institutionalized Research Relationships and Decolonizing Research Ethics," in *Indigenous and Decolonizing Studies in Education: Mapping the Long View*, ed. Linda T. Smith, Eve Tuck, and Wayne K. Yang (New York: Routledge, 2019): 146–158.
[18] Whetung and Wakefield, "Colonial Conventions," 146.
[19] Whetung and Wakefield, "Colonial Conventions," 146.

reconstructivist approaches to subaltern knowledge, but the indigenous are also kept from making impactful research into native cultures unless they adopt the position and profile of a colonizing researcher. Indigenous life is explained without significant input from those whose lives constitute the data. It omits the perspectives of those who live out the facts of the data.

Distortions of fact, refractions of reality, and reconstruction of narratives are consequences of these procedures. When magic is disregarded as an unrealistic or superstitious mode of evocative or generative force, it is because Western paradigms of thought have been superimposed over indigenous culture and its mode of reasoning. Approaches to indigenous life have taken a universal, Westocentric route that seeks to see everything in its own image. As a result, the indigenous see themselves from a Western vantage point, or in comparison to a Western model. One cannot overlook the implications of the way that Christianity interprets the manifestation of magic as evil, demonic, and paganistic. The structures that enabled the Enlightenment and Europe's civilizing missions to Africa have a strong Euro-Christian base.[20]

Europe's education of the African was an enterprise spearheaded by the Christian faith, supported and financed by Europe's orthodox churches. Teaching Africans in missionary schools was training for Africans to see the European modes of being, thought, and cultural progress as the dominant method of survival; both cultures were analyzed using frames of black and white, bucolic and civilized, pagan and holy, and atavistic and moral. The sanctions on African ideologies and patterns of cultural expression were justified by Christian modes of performing selfhood or nationhood. It is no wonder that Pentecostal churches, including those described in *Counting the Tiger's Teeth*, targeted indigenous spirituality; it was labeled superstitious, cultic, or magical in a derogatory sense. The earliest missionaries in Africa demonized African spirituality to achieve record numbers of indigenous persons converting to Christianity, jettisoning features of their native cultures on the road to redemption.

Indigenous life has been reduced to a data pool that is incapable of fashioning critical modes of cosmic or material understanding. Western critics are unable to accommodate African works of art as more than mere figurines, sculptures, or ornamental art, which displays their opposition to indigenous epistemology. Such insularity has rendered them unable to understand that the personal abode of an individual is an exhibitive space. When Eurocentric researchers misconstrue African arts as devoid of authorship,[21] or fail to recognize that "anonymous" is a category of aesthetic consideration, it is

---

[20] See Ogbu Kalu, "West African Christianity," in *The Collected Essays of Ogbu Uke Kalu*, vol. II: *Christian Missions in Africa: Success, Ferment, and Trauma*, ed. Nimi Wariboko, Toyin Falola, and Wilhelmina Kalu (Trenton: Africa World Press, Inc., 2010), 173–189.

[21] Yai, "Tradition"; Abiodun, "African Aesthetics."

because they are incapable of not equating Western art conventions with African ones.

The failure to appraise African art and worldviews within the context of their indigeneity – or the inability to understand that authorship and naming are observed differently in African (Yorùbá) art as a crucial part of artisanship – is due to a failure to situate criticism of African art within the linguistic and socioculturally informed conceptual frames that support it. To the African, naming carries or creates a synecdochical connection between an individual and the material thing made to share the name.

Authorial self-naming of artwork is not an absent tradition; its realization is conditioned by cultural realities specific to African art tradition. For the African, naming is a ritualized practice performed with tact, shrewdness, and diplomacy. Extreme caution is applied when naming something after oneself, which is predicated on the idea that a name provides direct access to one's Orí (essence). A name is comparable to an individual's fingerprint or access to their private property.

This cautionary approach to naming is not only used when identifying art, it is also observed when naming individuals; naming a child carries equal weight, if not greater. Names set persons apart, and Yorùbá ontology holds that naming or calling an individual's name can invoke or agitate a person's spiritual essence, making it vulnerable to benevolent or malevolent utterances. When a child is given a name, it is also believed that this name will influence the child's behavior.[22] Such ontological considerations determine to what extent and how self-authorship or authorial naming is applied within the Yorùbá art tradition. It is reductive to assume that self-naming is absent, which is one thing the chapters here correct in their unique but related strides. Recognition of artwork along authorial lines is culture specific; a community can identify a creator merely by engaging the creation. This level of cultural interconnectivity goes beyond Western performances of cultural collectivity.

The same thematic direction can be found in the essay on self in *A Mouth Sweeter than Salt*. Naming and the use of names are deliberate cultural actions, radically different from the nomenclatural procedures of the West. A name references itself and the history of its making – it is self-reflexive and a signifier of the extracontextual details or broader social conditions that attended its making. A name embodies an entire history; it also forebodes. A name relates the conditions that surround a birth or ancestry, or the place, lineage, or standing of an individual. This cultural practice is also observed in the names of places. Naming in Yorùbá culture goes beyond a sociolinguistic practice: it wields mythic, magical, and spiritual potency, and it carries historical and cultural basis. An insider's view, using an appropriate insider's

---

[22] Abiodun, "African Aesthetics."

perspective and frames of reasoning, is best positioned to uncover these dynamics without undue assumptions or reductive assertions.

In exploring narratives and art collections, the decolonial impulse driving the Africanization of knowledge is amplified above that of an echoing hum subsumed by postcolonial chatter. The autoethnographic leaning of these chapters provide an expansive take on Yorùbá culture – with implications for receiving all African culture in new ways – that rebuts existing notions, sensitizing beyond the apprehensions and affirmations of African culture made by Eurocentric authorities. It allows for an insider's view, taking a critical approach that provides the necessary, expansive perspective.

Engaging *A Mouth Sweeter than Salt* prompts the exploration and use of narrative as a means of assessing Nigerian reality. The dialectical function of a narrative, as contained in the material itself, provides channels through which *A Mouth Sweeter than Salt* can be probed to assess its cultural realities. The research voice, which belongs to an individual, contributes a counter-representation to the current understanding of the indigenous life within a national construct. Cultural consciousness and values are brought to bear without misrepresentation. The dominant task becomes the critical re-presentation of the sociocultural sphere's factual nature; the implication of this procedure is that Yorùbá cultural ideologies are accentuated and located within the epistemologies that support their existence.

Using narrative as a guidepost into cultural reality prompts reflections on narrative's place as media for cultural sensitization and folkloric communion in precolonial African life. Griots, bards, and performers are the souls of a community;[23] their folkloric art of singing, performance, and narration marks them as custodians of heritage, mores, beliefs, customs, and wisdom that make cultures distinctive. The position that a griot or bard holds, as a voice for the community, is reflected by the degree and type of recognition that their performances receive – they are seen as purveyors of knowledge, and their utterances are considered invaluable.

Griots are valued and exalted as "respected African historians and praise-singers ... keepers and purveyors of knowledge, including tribal history, family lineage, and news of births."[24] They engage in cultural historical transmission.[25] By viewing these holistically, the griot can be judged as a prompter of cultural provocation, doing what Krishnan describes as "calling

---

[23] Ruth Finnegan, *Oral Literature in Africa* (London: Oxford University Press, 1970); Frederick B. Akporobaro, *Introduction to African Oral Literature* (Lagos: Princeton Publishing Co., 2012).

[24] Becky Blanchard, "The Social Significance of Rap and Hip-Hop Culture," *Ethics of Development in a Global Environment(EDGE): Poverty and Prejudice: Media and Race* (1999), 21, https://web.stanford.edu/class/e297c/poverty_prejudice/mediarace/socialsignificance.htm

[25] Krishnan, "The Storyteller Function," 30.

upon a form of social responsibility and connectivity across society."[26] Narrative, as a cultural practice, had a pivotal role in instigating and retaining cultural memory. In the hands of professionals and skilled performers it attained its potential as a critical mode of observing and comprehending reality.

Because reality and fiction meet in narratives at the threshold of imagination, a narrative blurs the distinction between the two phenomena for specific purposes. Not only is the mode or medium acting in the capacity of a provocateur, it also instigates the type of awareness through which interventions can be made to reconcile people with important but overlooked aspects of their reality. Oral narratives of folkloric provenance had the mandate of provoking participation through imagination, the discourse they generated, or the instructive entertainment they provided. Narratives with such folkloric architecture had a duty to represent the ways, values, and ideologies of the people.

The structure of a folktale narrative, for example, instructs on the communal and collective ideology that bound people in acts, expressions, and thought – the tales have codas and stock phrases that require performer and audience participation.[27] Folkloric arts inform on the notions and principles guarding indigenous existence and framing culture, and the infusion of personal idiosyncrasies into narratives makes the imagination a defining feature of such oral arts.[28] It is imagination that allows the performer to modify tales and evoke the necessary emotions and affects within the audience, no matter how much he conforms to the fixed patterns, motifs, and elements of a generic story. Griots dealt in history and fiction, and reality and imagination, to achieve their aim of embodying and representing culture. They were their own critics, using performed stories to probe, search, and research – since narratives and performances are reenactments – indigenous life as a way to sustain their heritage.

The same impulse drives narratives explored in the essays of *Counting the Tiger's Teeth* and *A Mouth Sweeter than Salt*. The ancient tradition of oral narratives is maintained, applying them as modes of illumination and having raconteurs serve as custodians and performers who deal in history, imagination, and fact for cultural elevation. Not only do they merge history with reality as written works, but as written performances they also bring the same cultural charge to the fore that has distinguished African narrative performances as culture oriented. For example, in *A Mouth Sweeter than Salt* the Mèsìọ̀gọ̀ are given a right of place within the broader preoccupation of

---

[26] Krishnan, "The Storyteller Function," 30.

[27] Ropo Sekoni, "The Narrator, Narrative-Pattern and Audience Experience of Oral Narrative Performance," in *The Oral Performance in Africa*, ed. Isidore Okpewho (Ibadan: Spectrum Books, 1990): 139–159; Akporobaro, *African Oral Literature*.

[28] Akporobaro, *African Oral Literature*.

the narratives. The oral critics (*Gbẹ̀nugbẹ̀nu*) and aesthetes are allowed to shine, and they are accorded their dues as critically minded observers and connoisseurs of art in the chapter on sculpture; they are recovered from the margins of visibility where they had been placed by a Eurocentric take on Yorùbá art.

Yorùbá art not only reveals a vibrant culture, it displaces previous notions that African art is either for aesthetic or religious purposes. It can be for both. The dichotomy that the West creates when approaching African culture and art is resolved by exploring the artworks for their significations and how they bear representations of various cultural aspects. Submissions on Yorùbá art also negate observations that African art is devoid of defining aesthetics; such aesthetics form the basis of a distinct art tradition. One can also appreciate the industry of Yorùbá artistry, its patronage system, and the vibrant economy that developed ahead of pervasive, Eurocentric notions of commerce. Textiles and paintings continue to serve as visual markers of history in time and place. The African textiles that inspired Europe's sartorial industry have extended the range of their culture – their historical details are not only read from the textures and fabrics of Yorùbá clothing, but also resituated from the diversions imposed by Western revisionist machinery. The Yorùbá cloth industry is vibrant and active, continuing to influence designers who make fabrics for the African markets.

There are several corollaries accompanying attempts to experience culture through personal narratives and collected art. These attempts return the gaze to the individual culture and its dynamics; it also instructs readers to approach aspects of culture as foundational parts of the world created by the art. Gaze is a powerful phenomenon, determining the perception of reality and the assignment of power between the person gazing and the object gazed upon. In using an insider's gaze to explore culture through collected and self-created art, the artworks are set in their proper places to reflect a rich and wholesome culture, as they did in the past. In narrative and visual arts it is possible to observe essential details of culture such as its spiritual leanings, its deities, and its mythic foundations; visual encounters provoke histories of peoples. This activity also jogs cultural memories to enable interventionist recentering of indigenous history and folkloric practices from a world and knowledge system that fostered the dominance of Eurocentrism.

By applying these materials as magnifying lenses, we encounter what it means to be a Yorùbá. The autoethnographic approach and the chapters birthed from it form an intellectual force field – its gravitational pull is an ability to provoke reflections fostering an immersive return to old ways that had been made obscure by the continued Europeanization of African life. This includes knowledge forms, systems of thinking, and cultural space. The autoethnographic endeavor and its overarching ideologies are brought to bear as intercessional, opposing the Western tide that continually floods the African thought system and culture space. Reversing that tide will rescue indigenous patterns of thought and expression from the obscured margins of knowledge.

The benefits of an autoethnographic work are inexhaustible, including the rebuttal of dismissive and blatant lies. Western allegations – claiming that Africa was an abode of stark illiterates lacking education prior to European incursion – can hardly find traction in the face of autoethnographic research combining insider perspective, the rigors of critical intellectual thought, and the equal footing of history and narrative or history and art.

The process of educating an individual in the Yorùbá cultural setting starts from the formative years. It is extensive and expansive, with contributions from every member of the community. Collectivity, for the Yorùbá, belongs in no single domain. Each person, whether part of the *Agbo ilé* (clan/family ancestral abode), *Ẹbí* (extended kinship/family), *Ará* (kith/kin), or *Ará ita* (outsider) contributes in instructing, correcting, or chastising when it is deemed fitting.

The Yorùbá maxim "Agbà kìí wà l'ọ́jà kí orí ọmọ tuntun wọ́" (a child's head cannot be crooked in the marketplace in the presence of an elder) frames the collective efforts made in raising a child to become an ambassador of the culture, an *Ọmọlúàbí*. Educational achievements are not solely defined by the presence of a school's four walls or the ability to speak English. Correcting social vices, reforming errant individuals, punishing transgressions, and promoting laudable displays of virtue are not any single person's duty – every adult is the parent of a child or the keeper of his or her brethren and his or her brethren's offspring. This fact is well explored in *A Mouth Sweeter than Salt*, which narrates how community members suffering from inferiority complexes, desperate to achieve an illusory sense of belonging, saw Western education (merely a variant of knowledge) as the ticket to improving their social profile. They did not care whose ox was gored in the process:

> The racist Europeans and the "civilized Yorùbá" began to behave alike. The racist Europeans had used all sorts of offensive words to describe Africans. In turn, the civilized Yorùbá were using their advantages ... to turn others, because of their location outside the cities, into primitives, comparing them with monkeys, infantilizing their ideas, marginalizing their abodes.[29]

Educating youngsters is a cultural necessity achieved through multiple strategies that are accommodated by a dynamically constructed cultural pedagogy. Oral narratives have their roles to play alongside other aspects of folklore, such as fine arts. Sculptures and paintings manifest various aesthetics that uphold their duty to educate the public. The aesthetic of the cool is one such example that is duly explored in the chapters. The aesthetic informs aesthetes, artists,

---

[29] Falola, *A Mouth Sweeter than Salt*, 198.

and members of society that art is indeed functional. It provides templates for conditioning attitudes and behaviors through visual literacy. Portraits, painted or photographed, had vibrant cultural appeal for their visual emphasis on an individual's or subject's success at embracing cultural ideals. In portraits, proper conduct is exhibited through posture: moderation, cheerfulness, and measured self-expression are accepted methods of conduct for representing oneself.

Traditional portraits visually espouse accepted values.[30] Full regalia, when represented in portraits, informs on the value of clothing (Aṣọ) and dress sense (Ìmúra) as defining attributes for the Ọmọlúàbí, in contrast to a bucolic or slovenly person (Ọbùn). The tempered character associated with Yorùbá portraits is an exemplification of the aesthetic that shows why Inú tútù (gentleness) is expected of all Ọmọlúàbí. For the Yorùbá, coolness must manifest both internally and externally to show psychological and physical equilibrium. Little verbal instruction is required to impart education on appropriate conduct and expression.

Moderation, which is expected from everyone, is central to the Yorùbá moral system. Anti-aesthetics possess educative properties as culturally coded visual materials. They impart messages through the symptoms of pathology that they embody, which run counter to socially accepted representations of beauty and morals. They also educate through the conflict and irruption of normative definitions of aesthetics[31] that they provoke. It is not enough to assess artworks as mere products of cerebral activity, especially when they are informed by a context that is strongly anchored in cultural realities. It is reductive to interpret visual representations of kneeling women as an expression of subjugation, or worse, as manifestations of the presence of cultural hegemony.

Sculptures that portray women are appreciated for their signifying power; they embody the cultural principles of Ẹ̀bẹ̀ (supplication) and Ẹbọ (sacrifice). Images of women, expressed in various postures, are not a clear-cut symbol of oppression; the image can be a metaphor for the position of humans as wives of the deities or as a symbol of fecundity. These realities are visibly accentuated in sculpture, making it possible for the Western or outsider approach to arrive at unfounded generalizations about the culture.

Elevating African Epistemologies

Centering the indigenous self as the intelligence through which illumination is cast, striking obscured aspects of culture, is an act that encourages the sustenance of indigenous conceptual forms. These concepts lost their epistemic value

---

[30] Sprague, "How I See the Yoruba."
[31] Doris, "Symptoms and Strangeness."

at the dawn of forced European colonization, when indigenous patterns of expression in Africa were repressed and decentered.[32] Forcing European patterns of thought onto Africans and their cultural systems led to instances of epistemic violation and suicide. The colonization of Africa sought to eviscerate all evidences of indigeneity that sustained the agency of indigenous people, doing so on a scale that destroyed many forms of cultural expression and discredited others. Indigenous thought systems, principles, and value judgments lost their observing phenomena and the philosophical templates that enabled critical evaluations of character, morality, and society.

The linguistic or philosophical turn clamors to restore indigenous concepts and epistemologies for the evaluation of African life and culture. Autoethnographic research falls into this category. The chapters explore the sensitive connections between the indigenous self, the broader collective, and the material possessions reflecting both the indigenous self and the architecture of the culture, embodying and promoting this vision.

African philosophies exist, contrary to the opinion that African worldviews do not constitute philosophies. The arguments that African philosophy should not be compared with African worldviews – because the latter are not defined by the methodologies and theoretical practicalities of academia – reek of Eurocentrism. They also betray a level of provinciality anchored in Western approaches to knowledge. The question of what constitutes African philosophy distracts from more pertinent issues; definition of the matter at hand should not be limited to Western submissions on what constitutes "philosophy." To argue against indigenous worldviews as philosophies is to construct a taxonomy differentiating between philosophy in the popular sense and philosophy in the academic sense.[33] Scholars have hugged both sides of the divide: Anyanwu and More have opined that traditional African worldviews hold as authentic philosophies,[34] while others, such as Bodunrin, Wiredu, and Oladipo, eschew this line of thought.[35]

The dichotomy distracts from a pertinent issue: the purpose of African philosophizing and philosophy. It is not enough to demarcate philosophy in

---

[32] Anibal Quijano, "Coloniality and Modernity/Rationality," *Cultural Studies* 21, no. 2 (2010): 168–178.

[33] Philip Higgs, "Towards an Indigenous African Epistemology of Community in Education Research," *Procedia Social and Behavioral Sciences* 2 (2010): 2414–2421.

[34] See Kelechi C. Anyanwu, "The Problem of Method in African Philosophy," in *The Substance of African Philosophy*, ed. C. S. Momoh (Washington, DC: Brookings Institution, 1989), 122–130; Mabogo P. More, "African Philosophy Revisited," *Alternation* 3, no. 1 (1996): 109–129.

[35] See Peter O. Bodunrin, *Philosophy in Africa: Trends and Perspectives* (Ife: University of Ife Press, 1985); Kwasi Wiredu, *Philosophy and an African Culture* (Cambridge: Cambridge University Press, 2009; and Olusegun Oladipo, *The Idea of African Philosophy: A Critical Study of the Major Orientations in Contemporary African Philosophy* (Ibadan: Molecular Publishers, 1992).

a continent like Africa, populated with postcolonies, along lines of pure philosophy, applied or ethno-philosophy, and other categories.[36] Allowing these arguments to flourish is to neglect the pressing concern of the end of philosophy in Africa. The end of African philosophy should instigate the end of Western thought's dominance in the region.

Serequeberhan has argued that African philosophy should be an immersive, critical, and insightful enterprise through which the rethinking of African life and condition is achieved. This achievement would move these concepts away from the domineering presence of Western thought patterns and concepts.[37] To do this, indigenous concepts must be approached and used as philosophical tools and epistemological framing categories – we must see them for what they are and deploy them as such. Only then can there be a true philosophical turn. More so, only then can philosophy in Africa achieve its utmost significance and usefulness, which is to "contribute effectively towards the amelioration of the human condition, the lived and existing human condition."[38]

Each chapter has used or deployed African epistemic categories and concepts as philosophical mechanisms for exploring indigenous reality. The use and manner of philosophy in the West is significantly different, owing to disparities in cultural formation and history, meaning that the dynamics of philosophizing in Africa must maintain its African stripes. Instead of a perfectionist approach to theories and concepts, making them infallible as critical judgments of abstract reality – as is obtainable in the West – African philosophies should explore, comment on, and critique African social realities. African philosophy and its epistemologies cannot risk being merely a route to perfectionism of thought, and this references the functionality debate. Anyone familiar with African modes of reasoning understands that an emphasis on functionality does not ignore sophistication of thought. That is also one of the contentions of these chapters: even the aesthetic has its sociocultural and pedagogic value.

Several concepts threaded into the chapters for their philosophical components reflect on how African epistemologies aid critical and reflective observation of African life, especially in ways that sustain the defining characteristics of specific ethnicities or nations. The self, as a system of intelligence deploying these components, ensures that the imperative of using African epistemological frames and cultural concepts is sustained to show their bearing on African life; this supports their categorization as critical frames of cosmic and earthly comprehension. By using each self-narrative and art form – or each experience and collected item – as a prism to cast several hues of meaning, I am

---

[36] Higgs, "Indigenous African Epistemology."
[37] Tsenay Serequeberhan, *The Hermeneutics of African Philosophy: Horizon and Discourse* (New York: Routledge, 1994).
[38] Higgs, "Indigenous African Epistemology," 2416.

able to reflect on the cultural past based on which indigenous concept is set against what item. I can also situate the concepts to engender illuminations of collective Yorùbá life, displaying how power dynamics, cultural history, and the nitty-gritty of the Yorùbá reality function on a daily basis.

Are philosophical concepts useful to the development of African life? Do they have meanings that are of ethical, philosophical, and cultural importance? The chapters answer these questions explicitly. When *Inú tútù* as an aesthetic category to create an epistemic frame for understanding postures in sculptures, paintings, photographs, and drawings, or the *Ọmọlúàbí* cultural concept, is addressed, it is because lessons on acceptable behavior and morals takes these formats in the Yorùbá cultural system. Visual markers of moral standards manifest in several aspects of folkloric life. A composed, well-dressed subject in an image, complete with accessories, is a model to be followed by members of society. Visual literacy is elevated as a social means of education, and to dwell on these ideas critically, using personal experiences, is to accentuate their value.

It is possible to use the self as a refracting tool, harnessing the various energies floating within a space for proper cultural representation. The self can be a perspective, constructed to embrace the collective epistemologies necessary to discard the limiting definitions of culture imposed by outsiders. Epistemological materials and ethno-philosophies, such as Onaism, *Àjùmọ̀ṣe*, or *Ọmọlúàbí*, and principles like *Ìlùtí, Opọlọ pípé, Ìfarabalẹ̀, Ìtẹríba, Ìmúra*, and many others offer rich insights into the worldview, characterological functioning, and social composition of the culture. To sieve out instances through narrative, or to use several images for commenting on their manifestations, puts these philosophies on the map and recalls them from the peripheral spaces where they had been concealed as alternative, pseudo-philosophical materials. The self is the recording consciousness and probing voice that gives importance to the representation of culture, which means that it is not only critical but also reflective of culture. Other philosophical concepts, such as *Àyànmọ́, Orí, Ẹlẹ́dá*, and *Kádàrá* are succinct, complex, and critical takes on existential issues and predestination. They are given the robust treatment they deserve in the chapters, relating to the issues and materials treated therein.

Using Kant, Heidegger, or Sartre to explain *Orí* as the seat of individuality would not account for its ubiquitous role as the first part of the body to be molded by sculptors, nor would it explain why large heads on sculpted forms carry a significance that is knowable only to initiates. No such approach can account for abstract representations of the head as visual metaphors of the inner *Orí (Orí inú)* of the metaphysical world. They will not account for the *Orí*'s primacy as a spiritual, mystical, and biological phenomenon – discounting the head's susceptibility to malevolent and benevolent powers, dismissing its synecdochic status, and rejecting its ethereal significance along with its connection to the extraterrestrial world. These approaches are not suitable to accommodate an explanation, however critical, that involves an intersection of the spiritual plane with the physical.

To cite another example, Ọmọlúàbí is more than a submission on filial relationships or communalism. It is a defining bond that holds every Ẹbí, Ará, and Ìdílé together as systems within a system. It does not mean, as some have argued,[39] that the collective subsumes the individual. It is that the individual's unique voice, individualism, and agency still embodies the collective – even when acting autonomously and exercising free will. Higgs has correctly argued that it means "a person depends on others just as much as others depend on him or her. In fact, in terms of such a communitarian view, the individual's life and fulfillment is only to be found in community with others."[40] The concept of Ìwàlẹ̀wà (beauty as character) is yet another example that can only be appreciated for its full philosophical weight within the Yorùbá epistemic and cultural framework.

This does not deny the place of pluralism or the possibility of its universal appeal. The bone of contention is that these concepts and their ethno-philosophical leanings are more than enough to explore the self within the society and vice versa. No Western theory can adequately explain the complex, interesting, and robust Yorùbá culture as thoroughly as its indigenous epistemologies.

Resituating Knowledge

Autoethnographic endeavor and decolonial studies have, among others, one important shared feature: the repositioning of knowledge. In a world where Western cultural patterns and social practices are not only set as standards for other nations to adopt, but are now received as natural ways of existing, non-Western societies must turn to unusual methods of emphasizing and foregrounding their presence and agency. Autoethnography presents exciting and challenging ways of emphasizing the value of African epistemologies and contributions to world knowledge. It also offers productive ways of altering the way African knowledge is received and used by the global knowledge economy whose control centers are in the West. In providing dynamic avenues for members of subaltern cultures to critically make the case for African knowledge and knowledge sources or systems of codification, autoethnography eliminates the limitations against Africans and African knowledge representation. These limitations have capitalist, political, and cultural patterns, with strong influences in the centers of knowledge production such as academia.

---

[39] See Paulin J. Hountondji, *African Philosophy: Myth and Reality* (Bloomington: Indiana University Press, 1996).
[40] Higgs, "Indigenous African Epistemologies," 2417.

The taxonomic, curatorial, and transactional ways the West engages Africa and its knowledge are subverted and overtly rejected when the African critical gaze becomes the channel through which its cultural riches are presented to a global audience. African knowledge ceases to be packaged and branded as exotic, a terminology that collapses multiple traditions, rich in their diversities, into a monolithic whole for the benefit of the West, denying it its dynamism, vibrancy, and functionality.[41] Even in its most seemingly innocent connotations, the terminology reflects the dominance of the Western messianic complex in engaging African knowledge and in deciding how Africans are represented as knowledge producers.

The autoethnographic endeavor allows for the self to exist as a microcosm of culture and to speak for the culture, emphasizing patterns of knowledge encoding, dispersal, and retention in the process of centralizing the culture. The symbiosis between cultural ambassadors and cultural knowledge achieves heightened relevance through the critical avenues the former provides the latter to gain increased visibility. Through autoethnography, Africans in Western institutions can subvert the curricula, whose premises revolve around the idea of Africa uniqueness, greatness, or the lack of both. As explained earlier, autoethnography is about representation of knowledge that is critical through self-narratives with larger implications. This representation takes several forms whose decolonial imperative is expressly manifest.

A summary take on the premise of the works in this "collection of collections" is that they attempt to reconstruct the idea of Africa, especially as exotic or barbaric, that is woven into the modern consciousness by European travelers, Eurocentric ethnologists, and their modern apologists. The "heart of darkness" Conrad and his cohorts speak of, which has informed a great deal of opinions about modern Africa, is simply a fancy that tickles Western imagination and supports its messianic imperative. One important denigrating trope that has emanated from such discourses is the bucolic and unclothed precolonial African. The history of African textiles and sartorial culture influencing the European fabric industry and trade in Africa contradicts the exotic presentation of Africans as walking about in the nude or clothing themselves with leaves and twigs before the European arrival.[42] Traditional sources of knowledge corroborate the idea of Africans not only having cloth but also having a culture of being clothed.[43] Young ones would wear Bàntẹ̀ – which when worn over the genitals takes a triangular form – for play, while girls wore Tòbí, an apron-like garment.[44] Other dress types such as the Yẹrì and Ìlábírù

---

[41] Edward Said, *Orientalism* (New York: Vintage Books, 1978).
[42] Johnson, "Cotton Imperialism"; Nielsen, "History of Textiles"; Oyeniyi, "Dress and Identity."
[43] Oyeniyi, *Dress in the Making*; Lyndersay, *Nigerian Dress*.
[44] Oyeniyi, *Dress in the Making*.

have been identified as having been used as covers over the chest and undergarments respectively.⁴⁵ More so, Yorùbá clothing during this era had its functions as play clothes, work clothes, or clothes for social activities.

Other evidences of a preexisting sartorial culture in the Yorùbá social system are locatable in the *Ifá* corpus, an indigenous science of divination with epistemological, ontological, and spiritual significance that provides knowledge on all spheres of Yorùbá life. The *Òyèkú méjì* and *Òkànràn méjì*⁴⁶ provide narrative evidence of Yorùbá clothing tradition that contradicts fanciful tales of nudity and lack of sartorial awareness from colonialists and European writers. African sartorial taste would condition the choices of European designers and much of the European fabric industry, especially those that sought to break into the African market. The resist methods of the tie and dye (*Àdìrẹ*) were copied by European designers in creating the wax prints that eventually flourished within the African space.⁴⁷ A critical evaluation of clothes naturally yields these histories that redefine what has been projected about Africa. Artistic borrowing between the West and Africa has often been said to be top down, but assessing Yorùbá clothing as part of a collection, both personal and collective, unravels historical knowledge that negates these assumptions. Using cloth as a prism to critically scrutinize some of these preexisting conclusions and rebut Eurocentric opinions that have stereotyped Africa allows African knowledge anchored in African reality to shift to the center of global knowledge production.

The African contribution to global knowledge cannot be gainsaid. In areas of philosophy, religion, anthropology, music, culture, education, medicine, art, and resources (capital and human), Africa has remained a wellspring of influence. The history of global modernity provides evidences of this. Yet, the academia and knowledge-producing centers of the West have appropriated this knowledge source as theirs, rebranded it, and reoffered it back to Africa as global knowledge.⁴⁸ The centers in the West determine the trajectory, ethics, and end product of research, all of which do not favor Africa. They do this through grants and affiliations that determine what should be investigated and what body keeps the findings of the research activities. However, despite its Eurocentric connotations of "taking," research still remains one effective way in which Africans can change their position on the global knowledge-producing scale. Autoethnographic endeavors such as the chapter on textiles perform the necessary interventions.

For instance, engaging textiles as readable texts capable of offering insights into the economic history and industry of the Yorùbá clarifies misconceptions

---

⁴⁵ Oyeniyi, *Dress in the Making*.
⁴⁶ Oyeniyi, *Dress in the Making*.
⁴⁷ Steiner, "Another Image."
⁴⁸ See Smith, *Decolonizing Methodologies*; Overton, "Decolonizing Methodologies."

and also emphasizes ideas that have been associated with the people. Material things have always had a pride of place in Yorùbá cultural fabric. A cloth like *Sányán* is exotic, expensive, and worn by royalty. *Àlàárì* is also worn by kings and other royalty, especially to welcome guests. *Ẹtù* is considered functional cloth, while *Òfì* is considered as prestigious for being associated with elders.

These reveal the presence of an organized sociocultural system prior to colonialism. In addition, they depict the Yorùbá culture as structured, with its material reality reflecting on the philosophies that guide the social order. They contradict prejudicial conclusions by Eurocentric scholars that cultures like that of the Yorùbá were not advanced in politics, economy, or social affairs. European forms of politics, commerce, and education have been held as benchmarks of literacy and civility, so much so that the absence of these is taken as a sign of backwardness or ignorance. These conclusions gloss over the instructive power of folkloric practices. An adolescent can be taught about the social order and how the act of *Ìmúra* can signify one's position through songs about Yorùbá cloth types: "Kíjìpá aṣọ ọlẹ / Òfi aṣọ àgbà / Àgbà tí kì r'ówó r'òfì, kóra kíjìpá / Nítorípé sányán ni baba aṣọ, Ẹtù ni baba èwù / Àláárì ló tẹ le." The translation: *Kíjìpá*, a lazy man's cloth, *Òfì*, an elder's cloth / A poor elder who is incapable of buying *Òfì* should buy *Kíjìpá* / As *Sányán* is the best of cloth, *Ẹtù* is the father of garments / While *Àláárì* is the next in rank.[49] Orality, as an effective tool of education, remains vital to oral-based cultures like that of the Yorùbá.

The undue and reductive juxtaposition of orality with literacy in terms of its facilitation of learning has robbed orality of its efficacy. But, as has been argued by Finnegan, Okpewho, and Sterne, the "great divide," which pits orality and literacy against each other and holds up the latter as an improvement on the former, has only provided room for overgeneralizations and simplifications. Features that show orality as a communicative mode and means of facilitating learning and transfer of cultural literary forms are neither simplistic nor redundant, as has often been claimed.[50]

Some of these features, aiding the literariness of oral forms, have been found in (and to be core components of) print literatures.[51] More so, the rejection of orality as a capable means of philosophizing and educating is a function of the capacity of literacy to negatively affect its oral antecedents.[52] Claims like those

---

[49] See Oyeniyi, *Dress in the Making*, 74.

[50] Ruth Finnegan, "How Oral is Oral Literature?" *Bulletin of the School of Oriental and African Studies* 37, no. 1 (1974): 52–64.

[51] Moradewun Adejumobi, "Revenge of the Spoken Word? Writing, Performance, and New Media in Urban West Africa," *Oral Tradition* 26, no. 1 (2011): 3–26; Daniela Merolla, "Introduction: Orality and Technauriture of African Literatures," *Tydskrif vir Letterkunde* 51, no. 1 (2014): 80–90; Finnegan, *Oral literature in Africa*; Akporobaro, *African Oral Literature*.

[52] Walter Ong, *Orality and Literacy: The Technologizing of the Word* (London: Methuen & Co., 1982).

of Ong that "humanity cannot achieve its fullest potentials without writing"[53] show the ideological premises that have placed orality in a tertiary position in relation to literacy. Engaging writing and its standardization as the most important features in the history of communication[54] are ideologies fueling the Eurocentric rejection of orality, which depicts African societies as undeveloped in their communicative practices.

This could not be more untrue. As depicted in the song above, and others (chants, proverbs, songs) represented in several segments in the chapters in this collection, oral performances in precontact Yorùbá society are well-structured communicative forms. They not only convey African knowledge but instruct on ways in which it is dispersed and used in highlighting important aspects of cultural life. Knowledge not only comprises the non-material and transferable aspects of the social order. It is also made up of the institutions that create knowledge and organize the social order as well as the practices that sustain these institutions. African knowledge can be pushed to the center by engaging several aspects of the Yorùbá cultural and economic institutions, and using the cultural materials associated with each institution in highlighting the importance and dynamism of African knowledge forms, ontology, and epistemology.

This is why the song on laziness in *A Mouth Sweeter than Salt*[55] is an important exposé on the communal rejection of laziness; it also shows how young ones are made to see and are taught the pitfalls indolence. Another example is when women gather together at the workshop of the coiffeuse and exchange narratives, tales, and songs; this gathering is not wanton social behavior, but a practice in enculturation, solidarity, and in the creation of gender awareness. Hair and hair making and other associated practices are methods or ways of educating the Yorùbá in the benefits of civility, appearance, espousing sanctioned domestic qualities, and hair artistry. Some of these African hairstyles, such as *Dídì* (African braids) have gone on to have a pride of place in Western countries, with the essence of female bonding as cultural practices transported to black communities in the diaspora, where they continue to influence parallel non-black communities.

Aside from Africa contributing to the fabric of Western or global cultures – although under less-than-ideal and inhumane circumstances like slavery – it also adds to the global modern knowledge economy. It cannot be denied that Yorùbá cultural forms continue to influence the Western world. The *Ifá* system is being used across the diaspora. Yorùbá fabrics are also being used by Westerners. More so, Yorùbá designs have served as inspiration for Western

---

[53] Ong, *Orality and Literacy*, 14.
[54] Jonathan Sterne, "A Critic of Orality," *Canadian Journal of Communication* 36 (2011): 207–225.
[55] See Falola, *A Mouth Sweeter than Salt*, 426.

designers. Also, African markets such as the Yorùbá continue to influence the imagination and creativity of European designers. In repositioning African knowledge by focusing on its cultural dynamics and through its material components, the transactional ways the West engages with Africa are laid bare. Alongside these revelations are the consequences, among which is the continued denial of the agency of African communities as producers of knowledge. Globalization and glocalization are fanciful and covert ways of denying these agencies, because they remove the spotlight from subaltern communities (communities already trapped in the shadow of advanced economies) by placing them and their contributions in a larger (that is, global) framework of influence.

The force capable of driving the resituating of African knowledge must derive from within the culture's epistemological matrix. The self resides within the heart of the culture, and narratives remain expressive vehicles through which the self realizes itself. Narratives are natural to the human species.[56] Stories or narratives have held a pride of place especially in oral-based cultures, where they perform several didactic and social functions. Narrative is functional, providing coping mechanisms, vehicles of expressing certain philosophies, and means of indoctrinating, instructing or instilling fear. The efficacy of narratives as social-cultural apparatus of control can be seen in how ideas of affinity and solidarity are bound up in it, especially in its consequences as a strategic means of achieving desired ends.

The extent to which a narrative can be (re)constructed to be affective determines the range of its effect. Narratives appeal to the imagination, intellect, or emotions. People act on this, showing solidarity through response. For this reason, narratives are political. To this end, the self and its agenda can exist and be effective through narratives. On the one hand, the self and its actions, belongings, or ideologies are narratives already, considering that each person is a combination of actions, desires, and ideas that cohere to set them apart from others as part of statistics. George Monbiot agrees with this when he describes humans in the light of a "string of facts and figures."[57] On the other hand, the actions that constitute a narrative can be deliberate in order create a narrative politics. When this is done, the narrative becomes a rallying call.

The autoethnographic endeavor with its critical approach to using personal narratives to shed light on obscured broader cultural realities is a perfect domain for the realization of narrative politics. The situating of the self as a matrix of intelligence and setting up of mini-narratives such as artistic collections and memoirs against this critical consciousness to reflect on the culture is a rallying call. There is a mix of logical and emotional functions: personal narratives by default spring from a wealth of passionate experiences

[56] Abbott, "Story-Telling."
[57] Monbiot, "The New Political Story."

that have their defining essences in a larger cultural frame. More so, these experiences are laid out logically to have a boomerang effect on the cultural system that has created both the self and its narratives. In other words, the collection is a narrative that counters the master narratives of the West regarding Africa. The autoethnographic leaning of the narrative is its politics, and it is also anchored in shifting African knowledge to the center by reflecting on it from both the personal and the collective viewpoint.

Remaking the Case for African Art

To understand how an autoethnographic endeavor impacts indigenous culture, we must return to the matter of art and the self. African art has always been functional; its referential, mediumistic, and self-reflexive capacity marks it as a channel for social awareness, cultural elevation, and a fitting tool for autoethnographic purposes. African art, whether narrative, poetry, sculpture, painting, photography, or storytelling, carries society as its direct referent. The consciousness that constructs the art is a representative of the broader culture. This constructive self is a product of the currents that define the culture as a system. In this sense, the self is an aesthetic construct.[58] As a creation of multiple levels of interaction between sociocultural forces, the self is always caught in a process of constant development, progression, and renewal.[59] Its meaning as an essence is always deferred, from one plane of meaning to another and from one social structure to another. This condition marks the self as a narrative, progressive structure whose essence is spread across different points in time and place, or as a collage of all these manifestations.

In this sense, the self must be appreciated in its entirety; it must be viewed as a consciousness fed by specific cultural currents. Inscriptions are made upon the consciousness of the self by shared principles and essential features of culture, and the self ultimately institutionalizes and standardizes aspects of reality to form a unique identity. Because the self is defined by the geospecific or ethnocentric patterns of expression that define its psychical construction, it uniquely acts out these patterns of being.

The self's uniqueness is defined by the degree to which it conforms to or diverges from collective standardized notions of belonging that define the cultural identity. Such a consciousness, creating or probing art, is engaging in patterns of expression that are specific to its culture. At the very least, the culture resonates in the process of creating or exploring art. The self, which is already a narrative, fosters its narrative potency and capabilities, meditational capacity, referentiality, and communicability with the produced art that continues these culture-specific patterns of expression. The art attains an elevated

---

[58] Crites, "Storytime."
[59] Polkinghorne, "Narrative and Self-Concept."

status because it bears these features: when it is critically set against its reference culture and probed by a culturally informed aesthete, critic, or researcher, it achieves its fullest potential. The art draws the concealed currents of its creation to the surface of the discourse, and for this reason African art is often seen as functional. Its aesthetics, on the other hand, are bound in the history of its creation and in its functionality.

Ideological and sociological underpinnings are evoked in the exploration of poems, memoirs, sculptures, paintings, and artworks. The artworks themselves are prisms that house cultural knowledge, while the probing self that engages with it is the illuminating light as an intelligence that ferrets out these meanings. Art's significance as a consolidation of cultural knowledge is reinforced when the probing self models personal experiences into art, applying artwork as lenses through which cultural realities are refracted, reflected, and explored.

Art holds significance on multiple levels: personal, artistic, and communal. Narrating the self or using material aspects of culture to define the self – as is the case with fine art – involves narrating the culture. This is far from the burden of literature that African narratives are said to bear. The self is written within the art, where it thrives and attains its significance. To the extent that every work of art is a narrative, capable of recounting cultural history in its own way, the objects in this study proffer levels of understanding beyond those achievable through self-reflection. By turning self-reflective endeavor into moments of cultural engagement, art has achieved its utmost potential of being relevant beyond itself, its creator, and its burden.

The poetological narration of self and nation are examples of art's refractive and illuminative capacity of when steered by the right mind. Instances where personal encounters intersect with cultural junctures are accentuated because they are the pillars that hold the fabric of cultural reality in place. If a reader encounters satire in a memoir, applied as a tool for social reconstruction, its significance does not stem from how the author has conceived of it or how the critics interpret it in light of the narrative subject's life – its significance stems from its reflections on how culture holds itself and its people accountable in unique ways. If the art and social implications of making hair is reflected in several coiffeurs, it is because the Yorùbá view artistry as an equal combination of cultural significance and artistic consideration.

Ojú inú (critical awareness) is not solely a test of quality or the critical orientation of an individual or an aesthete. It is the ability to decipher, to be patient as an individual, to be at equilibrium and to avoid being impulsive, to be teachable, and to have a sense of artistry. Only artwork can reveal this; all these can be attributed to a person after encountering their artistic handiwork, whether it be hair, painting, or oral rendition. The art becomes a gateway, explored by the chapter and the collection of artwork they engage.

Conclusion: The African and the Collection

Africans, especially the Yorùbá, are linked with their possessions – this cannot be overstated. In the context of culture, the material possessions of an indigenous Yorùbá person determine their standing or character. A collection of fine materials signifies that the Yorùbá is a person with an appreciable taste for fine things – a seeker of beauty, and beauty is character, as the Yorùbá maxim goes. It is more than a maxim; it is a philosophical take that has its epistemic value in the Yorùbá cultural concepts of *Orí*, *Ọmọlúàbí*, and *Àjùmọ̀ṣe*.

"Orí l'ẹwà ẹni" means that the head is one's beauty – damage to the head is damage to the body. The *Ọmọlúàbí* is one who demonstrates and upholds principles that are expected from a cultural ambassador. And the principle of *Àjùmọ̀ṣe* celebrates togetherness; the individual who seeks personal glory is not ambassadorial. A self-absorbed individual deserves censure; the person is an *Òbùrẹ̀wà* (bad/ugly person), being ugly is the opposite of possessing beauty, and beauty is character. This outlook is reflected in sayings such as "Èníyàn laṣọ mi" (humans are my clothing/cover), meaning that one who is alone is never beautiful; without the metaphoric covering, clothes, or material, the cooperative principle of *Àjùmọ̀ṣe* is absent. Having companions is a thing of beauty, and a Yorùbá person with metaphoric or actual materials that are beautiful is a proper Yorùbá. Of course, beauty is problematized in the Yorùbá cultural sphere. It means refinement, moderation, taste, and an appreciation for togetherness rather than referring to mere facial beauty or material extravagance.

The Yorùbá cannot be divorced from the duty or innate desire to collect beauty. In a collection of beautiful things, a person reaches back into the culture. When a person uses these materials as vehicles to reach back into the culture, they are acting as the "I" within a broader "We," fulfilling the cultural mandate that humans and their belongings must enrich the culture or fully represent it – such is the duty of an *Ọmọlúàbí*. "Èníyàn kan kìí jẹ́ àwa" instructs on the importance of this cultural imperative: one person is "I," not "We." The chapters have explored collected arts, poems, and personal narratives so the culture can be duly represented and its epistemologies can find space within the center. That the chapters are personal does not detract from their capacity, or the autoethnographic capacity, to appropriately reflect on culture. After all, the "I" in Yorùbá culture is actually the "We."

BIBLIOGRAPHY

Abbott, P. "Story-Telling and Political Theory." *Soundings: An Interdisciplinary Journal* 74, no. 3-4 (1991): 369-397.

Abiodun, R. "African Aesthetics." *The Journal of Aesthetic Education* 34, no. 4 (2001): 15-23.

———. "African Art Studies: The State of the Discipline." Paper presented at a symposium organized by the National Museum of African Art, Smithsonian Institution, Washington, DC, September 16, 1987.

———. "Ase: The Empowered Word Must Come to Pass." In *Yoruba Art and Language: Seeking the African in African Art*, 53-87. Cambridge: Cambridge University Press, 2014.

———. "We Greet Aso before we Greet its Wearer." In *Yoruba Art and Language: Seeking the African in African Art*, 142-177. Cambridge: Cambridge University Press, 2014.

Abodunrin, J. "Taxonomy of Painting Styles in Nigeria." *Africology: Journal of Pan-African Studies* 10, no. 3 (2017): 234-247.

———. "Thematic Concerns in 21st Century Paintings in Nigerian Art Schools." *Scholars Journals of Arts, Humanities and Social Sciences* 3, no. 3b (2015): 681-691.

Abodunrin, J. A. and A. A. Oladiti. "Growth and Development of Styles of Painting in Contemporary Nigeria." *Research on Humanities and Social Sciences* 5, no. 5 (2015): 190-198.

Abrams, M. H. *A Glossary of Literary Terms.* Fort Worth: Brace Jovanovich, 1993 [New York: Holt, Rinehart & Winston, 1981].

Adejumobi, M. "Revenge of the Spoken Word? Writing, Performance, and New Media in Urban West Africa." *Oral Tradition* 26, no. 1 (2011): 3-26.

Adekunle, G., A. Ogunbiyi, and O. Daramola. "Cutaneous Adornment in the Yoruba of South-Western Nigeria – Past and Present." *International Society of Dermatology* 45, no. 1 (2006): 23-27.

Adeniran, T. "The Dynamics of Peasant Revolt: A Conceptual Analysis of the Agbekoya Parapo Uprising in the Western State of Nigeria." *Journal of Black Studies* 4, no.4 (1974): 363-375.

Adesanya, A. *Carving Wood, Making History: The Fakeye Family, Modernity and Yoruba Woodcarving.* Trenton: Africa World Press, 2012.

Adiji, B. E., B. I. Oladunmiye, and T. I. Ibiwoye. "Visual Documentation of Traditional Nigerian Hair Styles and Designs as a Means of Expressing Social and Cultural Heritage through Photography." *Global Journal of Arts Humanities and Social Sciences* 3, no. 6 (2015): 23–33.

Adler, P. *African Majesty: The Textile Art of the Ashanti and Ewe.* New York: Thames & Hudson, 1995.

Ahmed-Gamgum, A. "Nigeria at 100 Years: The Process and Challenges of Nation Building." *Public Policy and Administration Research* 4, no. 8 (2014): 114–139.

Ajayi, A., O. Familugba, and O. Oyewale. "Agbekoya Protest: It's Implication on Cocoa Production in Western Nigeria, 1960–1968." *International Journal of Development and Sustainability* 7, no. 3 (2018): 1169–1177.

Ajayi, D. *A Woman's Body Is a Country.* Lagos: Ouida Books, 2017.

Ajayi, O. S. *Yoruba Dance: The Semiotics of Movement and Body Attitude in a Nigerian Culture.* Trenton: Africa World Press, 1998.

Akanbi, G. O. and A. A. Jekayinfa. "Reviving the African Culture of 'Omoluabi' in the Yoruba Race as a Means of Adding Value to Education in Nigeria." *International Journal of Modern Education Research* 3, no. 3 (2016): 13–19.

Akinbileje, T. "Symbolic Values of Clothing and Textiles Art in Traditional and Contemporary Africa." *International Journal of Development and Sustainability* 3, no. 4 (2014): 626–641.

Akingbe, N. "Speaking Denunciation: Satire as Confrontation Language in Contemporary Nigerian Poetry." *Afrika Focus* 27, no. 1 (2014): 47–67.

Akinyemi, A. *Orature and Yoruba Riddles.* New York: Palgrave Macmillan Civic Education, Peace Building and the Nigerian Youths. 2015. www.thetidenewsonline.com/2017/07/22/civiceducation-peace-building-and-the-nigerian-youths-2/.

Akporobaro, F. B. *Introduction to African Oral Literature.* Lagos: Princeton Publishing Co., 2012.

Alabi, A. *Telling Our Stories: Continuities and Divergences in Black Autobiographies.* New York: Palgrave, 2005.

Alade, M. "Ori, Ipin ati Kadara, Apa Kini." *Olokun* 10 (1972): 8–10.

Albrecht, M. C. "The Relationship of Literature and Society." *American Journal of Sociology* 59, no. 5 (1954): 425–436.

Aljohani, F. "Magical Realism and the Problem of Self-Identity as Seen in Three Postcolonial Novels." *Arab World English Journal* no. 4 (2016): 73–82.

Alpern, S. B. "What Africans Got for their Slaves: A Master List of European Trade Goods." *History in Africa* 22 (2005): 5–43.

Amole, B. and S. Folaranmi. "Architecture: Indigenous." In *Culture and Customs of the Yoruba,* ed. T. Falola and A. Akinyemi, 171–202. Austin: Pan-African University Press, 2017.

Anderson, B. *Imagined Communities: Reflections on the Origins and Spread of Nationalism.* London: Verso, 1983.

Anderson, T. "From Episodic Memory to Narrative in a Cognitive Architecture." In *Proceedings of the 6th Workshop on Computational Models of Narrative*, ed. M. Finlayson, B. Miller, and R. Ronfard, 1–11. Dagstuhl: Schloss Dagstuhl, 2015.

Andreatta, M. M. "Being a Vegan: A Performative Autoethnography." *Cultural Studies ↔ Critical Methodologies* 15, no. 6 (2015): 477–486.

Andrews, J. "The Photographic Stare." *Philosophy of Photography* 2, no. 1 (2011): 41–56.

Antia, O. *Akwa Ibom Cultural Heritage: Its Incursion by Western Culture and its Renaissance*. Uyo: Abbny Publishers, 2005.

Antze, P. and M. Lambek. "Introduction." In *Tense Past: Cultural Essays in Trauma and Memory*, ed. P. Antze and M. Lambek, xi–2. New York: Routledge, 1996.

Anyanwu, K. C. "The Problem of Method in African Philosophy." In *The Substance of African Philosophy*, ed. C. S. Momoh, 122–130. Washington, DC: Brookings Institution, 1989.

Anyidoho, K. "Ayi Kwei Armah and Our Journey of the Mind." In *Literature and National Consciousness*, ed. E. Emenyonu, 108–117. Ibadan: Heinemann, 1989.

Appiah, A. *The Ethics of Identity*. Princeton: Princeton University Press, 2005.

Aras, G. "Personality and Individual Differences: Literature in Psychology-Psychology in Literature." *Procedia – Social and Behavioral Sciences* 185 (2015): 250–257.

Aremu, P. S. O., N. Umoru-Oke, E. T. Ijisakin, and B. Banjo. "Re-defining Wall Painting of the Yoruba of South-west Nigeria for Cultural Tourism." *WIT Transactions on Ecology and the Environment* 161 (2012): 343–352. www.researchgate.net/publication/268191803.

Aronson, L. "Ijebu Yoruba Aso-Olona: A Contextual and Historical Overview." *African Arts* 25, no. 3 (1992): 52–62.

Arowosegbe, J. O. "African Studies and the Bias of Eurocentricism." *Social Dynamics* 40, no. 2 (2014): 308–321.

Arutyunova, N. D. "Metaphor and Discourse." In *Theory of Metaphor*, 5–33. Moscow: Progress, 1990.

Arva, E. L. "Writing the Vanishing Real: Hyperreality and Magical Realism." *Journal of Narrative Theory* 38, no. 1 (2008): 60–85.

Asakitipki, A. O. "Functions of Hand Woven Textiles among Yoruba Women in Southwestern Nigeria." *Nordic Journal of African Studies* 16, no. 1 (2007): 101–115.

Assmann, J. and J. Czaplicka. "Collective Memory and Cultural Identity." *New German Critique* no. 65 (1995): 125–133.

Atkinson, R. and R. Shiffrin. "Human Memory: A Proposed System and Its Control Processes." In *The Psychology of Learning and Motivation: Advances in Research and Theory*, II, ed. K. W. Spence, 89–195. New York: Academic Press, 1968.

Ayeni-Akeke, A. "Collective Violence in Nigeria: Patterns and Significance." *Institute of African Studies Research Review* 4, no. 2 (1988): 28–49.
Ayodele, J. A. "Time in Yoruba Thoughts." In *African Philosophy: An Introduction*, ed. R. Wright, 93–111. Boston: University Press of America, 1984.
Azeez, S. A. "Gender Dialectics of Yoruba Drum Poetry." *Rupkatha Journal on Interdisciplinary Studies on Humanities* 5, no. 2 (2013): 168–177.
Baddeley, A. and G. Hitch. "Working Memory." In *Recent Advances in Learning and Motivation*, VIII, ed. G. A. Bower, 47–90. New York: Academic Press, 1974.
Bailey, M. "The Meanings of Magic." *Magic, Ritual, and Witchcraft* 1, no. 1 (2006): 1–23.
Baker-Smith, D. "Literature and the Visual Arts." In *Encyclopedia of Literature and Criticism*, ed. M. Coyle, P. Garside, M. Kelsall, and J. Peck, 991–1003. London: Routledge, 1990.
Bakhtin, M. *The Dialogic Imagination: Four Essays*. Austin: University of Texas Press, 1982.
Bamberg, M. "Who am I? Narration and its Contribution to Self and Identity." *Theory & Psychology* 21, no. 1 (2010): 1–22.
Banjoko, C. H. *Visual Art Made Easy*. Lagos: Movic Publication Co., 2009.
Barrington, L. "Introduction." In *After Independence: Making and Protecting the Nation in Postcolonial and Postcommunist State*, ed. L. Barrington, 3–32. Ann Arbor: University of Michigan Press, 2003.
Barry, P. *Beginning Theory: An Introduction to Literary and Cultural Theory*. Manchester: Manchester University Press, 1995.
Barthes, R. *Camera Lucida*, trans. R. Howard. London: Vintage Books, 2000.
——— "Introduction to the Structural Analysis of Narrative." In *Image, Music, Text*, ed. R. Barthes, trans. S. Heath, 79–124. New York: Hill & Wang, 1977.
Bate, D. "Photography and the Colonial Vision." *Third Text* 7, no. 22 (1993): 81–91.
Becker, H. S. "Visual Sociology, Documentary Photography, and Photojournalism: It's (Almost) All a Matter of Context." *Visual Sociology* 10, no. 1–2 (1995): 5–14.
Bennett. J. *The Sage Encyclopedia of Intercultural Competence*. Thousand Oaks: Sage Publications, 2015.
Beoku-Betts, J. "Western Perceptions of African Women in the 19th and Early 20th Centuries." *Africana Research Bulletin* 6, no. 4 (1976): 86–113.
Bernard, C. "Patterns of Change: The Work of Loïs Mailou Jones' Technology in the Arts." Pittsburgh: Carnegie Mellon University. www.anyonecanflyfoundation.org/library/Bernard_on_Mailou_Jones.essay.html.
Bhabha, H. "DissemiNation: Time, Narrative, and the Margins of the Modern Nation." In *Nation and Narration*, ed. H. Bhabha, 291–322. New York: Routledge, 1990.
Blanchard, B. "The Social Significance of Rap and Hip-Hop Culture," *Ethics of Development in a Global Environment (EDGE): Poverty and Prejudice:*

Media and Race. https://web.stanford.edu/class/e297c/poverty_prejudice/mediarace/socialsignificance.htm.

Blom, I., K. Hagemann, and C. Hall, eds. *Nations: Nationalisms and Gender Order in the Long Nineteenth Century.* Oxford: Berg, 2002.

Bodunrin, P. O. *Philosophy in Africa: Trends and Perspectives.* Ife: University of Ife Press, 1985.

Boehmer, E. *Colonial and Postcolonial Literature.* Oxford: Oxford University Press, 1995.

Bolman, L. and T. Deal. *Modern Approaches to Understanding and Managing Organizations.* San Francisco: Jossey-Bass, 1984.

Boukes, M., H. G. Boomgaarden, M. Moorman, and C. H. de Vreese. "At Odds: Laughing and Thinking? The Appreciation, Processing, and Persuasiveness of Political Satire." *Journal of Communication* 65 (2015): 721–744.

Braide, O. O. "Stylistic Features of Contemporary Adire in Nigerian Textile Practice." *Journal of Humanities, Social Science, and Creative Arts* 11, nos. 1 and 2 (2016): 104–116.

Bray, J. M. "The Organization of Traditional Weaving in Iseyin, Nigeria." *Journal of the International African Institute* 38, no. 3 (1968): 270–280.

Brennan, T. "Antonio Gramsci and Postcolonial Theory: 'Southernism.'" *Diaspora: A Journal of Transnational Studies* 10, no. 2 (2001): 143–187.

Briones, V. "Unacala en el realismomágico," *Cuadernos Americanos* 166, no. 5 (1969): 230–235.

Brockmeier, J. "Autobiographical Time." *Narrative Inquiry* 10, no. 1 (2000): 51–73.

Brock-Utne, B. "Researching Language and Culture in Africa Using an Autoethnographic Approach." *International Review of Education* 64, no. 6 (2018): 713–735.

Bryant, C. "The Language of Resistance? Czech Jokes and Joke-Telling under Nazi Occupation, 1943–45." *Journal of Contemporary History* 41, no. 1 (2006): 133–151.

Buchler, J. *The Main of Light: On the Concept of Poetry.* New York: Oxford University Press, 1974.

Burnett, R. *How Images Think.* Cambridge, MA: MIT Press, 2004.

Bušková, K. "The Role of Literature in Reconciling Trauma on Personal and Social Level." *Bohemica Litteraria* 16, no. 2 (2003): 83–91.

Caldicott, E. and A. Fuchs. "Introduction." In *Cultural Memory: Essays on European Literature and History,* ed. E. Caldicott and A. Fuchs, 11–32. Oxford: Peter Lang, 2003.

Caldwell, P. M. "A Hair Piece: Perspectives on the Intersection of Race and Gender." In *Critical Race Theory: The Cutting Edge,* ed. R. Delgado and J. Stefancic, 275–285. Philadelphia: Temple University Press, 2000.

Calhoun, C. "Nationalism and Ethnicity." *Annual Review of Sociology* 19 (1993): 211–239.

Canizares, B. R. *Eshu-Eleggua Elegbara.* New York: Original Publications, 2000.

Carroll, K. K. and D. F. Jamison. "African-Centered Psychology, Education and the Liberation of African Minds: Notes on the Psycho-Cultural Justification for Reparations." *Race, Gender & Class* 18, no. 1-2 (2011): 52-72.

Casely-Hayford, G. "The Powerful Stories that Shaped Africa." Filmed August 2017 in Arusha. TED video, 19:54. www.ted.com/talks/gus_casely_hayford_ the_powerful_stories_that_shaped_africa

Chanady, A. B. *Magical Realism and the Fantastic: Resolved versus Unresolved Antinomy*. New York and London: Garland Publishing, 1985.

Chandrashekar, S. "Not a Metaphor: Immigrant of Color Autoethnography as a Decolonial Move." *Cultural Studies ↔ Critical Methodologies* 18, no. 1 (2018): 72-79.

Chang, H. *Autoethnography as Method*. Walnut Creek, CA: Left Coast Press, 2008.

Chappel, T. J. H. "A Woodcarving from Abeokuta." *African Arts* 15, no. 1 (1981): 38-43.

Chatterjee, M. *Philosophical Inquiries*. Delhi: Motilal Banarsidas, 1968.

Chawla, D. and A. Atay. "Introduction: Decolonizing Autoethnography." *Cultural Studies ↔ Critical Methodologies* 18, no.1 (2018): 3-8.

Chepkuto, P. K. and S. Kipsang. "The Social Sciences and Humanities in Africa: Which Way Forward?" *International Journal of Academic Research in Business and Social Sciences* 3, no. 12 (2013):66-78.

Cohen, B. B. *Writing about Literature*. Chicago: Scott, Foresmann & Co., 1973.

Cohen, P. "Theories of Myth." *Man* 4, no. 3 (1969): 337-353.

Connor, W. "A Nation is a Nation, is an Ethnic Group, is a . . . ." *Ethnic and Racial Studies* 1, no. 4 (1978): 379-400.

Cordwell, J. M. "The Arts and Aesthetics of the Yoruba." *African Arts* 16, no. 2 (1983): 56-100.

Cortes Santiago, I., N. Karimi, and Z. R. Arvelo Alicea. "Neoliberalism and Higher Education: A Collective Autoethnography of Brown Women Teaching Assistants." *Gender and Education* 29, no.1 (2017): 48-65.

Craig, B. "Selected Themes in the Literature on Memory and Their Pertinence to Archives." *The American Archivist* 65 (2002): 276-289.

Cresswell, T. *Place: A Short Introduction*. Oxford: Oxford University Press, 2004.

Crites, S. "Storytime: Recollecting the Past and Projecting the Future." In *Narrative Psychology: The Storied Nature of Human Conduct*, ed. T. R. Sarbin, 152-173. New York: Praeger, 1986.

Curtin, P. D. *The Image of Africa: British Ideas and Action, 1780-1850*. Madison: University of Wisconsin Press, 1964.

Danesi, M. *Messages, Signs, and Meaning*. Ontario: Canadian Scholars' Press Inc., 2004.

Dasylva, A. "The Archivist as Muse: Toyin Falọla's Experimentation with Alternative History in A Mouth Sweeter than Salt." In *Toyin Falola: The Man, the Mask, the Muse*, ed. N. Afolabi, 735-764. Durham: Carolina Academic Press, 2010.

Songs of Odamolugbe. Ibadan: Kraftgriots, 2006.

Davies, C. "Nationalism: Discourse and Practice." In *Practising Feminism: Identity, Difference and Power*, ed. N. Charles, and F. Hughes-Freeland, 156–179. New York: Routledge, 1996.

Davis, J. E. "Narratives and Social Movements: The Power of Stories." In *Stories of Change: Narrative and Social Movements*, 3–30. New York: State University of New York Press, 2002.

de Sousa, S. B. "General Introduction: Reinventing Social Emancipation: Toward New Manifestos." In *Democratizing Democracy: Beyond the Liberal Democratic Canon*, ed. S. B. de Sousa, I, xvii–xxxiii. London: Verso, 2005.

Dewan, M. "Understanding Ethnography: An 'Exotic' Ethnographer's Perspective." In *Asian Qualitative Research in Tourism*, ed. P. Mura and C. Khoo-Lattimore, 185–203. Singapore: Springer, 2018.

Dickinson, P. "'Orality in Literacy': Listening to Indigenous Writing," *Canadian Journal of Native Studies* 14, no. 2 (1994): 319–340.

Dickson, A. and K. Holland. "Hysterical Inquiry and Autoethnography: A Lacanian Alternative to Institutionalized Ethical Commandments." *Current Sociology* 65, no. 1 (2017): 133–148.

Doris, D. "Symptoms and Strangeness in Yoruba Anti-Aesthetics." *African Arts* 38, no. 4 (2005): 24–31.

"The Unfunctioning Baby and Other Spectacular Departures from the Human in Yoruba Visual Culture." *RES: Anthropology and Aesthetics* 49/50 (2006): 115–138.

Drewal, H. "Art and Perception of Women in Yoruba Culture." *Cahiers d'Études Africaines* 17, no. 68 (1977): 545–567.

"Arts and Ethos of the Ijebu." In *Yoruba: Nine Centuries of African Art and Thought*, ed. H. J. Drewal, J. Pemberton III, R. Abiodun, and A. Wardwell, 117–145. New York: Center for African Art and Harry N. Abrams Inc., 1989.

Drewal, H. J., J. Pemberton III, R. Abiodun, and A. Wardwell, eds. *Yoruba: Nine Centuries of African Art and Thought*. New York: Center for African Art and Harry N. Abrams Inc., 1989.

Dubey, A. "Literature and Society." *IOSR Journal of Humanities and Social Science (IOSR-JHSS)* 9, no. 6 (2013): 84–85.

Durant, S. "Fostering Coexistence between People and Nature." *ZSL Science Review* 17 (2016): 18–19.

Durkheim, E. *Incest: The Nature and the Origin of the Taboo*. New York: Lyle Stuart, 1963.

Dutta, M. J. "Autoethnography as Decolonization, Decolonizing Autoethnography: Resisting to Build our Homes." *Cultural Studies ↔ Critical Methodologies* 18, no. 1 (2018): 94–96.

Earl, M., ed. *Perspectives on Management*. Oxford: Oxford University Press, 1983.

Eco, U. *A Theory of Semiotics*. Bloomington: Indiana University Press, 1976.

Edensor, T. *National Identity, Popular Culture and Everyday Life*. Oxford: Berg, 2002.

Ekpo, D. "Africa without Africanism: Post-Africanism vs. Indigenous Knowledge Systems, Culture/Art." In *The Arts and Indigenous Knowledge Systems in a Modernized Africa*, ed. R. de Lange, I. Stevens, R. Kruger, and M. Sirayi, 1–28. Newcastle upon Tyne: Cambridge Scholars Publishing, 2018.

"From Negritude to Post-Africanism." *Third Text* 24, no. 2 (2010): 177–187.

"Towards a Post-Africanism: Contemporary African Thought and Postmodernism." *Textual Practice* 9, no. 1 (1995): 121–135.

Eliot, T. S. *The Sacred Wood: Essays on Poetry and Criticism.* 1921. www.startbinghamton.com.

"Tradition and the Individual Talent." *Perspecta* 19 (1982): 36–42.

Ellis, C. *The Ethnographic I: A Methodological Novel about Autoethnography.* Walnut Creek, CA: AltaMira Press, 2004.

Ellis, C., T. E. Adams, and A. P. Bochner. "Autoethnography: An Overview." *Historical Social Research/Historische Sozialforschung* 36, no. 4 (2011): 273–290.

Ellis, S. and G. ter Haar. "Religion and Politics: Taking African Epistemologies Seriously." *Journal of Modern African Studies* 45, no. 3 (2007): 385–401.

Epstein, J. "Why do we Read Biographies?" Presentation at Hillsdale College, Hillsdale, MI, January 2016; "'Why do we Read Biographies?' - Joseph Epstein," YouTube Video, 42:55. www.youtube.com/watch?v=IY_-S5_Lnbg.

Erikson, E. H. *Childhood and Society.* New York: Norton, 1963.

Erll, A. "Cultural Memory Studies: An Introduction." In *Cultural Memory Studies: An International and Interdisciplinary Handbook*, ed. A. Erll and A. Nünning, 1–18. Berlin and New York: De Gruyter, 2008.

Etuk, U. *Religion and Cultural Identity.* Ibadan: Hope Publications, 2002.

Falola, T. *The African Diaspora: Slavery, Modernity and Globalization.* Rochester: University of Rochester Press, 2013.

Colonialism and Violence in Nigeria. Indianapolis: Indiana University Press, 2009.

Counting the Tiger's Teeth: An African Teenager's Story. Ann Arbor: University of Michigan Press, 2016.

Culture and Customs of Nigeria. Westport: Greenwood Press, 2001.

The History of Nigeria. Westport: Greenwood Press, 1999.

Ibàdàn: Foundation Growth and Change 1830–1960. Ibadan: Bookcraft, 2012.

In Praise of Greatness: The Poetics of African Adulation. Durham: Carolina Academic Press, 2019.

Key Events in African History: A Reference Guide. Westport: Greenwood Press: 2002.

A Mouth Sweeter than Salt: An African Memoir. Ibadan: Bookcraft, 2013.

Nationalism and African Intellectuals. Rochester: University of Rochester Press, 2001.

The Power of African Culture. Rochester: University of Rochester Press, 2003.

Violence in Nigeria: The Crisis of Religious Politics and Secular Ideologies. Rochester: University of Rochester Press, 1998.

Yoruba Gurus: Indigenous Production of Knowledge in Africa. Trenton: Africa World Press Inc., 1999.

Falola, T. and A. Adesanya. *Etches on Fresh Waters*. Durham: Carolina Academic Press, 2008.

Falola, T. and V. Bahl. *Scoundrels of Deferral: Poems to Redeem Reflection*. Durham: Carolina Academic Press, 2006.

Faris, W. *Ordinary Enchantments: Magical Realism and the Remystification of Narrative*. Nashville: Vanderbilt University Press, 2004.

Fass, P. S. "The Memoir Problem." *Reviews in American History* 34, no. 1 (2006): 107–123.

Fayemi, A. D. "Time in Yoruba Culture." *al-Hikmat* 36 (2016): 27–41.

Fine, G. A. "Ten Lies of Ethnography: Moral Dilemmas of Field Research." *Journal of Contemporary Ethnography* 22, no. 3 (1993): 267–294.

Finnegan, R. "How Oral is Oral Literature?" *Bulletin of the School of Oriental and African Studies* 37, no. 1 (1974): 52–64.

Oral Literature in Africa. London: Oxford University Press, 1970.

Firth, R., ed. *Man and Culture: An Evaluation of the Work of Bronislaw Malinowski*, Malinowski Collected Works 10. London: Routledge & Kegan Paul, 1957.

Folaranmi, S. A. and A. N. Umoru-Oke. "Orí (Head) as an Expression of Yorùbá Aesthetic Philosophy." *Mediterranean Journal of Social Sciences* 4, no. 9 (2018): 59–70.

Foster, N. "Photography and The Gaze: The Ethics of Vision Inverted." *Parallax* 12, no. 2 (2008): 78–92.

Foucault, M. *Society Must Be Defended*. New York: Picador, 2003.

Foucault, M., M. Morris, and P. Patton. *Power, Truth, Strategy*. Sydney: Feral Publications, 1979.

Frazer, J. *The Golden Bough*. New York: Macmillan, 1950.

Freeman, M. "Culture, Narrative, and the Poetic Construction of Selfhood." *Journal of Constructivist Psychology* 12, no. 2 (2010): 99–116.

Rewriting the Self: History, Memory, Narrative. London: Routledge, 1993.

Furman, R. "Poetry and Narrative as Qualitative Data: Explorations into Existential Theory." *Indo-Pacific Journal of Phenomenology* 7 (2007): 1–9.

Gates, H. L. *The Signifying Monkey: A Theory of African-American Literary Criticism*. Oxford: Oxford University Press, 1988.

Gellner, E. *Nations and Nationalism*. Oxford: Basil Blackwell, 1983.

Glowacki-Dudka, M., M. Treff, and I. Usman. "Research for Social Change: Using Autoethnography to Foster Transformative Learning." *Adult Learning* 16, no. 3–4 (2005): 30–31.

Goldwasser, D. and X. Zhang. "Understanding Satirical Articles Using Common-Sense." *Transactions of the Association for Computational Linguistics* 4 (2016): 537–549.

Goodson, I. "The Rise of the Life Narrative." *Teacher Education Quarterly* 33 (2006): 7–21. www.researchgate.net/publication/253187338_The_Rise_of_the_Life_Narrative.

Greenfeld, L. "The Emergence of Nationalism in England and France: A Study in the Sociology of National Identity." *Research in Political Sociology* 5 (1991): 333–370.

Guerrero, A. L. "Narrative as Resource for the Display of Self and Identity: The Narrative Construction of an Oppositional Identity." *Colombian Applied Linguistic Journal* 13, no. 2 (2011): 88–99.

Guibernau, M. "Anthony D. Smith on Nation and National Identity: A Critical Assessment." *Nation and Nationalism* 10, no. 1 and 2 (2004).

Nationalisms: The Nation-State and Nationalism in the Twenty-First Century. Cambridge: Polity, 1996.

Gul, T. and T. Javed. "Humour and Satire in Urdu Literature." *The Dialogue* 7, no. 2 (2012): 178–185.

Gvozden, V. "Magical Realism and the Politics of Narrative: Historical Postmodernism in the Contemporary Serbian Novel." *World Literature Studies* 8 (2016): 64–75.

Hackett, J. I. "Yoruba: Nine Centuries of African Art and Thought by Henry John Drewal, John Pemberton, and Rowland Abiodun." *Journal of Religion in Africa* 21, no. 3 (1991): 280–283.

Halbwachs, M. *The Collective Memory*. New York: Harper & Row, 1980.

Hale, T. A. "Griottes: Female Voices from West Africa." *Research in African Literatures* 25, no. 3 (1994): 71–91.

Hall, S. "The Question of Cultural Identity." In *Modernity: An Introduction to Modern Societies*, ed. S. Hall, D. Held, D. Hubert, and K. Thompson, 595–634. Malden: Blackwell, 1996.

Hancock, G. "An Interview with Jack Hodgins." *Canadian Fiction Magazine* 32/33 (1980): 33–63.

Haraway, D. "Situated Knowledges: The Science Question in Feminism and the Privilege of Partial Perspective." *Feminist Studies* 14, no. 3 (1988): 575–599.

Harlow, B. *Resistance Literature*. New York: Methuen, 1987.

Hartman, G. *The Longest Shadow: In the Aftermath of the Holocaust*. Bloomington: Indiana University Press, 1996.

Haverkampf, A. "The Memory of Pictures: Roland Barthes and Augustine on Photography." *Comparative Literature* 45, no. 3 (1993): 258–279.

Hawkes, T. *Structuralism and Semiotics*. New York: Methuen, 1977.

Heaney, S. *The Redress of Poetry*. New York: Noonday Press, 1995.

Henrich, J., S. J. Heine, and A. Norenzayan. "The Weirdest People in the World?" *Behavioral and Brain Sciences* 33 (2010): 61–135.

Higgs, P. "Towards an Indigenous African Epistemology of Community in Education Research." *Procedia Social and Behavioral Sciences* 2 (2010): 2414–2421.

Hill, B. "Ben Jonson's Theory and Use of Satire in Comedy." MA thesis, Boston University, 1933. https://hdl.handle.net/2144/8267.
Hirsch, H. *Genocide and the Politics of Memory: Studying Death to Preserve Life*. Chapel Hill: University of North Carolina Press, 1995.
Hirschheim, R. and N. Newman. "Symbolism and Information Systems Development: Myth, Metaphor and Magic." *Information Systems Research* 2, no. 1 (1991): 29–62.
Hobsbawm, E. *Nations and Nationalism since 1780: Programme, Myth, Reality*. New York: Cambridge University Press, 1990.
Holden, L. *Encyclopedia of Taboos*. Oxford: ABC-CLIO Ltd., 2000.
Holman, H. *A Handbook of Literature*. Indianapolis: Odyssey Press, 1977.
Holman Jones, S. "Living Bodies of Thought: The 'Critical' in Critical Autoethnography." *Qualitative Inquiry* 22, no. 4 (2016): 228–237.
Honary, S. "Comics and Cultures: Narrating the Self and Other in Persepolis." *Nätverket* 18 (2013): 51–57.
Hopkins, A. G. *An Economic History of West Africa*. New York: Columbia University Press, 1973.
Hountondji, P. J. *African Philosophy: Myth and Reality*. Bloomington: Indiana University Press, 1996.
Hühn, P. "Transgeneric Narratology: Application to Lyric Poetry." In *The Dynamics of Narrative Form: Studies in Anglo-American Narratology*, ed. J. Pier, 139–158. Berlin and New York: De Gruyter, 2004.
Hyvärinen. M. "Analyzing Narratives and Story-Telling." *Alasuutari: Social Research Methods* (2009): 447–460.
"Foreword: Life Meets Narrative." In *Life and Narrative: The Risks and Responsibilities of Storying Experience*, ed. B. Schiff, A. E. McKim, and S. Patron, ix–xxv. New York: Oxford University Press, 2017.
Idang, G. "African Culture and Values." *Phronimon* 16, no. 2 (2015): 97–111.
Idowu, E. B. *Olódùmarè: God in Yoruba Belief*. Ibadan: Longmans, 1962.
Ikoro, E. A. "Painting and Society in Modern Nigeria." *International Journal of Arts and Humanities* 3, no. 11 (2015): 87–93.
Imbert, A. *El Realismomágico y Otrosensayos*. Caracas: Monte Avila, 1976.
Inac, H. and F. Unal. "The Construction of National Identity in Modern Times: Theoretical Perspective." *International Journal of Humanities and Social Science* 3, no. 11 (2013): 223–232.
Irivwieri, G. O. "Onaism: An Artistic Model of Yoruba Civilization in Nigeria." *An International Multi-Disciplinary Journal, Ethiopia* 4, no. 3a (2010): 234–246.
Isaacs, E. "Ethnography: Ellen Isaacs at TEDxBroadway." Filmed in March 2013 at Tedx Broadway. New York City. Video, 12:02. www.youtube.com/watch?v=nV0jY5VgymI.
Jameson, F. "Third-World Literature in the Era of Multinational Capitalism." *Social Text* 15 (1986): 65–88.
Jayawardene, S. M. and S. McDougal. "Francis Cress Welsing's Contributions to Africana Studies Epistemology." *Journal of Black Studies* 48, no. 1 (2017): 43–56.

Johnson, M. "Cotton Imperialism in West Africa." *African Affairs* 73, no. 291 (1974): 178–187.
Johnson, S. *The History of the Yorubas*. Lagos: CSS Bookshops, 1921.
Johnson, T. A., and T. Bankhead. "Hair It Is: Examining the Experiences of Black Women with Natural Hair." *Open Journal of Social Sciences* 2 (2014): 86–100.
Johnson, Z. "Teaching Prince as Critical Pedagogy: An Autoethnography." *Journal of African American Studies* 21, no. 3 (2017): 337–352.
Joselit, D. "Painting Beside Itself." *October* 130, no. 10 (2009): 125–134.
Julien, E. "African Literature." In *Africa*, ed. P. Martin and P. O'Meara, 295–312. Bloomington: Indiana University Press, 1995.
Kalliney, P. "East African Literature and the Politics of Global Reading." *Research in African Literatures* 39, no. 1 (2008): 1–23.
Kaman, L. J. ""Conceptual Patterns in Yoruba Culture." Paper presented at the Ninth International Congress of Anthropological and Ethnological Sciences, 1973; repr. in *Language and Thought*, ed. W. C. McCormack and S. A. Wurm, 359–389. The Hague: Mouton, 1977.
Kambon, K. K. K. and J. A. Baldwin. *The African Personality in America: An African-Centered Framework*. Tallahassee: Nubian Nation Publications, 1992.
Kasikhan, H. "The Absence of 'Paucity' & 'Momentariness': Two New Components of Magical Realism in Günter Grass's The Tin Drum." *Journal of Teaching Language Skills* 4, no. 2 (2012): 155–169.
Kesić, V. "Gender and Ethnic Identities in Transition." In *From Gender to Nation*, ed. E. Iveković and J. Mostov, 63–80. Ravenna: Longo Editore Ravenna, 2001.
Klein, K. "On the Emergence of Memory in Historical Discourse." *Representations* 69, Special Issue (2000): 127–150.
Klimkiewicz, A. "Self-Translation as Broken Narrativity: Towards an Understanding of the Self's Multilingual Dialogue." In *Self-Translation: Brokering Originality in Hybrid Culture*, ed. A. Cordingley, 189–201. London and New York: Bloomsbury, 2013.
Knipp, T. "English-Language Poetry." In *A History of Twentieth-Century African Literatures*, ed. O. Owomoyela, 105–137. Lincoln: University of Nebraska Press, 1993.
Koot, S. "Perpetuating Power through Autoethnography: My Research Unawareness and Memories of Paternalism among the Indigenous Hai// om in Namibia." *Critical Arts* 30, no. 6 (2016): 840–854.
Korotchenko, E. and V. Petrenko, "Metaphor as a Basic Mechanism of Art (Painting)." *Psychology in Russia: State of the Art* 1, no. 5 (2012): 532–567.
Krishnamurty, J. *The First and the Last Freedom*. Chennai: Krishnamurty Foundation India, 1954.
Krishnan, M. "The Storyteller Function in Contemporary Nigerian Narrative." *Journal of Commonwealth Literature* 49, no. 1 (2014): 29–45.

Kundera, M. *The Curtain*, trans. L. Asher. New York: HarperCollins, 2005.
Kuzmanic, M. "Collective Memory and Social Identity: A Social Psychological Exploration of the Memory of the Disintegration of Former Yugoslavia." *Horizons of Psychology* 17, no. 2 (2008): 5–26.
LaBrack, B. "Disciplinary Approaches to Culture: Anthropology." In *The Sage Encyclopedia of Intercultural Competence*, ed. J. M. Bennett, 245–248. Thousand Oaks, CA: Sage Publications, 2015.
Lakoff, G. and M. Johnson *Metaphors We Live by*. London: University of Chicago Press, 1980.
Laney, C. and E. Loftus. "Traumatic Memories Are Not Necessarily Accurate Memories." *Canadian Journal of Psychiatry* 50, no. 13 (2005): 823–828.
Laplanche, J. and J. Pontalis. *The Language of Psychoanalysis*, trans. Donald Nicholson Smith. London: Hogarth and Institute of Psychoanalysis, 1973.
Lawal, B. "Àwòrán: Representing the Self and Its Metaphysical Other in Yoruba Art." *The Art Bulletin* 83, no. 3 (2001): 498–526.
"The Living Dead: Art and Immortality among the Yoruba of Nigeria." *Journal of the International African Institute* 47, no. 1 (1977): 50–61.
"The Significance of the Head in Yoruba Sculpture." *Journal of Anthropological Research* 41, no.1 (1985): 91–103.
Leitch, V. B., ed. *The Norton Anthology of Theory and Criticism*. New York: W. W. Norton & Company, 2001.
Levinas, E. "Reality and its Shadow." In *The Levinas Reader*, ed. and trans. S. Hand, 129–143. Oxford: Blackwell, 1989.
Lewis, S. "The Racial Bias Built into Photography," *New York Times*, April 25, 2019. www.nytimes.com/2019/04/25/lens/sarah-lewis-racial-bias-photography.html
Liechti, O. and T. Ichikawa. "A Digital Photography Framework Enabling Affective Awareness in Home Communication." *Personal and Ubiquitous Computing* 4, no. 1 (2000): 232–239.
Lincoln, Y. S., and E. M. González y González. "The Search for Emerging Decolonizing Methodologies in Qualitative Research: Further Strategies for Liberatory and Democratic Inquiry." *Qualitative Inquiry* 14, no. 5 (2008): 784–805.
Lodge, D. *The Art of Fiction*. London: Vintage, 2011.
Lotfi, N. "A Unique Approach of Memory Narrative Therapy in Diasporic Contexts: An Analysis of *The Bonesetter's Daughter* and *The Kitchen God's Wife* by Amy Tan." *Theory and Practice in Language Studies* 4, no. 9 (2014): 1912–1917.
Lowenthal, D. *The Past Is a Foreign Country*. Cambridge: Cambridge University Press, 1985.
Lucaites, J. L. and C. M. Condit. "Reconstructing Narrative Theory: A Functional Perspective." *Journal of Communication* 35, no. 4 (1985): 90–108.
Luna, I. and A. Rosa. "Memory, History and Narrative: Shifts of Meaning when (Re)constructing the Past." *Europe's Journal of Psychology* 8, no. 2 (2012): 300–310.

Luyaluka, K. L. "An Essay on Naturalized Epistemology of African Indigenous Knowledge." *Journal of Black Studies* 47, no. 6 (2016): 497–523.
Lyndersay, D. *Nigerian Dress, the Body Honoured: The Costume Arts of Traditional Nigerian Dress from Early History to Independence.* Lagos: Centre for Black and African Arts and Culture, 2011.
Madden, F. "Creating Coexistence between Humans and Wildlife: Global Perspectives on Local Efforts to Address Human–Wildlife Conflict." *Human Dimensions of Wildlife* 9 (2004): 247–257.
Mai, N. "Mobile Orientations: An Autoethnography of Tunisian Professional Boyfriends." *Sexualities* 20, no. 4 (2017): 482–496.
Malinowski, B. *Magic, Science and Religion and Other Essays.* Boston: Beacon Press, 1948.
Mambrol, N. "The Textuality of History and the Historicity of Texts," Literariness, October 17, 2016. https://literariness.org/2016/10/17/the-textuality-of-history-and-the-historicity-of-texts/
Manyika, S. L. *In Dependence.* Abuja: Cassava Republic, 2008.
Maracle, L. *Oratory: Coming to Theory.* North Vancouver: Gallerie Publications, 1990.
Margolis, J. Z. "Towards a Speech Act Theory of Literary Discourse by Mary Louise Pratt." *Journal of Aesthetics and Art Criticism* 36, no. 2 (1977): 225–228.
Martín, A. "Humor and Violence in Cervantes." In *The Cambridge Companion to Cervantes*, ed. A. J. Cascardi, 160–185. Cambridge: Cambridge University Press, 2002.
Masaka, D. "The Prospects of Ending Epistemicide in Africa: Some Thoughts." *Journal of Black Studies* 49, no. 3 (2018): 284–301.
Mashiya, N. "Learning in Childhood: An Autoethnography of Girl Childrearing Practices and Identity Construction in Southern Africa." *Gender & Behaviour* 16, no. 1 (2018): 10739–1047.
Mayer, T., ed. *Gender Ironies of Nationalism: Sexing the Nation.* London and New York: Routledge, 2000.
Mazama, M. A. "Afrocentricity and African Spirituality." *Journal of Black Studies* 33, no. 2 (2002): 218–234.
Mbiti, J. *African Religions and Philosophy.* New York: Praeger, 1969.
McCall, D. "The Marvelous Chicken and Its Companion in Yoruba Art and Myth." *Paideuma* 24 (1978): 131–146.
McClintock, A. "Family Feuds: Gender, Nationalism and the Family." *Feminist Review* 44 (1993): 61–80.
McLuhan, M. *The Medium Is the Message: An Inventory of Effects.* New York: Bantam Books, 1967.
Medie, P. A. and A. J. Kang. "Power, Knowledge and the Politics of Gender in the Global South." *European Journal of Politics and Gender* 1, no. 1–2 (2018): 37–53.
Medina, J. "Toward a Foucaultian Epistemology of Resistance: Counter-Memory, Epistemic Friction, and Guerrilla Pluralism." *Foucault Studies* 12 (2011): 9–35.

Meehan, K. "Decolonizing Ethnography: Spirit Possession and Resistance in 'Tell my Horse.'" *Obsidian* 9, no. 1 (2008): 59–73.
Mercer, K. "Black Hair/Style Politics." In *Out There: Marginalization and Contemporary Cultures*, ed. R. Ferguson, M. Gever, T. T. Minh-ha, and C. West, 247–264. New York: New Museum of Contemporary Art, 1990.
Merolla, D. "Introduction: Orality and Technauriture of African Literatures." *Tydskrif vir Letterkunde* 51, no. 1 (2014): 80–90.
Meyerowitz, E. R. "Wood-Carving in the Yoruba Country To-day." *Journal of the International African Institute*. 14, no. 2 (1943): 66–70.
Microsoft. "Hair." Microsoft® Encarta®. Redmond: Microsoft Corporation, 2009.
Mignolo, W. "Cosmopolitanism and the De-Colonial Option." *Studies in Philosophy and Education* 29, no. 2 (2010): 111–127.
    The Darker Side of the Renaissance: Literacy, Territoriality, and Colonization. Ann Arbor: University of Michigan Press, 1995.
    Local Histories/Global Designs: Coloniality, Subaltern Knowledges, and Border Thinking. New York: Princeton University Press, 2000.
Mikics, D. "Derek Walcott and Alejo Carpentier: Nature, History, and the Caribbean Writer." In *Magical Realism: Theory, History, Community*, ed. L. Zamora and W. B. Faris, 371–404. Durham: Duke University Press, 1993.
Miller, G. A. *Psychology: The Science of Mental Life*. New York: Harper & Row, 1962.
Miller, T. R. "Hair in African Art and Culture." *American Anthropologist* 103, no. 1 (2001): 182–188.
Misztal, B. *Theories of Social Remembering*. Philadelphia: Open University Press, 2003.
Mohammed, K. "The Role of History, Historiography and Historian in Nation Building." *International Journal of Humanities and Social Science Invention* 2, no. 7 (2013): 50–57.
Monbiot, G. "The New Political Story That Could Change Everything." Filmed July 2019 in Edinburgh, Scotland. TED video, 15:07. www.ted.com/talks/george_monbiot_the_new_political_story_that_could_change_everything#t-10426.
Moors, A. "On Autoethnography." *Ethnography* 18, no.3 (2017): 387–389.
More, M. P. "African Philosophy Revisited." *Alternation* 3, no. 1 (1996): 109–129.
Morreira, S. "Steps towards Decolonial Higher Education in Southern Africa? Epistemic Disobedience in the Humanities." *Journal of Asian and African Studies* 52, no. 3 (2017): 287–301.
Mraz, W. "Albums as Archives." *History of Photography* 2, no. 2 (1978): 176–178.
Mugambi, M. "Forget Your Past, Thank Colonialism!" *The People: People's Digest*, January 23–29, 1998.
Mutiso, G. *Socio-Political Thought in African Literature*. New York: Barnes & Noble, 1974.
Ndlovu-Gatsheni, S. J. "Decoloniality as the Future of Africa: Decoloniality, Africa, Power, Knowledge, Being." *History Compass* 13, no. 10 (2015): 485–496.

Nelson, K. and R. Fivush. "The Emergence of Autobiographical Memory: A Social Cultural Developmental Theory." *Psychological Review* 111, no. 2 (2004): 486–511.

Ngwenya, T. H. "The Historical Dimension of South African Autobiography." *Alternation* 7, no. 1 (2000): 1–4.

Nicoll, A. *An Introduction to Dramatic Theory*. New York: Brentano's, 1924.

Nielsen, R. "The History and Development of Wax-Printed Textiles Intended for West Africa and Zaire." In *The Fabrics of Culture*, ed. J. M. Cordwell and R. A. Schwarz, 467–498. The Hague: Mouton, 1979.

Nora, P. "Between Memory and History: Les Lieux de Mémoire." *Representations* no. 26 (1989): 7–24.

Oberauer, K., C. Jarrold, S. Farrell, and S. Lewandowsky. "What Limits Working Memory Capacity?" *Psychological Bulletin* 142, no. 7 (2016): 758–799.

Obiechina, E. "Narrative Proverbs in the African Novel." *Oral Tradition* 7, no. 2 (1992): 197–230.

Ochs, E. and L. Capps. "Narrating the Self." *Annual Review of Anthropology* 25 (1996): 19–43.

Odita, O. "Theory and Practice in Contemporary African Art: Modernists or Skokian Aspect." *Journal of Multi-Cultural and Cross-Cultural Research in Art Education* 1, no. 1 (1983): 43–56.

Odumosu, J. *Ìwé Ìwòsàn*. Liverpool: n.p., n.d.

Oesterheld, C. "Humor and Satire: Precolonial, Colonial and Postcolonial." *Annual of Urdu Studies* 26 (2011): 64–86.

Ogbu, K. "West African Christianity." In *The Collected Essays of Ogbu Uke Kalu*, vol. II: *Christian Missions in Africa: Mission, Ferment, Trauma*, ed. N. Wariboko, T. Falola, and W. Kalu, 173–189. Trenton: Africa World Press, Inc., 2010.

Ogude, S. E. "African Literature and the Burden of History: Some Reflections." In *African Literature and African Historical Experiences*, ed. C. Ikonne, E. Oko, and P. Onwudinjo, 1–10. Ibadan: Heinemann Educational Books, Nigeria, 1991.

Ogunremi, D. and B. Adediran, eds. *Culture and Society in Yorubaland*. Ibadan: Rex Charles Publications, 1986.

Ojo, O. "'Heepa' (Hail) Òrìṣà: The Òrìṣà Factor in the Birth of Yoruba Identity." *Journal of Religion in Africa*. 39, no. 1 (2009): 30–59.

Okam, H. H. "The Novelist as Historian: Yambo Ouologuem's *Le Devior de Violence*." In *African Literature and African Historical Experiences*, ed. C. Ikonne, E. Oko, and P. Onwudinjo, 53–62. Ibadan: Heinemann Educational Books, Nigeria, 1991.

Okeke, U. "The Story of the Contemporary Art of Nigeria's Eastern States." *Ikoro: Bulletin of the Institute of African Studies, University of Nigeria, Nsukka* 1, no. 2 (1971): 35–46.

Okri, B. *The Famished Road*. London: Vintage, 2003.

Oladipo, O. *The Idea of African Philosophy: A Critical Study of the Major Orientations in Contemporary African Philosophy.* Ibadan: Molecular Publishers, 1992.

Olafioye, O. and N. Orji. "Number of Dead Persons Appointed by Nigerian President Buhari into Boards of Government Agencies has Increased to 8." *Sahara Reporters,* December 31, 2017. http://saharareporters.com/2017/12/31/number-of-dead-persons-appointed-by-nigerian-president-buhari-into-boards-of-government-agencies-has/.

Olajubu, O. "Yoruba Verbal Artists and their Works." *Journal of American Folklore* 91, no. 360 (1978): 675–690.

Olanipekun, O. V. "Omoluabi: Rethinking the Concept of Virtue in Yoruba Culture and Moral System." *Africology: The Journal of Pan African Studies* 10, no. 9 (2017): 217–231.

Olaoye, T. 2005. "Iwa: Symbolism and Significance in Sango Ritual Textiles." In *Yoruba Religious Textiles: Essays in Honour of Cornelius Adepegba,* ed. E. P. Renne and B. Agbaje-Williams, 129–155. Ibadan: Book Builders, 2005.

Olney, J. *Memory and Narrative: The Weave of Life-Writing.* Chicago: University of Chicago Press, 1998.

Omooboola, O. C. "An Overview of Taboo and Superstition among the Yoruba of Southwest of Nigeria." *Mediterranean Journal of Social Sciences* 4, no. 2 (2013): 221–226.

Ong, W. *Orality and Literacy: The Technologizing of the Word.* London: Methuen & Co., 1982.

Ono, I. "The Natural and Human Environment in Nigeria: Their Implication for Architecture." *Journal of Applied Science and Environmental Management* 12, no. 2 (2008): 67–74.

Onuoha, J. and M. Ugwueze. "Political Scientists and Nation-Building: The Nigerian Experience." *International Journal of Social Science and Humanities Research* 2, no. 4 (2014): 36–46.

Orimoloye, G. *Ona: Exhibition of Paintings/Drawings by Gbenga Orimoloye.* Lagos: Terra Kulture, 2012. www.orimoloye.com/wp-content/uploads/2016/08/ona_2012.pdf.

Oripeloye, H. "The Development of Exilic Poetry in Anglophone West Africa." *Tydskrif vir Letterkunde* 52, no. 1 (2015): 155–167.

Ormerod, B. "Magical Realism in Contemporary French Caribbean Literature: Ideology or Literary Diversion." *Australian Journal of French Studies* 34, no. 2 (1997): 216–226.

Ortega, M. "Decolonial Woes and Practices of Un-Knowing." *Journal of Speculative Philosophy* 31, no. 3 (2017): 504–516.

Osegi, P. N. "Contemporary African Art: The College-Trained Modernist." *Visual Art Research* 17, no. 2 (1991): 56–59.

Overton, J. "Decolonizing Methodologies: Research and Indigenous Peoples." *Development in Practice* 23, no. 4 (2013): 598–599.

Oyeniyi, A. B. "Dress and Identity in Yoruba Land, 1880–1980." Ph.D. thesis, Leiden University, 2012. http://hdl.handle.net/1887/20143.
Dress in the Making of African Identity: A Social and Cultural History of the Yoruba People. New York: Cambria Press, 2015.
Oyerinde, N. D. *Ìwé Ìtàn Ògbómọ̀ṣọ* Jos: Niger Press, 1934.
Palmenfelt, U. "Contemporary Uses of Narrative." *Elore* 16, no. 2 (2009): 1–12.
Pathak, A. "Musings on Postcolonial Autoethnography." In *Handbook of Autoethnography*, ed. S. Holman Jones, T. E. Adams, and C. Ellis, 595–608. New York: Routledge, 2013.
Patton, T. O. "Hey Girl, Am I More than my Hair? African American Women and their Struggles with Beauty, Body image and Hair." *NWSA Journal* 18, no. 2 (2006): 24–51.
p'Bitek, O. *Song of Lawino & Song of Ocol.* London: Heinemann, 1984.
Pieldner, P. "Magic Realism, Minimalist Realism and the Figuration of the Tableau in Contemporary Hungarian and Romanian Cinema." *Acta Universitatis Sapientiae, Film and Media Studies*, 12 (2016): 87–114.
Pierce, Y. "Slave Rebellions." In *American History through Literature 1820–1870*, ed. J. Gabler-Hover, et al., 1087–1090. Detroit: Charles Scribner's Sons, 2006.
Pitard, J. "A Journey to the Centre of Self: Positioning the Researcher in Autoethnography." *Forum: Qualitative Social Research* 18, no.3 (2017): 108–127.
Polkinghorne, D. *Narrative Knowing and the Human Sciences.* Albany: State University of New York Press, 1988.
"Narrative and Self-Concept." *Journal of Narrative and Life History* 1, no. 2–3 (1999): 135–153.
Quarcoo, A. K. "Yoruba Religious Carving: Pagan and Christian Sculpture in Nigeria and Dahomey by Kevin Carroll." *Journal of Religion in Africa* 4, no. 2 (1971): 137–141.
Quijano, A. "Coloniality and Modernity/Rationality." *Cultural Studies* 21, no. 2 (2010): 168–178.
Quintero, R. "Introduction: Understanding Satire." In *Companion to Satire*, ed. R. Quintero, 1–11. Oxford: Blackwell, 2007.
Raji, R. "A Hilly Affair." In *Ìbàdàn Mesìọgò: A Celebration of a City, its History and People*, ed. D. Adelugba, R. Raji, O. Segun, and B. Olayebi, 72–75. Ibadan: Bookcraft Ltd., 2001.
Ramirez, F. and J. Boli. "The Political Construction of Mass Schooling: European Origins and Worldwide Institutionalization." *Sociology of Education* 60 (1987): 2–17.
Reiff, R., and M. Scheerer. *Memory and Hypnotic Age Regression.* New York: International Universities Press, 1959.
Relph, E. "A Pragmatic Sense of Place." *Environmental and Architectural Phenomenology* 20, no. 3 (2009): 24–31.

Renan, E. "What Is a Nation?" In *Nationalism in Europe: 1815 to the Present*, ed. S. Woolf, 48-60. New York: Routledge, 1996.
Renne, E. P. *Cloth that Does Not Die: The Meaning of Cloth in Bunu Social Life*. Seattle: University of Washington Press, 1995.
Renne, E. P. and B. Agbaje-Williams, eds. *Yoruba Religious Textiles: Essays in Honour of Cornelius Adepegba*. Ibadan: Book Builders, 2005.
Richardson, L. *Fields of Play: Constructing an Academic Life*. New Brunswick: Rutgers University Press, 1997.
——. *Time and Narrative*. Chicago: University of Chicago Press, 1988.
Ricoeur, P. "Life in Quest of Narrative." In *On Paul Ricoeur: Narrative and Interpretation*, ed. D. Wood, 20-33. London: Routledge, 1991.
Rigby, K. "Ecocriticism." In *Introducing Criticism at the 21st Century*, ed. J. Wolfreys, 151-178. Edinburgh: Edinburgh University Press, 2002.
Rigney, A. "Portable Monuments: Literature, Cultural Memory, and the Case of Jeanie Deans." *Poetics Today* 25, no. 2 (2004): 361-396.
Roberts, K. *Religion in Sociological Perspective*. Belmont: Wadworth, 1995.
Robertson, L. T. "Memory and the Brain." *Journal of Dental Education* 66, no. 1 (2002): 30-42.
Rosenthal, A. "Raising Hair." *Eighteenth-Century Studies* 38, no. 1 (2004): 1-16.
Rueckert, W. "Metaphor and Reality: A Meditation on Man, Nature and Words." *KB Journal* 2, no. 2 (2006), https://kbjournal.org/rueckert.
Rusu, M. "History and Collective Memory: The Succeeding Incarnations of an Evolving Relationship." *Philobiblon* 18, no. 2 (2013): 260-282.
Said, E. W. *Orientalism*. New York: Vintage Books, 1978.
——. "Orientalism Reconsidered." *Race & Class* 27, no. 2 (1985): 1-15.
Salack, M. "An Unpredictable Sojourner." www.texasobserver.org/1751-an-unpredictable-sojourner-by-marcela-salack/.
Sankara, E. "History and the Production and Reception of Autobiography in Francophone Africa." *Canadian Review of Comparative Literature* 32, no. 3-4 (2005): 440-458.
Santos, M. "Memory and Narrative in Social Theory: The Contributions of Jacques Derrida and Walter Benjamin." *Time & Society* 10, no. 2-3 (2001): 163-189.
Sarbin, T. R. "The Poetics of the Identity." *Theory & Psychology* 7, no. 1 (1997): 68-82.
Sarkeesian, A. "Anita Sarkeesian at TEDxWomen 2012." December 2012. TEDxTalks. Filmed at TEDxWomen 2012. Video, 10:29. www.youtube.com/watch?v=GZAxwsg9J9Q.
Sartre, J. P. *Transcendence of the Ego*, trans. F. Williams and R. Kirkpatrick. New York: Noonday Press, 1962.
Saussure, F. *A Course in General Linguistics*. New York: McGraw-Hill, 1916.
Schiffrin, D. "Narrative as Self-Portrait: Socio-Linguistic Constructions of Identity." *Language in Society* 25 (1996): 167-203.

Schreiber, L. "Overcoming Methodological Elitism: Afrocentrism as a Prototypical Paradigm for Intercultural Research." *International Journal of Intercultural Relations* 24, no. 5 (2000): 651–671.

Schwandt, T. A. "Farewell to Criteriology." *Qualitative Inquiry* 2, no. 1 (1996): 58–72.

Seamon, D. and J. Sowers. "Place and Placelessness (1976): Edward Relph." In *Key Texts in Human Geography*, ed. P. Hubbard, R. Kitchin, and G. Valentine, 43–52. London: Sage, 2008.

Sekoni, R. "The Narrator, Narrative-Pattern and Audience Experience of Oral Narrative Performance." In *The Oral Performance in Africa*, ed. I. Okpewho, 139–159. Ibadan: Spectrum Books, 1990.

Serequeberhan, T. *The Hermeneutics of African Philosophy: Horizon and Discourse*. New York: Routledge, 1994.

Shome, R. and R. S. Hegde. "Postcolonial Approaches to Communication: Charting the Terrain, Engaging the Intersections." *Communication Theory* 12, no. 3 (2002): 249–270.

Sieber, R. and F. Herreman. "Hair in African Art and Culture." *African Arts* 33, no. 3 (2000): 54–96.

Simon, D. "Namibian Elections: SWAPO Consolidates Its Hold on Power." *Review of African Political Economy* 27, no. 83 (2000): 113–115.

Simpkins, S. "Magical Strategies: The Supplement of Realism." *Twentieth Century Literature* 34, no. 2 (1988): 140–154.

Siskind, M. *Cosmopolitan Desires: Global Modernity and World Literature in Latin America*. Evanston: Northwestern University Press, 2014.

Skrodzka, A. *Magic Realist Cinema in East Central Europe*. Edinburgh: Edinburgh University Press, 2012.

Slaymaker, W. "Echoing the Other(s): The Call of Global Green and Black African Responses." In *African Literature: Anthology of Theory and Criticism*, ed. T. Olaniyan and A. Quayson, 683–697. Malden: Blackwell, 2007.

Slemon, S. "Magic Realism as Postcolonial Discourse." In *Magical Realism: Theory, History, Community*, ed. L. Zamora and W. Faris, 9–24. Durham: Duke University Press, 1995.

Smith, A. *The Ethnic Origins of Nations*. Oxford: Blackwell, 1986.

National Identity. London: Penguin, 1991.

Smith, L. T. *Decolonizing Methodologies: Research and Indigenous Peoples*. London: Zed Books, 2012.

Smith, R. *Kingdoms of the Yoruba*. London: University of Wisconsin Press, 1969.

Sontag, S. *On Photography*. New York: Delta, 1973.

Soyinka, W. "The Fourth Stage: Through the Mysteries of Ogun to the Origin of Yoruba Tragedy." In *African Philosophy: An Anthology*, ed. E. C. Eze, 438–446. Oxford: Blackwell, 1998.

Sprague, S. "How I See the Yoruba See Themselves." *Studies in Visual Communication* 5, no. 1 (1978): 9–28.

Stahlke Wall, S. "Toward a Moderate Autoethnography." *International Journal of Qualitative Methods* 15, no. 1 (2016). https://doi.org/10.1177/16094069 16674966.

Stalin, J. "The Nation." In *Nationalism*, ed. J. Hutchinson and A. Smith, 18–20. Oxford: Oxford University Press, 1994.

Stark, R. "Reconceptualising Religion, Magic and Science." *Review of Religious Research* 43, no. 2 (2001): 101–120.

Steiner, C. B. "Another Image of Africa: Toward an Ethnohistory of European Cloth Marketed in West Africa, 1873–1960." *Ethnohistory* 32, no. 2 (1985): 91–110.

Stephen, N. "Magical Realism: Locating Its Contours in Postmodern Literature." *Indian Journal of Postcolonial Literature* 15, no. 2 (2015): 109–115.

Sterne, J. "A Critic of Orality." *Canadian Journal of Communication* 36 (2011): 207–225.

Stikkers, K. W. "An Outline of Methodological Afrocentrism, with Particular Application to the Thought of W. E. B. DuBois." *Journal of Speculative Philosophy* 22, no. 1 (2008): 40–49.

Strauss, D. "Metaphor: The Intertwinement of Thought and Language." *Koers* 76, no. 1 (2011): 11–31.

Strawson, G. "Against Narrativity." *Ratio* 17, no. 4 (2004): 428–452.

Stuhlmiller, C. M. "Narrative Picturing: Ushering Experiential Recall." *Nursing Inquiry* 3 (1996): 183–184.

Sullivan, D. A. *Cosmetic Surgery: The Cutting Edge of Commercial Medicine in America*. New Brunswick: Rutgers University Press, 2001.

Theokinda, I. B. "Let Pupils Speak Vernacular – Ngugi." *The Star*, February 7, 2019. www.the-star.co.ke/news/2019-02-07-let-pupils-speak-vernacular-ngugi/.

Thompson, R. F. "An Aesthetic of the Cool." *African Arts* 7, no. 1 (1973): 40–91.

——. *African Art in Motion*. Berkeley: University of California Press, 1974.

Thorpe, C. O. *Àwọn Èèwọ̀ Ilẹ̀ Yoruba*. Ibadan: Onibon-Oje Press, 1972.

Toyosaki, S. "Toward De/Postcolonial Autoethnography: Critical Relationality with the Academic Second Persona." *Cultural Studies ↔ Critical Methodologies* 18, no. 1 (2018): 32–42.

Tse, J. K. H. "Grounded Theologies: 'Religion' and the 'Secular' in Human Geography." *Progress in Human Geography* 38, no. 2 (2014): 201–220.

Tucker, S. M. *Verse Satire in England before the Renaissance*. New York. Columbia University Press, 1903.

Tulving, E. "Episodic and Semantic Memory." In *Organization of Memory*, ed. E. Tulving and W. Donaldson, 381–403. New York: Academic Press, 1972.

Tunç, T. E. "The Poetics of Self-Writing: Women and the National Body in the Works of Lucille Clifton." *Journal of Faculty of Letters* 26, no. 1 (2009): 187–200.

Turner, B. *The Body and Society: Explorations in Social Theory*. London: Sage, 1966.

United Nations. "United Nations Framework Convention on Climate Change." https://treaties.un.org/Pages/ViewDetailsIII.aspx?src=TREATY&mtdsg_no=XXVII-7&chapter=27&Temp=mtdsg3&clang=_en.

Utz, R. "Nations, Nation-Building, and Cultural Intervention: A Social Science Perspective." *Max Planck Yearbook of United Nations Law* 9 (2005): 615–647.

van der Geest, S. "How Can It Be!? Ethnography as Magical Realism and the Discovery of the Ordinary." *Medicine Anthropology Theory* 2, no. 2 (2015): 79–94.

van Dijck, J. "Digital Photography: Communication, Identity, Memory." *Visual Communication* 7 (2008): 57–76.

van Dijk, T. A., and W. Kintsch. *Strategies of Discourse Comprehension*. New York: Academic Press, 1983.

Van Katwyk, T. and Y. Seko. "Knowing through Improvisational Dance: A Collaborative Autoethnography." *Forum: Qualitative Social Research* 18, no. 2 (2017): 122–144.

Vansina, J. *Art History in Africa: An Introduction to Method*. London and New York: Longman, 1984.

Vansina, M., R. Poynor, and M. Harris. *History of Art in Africa*. New York: Harry N. Abrams, Inc., 2001.

Vendler, H. *Soul Says: On Recent Poetry*. Cambridge, MA: Harvard University Press, 1995.

Verovsek, P. "Memory, Narrative, and Rupture: The Power of the Past as a Resource for Political Change." *Memory Studies* 13, no. 2 (2020): 208–222.

Vogel, S., ed. *For Spirits and Kings: African Art from the Paul and Ruth Tishman Collection*. New York: Cosmopolitan Museum of Arts, 1981.

Vye, A. "The Role of Visual Artists in Society," *Work*, Demand Media, http://.work.chron.com/role-visual-artists-society-22517.html.

Walby, S. "The Myth of the Nation-State: Theorizing Society and Polities in a Global Era." *Sociology* 37, no. 3 (2003): 529–546.

Waldorf, C. W. "The Implications of Master Narrative Politics." In *To Shape Our World for Good: Master Narratives and Regime Change in U.S. Foreign Policy, 1900–2011*, 199–218. Ithaca: Cornell University Press, 2019.

Wallach, J. J. "Building a Bridge of Words: The Literary Autobiography as Historical Source Material." *Biography* 29, no. 3 (2006): 446–461.

Wandama, W. "Prospects of Studying Magical Realism in Nigerian Literature." *International Journal of Arts and Humanities* 5, no. 3 (2016): 1–12.

Wang, Q., Q. Song, and J. Koh. "Culture, Memory, and Narrative Self-Making." *Imagination, Cognition and Personality: Consciousness in Theory, Research, and Clinical Practice* 37, no. 2 (2017): 199–223.

Wa Thiong'o, N. *Decolonising the Mind: The Politics of Language in African Literature*. London: James Currey, 1986.

———. *Homecoming*. London: Heinemann Educational Books, 1972.

Weaver, S. "The 'Other' Laughs Back: Humour and Resistance in Anti-Racist Comedy." *Sociology* 44, no. 1 (2010): 31–48.

Weitz, R. "Women and their Hair: Seeking Power through Resistance and Accommodation." *Gender and Society* 15, no. 5 (2001): 667–686.
Wenk, S. "Gendered Representations of the Nation's Past and Future." In *Gendered Nations: Nationalisms and Gender Order in the Long Nineteenth Century*, ed. I. Blom, K. Hagemann, and C. Hall, 63–81. Oxford: Berg, 2000.
Whetung, M. and S. Wakefield. "Colonial Conventions: Institutionalized Research Relationships and Decolonizing Research Ethics." In *Indigenous and Decolonizing Studies in Education: Mapping the Long View*, ed. L. T. Smith, E. Tuck, and W. K. Yang, 146–158. New York: Routledge, 2019.
White, H. "The Fictions of Factual Representation." In *Tropics of Discourse: Essays in Cultural Criticism*, 121–134. Baltimore: Johns Hopkins University Press, 1978.
———. "The Historical Text as Literary Artifact." In *Tropics of Discourse: Essays in Cultural Criticism*, 81–100. Baltimore: Johns Hopkins University Press, 1978.
Willett, F. *African Art*. London: Thames & Hudson, 1971.
Williams, H. R. and P. J. Gloviczki. "Storytelling across Generations: A Collaborative Autoethnography." *Humanity & Society* 42, no. 2 (2018): 255–257.
Wilson, K. and C. French. "Magic and Memory: Using Conjuring to Explore the Effects of Suggestion, Social Influence, and Paranormal Belief on Eyewitness Testimony for an Ostensibly Paranormal Event." *Frontiers in Psychology* 5 (2014): 1–9.
Wilson, R. "Metamorphoses of Fictional Space: Magical Realism." In *Magical Realism: Theory, History, Community*, ed. L. Zamora and W. Faris, 209–233. Durham: Duke University Press, 1995.
Winkler, I. "Doing Autoethnography: Facing Challenges, Taking Choices, Accepting Responsibilities." *Qualitative Inquiry* 24, no. 4 (2018): 236–247.
Wolfe, M. "Memory for Narrative and Expository Text: Independent Influences of Semantic Associations and Text Organization." *Journal of Experimental Psychology* 31, no. 2 (2005): 359–364.
Wordsworth, W. "Preface to Lyrical Ballads, with Pastoral and Other Poems (1802)." In *The Norton Anthology of Theory and Criticism*, ed. V. B. Leitch, 648–668. New York: W. W. Norton & Company, 2001.
Worldometers. "Book Statistics." New Book Titles Published. www.worldometers.info/books/.
Wyatt, T. R. "Knowing when to Step Forward, Back, or Out: An Autoethnography of a White Researcher in Two Post-Colonial Educational Contexts." *Power and Education* 10, no. 3 (2018): 301–314.
Yai, B. O. "Tradition and the Yoruba Artist." *African Arts* 3, no. 1 (1999): 32–35.
Yarkoni, T., N. Speer, and J. Zacks. "Neural Substrates of Narrative Comprehension and Memory." *NeuroImage* 41 (2008): 1408–1425.
Yuval-Davis, N. *Gender and Nation*. London: Sage, 1997.
———. "Nationalist Projects and Gender Relations." *Nar. umjet*, 40, no. 1 (2003): 9–36.

Zamora, L. and W. Faris, eds. *Magical Realism: Theory, History, Community.* Durham: Duke University Press, 1995.

Zandberg, E. "The Right to Tell the (Right) Story: Journalism, Authority and Memory." *Media Culture Society* 32, no. 5 (2010): 5–24.

Zeleza, T. P. and G. Weare. *Rethinking Africa's Globalization*, vol. I: *The Intellectual Challenges.* Trenton: Africa World Press, 2003.

Zuern, E. "Memorial Politics: Challenging the Dominant Party's Narrative in Namibia." *Journal of Modern African Studies* 50, no. 3 (2012): 493–518.

Zwaan, R. A. "Situation Models: The Mental Leap into Imagined Worlds." *Current Directions in Psychological Science* 8, no. 1 (1999): 15–18.

INDEX

Abíọ́la, J.D.E, 189
Abọ̀kẹ̀, 68
Abrams, M. H, 282
Academic separatism, 32
Adelabu, Adegoke, 195
Adelakun, Abimbola A, 192
Adeoye, Tafa, 159
Àdìrẹ (tie and dye), 316
aesthetic of the cool, 16, 300, 336, 347
aesthetic tradition, 329, 333
Afolabi, Niyi, 130
Afọnja, Àarẹ Ọ̀nà Kakaǹfò, 54
African culture, 110, 180
African culture, beads in, 107
African Diaspora: Slavery, Modernity and Globalization, 196
African epistemologies, 9, 10, 11, 15, 27
African epistemologies, creative structures of, 27
African epistemology, 25, 453
African futurism, 198
African literary narrative, 103
African literature, Satire in, 154
African migrant fiction, 122
African narratives, 103, 480
African prints, 288
African sartorial taste, 475
African traditional knowledge, polemics of, 108
African traditional system, 108
Afrocentric research, 27, 28
Afrocentricity, 28
Afrofuturism, 84, 168, 198
Agbádá, 300
Àgbẹ́kọ̀yà
  collapse, 175
  group, 91
  revolt, 75, 78, 86, 91
Agere, 270
Ajileye, Yekini, 88
Àjùmọ̀ṣe, 354
Akufo, 80
Alaafin (Emperor), 54
Andrews, Jorella, 415, 439, 440, 441
Anglican Church, 93
anonymity, 242
anthropology, 45
  cultural, 22
Anti-Tax rebellion, 199
Apata Ganga, 58
archives, defined, 5
Aristotle, 128
Àrọ́bá, 74
Àrokò, 97
art criticism
  African, 240
  nature of, 250
  Western principles of, 232
  Yoruba, 239
artwork, 340, 353, 480
  authorial self-naming, 464
  authorial self-naming of, 241
  exhibition, 31
  hair, 395
  mutual intelligibility, 353
  statuettes, 25, 206
  Yoruba, 274
Àṣà, 251
  Àṣà ìmúra, 286, 291
Àṣẹ, 16, 253, 255
  and dressing, 299
  individual, 274, 412

Aṣọ-òkè, 324, See textiles
  modern usage, 321
  types, 323
Àtẹnujẹ, 181
autobiography, 29, 47
Autoethnographic literature, 39
auto-ethnographic research, 470
autoethnography
  analytic, 34
  collaborative, 36
  decoloniality of, xvii
Avoseh, Theophilus O., 191
Awolọwọ, Ọbafẹmi, 91
Àwòrán, 389, 390
  hair, 391, 395
Àyànmọ́, 66
Ayola Commission, 93
Azikiwe, Nnamdi, 50

babaláwo, 67
Babangida, Ibrahim, 118
Bahl, Vivek, 131
Baker-Smith, Dominic, 353
Bamberg, Michael, 130
Bàńtẹ́, 287
Barney, Edward, 47
Barthes, Roland, 45, 419, 432
  photograph, 419, 432
beads, 107
Becker, Howard, 415
Benin, 199, 289
Bible, 82, 119, 164, 170
Blyden, Edward W., 190
Boas, Franz, 22
Boehmer, Elleke, 86
border thinking, 32
Brain drain, 123
Bray, Jennifer, 296
Brazil, 198
Bread and Bullet, 119
Buoda Gebu, 166
burden of representation, 112
Burẹ̀wà (ugly), 261

Caldwell, Paulette, 383
capitalism, 9, 462
  Western, xv
capitalism-based research., 462
Captain Bower, 53

Card, Shirley, 430
Caroll, Kevin, 233
carvings, 14, 245, 266
  cult, 213
  expressionist, 268
  utilitarian, 267
  Yoruba, 205, 229, 263
Casely-Hayford, Gus, 188
causation, principle of, 437
China, 174
Christ, 164, 167
Christ-complex, 22
Christianity, 67, 162, 322, 463
  advent of, 52
  magical rites in, 82
  resistance of, 200
civilized Yoruba, 157
civilizing mission, 22
climate change, 121
Climbing the Kilimanjaro, 139
cloth-making, 289
cloud services. See distributed storage
Cocoa House, 442
Collective memory, 48, 75, 76, 78
collectivism, 62
  principle of, 48
College-trained modern artists, 248
Colling, R. G., 47
colonial matrix of power, 19, 20–22, 37, 39, 40, 461, 462
colonial subjectivity, 247
colonialism, 22, 50, 117, 157, 173
communalism, 16, 357, 454, 473
constructive imagination, 47
contentment, 132, 135
Cordwell, Justine, 328, 330, 339, 341, 350
Cosmopolitanism, 41
Counter Violence, 121
Counting the Tiger's Teeth (CTTT), 457
Crowther, Ajayi, 190
Cuba, 198
cubism, 370–371
cult associations, 213
cultural constructionism, 30
cultural differentiation, 224
cultural envelope, 206
cultural exploration, 460
cultural nationalism, 10

cultural relativism, 22
cultural renaissance, 291
cultural specificity, 242
cultural symbolism, 326, 345, 367, 370
cultural values, 351, 370
culturalism, 10
culture
   phonocentric, 247
Cybercrime, 119

Danesi, Marcus, 283
Dasylva, Ademola, 49
dates, 53
David, Doris, 209, 349, 389, 408, 454
decoloniality, xviii, 11, 21–22
   academic, 37
   challenge to, 37
   tool of, 38
defamiliarization, 95, 132
   concept of, 89
deforestation, 171
Dídán (luminosity), 370
digital media, 442
Dijck, Jose V., 420–421, 425
Dike, Kenneth O., 191
distributed storage, 442, 444
drum, 359
Drumming, 360
Du Bois, W.E.B, 191
Durant, Sarah, 149

Èèwọ̀, 62
Ẹgba rebellion, 199
Egúngún, 213
Egúngún festivals, 67, 359
Egúngún worship, 64
Egypt, 19
Ekpo, Denis, 20
Ẹkupeople, 55
El Salvador, 20
Elésin Elésin, 148
Eliot, Thomas S., 392
Ellis, Carolyn, 40
Emèrè, 65
employment, 47
England, 49
ephebism, 368–369
epistemic disobedience, 30
epistemic liberation, 41, 42

epistemic violence, 21
Equiano, Olaudah, 29
Escobar, Pablo, 87
Èṣù, 65, 86, 219, 270–274
Èṣù shrines, 217
Èṣù statuette, 218
Èṣù's cult, 274
Etches on Waters, 99
ethnic group, 100,
   African, 107
ethnics, relevance of, 100
ethnography
   fieldwork, 23
   modern, 23
   realist, 24
ethnography, anthropological, 40
ethno-religious conflicts, 199
Eurocentric
   art historians, 242
   biases, 240
   paradigms, 33
   pedagogy, 461
   perspectives, xvi, 19
   scholars, 247, 476
   scholarship, 15
Eurocentric epistemology, 22
Eurocentrism, 21, 232, 461
Eurocentrism, dominance of, 467
Eurocentricity, 19
Eurocentricity, academic, 21
European colonization, 19
European modernity, 20
European weavers, 287, 292, 293
Ẹwà (beauty), 323
exhibition, 339
Exo-autoethnography, 37
expressionism, 370–371
Èyọ̀ festival, 359–359

fact, 46
Fakeye, Lamidi, xix, 209
Falola, James A., 105
Family (*Ẹbí*), 310
Feminism, 488
feminism in Africa, 115
Fine Gary A., 24
folkloric arts, 466
Freeman, Mark, 126
From Isola's Grave, 140

Frye, Northrop, 345
Fulani, 54

Gandhi, Mahatma, 25, 162
gazing, 439
Gbẹ̀nàgbẹ̀nà, 206
Gbẹ̀nugbẹ̀nu, 26, 245
Gender Studies, 35
Germany, 188
Ghana, 166, 193
Ghost working, 176
Global South, 19
globalization, 19, 478
   narratives of, 187
glocalization, 478
gògò, 274
Greeting Codes, 56
greetings, Yoruba, 55

hair, 374
   cut, 409
   in spiritual realm, 413
   Yoruba cults, *391*
hair-making, *395, 407*
Halbwach, Maurice, 76
Haraway, Donna, 439, 440
Harlem of Africa. *See* Ibadan
Heaney, Seamus, 128
herbalists, 165
History of Nigeria, 192
Honor, Shame and Money, 110, 141
Horton, James A., 190
human consciousness, *127*
human dignity, *21*
human rituals, *88*
humanism, *30, 33, 40, 286*
humanistic approach, 26

Ibadan, *54, 58, 62, 169*
   Foundation Growth and Change 1830–1960, 194
   foundation of, 194
   hills, *58*
   people, 59, 68
   warriors, 172
Ibadan School of History, 191
Ìbejì (twins), *219*
Idán. See magic

ìdùnnú Ọbẹ́rẹ́kẹ́tẹ́, *147*
Ifá cult, 213
Ifá divination system, *82, 109*
ifarahàn (visibility), *370*
Ijebu, *197, 296*
ìjúbà (salutation), *105*
Ilà. *See* tribal marks
Ìlábìrù, 287
Ìlùti, 407
imagination, 46
In Praise of Yanbiọla, 130
indigenous languages, *160*
indigenous spirituality, *463*
individuation, *377, 457*
individuation, powers of, *314*
industrialization, *19, 197*
Interesting Life of Olaudah Equiano, The, 29
internet, 442
iṣẹ́ tínkó, 315
Iseyin, *289, 296*
Islam, *162, 322*
   influence of, *52*
Islamic fundamentalism, *200*
Islamization, *197*
Ìterìba, *210, 262*
Ìwé Ìtàn Ogbomọṣọ, 189
Iwin, 65
Ìya Lékuléja, *26*
Ìyá Mọ̀pó, 317, 328

Jesus, 119, 167
Johnson, James, 190
Jones, Robert, 444
Joselit, David, 327
Julien, Eileen, 104
Jung, Carl, 48

Kaduna, 200
Kano, 200
Katsina, 200
Ké Ẹ Pé, 148
Kèǹgbè Ọ̀rọ̀, 117
Kenyatta, Jomo, 50
Kíjìpá, 289
King, Martin L., 162
knowledge, 19–20
   constellation of, 40
   esoteric, 67

knowledge (cont.)
  pluriversalism of, 32
  subjugated, 74
Kundera, Milan, 166

language, use of, 198
Latin America, 87
Lawal, Babatunde, 220, 234, 260, 391
leadership, 118
  bad, 192
  failure of, 118
Lẹ́fù-Rete, 120
Leitch, Vincent, 129
Levecque, M, 295
liberalism, political, 50
Livingstone, David, 172
Locke, Alain, 22
Lodge, David, 59

Madden, Francine, 149
magic
  and science, 84
magic, defined, 81
Magical realism, defined, 87
Maitatsine riots, 200
Mali, 193
Malinowski, Bronislaw, 22
Mama, 117
Mandela, Nelson, 50
manneris, culturally-shaped, 160
Mapo Hall, 444
Maradona of Politics, the, 121
Martin, Adrienne, 160
Marxism, xviii, 10
  African, 191
master narrative, 12, 38, 40, 187
Mboya, Tom, 190
McCall, Daniel, 224
McLuhan, M, 424, 425
memory
  cultural, 74, 76
  declarative, 71
  reconstruction, 76
  social, 70
memory, defined, 70
mental images, 94, 421
Mercer, Kobena, 377
Mèsìọ̀gọ̀, 46
  ideology, 59

meta-schematics, 4
methodological reflexiveness, 28
mnemonic devices, 46, 47
Moloney, Alfred, 293
Monbiot, George, 183
monovocality, 129
moralist criticism, 345
Moremi, 114
Morgan lewis H., 22
Mother's Wisdom, 108
motifs, 317
  flora, 316
  horrifying, 343
  in paintings, 329
  mythic, 223
  Yoruba-centric, 330
Mouth Sweeter Than Salt, A, 49, 68, 69, 465
multiculturalism, 56, 69
myths, 85

names
  importance of, 57
  praise, 57
Namibia, 188
Narcos, 87
narrative intelligence, 79
narratives
  Slave, 49
  spiritual, 50
nation, 99–101
national allegories, 103
National Council of Nigeria and the Cameroons, 199
nationalism, 199
Nationalism and African Intellectuals, 191
nationalist historiography, 186, 193
natural disasters, 121
negritude, xviii, 104, 191
neo-colonialism, 117, 173, 175
neo-westernization, 193
neutral researcher, 26, 28
Nigerian Football Association, 179
Nigerian Railway Workers Union, 199
Nigerian Structural Adjustment Program, 118
Nigerian Union of Teachers, 199
Nkrumah, Kwame, 50
non-college-trained artists, 247

Odinga, Oginga, 50
Oduduwa, 226
Ogheneruemu, Irivwieri G., 330
Ògún, 66, 96
  invocation of, 90
  worship, 83
Ògún's Gift, 174
Okediji, Moyọ, 331
Okeebadan festival, 63, 166
Okri, Ben, 86
Olajide Olayode II, Ọba, 93
Old Ọyọ Empire, 54
Olódùmarè, 66
Olubadan, 54, 315, 443
omoluabi, 210, 453
  attributes, 469
Ọnà (arts and aesthetics), 330
Ọnà (crossroad), 16
Onaism, 330, 331
Ọpọlọ Àbéniyàn, 112, 140
oral narratives, 466, 468
orality, 17, 49, 476
  rejection of, 476
Ordinary Enchantments, 89
Orí, 16
orientalism, 22
Òrìṣàs, 216, 260
Ormerod, Beverley, 86
Orò cult, 213
Osogbo, 289, 317
Overton, John, 462
Oyerinde, N.D, 189

painting
  Yoruba, 328, 329, 338, 351, 354
paintings
  shrine, 343, 345
Pan-Africanism, 191
pan-Yoruba consciousness, 210
Park, Mungo, 172
Pásitò, 162
passionate detachment, 439
peasant rebellion, 9
Pentecostalism, 200
phallic signifiers, 272
photograph, 415
photographic stare, 428

photographs
  analogue, 421
  digital, 421
poems, 102
poems, incantatory, 97
Polkinghorne, Donald, 125
portraits
  traditional, 469
post-African Future, 198
postmodernism, 69, 74, 431
Power of African Cultures, The, 197
Prague, Stephen, 431
Pratt Mary L., 46
psychological Narrativity thesis, 125, 454
public health, 179

racism, 32, 119
Raji, Remi, 194
realism
  magical, 89
  Nigerian, 87
reductionist approach, 26
reformers, 174
reincarnation
  Yoruba belief in, 88
Reincarnation (poem), 150
religions
  African, 162, 163
  hypocrisy of, 163
Relph, Edward, 455
research
  Eurocentric, 20
  secularity of, 30
  separatism in, 26
restoration story, 185, 186, 187, 188
Ricoeur, Paul, 126
Roberts, Keith, 84
Roh, Franz, 87
Roland Barthes, 239
Rootedness, 455
Rọrọrọfọ, 121
Rosenthal, Angela, 374, 375
Ruth, Nielsen, 292
Rwanda, 174

Saluck, Marcela, 59
Salutation to Work, 121
sandwich problem, 21, 38

Ṣàngó, 66, 230
Ṣàngó cult, 213
Sarkeesian, Anita, 35
satura, 152
Scoundrel of Deferral, 136
self-awareness, 127
self-consciousness, 3
self-identity, 23, 129
  European, 20
self-identity, defined, 130
self-indulgent, 35, 38
self-indulgent articles, 40
self-introspection, 134
self-narratives, xvii, 474
self-negotiation, 129
Senegambia, 293
Serequeberhan, Tsenay, 471
singular self, ideology of, *48*
singular truth, 30, 31, 32, 40
situation model, 72
Slippery, 110
social constructivism, 30
social hierarchy, 263, 310, 385
socialism, 9, 94
South West Africa People's
  Organization (SWAPO), 188
Soyinka, Wole, 351
Spirit of Ancestors, the, 132
spiritual influence, 458
spiritual symbolism, 233, 371
staring, 427
Statue of Liberty, 114
stooping, 334
Strain Train, The, 123
superstitions, 60, 82
Suspended in Space, 139
symbolic interactionism, 31
symbolism
  fluidity of, 229

taboos, 61–62
  family, 61
Tanzania, 20
testimony, 27
textiles
  Yoruba, 282
Thiong'o, Ngugi wa, 161
Thompson, Robert, 250
Tító, 406

tòbi, 287
traditional pharmacology, 157, 180
Trailers III, 119
Trans-Atlantic slave trade, 117, 122
trans-culturalism, 69
traumatic events, 71, 77
Tree's Fell, the, 118, 122
tribal marking, 107
tribal marks, 107, 370
Tunisia, 35, 36
Tylor, E.B, 22

Ubuntu philosophy, 454
Ujamaa, 38
United Nations Framework
  Convention on Climate Change,
  121
United States of America, 20
Urhobo, 54, 196

vernacular, 198, *See* indigenous
  languages
*Violence in Nigeria: the Crisis of
  Religious Politics and Secular
  Ideologies*, 199
visual *Oríkì* (invocative praise), 208

Weitz, Rose, 402–403, 405
West's messianic approach, 431
Western academia, 23, 26
Western education, 157, 160
  importance of, 158
Western educational system, weakness
  of, 165
Western imperialism, 31
Western philosophy, 248
westernization, 108–109, 195
white mythology, 239
White, Hayden, *47*
Wòbìà (gluttony), 181
women, objectification of, 115
woodcarving, 205
  Yoruba, 240, 247
working memory, 81

Yai, Babalola, 27, 240, 242, 251, 411
Yello Sisi, 119
Yemoja, 171, 333
Yèrì, 287

Yoruba
　architecture, 362, 445
　cosmic belief, 64, 65, 67
　cultural philosophy, 125, 367
　food, 180
　linguistic concepts, 248
　mythology, 320, 365
　pantheon, 212, 218, 225
　sculptors, 255, 267, 274
　society, 285, 368, 477
　spiritual ontology, 225, 413
　woman, 386, 403, 410
Yoruba art, 16
　aesthetics, 367
　features of, 328
　religious symbolism of, 238
　spirituality of, 212
　theme in, 226
　vulnerability in, 212

Yoruba Gurus: Indigenous Production of Knowledge in Africa (1999), 189
Yoruba identity, 456
Yoruba language, 55
Yoruba sculptors, 206
Yoruba sculpture, 26, 277
　effective evangelization of, 237
　Orí in, 252, 259
　spirituality and, 213
　women in, 41, 275
Yoruba society, 17
Yoruba textile
　history of, 285
　language of, 283
　market, 294
　production, 295
Yorubaland, 52, 54, 266, 341, 367

Zaria, 200

www.ingramcontent.com/pod-product-compliance
Ingram Content Group UK Ltd.
Pitfield, Milton Keynes, MK11 3LW, UK
UKHW022131020325
455765UK00006B/37